THE
MICROECONOMY
TODAY

SIXTEENTH EDITION

Mc
Graw
Hill

The McGraw-Hill Series Economics

THE
MICROECONOMY
TODAY

SIXTEENTH EDITION

Bradley R. Schiller

Karen Gebhardt

Mc
Graw
Hill

THE MICROECONOMY TODAY, SIXTEENTH EDITION

Published by McGraw Hill LLC, 1325 Avenue of the Americas, New York, NY 10121. Copyright ©2022 by McGraw Hill LLC. All rights reserved. Printed in the United States of America. Previous editions ©2019, 2016, and 2013. No part of this publication may be reproduced or distributed in any form or by any means, or stored in a database or retrieval system, without the prior written consent of McGraw Hill LLC, including, but not limited to, in any network or other electronic storage or transmission, or broadcast for distance learning.

Some ancillaries, including electronic and print components, may not be available to customers outside the United States.

This book is printed on acid-free paper.

1 2 3 4 5 6 7 8 9 LWI 24 23 22 21

ISBN 978-1-264-27341-6 (bound edition)
MHID 1-264-27341-X (bound edition)
ISBN 978-1-264-27344-7 (loose-leaf)
MHID 1-264-27344-4 (loose-leaf)

Portfolio Manager: *Anke Weekes*
Lead Product Developer: *Kelly Delso*
Content Project Managers: *Kathryn D. Wright, Ann Courtney, and Emily Windelborn*
Senior Buyer: *Laura Fuller*
Senior Designer: *Matt Diamond*
Content Licensing Specialist: *Traci Vaske*
Cover Image: *city vector/Shutterstock*
Compositor: *Aptara®, Inc.*

All credits appearing on page are considered to be an extension of the copyright page.

Library of Congress Cataloging-in-Publication Data

Names: Schiller, Bradley R., 1943- author. | Gebhardt, Karen, author.
Title: The microeconomy today / Bradley R. Schiller, with Karen Gebhardt.
Description: Sixteenth edition. | New York, NY : McGraw Hill Education,
    [2022] | Includes index.
Identifiers: LCCN 2020047123 | ISBN 9781264273416 (hardcover) | ISBN
    9781264273447 (spiral bound)
Subjects: LCSH: Microeconomics.
Classification: LCC HB172 .S3625 2022 | DDC 338.5–dc23
LC record available at https://lccn.loc.gov/2020047123

Bradley R. Schiller has more than four decades of experience teaching introductory economics at American University, the University of Nevada, the University of California (Berkeley and Santa Cruz), and the University of Maryland. He has given guest lectures at more than 300 colleges ranging from Fresno, California, to Istanbul, Turkey. Dr. Schiller's unique contribution to teaching is his ability to relate basic principles to current socioeconomic problems, institutions, and public policy decisions. This perspective is evident throughout *The Microeconomy Today.*

Dr. Schiller derives this policy focus from his extensive experience as a Washington consultant. He has been a consultant to most major federal agencies, many congressional committees, political candidates, and presidents. In addition, he has evaluated scores of government programs and helped design others. His studies of poverty, discrimination, training programs, tax reform, pensions, welfare, Social Security, and lifetime wage patterns have appeared in both professional journals and popular media. Dr. Schiller is also a frequent commentator on economic policy for television and radio, and his commentary has appeared in *The Wall Street Journal, The Washington Post, The New York Times,* and *Los Angeles Times,* among other major newspapers.

Dr. Schiller received his Ph.D. from Harvard and his B.A. degree, with great distinction, from the University of California (Berkeley). On his days off, Dr. Schiller is on the tennis courts, the ski slopes, or the crystal-blue waters of Lake Tahoe.

Courtesy of Bradley R. Schiller

Dr. Karen Gebhardt is a faculty member in the Department of Economics and is the Director of the Online Economics Program at the University of Colorado Boulder. Dr. Gebhardt has a passion for teaching economics. She regularly instructs courses in all modalities (online, on campus, hybrid, remote) from introductory courses in macro- and microeconomics, to upper-division courses in microeconomics, international trade, and managerial economics and graduate courses in environmental economics and public finance.

She is an early adopter of teaching with technology and advocates strongly for it because she sees the difference it makes in student engagement and learning. Dr. Gebhardt was the recipient of the Water Pik Excellence in Education Award in 2006 and was awarded the Best Teacher Award in 2015 while she was at Colorado State University.

Dr. Gebhardt's research interests, publications, and presentations involve the economics and online education and the economics of human–wildlife interaction. Before returning to academia, she worked as an economist at the U.S. Department of Agriculture/Animal and Plant Health Inspection Service/Wildlife Services/National Wildlife Research Center, conducting research related to the interactions of humans and wildlife. Her current research focuses on using data to improve student learning outcomes in economics education with an emphasis on improving grades and completion rates in online courses.

In her free time, Dr. Gebhardt enjoys learning about new teaching methods that integrate technology and going rock climbing and camping in the Colorado Rockies and beyond.

Courtesy of Karen Gebhardt

CURRENT, POLICY FOCUSED, READABLE

Every edition of *The Microeconomy Today* has offered a level of currency that no other text has matched. Maintaining that front-page advantage has been particularly important to this edition. First and foremost is the integration of the coronavirus pandemic into the narrative. The pandemic – and the responses to it – changed the behavior and performance of economies around the world. Among other things, the pandemic prompted breathtaking expansions in the scope of government intervention. It also focused more attention on the supply side of the economy, especially the potential for external shocks to shut down production and government subsidies to restore it. In micro, we have seen how the pandemic changed both consumer and producer behavior – and wreaked havoc on domestic and international financial markets. The pandemic also changed political priorities, contributing to President Biden's 2020 Election. This edition examines those developments and their implications for ongoing policy and personal decision-making. This 16th edition offers the latest data on U.S. economic performance, global comparisons, policy initiatives, court cases, and political controversies over economic policy and priorities. Among the more visible updates are the following:

The Microeconomy Today was one of the first economics textbooks to supplement the narrative with boxed illustrations of institutional and policy applications of core concepts. The goal has always been to help students see the relevance of studying economics to themselves and the world around them. Schiller and Gebhardt make sure students understand the challenges of economic policy and the consequences of specific actions like tariffs, regulation, and tax reform. They provide a balanced discussion of these issues, allowing students to recognize and assess different perspectives on critical issues. This Policy focus is reinforced by (a) attaching explanatory captions to every boxed insert, (b) referencing all of the boxed material in the body of the text, and (c) referencing the boxed material in end-of-chapter discussions questions and problems. Even the photos are captioned, to assure that students see their relevance.

Front Page Economics. The *Front Page Economics* boxes are used to illustrate domestic applications of core concepts that make economics ever more relevant today. Student-focused examples cover everything from Starbucks price hikes, COVID-19 externalities, antitrust lawsuits, and Disney+ subscription pricing to the CARES Act and Mike Trout's $426 million baseball contract. Some of the 20 new *Front Page Economics* stories are:

- "COVID-19 Cases Surpass 1 Million" illustrates externalities in Chapter 4.
- "Risky Business: Start-ups Face High Failure Rates" emphasizes entrepreneurial risk in Chapter 8.
- "Streaming Wars Heat Up" illustrates how competition evolves in Chapter 11.
- "House approves $15 minimum wage" highlights pros and cons of wage floors in Chapter 16.
- "Taxes: Bernie vs. Biden" showcases the difference between nominal and effective tax rates in Chapter 19.

Current

Policy Focused

World View. The *World View* boxes focus on global illustrations of core concepts that allow students to see economics in action beyond U.S. borders to help them become an educated global citizen. Among the 16 new *World View* boxes in this edition are:

- "Venezuela's Food Crisis" illustrates how price controls cause market shortages in Chapter 3.
- "Tesla Starts Rolling Out Cars from Shanghai Gigafactory" highlights investment vs. production decisions in Chapter 7.
- "Nations Scrambling to End Oil-Price War" emphasizes the need for coordination in oligopoly in Chapter 11.
- "JetBlue Looks to London" describes how landing slots are an entry barrier in Chapter 13.
- "Imported WineSqueezes U.S. Vintners" explains the resistance to free trade in Chapter 21.

Decisions for Tomorrow. At the end of every chapter, students are challenged to use critical thinking skills to apply core concepts to a real-world phenomenon. The challenges may relate to public policy issues or life situations. All of these provocative questions not only challenge students to apply critical thinking but also to recognize the relevancy of core principles to the real world. Notice that all of the *Decisions* are posed as questions. The intent here is to encourage classroom discussion and debate. Among the *Decisions* challenges in this edition are:

- "What Is the Cost of Going Green?," in Chapter 1, explores opportunity costs.
- "Do 'Influencers' Really Matter?" questions how consumers make decisions in Chapter 5.
- "$29 AirPods?" emphasizes the power of competition to drive innovation and prices in Chapter 9.
- "Do We Need a Billionaire's Tax?" examines the pros and cons of taxation in Chapter 19.
- "Who Wins Trade Wars?" looks at the impacts of trade wars in Chapter 21.

All of the *Decisions* are posed as questions to encourage classroom discussion.

Questions for Discussion. End-of-chapter questions are common in textbooks. What distinguishes the *questions* in *The Microeconomy Today* is their explicit integration with the core narrative and the boxed features in each chapter. There are 80 new questions in this 16th edition.

Problems. *Problems* are also provided at the end of each chapter. Like the *Questions for Discussion,* the *Problems* are closely integrated with chapter material and often require the student to review a boxed feature and apply data contained therein. There are 227 new problems (!) in this 16th edition.

Readable

The one adjective invariably used to describe *The Microeconomy Today* is "readable." Professors often express a bit of shock when they realize that students actually enjoy reading the text. The writing style is lively and issue-focused. Unlike any other text on the market, every boxed feature, every graph, and every table is explained and analyzed. Every feature is also referenced in the text, so students actually learn the material rather than skipping over it. Because readability is ultimately in the eye of the beholder, you might ask a couple of students to read and compare a parallel chapter in *The Microeconomy Today* and in another text. This is a test *The Microeconomy Today* usually wins.

Connect is designed to support teaching and learning goals through providing graded and ungraded activities that can be integrated into a lecture, or assigned as part of a discussion board or problem set. Activities such as assignable discussion, graphing, and algorithmic problems; interactive graphs; and videos make it easy to enhance learning with just a few clicks. One unique feature of this text is that Schiller and Gebhardt personally have created the text-specific Connect content, leveraging their combined 60 years of teaching undergraduate face-to-face, online, hybrid, and remote courses to help you improve *your* students' learning. The author team assures that the text and all supplemental materials are harmonized and robustly integrated with Connect, providing peace of mind for both the professor and students.

Robust Integration with Connect

Remote Proctoring & Browser-Locking Capabilities

New remote proctoring and browser-locking capabilities, hosted by Proctorio within Connect, provide control of the assessment environment by enabling security options and verifying the identity of the student.

Seamlessly integrated within Connect, these services allow instructors to control students' assessment experience by restricting browser activity, recording students' activity, and verifying students are doing their own work.

Instant and detailed reporting gives instructors an at-a-glance view of potential academic integrity concerns, thereby avoiding personal bias and supporting evidence-based claims.

CHAPTER-BY-CHAPTER CHANGES: PURPOSE, APPROACH, AND UPDATES

Every chapter of this edition has been thoroughly reviewed and subjected to careful revision, editing, and updating. The following paragraphs provide a quick overview of each chapter and a list of the most notable updates.

Chapter 1: Economics: The Core Issues introduces the core issues of What, How, and For Whom goods and services are produced. It also highlights debates of how those decisions are made—by free markets, by governments, or by some mix of both. The intent is to give students a sense that "the economy" is not an abstract phenomenon but instead a vital determinant of our collective well-being. Heritage Organization "free market" 2020 rankings illustrate how different economies are structured and global military spending levels illustrate some of the "guns vs. butter" outcomes that result. A new "Decisions for Tomorrow" feature highlights the goals and trade-offs of the "Green revolution."

Chapter 2: The U.S. Economy: A Global View is uniquely designed to give students an empirical perspective on the dimensions of the U.S. economy—specifically, what we produce, how we produce, and for whom we produce. Within each of these dimensions, comparisons are provided to the rest of the world, giving students a truly global view of how the U.S. economy stacks up. This is a critical foundation for informing students about the economic world we want them to understand.

Chapter 3: Supply and Demand introduces the core elements of the market mechanism. It does this in a much more empirical context, however, than most texts. Illustrations include a Front Page Economics story on the pricing of Disney+ subscriptions, a World View on the supply shifts due to the 2019 missile attacks on Saudi oil fields, a World View on Venezuelan price controls, and a discussion of how the coronavirus pandemic prompted alleged price gouging. The end-of-chapter Decisions for Tomorrow feature confronts students with the deadly consequences of prohibiting the purchase and sale of human organs.

Chapter 4: The Role of Government focuses on the justifications for government intervention and the institutions—federal, state, and local—that have been developed to perform those functions. The chapter not only details the scope of government(s) but also looks at public perceptions about how well the public sector performs. A World View on Israel's "Iron Dome" missile defense (a public good), a Front Page Economics on vaping bans (externalities), and a Front Page Economics on public confidence in government enliven the discussion. The end-of-chapter Decisions for Tomorrow feature highlights the shortcomings of collective decision making, including public choice theory.

Chapter 5: Consumer Choice introduces consumer choice by first contrasting sociopsychiatric and economic explanations of consumer behavior, thereby highlighting the differences between the desire for goods and the demand for goods. Utility theory, consumer surplus, price discrimination, and consumer choice are all covered. The Decisions for Tomorrow feature looks at how "influencers" affect consumer choices.

Chapter 6: Elasticity explores price, income, and cross-price elasticities with illustrations of Netflix price hikes, iPhone sales, and California's increased tax on cigarettes. The Decisions for Tomorrow feature ponders how falling gasoline prices will affect consumers' demand for electric vehicles.

Chapter 7: The Costs of Production introduces students to the supply side of markets. The production function is discussed in detail, emphasizing the embryotic relationship between productivity and cost measures. Changes in ATC are illustrated with the volume of Uber rides, and economies of scale are illustrated with a World View on Tesla's Shanghai gigafactory. The Decisions for Tomorrow feature examines the substance of President Trump's accusation of "unfair" competition from foreign producers.

Chapter 8: The Competitive Firm starts by looking at the nature of profits and public (mis)perceptions about their scope and origins. It then illustrates the spectrum of market power, ranging from the perfectly competitive firm to monopoly. With this foundation, the chapter proceeds to examine the production decisions of perfectly competitive firms in the context of static equilibrium. Front Page Economics on start-up failure rates, public views of profits, and corporate shutdown decisions provide illustrative context.

Chapter 9: Competitive Markets is a unique, second chapter on competition that focuses on the dynamics of competitive markets—the heart and soul of market economies. The core story traces the evolution of the personal computer industry from the original Apple 1 to the latest iPhone. The emphasis is on how the profit motive drives innovation, entry, cost reductions, price cuts, and even exit in low-barrier markets. The Decisions for Tomorrow feature applies these insights to the current competition in AirPods.

Chapter 10: Monopoly takes students to the other end of the market structure spectrum and shows how monopoly decision making and outcomes differ from those of perfect competition. A unique, step-by-step contrast of behavior patterns drives the message home. The 2020 Justice Department suit against Live Nation and the continuing EU antitrust actions against Google should spark student interest.

Chapter 11: Oligopoly starts by showing how common oligopoly is in familiar product markets, using product-specific concentration ratios found in no other text. This empirical base is followed by an analysis of how oligopolies would like to behave (replicating monopoly outcomes), the mechanisms they use in pursuit of that goal, and the obstacles they confront. Front Page Economics on the ongoing streaming wars, the 2020 oil-price war, the T-Mobile–Sprint merger, and Dr Pepper's "Fansville" ad campaign enliven the theoretical analysis. The Decisions for Tomorrow feature examines recent proposals to break up Big Tech companies.

Chapter 12: Monopolistic Competition stresses the unique structure, behavior, and outcomes of this common industry structure. Data on brand values and ad spending underscore the importance of product differentiation in monopolistic competition. The Front Page Economics on the latest Starbucks price hike illustrates the low price elasticity of demand that brand loyalty creates. The Decisions for Tomorrow feature considers proposals for requiring truth in advertising.

Chapter 13: Natural Monopolies: (De)Regulation? goes beyond the depiction of this unique industry structure to explore the regulatory dilemmas that result. Quite simply, how can regulators compel natural monopolies to deliver the benefits of economies of scale without stifling innovation and productivity advance? And how much will regulation cost? These questions are illustrated in the trucking, airline, cable, and electricity industries. A World View on landing rights at Heathrow airport highlights the importance of entry barriers in sheltering natural monopolies from potential competition.

Chapter 14: Environmental Protection addresses one of the world's greatest challenges—namely, saving the planet. The role of market incentives in both environmental degradation and, potentially, environmental protection is emphasized. Also discussed are the pros and cons of several nonmarket approaches. Front Page Economics on pollution-induced deaths, the 2021 closing of New York's nuclear plant, and California's cap-and-trade program enliven the discussion. The Decisions for Tomorrow feature assesses the costs of the Green New Deal.

Chapter 15: The Farm Problem looks at the unique circumstances of the farm sector that have motivated government interventions. Low price and income elasticities combine with the vagaries of the weather to keep farm prices and incomes volatile. The history of farm incomes and subsidies is depicted, including a summary of the 2018 Farm Act. A World View on the U.S.–China trade war points to another source of income instability on the farm.

Chapter 16: The Labor Market analyzes the determinants of labor demand and supply, and then shows how they interact to set market wages and employment levels. The issues of wage inequality and minimum wage floors are discussed at length. A critical distinction between *effective* and *ineffective* legislated wage hikes helps resolve empirical disputes. Front Page stories on Amazon's Career Day, Mike Trout's $426 million baseball contract, and the proposed "Raise the Wage Act" drive home the relevance of this chapter. The Decisions feature examines proposals for capping CEO pay.

Chapter 17: Labor Unions looks at the character, history, and prevalence of labor unions. The core of the chapter focuses on union wage/employment goals and their strategies for achieving them. Monopsonist strategies are also described and the parameters of collective bargaining established. A Front Page Economics on the 2019 UAW strike against GM illustrates the breadth of bargaining issues.

Chapter 18: Financial Markets emphasizes the economic function of financial markets in reallocating resources to new ventures and products. The stock, bond, and venture-capital markets are all analyzed. Examples range from the financing of Columbus's expedition to the Uber IPO. Stock market data on Apple, Google, and Uber are used to illustrate risk and present values.

Chapter 19: Taxes: Equity versus Efficiency sheds critical light on continuing debates about tax policy. The discussion begins with a look at the U.S. pre-tax and post-tax distributions of income. Actual tax burdens are illustrated with the tax returns of Joe Biden and Bernie Sanders (President Trump declined to provide his tax returns for this analysis) and 2020 tax brackets. Trump's tax cuts and Biden's proposed tax hikes are reviewed. The Decisions feature assesses billionaires' tax proposals.

Chapter 20: Transfer Payments: Welfare and Social Security focuses on the second tool of income redistribution. The discussion emphasizes the same trade-off between equity and efficiency that permeates tax policy. Welfare and social security illustrations showcase implicit marginal tax rates and their impact on labor-supply behavior.

Chapter 21: International Trade not only explains the theory of comparative advantage but also examines the opposition to free trade and the trade barriers that result. President Trump's trade wars with China and his national security argument about TikTok are discussed, followed by a Decisions feature on "Who Wins Trade Wars?" The USMCA is reviewed, as are the latest data on trade flows. World Views on the dumping of Korean cigarettes and competition from wine imports and a Front Page Economics on the cost of sugar quotas keep the discussion lively.

Chapter 22: International Finance goes beyond the mechanics of exchange-rate determination to identify the gainers and losers from exchange-rate fluctuations. A World

View on the effects of the 2014–2020 appreciation of the U.S. dollar helps illustrate those redistributive effects (and the opposition thereto). The collapse of the Venezuelan bolivar adds further insight. A World View on the weakest global currencies is insightful as well.

Chapter 23: Global Poverty draws attention to the persistent depravation that still afflicts nearly 40 percent of the world's population. The discussion begins with a comparison of U.S. poverty thresholds with official global poverty measures. A survey of global poverty incidence is followed by an analysis of causation and potential remedies.

Student Problem Set

We firmly believe that students must *work* with key concepts in order to really learn them. Weekly homework assignments are *de rigueur* in our own classes. To facilitate homework assignments, we have prepared the student problem set at the end of each chapter. These sets include built-in numerical and graphing problems that build on the tables, graphs, and boxed material that align with each chapter's learning objectives. Students cannot complete all the problems without referring to material in the chapter. This increases the odds of students actually *reading* the chapter, the tables, and the boxed applications.

The student problem set at the end of each chapter is reproduced in Connect. This really helps students transition between the written material and online supplements. It also means that the online assignments are totally book-specific.

NEW AND IMPROVED SUPPLEMENTS

The following ancillaries are available for quick download and convenient access via the Instructor Resource material available through McGraw-Hill Connect: PowerPoint Presentations, Accessible PowerPoint Presentations, Instructor's Manual, Solution's Manual, and Test Builder Access.

ACKNOWLEDGMENTS

This 16th edition of *The Microeconomy Today* represents a continuing commitment to disseminate the core principles of economics to a broad swath of college students.

Like earlier editions, it has benefited greatly from the continuing stream of ideas and suggestions from both instructors and students. For all that feedback we are most grateful. Among those who have contributed to this and prior editions are the following instructors:

Reviewers

Cynthia E. Abadie
Southwest Tennessee Community College

Mark Abajian
San Diego Mesa College

Steve Abid
Grand Rapids Community College

Ercument G. Aksoy
Los Angeles Valley College

Mauro Cristian Amor
Northwood University

Catalina Amuedo-Dorantes
San Diego State University

Dr. Michael Aubry
Cuyamaca College

Gerald Baumgardner
Penn College

Mack A. Bean
Franklin Pierce University

Adolfo Benavides
Texas A&M University-Corpus Christi

Anoop Bhargava
Finger Lakes Community College

Joerg Bibow
Skidmore College

Eugenie Bietry
Pace University

John Bockino
Suffolk County Community College

Peter Boelman
Norco College

Walter Francis Boyle
Fayetteville Technical Community College

Amber Brown
Grand Valley State University

Don Bumpass
Sam Houston State University

Suparna Chakraborty
Baruch College, CUNY

Stephen J. Conroy
University of San Diego

Sherry L. Creswell
Kent State University

Manabendra Dasgupta
University of Alabama-Birmingham

Antony Davies
Duquesne University

Diane de Freitas
Fresno City College

Diana Denison
Red Rocks Community College

Alexander Deshkovski
North Carolina Central University

John A. Doces
Bucknell University

Ishita Edwards
Oxnard College

Eric R. Eide
Brigham Young University

Yalcin Ertekin
Trine University

Ali Faegh
Houston Community College-Northwest

Kelley L. Fallon
Owensboro Community & Technical College

Frank Garland
Tri-County Technical College

Leroy Gill
The Ohio State University

Michael G. Goode
Central Piedmont Community College

Paul Graf
Indiana University

Barnali Gupta
Miami University

Sheila Amin Gutierrez de Pineres
University of Texas-Dallas

Jonatan Jelen
City College of New York

Hyojin Jeong
Lakeland Community College

Barbara Heroy John
University of Dayton

Ken Knox, Ph.D.
Eastern Gateway Community College

Tim Kochanski
Portland State University

David E. Laurel
South Texas College

Raymond Lawless
Quinsigamond Community College

Richard B. Le
Cosumnes River College

Jim Lee
Texas A&M University-Corpus Christi

Sang H. Lee
Southeastern Louisiana University

Minghua Li
Franklin Pierce University

Yan Li
University of Wisconsin-Eau Claire

Paul Lockard
Black Hawk College

Rotua Lumbantobing
North Carolina State University

Paula Manns
Atlantic Cape Community College

Shah Mehrabi
Montgomery College

Jeanette Milius
Iowa Western Community College

Norman C. Miller
Miami University

Stanley Robert Mitchell
McLennan Community College

Dr. Victor Moussoki
Lone Star College

Stephen K. Nodine
Tri-County Technical College

Phacharaphot Nuntramas
San Diego State University

Seth Ari Roberts
Frederick Community College

Michael J. Ryan
Western Michigan University

Craig F. Santicola
Westmoreland County Community College

Rolando A. Santos
Lakeland Community College

Theodore P. Scheinman
Mt. Hood Community College

James K. Self
Indiana University-Bloomington

Warren Smith
Palm Beach State College-Lake Worth

Marilyn K. Spencer
Texas A&M University-Corpus Christi

Irina Nikolayevna Strelnikova
Red Rocks Community College

Michael Swope
Wayne County Community College

Gary Lee Taylor
South Dakota State University

Deborah L. Thorsen
Palm Beach State College

Ngoc-Bich Tran
San Jacinto College

Markland Tuttle
Sam Houston State University

Roger E. Wehr
University of Texas-Arlington

Kenneth Lewis Weimer
Kellogg Community College

Selin Yalcindag
Mercyhurst College

Erik Zemljic
Kent State University

We would like to express our sincere appreciation to Gregory Gilpin of Montana State University and Christina Esparza-Luna at Hartnell College for preparing the PowerPoint Presentations, Christopher Blake of Emory University, Deborah Thorsen of Palm Beach State College, Emily Bello, and Stephen Slice of University of South Carolina for their contributions in revising the Testbank, Dan Mizak of Frostburg University for authoring the Instructor's Manual, and Jody Lotz for her detailed edit of the Connect content, as well as Mark Wilson of West Virginia State University, Joseph Euculano of Wilmington University, and Susan Bell of Seminole State College for their careful accuracy review. The text itself and all the accompanying supplements could not make it to the marketplace without the prodigious efforts of the production team at McGraw-Hill. In this regard, we want to extend special thanks to Kelly Delso, who managed the product development process required to produce a text today. Anke Weekes served once again as a valued portfolio director of the entire project. Let us conclude by thanking all the instructors and students who are going to use *The Microeconomy Today* as an introduction to economic principles. We will welcome any reactions and suggestions you'd like to pass on for future editions.

—**Bradley R. Schiller**

—**Karen Gebhardt**

Instructors: Student Success Starts with You

Tools to enhance your unique voice

Want to build your own course? No problem. Prefer to use our turnkey, prebuilt course? Easy. Want to make changes throughout the semester? Sure. And you'll save time with Connect's auto-grading too.

65%
Less Time Grading

Study made personal

Incorporate adaptive study resources like SmartBook® 2.0 into your course and help your students be better prepared in less time. Learn more about the powerful personalized learning experience available in SmartBook 2.0 at **www.mheducation.com/highered/connect/smartbook**

Laptop: McGraw Hill; Woman/dog: George Doyle/Getty Images

Affordable solutions, added value

Make technology work for you with LMS integration for single sign-on access, mobile access to the digital textbook, and reports to quickly show you how each of your students is doing. And with our Inclusive Access program you can provide all these tools at a discount to your students. Ask your McGraw Hill representative for more information.

Padlock: Jobalou/Getty Images

Solutions for your challenges

A product isn't a solution. Real solutions are affordable, reliable, and come with training and ongoing support when you need it and how you want it. Visit **www. supportateverystep.com** for videos and resources both you and your students can use throughout the semester.

Checkmark: Jobalou/Getty Images

Students: Get Learning that Fits You

Effective tools for efficient studying

Connect is designed to make you more productive with simple, flexible, intuitive tools that maximize your study time and meet your individual learning needs. Get learning that works for you with Connect.

Study anytime, anywhere

Download the free ReadAnywhere app and access your online eBook or SmartBook 2.0 assignments when it's convenient, even if you're offline. And since the app automatically syncs with your eBook and SmartBook 2.0 assignments in Connect, all of your work is available every time you open it. Find out more at
www.mheducation.com/readanywhere

> *"I really liked this app—it made it easy to study when you don't have your textbook in front of you."*
>
> - Jordan Cunningham,
>   Eastern Washington University

Calendar: owattaphotos/Getty Images

Everything you need in one place

Your Connect course has everything you need—whether reading on your digital eBook or completing assignments for class, Connect makes it easy to get your work done.

Learning for everyone

McGraw Hill works directly with Accessibility Services Departments and faculty to meet the learning needs of all students. Please contact your Accessibility Services Office and ask them to email accessibility@mheducation.com, or visit
www.mheducation.com/about/accessibility
for more information.

Because learning changes everything.®

Connect Economics Asset Alignment with Bloom's Taxonomy

Schiller/Gebhardt The Microeconomy Today 16e

We Take Students Higher

As a learning science company, we create content that supports higher order thinking skills. Within Connect®, we tag assessments accordingly so you can filter your search, assign it, and receive reporting on it. These content asset types can be associated with one or more levels of Bloom's Taxonomy.

The chart below shows a few of the key assignable economics assets with *McGraw Hill Connect* aligned with Bloom's Taxonomy. Take your students higher by assigning a variety of applications, moving them from simple memorization to concept application.

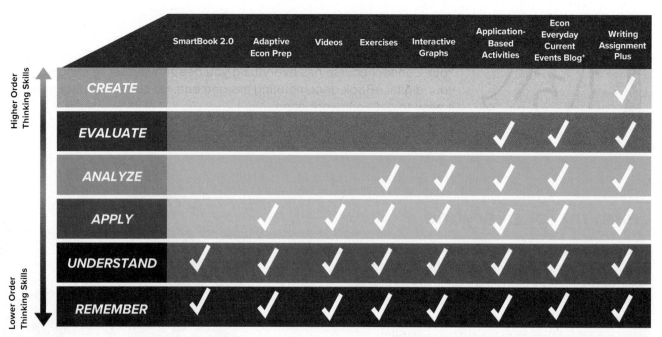

	SmartBook 2.0	Adaptive Econ Prep	Videos	Exercises	Interactive Graphs	Application-Based Activities	Econ Everyday Current Events Blog*	Writing Assignment Plus
CREATE								✓
EVALUATE						✓	✓	✓
ANALYZE				✓	✓	✓	✓	✓
APPLY		✓	✓	✓	✓		✓	✓
UNDERSTAND	✓	✓	✓	✓	✓	✓	✓	✓
REMEMBER	✓	✓	✓	✓	✓	✓	✓	✓

Higher Order Thinking Skills

Lower Order Thinking Skills

* Outside of Connect.

SmartBook 2.0

Adaptively aids students to study more efficiently by highlighting where in the chapter to focus, asking review questions and pointing them to passages in the text until they understand. Assignable and assessable

Adaptive Econ Prep

Math and graphing preparedness assignments help students refresh important prerequisite topics necessary to be successful in economics. New Adaptive Econ Prep Tool provides students just-in-time math and graphing remediation that are prerequisite to success in Economics courses and adapt to each student.

Videos

Tutorial videos provide engaging explanations to help students grasp challenging concepts. Application videos bring economics to life with relevant, real world examples. All videos include closed captioning for accessibility and are assignable with assessment questions for improved retention.

Exercises

Exercises with algorithmic variations provide ample opportunities for students to practice and hone quantitative skills. Graphing Exercises provide opportunities for students to draw, interact with, manipulate, and analyze graphs.

Interactive Graphs

Interactive Graphs provide visual displays of real data and economic concepts for students to manipulate. All graphs are accompanied by assignable Assessment questions and feedback to guide students through the experience of learning to read and interpret graphs and data.

Application-Based Activities

Immersive real-life scenarios engage students and put them in the role of everyday economists. Students practice their economic thinking and problem-solving skills as they apply course concepts and see the implications of their decisions as they go. Each activity is designed as a 15-minute experience, unless students eagerly replay for a better outcome.

ECON Everyday Current Events Blog

Our Econ Everyday blog saves instructors time bringing current, student-centered content into their course all semester long. Short articles, written for principles-level students, is tagged by topic to bring currency into your course. We also provide discussion questions to help you drive the conversation forward. Visit www.econeveryday.com and subscribe for updates.

Writing Assignment Plus

Writing Assignment Plus delivers a learning experience that helps students improve their written communication skills and conceptual understanding. Faculty can assign, monitor, grade, and provide feedback on writing projects efficiently. Built-in grammar and writing review helps students improve writing quality while an originality check helps students correct central plagiarism before submission. End result? Improved workplace skills of writing in critical thinking.

For more information, please visit: **www.mheducation.com/highered/economics**

CONTENTS

THE

MICROECONOMY
TODAY

SIXTEENTH EDITION

Mc
Graw
Hill

PART 1

THE ECONOMIC CHALLENGE

People in Equatorial Guinea want more food, better shelter, and access to safe drinking water. Will they get it? That depends on how well their economy grows and how the fruits of economic growth are distributed. The same is true for middle-class Americans. We want better homes, newer cars, stylish clothes, the latest tech toys, more exotic vacations, and effective vaccines. Will we get these things? Again, that depends on how well the economy grows and how the fruits of economic growth are distributed.

These first few chapters look at what "the economy" is and how it grows. What are the *limits* to the production of goods and services? How does the interplay of market forces and government policy determine how much output will actually be produced and who will get it? How does a nation's capacity to produce goods and services *increase*—so that we can have *more* of the things we want? How will those goods be distributed?

1

"The Economist in Chief"

ZUMA Press, Inc./Alamy Stock Photo

CHAPTER 1

Economics: The Core Issues

People understand that the president of the United States is the Commander in Chief of the armed forces. The president has the ultimate responsibility to decide when and how America's military forces will be deployed. He issues the orders that military officers must carry out. He is given credit for military successes and blame for military failures. He can't "pass the buck" down the line of command.

Less recognized is the president's role as "Economist in Chief." The president is held responsible not just for the *military* security of the United States, but for its *economic* security as well. Although he doesn't have the command powers in the economic arena that he has in the military arena, people expect him to take charge of the economy. They expect the Economist in Chief to keep the economy growing, to create jobs for everyone who wants one, and to prevent prices from rising too fast. Along the way, they expect the Economist in Chief to protect the environment, assure economic justice for all, and protect America's position in the global economy.

That is a tall order, especially in view of the president's limited constitutional powers to make economic policy decisions. The president can propose tax changes, spending priorities, and international trade deals, but the U.S. Congress must approve those policies. The economy is also buffeted by international and natural forces that no president can control. This was abundantly clear in 2020 when the "invisible enemy" of COVID-19 attacked the U.S. and derailed an otherwise prosperous economy. But no matter. Voters hold the Economist in Chief responsible for economic misfortunes, whether or not he is able to single-handedly prevent them, and give him credit for economic success.

What everyone ultimately wants is a prosperous and growing economy: an economy in which people can find good jobs, enjoy rising living standards and wealth, get the education they desire, and enjoy an array of creature comforts. And we want to enjoy this good life while protecting the environment, caring for the poor, and pursuing world peace.

How are we going to get all this? Is "the economy" some sort of perpetual motion machine that will keep churning out more goods and services every year? Clearly not. During the Great Recession of 2008-2009, the economy churned out less output, eliminated jobs, and reduced living standards and wealth. A lot of college graduates had to move back home when they couldn't find jobs. What went wrong?

Even after the Great Recession ended in June 2009, economic pain persisted. The growth of the economy was agonizingly slow, and unemployment remained high for another six years. Was that much distress really necessary? Couldn't the Economist in Chief have fixed these problems? These questions were debated intensely in the 2016 presidential election. Donald Trump promised "to make America great again" by creating more jobs, building more bridges and roads, strengthening the armed forces, and limiting both illegal immigration and unfair foreign competition. Voters decided to give him the opportunity to serve as an Economist in Chief.

The 2020 elections were largely a referendum on President Trump's performance as Economist in Chief. Voters gave Trump high marks for the growth of the economy during his first three years in office. Millions of new jobs had been created, incomes were up, wages were higher, and unemployment had fallen to record lows. Unfortunately, the coronavirus pandemic that swept across the world in early 2020 wiped out nearly all of those prior gains. In November 2020 the U.S. economy was still struggling to regain its footing: millions of Americans were still out of work, incomes were depressed, and people were fearful of a COVID-19 resurgence. They decided to vote for a new Economist in Chief.

The challenge for President Biden is to accelerate the economic recovery, while assuring people that the U.S. is well prepared to deal with any future viral attacks.

To succeed requires a knowledge of what makes an economy tick. How are prices, wages, employment, and other economic outcomes actually determined? Does Wall Street run the system? How about selfish, greedy capitalists? The banks? Or maybe foreign nations? Are incompetent bureaucrats and self-serving politicians the root of our occasional woes? Who, in fact, calls the shots?

The goal of this course is to understand how the economy works. To that end, we want to determine how *markets*—the free-wheeling exchange of goods and services—shape economic outcomes—everything from the price of this text to the national unemployment rate. Then we want to examine the role that government can and does play in (re)shaping economic performance. Do we need the government to assure adequate wages, fair prices, access to health care, or equal educational opportunities? Or can market forces alone give us these desirable outcomes? Once we've explored these issues, we'll be in a better position to evaluate what the Economist in Chief *can* do—and what he *should* do. We'll also better understand how we can make better economic decisions for ourselves.

Limited Resources

We'll start our inquiry with some harsh realities. In a world of unlimited resources, we could have all the goods we desired. We'd have time to do everything we wanted and enough money to buy everything we desired. We could produce enough to make everyone rich while protecting the environment and exploring the universe. The Economist in Chief could deliver everything voters asked for. Unfortunately, we don't live in that utopia: **We live in a world of limited resources.** Those limits are the root of our economic problems. They force us to make difficult decisions about how *best* to use our time, our money, and our resources. These are *economic* decisions.

In this first chapter, we'll examine how the problem of limited resources arises and the kinds of choices it forces us to make. As we'll see, **three core choices confront every nation:**

- **WHAT to produce with our limited resources.**
- **HOW to produce the goods and services we select.**
- **FOR WHOM goods and services are produced—that is, who should get them.**

We also have to decide who should answer these questions. Should people take care of their own health and retirement, or should the government provide a safety net of health care and pensions? Should the government regulate airfares or let the airlines set prices? Should Microsoft decide what features get included in a computer's operating system, or should the government make that decision? Should Facebook decide what personal information is protected, what posts should be permitted, or which ads can be targeted, or should the government make those decisions? Should interest rates be set by private banks alone, or should the government try to control interest rates? The battle over *who* should answer the core questions is often as contentious as the questions themselves.

THE ECONOMY IS US

To learn how the economy works, let's start with a simple truth: *The economy is us.* "The economy" is simply an abstraction referring to the grand sum of all our production and consumption activities. What we collectively produce is what the economy produces; what we collectively consume is what the economy consumes. In this sense, the concept of "the economy" is no more difficult than the concept of "the family." If someone tells you that the Jones family has an annual income of $42,000, you know that the reference is to the collective earnings of all the Joneses. Likewise, when someone reports that the nation's income is $22 trillion per year—as it now is—we should recognize that the reference is to the grand total of everyone's income. If we work fewer hours or get paid less, both family income *and* national income decline.

The same relationship between individual behavior and aggregate behavior applies to specific outputs. If we as individuals insist on driving cars rather than taking public transportation, the economy will produce millions of cars each year and consume vast quantities of oil. If we prefer to stream movies rather than watch them in theaters, then the economy will build fewer theaters and expand streaming services. If more consumers choose plant-based burgers rather than beef burgers, then cattle farms will shrink and plant processing expands. We also make choices on a collective level. We "produce" over $700 billion of national defense (e.g., military personnel, ships, planes, etc.) every year. This is a *choice* we make. If we want a different outcome, then we have to make a different choice. In each case, the output of the economy reflects the collective behavior of the 340 million individuals who participate in the U.S. economy.

We may not always be happy with the output of the economy, but we can't ignore the link between individual action and collective outcomes. If the highways are clogged and the air is polluted, we can't blame someone else for the transportation choices we made.

SCARCITY: THE CORE PROBLEM

Although we can change economic outcomes, we can't have everything we want. If you go to the mall with $20 in your pocket, you can buy only so much. The money in your pocket sets a *limit* to your spending.

The output of the entire economy is also limited. The limits in this case are set not by the amount of money in people's pockets, but by the resources available for producing goods and services. Everyone wants more housing, new schools, better transit systems, and a new car. We also want to explore space and bring safe water to the world's poor. But even a country as rich as the United States can't produce everything people want. So, like every other nation, we have to grapple with the core problem of **scarcity**—the fact that **there aren't enough resources available to satisfy all our desires.**

scarcity: Lack of enough resources to satisfy all desired uses of those resources.

Factors of Production

The resources used to produce goods and services are called **factors of production.** *The four basic factors of production are*

- *Land.*
- *Labor.*
- *Capital.*
- *Entrepreneurship.*

factors of production: Resource inputs used to produce goods and services, e.g., land, labor, capital, entrepreneurship.

These are the *inputs* needed to produce desired *outputs.* To produce this text, for example, we needed paper, printing presses, a building, and lots of labor. We also needed people with good ideas who could put it together. To produce the education you're getting in this class, we need not only a text but a classroom, a teacher, a blackboard, and maybe a computer as well. **Without factors of production, we simply can't produce anything.**

Land. The first factor of production, land, refers not just to the ground but to all natural resources. Crude oil, water, air, and minerals are all included in our concept of "land."

Labor. Labor too has several dimensions. It's not simply a question of how many bodies there are. When we speak of labor as a factor of production, we refer to the skills and abilities to produce goods and services. Hence, both the quantity and the quality of human resources are included in the "labor" factor.

Capital. The third factor of production is capital. In economics the term **capital** refers to final goods produced for use in further production. The residents of fishing villages in southern Thailand, for example, braid huge fishing nets. The sole purpose of these nets is to catch more fish. The nets themselves become a factor of production in obtaining the final goods (fish) that people desire. Thus, they're regarded as *capital.* Blast furnaces used to make steel and desks used to equip offices are also capital inputs.

capital: Final goods produced for use in the production of other goods, such as equipment and structures.

Entrepreneurship. The more land, labor, and capital we have, the more we can produce potential output. A farmer with 10,000 acres, 12 employees, and six tractors can grow more crops than a farmer with half those resources. But there's no guarantee that he will. The farmer with fewer resources may have better ideas about what to plant, when to irrigate, or how to harvest the crops. *It's not just a matter of what resources you have but also of how well you use them.* This is where the fourth factor of production—**entrepreneurship**—comes in. The entrepreneur is the person who sees the opportunity for new or better products and brings together the resources needed for producing them. If it weren't for entrepreneurs, Thai fishers would still be using sticks to catch fish. Without entrepreneurship, farmers would still be milking their cows by hand. If someone hadn't thought of a way to miniaturize electronic circuits, you wouldn't be able to text your friends.

entrepreneurship: The assembling of resources to produce new or improved products and technologies.

The role of entrepreneurs in economic progress is a key issue in the market versus government debate. The British economist John Maynard Keynes argued that free markets unleash the "animal spirits" of entrepreneurs, propelling innovation, technology, and growth. Critics of government regulation argue that government interference in the marketplace, however well intentioned, tends to stifle those very same animal spirits.

Limits to Output

No matter how an economy is organized, there's a limit to how much it can produce. The most evident limit is the amount of resources available for producing goods and services. One reason the United States can produce so much is that it has nearly 4 million square miles of land. Tonga, with less than 300 square miles of land, will never produce as much. The United States also has a population of more than 340 million people. That's a lot less than China (1.4 billion) but far larger than 200 other nations (Tonga has a population of less than 110,000). So an abundance of raw resources gives us the potential to produce a lot of output. But that greater production capacity isn't enough to satisfy all our desires. We're constantly scrambling for additional resources to build more houses, make better movies, and provide more health care. That imbalance between available resources and our wish list is one of the things that make the job of Economist in Chief so difficult: He can't deliver everything people want.

The science of **economics** helps us frame these choices. In a nutshell, economics is the study of how people use scarce resources. How do you decide how much time to spend studying? How does Google decide how many workers to hire? How does Tesla decide whether to use its factories to produce sport utility vehicles or sedans? What share of a nation's resources should be devoted to space exploration, the delivery of health care services, or pollution control? In every instance, **alternative ways of using scarce labor, land, and capital resources are always available, and we have to choose one use over another.**

economics: The study of how best to allocate scarce resources among competing uses.

OPPORTUNITY COSTS

Scientists have long sought to explore every dimension of space. President Kennedy initiated a lunar exploration program that successfully landed men on the moon on July 20, 1969. That only whetted the appetite for further space exploration. President George W. Bush initiated a program to land people on Mars, using the moon as a way station. Scientists believe that the biological, geophysical, and technical knowledge gained from the exploration of Mars will improve life here on Earth. But should we do it? In a world of unlimited resources, the answer would be an easy "yes." But we don't live in that world.

Every time we use scarce resources in one way, we give up the opportunity to use them in other ways. If we use more resources to explore space, we have fewer resources available for producing earthly goods. The forgone earthly goods represent the **opportunity costs** of a Mars expedition. *Opportunity cost is what is given up to get something else.* Even a so-called free lunch has an opportunity cost. The resources used to produce the lunch could have been used to produce something else. A trip to Mars has a much higher opportunity cost. President Obama decided those opportunity costs were too high: He scaled back the Mars programs to make more resources available for Earthly uses (like education, highway construction, and energy development). President Trump agreed. While calling space exploration "wonderful," he observed, "Right now, we have bigger problems—we've got to fix our potholes." He reallocated scarce resources from space exploration to domestic infrastructure (roads, bridges, airports).

Your economics class also has an opportunity cost. The building space used for your economics class can't be used to show movies at the same time. Your professor can't lecture (produce education) and repair motorcycles simultaneously. The decision to use these scarce resources (capital, labor) for an economics class implies producing less of other goods.

Even reading this text is costly. That cost is not measured in dollars and cents. The true (economic) cost is, instead, measured in terms of some alternative activity. What would you like to be doing right now? The more time you spend reading this text, the less time you have available for other uses of your time. The opportunity cost of reading this text is the best alternative use of your scarce time. If you are missing your favorite TV show, we'd say that show is the opportunity cost of reading this text. It is what you gave up to do this assignment. Hopefully, the benefits you get from studying will outweigh that cost. Otherwise, this wouldn't be the best way to use your scarce time.

Guns vs. Butter

One of the most difficult choices nations must make about resource use entails defense spending. After the September 11, 2001, terrorist attacks on the World Trade Center and Pentagon, American citizens overwhelmingly favored an increase in military spending. Even the unpopularity of the wars in Iraq and Afghanistan didn't quell the desire for more national defense. But national defense, like Mars exploration, requires the use of scarce resources; Americans wanted to feel *safe*. But there is a *cost* to assuring safety: The 1.4 million men and women who serve in the armed forces aren't available to build schools, program computers, or teach economics. Similarly, the land, labor, capital, and entrepreneurship devoted to producing military hardware aren't available for producing civilian goods. An *increase* in national defense implies more sacrifices of civilian goods and services. How many schools, hospitals, or cars are we willing to sacrifice in order to "produce" more national security? This is the "guns versus butter" dilemma that all nations confront.

PRODUCTION POSSIBILITIES

The opportunity costs implied by our every choice are easy to visualize. Suppose a nation can produce only two goods, trucks and tanks. To keep things simple, assume that labor (workers) is the only factor of production needed to produce either good. Although other

opportunity cost: The most desired goods or services that are forgone in order to obtain something else.

	Production Options	
	Output of Trucks per Day	Output of Tanks per Day
Option A	5	0
Option B	4	2.0
Option C	3	3.0
Option D	2	3.8
Option E	1	4.5
Option F	0	5.0

TABLE 1.1

A Production Possibilities Schedule

As long as resources are limited, their use entails an opportunity cost. In this case, resources (labor) used to produce trucks can't be used for tank assembly at the same time. Hence, the forgone tanks are the opportunity cost of additional trucks. If all our resources were used to produce trucks (*Option A*), no tanks could be assembled. To produce tanks, we have to reduce truck production.

factors of production (land, machinery) are also needed in actual production, ignoring them for the moment does no harm. Assume further that we have a total of only 10 workers available per day to produce either trucks or tanks. That's a tiny workforce, but it makes the math a lot easier.

Our initial problem is to determine the *limits* of output. How many trucks or tanks *can* be produced in a day with available resources (our 10 workers)?

Before going any further, notice how opportunity costs emerge. If we use all 10 workers to manufacture trucks, how can we produce any tanks? All our workers will be busy building trucks; no one will be available to assemble tanks. In this case, forgone tanks would be the *opportunity cost* of a decision to employ all our resources in truck production.

We still don't know how many trucks could be produced with 10 workers or exactly how many tanks would be forgone by such a decision. To get these answers, we need more details about the production processes involved—specifically, how many workers are required to manufacture either good.

The Production Possibilities Curve

Table 1.1 summarizes the hypothetical choices, or **production possibilities,** that we confront in this case. Suppose we wanted to produce only trucks (i.e., no tanks). Row *A* of the table shows the *maximum* number of trucks we could produce. We have 10 workers available. Suppose it takes 2 workers to manufacture a truck in a day. Then, the *maximum* number of trucks we can produce is 5 per day.

Producing five trucks per day leaves no workers available to produce tanks. Our 10 available workers are all being used to produce trucks. Look at option *A* of Table 1.1; we've got "butter" (trucks) but no "guns" (tanks). If we want tanks, we roll back truck production. The remainder of Table 1.1 illustrates the trade-offs we confront in this simple case. By cutting truck production from five to four trucks per day (Option *B*), we reduce labor use in truck production from 10 workers to 8. That leaves 2 workers available for other uses, including the production of tanks.

If we employ these 2 workers to assemble tanks, we can build two tanks a day. We would then end up on row *B* of the table with four trucks and two tanks per day. What's the opportunity cost of these two tanks? It's the one additional truck (the fifth truck) that we could have produced but didn't.

As we proceed down the rows of Table 1.1, the nature of opportunity costs becomes apparent. Each additional tank built implies the loss (opportunity cost) of truck output. Likewise, every truck produced implies the loss of some tank output.

Choices, Choices These trade-offs between truck and tank production are illustrated in the production possibilities curve of Figure 1.1. *Each point on the production possibilities curve depicts an alternative mix of output* that could be produced. In this case, each point represents

production possibilities: The alternative combinations of final goods and services that could be produced in a given period with all available resources and technology.

FIGURE 1.1

A Production Possibilities Curve

A production possibilities curve (PPC) describes the various output combinations that could be produced in a given time period with available resources and technology. It represents a menu of output choices an economy confronts.

Point *B* indicates that we could produce a *combination* of four trucks and two tanks per day. Alternatively, we could produce one less truck and a third tank by moving to point *C*.

Points *A, D, E,* and *F* illustrate still other output combinations that *could* be produced. This curve is a graphic illustration of the production possibilities schedule in Table 1.1.

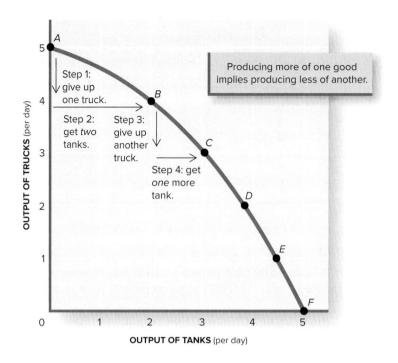

a different combination of trucks and tanks that we could produce in a single day using all available resources (10 workers in this case).

Notice in particular how points *A* through *F* in Figure 1.1 represent the choices described in each row of Table 1.1. At point *A*, we're producing five trucks per day and no tanks. As we move down the curve from point *A*, we're producing fewer trucks and more tanks. At point *B*, truck production has dropped from five to four vehicles per day while tank assembly has increased from zero to two. In other words, we've given up one truck to get two tanks assembled. The opportunity cost of those tanks is the one truck that is given up. A production possibilities curve, then, is simply a graphic summary of production possibilities, as described in Table 1.1. As such, *the production possibilities curve illustrates two essential principles:*

- *Scarce resources.* There's a limit to the amount of output we can produce in a given time period with available resources and technology. In this case, we can't produce more than 5 tanks or 5 trucks.

- *Opportunity costs.* We can obtain additional quantities of any particular good only by reducing the potential production of another good. To get more trucks, we have to produce fewer tanks, and vice versa.

In an economy as vast as the United States, we can, of course, produce millions of trucks and millions of tanks. But that doesn't change the basic principles. Every tank produced uses resources that could have been used to produce something else. This principle helps explain why both presidents Obama and Trump chose to devote fewer resources to space exploration. They felt the opportunity costs (such as reduced education or less infrastructure) were simply too high.

Opportunity costs made headlines again in 2020. When the potential severity of the COVID-19 pandemic became evident, there was a sense of desperation about the availability of ventilators, the breathing machines that severely ill patients needed. The availability of hand sanitizers was also an urgent concern. How could we get *more* of these essential medical supplies? The answer in part was to change the *mix* of output. Auto companies altered their production lines to produce ventilators. Distilleries altered their whiskey-making process in order to produce more high-proof ethanol, the key ingredient in hand sanitizers. By changing production in these ways, the nation moved to a more desirable mix of output (the WHAT outcome).

Increasing Opportunity Costs

The shape of the production possibilities curve reflects another limitation on our choices. Notice how opportunity costs increase as we move along the production possibilities curve. When we cut truck output from five to four (step 1, Figure 1.1), we get two tanks (step 2). When we cut truck production further, however (step 3), we get only one tank per truck given up (step 4). The opportunity cost of tank production is increasing. This process of increasing opportunity cost continues. By the time we give up the last truck (row *F*), tank output increases by only 0.5: We get only half a tank for the last truck given up. These increases in opportunity cost are reflected in the outward bend of the production possibilities curve.

Why do opportunity costs increase? Mostly because it's difficult to move resources from one industry to another. It's easy to transform trucks to tanks on a blackboard. In the real world, however, resources don't adapt so easily. Workers who assemble trucks may not have the right skills for tank assembly. As we continue to transfer labor from one industry to the other, we start getting fewer tanks for every truck we give up.

The difficulties entailed in transferring labor skills, capital, and entrepreneurship from one industry to another are so universal that we often speak of the *law* of *increasing opportunity cost.* This law says that we must give up ever-increasing quantities of other goods and services in order to get more of a particular good. The law isn't based solely on the limited versatility of individual workers. The *mix* of factor inputs makes a difference as well. Truck assembly requires less capital than tank assembly. In a pinch, wheels can be mounted on a truck almost completely by hand, whereas tank treads require more sophisticated machinery. As we move labor from truck assembly to tank assembly, available capital may restrict our output capabilities.

The Cost of North Korea's Military

The production possibilities curve illustrates why the core economic decision about WHAT to produce is so difficult: We can't have everything we want and, worse yet, getting more of one thing implies getting less of something else. We are forced to make difficult choices.

Consider, for example, North Korea's decision to maintain a large military. North Korea is a relatively small country: Its population of 26 million ranks 50th in the world. Yet North Korea maintains the fourth-largest army in the world and continues to develop a nuclear weapons capability. To do so, it allocates as much as 20 percent of all its resources to feeding, clothing, and equipping its military forces. As a consequence, there aren't enough resources available to produce food. Without adequate machinery, seeds, fertilizer, or irrigation, North Korea's farmers can't produce enough food to feed the population (see World View "North Korean Food Rations Cut"). As Figure 1.2 illustrates, the opportunity cost of "guns" in Korea is a lot of needed "butter."

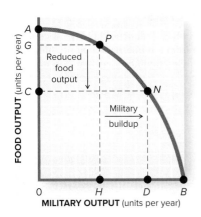

FIGURE 1.2

The Cost of War

North Korea devotes as much as 20 percent of its output to the military. The opportunity cost of this decision is reduced output of food. As the military expands from 0H to 0D, food output drops from 0G to 0C.

WORLD VIEW

WORLD'S LARGEST ARMIES

Rank	Country	Active Military
1	China	2,183,000
2	India	1,362,000
3	United States	1,282,000
4	North Korea	1,280,000
5	Russia	1,014,000
6	Pakistan	654,000
7	South Korea	525,000
8	Iran	523,000
9	Turkey	510,600
10	Vietnam	482,000

Source: U.S. Central Intelligence Agency 2019.

CRITICAL ANALYSIS: Nations "produce" national defense by employing land, labor, and capital in their armed forces. The **opportunity cost** of those "guns" is less "butter."

What is the opportunity cost of North Korea's army?

Ed Jones/AFP/Getty Images

During World War II, the United States confronted a similar trade-off. In 1944 nearly 40 percent of all U.S. output was devoted to the military. Civilian goods were so scarce that they had to be rationed. Staples like butter, sugar, and gasoline were doled out in small quantities. Even golf balls were rationed. In North Korea, golf balls would be a luxury even without a military buildup. As the share of North Korea's output devoted to the military increased, even basic food production became more difficult. (See World View "North Korean Food Rations Cut.")

WORLD VIEW

NORTH KOREAN FOOD RATIONS CUT

The United Nations estimates that 40 percent of North Korea's population—10.4 million people—experienced "food insecurity" in 2019. Most North Koreans depend on government-supplied food rations of rice, potatoes, and kimchi (fermented cabbage). Due to the worst harvests in a decade, however, the government slashed daily food rations from 380 grams (13.4 ounces) of food to only 300 grams (10.6 ounces). That is only half of the U.N. recommendation of at least 600 grams per day.

Source: United Nations Food and Agriculture Organization and news reports of May–November 2019.

NORTH KOREA RESUMES MISSILE LAUNCHES

After an 18-month hiatus, North Korea resumed ballistic missile launches in May. Since then, they have fired off seven more missiles, including one from a reputed submarine. Although keeping his promise not to test long-range missiles while continuing nuclear negotiations with President Trump, Kim Jong-un has vowed to strengthen North Korea's military capabilities. Analysts estimate that North Korea is now spending close to $2 billion a year on its nuclear and missile programs.

Source: Media reports, May–December 2019.

CRITICAL ANALYSIS: North Korea's inability to feed itself is partly due to maintaining its large army: Resources used for the military aren't available for producing food (**opportunity costs**).

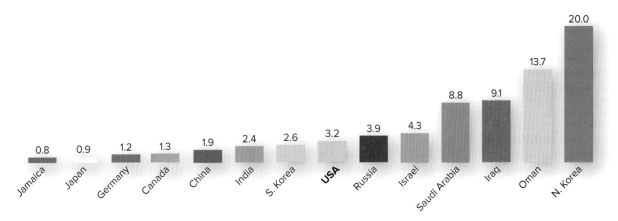

Percentage of Output Allocated to Military

FIGURE 1.3

The Military Share of Output

The share of total output allocated to the military indicates the opportunity cost of maintaining an army. North Korea has the highest cost, using one-fifth of its resources for military purposes. Although China and the United States have much larger armies, their military share of output is much smaller.

Source: Stockholm International Peace Research Institute and U.S. Central Intelligence Agency (2018 data).

Figure 1.3 illustrates how other nations divide available resources between military and civilian production. The $650 billion the United States now spends on national defense absorbs only 3.2 percent of total output. This made the opportunity costs of the post-9/11 military buildup and the wars in Iraq and Afghanistan less painful. By contrast, North Korea's commitment to military spending (20 percent) implies a very high opportunity cost.

Efficiency

Not all of the choices on the production possibilities curve are equally desirable. They are, however, all *efficient*. **Efficiency** means squeezing *maximum* output out of available resources. Every point of the PPC satisfies this condition. Although the *mix* of output changes as we move around the production possibilities curve (Figures 1.1 and 1.2), at every point we are getting as much *total* output as physically possible. Because efficiency in production means simply getting the most from what you've got, **every point on the production possibilities curve is efficient.** At every point on the curve, we are using all available resources in the best way we know how.

efficiency: Maximum output of a good from the resources used in production.

Inefficiency

There's no guarantee, of course, that we'll always use resources so efficiently. *A production possibilities curve shows* **potential** *output,* **not** *actual output.* If we're inefficient, actual output will be less than that potential. This happens. In the real world, workers sometimes loaf on the job. Or they call in sick and go to a baseball game instead of working. Managers don't always give the clearest directions or stay in touch with advancing technology. Even students sometimes fail to put forth their best effort on homework assignments. This kind of slippage can prevent us from achieving maximum production. When that happens, we end up *inside* the PPC rather than *on* it.

Point *Y* in Figure 1.4 illustrates the consequences of inefficient production. At point *Y*, we're producing only three trucks and two tanks. This is less than our potential. We could assemble a third tank without cutting back truck production (point *C*). Or we could get an extra truck without sacrificing any tank output (point *B*). Instead we're producing *inside* the production possibilities curve at point *Y*. **Whenever we're producing inside the production possibilities curve, we are forgoing the opportunity of producing (and consuming) additional output.**

FIGURE 1.4

Points Inside and Outside the PPC Curve

Points outside the production possibilities curve (point *X*) are unattainable with available resources and technology. Points inside the PPC (point *Y*) represent the incomplete use of available resources. Only points on the PPC (*A, B, C*) represent maximum use of our production capabilities.

All points on the PPC fully utilize available resources.

Unemployment

We can end up inside the production possibilities curve by utilizing resources inefficiently or simply by not using all available resources. This happened repeatedly in the Great Recession of 2008–2009. In October 2009, more than 15 million Americans were unemployed (see Front Page Economics "Jobless Workers Outnumber Manufacturing Workers"). These men and women were ready, willing, and available to work, but no one hired them. As a result, we were stuck *inside* the PPC, producing less output than we could have (like point *Y* in Figure 1.4). The same problem surfaced in 2020 when the COVID-19 pandemic threw millions of Americans out of work and pushed the economy well below its production possibilities. The goal of U.S. economic policy is to create more jobs and keep the United States on its production possibilities curve.

Economic Growth

The challenge of getting to the production possibilities curve increases with each passing day. People are born every day. As they age, they enter the labor force as new workers. In the United States, over 1 million new workers enter the marketplace every year. They want jobs,

FRONT PAGE ECONOMICS

JOBLESS WORKERS OUTNUMBER MANUFACTURING WORKERS

The number of jobless workers last month surpassed 15 million, according to the U.S. Bureau of Labor Statistics. The number of unemployed persons has risen every month since mid-2007 and is now double the level of unemployment that existed when the Great Recession started. Those 15 million *unemployed* workers now exceed the number of workers actually holding jobs in U.S. manufacturing.

Source: U.S. Bureau of Labor Statistics, October 2009.

CRITICAL ANALYSIS: In 2009 the U.S. economy was producing inside its production possibilities curve (like point *Y* in Figure 1.4), leaving millions of workers jobless and total output well below its potential. Our goal is to produce at a point on the PPC (**efficiency**).

FIGURE 1.5
Growth: Increasing Production Possibilities

A production possibilities curve is based on *available* resources and technology. If more resources or better technology becomes available, production possibilities will increase. This economic growth is illustrated by the *shift* from *PP*₁ to *PP*₂.

and we want the output they can produce. Technology keeps advancing every year, too. That means every worker can produce *more* output. These increases in available labor and technology keep pushing the production possibilities curve outward. This **economic growth** is a good thing in the sense that it allows us to produce more goods and raise living standards. With economic growth, countries can have more guns *and* more butter (see Figure 1.5). But to get the benefits of that growth, we have to keep creating more and more jobs: We are always chasing a moving target. Nations that fail to achieve that growth risk declining living standards, as population growth exceeds output growth. That is a common problem in many of the world's poorest nations.

economic growth: An increase in output (real GDP); an expansion of production possibilities.

THREE BASIC DECISIONS

Production possibilities define the output choices that a nation confronts. From these choices, every nation must make some basic decisions. As we noted at the beginning of this chapter, the three core economic questions are

- *WHAT to produce.*
- *HOW to produce.*
- *FOR WHOM to produce.*

What

There are millions of points along a production possibilities curve, and each one represents a different mix of output. Unfortunately, we can choose only *one* of these points at any time. The point we choose determines what mix of output actually gets produced. That choice determines how many guns are produced, and how much butter—or how many space expeditions are taken and how many sewage treatment facilities get built.

The production possibilities curve itself doesn't tell us which mix of output is best; it just lays out a menu of available choices. It's up to us to pick out the one and only mix of output that will be produced at a given time. This WHAT decision is a fundamental decision every nation must make.

How

Decisions must also be made about HOW to produce. Should we generate electricity by burning coal, smashing atoms, or harnessing solar power? Should we harvest ancient forests even if that destroys endangered owls or other animal species? Should we dump municipal and industrial waste into nearby rivers, or should we dispose of it in some other way? Should we use children to harvest crops and stitch clothes, or should we use only adult labor? There are lots of different ways of producing goods and services, and someone has to make a decision about which production methods to use. The HOW decision is a question not just of efficiency but of social values as well.

For Whom

After we've decided what to produce and how, we must address a third basic question: FOR WHOM? Who is going to get the output produced? Should everyone get an equal share? Should everyone wear the same clothes and drive identical cars? Should some people get to enjoy seven-course banquets while others forage in garbage cans for food scraps? How should the goods and services an economy produces be distributed? Are we satisfied with the way output is now distributed?

THE MECHANISMS OF CHOICE

Answers to the questions of WHAT, HOW, and FOR WHOM largely define an economy. But who formulates the answers? Who actually decides which goods are produced, what technologies are used, or how incomes are distributed?

The Invisible Hand of a Market Economy

Adam Smith had an answer back in 1776. In his classic work *The Wealth of Nations,* the Scottish economist Smith said the "invisible hand" determines what gets produced, how, and for whom. The invisible hand he referred to wasn't a creature from a science fiction movie but, instead, a characterization of the way markets work.

Consider the decision about how many cars to produce in the United States. Who makes that decision? There's no "auto czar" who dictates how many vehicles will be produced this year. Not even General Motors can make such a decision. Instead, the *market* decides how many cars to produce. Millions of consumers signal their desire to have a car by browsing the Internet, visiting showrooms, and buying cars. Their purchases flash a green light to producers, who see the potential to earn more profits. To do so, they'll increase auto output. If consumers stop buying cars, profits will disappear. Producers will respond by reducing output, laying off workers, and even closing factories, as they did during the recession of 2008–2009 and again in 2020.

Notice how the invisible hand moves us along the production possibilities curve. If consumers demand more cars, the mix of output will include more cars and fewer of other goods. If auto production is scaled back, the displaced autoworkers will end up producing other goods and services, changing the mix of output in the opposite direction. In this scenario, consumers and producers are collectively deciding WHAT the economy will produce.

Adam Smith's invisible hand is now called the **market mechanism.** Notice that it doesn't require any direct contact between consumers and producers. Communication is indirect, transmitted by market prices and sales. Indeed, *the essential feature of the market mechanism is the price signal.* If you want something and have sufficient income, you can buy it. If enough people do the same thing, the total sales of that product will rise, and perhaps its price will as well. Producers, seeing sales and prices rise, will want to exploit this profit potential. To do so, they'll attempt to acquire a larger share of available resources and use it to produce the goods we desire. That's how the "invisible hand" works.

The market mechanism can also answer the HOW question. To maximize their profits, producers seek the lowest-cost method of producing a good. By observing prices in the marketplace, they can identify the cheapest method and adopt it.

The market mechanism can also resolve the FOR WHOM question. A market distributes goods to the highest bidder. Individuals who are willing and able to pay the most for a product tend to get it in a pure market economy. That's why someone else—not you—is driving the newest McLaren 720S.

market mechanism: The use of market prices and sales to signal desired outputs (or resource allocations).

How does the market decide who gets this car?

somchai choochat/Shutterstock

Adam Smith was so impressed with the ability of the market mechanism to answer the basic WHAT, HOW, and FOR WHOM questions that he urged government to "leave it alone" (laissez faire). **Adam Smith believed the price signals and responses of the marketplace were likely to do a better job of allocating resources than any government could.**

laissez faire: The doctrine of "leave it alone," of nonintervention by government in the market mechanism.

Government Intervention

The laissez-faire policy Adam Smith favored has always had its share of critics. The German economist Karl Marx emphasized how free markets tend to concentrate wealth and power in the hands of the few at the expense of the many. As he saw it, unfettered markets permit the capitalists (those who own the machinery and factories) to enrich themselves while the proletariat (the workers) toil long hours for subsistence wages. **Marx argued that the government not only had to intervene but had to *own* all the means of production**—the factories, the machinery, the land—in order to avoid savage inequalities. In *Das Kapital* (1867) and the revolutionary *Communist Manifesto* (1848), he laid the foundation for a communist state in which the government would be the master of economic outcomes.

The British economist John Maynard Keynes offered a less drastic solution. The market, he conceded, was pretty efficient in organizing production and building better mousetraps. However, individual producers and workers had no control over the broader economy. The cumulative actions of so many economic agents could easily tip the economy in the wrong direction. A completely unregulated market might veer off in one direction and then another as producers all rushed to increase output at the same time or throttled back production in a herdlike manner. The government, Keynes reasoned, could act like a pressure gauge, letting off excess steam or building it up as the economy needed. With the government maintaining overall balance in the economy, the market could live up to its performance expectations. While assuring a stable, full-employment environment, the government might also be able to redress excessive inequalities. **In Keynes's view, government should play an active but not all-inclusive role in managing the economy.**

Conservatives vs. Liberals

These historical views shed perspective on today's political debates. The core of most debates is some variation of the WHAT, HOW, or FOR WHOM questions. Much of the debate is how these questions should be answered. Conservatives favor Adam Smith's laissez-faire approach, with minimal government interference in the markets. Liberals, by contrast, think government intervention is needed to improve market outcomes. Conservatives resist workplace regulation, price controls, and minimum wages because such interventions might impair market efficiency. Liberals argue that such interventions temper the excesses of the market and promote both equity and efficiency.

World Opinion. The debate over how best to manage the economy is not unique to the United States. **Countries around the world confront the same choice between reliance on the market and reliance on the government.** Public opinion clearly favors the market system, as World View "Market Reliance vs. Government Reliance?" documents. Yet few countries have ever relied exclusively on either the markets or the government to manage their economy.

Degrees of Market Reliance. The World View "Index of Economic Freedom" categorizes nations by the extent of their actual market reliance. Hong Kong scores high on this index because its tax rates are relatively low, the public sector is comparatively small, and there are few restrictions on private investment or trade. By contrast, North Korea scores extremely low because the government owns all property, directly allocates resources, sets wages, rations food, and limits trade. In other words, Hong Kong is the most market-reliant; North Korea is the most government-reliant.

WORLD VIEW

MARKET RELIANCE VS. GOVERNMENT RELIANCE?

A public opinion poll conducted in countries from around the world found a striking global consensus that the free market economic system is best. In all but one country polled, a majority or plurality agreed with the statement that "the free enterprise system and free market economy is the best system on which to base the future of the world."

Source: GlobeScan Toronto–London–San Francisco 2010.

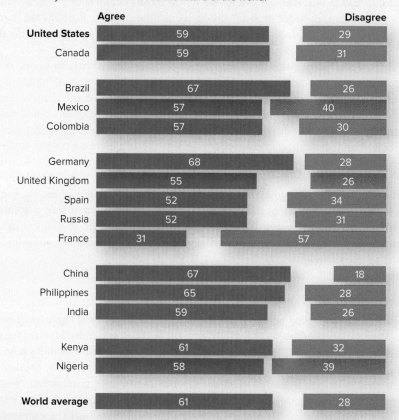

The free enterprise system and free market economy is the best system on which to base the future of the world.

	Agree	Disagree
United States	59	29
Canada	59	31
Brazil	67	26
Mexico	57	40
Colombia	57	30
Germany	68	28
United Kingdom	55	26
Spain	52	34
Russia	52	31
France	31	57
China	67	18
Philippines	65	28
India	59	26
Kenya	61	32
Nigeria	58	39
World average	61	28

CRITICAL ANALYSIS: Most people around the world believe that markets do a good job of answering the core questions of WHAT, HOW, and FOR WHOM. They favor a **laissez-faire** approach, albeit with government safeguards.

The Heritage rankings simply *describe* differences in the extent of market/government reliance across different nations. By themselves, they don't tell us which mix of market and government reliance is best. Moreover, the individual rankings change over time. In 1989 Russia began a massive transformation from a state-controlled economy to a more market-oriented economy. Some of the former Soviet republics (e.g., Estonia) became relatively free, while others (e.g., Turkmenistan) still rely on extensive government control of the economy. China has greatly expanded the role of private markets in the last 20 years, and Cuba is grudgingly moving in the same direction in fits and starts. Venezuela has moved in the opposite direction, with sharply increased government control of production and prices.

WORLD VIEW

INDEX OF ECONOMIC FREEDOM

Singapore ranks number one among the world's nations in economic freedom. It achieves that status with low tax rates, free-trade policies, minimal government regulation, and secure property rights. These and other economic indicators place Singapore at the top of the Heritage Foundation's 2020 country rankings by the degree of "economic freedom." The "most free" and the "least free" (repressed) economies on the list of 186 countries are listed here:

Greatest Economic Freedom	Least Economic Freedom
Singapore	North Korea
Hong Kong	Venezuela
New Zealand	Cuba
Australia	Eritrea
Switzerland	Republic of Congo
Ireland	Bolivia
United Kingdom	Zimbabwe
Denmark	Sudan

Source: *2020 Index of Economic Freedom*, Washington, DC: Heritage Foundation, 2020.

CRITICAL ANALYSIS: Nations differ in how much they rely on the **market mechanism** or government intervention to shape economic outcomes. Nations that rely the least on government intervention score highest ("most free") on this Index of Economic Freedom.

Notice that the United States is not on the World View list. Although the United States relies heavily on private markets to make WHAT, HOW, and FOR WHOM decisions, it lags behind Hong Kong, Canada, and other nations on the Heritage Index. In 2020 the United States came in 17th, down a notch from earlier years. That modest decline was largely due to the increased international trade barriers erected by President Trump. This tug-of-war between more government regulation and more market reliance continues—in both public opinion and the U.S. Congress.

A Mixed Economy

No one advocates *complete* dependence on markets, nor *total* government control of economic resources. Neither Adam Smith's invisible hand nor the governments' very visible hand always works perfectly. As a result, *the United States, like most nations, uses a combination of market signals and government directives to direct economic outcomes.* The resulting compromises are called **mixed economies.**

The reluctance of countries around the world to rely exclusively on either market signals or government directives is due to the recognition that both mechanisms can and do fail on occasion. As we've seen, market signals are capable of answering the three core questions of WHAT, HOW, and FOR WHOM. But the answers may not be the best possible ones.

mixed economy: An economy that uses both market signals and government directives to allocate goods and resources.

Market Failure

When market signals don't give the best possible answers to the WHAT, HOW, and FOR WHOM questions, we say that the market mechanism has *failed.* Specifically, **market failure** means that the invisible hand has failed to achieve the best possible outcomes. If the market fails, we end up with the wrong (*sub*optimal) mix of output, too much unemployment, polluted air, or an inequitable distribution of income.

market failure: An imperfection in the market mechanism that prevents optimal outcomes.

In a market-driven economy, for example, producers will select production methods based on cost. Cost-driven production decisions, however, may encourage a factory to spew pollution into the environment rather than to use cleaner but more expensive methods of production. The resulting pollution may be so bad that society ends up worse off as a result of the extra production. In such a case we may need government intervention to force better answers to the WHAT and HOW questions.

We could also let the market decide who gets to consume cigarettes. In that laissez-faire situation, anyone with enough money to buy a pack of cigarettes would then be entitled to smoke. What if, however, children aren't experienced enough to balance the risks of smoking against the pleasures? What if nonsmokers are harmed by secondhand smoke? In this case as well, the market's answer to the FOR WHOM question might not be optimal.

After the experience with the coronavirus in 2020, nearly everyone recognized that markets alone cannot assure optimal outcomes. While secondhand smoke is a significant problem for unregulated markets, COVID-19 contagion is far more deadly. If we had relied on free choice to determine how much social distancing or treatment was undertaken, many more people would have died from COVID-19. There was near universal consensus that government intervention (regulation, subsidized care, etc.) was needed to get better results.

Then there is the question of fairness. What if the market mechanism distributed incomes so unequally that some people couldn't afford basic necessities while others engaged in conspicuous consumption? Would that be *fair?* The market itself doesn't worry about fairness, but society might. In that event, we might want the government to intervene to change the answer to the FOR WHOM question.

Government Failure

Clearly, government intervention might be needed to correct market failures. If successful, the resulting mix of market signals and government directives would be an improvement over a purely market-driven economy. But government intervention may fail as well. **Government failure** occurs when government intervention fails to improve market outcomes or actually makes them worse.

Government failure often occurs in unintended ways. For example, the government may intervene to force an industry to clean up its pollution. The government's directives may impose such high costs that the industry closes factories and lays off workers. Some cutbacks in output might be appropriate, but they could also prove excessive. The government might also mandate pollution control technologies that are too expensive or even obsolete. None of this has to happen, but it might. If it does, government failure will have worsened economic outcomes.

The government might also fail if it interferes with the market's answer to the FOR WHOM question. For 50 years, communist China distributed goods by government directive, not market performance. Incomes were more equal, but uniformly low. To increase output and living standards, China turned to market incentives. As entrepreneurs responded to these incentives, living standards rose dramatically—even while inequality increased. That surge in living standards made the vast majority of Chinese believers in the power of free markets (see the World View appearing earlier in this chapter).

Excessive taxes and transfer payments can also worsen economic outcomes. If the government raises taxes on the rich to pay welfare benefits for the poor, neither the rich nor the poor may see much purpose in working. In that case, the attempt to give everybody a "fair" share of the pie might end up shrinking the size of the pie. If that happened, society could end up worse off.

Seeking Balance

None of these failures has to occur. But they might. ***The challenge for any society is to minimize economic failures by selecting the appropriate balance of market signals and government directives.*** This isn't an easy task. To begin with, it requires that we share some common perspectives about what mix of output is best, what the balance between production and environmental

government failure:
Government intervention that fails to improve economic outcomes.

protection should be, and how much inequality is fair. On a more mundane level, it also requires that we know how markets work and why they sometimes fail. We also need to know what policy options the government has and how and when they might work. That's a lot to ask for.

WHAT ECONOMICS IS ALL ABOUT

Understanding how economies function is the basic purpose of studying economics. We seek to know how an economy is organized, how it behaves, and how successfully it achieves its basic objectives. Then, if we're lucky, we can discover better ways of attaining those same objectives.

Ends vs. Means

Economists don't formulate an economy's objectives. Instead they focus on the *means* available for achieving given *goals.* In 1978, for example, the U.S. Congress identified "full employment" as a major economic goal. Congress then directed future presidents (and their economic advisers) to formulate policies that would enable us to achieve full employment. The economist's job is to help design policies that will best achieve this and other economic goals.

The same distinction between ends and means is integral to your own life. Your *goal* (the ends) may be to achieve a specific career. The immediate question is how best to achieve that goal (the means). Should you major in economics? Take computer science? Study art history? Surely, you hope that the course choices you make will best help you attain your career goals. Economists can help select those courses based on studies of other students, their majors, and their career outcomes.

Normative vs. Positive Analysis

The distinction between ends and means is mirrored in the difference between *normative* analysis and *positive* analysis. Normative analysis incorporates subjective judgments about what *ought* to be done. Positive analysis focuses on how things might be done without subjective judgments of what is "best." The Heritage Index of Economic Freedom (World View), for example, constitutes a *positive* analysis to the extent that it objectively describes global differences in the extent of market reliance. That effort entails collecting, sorting, and ranking mountains of data. Heritage slides into *normative* analysis when it suggests that market reliance is tantamount to "economic freedom" and inherently superior to more government intervention—that markets are good and governments are bad.

Debates over the core FOR WHOM question likewise reflect both positive and normative analysis. A positive analysis would observe that the U.S. incomes are very "unequal," with the richest 20 percent of the population getting half of all income (see table in Figure 2.3). That's an observable fact—that is, positive analysis. To characterize that same distribution as "inequitable" or "unfair" is to transform (positive) fact into (normative) judgment. Economists are free, of course, to offer their judgments but must be careful to distinguish positive and normative perspectives.

Macro vs. Micro

The study of economics is typically divided into two parts: macroeconomics and microeconomics. **Macroeconomics** focuses on the behavior of an entire economy—the "big picture." In macroeconomics we worry about such national goals as full employment, control of inflation, and economic growth, without worrying about the well-being or behavior of specific individuals or firms. The essential concern of macroeconomics is to understand and improve the performance of the economy as a whole.

Microeconomics is concerned with the details of this big picture. In microeconomics we focus on the individuals, firms, and government agencies that actually compose the larger economy. Our interest here is in the behavior of individual economic actors. What are their goals? How can they best achieve these goals with their limited resources? How will they respond to various incentives and opportunities?

macroeconomics: The study of aggregate economic behavior, of the economy as a whole.

microeconomics: The study of individual behavior in the economy, of the components of the larger economy.

A primary concern of *macro*economics, for example, is to determine how much money, *in total,* consumers will spend on goods and services. In *micro*economics, the focus is much narrower. In micro, attention is paid to purchases of *specific* goods and services rather than just aggregated totals. Macro likewise concerns itself with the level of *total* business investment, while micro examines how *individual* businesses make their investment decisions.

Although they operate at different levels of abstraction, macro and micro are intrinsically related. Macro (aggregate) outcomes depend on micro behavior, and micro (individual) behavior is affected by macro outcomes. One can't fully understand how an economy works until one understands how all the individual participants behave. But just as you can drive a car without knowing how its engine is constructed, you can observe how an economy runs without completely disassembling it. In macroeconomics we observe that the car goes faster when the accelerator is depressed and that it slows when the brake is applied. That's all we need to know in most situations. At times, however, the car breaks down. When it does, we have to know something more about how the pedals work. This leads us into micro studies. How does each part work? Which ones can or should be fixed?

Our interest in microeconomics is motivated by more than our need to understand how the larger economy works. The "parts" of the economic engine are people. To the extent that we care about the well-being of individuals, we have a fundamental interest in microeconomic behavior and outcomes. In this regard, we examine how individual consumers and business firms seek to achieve specific goals in the marketplace. The goals aren't always related to output. Gary Becker won the 1992 Nobel Prize in Economics for demonstrating how economic principles also affect decisions to marry, to have children, to engage in criminal activities—or even to complete homework assignments in an economics class.

Theory vs. Reality

The economy is much too vast and complex to describe and explain in one course (or one lifetime). We need to simplify it. To do so, we focus on basic relationships, ignoring annoying details. We develop basic principles of economic behavior and then use those principles to predict and explain economic events. This means that we formulate theories, or *models,* of economic behavior and then use those theories to evaluate and design economic policy.

Our model of consumer behavior assumes, for example, that people buy less of a good when its price rises. In reality, however, people *may* buy *more* of a good at increased prices, especially if those high prices create a certain snob appeal or if prices are expected to increase still further. In predicting consumer responses to price increases, we typically ignore such possibilities by *assuming* that the price of the good in question is the *only* thing that changes. This assumption of "other things remaining equal" (unchanged) (in Latin, ***ceteris paribus***) allows us to make straightforward predictions. If instead we described consumer responses to increased prices in any and all circumstances (allowing everything to change at once), every prediction would be accompanied by a book full of exceptions and qualifications. We'd look more like lawyers than economists.

Although the assumption of *ceteris paribus* makes it easier to formulate economic theory and policy, it also increases the risk of error. If other things do change in significant ways, our predictions (and policies) may fail. But like weather forecasters, we continue to make predictions, knowing that occasional failure is inevitable. In so doing, we're motivated by the conviction that it's better to be approximately right than to be dead wrong.

Imperfect Knowledge. One last word of warning before you read further. Economics claims to be a science in pursuit of basic truths. We want to understand and explain how the economy works without getting tangled up in subjective value judgments. This may be an impossible task. First, it's not clear where the truth lies. For more than 200 years economists have been arguing about what makes the economy tick. None of the competing theories has performed spectacularly well. Indeed, few economists have successfully predicted major economic events with any consistency. Even annual forecasts of inflation, unemployment,

ceteris paribus: The assumption of nothing else changing.

and output are regularly in error. Worse still, never-ending arguments about what caused a major economic event continue long after it occurs. In fact, economists are still arguing over the primary causes of the Great Depression of the 1930s!

In view of all these debates and uncertainties, don't expect to learn everything there is to know about the economy today in this text or course. Our goals are more modest. We want to develop a reasonable perspective on economic behavior, an understanding of basic principles. With this foundation, you should acquire a better view of how the economy works. Daily news reports on economic events should make more sense. Congressional debates on tax and budget policies should take on more meaning. You may even develop some insights that you can apply toward running a business, planning a career, or simply managing your scarce time and money more efficiently.

DECISIONS FOR TOMORROW

What Is the Cost of Going Green?

People are worried about the future of the planet. Continued population and production growth have raised concerns about global warming. The earth's temperature has risen over time, and scientists are worried that the warming trend is accelerating. In 2018, the United Nations warned that weather patterns will become more extreme, droughts will spread, and the solar ice field will melt if we don't curb the greenhouse gas emissions that are a root cause of global warming. Those warnings have spawned calls for "going green," that is, replacing carbon-based energy sources with clean, renewable, and zero-emissions energy sources like wind and solar. A proposed Green New Deal calls for the complete elimination of carbon-based energy by 2030.

Are wind farms a free good?

xxlphoto/123RF

That is a tall order. The United States now gets 80 percent of its energy from coal, petroleum, and natural gas—all carbon-based fuels. We get another 10 percent from nuclear power. Only 10 percent or so comes from renewable sources like wind and solar. So, while everyone might share the goal of an emissions-free future, we have to ask how we get from here to there.

Opportunity Costs. It's easy to get excited about a solar-powered future. But before we jump on the solar bandwagon, we have to at least consider the costs involved. Sure, the sun's rays are free. But you need a lot of capital investment to harness that solar power. Solar panels on the roof don't come free. Nor do solar-powered electrical charging stations, solar power plants, or the electrical grids that distribute electricity to users. To develop a nationwide, complete solar power infrastructure would cost *trillions* of dollars. That's only the beginning. We'd also have to change the technology embedded in our transportation systems, office buildings, homes, and even farms. Retrofitting existing infrastructure would cost billions of dollars. Building new transportation systems would cost even more. The dollar cost of "going green" would be tens of trillions.

In economics we don't think in terms of papers dollars, but instead in terms of opportunity costs. Paper money doesn't build solar panels; it takes real factors of production—land, labor, capital, and entrepreneurship. Those resources—worth trillions of dollars—could be used to produce something else. If we invested that many resources in medical technology, we might cure cancer, find an antidote for the COVID-19 virus, and maybe even eradicate the flu. Investing that many resources in education might make college not only more enjoyable but a lot more productive as well. To invest all those resources in renewable energy implies that "going green" trumps all other social goals. That's a *normative* judgment that not everyone embraces. Many people worry more about their education, their homes, national defense, and the nation's infrastructure than the harm that conventional energy sources inflict on the environment. In deciding whether and how intensively to develop clean energy, we have to assess opportunity costs—what goods and services we implicitly forsake in order to "go green."

SUMMARY

- Scarcity is a basic fact of economic life. Factors of production (land, labor, capital, entrepreneurship) are scarce in relation to our desires for goods and services. **LO1-1**
- All economic activity entails opportunity costs. Factors of production (resources) used to produce one output cannot simultaneously be used to produce something else. When we choose to produce one thing, we forsake the opportunity to produce some other good or service. **LO1-2**
- A production possibilities curve (PPC) illustrates the limits to production—the various combinations of goods and services that could be produced in a given period if all available resources and technology are used efficiently. The PPC also illustrates opportunity costs—what is given up to get more of something else. **LO1-3**
- The bent shape of the PPC reflects the law of increasing opportunity costs: Increasing quantities of any good can be obtained only by sacrificing ever-increasing quantities of other goods. **LO1-3**
- Inefficient or incomplete use of resources will fail to attain production possibilities. Additional resources or better technologies will expand them. This is the essence of economic growth. **LO1-3**
- Every country must decide WHAT to produce, HOW to produce, and FOR WHOM to produce with its limited resources. **LO1-4**
- The study of economics focuses on the broad question of resource allocation. Macroeconomics is concerned with allocating the resources of an entire economy to achieve aggregate economic goals (e.g., full employment). Microeconomics focuses on the behavior and goals of individual market participants. **LO1-4**
- The WHAT, HOW, and FOR WHOM choices can be made by the market mechanism or by government directives. Most nations are mixed economies, using a combination of these two choice mechanisms. **LO1-5**
- Market failure exists when market signals generate suboptimal outcomes. Government failure occurs when government intervention worsens economic outcomes. The challenge for economic theory and policy is to find the mix of market signals and government directives that best fulfills our social and economic goals. **LO1-5**

Key Terms

scarcity	production possibilities	market failure
factors of production	efficiency	government failure
capital	economic growth	macroeconomics
entrepreneurship	market mechanism	microeconomics
economics	laissez faire	*ceteris paribus*
opportunity cost	mixed economy	

Questions for Discussion

1. What opportunity costs did you incur in reading this chapter? If you read another chapter today, would your opportunity cost (per chapter) increase? Explain. **LO1-2**
2. How much time *could* you spend on homework in a day? How much do you spend? How do you decide? **LO1-2**
3. What's the real cost of a "free lunch," as mentioned in the discussion of "Opportunity Costs?" **LO1-2**
4. How might a nation's production possibilities be affected by the following? **LO1-3**
   (*a*) Discovery of a new oil field.
   (*b*) A decrease in immigration.
   (*c*) An increase in military spending.
   (*d*) More job training.
5. What was the opportunity cost of more hand sanitizers during the COVID-19 crisis? **LO1-2**
6. Who would go to college in a completely private (market) college system? How does government intervention change this FOR WHOM outcome? **LO1-4**
7. Why do people around the world have so much faith in free markets (World View "Market Reliance vs. Government Reliance?")? **LO1-5**
8. What is the connection between North Korea's missile program and its hunger problem? (World View "North Korean Food Rations Cut") **LO1-2**
9. Explain why there are limits to output and how these limits force economies to make trade-offs. **LO1-1**
10. If climate change was in fact the greatest threat to society, should all our resources be used to combat it? What percentage of our output should be devoted to the pursuit of a carbon-neutral economy? **LO1-2**

PROBLEMS FOR CHAPTER 1

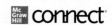

LO1-2 1. According to Table 1.1 (or Figure 1.1), what is the opportunity cost of the second truck produced?

LO1-3 2. (a) Compute the opportunity cost in forgone consumer goods (millions of pounds of butter) for each additional unit of military output produced (number of planes):

Military output	0	1	2	3	4	5
Consumer goods output	100	95	80	60	35	0
Opportunity cost		—	—	—	—	—

    (b) As military output increases, are opportunity costs increasing, decreasing, or remaining constant?

LO1-3 3. According to Figure 1.2, how much food production is sacrificed when North Korea moves from point *P* to point *N*?

LO1-2 4. (a) If the average North Korean farmer produces 1,500 pounds of food per year, what is the opportunity cost, in pounds of food, of North Korea's army (World View "World's Largest Armies")?

    (b) If a person needs at least 500 pounds of food per year to survive, how many people could have been fed with the forgone food output?

LO1-2 5. What is the opportunity cost (in civilian output) of a defense buildup that raises military spending from 3.2 to 3.4 percent of a $22 trillion economy?

LO1-5 6. According to Figure 1.3, what percent of output consists of nonmilitary goods in

    (a) Jamaica?

    (b) Russia?

LO1-3 7. According to the figure below (similar to Figure 1.4),

    (a) At which point(s) is this society producing some of each type of output but producing inefficiently?

    (b) At which point(s) is this society producing the most output possible with the available resources and technology?

    (c) At which point(s) is the output combination unattainable with available resources and technology?

    (d) Show the change that would occur if the resources of this society increased. Label this curve PPC_2.

    (e) Show the change that would occur with a huge natural disaster that destroyed one-third of production capacity. Label this curve PPC_3.

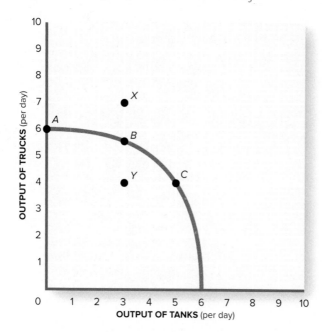

PROBLEMS FOR CHAPTER 1 (cont'd)

LO1-3 8. You have only 20 hours per week to use for either study time or fun time. Suppose the relationship between study time, fun time, and grades is shown in this table:

Fun time (hours per week)	16	12	8	4	0
Study time (hours per week)	0	4	8	12	16
Grade point average	*0*	*1.0*	*2.0*	*3.0*	*4.0*

    (*a*) Draw the (linear) production possibilities curve on a graph that represents the alternative uses of your time.

    (*b*) On the same graph, show the combination of study time and fun time that would get you a 2.0 grade average.

    (*c*) What is the cost, in lost fun time, of raising your grade point average from 2.0 to 3.0?

LO1-5 9. According to the World View "Market Reliance vs. Government Reliance?," which nation has

    (*a*) The highest level of faith in the market system?

    (*b*) The lowest level of faith in the market system?

LO1-2 10. If a student literally had "nothing else to do,"

    (*a*) What would be the opportunity cost of doing this homework?

    (*b*) What is the likelihood of that?

LO1-1 11. According to the World View "World's Largest Armies," what percent of the total population is serving in the military in

    (*a*) The United States (population = 340 million)?

    (*b*) North Korea (population = 25 million)?

    (*c*) China (population = 1.4 billion)?

LO1-2 12. *Decisions for Tomorrow:* What is the opportunity cost of investing $1 trillion in clean energy technology?

APPENDIX

....

USING GRAPHS

Economists like to draw graphs. In fact, we didn't even make it through the first chapter without a few graphs. This appendix looks more closely at the way graphs are drawn and used. The basic purpose of a graph is to illustrate a relationship between two *variables*. Consider, for example, the relationship between grades and studying. In general, we expect that additional hours of study time will lead to higher grades. Hence, we should be able to see a distinct relationship between hours of study time and grade point average.

Suppose that we actually surveyed all the students taking this course with regard to their study time and grade point averages. The resulting information can be compiled in a table such as Table A.1.

According to the table, students who don't study at all can expect an F in this course. To get a C, the average student apparently spends 8 hours a week studying. All those who study 16 hours a week end up with an A in the course.

These relationships between grades and studying can also be illustrated on a graph. Indeed, the whole purpose of a graph is to summarize numerical relationships.

We begin to construct a graph by drawing horizontal and vertical boundaries, as in Figure A.1. These boundaries are called the *axes* of the graph. On the vertical axis (often called the *y*-axis), we measure one of the variables; the other variable is measured on the horizontal axis (the *x*-axis).

In this case, we shall measure the grade point average on the vertical axis. We start at the *origin* (the intersection of the two axes) and count upward, letting the distance between horizontal lines represent half (0.5) a grade point. Each horizontal line is numbered, up to the maximum grade point average of 4.0.

TABLE A.1

Hypothetical Relationship of Grades to Study Time

Study Time (Hours per Week)	Grade Point Average
16	4.0 (A)
14	3.5 (B+)
12	3.0 (B)
10	2.5 (C+)
8	2.0 (C)
6	1.5 (D+)
4	1.0 (D)
2	0.5 (F+)
0	0.0 (F)

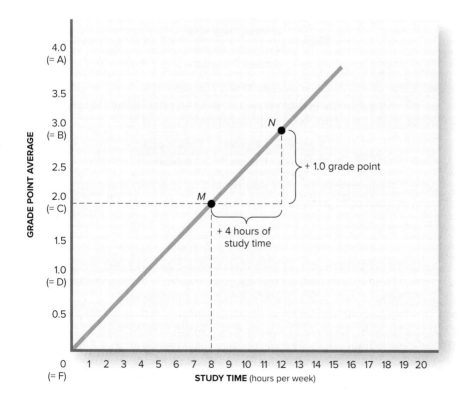

FIGURE A.1

The Relationship of Grades to Study Time

The upward (positive) slope of the curve indicates that additional studying is associated with higher grades. The average student (2.0, or C grade) studies 8 hours per week. This is indicated by point *M* on the graph.

The number of hours each week spent doing homework is measured on the horizontal axis. We begin at the origin again and count to the right. The *scale* (numbering) proceeds in increments of 1 hour, up to 20 hours per week.

When both axes have been labeled and measured, we can begin illustrating the relationship between study time and grades. Consider the typical student who does 8 hours of homework per week and has a 2.0 (C) grade point average. We illustrate this relationship by first locating 8 hours on the horizontal axis. We then move up from that point a distance of 2.0 grade points, to point *M*. Point *M* tells us that 8 hours of study time per week are typically associated with a 2.0 grade point average.

The rest of the information in Table A.1 is drawn (or *plotted*) on the graph the same way. To illustrate the average grade for people who study 12 hours per week, we move upward from the number 12 on the horizontal axis until we reach the height of 3.0 on the vertical axis. At that intersection, we draw another point (point *N*).

Once we've plotted the various points describing the relationship of study time to grades, we may connect them with a line or curve. This line (curve) is our summary. In this case, the line slopes upward to the right—that is, it has a *positive* slope. This slope indicates that more hours of study time are associated with *higher* grades. Were higher grades associated with *less* study time, the curve in Figure A.1 would have a *negative* slope (downward from left to right).

Slopes

The upward slope of Figure A.1 tells us that higher grades are associated with increased amounts of study time. That same curve also tells us *by how much* grades tend to rise with study time. According to point *M* in Figure A.1, the average student studies 8 hours per week and earns a C (2.0 grade point average). To earn a B (3.0 average), students apparently need to study an average of 12 hours per week (point *N*). Hence, an increase of 4 hours of study time per week is associated with a 1-point increase in grade point average. This relationship between *changes* in study time and *changes* in grade point average is expressed by the steepness, or *slope,* of the graph.

The slope of any graph is calculated as

$$\text{Slope} = \frac{\text{Vertical distance between two points}}{\text{Horizontal distance between two points}}$$

In our example, the vertical distance between *M* and *N* represents a change in grade point average. The horizontal distance between these two points represents the change in study time. Hence, the slope of the graph between points *M* and *N* is equal to

$$\text{Slope} = \frac{3.0 \text{ grade} - 2.0 \text{ grade}}{12 \text{ hours} - 8 \text{ hours}} = \frac{1 \text{ grade point}}{4 \text{ hours}}$$

In other words, a 4-hour increase in study time (from 8 to 12 hours) is associated with a 1-point increase in grade point average (see Figure A.1).

Shifts

The relationship between grades and studying illustrated in Figure A.1 isn't inevitable. It's simply a graphical illustration of student experiences, as revealed in our hypothetical survey. The relationship between study time and grades could be quite different.

Suppose that the university decided to raise grading standards, making it more difficult to achieve higher grades. To achieve a C, a student now would need to study 12 hours per week, not just 8 (as in Figure A.1). Whereas students could previously get a B by studying 12 hours per week, now they'd have to study 16 hours to get that grade.

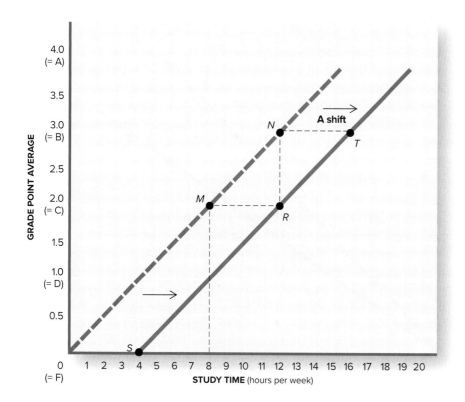

FIGURE A.2
A Shift

When a relationship between two variables changes, the entire curve *shifts*. In this case, a tougher grading policy alters the relationship between study time and grades. To get a C, one must now study 12 hours per week (point *R*), not just 8 hours (point *M*).

Figure A.2 illustrates the new grading standards. Notice that the new curve lies to the right of the earlier curve. We say that the curve has *shifted* to reflect a change in the relationship between study time and grades. Point *R* indicates that 12 hours of study time now "produce" a C, not a B (point *N* on the old curve). Students who now study only 4 hours per week (point *S*) will fail. Under the old grading policy, they could have at least gotten a D. ***When a curve shifts, the underlying relationship between the two variables has changed.***

A shift may also change the slope of the curve. In Figure A.2, the new grading curve is parallel to the old one; it therefore has the same slope. Under either the new grading policy or the old one, a 4-hour increase in study time leads to a 1-point increase in grades. Therefore, the slope of both curves in Figure A.2 is

$$\text{Slope} = \frac{\text{Vertical change}}{\text{Horizontal change}} = \frac{1}{4}$$

This too may change, however. Figure A.3 illustrates such a possibility. In this case, zero study time still results in an F. But now the payoff for additional studying is reduced. Now it takes 6 hours of study time to get a D (1.0 grade point), not 4 hours as before. Likewise, another 4 hours of study time (to a total of 10) raise the grade by only two-thirds of a point. It takes 6 hours to raise the grade a full point. The slope of the new line is therefore

$$\text{Slope} = \frac{\text{Vertical change}}{\text{Horizontal change}} = \frac{1}{6}$$

The new curve in Figure A.3 has a smaller slope than the original curve and so lies below it. What all this means is that it now takes a greater effort to improve your grade.

FIGURE A.3

A Change in Slope

When a curve shifts, it may change its slope as well. In this case, a new grading policy makes each higher grade more difficult to reach. To raise a C to a B, for example, one must study 6 additional hours (compare points *J* and *K*). Earlier it took only 4 hours to move the grade scale up a full point. The slope of the line has declined from 0.25 (= 1 ÷ 4) to 0.17 (= 1 ÷ 6).

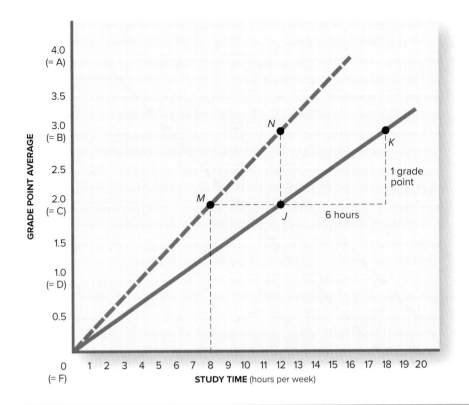

Linear vs. Nonlinear Curves

In Figures A.1–A.3 the relationship between grades and studying is represented by a straight line—that is, a *linear curve.* A distinguishing feature of linear curves is that they have the same (constant) slope throughout. In Figure A.1 it appears that *every* 4-hour increase in study time is associated with a 1-point increase in average grades. In Figure A.3 it appears that every 6-hour increase in study time leads to a 1-point increase in grades. But the relationship between studying and grades may not be linear. Higher grades may be more difficult to attain. You may be able to raise a C to a B by studying 4 hours more per week. But it may be harder to raise a B to an A. According to Figure A.4, it takes an additional 8 hours of studying to raise a B to an A. Thus, the relationship between study time and grades is *nonlinear* in Figure A.4; the slope of the curve changes as study time increases. In this case, the slope decreases as study time increases. Grades continue to improve, but not so fast, as more and more time is devoted to homework. You may know the feeling.

Causation

Figure A.4 doesn't by itself guarantee that your grade point average will rise if you study 4 more hours per week. In fact, the graph drawn in Figure A.4 doesn't prove that additional study ever results in higher grades. The graph is only a summary of empirical observations. It says nothing about cause and effect. It could be that students who study a lot are smarter to begin with. If so, then less able students might not get higher grades if they studied harder. In other words, the *cause* of higher grades is debatable. At best, the empirical relationship summarized in the graph may be used to support a particular theory (e.g., that it pays to study more). Graphs, like tables, charts, and other statistical media, rarely tell their own story; rather, they must be *interpreted* in terms of some underlying theory or expectation.Appendix

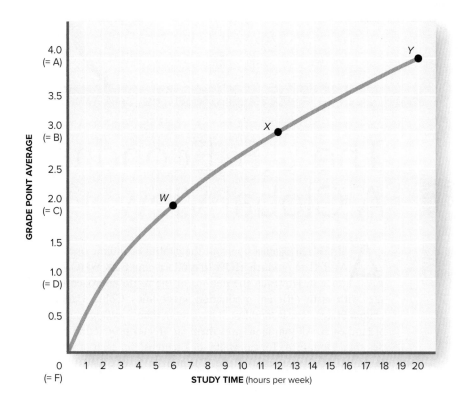

FIGURE A.4

A Nonlinear Relationship

Straight lines have a constant slope, implying a constant relationship between the two variables. But the relationship (and slope) may vary. In this case, it takes 6 extra hours of study to raise a C (point *W*) to a B (point *X*) but 8 extra hours to raise a B to an A (point *Y*). The slope decreases as we move up the curve.

Design Credit: Shutterstock

Jeff Chiu/AP Images

Glow Images   Pe3k/Shutterstock

The economy produces diverse goods and services.

CHAPTER 2

The U.S. Economy: A Global View

All nations must confront the central economic questions of WHAT to produce, HOW to produce, and FOR WHOM to produce it. However, the nations of the world approach these issues with vastly different production possibilities. China, Canada, the United States, Russia, and Brazil have more than *3 million* square miles of land each. All that land gives them far greater production possibilities than Dominica, Tonga, Malta, or Lichtenstein, each of which has less than 300 square miles of land. The population of China totals more than 1.4 billion people, nearly five times that of the United States, and 25,000 times the population of Greenland. Obviously, these nations confront very different output choices.

In addition to vastly uneven production possibilities, the nations of the world use different mechanisms for deciding WHAT, HOW, and FOR WHOM to produce. Belarus, Romania, North Korea, and Cuba still rely heavily on central planning. By contrast, Singapore, New Zealand, Ireland, and the United States permit the market mechanism to play a dominant role in shaping economic outcomes.

With different production possibilities and mechanisms of choice, you'd expect economic outcomes to vary greatly across nations. And they do. This chapter assesses how the U.S. economy stacks up. Specifically,

- **WHAT goods and services does the United States produce?**
- **HOW is that output produced?**
- **FOR WHOM is the output produced?**

In each case, we want to see not only how the United States has answered these questions but also how America's answers compare with those of other nations.

WHAT AMERICA PRODUCES

The United States has less than 5 percent of the world's population and only 12 percent of the world's arable land, yet it produces 20 percent of the world's output.

GDP Comparisons

World View "Comparative Output (GDP)" shows how total U.S. production compares with that of other nations. Every country produces a different mix of output. So, it's impossible to compare output in purely *physical* terms (e.g., so many cars, so many fish, etc.). But we can make comparisons based on the *value* of output. We do this by computing the

WORLD VIEW

COMPARATIVE OUTPUT (GDP)

The United States is by far the world's largest economy. Its annual output of goods and services is one and a half times larger than China's, three times Japan's, and more than all of the European Union's. The output of Third World countries is only a tiny fraction of U.S. output.

Source: The World Bank (Atlas method).

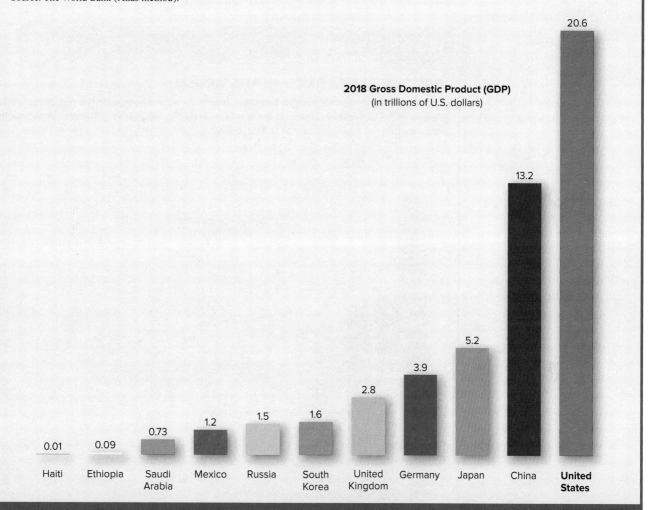

2018 Gross Domestic Product (GDP)
(in trillions of U.S. dollars)

Haiti	Ethiopia	Saudi Arabia	Mexico	Russia	South Korea	United Kingdom	Germany	Japan	China	United States
0.01	0.09	0.73	1.2	1.5	1.6	2.8	3.9	5.2	13.2	20.6

CRITICAL ANALYSIS: The market value of output (**GDP**) is a basic measure of an economy's size. The U.S. economy is far larger than any other and accounts for more than one-fifth of the entire world's output of goods and services.

total market value of all the goods and services a nation produces in a year—what we call **gross domestic product (GDP).** In effect, GDP is the "pie" of output we bake each year.

In 2019 the U.S. economy baked a huge pie—one containing more than $21 trillion worth of goods and services. That was far more output than any other nation produced. The second-largest economy, China, produced only two-thirds that much. Japan came in third, with about a third of U.S. output. Cuba, by contrast, produced less than $100 *billion* of output, less than the state of Mississippi. Russia, which is regarded as a superpower, produced only $1.5 trillion. The entire 27-member European Union produces less output than the United States.

Per Capita GDP. What makes the U.S. share of world output so remarkable is that we do it with so few people. The U.S. population of 340 million amounts to less than 5 percent of

gross domestic product (GDP): The total market value of all final goods and services produced within a nation's borders in a given time period.

the world's total (7.8 billion). Yet we produce more than 20 percent of the world's output. That means we're producing a lot of output *per person*. China, by contrast, has the opposite ratios: 18 percent of the world's population producing 17 percent of the world's output. So China is producing a lot of output but relatively less *per person*.

This people-based measure of economic performance is called **per capita GDP.** Per capita GDP is simply a nation's total output divided by its total population. It doesn't tell us how much any specific person gets. ***Per capita GDP is an indicator of how much output the average person would get if all output were divided evenly among the population.*** In effect, GDP per capita tells us how large a slice of the GDP pie the average citizen gets.

per capita GDP: The dollar value of GDP divided by total population; average GDP.

WORLD VIEW

GDP PER CAPITA AROUND THE WORLD

The American standard of living is five times higher than the average for the rest of the world. People in the poorest nations of the world (e.g., Haiti, Ethiopia) barely survive on per capita incomes that are a tiny fraction of U.S. standards.

Source: The World Bank.

GDP per Capita (2018)
(in U.S. dollars)

Country	GDP per Capita
United States	63,080
Germany	47,090
Canada	44,940
Japan	41,310
South Korea	30,600
Saudi Arabia	21,600
World average	11,124
Russia	10,230
China	9,460
Mexico	9,180
Cuba	7,480
India	2,020
Nigeria	1,960
Haiti	800
Ethiopia	790

CRITICAL ANALYSIS: Per capita GDP is a measure of output that reflects average living standards. America's exceptionally high **per capita GDP** implies access to far more goods and services than people in other nations have.

In 2019 per capita GDP in the United States was roughly $64,000. That means the average U.S. citizen could have consumed $64,000 worth of goods and services. That's a staggering amount by global standards—five times the average for the rest of the world. World View "GDP per Capita around the World" provides a global perspective on just how "rich" America is. Notice how much more output the average American has than a person in India or, worse yet, Haiti. The gap between U.S. living standards and those in other nations is startling. According to the World Bank, 40 percent of the people on Earth subsist on incomes of less than $3 a day—a level completely unimaginable to the average American. *Homeless* people in the United States enjoy a higher living standard than billions of poor people in other nations (see chapter titled "Global Poverty"). In this context, it's easy to understand why the rest of the world envies (and sometimes resents) America's prosperity.

GDP Growth. What's even more startling about global comparisons is that the GDP gap between the United States and the world's poor nations keeps growing. The reason for that is **economic growth.** With few exceptions, U.S. output increases nearly every year: The pie keeps getting larger. *On average, U.S. output has grown by roughly 3 percent a year, nearly three times faster than population growth (1 percent).* So the U.S. pie is growing faster than the number of people coming to the table. Hence, not only does *total* output keep rising, but *per capita* output keeps rising as well (see Figure 2.1). Even the Great Recession of 2008–2009 and the 2020 coronavirus pandemic hardly made a dent in this pattern of ever-rising incomes.

Poor Nations. People in the world's poorest countries aren't so fortunate. China's economy has grown exceptionally fast in the last 20 years, propelling it to second place in the global GDP rankings. But in many other nations, total output has actually *declined* year after year, further depressing living standards. Notice in Table 2.1, for example, what's been happening in Libya. From 2000 to 2018, Libya's output of goods and services (GDP) *declined* by an average of 1.2 percent a year. As a result, total Libyan output in 2018 was 25 percent *smaller* than in 2000. During those same years, the Libyan population kept growing—by 1.2 percent a year. So the Libyan pie was shrinking every year even as the number of people coming to the table was increasing. As a result, Libya's per capita GDP fell below $7,000 a year.

economic growth: An increase in output (real GDP); an expansion of production possibilities.

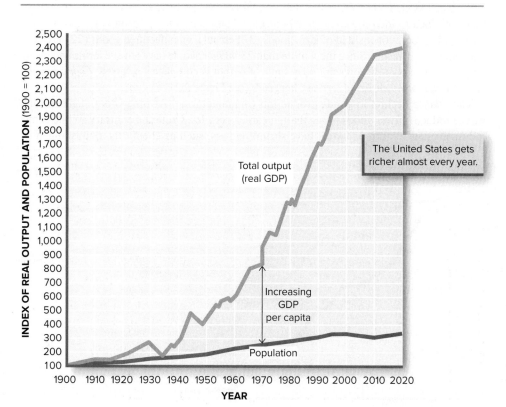

FIGURE 2.1

U.S. Output and Population Growth Since 1900

Over time, the growth of output in the United States has greatly exceeded population growth. As a consequence, GDP per capita has grown tremendously. GDP per capita was five times higher in 2000 than in 1900.

Source: U.S. Department of Labor.

TABLE 2.1

GDP Growth vs. Population Growth

The relationship between GDP growth and population growth is very different in rich and poor countries. The populations of rich countries are growing very slowly, and gains in per capita GDP are easily achieved. In the poorest countries, the population is still increasing rapidly, making it difficult to raise living standards. Notice how per capita incomes are *declining* in some lower-income countries (such as Libya and Haiti).

	Average Growth Rate (2000–2018) of		
	GDP	Population	Per Capita GDP
High-income countries			
United States	1.7	0.8	0.9
Canada	1.9	1.0	0.9
Japan	0.7	0.0	0.7
France	1.1	0.6	0.5
Middle-income countries			
China	9.5	0.5	9.0
India	6.8	1.4	5.4
Libya	−1.2	1.2	−2.4
Low-income countries			
Burundi	3.1	3.1	0.0
Haiti	1.4	1.5	−0.1
Ethiopia	9.8	2.8	7.0

Source: The World Bank, data.worldbank.org.

Burundi is another interesting case study of the relationship between output growth and population growth. Notice in Table 2.1 that Burundi's economy grew nearly twice as fast as the U.S. economy for 20 years. But Burundi's population increased just as fast as GDP. As a result, Burundians experienced *zero* improvement in living standards, while American per capita GDP was increasing at a 0.9 percent annual clip.

The Mix of Output

Regardless of how much output a nation produces, the *mix* of output always includes both *goods* (such as cars, big-screen TVs, and potatoes) and *services* (like this economics course, visits to a doctor, video streaming, or a professional baseball game). A century ago, about two-thirds of U.S. output consisted of farm goods (37 percent), manufactured goods (22 percent), and mining (9 percent). Since then, more than 25 *million* people have left the farms and taken jobs in other sectors. As a result, today's mix of output is completely reversed: ***Eighty percent of U.S. output now consists of services, not goods*** (see Figure 2.2).

The *relative* decline in goods production (manufacturing, farming) doesn't mean that we're producing *fewer* goods today than in earlier decades. Quite the contrary. While some industries such as iron and steel have shrunk, others, such as chemicals, publishing, and

FIGURE 2.2

The Changing Mix of Output

Two hundred years ago, almost all U.S. output came from farms. Today 80 percent of output consists of services, not farm or manufactured goods.

Source: U.S. Department of Commerce.

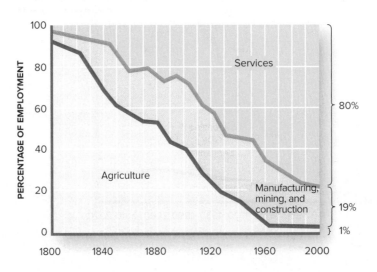

telecommunications equipment, have grown tremendously. The result is that manufacturing output has increased fourfold since 1950. The same kind of thing has happened in the farm sector, where output keeps rising even though agriculture's *share* of total output has declined. It's just that our output of *services* has increased so much faster.

Development Patterns. The transformation of the United States into a service economy is a reflection of our high incomes. In Ethiopia, where the most urgent concern is to keep people from starving, more than 50 percent of output still comes from the farm sector. Poor people don't have enough income to buy dental services, vacations, or even an education, so the mix of output in poor countries is weighted toward goods, not services.

HOW AMERICA PRODUCES

Regardless of how much output a nation produces, every nation ultimately depends on its resources—its **factors of production**—to produce goods and services. So *differences* in GDP must be explained in part by HOW those resources are used.

> **factors of production:** Resource inputs used to produce goods and services, e.g., land, labor, capital, entrepreneurship.

Human Capital

We've already observed that America's premier position in global GDP rankings isn't due to the number of humans within our borders. We have far fewer bodies than China or India, yet we produce far more output than either of those nations. What counts for production purposes is not just the *number* of workers a nation has, but the *skills* of those workers—what we call **human capital.**

> **human capital:** The knowledge and skills possessed by the workforce.

Over time, the United States has invested heavily in human capital. In 1940 only 1 out of 20 young Americans graduated from college; today more than 40 percent of young people are college graduates. High school graduation rates have jumped from 38 percent to more than 85 percent in the same period. In the poorest countries, fewer than half of youth ever *attend* high school, much less graduate (see World View "The Education Gap between Rich and Poor Nations"). As a consequence, the United Nations estimates that 1.2 billion people—a sixth of

---

WORLD VIEW

THE EDUCATION GAP BETWEEN RICH AND POOR NATIONS

Virtually all Americans attend high school and roughly 85 percent graduate. In poor countries, relatively few workers attend high school and even fewer graduate. Half the workers in the world's poorest nations are illiterate.

Source: The World Bank, WDI2017 Data Set, data.worldbank.org.

Enrollment in Secondary Schools (percentage of school-age youth attending secondary schools)

Low-income countries	41%
Middle-income countries	76%
High-income countries	100%

CRITICAL ANALYSIS: The high productivity of the American economy is explained in part by the quality of its labor resources, its **human capital.** Workers in poorer, less-developed countries get much less education and training.

Critical analysis: An abundance of capital equipment and advanced technology make American farmers and workers far more **productive** than workers in poor nations.
(*left*): Barry Barker/McGraw Hill; (*right*): Photo by Jeff Vanuga, USDA Natural Resources Conservation Service

humanity—are unable to read a book or even write their own names. Without even functional literacy, such workers are doomed to low-productivity jobs. Despite low wages, they are not likely to "steal" many jobs from America's highly educated and trained workforce.

Capital Stock

America has also accumulated a massive stock of capital—more than $80 *trillion* worth of machinery, factories, and buildings. As a result of all this prior investment, U.S. production tends to be very **capital-intensive.** The contrast with *labor-intensive* production in poorer countries is striking. A farmer in India still works mostly with his hands and crude implements, whereas a U.S. farmer works with computers, automated irrigation systems, and mechanized equipment (see the photos above). Russian business managers don't have the computer networks or telecommunications systems that make U.S. business so efficient. In Haiti and Ethiopia, even telephones, indoor plumbing, and dependable sources of power are scarce.

capital-intensive: Production processes that use a high ratio of capital to labor inputs.

High Productivity

When you put educated workers together with sophisticated capital equipment, you tend to get more output. This relationship largely explains why the United States has such a lead in worker **productivity**—the amount of output produced by the average worker. *American households are able to consume so much because American workers produce so much.* It's really that simple.

The huge output of the United States is thus explained not only by a wealth of resources but by their quality as well. *The high productivity of the U.S. economy results from using highly educated workers in capital-intensive production processes.*

productivity: Output per unit of input—for example, output per labor-hour.

Factor Mobility. Our continuing ability to produce the goods and services that consumers demand also depends on our agility in *reallocating* resources from one industry to another. Every year, some industries expand and others contract. Thousands of new firms start up each year, and almost as many others disappear. In the process, land, labor, capital, and entrepreneurship move from one industry to another in response to changing demands and technology. In 1975 Federal Express, Dell Computer, Staples, Oracle, and Amgen didn't exist. Walmart was still a small retailer. Starbucks was selling coffee on Seattle street corners, and the founders of Google, Facebook, and Snapchat weren't even born. Today these companies employ millions of people. These workers came from other firms and industries that weren't growing as fast.

Technological Advance. One of the forces that keep shifting resources from one industry to another is continuing advances in technology. Advances in technology can be as sophisticated as microscopic miniaturization of electronic circuits or as simple as the reorganization of production processes. Either phenomenon increases the productivity of the workforce and potential output. *Whenever technology advances, an economy can produce more output with existing resources;* its **production possibilities** curve shifts outward (see Figure 1.5).

Outsourcing and Trade. The same technological advances that fuel economic growth also facilitate *global* resource use. Telecommunications have become so sophisticated and inexpensive that phone workers in India or Grenada can answer calls directed to U.S. companies. Likewise, programmers in India can work online to write computer code, develop software, or perform accounting chores for U.S. corporations. Although such "outsourcing" is often viewed as a threat to U.S. jobs, it is really another source of increased U.S. output. By outsourcing routine tasks to foreign workers, U.S. workers are able to focus on higher-value jobs. U.S. computer engineers do less routine programming and more systems design. U.S. accountants do less cost tabulation and more cost analysis. By utilizing foreign resources in the production process, U.S. workers are able to pursue their *comparative advantage* in high-skill, capital-intensive jobs. In this way, both productivity and total output increase. Although some U.S. workers suffer temporary job losses in this process, the overall economy gains.

Role of Government

In assessing HOW goods are produced and economies grow, we must also take heed of the role the government plays. As we noted in Chapter 1, the amount of economic freedom varies greatly among the 200-plus nations of the world. Moreover, the Heritage Foundation has documented a positive relationship between the degree of economic freedom and economic growth. Quite simply, when entrepreneurs are unfettered by regulation or high taxes, they are more likely to design and produce better mousetraps. When the government owns the factors of production, imposes high taxes, or tightly regulates output, there is little opportunity or incentive to design better products or pursue new technology. This is one reason why more market-reliant economies grow faster than others.

Recognizing the importance of market incentives doesn't force us to reject all government intervention. No one really advocates the complete abolition of government. On the contrary, the government plays a critical role in establishing a framework in which private businesses can operate. Among its many roles are these:

* *Providing a legal framework.* One of the most basic functions of government is to establish and enforce the rules of the game. In some bygone era, maybe a person's word was sufficient to guarantee delivery or payment. Businesses today, however, rely more on written contracts. The government gives legitimacy to contracts by establishing the rules for such pacts and by enforcing their provisions. In the absence of contractual rights, few companies would be willing to ship goods without prepayment (in cash). Even the incentive to write texts would disappear if government copyright laws didn't forbid unauthorized photocopying. By establishing ownership rights, contract rights, and other rules of the game, the government lays the foundation for market transactions.
* *Protecting the environment.* The government also intervenes in the market to protect the environment. The legal contract system is designed to protect the interests of a buyer and a seller who wish to do business. What if, however, the business they contract for harms third parties? How are the interests of persons who *aren't* party to the contract to be protected?

  Numerous examples abound of how unregulated production may harm third parties. Earlier in the century, the steel mills around Pittsburgh blocked out the sun with clouds of sulfurous gases that spewed out of their furnaces. Local residents were harmed every time they inhaled. In the absence of government intervention, such side effects would be common. Decisions on how to produce would be based on costs alone, not on how the environment is affected. However, such negative **externalities**—spillover costs imposed on the broader community—affect our collective well-being.

production possibilities: The alternative combinations of final goods and services that could be produced in a given period with all available resources and technology.

externalities: Costs (or benefits) of a market activity borne by a third party; the difference between the social and private costs (benefits) of a market activity.

To reduce the external costs of production, the government limits air, water, and noise pollution and regulates environmental use.

- ***Protecting consumers.*** The government also uses its power to protect the interests of consumers. One way to do this is to prevent individual business firms from becoming too powerful. In the extreme case, a single firm might have a **monopoly** on the production of a specific good. As the sole producer of that good, a monopolist could dictate the price, the quality, and the quantity of the product. In such a situation, consumers would likely end up paying too much for too little.

    To protect consumers from monopoly exploitation, the government tries to prevent individual firms from dominating specific markets. Antitrust laws prohibit mergers or acquisitions that would threaten competition. The U.S. Department of Justice and the Federal Trade Commission also regulate pricing practices, advertising claims, and other behavior that might put consumers at an unfair disadvantage in product markets.

    Government also regulates the safety of many products. Consumers don't have enough expertise to assess the safety of various medicines, for example. If they rely on trial and error to determine drug safety, they might not get a second chance. To avoid this calamity, the government requires rigorous testing of new drugs, food additives, and other products.

- ***Protecting labor.*** The government also regulates how labor resources are used in the production process. In most poor nations, children are forced to start working at very early ages, often for minuscule wages. They often don't get the chance to go to school or to stay healthy. In Africa, 40 percent of children under age 14 work to survive or to help support their families. In the United States, child labor laws and compulsory schooling prevent minor children from being exploited. Government regulations also set standards for workplace safety, minimum wages, fringe benefits, and overtime provisions.

Striking a Balance

All these and other government interventions are designed to change the way resources are used. Such interventions reflect the conviction that the market alone might not always select the best possible way of producing goods and services. There's no guarantee, however, that government regulation of HOW goods are produced always makes us better off. Excessive regulation may inhibit production, raise product prices, and limit consumer choices. As noted in Chapter 1, *government* failure might replace *market* failure, leaving us no better off—possibly even worse off. This possibility underscores the importance of striking the right balance between market reliance and government regulation.

FOR WHOM AMERICA PRODUCES

As we've seen, America produces a huge quantity of output, using high-quality labor and capital resources. That leaves one basic question unanswered: FOR WHOM is all this output produced?

How many goods and services one gets largely depends on how much income one has to spend. The U.S. economy uses the market mechanism to distribute most goods and services. Those who receive the most income get the most goods. This goes a long way toward explaining why millionaires live in mansions and homeless people seek shelter in abandoned cars. This is the kind of stark inequality that fueled Karl Marx's denunciation of capitalism. Even today, people wonder how some Americans can be so rich while others are so poor.

U.S. Income Distribution

Figure 2.3 illustrates the actual distribution of income in the United States. For this illustration the entire population is sorted into five groups of equal size, ranked by income. In this depiction, all the rich people are in the top **income quintile**; the poor are in the lowest quintile. To be in the top quintile in 2019, a household needed at least $143,000 of income. All the households in the lowest quintile had incomes under $28,000.

monopoly: A firm that produces the entire market supply of a particular good or service.

income quintile: One-fifth of the population, rank-ordered by income (e.g., top fifth).

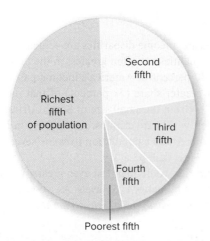

FIGURE 2.3
The U.S. Distribution of Income
The richest fifth of U.S. households gets half of all the income—a huge slice of the income pie. By contrast, the poorest fifth gets only a sliver.

Income Quintile	2019 Income	Average Income	Share of Total Income (%)
Highest fifth	Above $143,000	$254,400	51.9
Second fifth	$86,000–143,000	$111,100	22.7
Third fifth	$54,000–86,000	$ 68,900	14.1
Fourth fifth	$28,000–54,000	$ 40,700	8.3
Lowest fifth	$0–28,000	$ 15,300	3.1

Source: U.S. Department of Commerce, Bureau of the Census (averages rounded to thousands of dollars; 2019 data).

The most striking feature of Figure 2.3 is how large a slice of the income pie rich people get: *The top 20 percent (quintile) of U.S. households get half of all U.S. income.* By contrast, the poorest 20 percent (quintile) of U.S. households get only a sliver of the income pie—about 3 percent. Those grossly unequal slices explain why nearly half of all Americans believe the nation is divided into "haves" and "have nots." In the 2020 presidential campaigns, there was a lot of talk about changing the answer to the FOR WHOM question with new taxes on the rich and more subsidies and wage floors for the poor.

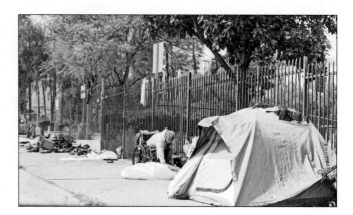

Critical analysis: The market distributes income (and, in turn, goods and services) according to the resources an individual owns and how well they are used. If the resulting inequalities are too great, government intervention may be desired to change the **FOR WHOM** outcome.
TerryJ/Getty Images; Philip Pilosian/Shutterstock

Global Inequality

As unequal as U.S. incomes are, income disparities are actually greater in many other countries. Ironically, income inequalities are often greatest in the poorest countries. The richest *tenth* of U.S. families gets 30 percent of America's income pie. The richest tenth of South Africa's families gets a far greater share (51 percent) of that nation's income (see World View "Global Inequalities"). Given the small size of South Africa's pie, the *bottom* tenth of South African families is left with mere crumbs. As we'll see in the chapter titled "Global Poverty," 40 percent of South Africa's population lives in "severe poverty," defined by the World Bank as an income of less than $3 a day.

Comparisons across countries would manifest even greater inequality. As we saw earlier, Third World GDP per capita is far below U.S. levels. As a consequence, even *poor people in the United States receive far more goods and services than the* average *household in most low-income countries.*

WORLD VIEW

GLOBAL INEQUALITIES

Inequality tends to diminish as a country develops. In poor, developing nations, the richest tenth of the population typically gets 40 to 50 percent of all income. In developed countries, the richest tenth gets 20 to 30 percent of total income.

Source: The World Bank, 2020.

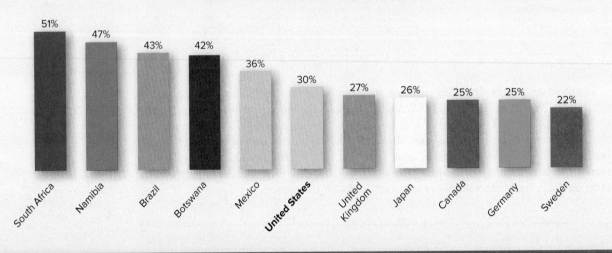

Share of Total Income Received by Top Tenth

South Africa	Namibia	Brazil	Botswana	Mexico	United States	United Kingdom	Japan	Canada	Germany	Sweden
51%	47%	43%	42%	36%	30%	27%	26%	25%	25%	22%

CRITICAL ANALYSIS: The **FOR WHOM** question is reflected in the distribution of income. Although the U.S. distribution of income is unequal, inequalities are much more severe in most poor nations.

DECISIONS FOR TOMORROW

Can We Eliminate Global Poverty?

Global answers to the basic questions of WHAT, HOW, and FOR WHOM have been shaped by market forces and government intervention. Obviously, the answers aren't fully satisfactory.

Millions of Americans still struggle to make ends meet. Worse yet, nearly 3 *billion* people around the world live in abject poverty—with incomes of less than $3 a day. More

Continued

than a sixth of the world's population are illiterate, nearly half have no access to sanitation facilities, and a fifth are chronically malnourished.

Then there is a staggering amount of pollution, rampant inequalities, inadequate education, and insufficient health care for billions of people.

The United Nations wants us to fashion better answers for the WHAT, HOW, and FOR WHOM questions. In September 2015 the U.N. adopted a set of 17 specific goals for sustainable development and a 15-year timeline for achieving them. Ending world poverty and eliminating world hunger are the first two on the list. High on the list is also the goal of reducing inequalities across income groups, gender, and race. Protecting the environment and slowing climate change are additional goals.

Can the world meet all these goals? Perhaps. But it will take a lot of resources and even more political will. Consider just the first goal of ending global poverty.

The rich nations of the world have enough resources to wipe out global poverty. But they're not willing to give them up. People in rich nations also have aspirations: They want higher living standards in the economy tomorrow. They already enjoy more comforts than people in poor nations even dream of. But that doesn't stop them from wanting more consumer goods, better schools, improved health care, a cleaner environment, and greater economic security. So the needs of the world's poor typically get lower priority.

How about the poor nations themselves? Couldn't they do a better job of mobilizing and employing their own resources to accelerate economic growth? Governments in many poor nations are notoriously self-serving and corrupt. Private property is often at risk of confiscation and contracts hard to enforce. This discourages the kind of investment poor nations desperately need. The unwillingness of rich nations to open their markets to the exports of poor nations also puts a lid on income growth.

In reality, an array of domestic and international policies has perpetuated global poverty. Developing a better mix of market-based and government-directed policies is the prerequisite for ending global poverty. Although some progress has been made in reducing poverty in the last few years, few believe that we will achieve the goal of eradicating extreme poverty in the next 10 years. In 2019, the U.N. itself projected that 6 percent of the world's population will still be in extreme poverty in the year 2030. Can we do better than that? How?

SUMMARY

- Answers to the core WHAT, HOW, and FOR WHOM questions vary greatly across nations. These differences reflect varying production possibilities, productivity, and values. **LO2-1, LO2-3, LO2-4**

- Gross domestic product (GDP) is the basic measure of how much an economy produces. The United States produces roughly $20 trillion of output per year, more than one-fifth of the world's total. **LO2-1**

- Per capita GDP is a nation's total output divided by its population. It indicates the average standard of living. The U.S. GDP per capita is five times the world average. **LO2-1**

- The high level of U.S. per capita GDP reflects the high productivity of U.S. workers. Abundant capital, education, technology, training, and management all contribute to high productivity. The relatively high degree of U.S. economic freedom (market reliance) is

also an important cause of superior economic growth. **LO2-3**

- More than 80 percent of U.S. output consists of services, including government services. This is a reversal of historical ratios and reflects the relatively high incomes in the United States. Poor nations produce much higher proportions of food and manufactured goods. **LO2-2**

- U.S. incomes are distributed very unequally, with households in the highest income class (quintile) receiving more than 10 times more income than low-income households. Incomes are even less equally distributed in most poor nations. **LO2-4**

- The mix of output, production methods, and the income distribution continues to change. The WHAT, HOW, and FOR WHOM answers in tomorrow's economy will depend on the continuing interplay of (changing) market signals and (changing) government policy. **LO2-2, LO2-3, LO2-4**

Key Terms

gross domestic product (GDP)
per capita GDP
economic growth
factors of production

human capital
capital-intensive
productivity
production possibilities

externalities
monopoly
income quintile

Questions for Discussion

1. Americans already enjoy living standards that far exceed world averages. Do we have enough? Should we even try to produce more? **LO2-1**

2. Why is per capita GDP so much higher in the United States than in Haiti? **LO2-3**

3. Can we continue to produce more output every year? Is there a limit? **LO2-3**

4. The U.S. farm population has shrunk by more than 25 million people since 1900. Where did all the people go? Why did they move? **LO2-2**

5. Is the relative decline in U.S. farming and manufacturing (Figure 2-2) a good thing or a bad thing? **LO2-2**

6. How many people are employed by your local or state government? Are they producing goods or services? Can you name some? What is the opportunity cost of that output? **LO2-1**

7. Where do growing companies like Netflix and Peloton get their employees? What were those workers doing before? **LO2-2**

8. Should the government try to equalize incomes more by raising taxes on the rich and giving more money to the poor? How might such redistribution affect total output and growth? **LO2-4**

9. Why are incomes so much more unequal in poor nations than in rich ones? **LO2-4**

10. What more can be done to reduce global poverty? **LO2-3**

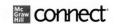

LO2-1   1. In 2018 the world's total output (real GDP) was roughly $84 trillion. What percent of this total was produced
   (*a*) By the three largest economies (World View "Comparative Output (GDP)")?
   (*b*) By the three smallest economies in that World View?

LO2-1   2. According to the World View "GDP per Capita around the World," how does per capita GDP in the following countries "stack up" against America's (in percentage terms)
   (*a*) Canada
   (*b*) Mexico
   (*c*) India

LO2-4   3. In 1980, America's GDP per capita was approximately $30,000 (measured in today's dollars). How much higher in percentage terms was America's GDP per capita in 2018 (see World View "GDP per Capita around the World")?

LO2-3   4. (*a*) How much more output does the $22 trillion U.S. economy produce when GDP increases by 1.0 percent?
   (*b*) By how much does this increase per capita income if the population is 340 million?

LO2-1   5. According to Table 2.1, how fast does total output (GDP) have to grow each year in order to increase per capita GDP in
   (*a*) the United States?
   (*b*) Japan?
   (*c*) Burundi?

LO2-3   6. (*a*) If Haiti's per capita GDP of $800 were to DOUBLE every decade (an annual growth rate of 7.2 percent), what would Haiti's per capita GDP be in 30 years?
   (*b*) Compare (a) to the U.S. per capita GDP in 2018 (World View "GDP per Capita around the World)?

LO2-2   7. U.S. real gross domestic product increased from $13 trillion in 2000 to $19 trillion in 2019. During that same time period, the share of manufactured goods (e.g., cars, appliances) fell from 16 percent to 11 percent. What was the dollar value of manufactured output
   (*a*) In 2000?
   (*b*) In 2019?
   (*c*) In percentage terms, by how much did the dollar value of manufacturing output change?

LO2-4   8. Using the data in Figure 2.3,
   (*a*) Compute the average income of U.S. households.
   If all incomes were equalized by government taxes and transfer payments,
   (*b*) How much would the average household in the highest income quintile pay in taxes?
   (*c*) What *percent* of income would the average household in the highest income quintile pay in tax?
   (*d*) How much would the average household in the lowest quintile receive in transfer payments?

LO2-3   9. If 160 million workers produced America's GDP in 2018 (World View "Comparative Output (GDP)"), how much output did the average worker produce?

LO2-1 10. Assuming the 2019 per capita GDP growth rate is equal to the average growth rate (2000–2018) provided in Table 2.1, estimate 2019 per capita GDP for each of the following countries using data from World View "GDP per Capita around the World."
   (*a*) China
   (*b*) Canada
   (*c*) Haiti

PROBLEMS FOR CHAPTER 2 (cont'd)

LO2-2 11. Using the data from the Data Tables, calculate
       (*a*) the federal government's share of total output in 1998, 2008, and 2018.
       (*b*) the state and local government's share of total output in 1998, 2008, and 2018.

LO2-2 12. ***Decisions for Tomorrow:*** How much more output per year will have to be produced in the world
       just to provide the 3 billion "severely" poor population with $1 more income per day?

Design Credit: Shutterstock

LADO/Shutterstock

Supply and Demand

LEARNING OBJECTIVES

After reading this chapter, you should know

LO3-1 The nature and determinants of market demand.

LO3-2 The nature and determinants of market supply.

LO3-3 How market prices and quantities are established.

LO3-4 What causes market prices to change.

LO3-5 How government price controls affect market outcomes.

On Saturday, September 14, 2019, ten unmanned drones attacked the Saudi Arabian oil facilities in Abqaiq. The resulting damage temporarily crippled Saudi Arabia's production capabilities—taking out 5.7 million barrels of oil per day. That damage represented about 50 percent of Saudi Arabia's daily production and about 5 percent of the entire world's capacity. Overnight, the U.S. price of unleaded, regular gasoline jumped by 3 cents, to $2.59 a gallon. A week later, the price was higher still, at $2.65 a gallon. The outcry from American motorists over "price gouging" was immediate: They thought it unfair for oil companies to charge higher prices. Those outcries prompted President Trump to announce that he was authorizing the sale of oil from America's Strategic Petroleum Reserve, an underground store of 645 million barrels of oil.

A similar price spike occurred when the World Health Organization declared a worldwide coronavirus pandemic on January 30, 2020. That declaration prompted people to stock up on surgical masks and hand sanitizers that might reduce the chances of COVID-19 infections. Within days, the price of an 8-ounce bottle of Purell hand sanitizer shot up from $3 to $16. The price of surgical masks increased as much as 166 percent on Amazon. Here again, a market shock had thrown demand and supply temporarily out of kilter. To restrain the resulting price hikes, the Surgeon General of the United States said that most people didn't need surgical masks (demand) and the federal government started selling surgical masks from its emergency medical stockpiles (supply). Mask manufacturers also increased production. As the market adjusted to the coronavirus threat, mask and sanitizer prices receded.

Economists took the spike in gasoline prices in stride. They pointed out that the price increase was the natural result of "supply and demand." The world was *demanding* just as much oil on Sunday, September 15 (about 100 million barrels per day) as it had on September 14. But the drone attacks had reduced the *supply* of oil by 5.7 million barrels. A price increase was inevitable. But economists also pointed out that the price jump was likely to be temporary. The Saudis would soon repair their production facilities and other nations (including the United States) would increase production to cover the Saudi shortfall. And that's exactly what happened. By the end of 2019, gasoline prices had fallen back to $2.49 a gallon. No oil had been taken out of the Strategic Petroleum Reserve. No congressional hearings had been conducted. And no oil companies had been charged with price gouging. The market forces of supply and demand had simply adjusted to changing circumstances.

The goal of this chapter is to explain how supply and demand really work. How do *markets* establish the prices of gasoline, surgical masks, and other products? Why do prices change so often? More broadly, how does the market mechanism decide WHAT to produce, HOW to produce, and FOR WHOM to produce? Specifically,

- **What determines the price of a good or service?**
- **How does the price of a product affect its production and consumption?**
- **Why do prices and production levels often change?**

Once we've seen how unregulated markets work, we'll observe how government intervention may alter market outcomes—for better or worse.

MARKET PARTICIPANTS

A good way to start figuring out how markets work is to see who participates in them. The answer is simple: just about every person and institution on the planet. Domestically, nearly 340 million consumers, about 25 million business firms, and tens of thousands of government agencies participate directly in the U.S. economy. Millions of international buyers and sellers also participate in U.S. markets.

Maximizing Behavior

All these market participants enter the marketplace to pursue specific goals. Consumers, for example, come with a limited amount of income to spend. Their objective is to buy the most desirable goods and services that their limited budgets will permit. We can't afford *everything* we want, so we must make *choices* about how to spend our scarce dollars. Our goal is to *maximize* the utility (satisfaction) we get from our available incomes.

Businesses also try to maximize in the marketplace. In their case, the quest is for maximum *profits*. Business profits are the difference between sales receipts and total costs. To maximize profits, business firms try to use resources efficiently in producing products that consumers desire.

The public sector also has maximizing goals. The economic purpose of government is to use available resources to serve public needs. The resources available for this purpose are limited too. Hence, local, state, and federal governments must use scarce resources carefully, striving to maximize the general welfare of society. International consumers and producers pursue these same goals when participating in our markets.

Market participants sometimes lose sight of their respective goals. Consumers sometimes buy impulsively and later wish they'd used their income more wisely. Likewise, a producer may take a two-hour lunch, even at the sacrifice of maximum profits. And elected officials sometimes put their personal interests ahead of the public's interest. In all sectors of the economy, however, *the basic goals of utility maximization, profit maximization, and welfare maximization explain most market activity.*

Specialization and Exchange

We are driven to buy and sell goods and services in the market by two simple facts. First, most of us are incapable of producing everything we want to consume. Second, even if we *could* produce all our own goods and services, it would still make sense to *specialize,* producing only one product and *trading* it for other desired goods and services.

Suppose you were capable of growing your own food, stitching your own clothes, building your own shelter, and even writing your own economics text. Even in this little utopia, it would still make sense to decide how *best* to expend your limited time and energy, relying on others to fill in the gaps. If you were *most* proficient at growing food, you would be best off spending your time farming. You could then *exchange* some of your food output for the clothes, shelter, and books you wanted. In the end, you'd be able to consume *more* goods than if you'd tried to make everything yourself.

Our economic interactions with others are thus necessitated by two constraints:

1. Our absolute inability as individuals to produce all the things we need or desire.
2. The limited amount of time, energy, and resources we have for producing those things we could make for ourselves.

Together these constraints lead us to *specialize* and interact. Most of the interactions that result take place in the market.

International Trade. The same motivations foster international trade. The United States is *capable* of producing just about everything. But we've learned that it's cheaper to import bananas from Ecuador than to grow them in hothouses in Idaho. So we *specialize* in production, exporting tractors to Ecuador in exchange for imported bananas. Both nations end up consuming more products than they could if they had to produce everything themselves. That's why *global* markets are so vital to economic prosperity.

THE CIRCULAR FLOW

Figure 3.1 summarizes the kinds of interactions that occur among market participants. Note first that the figure identifies four separate groups of participants. Domestically, the rectangle labeled "Consumers" includes all 340 million consumers in the United States. In the "Business firms" box are grouped all the domestic business enterprises that buy and sell goods and services. The third participant, "Governments," includes the many separate agencies of the federal government, as well as state and local governments. Figure 3.1 also illustrates the role of global actors.

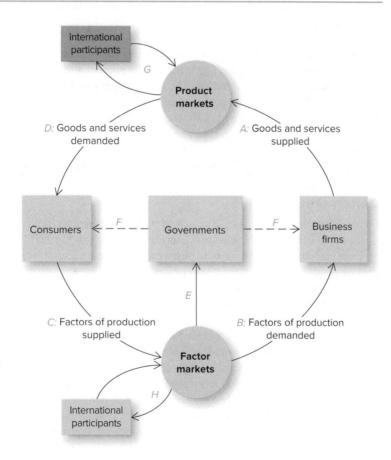

FIGURE 3.1

The Circular Flow

- *Business firms* supply goods and services to product markets (point *A*) and purchase factors of production in factor markets (*B*).

- *Individual consumers* supply factors of production such as their own labor (*C*) and purchase final goods and services (*D*).

- Federal, state, and local *governments* acquire resources in factor markets (*E*) and provide services to both consumers and business (*F*).

- *International participants* also take part by supplying imports, purchasing exports (*G*), and buying and selling factors of production (*H*).

The Two Markets

The easiest way to keep track of all this activity is to distinguish two basic markets. Figure 3.1 makes this distinction by portraying separate circles for product markets and factor markets. In **factor markets,** factors of production are exchanged. Market participants buy or sell land, labor, or capital that can be used in the production process. When you go looking for work, for example, you're making a factor of production—your labor—available to producers. The producers will hire you—purchase your services in the factor market—if you're offering the skills they need at a price they're willing to pay.

Interactions within factor markets are only half the story. At the end of a hard day's work, consumers go to the grocery store (or to a virtual store online) to buy desired goods and services—that is, to buy *products.* In this context, consumers again interact with business firms, this time purchasing goods and services those firms have produced. These interactions occur in **product markets.** Foreigners also participate in the product market by supplying goods and services (imports) to the United States and buying some of our output (exports).

The government sector also supplies services (e.g., education, national defense, highways). Most government services aren't explicitly sold in product markets, however. Typically, they're delivered "free," without an explicit price (e.g., public elementary schools, highways). This doesn't mean government services are truly free, though. There's still an **opportunity cost** associated with every service the government provides. Consumers and businesses pay that cost indirectly through taxes rather than directly through market prices.

In Figure 3.1, the arrow connecting product markets to consumers (*D*) emphasizes the fact that consumers, by definition, don't supply products. When individuals produce goods and services, they do so within the government or business sector. For instance, a doctor, a dentist, or an economic consultant functions in two sectors. When selling services in the market, this person is regarded as a "business"; when away from the office, he or she is regarded as a "consumer." This distinction is helpful in emphasizing that *the consumer is the final recipient of all goods and services produced.*

Locating Markets. Although we refer repeatedly to two kinds of markets in this text, it would be a little foolish to go off in search of the product and factor markets. Neither market is a single, identifiable structure. The term *market* simply refers to a place or situation where an economic exchange occurs—where a buyer and seller interact. The exchange may take place on the street, in a taxicab, over the phone, by mail, or in cyberspace. In some cases, the market used may in fact be quite distinguishable, as in the case of a Walmart store, the Chicago Commodity Exchange, or a state employment office. But whatever it looks like, *a market exists wherever and whenever an exchange takes place.*

Dollars and Exchange

Figure 3.1 neglects one critical element of market interactions: dollars. Each arrow in the figure actually has two dimensions. Consider again the arrow (*D*) linking consumers to product markets: It's drawn in only one direction because consumers, by definition, don't provide goods and services directly to product markets. But they do provide something: dollars. If you want to obtain something from a product market, you must offer to pay for it (typically with cash, check, or debit or credit card). Consumers exchange dollars for goods and services in product markets.

The same kinds of exchange occur in factor markets. When you go to work, you exchange a factor of production (your labor) for income, typically a paycheck. Here again, the path connecting consumers to factor markets (*C*) really goes in two directions: one of real resources, the other of dollars. Consumers receive wages, rent, and interest for the labor, land, and capital they bring to the factor markets. Indeed, nearly *every market transaction involves an exchange of dollars for goods (in product markets) or resources (in factor markets).* Money is thus critical in facilitating market exchanges and the specialization the exchanges permit.

factor market: Any place where factors of production (e.g., land, labor, capital) are bought and sold.

product market: Any place where finished goods and services (products) are bought and sold.

opportunity cost: The most desired goods or services that are forgone in order to obtain something else.

In markets people exchange money for products.

Ariel Skelley/Blend Images/Getty Images

Supply and Demand

In every market transaction, there must be a buyer and a seller. The seller is on the **supply** side of the market; the buyer is on the **demand** side. As noted earlier, we *supply* resources to the market when we look for a job—that is, when we offer our labor in exchange for income. We *demand* goods when we shop in a supermarket—that is, when we're prepared to offer dollars in exchange for something to eat. Business firms may *supply* goods and services in product markets at the same time they're *demanding* factors of production in factor markets. Whether one is on the supply side or the demand side of any particular market transaction depends on the nature of the exchange, not on the people or institutions involved.

> **supply:** The ability and willingness to sell (produce) specific quantities of a good at alternative prices in a given time period, *ceteris paribus*.

> **demand:** The willingness and ability to buy specific quantities of a good at alternative prices in a given time period, *ceteris paribus*.

DEMAND

To get a sense of how the demand side of market transactions works, we'll focus first on a single consumer. Then we'll aggregate to illustrate *market* demand.

Individual Demand

We can begin to understand how market forces work by looking more closely at the behavior of a single market participant. Let us start with Tom, a senior at Clearview College. Tom has majored in everything from art history to government in his five years at Clearview. He didn't connect to any of those fields and is on the brink of academic dismissal. To make matters worse, his parents have threatened to cut him off financially unless he gets serious about his course work. By that, they mean he should enroll in courses that will lead to a job after graduation. Tom thinks he has found the perfect solution: web design. Everything associated with the Internet pays big bucks. Or at least so Tom thinks. And his parents would definitely approve. So Tom has enrolled in web design courses.

Unfortunately for Tom, he never developed computer skills. Until he got to Clearview College, he thought mastering Sony's latest alien-attack video game was the pinnacle of electronic wizardry. Tom didn't have a clue about "cookies," "wireframe," "responsive design," or the other concepts the web design instructor outlined in the first lecture.

Given his circumstances, Tom was desperate to find someone who could tutor him in web design. But desperation is not enough to secure the services of a web architect. In a market-based economy, you must also be willing to *pay* for the things you want. Specifically, *a demand exists only if someone is willing and able to pay for the good*—that is, exchange dollars for a good or service in the marketplace. Is Tom willing and able to *pay* for the tutoring he so obviously needs?

Desiring a Gucci bag is not the same as demanding one.

gilaxia/Getty Images

Let us assume that Tom has some income and is willing to spend some of it to get a tutor. With these assumptions, we can claim that Tom is a participant in the *market* for web design services; he is a potential consumer.

But how much is Tom willing to pay? Surely Tom is not prepared to exchange *all* his income for help in mastering web design. After all, Tom could use his income to buy more desirable goods and services. If he spent all his income on a web tutor, that help would have an extremely high *opportunity cost.* He would be giving up the opportunity to spend that income on things he really likes. He'd pass his web design class but have little else. It doesn't sound like a good idea.

It seems more likely that there are *limits* to the amount Tom is willing to pay for web design tutoring. These limits will be determined by how much income Tom has to spend and how many other goods and services he must forsake to pay for a tutor.

Tom also knows that his grade in web design will depend in part on how much tutoring service he buys. He can pass the course with only a few hours of design help. If he wants a better grade, however, the cost is going to escalate quickly.

Naturally, Tom wants it all: an A in web design and a ticket to higher-paying jobs. But here again, the distinction between *desire* and *demand* is relevant. He may *desire* to master web design, but his actual proficiency will depend on how many hours of tutoring he is willing to *pay* for.

The Demand Schedule

demand schedule: A table showing the quantities of a good a consumer is willing and able to buy at alternative prices in a given time period, *ceteris paribus.*

We assume, then, that when Tom starts looking for a tutor, he has some sense of how much money he is willing to spend. He might have in mind some sort of **demand schedule,** like that described in Figure 3.2. According to row *A* of this schedule, Tom is willing and able to buy only 1 hour of tutoring service per semester if he must pay $50 an hour. At such a high price, he will learn just enough web design to pass the course.

At lower prices, Tom would behave differently. According to Figure 3.2, Tom would purchase *more* tutoring services if the price per hour were *less*. Indeed, we see from row *I* of the demand schedule that Tom is willing to purchase 20 hours per semester—the whole bag of design tricks—if the price of tutoring gets as low as $10 per hour.

Notice that the demand schedule doesn't tell us anything about *why* this consumer is willing to pay specific prices for various amounts of tutoring. Tom's expressed willingness to pay for web design tutoring may reflect a desperate need to finish a web design course, a lot of income to spend, or a relatively small desire for other goods and services. All the demand schedule tells us is what the consumer is *willing and able* to buy, for whatever reasons.

Also, observe that the demand schedule doesn't tell us how many hours of design help the consumer will *actually* buy. Figure 3.2 simply states that Tom is *willing and able* to pay for 1 hour of tutoring per semester at $50 per hour, for 2 hours at $45 each, and so on. How much tutoring he purchases will depend on the actual price of such services in the market. Until we know that price, we cannot tell how much service will be purchased. Hence, *"demand" is an expression of consumer buying intentions, of a willingness to buy, not a statement of actual purchases.*

The Demand Curve

demand curve: A curve describing the quantities of a good a consumer is willing and able to buy at alternative prices in a given time period, *ceteris paribus.*

A convenient summary of buying intentions is the **demand curve,** a graphical illustration of the demand schedule. The demand curve in Figure 3.2 tells us again that this consumer is willing to pay for only 1 hour of tutoring per semester if the price is $50 per hour (point *A*), for 2 if the price is $45 (point *B*), for 3 at $40 an hour (point *C*), and so on. Once we know what the market price of tutoring actually is, a glance at the demand curve tells what quantity a consumer will buy at any given price.

A common feature of demand curves is their downward slope. *As the price of a good falls, people purchase more of it.* In Figure 3.2, the quantity of tutoring demanded increases (moves rightward along the horizontal axis) as the price per hour decreases (moves down the vertical axis). This inverse relationship between price and quantity is so common that

Tom's Demand Schedule		
	Price of Tutoring (per Hour)	Quantity of Tutoring Demanded (Hours per Semester)
A	$50	1
B	45	2
C	40	3
D	35	5
E	30	7
F	25	9
G	20	12
H	15	15
I	10	20

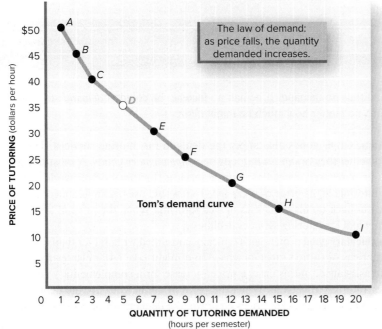

The law of demand: as price falls, the quantity demanded increases.

Tom's demand curve

FIGURE 3.2

A Demand Schedule and Curve

A demand schedule indicates the quantities of a good a consumer is able and willing to buy at alternative prices (*ceteris paribus*). The **demand schedule** here indicates that Tom would buy 5 hours of web tutoring per semester if the price were $35 per hour (row *D*). If web tutoring were less expensive (rows *E–I*), Tom would purchase a larger quantity.

A **demand curve** is a graphical illustration of a demand schedule. Each point on the curve refers to a specific quantity that will be demanded at a given price. If, for example, the price of web tutoring were $35 per hour, this curve tells us the consumer would purchase 5 hours per semester (point *D*). If web tutoring cost $30 per hour, 7 hours per semester would be demanded (point *E*). Each point on the curve corresponds to a row in the schedule.

we refer to it as the **law of demand.** Disney used this law to assure that its launch of the Disney+ streaming service would be a success (see Front Page Economics "Pricing Disney+").

law of demand: The quantity of a good demanded in a given time period increases as its price falls, *ceteris paribus*.

Determinants of Demand

The demand curve in Figure 3.2 has only two dimensions—quantity demanded (on the horizontal axis) and price (on the vertical axis). This seems to imply that the amount of tutoring demanded depends only on the price of that service. This is surely not the case. A consumer's willingness and ability to buy a product at various prices depend on a variety of forces. *The determinants of market demand include*

- *Tastes* (desire for this and other goods).
- *Income* (of the consumer).
- *Other goods* (their availability and price).
- *Expectations* (for income, prices, tastes).
- *Number of buyers.*

Tastes and Incomes. Tom's "taste" for tutoring has nothing to do with taste buds. *Taste* is just another word for desire. In this case, Tom's taste for web design services is clearly acquired. If he didn't have to pass a web design course, he would have no desire for related

FRONT PAGE ECONOMICS

PRICING DISNEY+

Disney decided it wanted to provide streaming services directly to customers, rather than renting its library of films and television shows to other streaming services like Netflix. But how successful would a streaming service be? In other words, what did the demand for a "Disney+" streaming service look like? Disney knew that the number of subscribers would depend not just on the attractiveness of the Disney archives, but also on the subscription price. After doing some market research, Disney decided to launch Disney+ at a price of $6.99 a month (or $69.99 per year). When Disney+ was launched on November 12, 2019, 10 million people signed up on the first day—a resounding success!

Source: News reports October–December 2019.

CRITICAL ANALYSIS: The **law of demand** dictates that a larger quantity will be demanded at lower prices. To secure millions of initial subscribers, Disney priced its streaming service low.

---

services and thus no demand. If he had no **income,** he couldn't *demand* any web design tutoring either, no matter how much he might *desire* it.

Other Goods. Other goods also affect the demand for tutoring services. Their effect depends on whether they're *substitute* goods or *complementary* goods. A **substitute good** is one that might be purchased instead of tutoring services. In Tom's simple world, pizza is a substitute for tutoring. If the price of pizza fell, Tom would use his limited income to buy more pizzas and cut back on his purchases of web tutoring. When the price of a substitute good falls, the demand for tutoring services declines.

A **complementary good** is one that's typically consumed with, rather than instead of, tutoring. If text prices or tuition rates increase, Tom might take fewer classes and demand *less* web design assistance. In this case, a price increase for a complementary good causes the demand for tutoring to decline. When the price of coffee goes up, the demand for cream goes down. When theater ticket prices go down, the demand for popcorn goes up.

Expectations. Expectations also play a role in consumer decisions. If Tom expected to flunk his web design course anyway, he probably wouldn't waste any money getting tutorial help; his demand for such services would disappear. On the other hand, if he expects a web tutor to determine his college fate, he might be more willing to buy such services.

Number of Buyers. Tom may not be the only one in need of tutoring. The demand for tutoring depends on the number of students who are in a similar situation.

Ceteris Paribus

If demand is in fact such a multidimensional decision, how can we reduce it to only the two dimensions of price and quantity? In Chapter 1 we first encountered this *ceteris paribus* trick. To simplify their models of the world, economists focus on only one or two forces at a time and *assume* nothing else changes. We know a consumer's tastes, income, other goods, and expectations all affect the decision to hire a tutor. But we want to focus on the relationship between quantity demanded and price. That is, we want to know what *independent* influence price has on consumption decisions. To find out, we must isolate that one influence, price, and assume that the determinants of demand remain unchanged.

The *ceteris paribus* assumption is not as farfetched as it may seem. People's tastes, income, and expectations do not change quickly. Also, the prices and availability of other goods don't change all that fast. Hence, a change in the *price* of a product may be the only factor that prompts an immediate change in quantity demanded.

---

substitute goods: Goods that substitute for each other; when the price of good *x* rises, the demand for good *y* increases, *ceteris paribus*.

complementary goods: Goods frequently consumed in combination; when the price of good *x* rises, the demand for good *y* falls, ceteris paribus.

ceteris paribus: The assumption of nothing else changing.

The ability to predict consumer responses to a price change is important. What would happen, for example, to enrollment at your school if tuition doubled? Must we guess? Or can we use demand curves to predict how the quantity of applications will change as the price of college goes up? *Demand curves show us how changes in market prices alter consumer behavior.* We used the demand curve in Figure 3.2 to predict how Tom's web design ability would change at different tutorial prices. Disney used its knowledge of consumer demand to set the subscription price for Disney+ (see Front Page Economics "Pricing Disney+").

Shifts in Demand

Although demand curves are useful in predicting consumer responses to market signals, they aren't infallible. The problem is that *the determinants of demand can and do change.* When they do, a specific demand curve may become obsolete. A *demand curve (schedule) is valid only so long as the underlying determinants of demand remain constant.* If the *ceteris paribus* assumption is violated—if tastes, income, other goods, or expectations change—the ability or willingness to buy will change. When this happens, the demand curve will **shift** to a new position.

Suppose, for example, that Tom won $1,000 in the state lottery. This windfall would increase his ability to pay for tutoring services. Figure 3.3 shows the effect on Tom's demand. The old demand curve, D_1, is no longer relevant. Tom's lottery winnings enable him to buy *more* tutoring at any price, as illustrated by the new demand curve, D_2. According to this

shift in demand: A change in the quantity demanded at any (every) price.

Demand *shifts* when tastes, income, other goods, or expectations change.

	Quantity Demanded (Hours per Semester)		
	Price (per Hour)	**Initial Demand**	**After Increase in Income**
A	$50	1	8
B	45	2	9
C	40	3	10
D	35	5	12
E	30	7	14
F	25	9	16
G	20	12	19
H	15	15	22
I	10	20	27

FIGURE 3.3

Shifts vs. Movements

A demand curve shows how a consumer responds to price changes. If the determinants of demand stay constant, the response is a *movement* along the curve to a new quantity demanded. In this case, when price falls from $35 to $20 per hour, the quantity demanded increases from 5 (point d_1), to 12 (point g_1).

If the determinants of demand *change,* the entire demand curve *shifts.* In this case, a rise in income increases demand. With more income, Tom is willing to buy 12 hours at the initial price of $35 (point d_2), not just the 5 hours he demanded before the lottery win (point d_1).

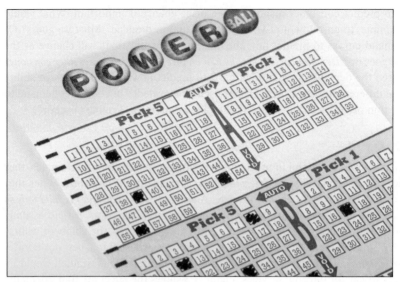

What would you buy if you won?
McGraw Hill

new curve, lucky Tom is now willing and able to buy 12 hours per semester at the price of $35 per hour (point d_2). This is a large increase in demand; previously (before winning the lottery), he demanded only 5 hours at that price (point d_1).

With his higher income, Tom can buy more tutoring services at every price. Thus, *the entire demand curve shifts to the right when income goes up.* Figure 3.3 illustrates both the old (pre-lottery) and new (post-lottery) demand curves.

Income is only one of the basic determinants of demand. Changes in any of the other determinants of demand would also cause the demand curve to shift. Tom's taste for web tutoring might increase dramatically, for example, if his parents promised to buy him a new car for passing web design. In that case, he might be willing to forgo other goods and spend more of his income on tutors. *An increase in taste (desire) also shifts the demand curve to the right.*

Pizza and Politics. A similar demand shift occurs at the White House when a political crisis erupts. On an average day, White House staffers order about $300 worth of pizza from the nearby Domino's. When a crisis hits, however, staffers work well into the night and their demand for pizza soars. On the evening of the November 2020 presidential elections, White House staffers ordered more than $1,000 worth of pizza! Political analysts now use pizza deliveries to predict major White House announcements.

Movements vs. Shifts

It's important to distinguish shifts of the demand curve from movements along the demand curve. *Movements along a demand curve are a response to price changes for that good.* Such movements assume that determinants of demand are unchanged. By contrast, *shifts of the demand curve occur when the determinants of demand change.* When tastes, income, other goods, or expectations are altered, the basic relationship between price and quantity demanded is changed (shifts).

For convenience, movements along a demand curve and shifts of the demand curve have their own labels. Specifically, take care to distinguish

- *Changes in quantity demanded:* movements along a given demand curve in response to price changes of that good.
- *Changes in demand:* shifts of the demand curve due to changes in tastes, income, other goods, or expectations.

Tom's behavior in the web tutoring market will change if either the price of tutoring changes (a movement) or the underlying determinants of his demand are altered (a shift).

Notice in Figure 3.3 that he ends up buying 12 hours of web tutoring if either the price of tutoring falls (to $20 per hour, leading him to point d_1) or his income increases (leading him to point d_2). Demand curves help us predict those market responses.

Market Demand

Whatever we say about demand for web design tutoring on the part of one wannabe web master, we can also say about every student at Clearview College (or, for that matter, about all consumers). Some students have no interest in web design and aren't willing to pay for related services: They don't participate in the web tutoring market. Other students want such services but don't have enough income to pay for them: They too are excluded from the web tutoring market. A large number of students, however, not only have a need (or desire) for web tutoring but also are willing and able to purchase such services.

What we start with in product markets, then, is many individual demand curves. Fortunately, it's possible to combine all the individual demand curves into a single **market demand.** The aggregation process is no more difficult than simple arithmetic. Suppose that you would be willing to buy 1 hour of tutoring per semester at a price of $80 per hour. George, who is also desperate to learn web design, would buy 2 at that price; and I would buy none because my publisher (McGraw-Hill) creates a web page for my book. What would our combined (market) demand for hours of tutoring be at that price? Collectively, we would be willing to buy a total of 3 hours of tutoring per semester if the price were $80 per hour. Our combined willingness to buy—our collective market demand—is nothing more than the sum of our individual demands. The same kind of aggregation can be performed for all consumers, leading to a summary of the total *market* demand for a specific good or service. Thus, *market demand is determined by the number of potential buyers and their respective tastes, incomes, other goods, and expectations.*

market demand: The total quantities of a good or service people are willing and able to buy at alternative prices in a given time period; the sum of individual demands.

The Market Demand Curve

Figure 3.4 provides the basic market demand schedule for a situation in which only three consumers participate in the market. It illustrates the same market situation with demand curves. The three individuals who participate in the market demand for web tutoring at Clearview College obviously differ greatly, as suggested by their respective demand schedules. Tom's demand schedule is portrayed in the first column of the table (and is identical to the one we examined in Figure 3.2). George is also desperate to acquire some job skills and is willing to pay relatively high prices for web design tutoring. His demand is summarized in the second column under Quantity Demanded in the table.

The third consumer in this market is Lisa. Lisa already knows the nuts and bolts of web design, so she isn't so desperate for tutorial services. She would like to upgrade her skills, however, especially in animation and e-commerce applications. But her limited budget precludes paying a lot for help. She will hire a tutor only if the price falls to $30 per hour. Should tutors cost less, she'd even buy quite a few hours of web design tutoring.

The differing circumstances of Tom, George, and Lisa are expressed in their individual demand schedules (Figure 3.4). To determine the *market* demand for tutoring from this information, we simply add these three separate demands. The end result of this aggregation is, first, a *market* demand schedule (last column in the table) and, second, the resultant *market* demand curve (Figure 3.4*d*). These market summaries describe the various quantities of tutoring that Clearview College students are *willing and able* to purchase each semester at various prices.

What price? How much web tutoring will be purchased each semester? Knowing how much help Tom, George, and Lisa are willing to buy at various prices doesn't tell you how much they're *actually* going to purchase. To determine the actual consumption of web tutoring, we have to know something about prices and supplies. Which of the many different prices illustrated in Figures 3.3 and 3.4 will actually prevail? How will that price be determined?

FIGURE 3.4

Construction of the Market Demand Curve

Market demand represents the combined demands of all market participants.

To determine the total quantity of web tutoring demanded at any given price, we add the separate demands of the individual consumers. Row *G* of this schedule indicates that a *total* quantity of 39 hours per semester will be demanded at a price of $20 per hour.

This same conclusion is reached by adding the individual demand curves, leading to point *G* on the market demand curve (see graph *d*).

	Price (per Hour)	Quantity of Tutoring Demanded (Hours per Semester)				
		Tom	+ George	+ Lisa	=	Market Demand
A	$50	1	4	0		5
B	45	2	6	0		8
C	40	3	8	0		11
D	35	5	11	0		16
E	30	7	14	1		22
F	25	9	18	3		30
G	20	12	22	5		39
H	15	15	26	6		47
I	10	20	30	7		57

SUPPLY

market supply: The total quantities of a good that sellers are willing and able to sell at alternative prices in a given time period, *ceteris paribus.*

To understand how the price of web tutoring is established, we must also look at the other side of the market: the *supply* side. We need to know how many hours of tutoring services people are willing and able to *sell* at various prices—that is, the **market supply.** As on the demand side, the *market supply* depends on the behavior of all the individuals willing and able to supply web tutoring at some price.

Determinants of Supply

Let's return to the Clearview campus for a moment. What we need to know now is how much tutorial help people are willing and able to provide. Generally speaking, web design can be fun, but it can also be drudge work, especially when you're doing it for someone else. Hosting services like Weebly, Squarespace, and GoDaddy have made setting up a website easier and more creative. And the cloud and Wi-Fi access have made the job more convenient. But teaching someone else to design web pages is still work. So why does anyone do it? Easy answer: for the money. People offer (supply) tutoring services to earn income that they, in turn, can spend on the goods and services *they* desire.

How much money must be offered to induce web designers to do a little tutoring depends on a variety of things. The *determinants of market supply include*

- *Technology.*
- *Factor costs.*
- *Other goods.*
- *Taxes and subsidies.*
- *Expectations.*
- *Number of sellers.*

Technology. The technology of web design, for example, is always getting easier and more creative. With a program like Weebly, for example, it's very easy to create a bread-and-butter web page. A continuous stream of new software programs (e.g., Wordpress, DreamWeaver) keeps stretching the possibilities for graphics, animation, interactivity, and content. These technological advances mean that web design services can be supplied more quickly and cheaply. They also make *teaching* web design easier. As a result, they induce people to supply *more* tutoring services at every price.

Factor Costs. How much web design service is offered at any given price also depends on the cost of factors of production. If the software programs needed to create web pages are cheap (or, better yet, free), web designers can afford to charge lower prices. If the required software inputs are expensive, however, they will have to charge more for their services.

Other Goods. Other goods can also affect the willingness to supply web design services. If you can make more income waiting tables than you can tutoring lazy students, why would you even boot up the computer? As the prices paid for other goods and services change, they will influence people's decision about whether to offer web services.

Taxes. In the real world, the decision to supply goods and services is also influenced by the long arm of Uncle Sam. Federal, state, and local governments impose **taxes** on income earned in the marketplace. When tax rates are high, people get to keep less of the income they earn. Once taxes start biting into paychecks, some people may conclude that tutoring is no longer worth the hassle and withdraw from the market.

Expectations. Expectations are also important on the supply side of the market. If web designers expect higher prices, lower costs, or reduced taxes, they may be more willing to learn new software programs. On the other hand, if they have poor expectations about the future, they may just find something else to do.

Number of Sellers. Finally, we note that the number of potential sellers will affect the quantity of service offered for sale at various prices. If there are lots of willing tutors on campus, a lot of tutorial service will be available at reasonable prices.

All these considerations—factor costs, technology, taxes, expectations—affect the decision to offer web services at various prices. In general, we assume that web architects will be willing to provide more tutoring if the per-hour price is high and less if the price is low. In other words, there is a **law of supply** that parallels the law of demand. *The law of supply says that larger quantities will be offered for sale at higher prices.* Here again, the laws rest on the *ceteris paribus* assumption: The quantity supplied increases at higher prices *if* the determinants of supply are constant. *Supply curves are upward-sloping to the right,* as shown in Figure 3.5. Note how the *quantity supplied* jumps from 39 hours (point *d*) to 130 hours (point *h*) when the price of web service doubles (from $20 to $40 per hour).

law of supply: The quantity of a good supplied in a given time period increases as its price increases, *ceteris paribus.*

FIGURE 3.5

Market Supply

The **market supply curve** indicates the *combined* sales intentions of all market participants—that is, the total quantities they are willing and able to sell at various prices.

If the price of tutoring were $45 per hour (point *i*), the *total* quantity of services supplied would be 140 hours per semester. This quantity is determined by adding the supply decisions of all individual producers. In this case, Ann supplies 93 hours, Bob supplies 33, and Carlos supplies the rest.

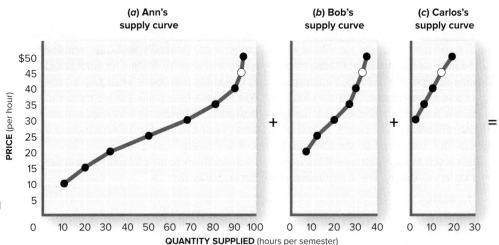

(a) Ann's supply curve   +   (b) Bob's supply curve   +   (c) Carlos's supply curve   =

The law of supply: quantity supplied increases as price rises.

	Price per Hour	Ann	+	Bob	+	Carlos	=	Market
				Quantity of Tutoring Supplied by				
j	$50	94		35		19		148
i	45	93		33		14		140
h	40	90		30		10		130
g	35	81		27		6		114
f	30	68		20		2		90
e	25	50		12		0		62
d	20	32		7		0		39
c	15	20		0		0		20
b	10	10		0		0		10

Market Supply

Figure 3.5 also illustrates how *market* supply is constructed from the supply decisions of individual sellers. In this case, only three web masters are available. Ann is willing to provide a lot of tutoring at low prices, whereas Bob requires at least $20 an hour. Carlos won't talk to students for less than $30 an hour.

By adding the quantity each tutor is willing to offer at every price, we can construct the market supply curve. Notice in Figure 3.5 how the quantity supplied to the market at $45 (point *i*) comes from the individual efforts of Ann (93 hours), Bob (33 hours), and Carlos (14 hours). *The market supply curve is just a summary of the supply intentions of all producers.*

None of the points on the market supply curve (Figure 3.5) tells us how much web tutoring is *actually* being sold on the Clearview campus. **Market supply is an expression of sellers' intentions— an offer to sell—not a statement of actual sales.** My next-door neighbor may be willing to sell his 2014 Honda Civic for $18,000, but most likely he'll never find a buyer at that price. Nevertheless, his *willingness* to sell his car at that price is part of the *market supply* of used cars.

Shifts of Supply

As with demand, there's nothing sacred about any given set of supply intentions. Supply curves *shift* when the underlying determinants of supply change. Thus, **it is important to distinguish**

- *Changes in quantity supplied:* movements along a given supply curve in response to price changes of that good.
- *Changes in supply:* shifts of the supply curve due to changes in technology, factor costs, other goods, taxes and subsidies, or expectations.

Our Latin friend *ceteris paribus* is once again the decisive factor. If the price of a product is the only variable changing, then we can **track changes in quantity supplied along the supply curve.** But if *ceteris paribus* is violated—if technology, factor costs, the profitability of producing other goods, tax rates, expectations, or the number of sellers changes—then **changes in supply are illustrated by shifts of the supply curve.**

The World View "Gas Prices Jump in Wake of Saudi Attack" illustrates how a supply shift pushed up gasoline prices in September 2019. As noted at the beginning of this chapter, drone strikes on Saudi oil facilities reduced Saudi Arabia's ability to produce (supply) oil. As the market supply curve shifted to the left, the price of gasoline rose.

WORLD VIEW

GAS PRICES JUMP IN WAKE OF SAUDI ATTACK

The Saudi Arabian oil processing plants in Abqaiq were hit by drone strikes, shutting down about half of the Kingdom's production capacity. Early estimates put the damage at about 5.7 million barrels of oil per day, roughly half of Saudi output. Crude oil prices jumped as much as $8 per barrel and U.S. gasoline prices jumped by 9 cents a gallon, according to the U.S. Energy Information Agency.

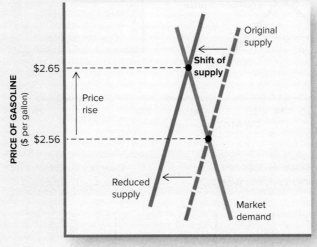

Source: News reports, September–December 2019.

CRITICAL ANALYSIS: When factor costs or availability worsens, the supply curve **shifts** to the left. Such leftward supply-curve shifts push prices up the market demand curve.

The coronavirus outbreak in 2020 had similar effects across a broad spectrum of industries. Thousands of American companies import needed components and materials from China. General Electric, for example, imports critical parts for its production of aircraft engines, CT scanners, X-ray machines, and other products. Pharmaceutical companies get critical ingredients from China to produce blood pressure, depression, and Alzheimer's disease medicines. Phantom Fireworks, a small company in Youngstown, Ohio, needs Chinese rockets and firecrackers for its July 4 celebrations. When the coronavirus shut down production facilities in China, the *market supply* of these products was reduced. The resulting leftward supply shift raised input prices and reduced production in U.S. factories.

EQUILIBRIUM

That spike in gasoline prices after the Saudi attacks offers some clues to how the forces of supply and demand set—and change—market prices. For a closer look at how those forces work, we'll return to Clearview College for a moment. How did supply and demand resolve the WHAT, HOW, and FOR WHOM questions in that web tutoring market?

Figure 3.6 helps answer that question by bringing together the market supply and demand curves we've already examined (Figures 3.4 and 3.5). When we put the two curves together, we see that *only one price and quantity combination is compatible with the intentions of both buyers and sellers. This equilibrium occurs at the intersection of the supply and demand curves.*

FIGURE 3.6

Equilibrium Price

The intersection of the demand and supply curves establishes the *equilibrium* price and quantity. Only at equilibrium is the quantity demanded equal to the quantity supplied. In this case, the equilibrium price is $20 per hour, and 39 hours is the equilibrium quantity.

At above-equilibrium prices, a market *surplus* exists—the quantity supplied exceeds the quantity demanded. At prices below equilibrium, a market *shortage* exists.

Price (per Hour)	Quantity Supplied (Hours per Semester)		Quantity Demanded (Hours per Semester)	
$50	148		5	
45	140		8	
40	130	Market surplus	11	Nonequilibrium prices create surpluses or shortages.
35	114		16	
30	90		22	
25	62		30	
20	39	Equilibrium	39	
15	20	Market shortage	47	
10	10		57	

Notice in Figure 3.6 where that intersection occurs—at the price of $20 and the quantity of 39 hours. So $20 is the **equilibrium price:** Campus tutors will sell a total of 39 hours of tutoring per semester—the same amount that students wish to buy at that price. Those 39 hours of tutoring service will be part of WHAT is produced in the economy.

Market Clearing

An equilibrium doesn't imply that everyone is happy with the prevailing price or quantity. Notice in Figure 3.6, for example, that some students who want to buy tutoring services don't get any. These would-be buyers are arrayed along the demand curve *below* the equilibrium. Because the price they're *willing* to pay is less than the equilibrium price of $20, they don't get any web design help. The market's FOR WHOM answer includes only those students willing and able to pay the equilibrium price.

Likewise, some would-be sellers are frustrated by this market outcome. These wannabe tutors are arrayed along the supply curve *above* the equilibrium. Because they insist on being paid *more* than the equilibrium price of $20 per hour, they don't actually sell anything.

Although not everyone finds satisfaction in the market equilibrium, that unique outcome is efficient. *The equilibrium price and quantity reflect a compromise between buyers and sellers. No other compromise yields a quantity demanded that's exactly equal to the quantity supplied.*

The Invisible Hand. The equilibrium price isn't determined by any single individual. Rather, it's determined by the collective behavior of many buyers and sellers, each acting out his or her own demand or supply schedule. It's this kind of impersonal price determination that gave rise to Adam Smith's characterization of the market mechanism as "the invisible hand." In attempting to explain how the **market mechanism** works, the famed 18th-century economist noted a remarkable feature of market prices. The market behaves as if some unseen force (the invisible hand) were examining each individual's supply or demand schedule and then selecting a price that assured an equilibrium. In practice, the process of price determination isn't so mysterious: It's a simple process of trial and error.

Disequilibrium: Surplus and Shortage

Market Surplus. To appreciate the power of the market mechanism, consider interference in its operation. Suppose, for example, that campus tutors banded together and agreed to charge a minimum price of $25 per hour, five dollars more than the equilibrium price. By establishing a **price floor,** a minimum price for their services, the tutors hope to increase their incomes. Their goal won't be achieved. Figure 3.6 illustrates the consequences of this *dis*equilibrium pricing. At $25 per hour, campus tutors would be offering more than 39 hours of tutoring. How much more? Move up the market supply curve from the equilibrium price until you hit the price of $25. At that price, tutors are prepared to offer the quantity indicated by point *y*. What's wrong with that point? Students in need of tutoring aren't willing to buy that much tutoring at that price. The market demand curve tells us Tom, George, and Lisa are willing to buy only the smaller quantity indicated by point *x* at the price of $25 per hour. We have a discrepancy between the quantity suppliers want to sell and the quantity consumers want to buy. This is a *dis*equilibrium.

In this case, the disequilibrium creates a **market surplus:** More tutoring is being offered for sale than consumers are willing to purchase at the available price. As Figure 3.6 indicates, at a price of $25 per hour, a market surplus of 32 hours per semester exists. Under these circumstances, campus tutors would be spending many idle hours at their keyboards waiting for customers to appear. Their waiting will be in vain because the quantity of web tutoring demanded will not increase until the price of tutoring falls. That is the clear message of the demand curve. As would-be tutors get this message, they'll reduce their prices. They really have no other choice.

As sellers' asking prices decline, the quantity demanded will increase. This concept is illustrated in Figure 3.6 by the movement along the demand curve from point *x* to lower prices and greater quantity demanded. As we move down the market demand curve, the *desire* for web design help doesn't change, but the quantity people are *able and willing to buy* increases. When the price falls to $20 per hour, the quantity demanded will finally equal the quantity supplied. This is the *equilibrium* illustrated in Figure 3.6.

equilibrium price: The price at which the quantity of a good demanded in a given time period equals the quantity supplied.

market mechanism: The use of market prices and sales to signal desired outputs (or resource allocations).

price floor: Lower limit set for the price of a good.

market surplus: The amount by which the quantity supplied exceeds the quantity demanded at a given price; excess supply.

Market Shortage. A very different sequence of events would occur if a market shortage existed. Suppose someone were to spread the word that web tutoring services were available at only $15 per hour. Tom, George, and Lisa would be standing in line to get tutorial help, but campus web designers wouldn't be willing to supply the quantity demanded at that price. As Figure 3.6 confirms, at $15 per hour, the quantity demanded (47 hours per semester) greatly exceeds the quantity supplied (20 hours per semester). In this situation, we speak of a **market shortage**—that is, an excess of quantity demanded over quantity supplied. At a price of $15 an hour, the shortage amounts to 27 hours of tutoring services.

When a market shortage exists, not all consumer demands can be satisfied. Some people who are *willing* to buy web help at the going price ($15) won't be able to do so. To get the help they want, Tom, George, Lisa, or some other consumer will offer to pay a *higher* price, thus initiating a move up the demand curve in Figure 3.6. The higher prices offered will in turn induce enterprising tutors to work more hours, thus ensuring an upward movement along the market supply curve. Notice, again, that the *desire* to tutor web design hasn't changed; only the quantity supplied has responded to a change in price. As this process continues, the quantity supplied will eventually equal the quantity demanded (39 hours in Figure 3.6).

Price Gouging? In the midst of a crisis, it is often difficult to wait for the market to adjust to an abrupt disequilibrium. Consider what happened to the price of hand sanitizers when the coronavirus swept across the country. Suddenly, everyone wanted hand sanitizers to ward off the COVID-19 virus. The explosion of demand sent the price of hand sanitizers soaring. Consumers cried foul and asked the government to step in and prevent price gouging.

Economists would argue that the price hikes were an important step in satisfying consumer demands. On the demand side, the higher price discouraged people from buying more sanitizer than they needed (hoarding). More importantly, the high prices were an incentive for producers to increase the quantity supplied. Soap companies increased production, while companies that had never produced sanitizers before (like Jim Beam, the whiskey distiller) jumped into the market. If the government prohibited price gouging,

market shortage: The amount by which the quantity demanded exceeds the quantity supplied at a given price; excess demand.

WORLD VIEW

VENEZUELA'S FOOD CRISIS

Venezuelans are starving. According to the Food and Agriculture Organization (FAO), 21.2 percent of Venezuelans are suffering from hunger. Thirty percent of children are malnourished. There simply isn't enough food to go around.

Price controls are a major culprit. In 2003, then-president Hugo Chavez declared war on "speculators" who were increasing food prices. He imposed price controls on basic foods and medicines. Price controls were tightened by his successor, Nicolas Maduro, in the Fair Prices Act of 2014 and again in the Constitutional Law of Agreed Prices passed in November 2017.

The price ceilings make food seem affordable. But food is hard to find. The price ceilings make production and importation of food unprofitable. The government distributes some basic food rations every month. But people have to wait hours in line to get access to more food, often in vain. Rice, flour, coffee, toilet paper, diapers, sugar, and medicine are in short supply. Black markets, occasional food riots, and cross-border smuggling bring some relief but not enough. Over four million Venezuelans have fled the country since 2014. Those left behind are hungry all the time.

Source: News reports of 2017–2019.

CRITICAL ANALYSIS: Price controls increase the quantity demanded but reduce the quantity supplied. The end result is a **market shortage** that leaves consumers frustrated (and hungry).

those market adjustments wouldn't have occurred and the sanitizer shortage would have persisted longer.

In Venezuela, the government's determination to prevent any sort of price gouging has had debilitating effects. The socialist government has tried to keep food prices low by imposing **price ceilings** on everything from rice to sanitary napkins. As the accompanying World View "Venezuela's Food Crisis" notes, those price controls have led to widespread hunger.

Self-Adjusting Prices. What we observe, then, is that *whenever the market price is set above or below the equilibrium price, either a market surplus or a market shortage will emerge.* To overcome a surplus or shortage, buyers and sellers will change their behavior. Sellers will have to compete for customers by reducing prices when a market surplus exists. If a shortage exists, buyers will compete for service by offering to pay higher prices. Only at the *equilibrium* price will no further adjustments be required.

Sometimes the market price is slow to adjust, and a disequilibrium persists. This is often the case with tickets to rock concerts, football games, and other one-time events. People initially adjust their behavior by standing in ticket lines for hours, or hopping on the Internet, hoping to buy a ticket at the below-equilibrium price. The tickets are typically resold ("scalped"), however, at prices closer to equilibrium. This is a common occurrence at major college sporting events such as the Final Four basketball championships (see Front Page Economics "March Madness Becomes Sadness").

FRONT PAGE ECONOMICS

MARCH MADNESS BECOMES SADNESS

Ticket prices for the college basketball championships always skyrocket when the 68-team draw is announced. And they jump even further as the Final Four teams emerge. The year 2020 was no different. The 700 floor seats that are sold to students for $40 apiece were already reselling for as much as $4,670 in early January. If the history of March Madness is a guide, those tickets could have sold for more than $10,000 each once the Final Four teams were known. In 2020, however, there wasn't a Final Four: Fear of the coronavirus convinced the NCAA to cancel that year's tournament. The only madness was among those fans that paid scalpers' prices for tickets that got only $40 refunds.

Source: Media reports, March 10–14, 2020.

CRITICAL ANALYSIS: When tickets are sold initially at below-equilibrium prices, a market **shortage** is created. Scalpers resell tickets at prices closer to equilibrium, reaping a profit in the process.

Business firms can discover equilibrium prices by trial and error. If consumer purchases aren't keeping up with production, a firm may conclude that its price is above the equilibrium price. To get rid of accumulated inventory, the firm will have to lower its price. In the happier situation where consumer purchases are outpacing production, a firm might conclude that its price was a trifle too low and give it a nudge upward. In either case, the equilibrium price can be established after a few trials in the marketplace.

Changes in Equilibrium

No equilibrium price is permanent. The equilibrium price established in the Clearview College tutoring market, for example, was the unique outcome of specific demand and supply schedules. Those schedules themselves were based on our assumption of *ceteris paribus.* We assumed that the "taste" (desire) for web design assistance was given, as were consumers'

Why do stores ever have sales?
Ron Zmiri/123RF

incomes, the price and availability of other goods, and expectations. Any of these determinants of demand could change. When one does, the demand curve has to be redrawn. Such a shift of the demand curve will lead to a new equilibrium price and quantity. Indeed, *the equilibrium price will change whenever the supply or demand curve shifts.*

A Demand Shift We can illustrate how equilibrium prices change by taking one last look at the Clearview College tutoring market. Our original supply and demand curves, together with the resulting equilibrium (point E_1), are depicted in Figure 3.7. Now suppose that all the professors at Clearview begin requiring class-specific web pages from each student. The

FIGURE 3.7

Changes in Equilibrium

If demand or supply changes (shifts), market equilibrium will change as well.

 Demand shift: In (*a*), the rightward shift of the demand curve illustrates an increase in demand. When demand increases, the equilibrium price rises (from E_1 to E_2).

 Supply shift: In (*b*), the leftward shift of the supply curve illustrates a decrease in supply. This raises the equilibrium price to E_3.

 Demand and supply curves shift only when their underlying determinants change—that is, when *ceteris paribus* is violated.

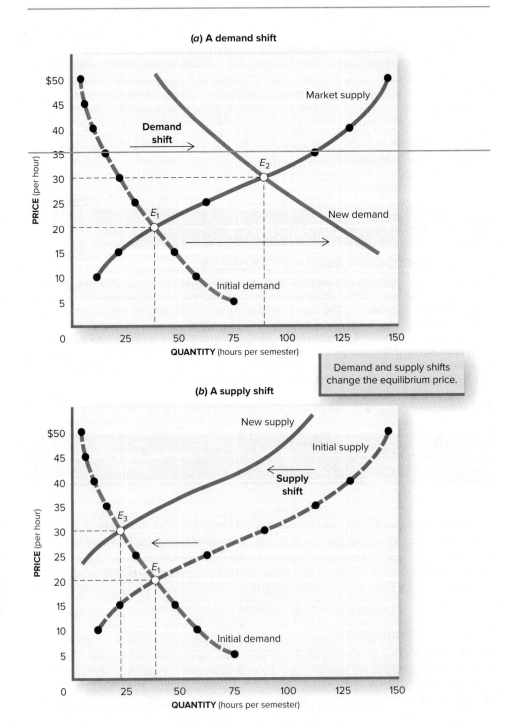

(*a*) A demand shift

(*b*) A supply shift

Demand and supply shifts change the equilibrium price.

increased need (desire) for web design ability will affect market demand. Tom, George, and Lisa will be willing to buy more web tutoring at every price than they were before. That is, the *demand* for web services has increased. We can represent this increased demand by a rightward *shift* of the market demand curve, as illustrated in Figure 3.7a.

Note that the new demand curve intersects the (unchanged) market supply curve at a new price (point E_2); the equilibrium price is now $30 per hour and 90 hours of tutoring are bought. This new equilibrium price will persist until either the demand curve or the supply curve shifts again.

A Supply Shift. Figure 3.7b illustrates a *supply* shift. The decrease (leftward shift) in supply might occur if some on-campus tutors got sick. Or approaching exams might convince would-be tutors that they have no time to spare. ***Whenever supply decreases (shifts left), price tends to rise,*** as in Figure 3.7b.

Lots of Shifts. In the real world, demand and supply curves are constantly shifting. A change in the weather can alter the supply and demand for food, vacations, and baseball games. A new product can change the demand for old products. A foreign crisis can alter the supply, demand, and price of oil (see World View "Gas Prices Jump in Wake of Saudi Attack"). And a virus can lead to extreme changes in ticket prices to sporting events (see Front Page Economics "March Madness Becomes Sadness"). Look for and remember these shifts:

Type of Shift	Name	Effect on Price	Effect on Quantity
Rightward shift of demand	"Increase in demand"	Price increase	Quantity increase
Leftward shift of demand	"Decrease in demand"	Price decrease	Quantity decrease
Rightward shift of supply	"Increase in supply"	Price decrease	Quantity increase
Leftward shift of supply	"Decrease in supply"	Price increase	Quantity decrease

When you see a price change, one or more of these shifts must have occurred.

MARKET OUTCOMES

Notice how the market mechanism resolves the basic economic questions of WHAT, HOW, and FOR WHOM.

WHAT

The WHAT question refers to the mix of output society produces. How much web tutorial service will be included in that mix? The answer at Clearview College was 39 hours of tutoring per semester. This decision wasn't reached in a referendum, but instead in the market equilibrium (Figure 3.6). In the same way but on a larger scale, millions of consumers and a handful of auto producers decide to include 17 million or so cars and trucks in each year's mix of output. Auto manufacturers use rebates, discounts, and variable interest rates to induce consumers to buy the same quantity that auto manufacturers are producing.

HOW

The market mechanism also determines HOW goods are produced. Profit-seeking producers will strive to produce web designs and automobiles in the most efficient way. They'll use market prices to decide not only WHAT to produce but also what resources to use in the production process. If new software simplifies web design—and is priced low enough—tutors will use it. Likewise, auto manufacturers will use robots rather than humans on the assembly line if robots reduce costs and increase profits.

FOR WHOM

Finally, the invisible hand of the market will determine who gets the goods produced. At Clearview College, who got web tutoring? Only those students who were willing and able to pay $20 per hour for that service. FOR WHOM are all those automobiles produced each year? The answer is the same: those consumers who are willing and able to pay the market price for a new car.

Optimal, Not Perfect

Not everyone is happy with these answers, of course. Tom would like to pay only $10 an hour for a tutor. And some of the Clearview students don't have enough income to buy any tutoring. They think it's unfair that they have to design their own web pages while rich students can have someone else do their design work for them. Students who can't afford cars are even less happy with the market's answer to the FOR WHOM question.

Although the outcomes of the marketplace aren't perfect, they're often optimal. Optimal outcomes are the best possible given our incomes and scarce resources. Sure, we'd like everyone to have access to tutoring and to drive a new car. But there aren't enough resources available to create such a utopia. So we have to ration available tutors and cars. The market mechanism performs this rationing function. People who want to supply tutoring or build cars are free to make that choice. And consumers are free to decide how they want to spend their income. In the process, we expect market participants to make decisions that maximize their own well-being. If they do, then we conclude that everyone is doing as well as possible, given their available resources.

DECISIONS FOR TOMORROW

Should We Allow the Sale of Human Organs?

As you were reading this chapter, dozens of Americans were dying from failed organs. More than 100,000 Americans are waiting for life-saving kidneys, livers, lungs, and other vital organs. They can't wait long, however. Every day at least 20 of these organ-diseased patients die. The clock is always ticking.

Modern technology can save most of these patients. Vital organs can be transplanted, extending the life of diseased patients. How many people are saved, however, depends on how well the organ "market" works.

The Supply of Organs. The only cure for liver disease and some other organ failures is a replacement organ. More than 50 years ago, doctors discovered that they could transplant an organ from one individual to another. Since then, medical technology has advanced to the point where organ transplants are exceptionally safe and successful. The constraint on this life-saving technique is the *supply* of transplantable organs.

Although more than 2 million Americans die each year, most deaths do not create transplantable organs. Only 20,000 or so people die in circumstances—such as brain death after a car crash—that make them suitable donors for life-saving transplants. Additional kidneys can be "harvested" from live donors (we have two kidneys but can function with only one; this is not true for liver, heart, or pancreas).

You don't have to die to supply an organ. Instead, you become a donor by agreeing to release your organs after death. The agreement is typically certified on a driver's license and sometimes on a bracelet or "dog tag." This allows emergency doctors to identify potential organ supplies.

People become donors for many reasons. Moral principles, religious convictions, and humanitarianism all play a role in the donation decision. It's the same with blood donations: People give blood (while alive!) because they want to help save other individuals.

Continued

Market Incentives. Monetary incentives could also play a role. When blood donations are inadequate, hospitals and medical schools *buy* blood in the marketplace. People who might not donate blood come forth to *sell* blood when a price is offered. In principle, the same incentive might increase the number of *organ* donors. If offered cash now for a postmortem organ, would the willingness to donate increase? The law of supply suggests it would. Offer $1,000 in cash for signing up, and potential donors will start lining up. Offer more, and the quantity supplied will increase further.

Zero Price Ceiling. The government doesn't permit this to happen. In 1984 Congress forbade the purchase or sale of human organs in the United States (the National Organ Transplantation Act). In part, the prohibition was rooted in moral and religious convictions. It was also motivated by equity concerns—the FOR WHOM question. If organs could be bought and sold, then the rich would have a distinct advantage in living.

The prohibition on market sales is effectively a **price ceiling** set at zero. As a consequence, the only available organs are those supplied by altruistic donors—people who are willing to supply organs at a zero price. The quantity supplied can't be increased with (illegal) price incentives. In general, *price ceilings have three predictable effects: they*

> **price ceiling:** An upper limit imposed on the price of a good.

- *Increase the quantity demanded.*
- *Decrease the quantity supplied.*
- *Create a market shortage.*

The Deadly Shortage Figure 3.8 illustrates the consequences of this price ceiling. At a price of zero, only the quantity q_a of "altruistic" organs is available (roughly one-third of the potential supply). But the quantity q_d is demanded by all the organ-diseased individuals. The market shortage $q_d - q_a$ tells us how many patients will die.

Economists contend that many of these deaths are unnecessary. A University of Pennsylvania study showed that the quantity of organs supplied *doubled* when payment was offered. Without the government-set price ceiling, more organ-diseased patients would live. Figure 3.8 shows that q_E people would get transplants in a market-driven system. In the government-regulated system, only the quantity of q_a of transplants can occur.

Why does the government impose price controls that condemn more people to die? Because it feels the market unfairly distributes available organs. Only people who can afford the price p_E end up living in the market-based system—a feature regulators say is unfair. In the absence of the market mechanism, however, the government must set other rules for who gets the even smaller quantity of organs supplied. That rationing system may be unfair as well.

Would the market supply more organs?

ERproductions Ltd/Blend Images LLC

FIGURE 3.8

Organ Transplant Market

A market in human organs would deliver the quantity q_E at a price of p_E. The government-set price ceiling ($p = 0$) reduces the quantity supplied to q_a.

SUMMARY

- People participate in the marketplace by offering to buy or sell goods and services, or factors of production. Participation is motivated by the desire to maximize utility (consumers), profits (business firms), or the general welfare (government) from the limited resources each participant has.   **LO3-1, LO3-2**
- All market transactions involve the exchange of either factors of production or goods and services. Although the actual exchanges can occur anywhere, they take place in product markets or factor markets, depending on what is being exchanged.   **LO3-1, LO3-2**
- People willing and able to buy a particular good at some price are part of the market demand for that product. All those willing and able to sell that good at some price are part of the market supply. Total market demand or supply is the sum of individual demands or supplies.   **LO3-1, LO3-2**
- Supply and demand curves illustrate how the quantity demanded or supplied changes in response to a change in the price of that good, if nothing else changes (*ceteris paribus*). Demand curves slope downward; supply curves slope upward.   **LO3-1, LO3-2**
- Determinants of market demand include the number of potential buyers and their respective tastes (desires), incomes, other goods, and expectations. If any of these determinants changes, the demand curve shifts. Movements along a demand curve are induced only by a change in the price of that good.   **LO3-4**
- Determinants of market supply include factor costs, technology, profitability of other goods, expectations, tax rates, and number of sellers. Supply shifts when these underlying determinants change.   **LO3-4**
- The quantity of goods or resources actually exchanged in each market depends on the behavior of all buyers and sellers, as summarized in market supply and demand curves. At the point where the two curves intersect, an equilibrium price—the price at which the quantity demanded equals the quantity supplied—is established.   **LO3-3**
- A distinctive feature of the market equilibrium is that it's the only price-quantity combination acceptable to buyers and sellers alike. At higher prices, the quantity supplied is more than buyers are willing to purchase (a market surplus); at lower prices, the amount demanded exceeds the quantity supplied (a market shortage). Only the equilibrium price clears the market.   **LO3-3**
- Price ceilings are disequilibrium prices imposed on the marketplace. Such price controls create an imbalance between quantities demanded and supplied, resulting in market shortages.   **LO3-5**

Key Terms

factor market	law of demand	law of supply
product market	substitute goods	equilibrium price
opportunity cost	complementary goods	market mechanism
supply	*ceteris paribus*	price floor
demand	shift in demand	market surplus
demand schedule	market demand	market shortage
demand curve	market supply	price ceiling

Questions for Discussion

1. In our story of Tom, the student confronted with a web design assignment, we emphasized the great urgency of his desire for web tutoring. Many people would say that Tom had an "absolute need" for web help and therefore was ready to "pay anything" to get it. If this were true, what shape would his demand curve have? Why isn't this realistic?   **LO3-1**
2. If Disney+ had been priced at $9.99 instead of $6.99 what would have happened to (a) market demand, (b) the quantity demanded? Why was the initial price so important? (see Front Page Economics "Pricing Disney+")?   **LO3-1**
3. With respect to the demand for college enrollment, which of the following would cause (1) a movement along the demand curve or (2) a shift of the demand curve?   **LO3-4**
   a. An increase in incomes.
   b. Lower tuition.
   c. More student loans.
   d. An increase in textbook prices.
4. What happens to Netflix subscriptions when the price of Amazon Prime changes?   **LO3-5**
5. Why are scalpers typically able to resell tickets to the Final Four basketball games at such high prices (Front

Page Economics "March Madness Becomes Sadness")? **LO3-2**

6. In Figure 3.8, why is the organ demand curve downward-sloping rather than vertical? **LO3-1**

7. The shortage in the organ market (Figure 3.8) requires a nonmarket rationing scheme. Who should get the available (q_a) organs? Is this fairer than the market-driven distribution? **LO3-5**

8. What would happen in the apple market if the government set a *minimum* price of $10.00 per apple? What might motivate such a policy? **LO3-5**

9. When the price of hand sanitizers shot up in March 2020, the attorneys general of 33 states demanded that sellers stop price gouging. How would a price ceiling have affected the availability and distribution of hand sanitizers, compared to an uncontrolled market? **LO3-5**

10. Is there a shortage of on-campus parking at your school? How might the shortage be resolved? **LO3-3**

PROBLEMS FOR CHAPTER 3

LO3-1   1. According to Figure 3.3, at what price would Tom buy 12 hours of web tutoring?
(*a*) Without a lottery win.
(*b*) With a lottery win.

LO3-3   2. According to Figures 3.5 and 3.6, what would the new equilibrium price of tutoring services be if Ann decided to stop tutoring?

LO3-1   3. Suppose Disney+ changes its monthly subscription price from $7 to $9 per month. Graphically show the impact of this price change in the following markets:
(*a*) Popcorn, pizza, and other movie snacks.
(*b*) Netflix.

LO3-3   4. If the quantity demanded increases by 2 million for every $1 reduction in the subscription price,
(*a*) How many initial subscribers would Disney+ have gotten at a price of $8.99 (see Front Page Economics "Pricing Disney+")?
(*b*) Is this a movement along the demand curve or a shift in demand?

       5. If Netflix loses 4 million subscribers for every $1 reduction in the Disney+ subscription price,
(*a*) How many more subscribers would Netflix have lost if Disney+ were initially priced at $4.99 a month (see Front Page Economics "Pricing Disney+")?
(*b*) Is this a movement along the demand curve or a shift in demand?

LO3-3   6. According to Front Page Economics "March Madness Becomes Sadness"
(*a*) What was the initial student price of a ticket to the NCAA finals?
(*b*) In January 2020, was there an equilibrium, a shortage, or a surplus of tickets?
(*c*) In March 2020, was there an equilibrium, a shortage, or a surplus of tickets?

LO3-3   7. Given the following data on gasoline supply and demand,
(*a*) What is the equilibrium price?
(*b*) Suppose the current price is $4. At this price, how much of a shortage or surplus exists?

Price per gallon	$5.00	$4.00	$3.00	$2.00	$1.00		$5.00	$4.00	$3.00	$2.00	$1.00
Quantity demanded (gallons per day)						**Quantity supplied (gallons per day)**					
Al	1	2	3	4	5	Firm A	3	3	2	2	1
Betsy	0	1	1	1	2	Firm B	7	5	3	3	2
Casey	2	2	3	3	4	Firm C	6	4	3	3	1
Daisy	1	3	4	4	6	Firm D	6	5	3	2	0
Eddie	<u>1</u>	<u>2</u>	<u>2</u>	<u>3</u>	<u>5</u>	Firm E	<u>4</u>	<u>2</u>	<u>2</u>	<u>2</u>	<u>1</u>
Market total	—	—	—	—	—	Market total	—	—	—	—	—

LO3-2   8. Illustrate using a supply and demand graph what happened to gasoline prices in World View "Gas Prices Jump in Wake of Saudi Attack."
(*a*) Which curve shifted?
(*b*) Which direction did that curve shift (left or right)?
(*c*) Did price increase or decrease?
(*d*) Did quantity increase or decrease?

LO3-4   9. Illustrate using a supply and demand graph what happened to Netflix resulting from new competition (see Front Page Economics "Pricing Disney+").
(*a*) Which curve shifted?
(*b*) Which direction did that curve shift (left or right)?
(*c*) Did price increase or decrease?
(*d*) Did quantity increase or decrease?

PROBLEMS FOR CHAPTER 3 (cont'd)

LO3-5 10. Which curve shifts and in which direction when the following events occur in the domestic car market?
- (*a*) The U.S. economy falls into a recession.
- (*b*) U.S. autoworkers go on strike.
- (*c*) Imported cars become more expensive.
- (*d*) The price of gasoline increases.

LO3-5 11. Use the following data to draw supply and demand curves and illustrate the answers for (*a*)–(*c*) on your graph.

Price	$ 8	7	6	5	4	3	2	1
Quantity demanded	2	3	4	5	6	7	8	9
Quantity supplied	10	9	8	7	6	5	4	3

- (*a*) What is the equilibrium price?
- (*b*) Suppose the current price is $7,
    - (*i*) What kind of disequilibrium situation results?
    - (*ii*) How large is this surplus or shortage?
- (*c*) Suppose the current price is $3,
    - (*i*) What disequilibrium situation results?
    - (*ii*) How large is this surplus or shortage?

LO3-5 12. *Decisions for Tomorrow:* In Figure 3.8, when a price ceiling of zero is imposed, does
- (*a*) The quantity of organs demanded increase?
- (*b*) The market demand increase?
- (*c*) The quantity of organs supplied decrease?
- (*d*) The market supply increase?
- (*e*) The equilibrium price change?

LO3-5 13. *Decisions for Tomorrow:* According to Figure 3.8,
- (*a*) How many organs are supplied at a zero price?
- (*b*) How many people die in the government-regulated economy where there is a price ceiling = $0?
- (*c*) How many people die in the market-driven economy?

Design Credit: Shutterstock

CHAPTER 4

The Role of Government

The market has a keen ear for private wants, but a deaf ear for public needs.

—**Robert Heilbroner**

LEARNING OBJECTIVES

After reading this chapter, you should know

LO4-1 The nature and causes of market failure.

LO4-2 How the public sector has grown.

LO4-3 Which taxes finance state, local, and federal governments.

LO4-4 The meaning of government failure.

Governments play a huge role in the economy today—not just the massive federal government, but also the 50 state governments, the 3,142 county governments, the 35,000 city governments, and thousands of school, sanitation, transportation, utility, and other special districts. Together, these various governments directly account for more than a fifth of our economic output and exercise significant influence on all WHAT, HOW, and FOR WHOM answers.

Public opinion polls consistently reveal that Americans feel that the government sector has grown too large. Yet, the same polls show that people want the government to do more things, fix more problems, and regulate more activities. To decide whether the government sector should be larger or smaller, we've got to understand its economic functions better. That is the goal of this chapter.

Laissez faire? We know by now that markets do work: The interaction of supply and demand in product markets *does* generate goods and services. Likewise, the interaction of supply and demand in labor markets *does* yield jobs, wages, and a distribution of income. As we've observed, the market is capable of determining WHAT goods to produce, HOW, and FOR WHOM.

But are the market's answers good enough? Is the mix of output produced by unregulated markets the best possible mix? Will producers choose the production process that protects the environment? Will the market-generated distribution of income be fair enough? Will there be enough jobs for everyone who wants one?

In reality, markets don't always give us the best possible outcomes. Markets dominated by a few powerful corporations may charge excessive prices, limit output, provide poor service, or even retard technological advance. In the quest for profits, producers may sacrifice the environment for cost savings. In unfettered markets, some people may not get life-saving health care, basic education, or even adequate nutrition. When markets generate such undesirable outcomes, government intervention may be needed to ensure better answers to the WHAT, HOW, and FOR WHOM questions.

This chapter identifies the circumstances under which such government intervention is desirable. To this end, we answer the following questions:

- **Under what circumstances do markets fail?**
- **How can government intervention help?**
- **How much government intervention is desirable?**

As we'll see, there's substantial agreement about how and when markets fail to give us the best WHAT, HOW, and FOR WHOM answers. But there's much less agreement about whether government intervention improves the situation. Indeed, an overwhelming majority of Americans are ambivalent about government intervention. They want the government to "fix" the mix of output, protect the environment, and ensure an adequate level of income for everyone. But voters are equally quick to blame government meddling for many of our economic woes.

laissez faire: The doctrine of "leave it alone," of non-intervention by government in the market mechanism.

MARKET FAILURE

We can visualize the potential for government intervention by focusing on the WHAT question. Our goal is clear: produce the best possible mix of output with existing resources. We illustrated this goal earlier with production possibilities curves. Figure 4.1 assumes that of all the possible combinations of output we could produce, the unique combination at point X represents the most desirable one. In other words, it's the **optimal mix of output,** the one that maximizes our collective social utility. We haven't yet figured out how to pinpoint that optimal mix; we're simply using the arbitrary point X in Figure 4.1 to represent that best possible outcome.

Ideally, the **market mechanism** would lead us to point X. Price signals in the marketplace are supposed to move factors of production from one industry to another in response to consumer demands. If we demand more health care—offer to buy more at a given price—more resources (labor) will be allocated to health care services. Similarly, a fall in demand will encourage health care practitioners (doctors, nurses, and the like) to find jobs in another industry. *Changes in market prices direct resources from one industry to another, moving us along the perimeter of the production possibilities curve.*

Where will the market mechanism take us? Will it move resources around until we end up at the optimal point X? Or will it leave us at another point on the production possibilities curve with a *sub*optimal mix of output? (If point X is the *optimal,* or best possible, mix, all other output mixes must be *sub*optimal.)

We use the term **market failure** to refer to situations in which the market generates imperfect (suboptimal) outcomes. If the invisible hand of the marketplace produces a mix of output that's different from the one society most desires, then it has failed. *Market failure implies that the forces of supply and demand haven't led us to the best point on the*

optimal mix of output: The most desirable combination of output attainable with existing resources, technology, and social values.

market mechanism: The use of market prices and sales to signal desired outputs (or resource allocations).

market failure: An imperfection in the market mechanism that prevents optimal outcomes.

FIGURE 4.1

Market Failure

We can produce any mix of output on the production possibilities curve. Our goal is to produce the optimal (best possible) mix of output, as represented by point X. Market forces, however, might produce another combination, like point M. In that case, the market fails—it produces a *sub*optimal mix of output.

production possibilities curve. Such a failure is illustrated by point *M* in Figure 4.1. Point *M* is assumed to be the mix of output generated by market forces. Notice that the market mix (*M*) doesn't represent the optimal mix, which is assumed to be at point *X.* We get less health care and more of other goods than are optimal. The market in this case *fails;* we get the wrong answer to the WHAT question.

Market failure opens the door for government intervention. If the market can't do the job, we need some form of *nonmarket* force to get the right answers. In terms of Figure 4.1, we need something to change the mix of output—to move us from point *M* (the market mix of output) to point *X* (the optimal mix of output). Accordingly, *market failure establishes a basis for government intervention.* We look to the government to push market outcomes closer to the ideal.

Causes of Market Failure. Because market failure is the justification for government intervention, we need to know how and when market failure occurs. *The four specific sources of market failure are*

* *Public goods.*
* *Externalities.*
* *Market power.*
* *Inequity.*

We will first examine the nature of these problems, then see why government intervention is called for in each case.

Public Goods

The market mechanism does a good job of signaling consumer demands for various goods and services. By offering to pay for goods, we express our preferences about WHAT to produce. However, this mode of communication is socially efficient only if the benefits of consuming a particular good are available only to the individuals who purchase that product.

Consider doughnuts, for example. When you eat a doughnut, you alone get the satisfaction from its sweet, greasy taste—that is, you derive a private benefit. No one else benefits from your consumption of a doughnut: The doughnut you purchase in the market is yours alone to consume; it's a **private good.** Accordingly, your decision to purchase the doughnut will be determined only by your anticipated satisfaction, your income, and your opportunity costs.

No Exclusion. Most of the goods and services produced in the public sector are different from doughnuts—and not just because doughnuts look, taste, and smell different from "star wars" missile shields. When you buy a doughnut, you exclude others from consumption of that product. If Dunkin' Donuts sells you a particular pastry, it can't supply the same pastry to someone else. If you devour it, no one else can. In this sense, the transaction and product are completely private.

The same exclusiveness is not characteristic of national defense. If you buy a missile defense system to thwart enemy attacks, there's no way you can exclude your neighbors from the protection your system provides. Either the missile shield deters would-be attackers—like Israel's "Iron Dome" (see World View "Israel's 'Iron Dome' 86 Percent Effective")—or it doesn't. In the former case, both you and your neighbors survive happily ever after; in the latter case, we're all blown away together. In that sense, you and your neighbors consume the benefits of a missile shield *jointly.* National defense isn't a divisible service. There's no such thing as exclusive consumption here. The consumption of nuclear defenses is a communal feat, no matter who pays for them. Accordingly, national defense is regarded as a **public good** in the sense that *consumption of a public good by one person doesn't preclude consumption of the same good by another person.* By contrast, a doughnut is a private good because if I eat it, no one else can consume it.

private good: A good or service whose consumption by one person excludes consumption by others.

public good: A good or service whose consumption by one person does not exclude consumption by others.

WORLD VIEW

ISRAEL'S "IRON DOME" 86 PERCENT EFFECTIVE

The fragile peace between Israel and its Arab neighbors never lasts very long. The surest sign of a peace breakdown is a barrage of rockets fired by Hamas into Israel. Since 2011, however, Israel has had the advantage in these skirmishes. Its "Iron Dome" defense system is designed to intercept and destroy incoming missiles and mortars. Between 2011 and 2019, Israel claims to have intercepted and destroyed 1,500 incoming projectiles. In May 2019 Israel successfully intercepted 86 percent of a one-day, 600-rocket barrage fired off by Hamas. This defense doesn't come cheap, however: Each interceptor costs about $100,000.

Source: News reports, May 2019.

CRITICAL ANALYSIS: An air-defense system is a **public good,** as consumption of its services by one individual does not preclude consumption by others. Nonpayers cannot be excluded from its protection.

The Free-Rider Dilemma. The communal nature of public goods creates a dilemma. If you and I will *both* benefit from nuclear defenses, which one of us should buy the missile shield? I'd prefer that *you* buy it, thereby giving me protection at no direct cost. Hence, I may profess no desire for a missile shield, secretly hoping to take a **free ride** on your market purchase. Unfortunately, you too have an incentive to conceal your desire for national defenses. As a consequence, neither one of us may step forward to *demand* a missile shield in the marketplace. We'll both end up defenseless.

Flood control is also a public good. No one in the valley wants to be flooded out. But each landowner knows that a flood control dam will protect *all* the landowners, regardless of who pays. Either the entire valley is protected or no one is. Accordingly, individual farmers and landowners may say they don't want a dam and aren't willing to pay for it. Everyone is waiting and hoping that someone else will pay for flood control. In other words, everyone wants a *free ride.* Thus, if we leave it to market forces, no one will *demand* flood control, and all the property in the valley will be washed away.

The difference between public goods and private goods rests on *technical considerations,* not political philosophy. ***The central question is whether we have the technical capability to exclude nonpayers.*** In the case of national defense or flood control, we simply don't have that capability. Even city streets have the characteristics of public goods. Although theoretically we could restrict the use of streets to those who paid to use them, a tollgate on every corner would be exceedingly expensive and impractical. Here again, joint or public consumption appears to be the only feasible alternative. As Front Page Economics "Firefighters Watch as Home Burns to the Ground" on local firefighting emphasizes, the technical capability to exclude nonpayers is the key factor in identifying "public goods."

To the list of public goods we could add snow removal, the administration of justice (including prisons), the regulation of commerce, the conduct of foreign relations, airport security, and even Fourth of July fireworks. These services—which cost tens of *billions* of dollars and employ thousands of workers—provide benefits to everyone, no matter who pays for them. In each instance it's technically impossible or prohibitively expensive to exclude nonpayers from the services provided.

Underproduction of Public Goods. The free riders associated with public goods upset the customary practice of paying for what you get. If I can get all the national defense, flood control, and laws I want without paying for them, I'm not about to complain. I'm perfectly happy to let you pay for the services while we all consume them.

You may feel the same way. Why should you pay for these services if you can consume just as much of them when your neighbors foot the whole bill? It might seem selfish not to pay

free rider: An individual who reaps direct benefits from someone else's purchase (consumption) of a public good.

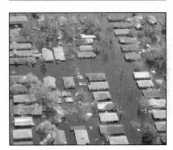

Flood control is a public good.

Department of Commerce/NOAA

FRONT PAGE ECONOMICS

FIREFIGHTERS WATCH AS HOME BURNS TO THE GROUND

OBION COUNTY, Tenn.—Imagine your home catches fire, but the local fire department won't respond, then watches it burn. That's exactly what happened to a local family tonight.

A local neighborhood is furious after firefighters watched as an Obion County, Tennessee, home burned to the ground.

The homeowner, Gene Cranick, said he offered to pay whatever it would take for firefighters to put out the flames but was told it was too late. They wouldn't do anything to stop his house from burning.

Each year, Obion County residents must pay $75 if they want fire protection from the city of South Fulton. But the Cranicks did not pay.

The mayor said if homeowners don't pay, they're out of luck.

—Jason Hibbs

WPSD Local 6/AP Images

©WPSD Local 6, Paducah, KY, September 30, 2010. Used with permission.

CRITICAL ANALYSIS: A product is a **public good** only if nonpayers *cannot* be excluded from its consumption. Firefighters in Tennessee proved that fire protection is not inherently a public good: They let the nonpaying homeowner's house burn down!

your share of the cost of providing public goods. But you'd be better off in a material sense if you spent your income on doughnuts, letting others pick up the tab for public services.

Because the link between paying and consuming is broken, public goods can't be peddled in the supermarket. People are reluctant to buy what they can get free. Hence, *if public goods were marketed like private goods, everyone would wait for someone else to pay.* The end result might be a total lack of public services. This is the kind of dilemma Robert Heilbroner had in mind when he spoke of the market's "deaf ear" (see the quote at the beginning of this chapter).

The production possibilities curve in Figure 4.2 illustrates the dilemma created by public goods. Suppose that point *A* represents the optimal mix of private and public goods. It's the mix of goods and services we'd select if everyone's preferences were known and reflected in production decisions. The market mechanism won't lead us to point *A,* however, because the *demand* for public goods will be hidden. If we rely on the market, nearly everyone will withhold demand for public goods, waiting for a free ride to point *A.* As a result, we'll get a smaller quantity of public goods than we really want. The market mechanism will leave us at point *B,* with few, if any, public goods. Because point *A* is assumed to be optimal, point *B* must be *suboptimal* (inferior to point *A*). The market fails: We can't rely on the market mechanism to allocate enough resources to the production of public goods, no matter how much they might be desired.

Note that we're using the term "public good" in a peculiar way. To most people, "public good" refers to any good or service the government produces. In economics, however, the meaning is much more restrictive. The term "public good" refers only to those nonexcludable goods and services that must be consumed jointly, both by those who pay for them and by those who don't. Public goods can be produced by either the government or the private sector. Private goods can be produced in either sector as well. The problem is that *the market tends to underproduce public goods and overproduce private goods.* If we want more public goods, we need a *nonmarket* force—government intervention—to get them. The government will have to force people to pay taxes, then use the tax revenues to pay for the production of national defense, flood control, snow removal, and other public goods.

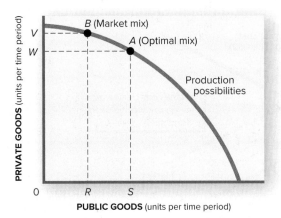

FIGURE 4.2

Underproduction of Public Goods

Suppose point *A* represents the optimal mix of output—that is, the mix of private and public goods that maximizes society's welfare. Because consumers won't demand purely public goods in the marketplace, the price mechanism won't allocate so many resources to their production. Instead the market will tend to produce a mix of output like point *B*, which includes fewer public goods (*0R*) than are optimal (*0S*).

Externalities

The free-rider problem associated with public goods is an important justification for government intervention. It's not the only justification, however. A second justification for intervention arises from the tendency of costs or benefits of some market activities to "spill over" onto third parties.

Consider the case of cigarettes. The price someone is willing to pay for a pack of cigarettes reflects the amount of satisfaction a smoker anticipates from its consumption. If that price is high enough, tobacco companies will produce the cigarettes demanded. That is how market-based price signals are supposed to work. In this case, however, the price paid isn't a satisfactory signal of the product's desirability. The smoker's pleasure is offset in part by nonsmokers' *dis*pleasure. In this case, smoke literally spills over onto other consumers, causing them discomfort, ill health, and even death (see World View "Secondhand Smoke Kills 600,000 People a Year"). Yet their loss isn't reflected in the market price: The harm caused to nonsmokers is *external* to the market price of cigarettes.

The term **externalities** refers to all costs or benefits of a market activity borne by a third party—that is, by someone other than the immediate producer or consumer. *Whenever externalities are present, market prices aren't a valid measure of a good's value to society.* As a

externalities: Costs (or benefits) of a market activity borne by a third party; the difference between the social and private costs (benefits) of a market activity.

WORLD VIEW

SECONDHAND SMOKE KILLS MORE THAN 600,000 PEOPLE A YEAR

Secondhand smoke globally kills more than 600,000 people each year, accounting for 1 percent of all deaths worldwide.

Researchers estimate that annually secondhand smoke causes about 379,000 deaths from heart disease, 165,000 deaths from lower respiratory disease, 36,900 deaths from asthma, and 21,400 deaths from lung cancer.

Hannah Maule-Finch/Image Source/Corbis

Children account for about 165,000 of the deaths. Forty percent of children and 30 percent of adults regularly breathe in secondhand smoke.

Source: World Health Organization

CRITICAL ANALYSIS: The health risks imposed on nonsmokers via passive smoke represent an **external cost.** The market price of cigarettes doesn't reflect costs borne by third parties.

FIGURE 4.3
Externalities

The market responds to consumer demands, not externalities. Smokers demand q_M cigarettes at the equilibrium price of $7. But external costs on nonsmokers ($2 per pack) imply that the *social* demand for cigarettes is less than (below) *market* demand. The socially optimal level of output is q_O, less than the market output q_M.

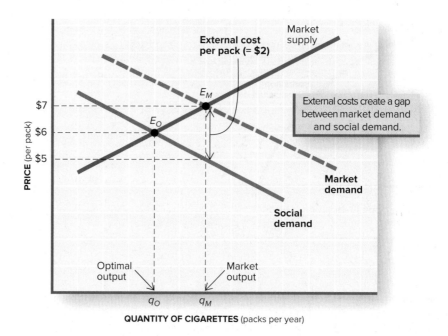

consequence, the market will fail to produce the right mix of output. Specifically, *the market will underproduce goods that yield external benefits and overproduce those that generate external costs.*

External Costs. Figure 4.3 shows how external costs—*negative* externalitites—cause the market to overproduce cigarettes. The market demand curve includes only the wishes of smokers—that is, people who are willing and able to purchase cigarettes. The forces of market demand and supply result in an equilibrium at E_M in which Q_M cigarettes are produced and consumed. The market price of $7 reflects the value of those cigarettes to smokers.

The well-being of *non*smokers isn't reflected in the market equilibrium. To take the *non*smokers' interests into account, we must subtract the external costs imposed on *them* from the value that *smokers* put on cigarettes. In general,

$$\text{Social demand} = \text{Market demand} \pm \text{Externalities}$$

In this case, the externality is a *cost,* so we must *subtract* the external cost from market demand to get a full accounting of social demand. Suppose that the external costs associated with secondhand smoke work out to $2 a pack. That implies that the social value of a pack of cigarettes is $5.

$$
\begin{array}{ccccc}
\text{Social value} & = & \text{Market value} & - & \text{External Costs} \\
\$5 & = & \$7 & - & \$2
\end{array}
$$

Yet, the market equilibrium depicted in Figure 4.3 doesn't reflect this social calculation.

What we need is a *second* demand curve, one that takes into account the well-being of both the smokers and the nonsmokers. We call this second curve the "social demand" curve. To locate this curve in Figure 4.3, we subtract the amount of external cost ($2) from every price on the market demand curve. Hence, the social demand curve lies below the market demand curve in this case. What the social demand curve tells us is how much society would be willing and able to pay for cigarettes if the preferences of *both* smokers and nonsmokers were taken into account.

The social demand curve in Figure 4.3 creates a social equilibrium at E_O. At this juncture, we see that the socially *optimal* quantity of cigarettes is q_O, not the larger market-generated level at q_M. In this sense, the market produces too many cigarettes.

Many people have tried to extend the restrictions on cigarettes to vaping. At first blush, the argument seems plausible, as vape (aerosol) clouds look like exhaled smoke. But studies have concluded that vape clouds might be a nuisance, but they don't pose secondhand health risks (see Front Page Economics "The Health Risks of Vaping"). So vaping restrictions have to be based on other market-failure arguments.

FRONT PAGE ECONOMICS

THE HEALTH RISKS OF VAPING

Vaping has become a popular alternative to smoking, especially among teenagers. In 2019, roughly one out of three teenagers reported vaping. Most teens used flavored pods or cartridges, especially mint-flavored ones produced by JUUL, the industry leader. Concerned with the health risks of vaping, several cities and states sought bans on vaping. Even President Trump suggested that flavored pods should be prohibited.

These government interventions aren't based on the externalities argument, however. Vape clouds do contain some nicotine, fine particles, and trace amounts of toxins associated with cancer. But the levels of these contaminants are so low that they pose no risk to third parties. The bans on vaping are motivated by the health risks to vapers themselves, not to nonvapers.

Source: News reports of September–November 2019.

CRITICAL ANALYSIS: The **externality** explanation for market failure focuses on third-party effects of market transactions. Vaping doesn't pose significant secondhand risks.

Negative externalities also exist in production. A power plant that burns high-sulfur coal damages the surrounding environment. Yet the damage inflicted on neighboring people, vegetation, and buildings is external to the cost calculations of the firm. Because the cost of such pollution is not reflected in the price of electricity, the firm will tend to produce more electricity (and pollution) than is socially desirable. To reduce this imbalance, the government has to step in and change market outcomes.

External Benefits. Externalities can also be beneficial. A product may generate external *benefits* rather than external *costs*. Your college is an example. The students who attend your school benefit directly from the education they receive. That's why they (and you) are willing to pay for tuition, books, and other services. The students in attendance aren't the only beneficiaries of this educational service, however. The research that a university conducts may yield benefits for a much broader community. The values and knowledge students acquire may also be shared with family, friends, and coworkers. These benefits would all be *external* to the market transaction between a paying student and the school. Positive externalities also arise from immunizations against infectious diseases: The person getting immunized obviously benefits, but so do all the people with whom that person comes into contact. Other people (third parties) benefit when you get vaccinated.

If a product yields external benefits, the social demand is greater than the market demand. In this case, the social value of the good *exceeds* the market price (by the amount of external benefit). Accordingly, society wants *more* of the product than the market mechanism alone will produce at any given price. To get that additional output, the government may have to intervene with subsidies or other policies. We conclude then that *the market fails by*

- *Overproducing goods that have external costs.*
- *Underproducing goods that have external benefits.*

If externalities are present, the market won't produce the optimal mix of output. To get that optimal mix, we need government intervention.

The need for government intervention was dramatically apparent during the coronavirus pandemic. The coronavirus pandemic that started in Wuhan, China, in December 2019 swept across the globe like wildfire. Within three months' time, over 1 million cases were reported in 151 nations (see Front Page Economics "COVID-19 Cases Surpass 1 Million"). One of the most critical factors in the spread of the COVID-19 virus was its contagiousness: People with the virus were infecting others with whom they came into contact. More often than not, the people harboring the virus didn't even know they were affected, much less contagious. So, they weren't likely to pay for tests or treatments or voluntarily take precautions that would reduce the spread of the virus. Yet, tests, self-isolation, and treatment would generate a positive—life-saving—externality. But too few people were willing to do it on their own. This was a deadly situation. In response, governments everywhere mandated "social distancing" to reduce infectious contact and offered free tests and treatments. Many governments also ordered people to shelter in place. The motivation there was not only to protect affected individuals, but also to prevent individuals from spreading the virus to others—that is, create positive externalities.

FRONT PAGE ECONOMICS

COVID-19 CASES SURPASS 1 MILLION

Confirmed cases of the coronavirus worldwide surpassed one million this week. Data collected by researchers at the Johns Hopkins University reveal that the number of confirmed cases has risen to 1,011,490 worldwide, with 52,863 confirmed deaths. In the United States, the case count stands at 242,182, with 5,850 deaths. Experts say the number of confirmed cases likely understates the actual incidence of COVID-19 infections due to incomplete reporting. They also expect the case and death tolls to rise in the coming weeks despite increasingly stringent mitigation efforts.

Source: Media reports of April 2–5, 2020.

CRITICAL ANALYSIS: An infectious disease is a classic case of an **externality.** If people isolate themselves or take other preventive measures, they are benefiting third parties. When market participants won't exercise enough caution, the government can force behavior changes that create positive externalities.

Market Power

In the case of both public goods and externalities, the market fails to achieve the optimal mix of output because the price signal is flawed. The price consumers are willing and able to pay for a specific good doesn't reflect all the benefits or cost of producing that good.

The market may fail, however, even when the price signals are accurate. The *response* to price signals, rather than the signals themselves, may be flawed.

Restricted Supply. Market power is often the cause of a flawed response. Suppose that there were only one airline company in the world. This single seller of airline travel would be a **monopoly**—that is, the only producer in that industry. As a monopolist, the airline could charge extremely high prices without worrying that travelers would flock to a competing airline. At the same time, the high prices paid by consumers would express the importance of that service to society. Ideally, those high prices would act as a signal to producers to build and fly more planes—to change the mix of output. But a monopolist doesn't have to cater to every consumer's whim. It can rake in those high prices without increasing service, thereby obstructing our efforts to achieve an optimal mix of output.

Monopoly is the most severe form of **market power.** More generally, market power refers to any situation in which a single producer or consumer has the ability to alter the market

monopoly: A firm that produces the entire market supply of a particular good or service.

market power: The ability to alter the market price of a good or service.

price of a specific product. If the publisher (McGraw-Hill) charges a high price for this book, you'll have to pay the tab. McGraw-Hill has market power because there are relatively few economics texts and your professor has required you to use this one. You don't have power in the textbook market because your decision to buy or not won't alter the market price of this text. You're only one of the million students who are taking an introductory economics course this year.

The market power McGraw-Hill possesses is derived from the copyright on this text. No matter how profitable textbook sales might be, no one else is permitted to produce or sell this particular book. Patents are another common source of market power because they also preclude others from making or selling a specific product. Market power may also result from control of resources, restrictive production agreements, or efficiencies of large-scale production.

Whatever the source of market power, the direct consequence is that one or more producers attain discretionary power over the market's response to price signals. They may use that discretion to enrich themselves rather than to move the economy toward the optimal mix of output. In this case, the market will again fail to deliver the most desired goods and services.

The mandate for government intervention in this case is to prevent or dismantle concentrations of market power. That's the basic purpose of **antitrust** policy. Another option is to *regulate* market behavior. This was one of the goals of the antitrust case against Microsoft. The government was less interested in breaking Microsoft's near monopoly on operating systems than in changing the way Microsoft behaved. Google is now under the same kind of pressure to change its search protocols in order to permit greater competition.

In some cases, it may be economically efficient to have one large firm supply an entire market. Such a situation arises in **natural monopoly,** where a single firm can achieve economies of scale over the entire range of market output. Utility companies, local telephone service, subway systems, and cable all exhibit such scale (size) efficiencies. In these cases, a monopoly *structure* may be economically desirable. The government may have to regulate the *behavior* of a natural monopoly, however, to ensure that consumers get the benefits of that greater efficiency.

Inequity

Public goods, externalities, and market power all cause resource misallocations. Where these phenomena exist, the market mechanism will fail to produce the optimal mix of output in the best possible way.

Beyond the questions of WHAT and HOW to produce, we're also concerned about FOR WHOM output is produced. The market answers this question by distributing a larger share of total output to those with the most income. Although this result may be efficient, it's not necessarily equitable. As we saw in Chapter 2, the market mechanism may enrich some people while leaving others to seek shelter in abandoned cars. If such outcomes violate our vision of equity, we may want the government to change the market-generated distribution of income.

Taxes and Transfers. The tax-and-transfer system is the principal mechanism for redistributing incomes. The idea here is to take some of the income away from those who have "too much" and give it to those whom the market has left with "too little." Taxes are levied to take back some of the income received from the market. Those tax revenues are then redistributed via transfer payments to those deemed needy, such as the poor, the aged, and the unemployed. **Transfer payments** are income payments for which no goods or services are exchanged. They're used to bolster the incomes of those for whom the market itself provides too little. In the 2020 presidential campaigns, Democrats championed the notion of changing the market's answer to the FOR WHOM question with higher taxes on the rich and more transfers to the poor.

Merit Goods. Often our vision of what is "too little" is defined in terms of specific goods and services. There is a widespread consensus in the United States that everyone is entitled to some minimum levels of shelter, food, and health care. These are regarded as **merit goods,** in the

With nearly 90 percent of the online search market, Google has great market power.

Annette Shaff/Shutterstock

antitrust: Government intervention to alter market structure or prevent abuse of market power.

natural monopoly: An industry in which one firm can achieve economies of scale over the entire range of market supply.

transfer payments: Payments to individuals for which no current goods or services are exchanged, like Social Security, welfare, and unemployment benefits.

merit good: A good or service society deems everyone is entitled to some minimal quantity of.

sense that everyone merits at least some minimum provision of such goods. When the market does not distribute that minimum provision, the government is called on to fill the gaps. In this case, the income transfers take the form of *in-kind* transfers (e.g., food stamps, housing vouchers, Medicaid) rather than *cash* transfers (e.g., welfare checks, Social Security benefits).

Some people argue that we don't need the government to help the poor—that private charity alone will suffice. Unfortunately, private charity alone has never been adequate. One reason private charity doesn't suffice is the "free-rider" problem. If I contribute heavily to the poor, you benefit from safer streets (fewer muggers), a better environment (fewer slums and homeless people), and a clearer conscience (knowing that fewer people are starving). In this sense, the relief of misery is a *public* good. Were I the only taxpayer to benefit substantially from the reduction of poverty, then charity would be a private affair. As long as income support substantially benefits the public at large, then income redistribution is a *public* good, for which public funding is appropriate. This is the *economic* rationale for public income redistribution activities. To this rationale one can add such moral arguments as seem appropriate.

Macro Instability

The micro failures of the marketplace imply that we may end up at the wrong point on the production possibilities curve or inequitably distributing the output produced. There's another basic question we've swept under the rug, however. How do we get to the production possibilities curve in the first place? To reach the curve, we must utilize all available resources and technology. Can we be confident that the invisible hand of the marketplace will use all available resources? That confidence was shattered in 2008–2009 when total output contracted and **unemployment** soared. Millions of people who were willing and able to work but unable to find jobs demanded that the government intervene to increase output and create more jobs. The market had failed.

And what about prices? Price signals are a critical feature of the market mechanism. But the validity of those signals depends on some stable measure of value. What good is a doubling of salary when the price of everything you buy doubles as well? Generally, rising prices will enrich people who own property and impoverish people who rent. That's why we strive to avoid **inflation**—a situation in which the *average* price level is increasing.

Historically, the marketplace has been wracked with bouts of both unemployment and inflation. These experiences have prompted calls for government intervention at the macro level. *The goal of macro intervention is to foster economic growth—to get us on the production possibilities curve (full employment), maintain a stable price level (price stability), and increase our capacity to produce (growth).*

unemployment: The inability of labor force participants to find jobs.

inflation: An increase in the average level of prices of goods and services.

GROWTH OF GOVERNMENT

The potential micro and macro failures of the marketplace provide specific justifications for government intervention. We do need government to provide public goods, compensate for externalities, limit the excesses of market power, and redistribute incomes more fairly. We can't rely completely on a private, market-based economy to generate optimal answers to the WHAT, HOW, and FOR WHOM questions.

The question then becomes, "How well does the government respond to these needs?" We'll start answering this question by looking at what the government now does and how it has grown.

Federal Growth

Until the 1930s the federal government's role was largely limited to national defense (a public good), enforcement of a common legal system (also a public good), and provision of postal service (equity). The Great Depression of the 1930s spawned a new range of government activities, including welfare and Social Security programs (equity), minimum wage laws and workplace standards (regulation), and massive public works (public goods and externalities). In the 1950s the federal government also assumed a greater role in maintaining macroeconomic stability (macro failure), protecting the environment (externalities), and safeguarding the public's health (externalities and equity).

These increasing responsibilities have greatly increased the size of the public sector. In 1902 the federal government employed fewer than 350,000 people and spent a mere $650 *million.* Today, the federal government employs nearly 4 million people and spends nearly $5 *trillion* a year.

Direct Expenditure. Figure 4.4 summarizes the growth of the public sector since 1930. Let's focus on the federal government, depicted with the orange line. Back in 1930 the federal share of total spending was close to zero. That share grew in the 1930s and skyrocketed during World War II. Federal purchases of goods and services for the war accounted for more than 40 percent of total output during the 1943–1944 period. The federal share of total U.S. output fell abruptly after World War II, rose again during the Korean War (1950–1953), and has declined slightly since then.

The decline in the federal share of total output is somewhat at odds with most people's perception of government growth. This discrepancy is explained by two phenomena. First, people see the *absolute* size of the government growing every year. But we're focusing here on the *relative* size of the public sector. From 1950 until 2008, the public sector grew a bit more slowly than the private sector, slightly reducing its relative size. The trend was interrupted in 2008–2011, when the private sector shrank and the federal government undertook massive stimulus spending. Since then, the federal government's share of total output has hovered around 6.5 percent. President Trump's stepped-up spending on national defense has increased that share by only one decimal point.

Income Transfers. The federal share of output depicted in Figure 4.4 looks small (6.6 percent) because it doesn't include *all* federal spending. As noted above, Uncle Sam *spends* nearly $5 trillion a year. But the majority of that spending is for income transfers, not direct

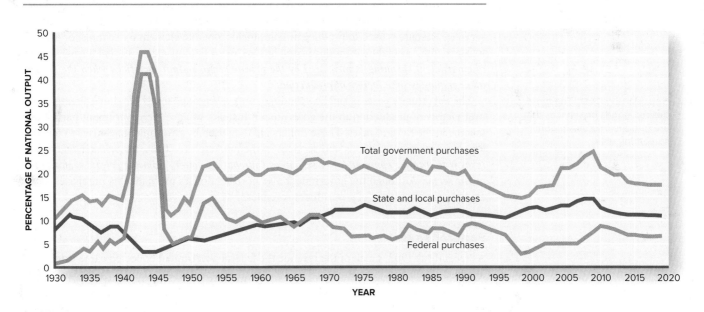

FIGURE 4.4

Government Growth

During World War II the public sector purchased nearly half of the total U.S. output. Since the early 1950s the public sector share of total output has been closer to 20 percent. Within the public sector, however, there's been a major shift: Since 1970,

state and local claims on resources (now 11 percent) have exceeded the federal share (now 6.5 percent).

Source: U.S. Bureau of Economic Analysis.

expenditure on goods and services. Figure 4.4 only counts direct expenditure on things like national defense, transportation systems, education, and other real goods—the things that are included in the WHAT outcome of the economy. By contrast, income transfers go to people who themselves decide how to spend that money—and thus what gets produced. Hence, income transfers don't directly alter the mix of output. Their effect is primarily *distributional* (the FOR WHOM question), not *allocative* (the WHAT question). Were income transfers included, the relative size and growth of the federal government would be larger than Figure 4.4 depicts. This is because *most of the growth in federal spending has come from increased income transfers, not purchases of goods and services.*

State and Local Growth

State and local spending on goods and services has followed a very different path. Prior to World War II, state and local governments dominated public sector spending. During the war, however, the share of total output going to state and local governments fell, hitting a low of 3 percent in that period (Figure 4.4).

State and local spending caught up with federal spending in the mid-1960s and has exceeded it ever since. Today *more than 80,000 state and local government entities buy much more output than Uncle Sam and employ five times as many people.* Education is a huge expenditure at lower levels of government. Most direct state spending is on colleges; most local spending is for elementary and secondary education. The fastest-growing areas for state expenditure are prisons (public safety) and welfare. At the local level, sewage and trash services are claiming an increasing share of budgets.

TAXATION

Whatever we may think of any specific government expenditure, we must recognize one basic fact of life: We pay for government spending. We pay not just in terms of tax *dollars* but in the more fundamental form of a changed mix of output. Government expenditures on goods and services absorb factors of production that could be used to produce consumer goods. The mix of output changes toward *more* public services and *fewer* private goods and services. Resources used to produce missile shields, operate elementary schools, or journey to Mars aren't available to produce cars, houses, or restaurant meals. In real terms, *the cost of government spending is measured by the private sector output sacrificed when the government employs scarce factors of production.*

opportunity cost: The most desired goods or services that are forgone in order to obtain something else.

The **opportunity costs** of public spending aren't always apparent. We don't directly hand over factors of production to the government. Instead, we give the government part of our income in the form of taxes. Those dollars are then used by government agencies to buy factors of production or goods and services in the marketplace. Thus, *the primary function of taxes is to transfer command over resources (purchasing power) from the private sector to the public sector.* Although the government also borrows dollars to finance its purchases, taxes are the primary source of government revenues.

Federal Taxes

As recently as 1902, much of the revenue the federal government collected came from taxes imposed on alcoholic beverages. The federal government didn't have authority to collect income taxes. As a consequence, *total* federal revenue in 1902 was only $653 million.

Income Taxes. All that changed, beginning in 1915. The Sixteenth Amendment to the U.S. Constitution granted the federal government authority to collect *income* taxes. The government now collects more than $1.8 *trillion* in that form alone each year. Although the federal government still collects taxes on alcoholic beverages, the individual income tax has become the largest single source of government revenue (see Figure 4.5).

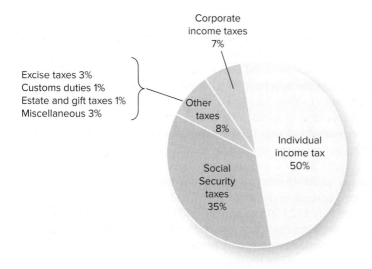

Corporate
income taxes
7%

Excise taxes 3%
Customs duties 1%
Estate and gift taxes 1%
Miscellaneous 3%

Other
taxes
8%

Individual
income tax
50%

Social
Security
taxes
35%

FIGURE 4.5

Federal Taxes

Taxes transfer purchasing power from the private sector to the public sector. The largest federal tax is the individual income tax. The second-largest source of federal revenue is the Social Security payroll tax.

Source: Office of Management and Budget, FY2020 data.

In theory, the federal income tax is designed to be **progressive**—that is, to take a larger *fraction* of high incomes than of low incomes. In 2020, for example, a single person with less than $9,875 of taxable income was taxed at 10 percent. People with incomes of $40,126–$85,525 confronted a 24 percent tax rate on their additional income. The marginal tax rate got as high as 37 percent for people earning more than $518,400 in income. Thus, *people with high incomes not only pay more taxes but also pay a larger* **fraction** *of their income in taxes.*

Social Security Taxes. The second major source of federal revenue is the Social Security payroll tax. People working now transfer part of their earnings to retired workers by making "contributions" to Social Security. There's nothing voluntary about these "contributions"; they take the form of mandatory payroll deductions. In 2020, each worker paid 7.65 percent of his or her wages to Social Security, and employers contributed an equal amount. As a consequence, the government collected more than $1.3 trillion from this tax.

At first glance, the Social Security payroll tax looks like a **proportional tax**—that is, a tax that takes the *same* fraction of every taxpayer's income. But this isn't the case. The Social Security (FICA) tax isn't levied on every payroll dollar. Incomes above a certain ceiling ($132,900 in 2020) aren't taxed. As a result, workers with *really* high salaries turn over a smaller fraction of their incomes to Social Security than do low-wage workers. This makes the Social Security payroll tax a **regressive tax.**

Corporate Taxes. The federal government taxes the profits of corporations as well as the incomes of consumers. But there are far fewer corporations (less than 2 million) than consumers (340 million), and their profits are small in comparison to total consumer income. In 2020, the federal government collected less than $300 billion in corporate income taxes, despite the fact that it imposed a top tax rate of 21 percent on corporate profits.

Excise Taxes. The last major source of federal revenue is excise taxes. Like the early taxes on whiskey, excise taxes are sales taxes imposed on specific goods and services. The federal government taxes not only liquor ($13.50 per gallon) but also gasoline (18.4 cents per gallon), cigarettes ($1.01 per pack), air fares (7.5 percent), firearms (10–11 percent), gambling (0.25 percent), and a variety of other goods and services. Such taxes not only discourage production and consumption of these goods by raising their price and thereby reducing the quantity demanded; they also raise a substantial amount of revenue.

State and Local Revenues

Taxes. State and local governments also levy taxes on consumers and businesses. In general, cities depend heavily on property taxes, and state governments rely heavily on sales

progressive tax: A tax system in which tax rates rise as incomes rise.

proportional tax: A tax that levies the same rate on every dollar of income.

regressive tax: A tax system in which tax rates fall as incomes rise.

taxes. Although nearly all states and many cities also impose income taxes, effective tax rates are so low (averaging less than 2 percent of personal income) that income tax revenues are much less than sales and property tax revenues.

Like the Social Security payroll tax, state and local taxes tend to be *regressive*—that is, they take a larger share of income from the poor than from the rich. Consider a 4 percent sales tax, for example. It might appear that a uniform tax rate like this would affect all consumers equally. But people with lower incomes tend to spend most of their income on goods and services. Thus, most of their income is subject to sales taxes. By contrast, a person with a high income can afford to save part of his or her income and thereby shelter it from sales taxes.

Consider a family that earns $40,000 and spends $30,000 of it on taxable goods and services. This family will pay $1,200 in sales taxes when the tax rate is 4 percent. In effect, then, they are handing over 3 percent of their *income* ($1,200 ÷ $40,000) to the state. Now consider a family that makes only $12,000 and spends $11,500 of it for food, clothing, and shelter. That family will pay $460 in sales taxes in the same state. Their total tax is smaller, but it represents a much larger *share* (3.8 versus 3.0 percent) of their income.

Local property taxes are also regressive because poor people devote a larger portion of their incomes to housing costs. Hence, a larger share of a poor family's *income* is subject to property taxes. State lotteries are also regressive for the same reason (see Front Page Economics "State Lotteries: A Tax on the Uneducated and the Poor"). Low-income players spend 1.4 percent of their incomes on lottery tickets while upper-income players devote only 0.1 percent of their income to lottery purchases.

FRONT PAGE ECONOMICS

STATE LOTTERIES: A TAX ON THE UNEDUCATED AND THE POOR

Americans now spend over $85 billion a year on lottery tickets. That's more than we spend on sporting events, books, video games, movies, and music *combined*. That spending works out to about $650 a household.

Poor people are proportionally the biggest buyers of lottery tickets. Households with less than $25,000 of income spend $1,100 a year on lottery tickets. By contrast, households with more than $50,000 of income buy only $300 of lottery tickets each year.

Education also affects lottery spending: 2.7 percent of high school dropouts are compulsive lottery players, while only 1.1 percent of college grads play compulsively. Because lottery games are a sucker's game to start with—payouts average less than 60 percent of sales—lotteries are effectively a regressive tax on the uneducated and the poor.

Source: Research on lottery sales.

CRITICAL ANALYSIS: Poor people spend a larger percentage of their income on lottery tickets than do rich people. This makes lotteries a **regressive** source of government revenue.

GOVERNMENT FAILURE

Some government intervention in the marketplace is clearly desirable. The market mechanism can fail for a variety of reasons, leaving a laissez-faire economy short of its economic goals. But how much government intervention is desirable? Communist nations once thought that complete government control of production, consumption, and distribution decisions was the surest path to utopia. They learned the hard way that *not only markets but governments as well can fail.* In this context, **government failure** means that government intervention fails to move us closer to our economic goals.

government failure:
Government intervention that fails to improve economic outcomes.

FIGURE 4.6
Government Failure

When the market produces a suboptimal mix of output like point *M*, the goal of government is to move output to the social optimum (point *X*). A move to G_4 would be an improvement in the mix of output. But government intervention *may* move the economy to points G_1, G_2, or G_3—all reflecting government failure.

Consider again our collective goal of producing the optimal mix of output. In Figure 4.6, this goal is again illustrated by point *X* on the production possibilities curve. Point *M* on the curve reminds us that the market may fail to generate that optimal answer to the WHAT question. This is why we want the government to intervene. We want the government to move the mix of output from point *M* to point *X*.

We have no guarantee that government intervention will yield the desired move. Government intervention might unwittingly move us to point G_1, making matters worse. Or the government might overreact, sending us to point G_2. Red tape and onerous regulation might even force us to point G_3, *inside* the production possibilities curve (with less total output than at point *M*). All those possibilities (G_1, G_2, G_3) represent government failure. **Government intervention is desirable only to the extent that it *improves* market outcomes** (e.g., G_4).

We face a similar risk when the government intervenes in the HOW and FOR WHOM questions. Regulations imposed on an industry may reduce output with little or no environmental improvements. Taxes and transfers intended to make the distribution of income fairer may actually have the opposite effect. These things won't necessarily happen, but they *could*. Even when outcomes improve, government failure may occur if the costs of government intervention exceed the benefits of an improved output mix, cleaner production methods, or a fairer distribution of income.

DECISIONS FOR TOMORROW

Can We Trust Government to Fix Things?

Two things are obvious from our discussion of the government sector. First, market failures provide an economic justification for government intervention. When the market alone gives us the wrong answers to the WHAT, HOW, and FOR WHOM questions, we need someone to adjust those answers. That "someone" is the government.

Second, we recognize that government intervention doesn't always succeed. The government may change market outcomes in the wrong direction, making things worse. Or it may generate a miniscule improvement in market outcomes, but at too high a price. In these cases, we end up with government failure—outcomes no better, and possibly worse, than the market alone would generate.

Public Opinion. Taxpayers seem to have strong opinions about government failure. A 2019 poll asked people how confident they were that the federal government could

Continued

Source: Gallup poll of September 3–15, 2019.

CRITICAL ANALYSIS: When people say they don't think the government can improve market outcomes, they are expecting **government failure.**

successfully tackle important problems. As Front Page Economics "Perceptions of Government Failure" reveals, 60 percent of Americans don't have such confidence. In other words, they *expect* government failure.

People also feel that the federal government *wastes* their tax dollars. The average taxpayer now believes that state governments waste 42 cents out of each dollar, while the federal government wastes 51 cents out of each tax dollar!

Government "waste" implies that the public sector isn't producing as many services as it could with the resources at its disposal. Such inefficiency implies that we're producing somewhere *inside* our production possibilities curve rather than on it (e.g., point G_3 in Figure 4.6). If the government is wasting resources this way, we can't possibly be producing the optimal mix of output.

Opportunity Cost

Even if the government wasn't wasting resources, it might still be guilty of government failure. Notice in Figure 4.6 that points G_1 and G_2 are on the production possibilities curve. So resources aren't being "wasted." But those points still represent suboptimal outcomes. In reality, *the issue of government failure encompasses two distinct questions:*

- *Efficiency:* Are we getting as much service as we could from the resources we allocate to government?
- *Opportunity cost:* Are we giving up too many private sector goods in order to get those services?

When assessing government's role in the economy, *we must consider not only what governments do but also what we give up to allow them to do it.* Everyone wants better schools, more access to health care, improved roads and transit systems, and secure national defenses. But each of those things comes with a price tag. When the government employs resources to produce goods that society wants, it takes resources from the production of other goods. Again, we are looking for the optimal *mix* of output, not just better schools, roads, and other public services.

Who Should Decide? You don't have to be a genius to find the optimal mix of output in Figure 4.6—it's clearly marked. In practice, establishing the optimal size of the public sector isn't so easy. We rarely have complete information about people's preferences, the social value of specific goods, or the precise opportunity costs incurred. So, while economists can talk in theoretical terms about the optimal mix of output, they aren't really equipped to locate it with any precision. Nor are they any better positioned to tell us which distribution of income is the most fair.

Ballot Box Economics. In practice, we rely on political mechanisms to decide what to produce in the public sector and how to redistribute incomes. *Voting mechanisms substitute for the market mechanism in allocating resources to the public sector and deciding how to use them.* Some people have even suggested that the variety and volume of public goods are determined by the most votes, just as the variety and volume of private goods are determined by the most dollars. Thus, governments choose the level and mix of output (and related taxation) that seem to command the most votes.

Sometimes the link between the ballot box and output decisions is very clear and direct. State and local governments, for example, are often compelled to get voter approval before building another highway, school, housing project, or sewage plant. *Bond referenda* are direct requests by a government unit for voter approval of specific public spending projects (e.g., roads, schools). In 2018, for example, nine state governments sought voter approval for $12 billion of new borrowing to finance specific public projects (schools, hospitals, etc.).

Bond referenda are more the exception than the rule. Bond referenda account for less than 1 percent of state and local expenditures (and no federal expenditures). As a consequence, voter control of public spending is typically much less direct. At best, voters get the opportunity every two years to elect congressional representatives and every four years a president. Promises about future spending and taxes typically play a major role in those elections. But election campaigns rarely get into the details of government spending and often fail to deliver on campaign promises.

Public Choice Theory. The tenuous link between the ballot box and economic policy creates another mechanism for decision making—namely, self-interest. In principle, government officials are supposed to serve the people. It doesn't take long, however, before officials realize that the public is indecisive about what it wants and takes little interest in government's day-to-day activities. With such latitude, government officials can set their own agendas. Those agendas may give higher priority to personal advancement than to the needs of the public. Agency directors may foster new programs that enlarge their mandate, enhance their visibility, and increase their prestige or income. Members of Congress may likewise pursue legislative favors like tax breaks for supporters more diligently than they pursue the general public interest. In such cases, the probability of attaining the socially optimal mix of output declines.

The theory of **public choice** emphasizes the role of self-interest in public decision making. Public choice theory essentially extends the analysis of market behavior to political behavior. Public officials are assumed to have specific personal goals (for example, power, recognition, wealth) that they'll pursue in office. *A central tenet of public choice theory is that bureaucrats are just as selfish (utility maximizing) as everyone else.*

Public choice theory provides a neat and simple explanation for public sector decision making. But critics argue that the theory provides a woefully narrow view of public servants. Some people do selflessly pursue larger, public goals, such critics argue, and ideas can overwhelm self-interest. Steven Kelman of Harvard, for example, argues that narrow self-interest can't explain the War on Poverty of the 1960s, the tax revolt of the 1970s, or the deregulation movement of the 1980s. These tidal changes in public policy reflect the power of ideas, not simple self-interest. Public choice theory tells us how many decisions about government are made; it doesn't tell us how they should be made. The role of government in the economy tomorrow will depend less on self-interest and more on how much we trust *markets* to generate optimal outcomes or trust government intervention to *improve* on market failures.

public choice: Theory of public sector behavior emphasizing rational self-interest of decision makers and voters.

SUMMARY

- Government intervention in the marketplace is justified by market failure—that is, suboptimal market outcomes. **LO4-1**
- The micro failures of the market originate in public goods, externalities, market power, and an inequitable distribution of income. These flaws deter the market from achieving the optimal mix of output or distribution of income. **LO4-1**
- Public goods are those that can't be consumed exclusively; they're jointly consumed regardless of who pays. Because everyone seeks a free ride, no one demands public goods in the marketplace. Hence, the market underproduces public goods. **LO4-1**
- Externalities are costs (or benefits) of a market transaction borne by a third party. Externalities create a divergence between social and private costs or benefits, causing suboptimal market outcomes. The market overproduces goods with external costs and underproduces goods with external benefits. **LO4-1**
- Market power enables a producer to thwart market signals and maintain a suboptimal mix of output. Antitrust policy seeks to prevent or restrict market power. The government may also regulate the behavior of powerful firms. **LO4-1**

- The market-generated distribution of income may be unfair. This inequity may prompt the government to intervene with taxes and transfer payments that redistribute incomes. **LO4-1**
- The macro failures of the marketplace are reflected in unemployment and inflation. Government intervention is intended to achieve full employment and price stability. **LO4-1**
- The federal government expanded greatly in the 1930s and during World War II, but its share of output has shrunk in recent decades. Recent growth in federal spending has been on income transfers, not output. **LO4-2**
- State and local governments purchase more output (11 percent of GDP) than the federal government (6.5 percent) and employ five times as many workers. **LO4-2**
- Income and payroll taxes provide most federal revenues. States get most revenue from sales taxes; local governments rely on property taxes. **LO4-3**
- Government failure occurs when intervention doesn't move toward the optimal mix of output (or income). Failure may result from outright waste (operational inefficiency) or from a misallocation of resources. **LO4-4**
- All government activity must be evaluated in terms of its opportunity cost—that is, the *private* goods and services forgone to make resources available to the public sector. **LO4-4**

Key Terms

laissez faire
optimal mix of output
market mechanism
market failure
private good
public good
free rider
externalities

monopoly
market power
antitrust
natural monopoly
transfer payments
merit good
unemployment
inflation

opportunity cost
progressive tax
proportional tax
regressive tax
government failure
public choice

Questions for Discussion

1. If vaping doesn't entail external costs, what is the theoretical basis for restricting vape consumption (see Front Page Economics "The Health Risks of Vaping")? **LO4-1**
2. If the United States wanted to build an "Iron Dome" missile system, how much would you willingly contribute to its cost? Could it be financed with crowd funding? (World View "Israel's 'Iron Dome' 86 Percent Effective") **LO4-1**
3. If everyone seeks a free ride, what mix of output will be produced in Figure 4.2? Why would anyone voluntarily contribute to the purchase of public goods like flood control or snow removal? **LO4-1**

4. Should the firefighters have saved the house in Front Page Economics "Firefighters Watch as Home Burns to the Ground"? What was the justification for their belated intervention? **LO4-1**
5. Why might Fourth of July fireworks be considered a public good? Who should pay for them? What about airport security? **LO4-1**
6. What is the specific market failure justification for government spending on (*a*) public universities, (*b*) health care, (*c*) trash pickup, (*d*) highways, (*e*) police, and (*f*) solar energy? Would a purely private economy produce any of these services? **LO4-1**

7. If smoking generates external costs, should smoking simply be outlawed? How about cars that pollute?   **LO4-1**

8. The government now spends more than $1 trillion a year on Social Security benefits. Why don't we leave it to individuals to save for their own retirement?   **LO4-1**

9. What government actions might cause failures like points G_1, G_2, and G_3 in Figure 4.6? Can you give examples?   **LO4-4**

10. How does Sirius Satellite deter nonsubscribers from listening to its transmissions? Does this make radio programming a private good or a public good?   **LO4-1**

11. Which taxes hit the poor hardest—those of local, state, or federal governments?   **LO4-3**

12. Why wouldn't market participants take the optimal amount of precautionary actions in a virus pandemic?   **LO4-1**

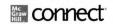

PROBLEMS FOR CHAPTER 4

LO4-1 1. In Figure 4.2, by how much is the market
(a) Overproducing private goods?
(b) Underproducing public goods?

LO4-1 2. (a) Use Figure 4.3 to illustrate on the accompanying production possibilities curve the optimal mix of output (X)

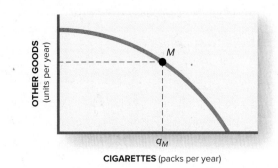

(b) Does the optimal mix include more or fewer "other goods"?

LO4-1 3. Assume that the product depicted below generates external costs in consumption of $3 per unit.
(a) What is the market price (market value) of the product?
(b) Draw the social demand curve.
(c) What is the socially optimal output?
(d) By how much does the market overproduce this good?

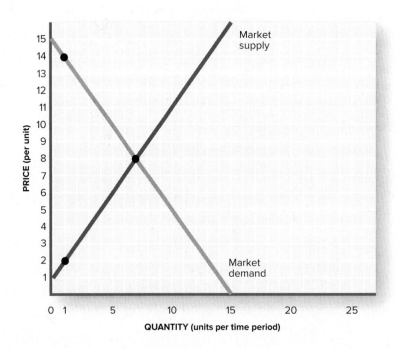

LO4-1 4. (a) Draw the market demand curve, social demand curve, and the supply curve for flu shots.
(b) Based on your graph, does society want more or less people to get a flu shot?

LO4-1 5. If the average adult produces $30,000 of output per year, how much global output is lost annually as a result of adult deaths from secondhand smoke, according to World View "Secondhand Smoke Kills More Than 600,000 People a Year?"

PROBLEMS FOR CHAPTER 4 (cont'd)

LO4-3 6. (a) Assuming an 8 percent sales tax is levied on all consumption, complete the following table:

Income	Consumption	Sales Tax	Percentage of Income Paid in Taxes
$10,000	$11,000	_____	_____
20,000	20,000	_____	_____
40,000	36,000	_____	_____
80,000	60,000	_____	_____

     (b) Is the sales tax progressive or regressive?

LO4-4 7. If a new home can be constructed for $150,000, what is the opportunity cost of federal defense spending, measured in terms of private housing? (Assume a defense budget of $750 billion.)

LO4-1 8. Suppose the following data represent the market demand for college education:

Tuition (per year)	$40,000	$35,000	$30,000	$25,000	$20,000	$15,000	$10,000	$5,000
Enrollment demanded (in millions per year)	1	2	3	4	5	6	7	8

     (a) If tuition is set at $15,000, how many students will enroll?

     Now suppose that society gets an external benefit of $5,000 for every enrolled student.

     (b) Draw the social and market demand curves for this situation on the graph below.
     (c) What is the socially optimal level of enrollment at the same tuition price of $15,000?
     (d) If the government were to intervene and subsidize college education, how large of a subsidy is needed per student each year to achieve this optimal outcome?

College Market

LO4-1 9. Suppose the market demand for cigarettes is given in the following table.

Price per pack	$10	$9	$8	$7	$6	$5	$4	$3
Quantity demanded (million packs per year)	2	4	6	8	10	12	14	16

Suppose further that smoking creates external costs valued at $2 per pack.

(*a*) Graph the social and market demand curves.

If cigarettes are priced at $7 a pack,
(*b*) What is the quantity demanded in the market?
(*c*) What is the socially optimal quantity?
(*d*) If the government were to intervene and tax cigarettes, how large of a tax is needed per pack to achieve this optimal outcome?

LO4-3 10. According to Front Page Economics "State Lotteries: A Tax on the Uneducated and the Poor," what percentage of income is spent on lottery tickets by
(*a*) A low-income family with income of $20,000 per year?
(*b*) An middle-income family with income of $60,000 per year?

LO4-3 11. *Decisions for Tomorrow:* The following production possibilities curve shows the trade-off between housing and all other goods.

PRODUCTION POSSIBILITIES CURVE

(*a*) If the market mix of output is at point *A* and the optimal mix of output is at point *D*, does a market failure exist?
(*b*) If the government has a laissez-faire approach, will it intervene?
(*c*) If the government intervenes and the economy moves to point *C*, is this a government failure?
(*d*) Suppose a politician has self-interest to keep the current mix of output despite the need for more housing in her district. If this is the case, and based on your knowledge of public choice theory, will the politician intervene?

Design Credit: Shutterstock

PRODUCT MARKETS: THE BASICS

The prices and products we see every day emerge from decisions made by millions of individual consumers and firms. A primary objective of microeconomic theory is to explain how those decisions are made. How high a price are consumers willing to pay for the products they want? Which products will consumers actually purchase—and in what quantities? We explore these dimensions of consumer *demand* in Chapters 5 and 6. We move to the *supply* side in Chapter 7, examining the costs that businesses incur in producing the products consumers demand.

Onoky/SuperStock

Michele Constantini/PhotoAlto Agency RF Collections/Getty Images

Rob Crandall/SCPhotos/Alamy Stock Photo

Onoky/SuperStock

CHAPTER 5

Consumer Choice

Steve Jobs knew he had a winner with the iPhone. Every time Apple added a feature to the iPod, sales picked up. Now Jobs had a product that combined cell phone services with wireless computing and audio and video download capabilities—all accessible on a touch screen. It was sure to be a hit. The only sticky question was *price*. What price should Apple put on its new iPhone? The company's goal was to sell 10 million iPhones in the first two years of production. If it set the price low enough, it could surely do that. But Apple didn't want to give away the iPhone—it wanted to make a nice profit. Yet if it set the price *too* high, sales would fall short of its sales target. What price should it charge? Apple's pricing committee had to know how many iPhones consumers would buy at different prices. In other words, they had to know the dimensions of *consumer demand*. After considerable deliberation, they set the initial price at $499 for the 4 GB iPhone, launched in January 2007.

Apple's iPhone pricing dilemma underscores the importance of *prices* in determining consumer behavior. Consumers "want," "need," and "just have to have" a vast array of goods and services. When decision time comes, however, product *prices* often dictate what consumers will actually buy. As we observed in Chapter 3, the quantity of a product *demanded* depends on its price.

This chapter takes a closer look at how product prices affect consumer decisions. We focus on three related questions:

- **How do we decide how much of any good to buy?**
- **Why do we feel so good about our purchases?**
- **Why do we buy certain products but not others?**

The law of demand (first encountered in Chapter 3) gives us some clues for answering these questions. But we need to look beyond that law to fashion more complete answers. We need to know what forces give demand curves their downward-sloping shape. We also need to know more about how to *use* demand curves to predict consumer behavior.

LEARNING OBJECTIVES

After reading this chapter, you should know

LO5-1 Why demand curves are downward sloping.

LO5-2 The nature and source of consumer surplus.

LO5-3 The meaning and use of price discrimination.

LO5-4 How consumers maximize utility.

DETERMINANTS OF DEMAND

In seeking explanations for consumer behavior, we have to recognize that the field of economics doesn't have all the answers. But it does offer a unique perspective that sets it apart from other fields of study.

The Sociopsychiatric Explanation

Consider first the explanations of consumer behavior offered by other fields of study. Psychiatrists and psychologists have had a virtual field day formulating such explanations. Freud was among the first to describe us humans as bundles of subconscious (and unconscious) fears, complexes, and anxieties. From a Freudian perspective, we strive for ever higher levels of consumption to satisfy basic drives for security, sex, and ego gratifications. Like the most primitive of people, we clothe and adorn ourselves in ways that assert our identity and worth. We eat and smoke too much because we need the oral gratifications and security associated with mother's breast. Oversized homes and cars give us a sense of warmth and security remembered from the womb. On the other hand, we often buy and consume some things we don't really want, just to assert our rebellious feelings against our parents (or parent substitutes). In Freud's view, it's the constant interplay of these id, ego, and superego drives that motivates us to buy, buy, buy.

Why does anyone want this car?

Siarhei Tsesliuk/Shutterstock

Sociologists offer additional explanations for our consumption behavior. They observe our yearning to stand above the crowd, to receive recognition from the masses. For people with exceptional talents, such recognition may come easily. But for the ordinary person, recognition may depend on conspicuous consumption. A sleek car, a newer fashion, a more exotic vacation become expressions of identity that provoke recognition, even social acceptance. We strive for ever higher levels of consumption—not just to keep up with the Joneses but to surpass them.

Not *all* consumption is motivated by ego or status concerns. Some food is consumed for the sake of self-preservation, some clothing worn for warmth, and some housing built for shelter. The typical U.S. consumer has more than enough income to satisfy these basic needs, however. In today's economy, most consumers also have *discretionary* income that can be used to satisfy psychological or sociological longings. Single women are able to spend a lot of money on clothes and pets, and men spend freely on entertainment, food, and drink (see Front Page Economics "Men vs. Women: How They Spend"). Teenagers assert their identity with purchases of electronic goods, cars, and clothes (see Figure 5.1).

FRONT PAGE ECONOMICS

MEN VS. WOMEN: HOW THEY SPEND

Are men really different from women? If spending habits are any clue, males do differ from females. That's the conclusion one would draw from the latest Bureau of Labor Statistics (BLS) survey of consumer expenditure. Here's what the BLS found out about the spending habits of young (under age 25) men and women who are living on their own:

Common Traits

- Young men have a lot more after-tax income to spend ($17,473 per year) than do young women ($13,365).
- Both sexes spend about $24,000 per year, much more than their income.
- Education is one of the biggest expenses for both men and women, although single women spend twice as much ($4,661) as single men ($2,108).
- Neither sex spends much on charity, reading, or health care.

Distinctive Traits

- Young men spend twice as much more on alcoholic beverages and smoking.
- Young men spend almost twice as much as women do on electronic equipment.
- Young women spend twice as much money on clothing, personal care items, and their pets.

Source: U.S. Bureau of Labor Statistics, 2018–2019, Consumer Expenditure Survey.

CRITICAL ANALYSIS: Consumer patterns vary by gender, age, and other characteristics. Economists try to isolate the common influences on consumer behavior and **demand**.

FIGURE 5.1

Affluent Teenagers

Teenagers spend nearly $300 billion a year. Much of this spending is for cars, technology, and other durables. The percentages of U.S. teenagers owning certain items are shown here.

Industry Reports, 2015–2017.

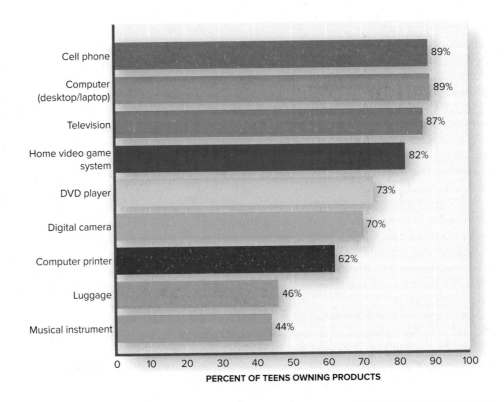

PERCENT OF TEENS OWNING PRODUCTS

demand: The willingness and ability to buy specific quantities of a good at alternative prices in a given time period, *ceteris paribus*.

The Economic Explanation

Although psychiatrists and sociologists offer intriguing explanations for our consumption patterns, their explanations fall a bit short. Sociopsychiatric theories tell us why teenagers, men, and women *desire* certain goods and services. But they don't explain which goods will actually be *purchased*. Desire is only the first step in the consumption process. To acquire goods and services, one must be willing and able to *pay* for one's wants. Producers won't give you their goods just to satisfy your Freudian desires. They want money in exchange for their goods. Hence, ***prices and income are just as relevant to consumption decisions as are more basic desires and preferences.***

In explaining consumer behavior, economists focus on the *demand* for goods and services. As we observed in Chapter 3, **demand** entails the *willingness and ability to pay* for goods and services. To say that someone *demands* a particular good means that he or she will offer to *buy* it at some price(s).

Determinants of Demand. What determines a person's willingness to buy a product at some price? Economists isolate four determinants of demand. We say ***an individual's demand for a specific product is determined by these four factors:***

- *Tastes* (desire for this and other goods).
- *Income* (of the consumer).
- *Expectations* (for income, prices, tastes).
- *Other goods* (their availability and prices).

Freud might have been content to focus on tastes or desires originating in infancy. But economists go several steps further. Tastes alone do not guarantee you'll buy a specific product. Income, expectations, and the price and availability of other goods also come into play at the cash register. All four determinants of demand play a role in the purchase decision.

The remainder of this chapter examines these determinants of demand. The objective is not only to explain consumer behavior but also to predict how consumption patterns change in response to *changes* in the price of a good or to *changes* in underlying tastes, income, prices or availability of other goods, or expectations.

THE DEMAND CURVE

The starting point for an economic analysis of demand is quite simple. Economists accept consumer tastes as the outcome of sociopsychiatric and cultural influences. They don't look beneath the surface to see how those tastes originated. They don't care if your desires originated in the womb or in some TV ad. Economists want to know only how those tastes (desires) affect consumption decisions.

Utility Theory

The first observation economists make is that the more pleasure a product gives us—for whatever reason—the higher the price we're willing to pay for it. If the oral sensation of buttered popcorn at the movies really turns you on, you're likely to be willing to pay dearly for it. If, on the other hand, you have no great taste or desire for popcorn, the theater might have to give it away before you'd eat it.

Total vs. Marginal Utility. Economists use the term **utility** to refer to the expected pleasure, or satisfaction, obtained from goods and services. If you really like popcorn, we say you get a lot of utility (satisfaction) from consuming it. Pretty simple. But we then go a step further in explaining your satisfaction by distinguishing between the *total* utility you get from eating popcorn and your *marginal* utility. **Total utility** refers to the amount of satisfaction obtained from your *entire* consumption of a product. By contrast, **marginal utility** refers to the amount of satisfaction you get from consuming the *last* (i.e., "marginal") unit of a product. More generally, note that

$$\text{Marginal utility} = \frac{\text{Change in total utility}}{\text{Change in quantity}}$$

Diminishing Marginal Utility. The concepts of total and marginal utility explain not only why we buy popcorn at the movies but also why we stop eating it at some point. Even people who love popcorn (i.e., derive great *total* utility from it) don't eat endless quantities of it. Why not? Presumably because the thrill diminishes with each mouthful. The first box of popcorn may bring sensual gratification, but the second or third box is likely to bring a stomachache. We express this change in perceptions by noting that the marginal utility of the first box of popcorn is higher than the additional or marginal utility derived from the second box.

The behavior of popcorn connoisseurs isn't abnormal. As a rule, the amount of additional utility we obtain from a product declines as we continue to consume it. The third slice of pizza isn't as desirable as the first, the sixth beer not as satisfying as the fifth, and so forth. Indeed, this phenomenon of diminishing marginal utility is so nearly universal that economists have fashioned a law around it. This **law of diminishing marginal utility** states that each successive unit of a good consumed yields less *additional* utility.

The law of diminishing marginal utility does *not* say that we won't like the second box of popcorn, the third pizza slice, or the sixth beer; it just says we won't like them as much as the ones we've already consumed. Time is also important here: If the first box of popcorn was eaten last year, the second box may now taste just as good. The law of diminishing marginal utility applies to short time periods.

The Popcorn Test. Let's put the law of diminishing marginal utility to a test—the popcorn test. The test measures how much popcorn you'd eat if it were absolutely free. To complete this test, we'll make up some numbers for total and marginal utility.

Let's start with the first box of popcorn. That first box is yummy. We'll assume an arbitrary number and say that first box delivers 20 units of utility. If we stopped there, at one box, our total utility would be 20 "utils" (units of utility).

But it's hard to stop munching on popcorn. So suppose we go for a *second* box (mini boxes, of course!). Will it taste good? If so, we say it has positive marginal utility; it adds to our pleasure.

utility: The pleasure or satisfaction obtained from a good or service.

total utility: The amount of satisfaction obtained from entire consumption of a product.

marginal utility: The change in total utility obtained by consuming one additional (marginal) unit of a good or service.

law of diminishing marginal utility: The marginal utility of a good declines as more of it is consumed in a given time period.

TABLE 5.1

The Satisfaction Meter

Marginal utility refers to the pleasure we get from one more unit of a good. Although marginal utility diminishes as we consume additional units, total utility keeps rising so long as *marginal* utility is positive.

Popcorn Consumption	Marginal Utility (in Units)	Total Utility
0	0	0
First box	20	20
Second box	15	35
Third box	9	44
Fourth box	5	49
Fifth box	1	50
Sixth box	−10	40

But here's the tough question: Is the second box as satisfying as the first? Probably not. So we have to acknowledge that the marginal utility of the second box is less than the marginal utility of the first box (20 utils). Let's assume the second box adds only 15 units of pleasure.

Notice where we're at on the satisfaction meter in Table 5.1. Our total utility is now at 35 utils, based on the pleasures of the first (20 utils) and second boxes (15 utils).

We'll keep moving up the satisfaction meter so long as we continue to enjoy munching popcorn—so long as the marginal utility of the next box is positive. Sooner or later, however, another box of popcorn isn't going to look so appetizing. At some point, another handful of popcorn might even look repulsive—that is, deliver *negative* marginal utility. In Table 5.1 this threshold is reached with the sixth box. Notice that the marginal utility of the sixth box is *negative*—if you eat it, you'll feel *worse* than if you don't. That's why you move down the satisfaction meter of *total* utility from 50 to 40 when you consume the sixth box.

Here's the popcorn test: Would you eat that sixth box, even if it were free? Hopefully not. Once you realize that the thrill of eating popcorn diminishes with each additional box, you will stop eating it at some point.

Figure 5.2 illustrates how we get to that point. As we consume boxes 1 through 5, we climb the utility staircase. Each step represents the marginal utility of the next box. Because marginal

FIGURE 5.2

Total vs. Marginal Utility

The *total utility* derived from consuming a product comes from the *marginal* utilities of each successive unit. The total utility curve shows how each of the first five boxes of popcorn contributes to total utility. Note that the utility staircase is rising, but each successive step is smaller. This reflects the law of diminishing marginal utility.

The sixth box of popcorn causes the total utility steps to descend; the sixth box actually *reduces* total utility. This means that the sixth box has *negative* marginal utility.

The marginal utility curve (*b*) shows the change in total utility with each additional unit. It's derived from the total utility curve. Marginal utility here is positive but diminishing for the first five boxes.

utility diminishes, each successive step gets shorter. So long as we are climbing, however, total utility is increasing. *As long as marginal utility is positive, total utility must be increasing.*

The situation changes with the sixth box of popcorn. As we have already noted, the good sensations associated with popcorn consumption are completely forgotten by the time the sixth box arrives. Nausea and stomach cramps take over. Indeed, the sixth box is absolutely *distasteful,* as reflected in the downturn of *total* utility and the *negative* value for marginal utility. We were happier—in possession of more total utility—with only five boxes of popcorn. The sixth box—yielding *negative* marginal utility—reduces total satisfaction. This is the kind of sensation you'd probably experience if you ate six hamburgers (see the cartoon below).

Analysis: No matter how much we like a product, marginal utility is likely to diminish as we consume more of it. If marginal utility becomes *negative* (as here), total satisfaction will decrease.

Not every good ultimately reaches negative marginal utility. Yet the more general principle of diminishing marginal utility is experienced daily. That is, *eventually additional quantities of a good yield increasingly smaller increments of satisfaction.*

Price and Quantity

Marginal utility is essentially a measure of how much we desire particular goods, our *taste.* But which ones will we buy? Clearly, we don't always buy the products we most desire. *Price* often holds us back. All too often we have to settle for goods that yield less marginal utility simply because they are available at a lower price. This explains why most people don't drive Porsches. Our desire ("taste") for a Porsche may be great, but its price is even greater. The challenge for most of us is to somehow reconcile our tastes with our bank balances.

In deciding whether to buy something, our immediate focus is typically on a single variable, namely *price.* Assume for the moment that a person's tastes, incomes, and expectations are set in stone, and that the prices of other goods are set as well. This is the ***ceteris paribus*** assumption we first encountered in Chapter 1. It doesn't mean that other influences on consumer behavior are unimportant. Rather, *ceteris paribus* simply allows us to focus on one variable at a time. In this case, we are focusing on price. What we want to know is how high a price a consumer is willing to pay for another unit of a product. This is the question Steve Jobs had to confront when Apple launched the first iPhone in 2007.

The concepts of marginal utility and *ceteris paribus* enable us to answer this question. *The more marginal utility a product delivers, the more a consumer will be willing to pay for it.* We also noted that marginal utility *diminishes* as increasing quantities of a product are consumed, suggesting that consumers are willing to pay progressively *less* for additional quantities of a product. The moviegoer willing to pay 50 cents for that first mouth-watering ounce of buttered popcorn may not be willing to pay so much for a second or third ounce. The same is true for a second pizza, the sixth beer, and so forth. *Because marginal utility declines, people are willing to buy additional quantities of a good only if its price falls.* In other words,

ceteris paribus: The assumption of nothing else changing.

FIGURE 5.3

An Individual's Demand Schedule and Curve

Consumers are generally willing to buy larger quantities of a good at lower prices. This demand schedule illustrates the specific quantities demanded at alternative prices. If popcorn sold for 25 cents per ounce, this consumer would buy 12 ounces per show (row *F*). At higher prices, less popcorn would be purchased.

A downward-sloping demand curve expresses the law of demand: The quantity of a good demanded increases as its price falls. Notice that points *A* through *J* on the curve correspond to the rows of the demand schedule.

Demand curve

The willingness to pay diminishes along with marginal utility.

Demand Schedule

	Price (per Ounce)	Quantity Demanded (Ounces per Show)
A	$0.50	1
B	0.45	2
C	0.40	4
D	0.35	6
E	0.30	9
F	0.25	12
G	0.20	16
H	0.15	20
I	0.10	25
J	0.05	30

law of demand: The quantity of a good demanded in a given time period increases as its price falls, *ceteris paribus*.

demand curve: A curve describing the quantities of a good a consumer is willing and able to buy at alternative prices in a given time period, *ceteris paribus*.

market demand: The total quantities of a good or service people are willing and able to buy at alternative prices in a given time period; the sum of individual demands.

as the marginal utility of a good diminishes, so does our willingness to pay. This **law of demand** is illustrated in Figure 5.3 with the downward-sloping **demand curve.**

The law of demand and the law of diminishing marginal utility tell us nothing about why we crave popcorn or why our cravings subside. Those explanations are reserved for psychiatrists, sociologists, and physiologists. The laws of economics simply describe our market behavior.

MARKET DEMAND

Our explanation of an individual's popcorn consumption applies to all products and all consumers. As we saw in Chapter 3, the **market demand** for popcorn is just the sum of all our individual demands for that product. The market demand curve resembles an individual's demand curve but differs in two important respects. First, the units of measurement are larger: The quantities on the horizontal axis are in hundreds, thousands, or possibly millions of units, not single digits. Second, the demand curve expresses the ability and willingness to pay of thousands of consumers, not just one individual.

CONSUMER SURPLUS

The presence of so many individuals on the market demand curve has some interesting implications for both consumers and producers. To see this, let's venture into another market—say, the new car market. Let's focus on a specific car, the Porsche 918 Spyder Hybrid, a sports car with a 608 horsepower V8 engine supplemented by two electrical engines, a top speed of 211 miles per hour, and 71 miles per gallon in all-electric mode.

Lots of people crave this car. But not everyone is willing and able to buy it at the Manufacturer's Suggested Retail Price (MSRP) of $847,975. In fact, most people who *desire* the car aren't prepared to pay anywhere near that much money. Some people are, however. Indeed, some Porsche fans would pay even a *higher* price to get their hands on a 918 Spyder. And it's not just a question of who is rich enough. Remember that there are *four* determinants of an individual's demand: tastes, income, expectations, and other goods (price and availability). So a rich person with little desire for speed might not demand a Spyder at the $847,975 price. On the other hand, a real speed freak with only a modest income might be willing to borrow money, rent out the house, and sell the kids to get behind the wheel of a 918 Spyder.

As individuals work their way through the determinants of demand, they will ultimately decide how much money they are willing to pay for a Porsche 918 Spyder. For those sorry souls who would never think of driving a Spyder, their price would be zero: They would not be part of the market demand for that car. Everyone else, however, would be deciding the *maximum* price they would be willing and able to pay for a new 918 Spyder. That decision will determine where they are positioned on the market demand curve.

Consider the positions depicted in Figure 5.4. Fred is positioned high up on the market demand curve because he is willing to pay as much as $1 million for a Spyder. Michel and Hua are also willing and able to shell out big bucks for the car. Blaise also wants a Spyder but can't or won't spend more than $650,000 to get one.

What we also see on the market demand curve is how many cars the Porsche dealer can sell at the MSRP of $847,975. At that price (point *A* on the graph), four Spyders will be demanded and therefore sold.

Fred will be particularly excited with this deal. We know that Fred would pay as much as $1 million for a 918 Spyder. But he has to pay only the $847,975 price set by the dealer. In his mind, he is getting a real bargain—getting the Spyder for a lot less money than the maximum price he would be willing to pay. We call this "bargain" his **consumer surplus.** Specifically, consumer surplus is the difference between the maximum price a person is *willing to pay* and the price paid:

You may *desire* a Porsche, but do you *demand* it?

Sean Gallup/Getty Images News/Getty Images

consumer surplus: The difference between the maximum price a person is willing to pay and the price paid.

$$\text{Consumer surplus} = \text{Maximum price willing to pay} - \text{Price actually paid}$$

FIGURE 5.4

Consumer Surplus

A person's position on the market demand curve expresses the maximum price he or she is willing to pay. The difference between that individualized maximum price and the price paid represents "consumer surplus." At the MSRP price of $847,975, Michel would have a consumer surplus of $102,025 (= $950,000 − $847,975).

FIGURE 5.5

Total consumer surplus

Every consumer who buys a product must be willing and able to pay *at least* the prevailing price. Therefore, all consumers buying the good reap some consumer surplus. Their collective consumer surplus is represented by the shaded area in the graph.

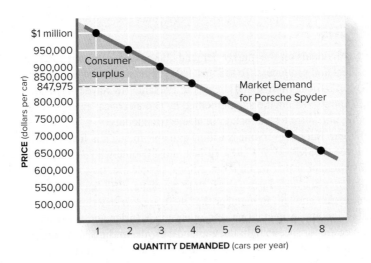

In Fred's case, that consumer surplus amounts to $152,025 (= $1 million − $847,975).

Michel enjoys a consumer surplus as well. Notice again in Figure 5.4, where she is on the market demand curve: She is willing to pay as much as $950,000 for a Spyder. So she enjoys a consumer surplus of $102,025 (= $950,000 − $847,975). She cannot wait to tell all her friends what a "bargain" she got.

In fact, everyone who buys a Spyder thinks she or he got a bargain! That is because *the only people who purchase a product are those whose maximum price equals or exceeds the market price.* In Figure 5.4 only the consumers at or above point *A* drive away in a new Spyder. Anyone *below* point *A* walks; John, Marty, Bob, and Blaise want a Porsche 918 Spyder but are not willing to pay $847,975 to get one.

Now you know why we love to shop. People do not buy things that are priced above their maximum price thresholds. We only buy those things priced at or below our maximum price threshold. So we are always getting some consumer surplus and bragging about the "bargains" we got. This collective consumer surplus is depicted in Figure 5.5.

PRICE DISCRIMINATION

Car dealers are well aware of this consumer surplus phenomenon and determined to profit from it. Consider their options. Figure 5.4 reveals that the dealer can sell four cars at the posted price of $847,975. That would generate **total revenue** (= price × quantity) of $3,391,180.

But he could do better than that if he priced each car separately rather than charging the *same* price for all four cars. Suppose he knew that Fred was willing and able to pay as much as $1 million for a Spyder. Instead of posting a uniform price of $847,975, the dealer could let Fred try to negotiate a price for himself. What is the *most* Fred would pay? $1 million. So the dealer could ask for $1.2 million and let Fred "bargain" his way down to $1 million. Fred would drive off in his Spyder, feeling smug about the "deal" he had struck. And the dealer would be smiling all the way to the bank.

If the dealer handled all the buyers in this way, he would bring in a lot more revenue from the sale of his four cars. He would sell the first car to Fred for $1 million, a car to Michel for $950,000, a car to Hua for $900,000, and one to Carlos for $850,000. His total revenue would be $3.7 million rather than the $3,391,900 he got with uniform pricing. Pretty nice deal.

What the dealer is doing here is practicing **price discrimination:** charging individual consumers different prices for the same good. In effect, the dealer is picking off consumers from their positions on the market demand curve and charging them the maximum price

---

total revenue: The price of a product multiplied by the quantity sold in a given time period: $p \times q$.

---

price discrimination: The sale of an individual good at different prices to different consumers.

each is willing to pay. If successful, the dealer will eliminate all consumer surplus and maximize his own revenue.

There is nothing illegal about this kind of price discrimination. And no one gets harmed. No one paid more for a Spyder than she or he was willing to pay. And the buyers might even feel good about their negotiating skills.

Divide and Conquer. The key to the dealer's success is the ability to negotiate each price individually. There is no transparency here. Car dealers typically conduct negotiations in small cubicles, isolated from other consumers. That way the dealer can probe to discover what maximum price each individual is willing to pay. So long as that price is above the uniform price threshold ($847,975 in this case), the dealer extracts some of that consumer surplus (and increases total revenue).

Price discrimination is rampant in the auto industry, but common in many other markets as well. Next time you are on an airplane, ask your seatmates how much they paid for their tickets. Odds are that it is not the same price you paid. The airlines use a variety of techniques to "divide and conquer" airline passengers. People who must travel on short notice and with uncertain schedules pay high "unrestricted" fares. Travelers who are further down the market demand curve are singled out with advance ticketing, nonrefundable purchases, and minimum-stay restrictions. They end up paying a lower price for the same flight. That is price discrimination.

Even colleges engage in price discrimination. Your school may have a seemingly uniform price for tuition. But schools adjust that price on an individual basis with scholarships and grants. In so doing, they hope to "sell" the school to applicants with exceptional academic or athletic potential who otherwise are not willing and able to pay the posted price.

Price discrimination is most effective when consumers don't have perfect information about market prices and there are few sellers. Price discrimination is also easier to practice in markets where individual consumers make only occasional purchases (e.g., new cars, vacations, college).

CHOOSING AMONG PRODUCTS

Our analysis of demand thus far has focused on the decision to buy a single product at varying prices. Actual consumer behavior is multidimensional, however, and therefore more complex. When we go shopping, our concern isn't limited to how much of one good to buy. Rather, we must decide *which* of many available goods to buy at their respective prices.

The presence of so many goods complicates consumption decisions. Our basic objective remains the same, however: We want to get as much satisfaction as possible from our available income. In striving for that objective, we have to recognize that the purchase of any single good means giving up the opportunity to buy more of other goods. In other words, consuming a Porsche 918 Spyder, popcorn, or any other good entails distinct **opportunity costs.**

opportunity cost: The most desired goods or services that are forgone in order to obtain something else.

Marginal Utility vs. Price

The economic explanation for consumer choice builds on the theory of marginal utility and the law of demand. Suppose you have a $10 gift card for music and video game downloads. The first proposition of consumer choice says you'll *prefer* the download that gives you the most satisfaction. Hardly a revolutionary proposition.

The second postulate of consumer choice takes into account market prices. Suppose you *prefer* a video game, but music downloads are cheaper. Under these circumstances, your budget may win out over your desires. There's nothing irrational about downloading a song instead of a more desirable video game when you have only a limited amount of income to spend. On the contrary, *rational behavior requires one to compare the anticipated utility of each expenditure with its price.* The smart thing to do, then, is to choose those products that promise to provide the most pleasure for the amount of income available.

Suppose your desire for a video game is *twice* as great as your desire to hear a tune. In economic terms, this means that the marginal utility of the first video game is two times that of the first music download. Which one should you download? Before hitting buttons on your smartphone, you'd better look at relative prices. What if a game costs $3 and a song costs only $1? In this case, you must pay *three* times as much for a video game that gives only *twice* as much pleasure. This isn't a good deal. You could get more utility *per dollar* by downloading music.

The same kind of principle explains why some rich people drive a Ford rather than a shiny new Porsche 918 Spyder. The marginal utility (MU) of driving a Spyder is substantially higher than the MU of driving a Ford. A nice Spyder, however, costs about 30 times as much as a basic Ford. A rich person who drives a Ford must feel that driving a Spyder is not 30 times as satisfying as driving a Ford. For such people, a Ford yields more *marginal utility per dollar spent.*

The key to utility maximization, then, isn't simply to buy the things you like best. Instead you must compare goods on the basis of their marginal utility *and* price. ***To maximize utility, the consumer should choose the good that delivers the most marginal utility per dollar.***

Utility Maximization

This basic principle of consumer choice is easily illustrated. Think about spending that $10 gift card on music or game downloads, the only available choices. Your goal, as always, is to get as much pleasure as possible from this limited income. That is, you want to maximize the *total* utility attainable from the expenditure of your income. The question is how to do it. What combination of songs and games will maximize the utility you get from $10?

We've already assumed that the marginal utility (MU) of the first game is two times higher than the MU of the first song. This is reflected in the second row of Table 5.2. The MU of the first video game has been set arbitrarily at 20 utils (units of utility). We don't need to know whether 20 utils is a real thrill or just a bit of amusement. Indeed, the concept of "utils" has little meaning by itself; it's only a useful basis for comparison. In this case, we want to compare the MU of the first game with the MU of the first song. Hence, we set the MU of the first game at 20 utils and the MU of the first song at 10 utils. The first game download is twice as satisfying as the first music download:

$$\text{MU game} = 2 \text{ MU song}$$

Diminishing Marginal Utility

The remainder of Table 5.2 indicates how marginal utility diminishes with increasing consumption of a product. Look at what happens to the sound of music. The marginal utility of the first song is 10, but the MU of the second song is only 9 utils. The third song generates even less MU ($= 8$). You started with your favorite song; now you're working down your hits list. By the time you get to a sixth song, music downloads aren't raising your spirits much (MU $= 4$). By the tenth song, you're tired of music (MU $= 0$).

Game downloads also conform to the law of diminishing marginal utility. You start with your favorite game (MU $= 20$), seeking a high score. The second game is fun, too, though not quite as much (MU $= 18$). As you keep playing, frustration rises and marginal utility diminishes. By the time you play a sixth game, your nerves are just about shot; the sixth game gives you only 1 util of marginal utility.

Finding the Best Mix

With these psychological insights to guide us, we can now determine how best to spend $10. What we're looking for is the combination of songs and video games that *maximizes* the total utility attainable from an expenditure of $10. We call this combination **optimal consumption**—that is, the mix of goods that yields the most utility for the available income.

optimal consumption: The mix of consumer purchases that maximizes the utility attainable from available income.

| Quantity Consumed | Amount of Utility (in Units of Utility, or Utils) | | | |
| | From Music Downloads | | From Game Downloads | |
	Total	Marginal	Total	Marginal
0	0	—	0	—
1	10	10	20	20
2	19	9	38	18
3	27	8	54	16
4	33	6	66	12
5	38	5	72	6
6	42	4	73	1
7	45	3		
8	47	2		
9	48	1		
10	48	0		

| Quantity | Example | |
	Total	Marginal
0	0	—
1	10	10
2	19	9
3	27	8

TABLE 5.2

Maximizing Utility

Q: How can you get the most satisfaction (utility) from $10 if you must choose between downloading songs at $1 apiece or video games at $3 apiece?

A: By playing two games and playing four songs. See the text for explanation.

We can start looking for the optimal mix of consumer purchases by assessing the utility of spending the entire $10 on video games. At $3 per play, we could buy three games. This would give us *total* utility of 54 utils (see Table 5.2). Plus we'd have enough change to download one song (MU = 10), for a grand utility total of 64 utils.

Alternatively, you could also spend the entire gift card on music downloads. With $10 to spend, you could buy 10 songs. However, this would generate only 48 utils of total utility. Hence, if you were forced to choose between *only* downloading songs or *only* playing video games, you'd pick the games.

Fortunately, we don't have to make such extreme choices. In reality, we can buy a *combination* of songs and video games. This complicates our decision making (with more choices) but permits us to attain higher levels of total satisfaction.

To reach the peak of satisfaction, consider spending your $10 in $3 increments. How should you spend the first $3? If you spend it on one game, you'll get 20 utils of satisfaction. On the other hand, $3 will buy your first three music downloads. The first song has an MU of 10 and the second song adds another 9 utils to your happiness. The third song brings in another 8 utils. Hence, by spending the $3 on songs, you reap 27 utils of total utility. This is superior to the pleasure of a first game, and it's therefore your first purchase.

Having downloaded three songs, you now can spend the second $3. How should it be spent? Your choice now is that first game or a fourth, fifth, and sixth song. That first unplayed game still promises 20 utils of real pleasure. By constrast, the MU of a fourth song is 6 utils. And the MU of a fifth song is only 5 utils. Together, then, the fourth, fifth, and sixth songs will increase your total utility by 15 utils, whereas a first game will give you 20 utils. You should spend the second $3 on a game download.

The decision on how to spend the remaining four dollars is made the same way. The final choice is to purchase either a second game (MU = 18) or the fourth, fifth, and sixth songs (MU = 15). The second game offers more marginal utility and is thus the correct decision.

Maximizing Utility

After working your way through these calculations, you'll end up downloading two games and four songs. Was it worth it? Do you end up with more total utility than you could have gotten from any other combination? The answer is yes. The *total* utility of two games (38 utils) and four songs (33 utils) is 71 units of utility. This is significantly better than the alternatives of spending your $10 on songs alone (total utility = 48) or three games and a song (total utility = 64). In fact, the combination of two games and four songs is the *best* one you can find. Because this combination maximizes the total utility of your income ($10), it represents *optimal consumption*.

Utility-Maximizing Rule

Optimal consumption refers to the mix of products that maximizes total utility for the limited amount of income you have to spend. The basic approach to utility maximization is to purchase the good next that delivers the most *marginal utility per dollar.* Marginal utility per dollar is simply the MU of the good divided by its price: MU ÷ P.

From Table 5.2 we know that a first game has an MU of 20 and a price of $3. It thus delivers a marginal utility per dollar of

$$\frac{\text{MU}_{\text{first game}}}{P_{\text{game}}} = \frac{20}{\$3} = 6.67 \text{ utils per dollar}$$

On the other hand, the first song has a marginal utility of 10 and a price of $1. It offers a marginal utility per dollar of

$$\frac{\text{MU}_{\text{first song}}}{P_{\text{song}}} = \frac{10}{\$1} = 10 \text{ utils per dollar}$$

From this perspective, the first song is a better deal than the first game and should be purchased.

Optimal consumption implies that the utility-maximizing combination of goods has been found. If this is true, you can't increase your total utility by trading one good for another. All goods included in the optimal consumption mix yield the *same* marginal utility per dollar. We know we've reached maximum utility when we've satisfied the following rule:

$$\text{Utility-maximizing rule:} \quad \frac{\text{MU}_x}{P_x} = \frac{\text{MU}_y}{P_y}$$

where *x* and *y* represent any two goods included in our consumption.

Rational consumer choice depends on comparisons of marginal utilities and prices. If a dollar spent on product *X* yields more marginal utility than a dollar spent on product *Y,* we should buy product *X*. To use this principle, of course, we have to know the amounts of utility obtainable from various goods and be able to perform a little arithmetic. By doing so, however, we can get the greatest satisfaction from our limited income.

Equilibrium Outcomes

All these graphs and equations make consumer choice look dull and mechanical. Economic theory seems to suggest that consumers walk through shopping malls with marginal utility tables and handheld computers. In reality, no one does this—not even your economics instructor. Yet economic theory is pretty successful in predicting consumer decisions. Consumers don't always buy the optimal mix of goods and services with their limited income. But after some trial and error, consumers adjust their behavior. What economic theory predicts is that the final choices—the *equilibrium* outcomes—will be the predicted optimal ones.

DECISIONS FOR TOMORROW

Do "Influencers" Really Matter?

LeBron James is paid more than $55 million a year to help convince us to buy Nike shoes, drink Sprite and Powerade, use Beats to listen to music, eat Dunkin' Doughnuts, drive a Kia, and buy Piguet watches. Do these sponsors know something economic theory doesn't? Economists *assume* consumers know what they want and will act rationally to get the most satisfaction they can. The companies that sponsor basketball star LeBron James don't accept that assumption. They think your tastes will follow LeBron's lead—that he is a valued "influencer." Your perception of the marginal utility associated with LeBron-endorsed products will increase.

Advertisers now spend more than $200 *billion* per year to change our perceptions. In the United States, this spending works out to more than $600 per consumer, one of the highest per capita advertising rates in the world. Some of this advertising (including product labeling) is intended to provide information about existing products or to bring new products to our attention. A great deal of advertising, however, is also designed to exploit our senses and lack of knowledge. Recognizing that we're guilt-ridden, insecure, and sex-hungry, advertisers promise exoneration, recognition, and love; all we have to do is buy the right products.

What are the right products? Well, of course, the ones the celebrity influencers are showcasing on blog posts or Instagram videos. Companies are now spending over $10 billion a year on product sponsorships by "influencers"—celebrities and noncelebrities alike. Marketing research indicates those investments deliver the customers.

Is this a shoe salesman?!
Kevin C. Cox/Staff/Getty Images

Why does anyone care about which cosmetics Kylie uses?
David Dee Delgado/Getty Images

Are Wants Created? Advertising can't be blamed for all of our foolish consumption. Even members of the most primitive tribes, uncontaminated by the seductions of advertising, adorned themselves with rings, bracelets, and pendants. Furthermore, advertising has grown to massive proportions only in the past 50 years, but consumption spending has been increasing throughout recorded history. Finally, a lot of advertising simply fails to change buying decisions. Accordingly, it's a mistake to attribute the growth or content of consumption entirely to the persuasions of advertisers.

This isn't to say that advertising has necessarily made us happier. The objective of all advertising is to alter the choices we make. Just as product images are used to attract us to particular products, so are pictures of hungry, ill-clothed children used to persuade us to give money to charity. In the same way, public relations gimmicks are employed to

Continued

shift in demand: A change in the quantity demanded at any (every) price.

sway our votes for public servants. In the case of consumer products, advertising seeks to increase tastes for particular goods and services and therewith our willingness to pay. *A successful advertising campaign is one that increases the perceived marginal utility of a product, thereby* **shifting the demand curve** *for that product to the right* (see Figure 5.6). Maybe I won't be able to jump 8 feet high if I wear Nike's LeBron 17 Monstars shoes, but I might *feel* better just knowing that LeBron wears the same shoes. By influencing our choices in this way, advertising will affect the consumption choices we make in the economy tomorrow. Advertising alone is unlikely to affect the total *level* of consumption, however.

FIGURE 5.6

The Impact of Advertising on a Demand Curve

Advertising seeks to increase our taste for a particular product. If our taste (the product's perceived utility) increases, so will our willingness to buy. The resulting change in demand is reflected in a rightward shift of the demand curve, often accompanied by diminished elasticity.

SUMMARY

- Our desires for goods and services originate in the structure of personality and social dynamics and aren't explained by economic theory. Economic theory focuses on *demand*—that is, our ability and willingness to buy specific quantities of a good at various prices.   **LO5-1**
- The determinants of demand include tastes (desires), income, other goods (price and availability), and expectations.   **LO5-1**
- Marginal utility measures the additional satisfaction obtained from consuming one more unit of a good. The law of diminishing marginal utility says that the more of a product we consume, the smaller the increments of pleasure we tend to derive from additional units of it. This is a basis for the law of demand.   **LO5-1**
- The determinants of demand establish the maximum price a consumer will pay for a good. That maximum price determines where an individual is positioned on the market demand curve.   **LO5-1**
- A person will buy a product only if its price is at or below the maximum price that person is willing and able to pay.

The difference between that maximum price threshold and the price paid is called "consumer surplus."   **LO5-2**
- Producers can extract some or all consumer surplus by charging different prices to individuals, based on their willingness to pay—a practice called "price discrimination."   **LO5-3**
- In choosing among alternative goods and services, a consumer compares the prices and anticipated satisfactions that they offer. To maximize utility with one's available income—to achieve an optimal mix of goods and services—one has to get the most utility for every dollar spent. To do so, one must choose those goods promising the most marginal utility per dollar.   **LO5-4**
- Advertising (including influencer marketing) seeks to change consumer tastes and thus the willingness to buy. If tastes do change, the demand curve for that product will shift.   **LO5-1**

Key Terms

demand
utility
total utility
marginal utility
law of diminishing marginal utility

ceteris paribus
law of demand
demand curve
market demand
consumer surplus

total revenue
price discrimination
opportunity cost
optimal consumption
shift in demand

Questions for Discussion

1. What does the demand for enrollments in your college look like? What is on the axes? How do tuition, enrollment, and total revenue interact? **LO5-1**

2. If the marginal utility of pizza never diminished, how many pizzas would you eat? **LO5-1**

3. How do total and marginal utility change as you spend more time tweeting your friends? **LO5-1**

4. Can you think of any product that violates the law of diminishing marginal utility? **LO5-1**

5. How did Apple decide what price to charge for its 10-year anniversary iPhone in 2017? Could it have charged a higher price? Should it have? **LO5-1**

6. When the producer price discriminates in Figure 5.4, what happens to unit sales? Total revenue? Total profit? **LO5-3**

7. Under what circumstances could a producer extract *the entire* consumer surplus in Figure 5.5? **LO5-2**

8. How does a car dealer determine where a buyer is on the market demand curve? **LO5-3**

9. Why do airlines charge different fares for the same flight? **LO5-3**

10. Why does anyone care what cosmetics Kylie Jenner uses? **LO5-4**

LO5-1 1. According to Table 5.1
   (*a*) With which box of popcorn does marginal utility first diminish?
   (*b*) With which box does marginal utility become negative?

LO5-2 2. In Figure 5.4, how much consumer surplus is received by
   (*a*) Fred?
   (*b*) Hua?
   (*c*) Carlos?

LO5-2 3. In Figure 5.4, if Bob's maximum price increased by 50 percent,
   (*a*) Would he buy a Spyder?
   (*b*) How much consumer surplus would he have?

LO5-2 4. If the price of a Spyder drops to $700,000 in Figure 5.4,
   (*a*) How many Spyders can be sold at that price?
   (*b*) How much consumer surplus will there be if all the cars are sold at that price?
   (*c*) How much revenue will the car dealer get if he sells all the cars at
       (i) the same price ($700,000)?
       (ii) the maximum price each buyer is willing to pay?

LO5-3 5. The following data reveal how much each consumer is willing to pay for an Alaskan cruise:

Amy	$ 900	Ed	$2,000
Bob	$1,100	Gigi	$1,300
Carol	$1,500	Hugo	$1,800
Eduardo	$ 400	Isabelle	$1,500

   (*a*) Draw the market demand for these eight consumers.
   (*b*) If the cruise costs $1,000, how many passengers will there be?
   (*c*) If the cruise costs $1,000, how much total revenue will be collected?
   (*d*) If the cruise costs $1,000, how much consumer surplus will those passengers enjoy?

LO5-4 6. Suppose movie downloads cost $2 apiece and game downloads cost $3. If the marginal utility of movie downloads at the optimal mix of consumption is 10 utils, what is the marginal utility of a game download?

LO5-1 7. Suppose the graph below depicts the demand for football tickets at Grand University.
   (*a*) If current demand is represented as Demand 2, what is total revenue at the price of $24?
   (*b*) If the price drops to $12, how many tickets would consumers purchase?
   (*c*) What is total revenue at that point?
   (*d*) If the team has a losing streak and the price is still $24, at what point do we end up?
   (*e*) What is total revenue at that point?

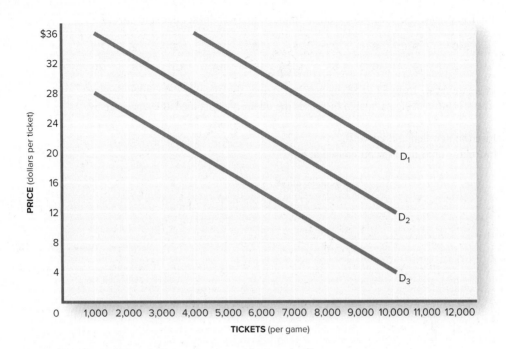

LO5-4 8. Suppose the following table reflects the total satisfaction derived from consumption of pizza slices and Pepsis. Assume that pizza costs $1 per slice and a large Pepsi costs $2. With $20 to spend, what consumption mix will maximize satisfaction?

Quantity consumed	1	2	3	4	5	6	7	8	9	10	11	12	13	14
Total units of pleasure from pizza slices	47	92	132	166	196	224	251	271	288	303	313	315	312	300
Total units of pleasure from Pepsis	111	200	272	336	386	426	452	456	444	408	340	217	92	−17

LO5-4 9. A consumer downloads 4 movies and 3 apps per week. Suppose the price is $5 per movie and $3 per app, and the marginal utility for this consumption level is 12 for a movie and 10 for an app.
(a) Calculate marginal utility per dollar.
(b) Is this optimal consumption?
(c) If not, how should the consumer change his consumption to maximize?

LO5-1   10. Decisions for Tomorrow: Use the following data to illustrate the relevant demand curve:

Price	$10	9	8	7	6	5	4	3	2	1
Quantity	2	4	6	8	10	12	14	16	18	20

(*a*) If the price increases from $4 to $8, by how much does the quantity demanded decline?

(*b*) If a successful advertising campaign increases the quantity demanded at every price by 4 units,

   (*i*) Draw the new demand curve D_2.

   (*ii*) How many units are now purchased at $8?

> # APPENDIX

....

INDIFFERENCE CURVES

A consumer's demand for any specific product is an expression of many forces. As we've observed, the actual quantity of a product demanded by a consumer varies inversely with its price. The price–quantity relationship is determined by

- *Tastes* (desire for this and other goods).
- *Income* (of the consumer).
- *Expectations* (for income, prices, tastes).
- *Other goods* (their availability and price).

Economic theory attempts to show how each of these forces affects consumer demand. Thus far, we've used two-dimensional demand curves to illustrate the basic principles of demand. We saw that, in general, a change in the price of a good causes a movement along the demand curve, whereas a change in tastes, income, expectations, or other goods shifts the entire demand curve to a new position.

We haven't looked closely at the origins of demand curves, however. We assumed that a demand curve could be developed from observations of consumer behavior, such as the number of boxes of popcorn that were purchased at various prices (Figure 5.3).

It's possible, however, to derive a demand curve without actually observing consumer behavior. In theory we can identify consumer *preferences* (tastes), then use those preferences to construct a demand curve. In this case, the demand curve is developed explicitly from known preferences rather than on the basis of market observations. The end result—the demand curve—is the same, at least so long as consumers' behavior in product markets is consistent with their preferences.

Indifference curves are a mechanism for illustrating consumer tastes. We examine their construction and use in this appendix. Indifference curves provide an explicit basis for constructing a demand curve. In addition, they are another way of viewing how consumption is affected by price, tastes, and income. Indifference curves are also a useful tool for explicitly illustrating consumer *choice*—that is, the decision to purchase one good rather than another.

Constructing an Indifference Curve

Suppose you're in an arcade and want to buy some Cokes and play video games but don't have enough money to buy enough of each. The income constraint compels you to make hard decisions. You have to consider the **marginal utility** each additional Coke or video game will provide, compare their respective prices, then make a selection. With careful introspection and good arithmetic you could select the optimal mix of Cokes and video games—that is, the combination that yields the most satisfaction (utility) for the income available. This process of identifying your **optimal consumption** was illustrated in Table 5.2 with downloads of music and video games.

Computing your optimal consumption is difficult because you must assess the marginal utility of each prospective purchase. In Table 5.2 we assumed that the marginal utility of the first music download was 10 utils, while the first game download had a marginal utility of 20. Then we had to specify the marginal utility of every additional music and game download. Can we really be so specific about our tastes?

Indifference curves require a bit less arithmetic. *Instead of trying to measure the marginal utility of each prospective purchase, we now look for combinations of goods that yield equal satisfaction.* In the arcade, this entails different combinations of Cokes and games. All we need is to determine that one particular combination of Cokes and video games is as satisfying as another. We don't have to say how many "units of pleasure" both combinations provide—it's sufficient that they're both equally satisfying.

marginal utility: The change in total utility obtained by consuming one additional (marginal) unit of a good or service.

optimal consumption: The mix of consumer purchases that maximizes the utility attainable from available income.

Equally Satisfying Combinations

Different combinations of two goods may be equally satisfying. In this case, we assume that the combinations *A, B,* and *C* all yield equal total utility. Hence, the consumer will be indifferent about which of the three combinations he or she receives.

Combination	Cokes	Video Games
A	1	8
B	2	5
C	3	4

The initial combination of 1 Coke and 8 video games is designated as combination *A* in Table 5A.1. This combination of goods yields a certain, but unspecified, level of total utility. What we want to do now is to find another combination of Cokes and games that's just as satisfying as combination *A*. Finding other combinations of equal satisfaction isn't easy, but it's at least possible. After a lot of soul searching, we decide that 2 Cokes and 5 video games would be just as satisfying as 1 Coke and 8 games.[1] This combination is designated as *B* in Table 5A.1.

Table 5A.1 also depicts a third combination of Cokes and video games that's as satisfying as the first. Combination *C* includes 3 Cokes and 4 games, a mix of consumption assumed to yield the same total utility as 1 Coke and 8 games (combination *A*).

Notice that we haven't said anything about how much pleasure combinations *A, B,* and *C* provide. We're simply asserting that these three combinations are *equally* satisfying.

Figure 5A.1 illustrates the information about tastes that we've assembled. Points *A, B,* and *C* represent the three equally satisfying combinations of Cokes and video games we've identified. By connecting these points, we create an **indifference curve.** The indifference curve illustrates all combinations of two goods that are equally satisfying. A consumer would be just as happy with any combination represented on the curve, so a choice among them would be a matter of indifference.

An Indifference Map. Not all combinations of Cokes and video games are as satisfying as combination *A*, of course. Surely 2 Cokes and 8 games would be preferred to only 1 Coke and 8 games. Indeed, *any combination that provided more of one good and no less of the other would be preferred.* Point *D* in Figure 5A.2 illustrates just one such combination. Combination *D* must yield more total utility than combination *A* because it includes one more Coke and no fewer games. A consumer wouldn't be indifferent to a choice between *A* and *D*; on the contrary, combination *D* would be preferred.

Combination *D* is also preferred to combinations *B* and *C*. How do we know? Recall that combinations *A, B,* and *C* are all equally satisfying. Hence, if combination *D* is better than *A*,

indifference curve: A curve depicting alternative combinations of goods that yield equal satisfaction.

FIGURE 5A.1

An Indifference Curve

An indifference curve illustrates the various combinations of two goods that would provide equal satisfaction. The consumer is assumed to be indifferent to a choice between combinations *A, B,* and *C* (and all other points on the curve) because they all yield the same total utility.

[1]The utility computations used here aren't based on Table 5.2; a different set of tastes is assumed.

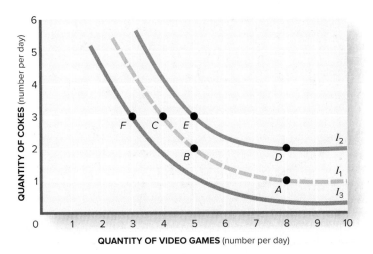

FIGURE 5A.2

An Indifference Map

All combinations of goods depicted on any given indifference curve (e.g., I_1) are equally satisfying. Other combinations are more or less satisfying, however, and thus lie on higher (I_2) or lower (I_3) indifference curves. An indifference map shows all possible levels of total utility (e.g., $I_1, I_2, I_3, \ldots, I_n$) and their respective consumption combinations.

it must also be better than *B* and *C*. Given a choice, a consumer would select combination *D* (2 Cokes, 8 games) in preference to *any* combination depicted on indifference curve I_1.

There are also combinations that are as satisfying as *D,* of course. These possibilities are illustrated on indifference curve I_2. All these combinations are equally satisfying and must therefore be preferred to any points on indifference curve I_1. In general, *the farther the indifference curve is from the origin, the more total utility it yields.*

The curve I_3 illustrates various combinations that are less satisfying. Combination *F,* for example, includes 3 Cokes and 3 games. This is 1 game less than the number available in combination *C*. Therefore, *F* yields less total utility than *C* and isn't preferred: A consumer would rather have combination *C* than *F.* By the same logic we just used, all points on indifference curve I_3 are less satisfying than combinations on curve I_2 or I_1.

Curves 1, 2, and 3 in Figure 5A.2 are the beginnings of an **indifference map**. An indifference map depicts all the combinations of goods that would yield various levels of satisfaction. A single indifference curve, in contrast, illustrates all combinations that provide a single (equal) level of total utility.

indifference map: The set of indifference curves that depicts all possible levels of utility attainable from various combinations of goods.

Utility Maximization

We assume that all consumers strive to maximize their utility. They want as much satisfaction as they can get. In the terminology of indifference curves, this means getting to the indifference curve that's farthest from the origin. The farther one is from the origin, the greater the total utility.

Although the goal of consumers is evident, the means of achieving it isn't so clear. Higher indifference curves aren't only more satisfying, they're also more expensive. We're confronted again with the basic conflict between preferences and prices. With a limited amount of income to spend, we can't attain infinite satisfaction (the farthest indifference curve). We have to settle for less (an indifference curve closer to the origin). The question is, How do we maximize the utility attainable with our limited income?

The Budget Constraint. For starters, we have to determine how much we have to spend. Suppose for the moment that we have only $2 to spend in the arcade and that Cokes and video games are still the only objects of our consumption desires. The price of a Coke is 50 cents; the price of a game is 25 cents. Accordingly, the maximum number of Cokes we could buy is 4 if we didn't play any video games. On the other hand, we could play as many as 8 games if we were to forsake Coke.

Figure 5A.3 depicts the limitations placed on our consumption possibilities by a finite income. The **budget constraint** illustrates all combinations of goods affordable with a given income. In this case, the outermost budget line illustrates the combinations of Cokes and video games that can be purchased with $2.

budget constraint: A line depicting all combinations of goods that are affordable with a given income and given prices.

FIGURE 5A.3

The Budget Constraint

Consumption possibilities are limited by available income. The budget constraint illustrates this limitation. The end points of the budget constraint are equal to income divided by the price of each good. All points on the budget constraint represent affordable combinations of goods.

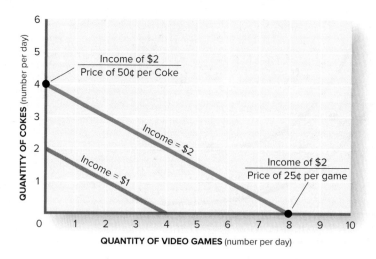

The budget line is easily drawn. The end points of the budget constraint are found by dividing one's income by the price of the good on the corresponding axis. Thus, the outermost curve begins at 4 Cokes ($2 ÷ 50 cents) and ends at 8 games ($2 ÷ 25 cents). All the other points on the budget constraint represent other combinations of Cokes and video games that could be purchased with $2.

A smaller income is also illustrated in Figure 5A.3. If we had only $1 to spend, we could afford fewer Cokes and fewer games. Hence, a smaller income is represented by a budget constraint that lies closer to the origin.

Optimal Consumption. With a budget constraint looming before us, the limitation on utility maximization is evident. We want to reach the highest indifference curve possible. Our limited income, however, restricts our grasp. We can go only as far as our budget constraint allows. In this context, *the objective is to reach the highest indifference curve that is compatible with our budget constraint.*

Figure 5A.4 illustrates the process of achieving optimal consumption. We start with an indifference map depicting all utility levels and product combinations. Then we impose a budget line that reflects our income. In this case, we continue to assume that Coke costs 50 cents, video games cost 25 cents, and we have $2 to spend. Hence, *we can afford only those consumption combinations that are on or inside the budget line.*

FIGURE 5A.4

Optimal Consumption

The optimal consumption combination—the one that maximizes the utility of spendable income—lies at the point where the budget line is tangent to (just touches) an indifference curve. In this case, point *M* represents the optimal mix of Cokes and video games because no other affordable combination lies on a higher indifference curve than I_c.

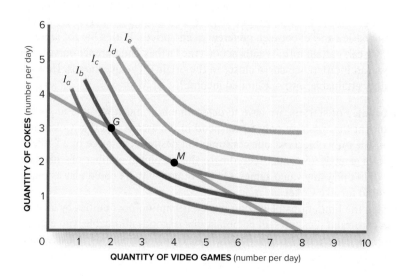

Which particular combination of Cokes and video games maximizes the utility of our $2? It must be 2 Cokes and 4 video games, as reflected in point M. Notice that point M isn't only on the budget line but also touches indifference curve I_c. No other point on the budget line touches I_c or any higher indifference curve. Accordingly, I_c represents the most utility we can get for $2 and is attainable only if we consume 2 Cokes and 4 video games. Any other affordable combination yields less total utility—that is, falls on a lower indifference curve. Point G, for example, which offers 3 Cokes and 2 video games for $2, lies on the indifference curve I_b. Because I_b lies closer to the origin than I_c, point G must be less satisfying than point M. We conclude, then, that *the point of tangency between the budget constraint and an indifference curve represents optimal consumption.* It's the combination we should buy if we want to maximize the utility of our limited income.

Marginal Utility and Price: A Digression. We earlier illustrated the utility-maximizing rule, which required a comparison of the ratios of marginal utilities to prices. Specifically, optimal consumption was represented as that combination of Cokes and video games that yielded

$$\frac{MU \text{ Coke}}{P \text{ Coke}} = \frac{MU \text{ games}}{P \text{ games}}$$

Does point M in Figure 5A.4 conform to this rule?

To answer this question, first rearrange the preceding equation as follows:

$$\frac{MU \text{ Coke}}{MU \text{ games}} = \frac{P \text{ Coke}}{P \text{ games}}$$

In this form, the equation says that the relative marginal utilities of Cokes and video games should equal their relative prices when consumption is optimal. In other words, if a Coke costs twice as much as a video game, then it must yield twice as much marginal utility if the consumer is to be in an optimal state. Otherwise, some substitution of Cokes for video games, or vice versa, would be desirable.

With this foundation, we can show that point M conforms to our earlier rule. Consider first the slope of the budget constraint, which is determined by the relative prices of Cokes and video games. In fact, *the (absolute) slope of the budget constraint equals the relative price of the two goods.* In Figure 5A.4 the slope equals the price of video games divided by the price of Cokes (25 cents ÷ 50 cents = ½). It tells us the rate at which video games can be exchanged for Cokes in the market. In this case, one video game is "worth" half a Coke.

The relative marginal utilities of the two goods are reflected in the slope of the indifference curve. Recall that the curve tells at what rate a consumer is willing to substitute one good for another, with no change in total utility. In fact, the slope of the indifference curve is called the **marginal rate of substitution**. It's equal to the relative marginal utilities of the two goods. Presumably one would be indifferent to a choice between 2 Cokes + 5 games and 3 Cokes + 4 games—as suggested in Table 5A.1—only if the third Coke were as satisfying as the fifth video game.

At the point of optimal consumption (M) in Figure 5A.4, the budget constraint is tangent to the indifference curve I_c, which means that the two curves must have the same slope at that point. In other words,

marginal rate of substitution: The rate at which a consumer is willing to exchange one good for another; the relative marginal utilities of two goods.

$$\frac{P \text{ games}}{P \text{ Coke}} = \frac{MU \text{ games}}{MU \text{ Coke}}$$

or alternatively,

$$\frac{\text{Rate of}}{\text{market exchange}} = \frac{\text{Marginal rate}}{\text{of substitution}}$$

Both indifference curves and marginal utility comparisons lead us to the same optimal mix of consumption.

FIGURE 5A.5

Changing Prices

When the price of a good changes, the budget constraint shifts, and a new consumption combination must be sought. In this case, the price of video games is changing. When the price of games increases from 25 cents to 50 cents, the budget constraint shifts inward and optimal consumption moves from point *M* to point *N*.

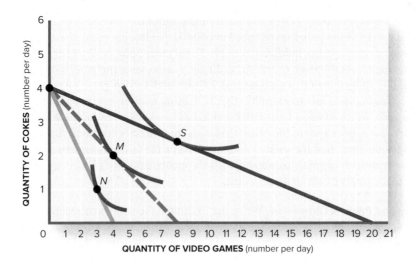

Deriving the Demand Curve

We noted at the beginning of this appendix that indifference curves not only give us an alternative path to optimal consumption but also can be used to derive a demand curve. To do this, we need to consider how the optimal consumption combination changes when the price of one good is altered. We can see what happens in Figure 5A.5.

Figure 5A.5 starts with the optimal consumption attained at point *M*, with income of $2 and prices of 50 cents for a Coke and 25 cents for a video game. Now we're going to change the price of video games and observe how consumption changes.

Suppose that the price of a video game doubles, from 25 cents to 50 cents. This change will shift the budget constraint inward: Our income of $2 now buys a maximum of 4 games rather than 8. Hence, the lower end point of the budget constraint moves from 8 games to 4 games. ***Whenever the price of a good changes, the budget constraint shifts.***

Only one end of the budget constraint is changed in Figure 5A.5. The budget line still begins at 4 Cokes because the price of Coke is unchanged. If only one price is changed, then only one end of the budget constraint is shifted.

Because the budget constraint has shifted inward, the combination *M* is no longer attainable. Two Cokes (at 50 cents each) and 4 games (at 50 cents each) now cost more than $2. We're now forced to accept a lower level of total utility. According to Figure 5A.5, optimal consumption is now located at point *N*. This is the point of tangency between the new budget constraint and a lower indifference curve. At point *N* we consume 1 Coke and 3 video games.

demand curve: A curve describing the quantities of a good a consumer is willing and able to buy at alternative prices in a given time period, *ceteris paribus.*

Consider what has happened here. The price of video games has increased (from 25 cents to 50 cents), and the quantity of games demanded has decreased. This is the kind of relationship that demand curves describe. **Demand curves** indicate how the quantity demanded of a good changes in response to a change in its price, given a fixed income and all other things held constant. Not only does Figure 5A.5 provide the same information, it also conforms to the **law of demand:** As the price of games increases, the quantity demanded falls.

Suppose the price of video games were to fall rather than increase. Specifically, assume that the price of a game fell to 10 cents. This price reduction would shift the budget constraint farther out on the horizontal axis because as many as 20 games could then be purchased with $2. As a result of the price reduction, we can now buy more goods and thus attain a higher level of satisfaction.

law of demand: The quantity of a good demanded in a given time period increases as its price falls, *ceteris paribus.*

Point *S* in Figure 5A.5 indicates the optimal combination of Cokes and video games at the new video game price. At these prices, we consume 8 video games and 2.4 Cokes (we may have to share with a friend). The law of demand is again evident: When the price of video games declines, the quantity demanded increases.

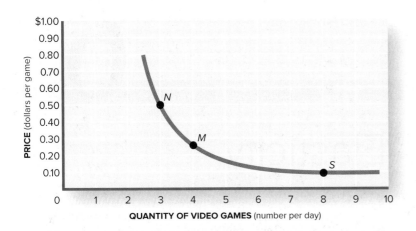

FIGURE 5A.6

The Demand for Video Games

Figure 5A.5 shows how optimal consumption is altered when the price of video games changes. From that figure we can determine the quantity of video games demanded at alternative prices, *ceteris paribus.* That information is summarized here in the demand schedule (below) and the demand curve (above).

Point	Price (per Game)	Quantity Demanded (Games per Day)
N	50 cents	3
M	25	4
S	10	8

The Demand Schedule and Curve. Figure 5A.6 summarizes the information we've acquired about the demand for video games. The demand schedule depicts the price–quantity relationships prevailing at optimal consumption points *N, M,* and *S* (from Figure 5A.5). The demand curve generalizes these observations to encompass other prices. What we end up with is a demand curve explicitly derived from our (assumed) knowledge of consumer tastes.

Key Terms

marginal utility
optimal consumption
indifference curve

indifference map
budget constraint
marginal rate of substitution

demand curve
law of demand

Michele Constantini/PhotoAlto Agency RF Collections/
Getty Images

6

Elasticity

LEARNING OBJECTIVES

After reading this chapter, you should know

LO6-1 How to compute price elasticity of demand.

LO6-2 The relationships between price changes, price elasticity, quantity demanded, and total revenue.

LO6-3 What the cross-price elasticity of demand measures.

LO6-4 What the income elasticity of demand tells us.

LO6-5 What the elasticity of supply measures.

S teve Jobs made a pricing mistake when he launched the 8 GB iPhone in June 2007. He knew all about consumer demand and its many determinants. And he could draw a downward-sloping demand curve just as well as any college economics major (even though he dropped out of Reed College after just one semester). But he overestimated the dimensions of market demand. The demand curve he drew projected that the quantity of iPhones demanded at the price of $599 would be far greater than it turned out to be. This mistake created an instant dilemma. If he kept the price of $599, iPhone sales would come in below publicized projections, and the phone would be deemed a failure. Apple's image of consistent success would be tarnished. Software writers might not develop the library of iPhone apps that would make the iPhone irresistible. So Jobs knew what he had to do: reduce the iPhone's price—fast!

But he couldn't afford to make another mistake. If he reduced the price too little, iPhone sales would still fall short of projections. If he reduced the price too much, sales would soar past production rates and market shortages would frustrate would-be buyers. On the second go-round, Steve Jobs had to pick the right price—the one that would increase the quantity demanded to match Apple's sales projections. The concept that could save him was the "price elasticity of demand"—a measure of how the quantity demanded *changes* in response to a *change* in price.

This chapter focuses on that *elasticity* concept. Among the questions we'll pursue are

- **How does a change in a product's price affect the quantity we purchase or the amount of money we spend on it?**
- **How do changes in the price of *other* products affect the amount of a product we buy?**
- **How do changes in income affect the quantity demanded of various goods and services?**

As we will see, the concept of "elasticity" is part of the answer to all these questions. We will also see how Steve Jobs salvaged the original iPhone with the same concept and how Apple used the concept again in 2020 to price the iPhone 12.

PRICE ELASTICITY

What Steve Jobs wanted to know in September 2007 was how much phone sales would *increase* if he *reduced* its price. The same question haunts movie theater owners. They make a big chunk of profit from the sale of popcorn, candy, and soda. People are always complaining about how expensive those snacks are. But will they buy more if prices are reduced? A *lot* more, or just a *little* more?

Like Apple, theater owners know all about the **law of demand** and the downward-sloping **demand curve.** But that law isn't greatly informative; it tells them only that the quantity demanded will increase when the price is reduced. That begs the critical question of *how much.* What the theater owner wants to know is *by how much* the quantity demanded will increase if the price is reduced. Steve Jobs wanted to know the same thing about the demand for iPhones: How many *more* iPhones would be purchased if he reduced its price?

The central question in all these decisions is the response of quantity demanded to a change in price. *The response of consumers to a change in price is measured by the price elasticity of demand.* Specifically, the **price elasticity of demand** refers to the *percentage* change in quantity demanded divided by the *percentage* change in price:

$$\text{Price elasticity} \ (E) = \frac{\text{\% change in quantity demanded}}{\text{\% change in price}}$$

What would the value of price elasticity be if air travel didn't change at all when airfares were cut by 5 percent? In that case, the price elasticity of demand would be

$$E = \frac{\text{\% change in quantity demanded}}{\text{\% change in price}}$$
$$= \frac{0}{5} = 0$$

But is this realistic? According to the law of demand, the quantity demanded goes up when price goes down. So we'd expect *somebody* to buy more airline tickets if fares fell by 5 percent. In a large market like air travel, we don't expect *everybody* to jump on a plane when airfares are reduced. But if *some* consumers fly more, the percentage change in quantity demanded will be larger than zero. Indeed, *the law of demand implies that the price elasticity of demand will always be greater than zero.*

Technically, the price elasticity of demand (*E*) is a negative number because quantity demanded and price always move in opposite directions (law of demand). For simplicity, however, *E* is typically expressed in absolute terms (without the minus sign). *The key question, then, is how much greater than zero E actually is.*

Computing Price Elasticity

To get a feel for the dimensions of elasticity, let's return to the popcorn counter at the movies that we first encountered in Chapter 5. We observed there that at a price of 45 cents an ounce, the average moviegoer demands 2 ounces of popcorn per show. This is illustrated again in Figure 6.1 at point *B.* At the lower price of 40 cents per ounce (point *C*), the quantity demanded jumps to 4 ounces per show.

Percentage Change in q. We can summarize this response with the price elasticity of demand. To do so, we have to calculate the *percentage* changes in quantity and price. Consider the percentage change in quantity first. In this case, the change in quantity demanded is 4 ounces − 2 ounces = 2 ounces. The *percentage* change in quantity is therefore

$$\text{\% change in quantity} = \frac{2}{q}$$

The computational problem is to transform the denominator *q* into a number. Should we use the quantity of popcorn purchased *before* the price reduction—that is, $q_1 = 2$? Or should we use the quantity purchased *after* the price reduction—that is, $q_2 = 4$? The choice of denominator will have a big impact on the computed percentage change. To ensure consistency, economists prefer to use the *average* quantity in the denominator:[1]

$$\text{\% change in quantity demanded} = \frac{\text{Change in quantity}}{\text{Average quantity}}$$

[1]This procedure is referred to as the *arc* (midpoint) elasticity of demand. If a single quantity (price) is used in the denominator, we refer to the *point* elasticity of demand.

law of demand: The quantity of a good demanded in a given time period increases as its price falls, *ceteris paribus.*

demand curve: A curve describing the quantities of a good a consumer is willing and able to buy at alternative prices in a given time period, *ceteris paribus.*

price elasticity of demand: The percentage change in quantity demanded divided by the percentage change in price.

How do prices affect popcorn sales?

D. Hurst/Alamy Stock Photo

FIGURE 6.1

Demand and Elasticity

We know from the law of demand that the quantity demanded increases when price is reduced. This demand curve (identical to Figure 19.3) informs us that when the price of popcorn falls from 45 cents per ounce to 25 cents, the quantity demanded increases from 2 (point *B*) to 12 ounces per show (point *F*).

What the price elasticity of demand tells us is how much, *in percentage terms,* the quantity demanded changes in response to various price changes.

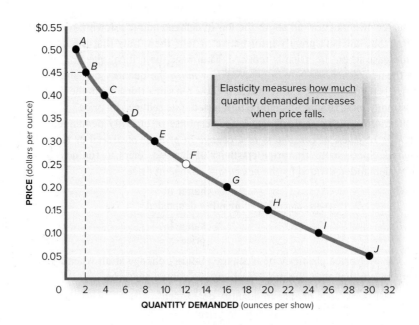

Elasticity measures how much quantity demanded increases when price falls.

	Price (per Ounce)	Quantity Demanded (Ounces per Show)
A	$0.50	1
B	0.45	2
C	0.40	4
D	0.35	6
E	0.30	9
F	0.25	12
G	0.20	16
H	0.15	20
I	0.10	25
J	0.05	30

Our first task is therefore to compute the *average* quantity: the average of the first (pre-price change) and second (post-price change) quantities. The formula for this calculation is

$$\text{Average quantity} = \frac{q_1 + q_2}{2} = \frac{2 + 4}{2} = 3 \text{ ounces}$$

(3 is the average value of 2 and 4).

We can now complete the calculation of the percentage change in quantity demanded. It is

$$\frac{\text{\% change in}}{\text{quantity demanded}} = \frac{\text{Change in quantity}}{\text{Average quantity}} = \frac{q_2 - q_1}{\frac{q_1 + q_2}{2}} = \frac{2}{3} = 0.667$$

Popcorn sales increased by an average of 67 percent when the price of popcorn was reduced from 45 cents to 40 cents per ounce.

Percentage Change in p. The computation of the percentage change in price is similar. We first note that the price of popcorn fell by 5 cents (40¢ − 45¢) when we move from point B to point C on the demand curve (Figure 6.1). We then compute the *average* price of popcorn in this range of the demand curve as

$$\text{Average price} \atop \text{of popcorn} = \frac{p_1 + p_2}{2} = \frac{45¢ + 40¢}{2} = 42.5 \text{ cents}$$

This *average* is the denominator we use in calculating the percentage price change. Using these numbers, we see that the absolute value of the percentage change is

$$\text{% change} \atop \text{in price} = \frac{\text{Change in price}}{\text{Average price}} = \frac{p_2 - p_1}{\dfrac{p_1 + p_2}{2}} = \frac{5}{42.5} = 0.118$$

The price of popcorn fell by 11.8 percent.

These calculations are a bit cumbersome, but they give us all the information required to compute the price elasticity of demand. In this case,

$$E = \frac{\text{% change in quantity demanded}}{\text{% change in price}} = \frac{0.667}{0.118} = 5.65$$

What we get from all these calculations is a very useful number. It says that the consumer response to a price reduction will be extremely large. Specifically, the quantity of popcorn consumed will increase 5.65 times as fast as price falls. A 1 percent reduction in price brings about a 5.65 percent increase in purchases. The theater manager can therefore boost popcorn sales greatly by lowering price a little. Steve Jobs would have been thrilled if the demand for the first iPhones had been that elastic.

Elastic vs. Inelastic Demand. We characterize the demand for various goods in one of three ways: *elastic, inelastic,* or *unitary elastic:*

- *If E is larger than 1, demand is elastic.* Consumer response is large relative to the change in price. This is clearly the case in the popcorn example above ($E = 5.65$).
- *If E is less than 1, demand is* **inelastic.** If demand is inelastic ($E < 1$), consumers aren't very responsive to price changes.
- *If E is equal to 1, demand is* **unitary** *elastic.* In this case, the percentage change in quantity demanded is exactly equal to the percentage change in price.

Consider the case of smoking. Many smokers claim they'd "pay anything" for a cigarette after they've run out. But would they? Would they continue to smoke just as many cigarettes if prices doubled or tripled? If so, the demand curve would be vertical (as in Figure 6.2*b*) rather than downward-sloping. Research suggests this is not the case: Higher cigarette prices *do* curb smoking. There is at least *some* elasticity in the demand for cigarettes. But the elasticity of demand is low; Table 6.1 indicates that the price elasticity of cigarette demand is only 0.4. Because 0.4 is less than 1.0, we say that cigarette demand is inelastic. But that doesn't mean smokers are completely unresponsive to cigarette prices. If the price goes up, they will buy fewer cigarettes, but not a *lot* fewer.

Although the average adult smoker is not very responsive to changes in cigarette prices, teen smokers apparently are. Research studies confirm that teen smoking drops by almost 7 percent when cigarette prices increase by 10 percent. Thus, the price elasticity of *teen* demand for smoking is

$$E = \frac{\text{Percentage drop in quantity demanded}}{\text{Percentage increase in price}} = \frac{7\%}{10\%} = 0.7$$

FIGURE 6.2

Extremes of Elasticity

If demand were perfectly elastic ($E = \infty$), the demand curve would be *horizontal*. In that case, any increase in price (e.g., p_1 to p_2) would cause quantity demanded to fall to zero.

A *vertical* demand curve implies that an increase in price won't affect the quantity demanded. In this situation of perfectly *in*elastic ($E = 0$) demand, consumers are willing to pay *any* price to get the quantity q_1.

In reality, elasticities of demand for goods and services lie between these two extremes (obeying the law of demand).

(a) Completely elastic ($E = \infty$)

(b) Completely inelastic ($E = 0$)

Hence, higher cigarette prices can be an effective policy tool for curbing teen smoking. The *tripling* of the federal excise tax on cigarettes in 2009 (from 39 cents to $1.01 per pack) raised the price of cigarettes by 13 percent and deterred 250,000 teens from smoking.

According to Table 6.1, the demand for airline travel is much more price-elastic than the demand for cigarettes. Whenever a fare cut is announced, the airlines get swamped with telephone and Internet inquiries. If fares are discounted by 25 percent, the number of passengers may increase by as many as 60 percent. As Table 6.1 shows, the elasticity of airline demand is 2.4, meaning that the percentage change in quantity demanded (60 percent) will be 2.4 times larger than the price cut (25 percent).

Product	Price Elasticity
Relatively elastic ($E > 1$)	
Airline travel, long run	2.4
Restaurant meals	2.3
Fresh fish	2.2
New cars, short run	1.2–1.5
Unitary elastic ($E = 1$)	
Private education	1.1
Radios and televisions	1.2
Shoes	0.9
Movies	0.9
Canned Tuna	0.9
Relatively inelastic ($E < 1$)	
Milk	0.6
Cigarettes	0.4
Coffee	0.3
Eggs	0.3
Gasoline, short run	0.2
Electricity (in homes)	0.1

TABLE 6.1

Elasticity Estimates

Price elasticities vary greatly. When the price of gasoline increases, consumers reduce their consumption only slightly ($E = 0.2$). When the price of fish increases, however, consumers cut back their consumption substantially ($E = 2.2$). These differences reflect the availability of immediate substitutes, the prices of the goods, and the amount of time available for changing behavior.

Sources: Hendrick S. Houthakker and Lester D. Taylor, *Consumer Demand in the United States, 1929–1970* (Cambridge: Harvard University Press, 1966); F. W. Bell, "The Pope and Price of Fish," *American Economic Review*, December 1968; Herbert Scarf and John Shoven, *Applied General Equilibrium Analysis* (New York: Cambridge University Press, 1984); and Michael Ward, "Product Substitutability and Competition in Long-Distance Telecommunications," *Economic Inquiry*, October 1999.

Steve Jobs was pleased to discover that the demand for iPhones was even more elastic than that. Two months after launching the 8 GB iPhone in 2007, he reduced its price from $599 to $399. Unit sales not only increased, they soared, as Front Page Economics "After iPhone Price Cut, Sales Are Up by 200 Percent" reports. Demand for the iPhone was very elastic.

FRONT PAGE ECONOMICS

AFTER IPHONE PRICE CUT, SALES ARE UP BY 200 PERCENT

Piper Gene Munster, the person responsible for a survey dedicated to Apple in which he "found" out an estimated number of iPhones that were sold, has come up with yet another interesting theory.

According to Munster and the past-week Apple announcement about 1 million iPhones sold, the calculations take to the conclusion that after the price cut, the sales increased up to 200 percent. . . .

By Munster's reckoning, Apple and AT&T were selling an average of 9,000 iPhones a day before the price reduction, which would have put their quarterly sales at 594,000 as of September 5.

By the end of the quarter, he believes Apple will have sold a total of 1.28 million iPhones.

Source: Mobilewhack.com, September 11, 2007.   McGraw Hill

CRITICAL ANALYSIS: If demand is **elastic,** unit sales increase by a larger percentage than price declines. The demand for iPhones was highly elastic.

Netflix Price Increase. Reed Hastings, the CEO of Netflix, was hoping in 2019 that the demand for that video-streaming service was *not* that elastic. Why? Because Netflix was *increasing* the price of monthly subscriptions. Hastings knew that some customers would quit the service if he raised the price: The law of demand applies to streaming services as well as cell phones and popcorn. But how many subscribers would Netflix lose? If the price elasticity of demand was low, few subscribers would quit. On the other hand, a high elasticity of demand would cause a huge loss of subscribers. After doing some market research, Netflix determined that the price elasticity of demand for streaming was probably low. And they were right. When Netflix increased the price of its popular monthly Standard Plan from $10.99 to $12.99 a month in May 2019, only 126,000 of its 58 million subscribers quit the service. Demand for Netflix was clearly inelastic.

Determinants of Elasticity

Why are consumers so price-sensitive ($E > 1$) with some goods and not ($E < 1$) with others? To answer that, we must go back to the demand curve itself. The elasticity of demand is computed between points on a given demand curve. Hence, *the price elasticity of demand is influenced by all the determinants of demand.* Four factors are particularly worth noting.

Necessities vs. Luxuries. Some goods are so critical to our everyday life that we regard them as "necessities." A hairbrush, toothpaste, and perhaps textbooks might fall into this category. Our "taste" for such goods is so strong that we can't imagine getting along without them. As a result, we don't change our consumption of "necessities" much when the price increases; *demand for necessities is relatively inelastic.*

A "luxury" good, by contrast, is something we'd *like* to have but aren't likely to buy unless our income jumps or the price declines sharply, such as vacation travel, new cars (that Porsche 918 Spyder!), and iPhones. We want them but can get by without them. That is, ***demand for luxury goods is relatively elastic.***

Availability of Substitutes. Our notion of which goods are necessities is also influenced by the availability of substitute goods. The high elasticity of demand for fish (Table 6.1) reflects the fact that consumers can eat chicken, beef, or pork if fish prices rise. On the other hand, most bleary-eyed coffee drinkers can't imagine any other product that could substitute for a cup of coffee. As a consequence, when coffee prices rise, consumers don't reduce their purchases much at all. Likewise, the low elasticity of demand for gasoline reflects the fact that most cars can't run on alternative fuels. In general, *the greater the availability of substitutes, the higher the price elasticity of demand.*

The availability of substitutes frustrated California's attempt to both reduce smoking and increase tax revenues when it hiked the state tax on cigarettes from 87 cents a pack to $2.87 a pack in 2017 (see Front Page Economics "Californians Vote to Triple Cigarette Tax"). Studies have shown conclusively that the price elasticity for cigarettes is low. But the demand for *California-taxed* cigarettes is much more elastic. Why? Because Californians can buy cigarettes in neighboring states or on Indian reservations, or even order them over the Internet. In New York, where the state tax is a whopping $4.35 per pack and the New York City tax is another $1.50, over half of all the cigarettes smoked are smuggled in from other jurisdictions. When Netflix raised its subscription price, it had few competitors. Later in that year, however, Disney and a couple of other big entertainment companies started streaming services. As more competition entered the streaming services market, Netflix would have to be much more careful about raising prices.

FRONT PAGE **ECONOMICS**

CALIFORNIANS VOTE TO TRIPLE CIGARETTE TAX

Sacramento, CA—Californians voted to more than triple the state tax on cigarettes from $0.87 a pack to $2.87 a pack, beginning April 1, 2017.

Anti-smoking groups say the higher price will reduce smoking in the state. They foresee the proportion of smokers falling from the current 11.6 percent of the population to as low as 7.1 percent by 2020.

The state treasurer is also applauding the higher price, but for different reasons. According to the state's Legislature Analyst's Office (LAO), the additional $2 per pack tax will bring in $1.27–$1.61 billion a year to the state treasury.

Michael Hierner/Alamy Stock Photo

Both groups were wrong. Californians continued to smoke about 800 million cigarettes a year, disappointing health advocates. And the state netted much less that $1 billion in new tax revenue, disappointing the state treasurer. These disappointments are due to the fact that Californians can easily purchase cheaper cigarettes in neighboring states, on Indian reservations, and from smuggled supplies.

Source: News reports, November 10, 2016.

CRITICAL ANALYSIS: Higher prices do discourage smoking. But smokers can obtain cigarettes from other jurisdictions **(availability of substitutes)** when a single city or state increases its tax.

Relative Price (to Income). Another important determinant of elasticity is the price of the good in relation to a consumer's income. Airline travel and new cars are quite expensive, so even a small percentage change in their prices can have a big impact on a consumer's budget

Age Group	Percent Decline in Smoking
12–17 years	5 %
18 years	4.5
19–39 years	4
40 years and older	1.5

Source: Congressional Budget Office, *Raising the Excise Tax on Cigarettes,* June 2012.

TABLE 6.2

Long-Run Price Elasticities for Cigarettes

The Congressional Budget Office (CBO) has estimated the following responses over a 10-year period to a 10 percent rise in cigarette prices.

and consumption decisions. The demand for such big-ticket items tends to be elastic. By contrast, coffee is so cheap that even a large *percentage* change in price doesn't affect consumer behavior much. That helps explain why demand for iPhones is more elastic than demand for Netflix.

Because the relative price of a good affects price elasticity, the value of E_1 *changes* along a given demand curve. At current prices the elasticity of demand for coffee is low. How would consumers behave, however, if coffee cost $5 a cup? Some people would still consume coffee. At such higher prices, however, the quantity demanded would be more sensitive to price changes. Accordingly, when we observe, as in Table 6.1, that the demand for coffee is price-inelastic, that observation applies only to the current range of prices. Were coffee prices dramatically higher, the price elasticity of demand would be higher as well. As a rule, *the price elasticity of demand declines as price moves down the demand curve.*

Time. Finally, time affects the price elasticity of demand. Car owners can't switch to electric autos every time the price of gasoline goes up. In the short run, the elasticity of demand for gasoline is quite low. With more time to adjust, however, consumers can buy more fuel-efficient cars, relocate their homes or jobs, and even switch fuels. As a consequence, *the long-run price elasticity of demand is higher than the short-run elasticity.* Nobel Prize–winning economist Gary Becker used the distinction between long-run and short-run elasticities to explain why a proposed increase in cigarette excise taxes wouldn't generate nearly as much revenue as President Clinton expected (see Front Page Economics "Professor Becker Rejects Clinton's Tax Math"). Table 6.2 depicts long-run price elasticities for smokers of various ages.

FRONT PAGE ECONOMICS

PROFESSOR BECKER REJECTS CLINTON'S TAX MATH

In seeking ways to balance the federal budget, President Clinton has seized on the excise tax on cigarettes. That tax, now at 24 cents per pack, brought in around $12 billion in federal revenue last year. President Clinton says that raising that tax by $1 a pack could generate another $53 billion over the next five years.

Chicago professor and Nobel laureate Gary Becker says the president is blowing smoke. A quadrupling of the excise tax will convince a lot of smokers to quit—or at least smoke less. Because smoking is addictive, the decline in smoking won't be immediate. In the short run, every 10 percent hike in the price of cigarettes will reduce consumption by only 4 percent. But in the long run, smoking will decline by about 7 percent. As a result, the tax hike will bring in only a fraction of what Clinton anticipates.

Source: Media reports, 1994.

CRITICAL ANALYSIS: It takes time for people to adjust their behavior to changed prices. Hence, the **short-run price elasticity** of demand is lower than the **long-run elasticity.**

PRICE ELASTICITY AND TOTAL REVENUE

The concept of price elasticity refutes the popular misconception that producers charge the "highest price possible." Were that true, Steve Jobs might have initially priced the iPhone at $8,996. Except in the very rare case of completely inelastic demand, this notion makes no sense. Indeed, higher prices not only reduce unit sales, but may actually reduce total sales revenue as well.

The **total revenue** of a seller is the amount of money received from product sales. It is determined by the quantity of the product sold and the price at which it is sold:

$$\text{Total revenue} = \text{Price} \times \text{Quantity sold}$$

In the movie theater example, if the price of popcorn is 40 cents per ounce and only 4 ounces are sold, total revenue equals $1.60 per show. This revenue is illustrated by the shaded rectangle in Figure 6.3. (The area of a rectangle is equal to its height [p] times its width [q].)

total revenue: The price of a product multiplied by the quantity sold in a given time period: $p \times q$.

FIGURE 6.3

Elasticity and Total Revenue

Total revenue is equal to the price of the product times the quantity sold. It is illustrated by the area of the rectangle formed by $p \times q$.

The shaded rectangle illustrates total revenue ($1.60) at a price of 40 cents and a quantity demanded of 4 ounces. When price is increased to 45 cents (point B), the rectangle and total revenue shrink (see the dashed lines) because demand is relatively elastic in that price range. Price hikes increase total revenue only if demand is inelastic.

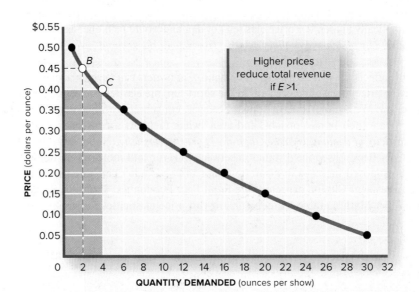

	Price	×	Quantity Demanded	=	Total Revenue
A	50¢		1		$0.50
B	45		2		0.90
C	40		4		1.60
D	35		6		2.10
E	30		8		2.40
F	25		12		3.00
G	20		16		3.20
H	15		20		3.00
I	10		25		2.50
J	5		30		1.50

If Demand Is	Effect on Total Revenue of	
	Price Increase	Price Reduction
Elastic (E > 1)	Decrease	Increase
Inelastic (E < 1)	Increase	Decrease
Unitary elastic (E = 1)	No change	No change

TABLE 6.3

Price Elasticity of Demand and Total Revenue

The impact of higher prices on total revenue depends on the price elasticity of demand. Higher prices result in higher total revenue only if demand is inelastic. If demand is elastic, *lower* prices result in *higher* revenues.

Now consider what happens to total revenue when the price of popcorn is increased. From the law of demand, we know that an increase in price will lead to a decrease in quantity demanded. But what about total revenue? The change in total revenue depends on *how much* quantity demanded falls when price goes up.

Suppose we raise popcorn prices again, from 40 cents back to 45 cents. What happens to total revenue? At 40 cents per box, 4 ounces are sold (see Figure 6.3) and total revenue equals $1.60. If we increase the price to 45 cents, only 2 ounces are sold and total revenue drops to 90 cents. In this case, an *increase* in price leads to a *decrease* in total revenue. This new and smaller total revenue is illustrated by the dashed rectangle in Figure 6.3.

Price increases don't always lower total revenue. If consumer demand was relatively *inelastic* (E < 1), a price increase would lead to *higher* total revenue. Thus, we conclude that

- *A price hike increases total revenue only if demand is inelastic (E < 1).*
- *A price hike reduces total revenue if demand is elastic (E > 1).*
- *A price hike does not change total revenue if demand is unitary elastic (E = 1).*

Table 6.3 summarizes these and other responses to price changes.

Changing Value of E. Once we know the price elasticity of demand, we can predict how consumers will respond to changing prices. We can also predict what will happen to the total revenue of the seller when the price is raised or reduced. Figure 6.4 shows how elasticity and total revenue change along a given demand curve. Demand for cigarettes is *elastic* (E > 1) at prices above $6 per pack but *inelastic* (E < 1) at lower prices.

The bottom half of Figure 6.4 shows how total revenue changes along the demand curve. At very high prices (e.g., $14 a pack), few cigarettes are sold and total revenue is low. As the price is reduced, however, the quantity demanded increases so much that total revenue *increases* despite the lower price. With each price reduction from $14 down to $6, total revenue increases.

Price cuts below $6 a pack continue to increase the quantity demanded (the law of demand). The increase in unit sales is no longer large enough, however, to offset the price reductions. Total revenue starts falling after the price drops below $6 per pack. The lesson to remember here is that *the impact of a price change on total revenue depends on the (changing) price elasticity of demand.*

Netflix Revenues. These elasticity principles fully explain why Netflix raised subscription prices in May 2019. At the time, Netflix had 58 million subscribers. When Netflix raised the monthly price from $10.99 to $12.99, it was sure to lose some customers. But what would happen to total revenue? It depended on the percent of subscribers lost relative to the percent increase in price. As it turned out, only 126,000 subscribers quit. That was a change in quantity demanded of only 0.2 percent. So, the percent change in quantity demanded was much smaller than the percentage change in price (16.7 percent). That is to say, the price elasticity of demand (.011) was *way* below 1.0. So, what happened to Netflix's total revenue? Revenue *increased* by nearly $1 billion a year!

FIGURE 6.4

Price Elasticity Changes along a Demand Curve

The concept of price elasticity can be used to determine whether people will spend more money on cigarettes when their price rises. The answer to this question is yes and no, depending on how high the price goes.

Notice in the table and the graphs that total revenue rises when the price of cigarettes increases from $2 to $4 a pack and again to $6. At low prices, the demand for cigarettes appears relatively inelastic: Price and total revenue move in the same direction.

As the price of cigarettes continues to increase, however, total revenue starts to fall. As the price is increased from $6 to $8 a pack, total revenue drops. At higher prices, the demand for cigarettes is relatively elastic: Price and total revenue move in *opposite directions*. Hence, the price elasticity of demand depends on where one is on the demand curve.

(a) The demand curve

(b) Total revenue

Price of Cigarettes	×	Quantity Demanded	=	Total Revenue	
$ 2		100		$200 ⎫	Low elasticity; E < 1
4		90		360 ⎬	(total revenue rises
6		70		420 ⎭	when price increases)
8		50		400 ⎫	High elasticity; E > 1
10		25		250 ⎬	(total revenue falls
12		10		120 ⎪	when price increases)
14		6		84 ⎭	

CROSS-PRICE ELASTICITY

The price elasticity of demand tells us how consumers will respond to a change in the price of a good under the assumption of *ceteris paribus*. But other factors do change, and consumption behavior may respond to those changes as well.

Shifts vs. Movements

We recognized this problem in Chapter 3 when we first distinguished *movements* along a demand curve from *shifts* of the demand curve. A movement along an unchanged demand curve represents consumer response to a change in the *price* of that specific good. The magnitude of that movement is expressed in the price elasticity of demand.

When the underlying determinants of demand change, the entire demand curve shifts. These shifts also alter consumer behavior. The *price* elasticity of demand is of no use in gauging these behavioral responses because it refers to price changes (movements along a constant demand curve) for that good only. Now we have to ask how consumers will respond when an underlying determinant of demand (tastes, income, other goods, or expectations) changes and the demand curve shifts.

A Change in Price of "Other Goods"

Let's sneak back into the movie theater for a moment and reconsider why we buy popcorn. Popcorn isn't the only treat at the concession stand; you can also purchase candy, soda, ice cream, and more. Thus, the decision to buy popcorn depends not only on *its* price but also on the price and availability of other goods.

Suppose for the moment that the prices of these other goods were to fall. Imagine that candy bars were put on sale for a quarter, rather than the usual dollar. Would this price reduction for candy affect the consumption of popcorn?

According to Figure 6.5, the demand for popcorn might *decrease* if the price of candy fell. The leftward shift of the demand curve from D_1 to D_2 tells us that consumers now demand less popcorn at every price. At 25 cents per ounce, consumers now demand only 8 ounces of popcorn (point R) rather than the previous 12 ounces (point F). In other words, a decline in the price of *candy* has caused a reduction in the demand for *popcorn*. We conclude that candy and popcorn are **substitute goods**—when the price of one declines, demand for the other falls.

Netflix vs. Disney+. The concept of cross-price elasticity raised concerns about Netflix subscriptions when Disney+ was launched in November 2019. Disney not only has a trove of popular movies in its archives but also chose to price its streaming subscriptions at a low $6.99 a month. Disney+ signed up 10 million subscribers in its first two days and projected that it would have close to 20 million subscribers by 2021. How would this affect the demand for Netflix? The availability of a new substitute good would undoubtedly restrain demand for Netflix. The effect would be a leftward shift of the Netflix demand curve, like the shift from D_1 to D_2 in Figure 6.5. But the shift turned out to be modest. The cross-price elasticity of demand was quite low.

Do soda prices affect popcorn sales?

Randy Faris/Getty Images

substitute goods: Goods that substitute for each other; when the price of good *x* rises, the demand for good *y* increases, *ceteris paribus.*

FIGURE 6.5

Substitutes and Complements

The curve D_1 represents the initial demand for popcorn, given the prices of other goods. Other prices may change, however. If a reduction in the price of another good (candy) causes a *reduction* in the demand for this good (popcorn), the two goods are *substitutes.* Popcorn demand shifts to the left (to D_2) when the price of a *substitute good* falls.

If a reduction in the price of another good (e.g., Pepsi) leads to an *increase* in the demand for this good (popcorn), the two goods are *complements.* Popcorn demand shifts to the right (to D_3) when the price of a *complementary good* falls.

complementary goods: Goods frequently consumed in combination; when the price of good *x* rises, the demand for good *y* falls, *ceteris paribus.*

How is SUV demand affected by gas prices?

Thinkstock Images/Getty Images

cross-price elasticity of demand: Percentage change in the quantity demanded of *X* divided by the percentage change in the price of *Y*.

Popcorn sales would follow a very different path if the price of soda fell. People like to wash down their popcorn with soda. When soda prices fall, moviegoers actually buy *more* popcorn. Here again, *a change in the price of one good affects the demand for another good.* In this case, however, we're dealing with **complementary goods** because a decline in the price of one good causes an *increase* in the demand for the other good.

The distinction between substitute goods and complementary goods is illustrated in Figure 6.5. Note that *in the case of substitute goods, the price of one good and the demand for the other move in the same direction.* (A *decrease* in candy prices causes a *decrease* in popcorn demand.) A price reduction by Disney+ will *increase* the demand for Verizon and other wireless services; streaming and wireless services are *complementary* goods. A Disney+ price cut would *reduce* the demand for Netflix; Disney+ and Netflix are *substitute* goods.

In the case of complementary goods (e.g., Pepsi and popcorn, cream and coffee), the price of one good and the demand for the other move in opposite directions. This helps explain why U.S. consumers bought more cars in 2019 when gasoline prices were falling and fewer SUVs in 2011 when gasoline prices were rising. The concept of complementary goods also explains why the demand for online apps increases when the price of smartphones drops.

Calculating Cross-Price Elasticity. The mathematical relationship between the price of one good and demand for another is summarized in yet another elasticity concept. The **cross-price elasticity of demand** is the *percentage* change in the quantity demanded of one good divided by the *percentage* change in the price of *another* good:

$$\text{Cross-price elasticity of demand} = \frac{\begin{array}{c}\text{\% change in quantity}\\ \text{demanded of good } X\\ \text{(at given price)}\end{array}}{\begin{array}{c}\text{\% change in price}\\ \text{of good } Y\end{array}}$$

What has changed here is the denominator. Now the denominator refers to a change in the price of *another* good rather than the *same* good.

Consider what happened to sales of the Samsung Galaxy when Apple cut the price of its 16 GB iPhone 5 back in 2014. The 16 GB iPhone 5s dropped in price from $199 to $99. We compute the *percentage* decline as

$$\frac{\text{\% change}}{\text{in iPhone price}} = \frac{\text{Change in price}}{\text{Average price}} = \frac{\$199 - \$99}{\$149} = -0.67$$

Galaxy sales *declined* by 20 percent. Hence, the cross-price elasticity of demand was

$$E_x = \frac{-0.20}{-0.67} = +0.30$$

Demand for Galaxys declined by 0.30 percent for every 1 percent decline in the iPhone price. A 67 percent iPhone price cut therefore caused a 20 percent decline in Galaxy demand.

Notice that the cross-price elasticity computed here is a *positive* number (+0.30). We saw earlier that the simple (same-product) price elasticity of demand is always a negative number, so we could ignore its sign. That's not the case with cross-price elasticities. In fact, the sign of the cross-price elasticity of demand is important.

If the cross-price elasticity is positive, the two goods are substitutes; if the cross-price elasticity is negative, the two goods are complements. Pepsi and popcorn are complements because a fall (−) in the price of one leads to an increase (+) in the demand for the other; in other words, the cross-price elasticity is negative.

INCOME ELASTICITY

Changes in the price of other goods aren't the only source of demand shifts. Each of the four determinants of demand is a potential shift factor. Suppose consumer incomes were to increase. How would popcorn consumption be affected? Figure 6.6 provides an answer. Before the change in income, consumers demanded 12 ounces of popcorn at a price of 25 cents

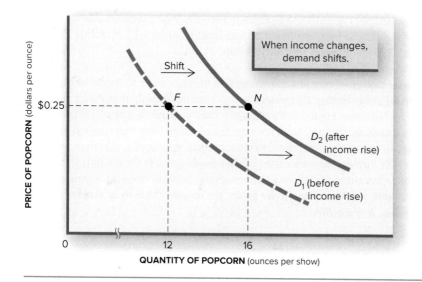

FIGURE 6.6

Income Elasticity

If income changes, the demand curve *shifts*. In this case, an increase in income enables consumers to buy more popcorn at every price. At a price of 25 cents, the quantity demanded increases from 12 ounces (point *F*) to 16 ounces (point *N*). The *income elasticity of demand* measures this response of demand to a change in income.

per ounce. With more income to spend, the new demand curve (D_2) suggests that consumers will now purchase a greater quantity of popcorn at every price. The increase in income has caused a rightward shift in demand. If popcorn continues to sell for 25 cents per ounce, consumers will now buy 16 ounces per show (point *N*) rather than only 12 ounces (point *F*).

It appears that changes in income have a substantial impact on consumer demand for popcorn. The graph in Figure 6.6 doesn't tell us, however, how large the change in income was. Will a *small* increase in income cause such a shift, or does popcorn demand increase only when moviegoers have a *lot* more money to spend?

Figure 6.6 doesn't answer these questions. But a little math will. Specifically, the **income elasticity of demand** relates the *percentage* change in quantity demanded to the *percentage* change in income:

$$\text{Income elasticity of demand} = \frac{\substack{\% \text{ change in} \\ \text{quantity demanded} \\ \text{(at given price)}}}{\substack{\% \text{ change in} \\ \text{income}}}$$

income elasticity of demand: Percentage change in quantity demanded divided by percentage change in income.

The similarity to the price elasticity of demand is apparent. In this case, however, the denominator is *income* (a determinant of demand), not *price*.

Computing Income Elasticity. As was the case with price elasticity, we compute income elasticity with *average* values for the changes in quantity and income. Suppose that the shift in popcorn demand illustrated in Figure 6.6 occurred when income increased from $110 per week to $120 per week. We would then compute

$$\text{Income elasticity} = \frac{\dfrac{\text{Change in quantity demanded}}{\text{Average quantity}}}{\dfrac{\text{Change in income}}{\text{Average income}}}$$

$$= \frac{\dfrac{16 \text{ ounces} - 12 \text{ ounces}}{14 \text{ ounces}}}{\dfrac{\$120 - \$110}{\$115}}$$

$$= \frac{4}{14} \div \frac{10}{115}$$

$$= \frac{0.286}{0.087} = 3.29$$

Popcorn purchases are very sensitive to changes in income. When incomes rise by 8.7 percent, popcorn sales increase by a whopping 28.6 percent (that is, 8.7% × 3.29). The computed elasticity of 3.29 summarizes this relationship.

Normal vs. Inferior Goods. Demand and income don't always move in the same direction. Popcorn is a **normal good** because consumers buy more of it when their incomes rise. People actually buy *less* of some goods, however, when they have more income. With low incomes, people buy discount clothes, used textbooks, and cheap beer, and they eat at home. With more money to spend, they switch to designer clothes, new books, premium beer, and restaurant meals. The former items are called **inferior goods** because the quantity demanded *falls* when income *rises.* Similarly, when incomes *decline,* people demand *more* spaghetti, pawnbrokers, and lottery tickets. *For inferior goods, the income elasticity of demand is negative; for normal goods, it is positive.*

> **normal good:** Good for which demand increases when income rises.

> **inferior good:** Goods for which demand decreases when income rises.

ELASTICITY OF SUPPLY

Sensitivity to changing prices is not just a consumer phenomenon. Producers, too, alter their behavior when prices change. We know from the **law of supply** (Chapter 3) that businesses will produce more output at higher prices. What we want to know is how much more they'll produce as prices go up. That is what the **price elasticity of supply** tells us. Like its counterpart on the demand side, the price elasticity of supply relates *percentage* changes in the quantity supplied to *percentage* changes in price:

> **law of supply:** The quantity of a good supplied in a given time period increases as its price increases, *ceteris paribus.*

> **price elasticity of supply:** The percentage change in quantity supplied divided by the percentage change in price.

$$\text{Price elasticity of supply} = \frac{\text{Percentage change in quantity supplied}}{\text{Percentage change in price}}$$

A high price elasticity of supply means that producers are very responsive to price changes; a low elasticity implies a sluggish response. As World View "Rebounding Oil Price Spurs More Rigs" reports, U.S. oil *production* responds to changes in oil *prices.*

WORLD VIEW

REBOUNDING OIL PRICE SPURS MORE RIGS

The recent spike in the price of oil has brought more rigs on line. According to the weekly Baker Hughes count, the number of active oil rigs has jumped 60 percent since last year. When oil prices were falling, the number of active U.S. rigs fell from 2,000 in 2015 to only 480 in 2016. The latest survey, for the week of March 10, 2017, put the number at 762. Higher-cost shale producers in the Permian basin are quick to respond to higher oil prices, acting as the marginal producer. Overall, economists estimate the elasticity of oil supply at around 0.1.

Source: Media reports of March 2017.

U.S. Coast Guard photo by Petty Officer 3rd Class Patrick Kelley

CRITICAL ANALYSIS: Higher oil prices spur additional drilling and production; the **price elasticity of supply** is significantly greater than zero.

DECISIONS FOR **TOMORROW**

Will EVs Replace Gas Guzzlers?

Electric cars have been a hit. Sales of battery-only (BEV) and plug-in hybrid (PHEV) electric cars have risen every year. Sales in the United States hit a record of 360,000 units in 2019. Some analysts predict that EV sales will surpass 500,000 a year by 2023. One EV producer, Tesla, built a lithium battery factory in Nevada that can produce 500,000 batteries a year.

One of the attractions of EVs is their environmental impact. The BEVs burn no gasoline and the PHEVs burn very little. They get mileage in the range of 100–120 miles per gallon, three or four times the mileage of gasoline-powered cars. Even when the pollution associated with electricity generation is factored in, EVs do less harm to the environment than do gasoline-powered autos. In view of this positive externality, both the federal government and several states offer substantial subsidies (tax credits and purchase rebates) for EV buyers.

For all their success, however, EVs are still a tiny fraction of new car sales. The record 360,000 EVs sold in 2019 pales in comparison to the 17.5 *million* gas guzzlers sold in the United States that year. EVs got only 1.5 percent of the market that year, and even the most optimistic forecasts of future sales envision a market share of 2.4 percent by 2025. So, EVs aren't about to overtake the gas guzzlers (a substitute good) anytime soon.

A couple of factors will materially affect future EV sales. The first, of course, is the price of the EVs themselves. Producers are hoping that advances in battery technology will bring down the cost of batteries, the most expensive ingredient in EVs. Lower battery prices (a complimentary good) will in turn lead to lower EV prices (and more sales via the price elasticity of demand).

EV producers also have to hope that the price of gasoline (another substitute good) keeps going up. The experience of the last decade shows that high gasoline prices sway consumers' decision to buy an EV. By contrast, when gasoline prices are low, consumers ignore EVs and opt to buy SUVs and bigger cars.

EV producers also have to worry about alternative technologies. Cars powered by natural gas or fuel cells may prove to be cheaper and more efficient. Then there is the prospect of more autonomous vehicles. Autonomous vehicles must be larger than EVs in order to store all the cameras, computers, and other technology embedded in self-driving cars. As these substitute goods become more popular—especially in ride-sharing services like Lyft and Uber—the demand for EVs may wane.

Last but not least, EV producers have to worry about those government subsidies. If the federal government or individual states terminate the tax credits and purchase rebates EV buyers now enjoy, the effective price of an EV will increase by a couple of thousand dollars. Will consumers pay higher prices to drive EVs?

SUMMARY

- The price elasticity of demand (*E*) is a numerical measure of consumer response to a change in price, *ceteris paribus.* It equals the percentage change in quantity demanded divided by the percentage change in price. **LO6-1**
- Demand for a product is *elastic* if *E* is greater than 1.0 or *inelastic* if *E* is less than 1.0. **LO6-1**
- The degree of price elasticity depends on the price of a good relative to income, the availability of substitutes, and time. **LO6-1**

- The effect of a price change on total revenue depends on price elasticity. Total revenue and price move in the *same* direction only if demand is price-inelastic ($E < 1$). **LO6-2**
- The shape and position of any particular demand curve depend on a consumer's income, tastes, expectations, and the price and availability of other goods. Should any of these factors change, the assumption of *ceteris paribus* will no longer hold, and the demand curve will *shift.* **LO6-3, LO6-4**

- Cross-price elasticity measures the response of demand for one good to a change in the price of another. The cross-price elasticity of demand is positive for substitute goods and negative for complementary goods.   **LO6-3**
- The income elasticity of demand measures the response of demand to a change in income. If demand increases (shifts right) with income, the product is a normal good. If demand declines (shifts left) when income rises, it's an inferior good.   **LO6-4**
- The price elasticity of supply is the percentage change in quantity *supplied* divided by the percentage change in price.   **LO6-5**

Key Terms

law of demand
demand curve
price elasticity of demand
total revenue

substitute goods
complementary goods
cross-price elasticity of demand
income elasticity of demand

normal good
inferior good
law of supply
price elasticity of supply

Questions for Discussion

1. Is the demand for enrollments in your college price-elastic? How could you find out?   **LO6-1**
2. If the price of gasoline doubled, how would consumption of (*a*) cars, (*b*) public transportation, and (*c*) restaurants be affected? How quickly would these adjustments be made?   **LO6-3**
3. Identify two goods each whose demand exhibits (*a*) high income elasticity, (*b*) low income elasticity, (*c*) high price elasticity, and (*d*) low price elasticity. What accounts for the differences in elasticity?   **LO6-4**
4. Why does the price elasticity of demand for cigarettes differ for teenagers and adults (see Table 6.2)?   **LO6-1**
5. In California, 15.7 percent of low-income households smoke, but only 9.4 percent of high-income households do so. So, the burden of higher cigarette taxes (Front Page Economics "Californians Vote to Triple Cigarette Tax") falls disproportionately on the poor. Is this fair?   **LO6-2**
6. If you owned a movie theater, would you want the demand for movies to be elastic or inelastic?   **LO6-2**
7. Why are the price and cross-price elasticities for Netflix so small?   **LO6-2, LO6-3**
8. If the elasticity of demand for coffee is so low (Table 6.1), why doesn't Starbucks raise the price of coffee to $10 a cup?   **LO6-2**
9. Is the demand for iPhones price inelastic or elastic? Why? Is income elasticity high or low?   **LO6-4**
10. Why did Disney+ price itself so low at the outset? Will the price go up?   **LO6-2**
11. What do oil producers have to do in order to increase the supply of oil (*a*) in the short run and (*b*) in the long run? Will they?   **LO6-5**

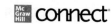
LO6-1   1. What was the quarterly price elasticity of demand for iPhones in 2007 (Front Page Economics "After iPhone Price Cut, Sales Are Up by 200 Percent" and section "Computing Price Elasticity")?

LO6-1   2. According to Professor Becker (Front Page Economics "Professor Becker Rejects Clinton's Tax Math"), by how much would cigarette prices have to rise to get a 20 percent reduction in smoking in
    (*a*) One year?
    (*b*) Three years?

LO6-1   3. What is the price elasticity of demand for cigarettes implied in Front Page Economics "Californians Vote to Triple Cigarette Tax" by
    (*a*) The state's legislative analyst office?
    (*b*) Anti-smoking advocates?
    If the actual price elasticity of demand for California-tax cigarettes is 0.8,
    (*c*) By how much will the quantity demanded decrease with the new tax?
    (*d*) How much additional revenue will the state take in?

LO6-1   4. Suppose consumers buy 40 million packs of cigarettes per month at a price of $5 per pack. If a $2 tax is added to that price,
    (*a*) By what percentage does price change? (Use the midpoint formula in "Computing Price Elasticity.")
    (*b*) By what percentage will cigarette sales decline in the short run? (See Table 6.1 for a clue.)
    (*c*) According to Gary Becker, by how much will sales decline in the long run? (See Front Page Economics "Professor Becker Rejects Clinton's Tax Math.")

LO6-2   5. From Figure 6.1, compute
    (*a*) The price elasticity between the points listed in the table.
    (*b*) The total revenue at each point listed in the table.

	Price Elasticity		Total Revenue
Point C to D	_____	At point C	_____
		D	_____
H to I	_____	H	_____
		I	_____

    (*c*) If there is a price decrease, will total revenue increase when demand is elastic or inelastic?

LO6-4   6. According to the calculation in the section "Income Elasticity," by how much will popcorn sales increase if average income goes up by 6 percent?

LO6-5   7. According to the World View "Rebounding Oil Price Spurs More Rigs," based on the estimated price elasticity of supply, calculate the change in the quantity of oil supplied if the price of oil increased by 20 percent.

LO6-3 8. If the cross-price elasticity of demand between printed textbooks and ebooks is +0.70,
    (*a*) Are ebooks and textbooks complementary or substitute goods?
    (*b*) If textbook prices increase by 10 percent, by how much will ebook demand change?

LO6-1 9. Suppose that in a week the price of Greek yogurt decreases from $1.75 to $1.25 per container. At the same time, the quantity of Greek yogurt demanded increases from 10,000 to 18,000 containers per week. What is the price elasticity of demand for Greek yogurt?

LO6-2 10. Use the following data to illustrate the demand curve and total revenue curve on the accompanying graphs:

Price	$10	9	8	7	6	5	4	3	2	1
Quantity	2	4	6	8	10	12	14	16	18	20

    (*a*) At what price is total revenue maximized?
    (*b*) At that price, what is the elasticity of demand?

(a) Demand curve

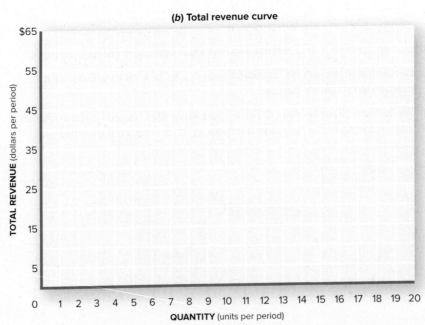

(b) Total revenue curve

PROBLEMS FOR CHAPTER 6 (cont'd)

LO6-3 11. Will demand for Netflix increase or decrease if
LO6-4

        (*a*) The price of Disney+ falls?

        (*b*) Cell phone providers offer lower-cost unlimited data plans?

        (*c*) The economy falls into a recession?

        (*d*) Cable TV becomes more expensive?

      12. ***Decisions for Tomorrow:*** In 2019, 360,000 electric vehicles (EVs) were sold in the United States.

LO6-1   (*a*) Suppose the average price of these cars was $40,000. Calculate price elasticity of demand if a $2,000 tax credit caused an increase in sales by 20,000 EVs.

LO6-3   (*b*) Calculate cross-price elasticity if a 20 percent increase in the price of gasoline caused an increase in sales of EVs by 30,000.

Design Credit: Shutterstock

Rob Crandall/SCPhotos/Alamy Stock Photo

LEARNING OBJECTIVES

After reading this chapter, you should know

LO7-1 What the production function represents.

LO7-2 What the law of diminishing returns means.

LO7-3 How the various measures of cost relate to each other.

LO7-4 How economic and accounting costs differ.

LO7-5 What (dis)economies of scale are.

CHAPTER 7

The Costs of Production

Last year U.S. consumers bought more than $2.5 *trillion* worth of imported goods, including Japanese cars, Italian shoes, and toys from China. As you might expect, this angers domestic producers, who frequently end up with unsold goods, half-empty factories, and unemployed workers. They, along with President Trump, rage against the "unfair" competition from abroad, asserting that producers in India, Brazil, and China can undersell U.S. producers because workers in these countries are paid dirt-poor wages.

But lower wages don't necessarily imply lower costs. You could pay me $2 per hour to type and still end up paying a lot for typing. Truth is, I type only about 10 words a minute, with lots of mistakes. The cost of producing goods depends not only on the price of inputs (e.g., labor) but also on how much they produce. Paying $10 an hour to someone who types 90 words a minute is a lot cheaper than paying $2 an hour to someone who types only 10 words a minute.

In this chapter we begin looking at the costs of producing the goods and services that market participants demand. We confront the following questions:

- **How much output *can* a firm produce?**
- **How do the *costs* of production vary with the rate of output?**
- **Do larger firms have a cost advantage over smaller firms?**

The answers to these questions are important not only to producers facing foreign competition but to consumers as well. The costs of producing a good have a direct impact on the prices we pay at the grocery store, the mall, or even the campus bookstore.

THE PRODUCTION FUNCTION

No matter how large a business is or who owns it, all businesses confront one central fact: It costs something to produce goods. To produce corn, a farmer needs land, water, seeds, equipment, and labor. To produce fillings, a dentist needs a chair, a drill, some space, and labor. Even the production of educational services such as this economics class requires the use of labor (your teacher), land (on which the school is built), and capital (the building, blackboard, computers). In short, unless you're producing unrefined, unpackaged air, you need **factors of production**—that is, resources that can be used to produce a good or service.

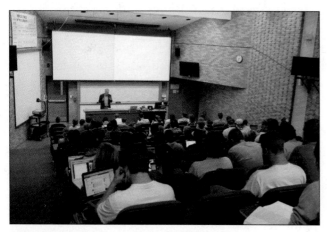

What are the costs to produce this class?

Aaron Roeth Photography

Factor Costs

These factors of production provide the basic measure of economic cost. The costs of your economics class, for example, are measured by the amounts of land, labor, and capital it requires. These are *resource* costs of production.

Best Practices

To assess the costs of production, we must first determine how many resources are actually needed to produce a given product. You could use a lot of resources to produce a product or use just a few. What we really want to know is how *best* to produce. What's the *smallest* amount of resources needed to produce a specific product? Or we could ask the same question from a different perspective: What's the *maximum* amount of output attainable from a given quantity of resources?

The answers to these questions are reflected in the **production function,** which tells us the maximum amount of good *X* producible from various combinations of factor inputs. With one chair and one drill, a dentist can fill a *maximum* of 32 cavities per day. With two chairs, a drill, and an assistant, a dentist can fill up to 55 cavities per day.

A production function is a technological summary of our ability to produce a particular good.[1] Table 7.1 provides a partial glimpse of one such function. In this case, the output is designer jeans, as produced by Low-Rider Jeans Corporation. The essential inputs in the production of jeans are land, labor (garment workers), and capital (a factory and sewing machines). With these inputs, Low-Rider Jeans Corporation can produce and sell hip-hugging jeans to style-conscious consumers.

Varying Input Levels

As in all production endeavors, we want to know how much output we can produce with available resources. To make things easy, we'll assume that the factory is already built, with fixed space dimensions. The only inputs we can vary are labor (the number of garment workers per day) and additional capital (the number of sewing machines we lease per day).

In these circumstances, the quantity of jeans we can produce depends on the amount of labor and capital we employ. ***The purpose of a production function is to tell us just how much***

factors of production: Resource inputs used to produce goods and services, e.g., land, labor, capital, entrepreneurship.

production function: A technological relationship expressing the maximum quantity of a good attainable from different combinations of factor inputs.

---

[1]By contrast, the production possibilities curve discussed in Chapter 1 expresses our ability to produce various *combinations* of goods, given the use of *all* our resources. The production possibilities curve summarizes the output capacity of the entire economy. A production function describes the capacity of a single firm.

Capital Input (Sewing Machines per Day)	Labor Input (Workers per Day)								
	0	1	2	3	4	5	6	7	8
	Jeans Output (Pairs per Day)								
0	0	0	0	0	0	0	0	0	0
1	0	15	34	44	48	50	51	51	47
2	0	20	46	64	72	78	81	82	80
3	0	21	50	73	83	92	99	103	103

productivity: Output per unit of input—for example, output per labor-hour.

output we can produce with varying amounts of factor inputs. Table 7.1 provides such information for jeans production.

Consider the simplest option—that of employing no labor or capital (the upper left corner in Table 7.1). An empty factory can't produce any jeans; maximum output is zero per day. Even though land, capital (an empty factory), and even denim are available, some essential labor and capital inputs are missing, and jeans production is impossible.

Suppose now that we employ some labor (a machine operator) but don't lease any sewing machines. Will output increase? Not according to the production function. The first row in Table 7.1 illustrates the consequences of employing labor without any capital equipment. Without sewing machines (or even needles, another form of capital), the operators can't make jeans. Maximum output remains at zero no matter how much labor is employed in this case.

The dilemma of machine operators without sewing machines illustrates a general principle of production: *The* **productivity** *of any factor of production depends on the amount of other resources available to it.* Industrious, hardworking machine operators can't make designer jeans without sewing machines.

We can increase the productivity of garment workers by providing them with machines. The production function again tells us by *how much* jeans output could increase. Suppose that we leased just one machine per day. Now the second row in Table 7.1 is the relevant one. It says jeans output will remain at zero if we lease one machine but employ no labor. If we employ one machine *and* one worker, however, the jeans will start rolling out the door. Maximum output under these circumstances (row 2, column 2) is 15 pairs of jeans per day. Now we're in business!

The remaining columns in row 2 tell us how many additional jeans we can produce if we hire more workers, still leasing only one sewing machine. With one machine and two workers, maximum output rises to 34 pairs per day. If a third worker is hired, output could increase to 44 pairs.

Table 7.1 also indicates how production would increase with additional sewing machines (capital). By reading down any column of the table, you can see how more machines increase potential jeans output.

Efficiency

The production function summarized in Table 7.1 underscores the essential relationship between resource *inputs* and product *outputs*. It's also a basic introduction to economic costs. To produce 15 pairs of jeans per day, we need one sewing machine, an operator, a factory, and some denim. All these inputs make up the *resource cost* of producing jeans.

Another feature of Table 7.1 is that it conveys the *maximum* output of jeans producible from particular input combinations. The standard garment worker and sewing machine, when brought together at Low-Rider Jeans Corporation, can produce *at most* 15 pairs of jeans per day. They could also produce a lot less. Indeed, a careless cutter can waste a lot of denim. A lazy or inattentive worker won't keep the sewing machines humming. As many a producer has learned, actual output can fall far short of the limits described in the production function. Jeans output will reach the levels in Table 7.1 only if the jeans factory operates with relative **efficiency**. This requires getting maximum output from the resources used in the production process. ***The production function represents maximum technical efficiency—that is, the most output attainable from any given level of factor inputs.***

We can always be inefficient, of course. This merely means getting less output than possible for the inputs we use. But this isn't a desirable situation. To a factory manager, it means less output for a given amount of input (cost). To society as a whole, inefficiency implies a waste of resources. If Low-Rider Jeans isn't producing efficiently, we're being denied some potential output. It's not only a question of having fewer jeans. We could also use the labor and capital now employed by Low-Rider Jeans to produce something else. Specifically, the **opportunity cost** of a product is measured by the most desired goods and services that could have been produced with the same resources. Hence, if jeans production isn't up to par, society is either (1) getting fewer jeans than it should for the resources devoted to jeans production or (2) giving up too many other goods and services in order to get a desired quantity of jeans. Neither outcome is desirable.

Although we can always do worse than the production function suggests, we can't do better, at least not in the short run. The production function represents the *best* we can do with our current technological know-how. For the moment, at least, there's no better way to produce a specific good. As our technological and managerial capabilities increase, however, we'll attain higher levels of future productivity. These advances in our productive capability will be represented by new production functions.

efficiency: Maximum output of a good from the resources used in production.

opportunity cost: The most desired goods or services that are forgone in order to obtain something else.

Short-Run Constraints

Let's step back from the threshold of scientific advance for a moment and return to Low-Rider Jeans. Forget about possible technological breakthroughs in jeans production (e.g., electronic sewing machines or robot operators) and concentrate on the economic realities of our modest endeavor. For the present we're stuck with existing technology. In fact, all the output figures in Table 7.1 are based on the use of a specific factory. Once we've purchased or leased that factory, we've set a limit to current jeans production. When such commitments to fixed inputs (e.g., the factory) exist, we're dealing with a **short-run** production problem. If no land or capital were in place—if we could build or lease any sized factory—we'd be dealing with a *long-run* decision.

short run: The period in which the quantity (and quality) of some inputs can't be changed.

Our short-run objective is to make the best possible use of the factory we've acquired. This entails selecting the right combination of labor and capital inputs to produce jeans. To simplify the decision, we'll limit the number of sewing machines in use. If we lease only one sewing machine, then the second row in Table 7.1 is the only one we have to consider. In this case, the single sewing machine (capital) becomes another short-run constraint on the production of jeans. With a given factory and one sewing machine, the short-run rate of output depends entirely on how many workers are hired.

Figure 7.1 illustrates the short-run production function applicable to the factory with one sewing machine. As noted before, a factory with a sewing machine but no machine operators produces no jeans. This was observed in Table 7.1 (row 1, column 0) and is now illustrated by point *A* in Figure 7.1. To get any jeans output, we need to hire some labor. In this simplified example, ***labor is the variable input that determines how much output we get from our fixed inputs (land and capital).*** By placing one worker in the factory, we can produce 15 pairs of jeans per day. This possibility is represented by point *B*. The remainder of the production function shows how many more jeans we get when we employ more workers in our single-machine factory.

FIGURE 7.1

Short-Run Production Function

In the short run, some inputs (e.g., land and capital) are fixed in quantity. Output then depends on how much of a variable input (e.g., labor) is used.

The short-run production function shows how output changes when more labor is used. This figure and the table below are based on the second (one-machine) row in Table 7.1.

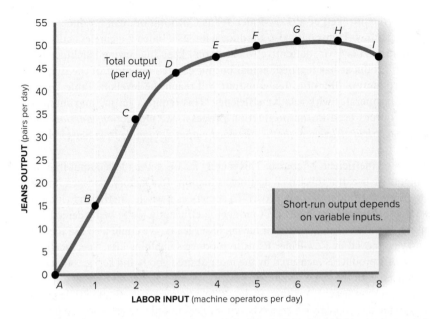

	A	B	C	D	E	F	G	H	I
Number of workers	0	1	2	3	4	5	6	7	8
Total output	0	15	34	44	48	50	51	51	47
Marginal physical product	—	15	19	10	4	2	1	0	−4

MARGINAL PRODUCTIVITY

The short-run production function not only defines the *limit* to output but also shows how much each worker contributes to that limit. Notice again that jeans output increases from zero (point *A* in Figure 7.2) to 15 pairs (point *B*) when the first machine operator is hired. In other words, total output *increases* by 15 pairs when we employ the first worker. This increase is called the **marginal physical product (MPP)** of that first worker—that is, the *change* in total output that results from employment of one more unit of (labor) input:

marginal physical product (MPP): The change in total output associated with one additional unit of input.

$$\text{Marginal physical product (MPP)} = \frac{\text{Change in total output}}{\text{Change in input quantity}}$$

With zero workers, total output was zero. When that first worker is employed, total output increases to 15 pairs of jeans per day. The MPP of the first worker is 15 pairs of jeans.

If we employ a second operator, jeans output more than doubles, to 34 pairs per day (point *C*). The 19-pair *increase* in output represents the marginal physical product of the *second* worker.

The higher MPP of the second worker raises a question about the first. Why was the first's MPP lower? Laziness? Is the second worker faster, less distracted, or harder working?

The second worker's higher MPP isn't explained by superior talents or effort. We assume, in fact, that all "units of labor" are equal—that is, one worker is just as good as another.[2] Their different marginal products are explained by the structure of the production process, not by their respective abilities. The first garment worker not only had to sew jeans but also had to unfold bolts of denim, measure the jeans, sketch out the patterns, and cut them to

[2]In reality, garment workers do differ greatly in energy, talent, and diligence. These differences can be eliminated by measuring units of labor in *constant-quality* units. A person who works twice as hard as everyone else would count as two *quality-adjusted* units of labor.

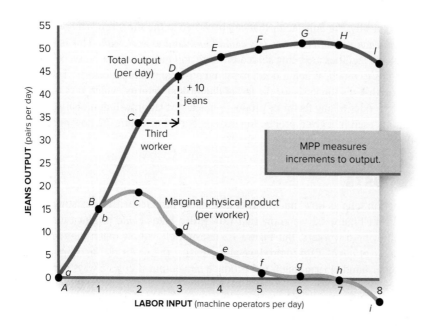

FIGURE 7.2

Marginal Physical Product (MPP)

Marginal physical product is the *change* in total output that results from employing one more unit of input. The *third* worker, for example, increases *total output* from 34 (point *C*) to 44 (point *D*). Hence, the *marginal* output of the third worker is 10 pairs of jeans (point *d*).

What's the MPP of the fourth worker? What happens to *total* output when this worker is hired?

approximate size. A lot of time was spent going from one task to another. Despite the worker's best efforts, this person simply couldn't do everything at once.

A second worker alleviates this situation. With two workers, less time is spent running from one task to another. While one worker is measuring and cutting, the other can continue sewing. This improved *ratio* of labor to other factors of production results in the large jump in total output. The second worker's superior MPP isn't unique to this person: It would have occurred even if we'd hired the workers in the reverse order.

Diminishing Marginal Returns

Unfortunately, total output won't keep rising so sharply as more workers are hired. Look what happens when a third worker is hired. Total jeans production continues to increase. But the increase from point *C* to point *D* in Figure 7.2 is only 10 pairs per day. Hence, the third worker's MPP (10 pairs) is *less* than that of the second (19 pairs). Marginal physical product is *diminishing*. This concept is illustrated by point *d* in Figure 7.2.

What accounts for this decline in MPP? The answer lies in the ratio of labor to other factors of production. A third worker begins to crowd our facilities. We still have only one sewing machine. Two people can't sew at the same time. As a result, some time is wasted as the operators wait for their turns at the machine. Even if they split up the various jobs, there will still be some "downtime" because measuring and cutting aren't as time-consuming as sewing. Consequently, we can't make full use of a third worker. The relative scarcity of other inputs (capital and land) constrains the third worker's marginal physical product.

Resource constraints are even more evident when a fourth worker is hired. Total output increases again, but the increase this time is very small. With three workers, we got 44 pairs of jeans per day (point *D*); with four workers, we get a maximum of 48 pairs (point *E*). Thus, the fourth worker's MPP is only 4 pairs of jeans. There simply aren't enough machines to make productive use of so much labor.

If a seventh worker is hired, the operators get in one another's way, argue, and waste denim. Notice in Figure 7.1 that total output doesn't increase at all when a seventh worker is hired (point *H*). The MPP of the seventh worker is zero (point *h*). Were an eighth worker hired, total output would actually *decline,* from 51 pairs (point *H*) to 47 pairs (point *I*). The eighth worker has a *negative* MPP (point *i* in Figure 7.2).

Law of Diminishing Returns. The problems of crowded facilities apply to most production processes. In the short run, a production process is characterized by a fixed amount of available

law of diminishing returns: The marginal physical product of a variable input declines as more of it is employed with a given quantity of other (fixed) inputs.

land and capital. Typically, the only factor that can be varied in the short run is labor. Yet *as more labor is hired, each unit of labor has less capital and land to work with.* This is simple division: The available facilities are being shared by more and more workers. At some point, this constraint begins to pinch. When it does, marginal physical product declines. This situation is so common that it's the basis for the **law of diminishing returns,** which says that the marginal physical product of any factor of production, such as labor, will diminish at some point as more of it is used in a given production setting. Notice in Figure 7.2 how diminishing returns set in when the third worker was hired.

RESOURCE COSTS

A production function tells us how much output a firm *can* produce with its existing plant and equipment. From Figure 7.2 we know that Low-Rider Jeans *could* produce up to 51 pairs per day, employing 6 workers. But Figure 7.2 doesn't tell us how much the firm will *want* to produce. A firm *might* want to produce at capacity if the profit picture were bright enough. On the other hand, a firm might not produce *any* output if costs always exceeded sales revenue. The most desirable rate of output is the one that maximizes total **profit**—the difference between total revenue and total costs. And *there is no reason to expect maximum profit to coincide with maximum output.*

profit: The difference between total revenue and total cost.

The production function therefore is just a starting point for supply decisions. To decide how much output to produce with that function, a firm must next examine the costs of production. How fast do costs rise when output increases?

The law of diminishing returns provides a clue to how fast costs rise. *The economic cost of a product is measured by the value of the resources needed to produce it.* What we've seen here is that those resource requirements eventually increase. Each additional sewing machine operator produces fewer and fewer jeans. In effect, then, each additional pair of jeans produced uses more and more labor.

Unit Labor Costs

Suppose we employ one sewing machine and one operator again, for a total output of 15 pairs of jeans per day; see point *b* in Figure 7.3a. Now look at production from another perspective—that of *costs*. The resource costs of producing jeans are measured by how much labor is used in the production process.

How much labor cost are we using at point *b* to produce one pair of jeans? We know that one worker is producing 15 pairs of jeans, so the labor input per pair of jeans must be one-fifteenth of a worker's day—that is, 0.067 unit of labor. This resource cost is illustrated by point 1/*b* in Figure 7.3b. All we're doing here is translating *output* data into related *input* (cost) data.

Marginal Resource Cost

The next question is, How do unit labor costs change when output increases? As point *c* in Figure 7.3a reminds us, total output increases by 19 pairs when we hire a second worker. What's the implied labor cost of those *additional* 19 pairs? By dividing one worker by 19 pairs of jeans, we observe that the labor cost of that extra output is one-nineteenth, or 0.053 of a worker's day; see point 1/*c* in Figure 7.3b.

When we focus on the *additional* costs incurred from increasing production, we're talking about *marginal* costs. Specifically, marginal cost (MC) refers to the *increase* in total costs required to get one additional unit of output. More generally,

$$\text{Marginal cost (MC)} = \frac{\text{Change in total cost}}{\text{Change in output}}$$

In this simple case—where labor is the only variable input—the marginal cost of the added jeans is

$$\text{Marginal cost of jeans} = \frac{1 \text{ additional worker}}{19 \text{ additional pairs}}$$
$$= 0.053 \text{ worker per pair}$$

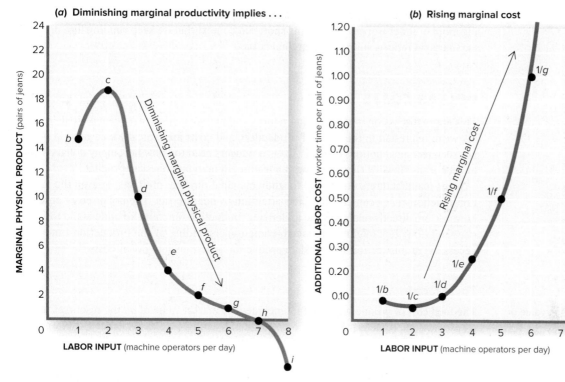

FIGURE 7.3

Falling MPP Implies Rising Marginal Cost

Marginal physical product (MPP) is the additional output obtained by employing one more unit of input. If MPP is falling, each additional unit of input is producing less additional output, which means the input cost of each unit of output is rising. The third worker's MPP is 10 pairs (point *d* in part *a*). Therefore, the labor cost of these additional jeans is approximately 1/10 unit of labor per pair (point 1/*d* in part *b*).

The amount 0.053 of labor represents the *change* in total resource cost when we produce one *additional* pair of jeans.

Notice in Figure 7.3*b* that the marginal labor cost of jeans production declines when the second worker is hired. Marginal cost falls from 0.067 unit of labor (plus denim) per pair (point 1/*b* in Figure 7.3*b*) to only 0.053 unit of labor per pair (point 1/*c*). It costs less labor *per pair* to use two workers rather than only one. This is a reflection of the second worker's increased MPP. ***Whenever MPP is increasing, the marginal cost of producing a good must be falling.*** This is illustrated in Figure 7.3 by the upward move from *b* to *c* in part *a* and the corresponding downward move from 1/*b* to 1/*c* in part *b*.

Unfortunately, marginal physical product typically declines at some point. As it does, the marginal costs of production rise. In this sense, each additional pair of jeans becomes more expensive—we need more and more labor per pair.

Figure 7.3 illustrates this inverse relationship between MPP and marginal cost. The third worker has an MPP of 10 pairs, as illustrated by point *d*. The marginal labor input of these extra 10 pairs is thus 1 ÷ 10, or 0.10 unit of labor. In other words, one-tenth of a third worker's daily effort goes into each pair of jeans. This additional labor cost *per unit* is illustrated by 1/*d* in part *b* of the figure.

Note in Figure 7.3 how marginal physical product declines after point *c* and how marginal costs rise after point 1/*c*. This is no accident. ***If marginal physical product declines, marginal cost increases.*** Thus, increasing marginal cost is as common as—and the direct result of—diminishing returns. These increasing marginal costs aren't the fault of any person or factor; they simply reflect the resource constraints found in any established production setting (i.e., existing and limited plants and equipment). In the short run, the quantity and

If MPP is falling, MC must be rising. MPP and MC move in opposite directions.

quality of land and capital are fixed, and we can vary only their intensity of use by employing more or fewer workers. It's in this short-run context that we keep running into diminishing marginal returns and rising marginal costs.

DOLLAR COSTS

This entire discussion of diminishing returns and marginal costs may seem a bit alien. After all, we're interested in the costs of production, and costs are typically measured in *dollars,* not such technical notions as MPP. Jeans producers need to know how many dollars it costs to keep jeans flowing; they don't want a lecture on marginal physical product.

Jeans manufacturers don't have to study marginal physical products, or even the production function. They can confine their attention to dollar costs. The dollar costs observed, however, are directly related to the underlying production function. To understand *why* costs rise—and how they might be reduced—some understanding of the production function is necessary. In this section we translate production functions into dollar costs.

Total Cost

> **total cost:** The market value of all resources used to produce a good or service.

The **total cost** of producing a product includes the market value of *all* the resources used in its production. To determine this cost, we simply identify all the resources used in production, determine their value, and then add up everything.

In the production of jeans, these resources included land, labor, and capital. Table 7.2 identifies these resources, their unit values, and the total dollar cost associated with their use. This table is based on an assumed output of 15 pairs of jeans per day, with the use of one worker and one sewing machine (point *B* in Figure 7.2). The rent on the factory is $100 per day, a sewing machine rents for $20 per day, and the wages of a garment worker are $80 per day. We'll assume Low-Rider Jeans Corporation can purchase bolts of denim for $30 apiece, with each bolt providing enough denim for 10 pairs of jeans. In other words, one-tenth of a bolt ($3 worth of material) is required for one pair of jeans. We'll ignore any other potential expenses. With these assumptions, the total cost of producing 15 pairs of jeans per day amounts to $245, as shown in Table 7.2.

Fixed Costs. Total costs will change, of course, as we alter the rate of production. But not *all* costs increase. In the short run, some costs don't increase at all when output is increased. These are **fixed costs** in the sense that they don't vary with the rate of output. The factory lease is an example. Once you lease a factory, you're obligated to pay for it whether or not you use it. The person who owns the factory wants $100 per day. Even if you produce no jeans, you still have to pay that rent. That's the essence of fixed costs.

> **fixed costs:** Costs of production that don't change when the rate of output is altered, such as the cost of basic plants and equipment.

The leased sewing machine is another fixed cost. When you rent a sewing machine, you must pay the rental charge. It doesn't matter whether you use it for a few minutes or all day long—the rental charge is fixed at $20 per day.

Variable Costs. Labor costs are another story altogether. The amount of labor employed in jeans production can be varied easily. If we decide not to open the factory tomorrow, we can

TABLE 7.2

The Total Costs of Production (Total Cost of Producing 15 Pairs of Jeans per Day)

The total cost of producing a good equals the market value of all the resources used in its production. In this case, the production of 15 pairs of jeans per day requires resources worth $245.

Resource Input	×	Unit Price of Input	=	Total Cost
1 factory		$100 per day		$100
1 sewing machine		20 per day		20
1 operator		80 per day		80
1.5 bolts of denim		30 per bolt		45
Total cost				$245

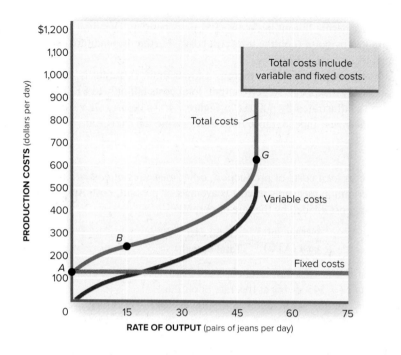

FIGURE 7.4

The Cost of Jeans Production

Total cost includes both fixed and variable costs.

Fixed costs must be paid even if no output is produced (point *A*). Variable costs start at zero and increase with the rate of output.

The total cost of producing 15 pairs of jeans (point *B*) includes $120 in fixed costs (rent on the factory and sewing machines) and $125 in variable costs (denim and wages). Total cost rises as output increases because additional variable costs must be incurred.

In this example, the short-run capacity is equal to 51 pairs (point *G*). If still more inputs are employed, costs will rise but not total output.

just tell our only worker to take the day off (without pay, of course!). We'll still have to pay rent, but we can cut back on wages. On the other hand, if we want to increase daily output, we can also hire additional workers easily and quickly. Labor is regarded as a **variable cost** in this line of work—that is, a cost that *varies* with the rate of output.

The denim itself is another variable cost. Denim not used today can be saved for tomorrow. Hence, how much we spend on denim today is directly related to how many jeans we produce. In this sense, the cost of denim input varies with the rate of jeans output.

Figure 7.4 illustrates how these various costs are affected by the rate of production. On the vertical axis are the costs of production in dollars per day. Notice that the total cost of producing 15 pairs per day is still $245, as indicated by point *B*. This cost figure consists of

variable costs: Costs of production that change when the rate of output is altered, such as labor and material costs.

DOLLAR COST OF PRODUCING 15 PAIRS

Fixed costs:		
Factory rent	$100	
Sewing machine rent	20	
Subtotal		$120
Variable costs:		
Wages to labor	$ 80	
Denim	45	
Subtotal		$125
Total costs		$245

If we increase the rate of output beyond these 15 pairs, total costs will rise. *How fast total costs rise depends on variable costs only,* however, because fixed costs remain at $120 per day. (Notice the horizontal fixed cost curve in Figure 7.4.)

Capacity. With one sewing machine and one factory, there's an absolute limit to daily jeans production. According to the production function in Figure 7.1, the capacity of a factory with one machine is roughly 51 pairs of jeans per day. If we try to produce more jeans than this by hiring additional workers, our total costs will rise, but our output won't. Recall that the seventh worker had a *zero* marginal physical product (Figure 7.2). In fact, we could fill the factory with garment workers and drive total costs sky-high. But the limits of space and one sewing machine don't permit output in excess of 51 pairs per day. This limit to productive capacity is represented by point *G* on the total cost curve. Further expenditure on inputs will increase production *costs* but not *output.*

Although there's no upper limit to costs, there is a lower limit. If output is reduced to zero, costs won't completely disappear. At zero output, total costs fall only to $120 per day, the level of fixed costs, as illustrated by point *A* in Figure 7.4. As before, ***there's no way to avoid fixed costs in the short run.*** Indeed, those fixed costs define the short run.

Average Costs

While Figure 7.4 illustrates *total* costs of production, other measures of cost are often desired. One of the most common measures of cost is average, or per-unit, cost. **Average total cost (ATC)** is simply total cost divided by the rate of output:

$$\text{Average total cost (ATC)} = \frac{\text{Total cost}}{\text{Total output}}$$

At an output of 15 pairs of jeans per day, total costs are $245. The average cost of production is thus $16.33 per pair ($= 245 \div 15$) at this rate of output.

The average cost of production is not a constant number. On the contrary, ***average total cost changes with the rate of output.*** So, when someone cites the average cost of producing something, they must have a specific quantity of output in mind.

Figure 7.5 shows how average costs change as the rate of output varies. Row *J* of the cost schedule, for example, again indicates the fixed, variable, and total costs of producing 15 pairs of jeans per day. Fixed costs are still $120; variable costs are $125. Thus, the total cost of producing 15 pairs per day is $245, as we saw earlier.

The rest of row *J* shows the average costs of jeans production. These figures are obtained by dividing each dollar total (columns 2, 3, and 4) by the rate of physical output (column 1). At an output rate of 15 pairs per day, **average fixed cost (AFC)** is $8 per pair, **average variable cost (AVC)** is $8.33, and *average total cost (ATC)* is $16.33. ATC, then, is simply the sum of AFC and AVC:

$$\text{ATC} = \text{AFC} + \text{AVC}$$

Falling AFC. At this relatively low rate of output, fixed costs are a large portion of total costs. The rent paid for the factory and sewing machines works out to $8 per pair ($120 \div 15$). This high average fixed cost accounts for nearly one-half of total average costs. This suggests that it's quite expensive to lease a factory and sewing machine to produce only 15 pairs of jeans per day. To reduce average costs, we must make fuller use of our leased plant and

average total cost (ATC):
Total cost divided by the quantity produced in a given time period.

average fixed cost (AFC):
Total fixed cost divided by the quantity produced in a given time period.

average variable cost (AVC):
Total variable cost divided by the quantity produced in a given time period.

How do costs change with the number of rides?

Sean Gallup/Getty Images

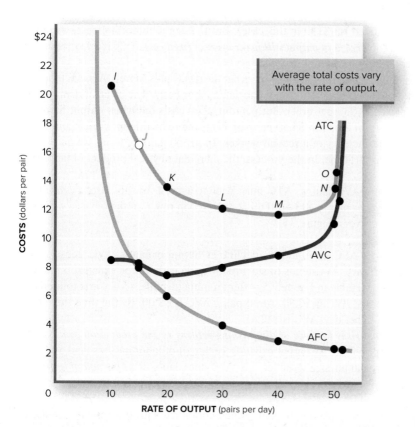

FIGURE 7.5

Average Total Costs (ATC)

Average total cost (ATC) in column 7 equals total cost (column 4) divided by the rate of output (column 1).

Because total cost includes both fixed (column 2) and variable (column 3) costs, ATC also equals AFC (column 5) plus AVC (column 6). This relationship is illustrated in the graph. The ATC of producing 15 pairs per day (point *J*) equals $16.33—the sum of AFC ($8) and AVC ($8.33).

Average total costs vary with the rate of output.

	(1)	(2)		(3)		(4)	(5)		(6)		(7)
	Rate of Output	Fixed Costs	+	Variable Costs	=	Total Cost	Average Fixed Cost	+	Average Variable Cost	=	Average Total Cost
H	0	$120		$ 0		$120	—		—		—
I	10	120		85		205	$12.00		$ 8.50		$20.50
J	15	120		125		245	8.00		8.33		16.33
K	20	120		150		270	6.00		7.50		13.50
L	30	120		240		360	4.00		8.00		12.00
M	40	120		350		470	3.00		8.75		11.75
N	50	120		550		670	2.40		11.00		13.40
O	51	120		633		753	2.35		12.41		14.76

equipment. That is one reason the Uber and Lyft drivers try to book so many trips; the more trips they have, the smaller the *average* total cost becomes as the fixed costs of the car and insurance are spread over more rides.

Notice what happens to average costs when the rate of output is increased to 20 pairs per day (row *K* in Figure 7.5). Average fixed costs go down to only $6 per pair. This sharp decline in AFC results from the fact that total fixed costs ($120) are now spread over more output. Even though our rent hasn't dropped, the *average* fixed cost of producing jeans has.

If we produce more than 20 pairs of jeans per day, AFC will continue to fall. Recall that

$$AFC = \frac{\text{Total fixed cost}}{\text{Total output}}$$

The numerator is fixed (at $120 in this case). But the denominator increases as output expands. Hence, *any increase in output will lower average fixed cost.* This is reflected in Figure 7.5 by the constantly declining AFC curve.

As jeans output increases from 15 to 20 pairs per day, AVC falls as well. AVC includes the price of denim used in a pair of jeans and associated labor costs. The price of denim is unchanged at $3 per pair ($30 per bolt). But per-unit *labor* costs fall when output increases from 15 to 20 pairs, from $5.33 to $4.50 per pair. Thus the reduction in AVC is completely due to the greater productivity of a second worker. To get 20 pairs of jeans, we had to employ a second worker part-time. In the process, the marginal physical product of labor rose and AVC fell.

With both AFC and AVC falling, ATC must decline as well. In this case, *average* total cost falls from $16.33 per pair to $13.50. This is reflected in row *K* in the table as well as in point *K* on the ATC curve in Figure 7.5.

Rising AVC. Although AFC continues to decline as output expands, AVC doesn't keep dropping. On the contrary, AVC tends to start rising quite early in the expansion process. Look at column 6 of the table in Figure 7.5. After an initial decline, AVC starts to increase. At an output of 20 pairs, AVC is $7.50. At 30 pairs, AVC is $8.00. By the time the rate of output reaches 51 pairs per day, AVC is $12.41.

Average variable cost rises because of diminishing returns in the production process. We discussed this concept before. As output expands, each unit of labor has less land and capital to work with. Marginal physical product falls. As it does, labor costs *per pair of jeans* rise, pushing up AVC.

U-Shaped ATC. The steady decline of AFC, when combined with the typical increase in AVC, results in a U-shaped pattern for average total costs. In the early stages of output expansion, the large declines in AFC outweigh any increases in AVC. As a result, ATC tends to fall. Notice that ATC declines from $20.50 to $11.75 as output increases from 10 to 40 pairs per day. This is also illustrated in Figure 7.5 with the downward move from point *I* to point *M*.

The battle between falling AFC and rising AVC takes an irreversible turn soon thereafter. When output is increased from 40 to 50 pairs of jeans per day, AFC continues to fall (row *N* in the table). But the decline in AFC (−60 cents) is overshadowed by the increase in AVC (+$2.25). Once rising AVC dominates, ATC starts to increase as well. ATC increases from $11.75 to $13.40 when jeans production expands from 40 to 50 pairs per day.

This and further increases in average total costs cause the ATC curve in Figure 7.5 to start rising. *The initial dominance of falling AFC, combined with the later resurgence of rising AVC, is what gives the ATC curve its characteristic U shape.*

Minimum Average Cost. Whew! There are a lot of numbers here. It's easy to get lost in this thicket of intertwined graphs and jumble of equations. A couple of landmarks will help guide us out, however. One of those is located at the very bottom of the U-shaped average total cost curve. Point *M* in Figure 7.5 represents *minimum* average total costs. By producing exactly 40 pairs per day, we minimize the amount of land, labor, and capital used per pair of jeans. For Low-Rider Jeans Corporation, point *M* represents least-cost production—the lowest-cost jeans. For society as a whole, point *M* also represents the lowest possible opportunity cost: At point *M,* we're minimizing the amount of resources used to produce a pair of jeans and therefore maximizing the amount of resources left over for the production of other goods and services.

As attractive as point *M* is, you shouldn't conclude that it's everyone's dream. The goal of producers is to maximize *profits.* We already noted that maximum *profits* and maximum *output* don't necessarily coincide. Now we'll see that **minimizing average total cost isn't necessarily the same thing as maximizing profit,** either.

Inputs Used to Produce 16th Pair of Jeans	×	Market Value of Input	=	Marginal Cost
0.053 unit of labor		0.053 × $80 per unit of labor		$4.24
0.1 bolt of denim		0.1 × $30 per bolt		3.00
				$7.24

TABLE 7.3

Resource Computation of Marginal Cost

Marginal cost refers to the value of the additional inputs needed to produce one more unit of output. To increase daily jeans output from 15 to 16 pairs, we need 0.053 units of labor and one-tenth of a bolt of denim. These extra inputs cost $7.24.

Marginal Cost

To get a firmer grip on profit maximization, we need to introduce one last cost concept. Indeed, this last concept is probably the most important one for production. It's *marginal cost*. We encountered this concept in our discussion of resource costs, where we noted that marginal cost refers to the value of the resources needed to produce one more unit of a good. To produce *one* more pair of jeans, we need the denim itself and a very small amount of additional labor. These are the extra or added costs of increasing output by one pair of jeans per day.

To compute the *dollar* value of these marginal costs, we could determine the market price of denim and labor and then add them up. Table 7.3 provides an example. In this case, we calculate that the additional or *marginal* cost of producing a sixteenth pair of jeans is $7.24. This is how much *total* costs will increase if we decide to expand jeans output by only one pair per day (from 15 to 16).

Table 7.3 emphasizes the link between resource costs and dollar costs. However, there's a much easier way to compute marginal cost. ***Marginal cost refers to the change in total costs associated with one more unit of output.*** Accordingly, we can simply observe *total* dollar costs before and after the rate of output is increased. The difference between the two totals equals the *marginal cost* of increasing the rate of output. This technique is much easier for jeans manufacturers who don't know much about marginal resource utilization but have a sharp eye for dollar costs. It's also a lot easier for economics students, of course. But they have an obligation to understand the resource origins of marginal costs and what causes marginal costs to rise or fall. As we noted before, ***diminishing returns in production cause marginal costs to increase as the rate of output is expanded.***

Figure 7.6 shows what the marginal costs of producing jeans look like. At each output rate, marginal cost is computed as the *change* in total cost divided by the *change* in output. When output increases from 20 jeans to 30 jeans, total cost rises by $90. Dividing this change in costs by 10 (the change in output) gives us a marginal cost of $9, as illustrated by point *s*.

Increasing MC. Notice in Figure 7.6 how the marginal cost curve starts climbing upward after 20 units of output have been produced. This rise in marginal costs reflects the law of diminishing returns. As increases in output become more difficult to achieve, they also become more expensive. Each additional pair of jeans beyond 20 requires a bit more labor than the preceding pair and thus entails rising marginal cost. After output passes 40 pairs, marginal costs really shoot upward.

A Cost Summary

All these cost calculations can give you a real headache. They can also give you second thoughts about jumping into Low-Rider Jeans or any other business. There are tough choices to be made. A given firm can produce many different rates of output, each of which entails a distinct level of costs. ***The output decision has to be based not only on the capacity to produce (the production function) but also on the costs of production (the cost functions).*** Only those who make the right decisions will succeed in business.

FIGURE 7.6

Marginal Costs

Marginal cost is the change in total cost that occurs when more output is produced. MC equals $\Delta TC/\Delta q$.

When diminishing returns set in, MC begins rising, as it does here after the output rate of 20 pairs per day is exceeded.

Rate of Output	Total Cost	$\dfrac{\Delta TC}{\Delta q}$ = MC
0	$120	—
p	10	205	$85/10 = $8.5
q	15	245	$40/5 = $8.0
r	20	270	$25/5 = $5.0
s	30	360	$90/10 = $9.0
t	40	470	$110/10 = $11.0
u	50	670	$200/10 = $20.0
v	51	753	$83/1 = $83.0

The decision-making process is made a bit easier with the glossary in Table 7.4 and the generalized cost curves in Figure 7.7. As before, we're concentrating on a short-run production process, with fixed quantities of land and capital. In this case, however, we've abandoned the Low-Rider Jeans Corporation and provided hypothetical costs for an idealized production process. The purpose of these figures is to provide a more general view of how

TABLE 7.4

A Guide to Costs

A quick reference to key measures of cost.

Total costs of production are made up of fixed costs and variable costs:

$$TC = FC + VC$$

Dividing total costs by the quantity of output yields the average total cost:

$$ATC = \frac{TC}{q}$$

which also equals the sum of average fixed cost and average variable cost:

$$ATC = AFC + AVC$$

The most important measure of changes in cost is marginal cost, which equals the increase in total costs when an additional unit of output is produced:

$$MC = \frac{\text{Change in total cost}}{\text{Change in output}}$$

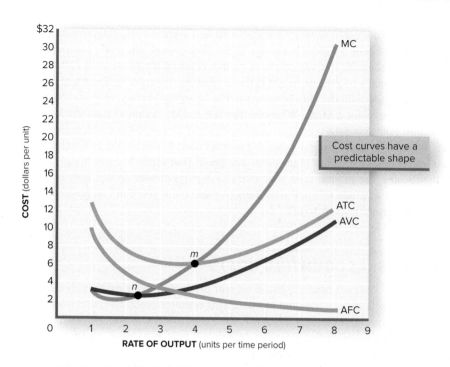

FIGURE 7.7
Basic Cost Curves

With total cost and the rate of output, all other cost concepts can be computed.

The resulting cost curves have several distinct features. The AFC curve always slopes downward. The MC curve typically rises, sometimes after a brief decline.

The ATC curve has a U shape. And the MC curve will always intersect both the ATC and AVC curves at their lowest points (*m* and *n*, respectively).

Rate of Output	TC	MC	ATC	AFC	AVC
0	$10.00	—	—	—	—
1	13.00	$ 3.00	$13.00	$10.00	$ 3.00
2	15.00	2.00	7.50	5.00	2.50
3	19.00	4.00	6.33	3.33	3.00
4	25.00	6.00	6.25	2.50	3.75
5	34.00	9.00	6.80	2.00	4.80
6	48.00	14.00	8.00	1.67	6.33
7	68.00	20.00	9.71	1.43	8.28
8	98.00	30.00	12.25	1.25	11.00

the various cost concepts relate to each other. Note that MC, ATC, AFC, and AVC can all be computed from total costs. All we need, then, are the first two columns of the table in Figure 7.7, and we can compute and graph all the rest of the cost figures.

MC–ATC Intersection. The centerpiece of Figure 7.7 is the U-shaped ATC curve (in green). Of special significance is its relationship to marginal costs. Notice that *the MC curve intersects the ATC curve at its lowest point* (point *m*). This will always be the case. So long as the marginal cost of producing one more unit is less than the previous average cost, average costs must fall. *Thus, average total costs decline as long as the marginal cost curve lies below the average cost curve,* as to the left of point *m* in Figure 7.7.

We already observed, however, that marginal costs rise as output expands, largely because additional workers reduce the amount of land and capital available to each worker (in the short run, the size of plant and equipment is fixed). Consequently, at some point (*m* in Figure 7.7) marginal costs will rise to the level of average costs.

As marginal costs continue to rise beyond point *m,* they begin to pull average costs up, giving the average cost curve its U shape. *Average total costs increase whenever marginal costs exceed average costs.* This is the case to the right of point *m* because the marginal cost curve always lies above the average cost curve in that part of Figure 7.7.

To visualize the relationship between marginal cost and average cost, imagine computing the average height of people entering a room. If the first person who comes through the door is six feet tall, then the average height of people entering the room is six feet at that point. But what happens to average height if the second person entering the room is only three feet tall? *Average* height declines because the last (marginal) person entering the room is shorter than the previous average. Whenever the last entrant is shorter than the average, the average must fall.

The relationship between marginal costs and average costs is also similar to that between your grade in this course and your grade point average. If your grade in economics is better (higher) than your other grades, then your overall grade point average will rise. In other words, a high *marginal* grade will pull your *average* grade up. If you don't understand this, your grade point average is likely to fall.

ECONOMIC VS. ACCOUNTING COSTS

The cost curves we observed here are based on *real* production relationships. The dollar costs we compute are a direct reflection of underlying resource costs: the land, labor, and capital used in the production process. Not everyone counts this way. On the contrary, accountants and businesspeople typically count dollar costs only and ignore any resource use that doesn't result in an explicit dollar cost.

Return to Low-Rider Jeans for a moment to see the difference. When we computed the dollar cost of producing 15 pairs of jeans per day, we noted the following resource inputs:

INPUTS	COST PER DAY
1 factory rent	$100
1 machine rent	20
1 machine operator	80
1.5 bolts of denim	45
Total cost	$245

The total value of the resources used in the production of 15 pairs of jeans was thus $245 per day. But this figure needn't conform to *actual* dollar costs. Suppose the owners of Low-Rider Jeans decided to sew jeans themselves. Then they wouldn't have to hire a worker and pay $80 per day in wages. **Explicit costs**—the *dollar* payments—would drop to $165 per day. The producers and their accountant would consider this a remarkable achievement. They might assert that the cost of producing jeans had fallen.

explicit costs: A payment made for the use of a resource.

Economic Cost

An economist would draw no such conclusions. *The essential economic question is how many resources are used in production.* This hasn't changed. One unit of labor is still being employed at the factory; now it's simply the owner, not a hired worker. In either case, one unit of labor is not available for the production of other goods and services. Hence, society is still paying $245 for jeans, whether the owners of Low-Rider Jeans write checks in that amount or not. The only difference is that we now have an **implicit cost** rather than an explicit one. We really don't care who sews jeans—the essential point is that someone (i.e., a unit of labor) does.

The same would be true if Low-Rider Jeans owned its own factory rather than rented it. If the factory were owned rather than rented, the owners probably wouldn't write any rent checks. Hence, *accounting* costs would drop by $100 per day. But the factory would still be in use for jeans production and therefore unavailable for the production of other goods and services. The economic (resource) cost of producing 15 pairs of jeans would still be $245.

The distinction between an economic cost and an accounting cost is essentially one between resource and dollar costs. *Dollar cost* refers to the explicit dollar outlays made by a producer; it's the lifeblood of accountants. **Economic cost,** in contrast, refers to the *value* of

implicit cost: The value of resources used, for which no direct payment is made.

economic cost: The value of all resources used to produce a good or service; opportunity cost.

all resources used in the production process; it's the lifeblood of economists. In other words, economists count costs as

$$\text{Economic cost} = \text{Explicit costs} + \text{Implicit costs}$$

As this formula suggests, *economic and accounting costs will diverge whenever any factor of production is not paid an explicit wage (or rent, etc.).*

The Cost of Homework. These distinctions between economic and accounting costs apply also to the "production" of homework. You can pay people to write term papers for you or buy them off the Internet. At large schools you can often buy lecture notes as well. But most students do their own homework so they'll learn something and not just turn in required assignments.

Doing homework is expensive, however, even if you don't pay someone to do it. The time you spend reading this chapter is valuable. You could be doing something else if you weren't reading right now. What would you be doing? That forgone activity—the best alternative use of your time—represents the economic cost of doing homework. Even if you don't pay yourself for reading this chapter, you'll still incur that *economic* cost.

LONG-RUN COSTS

We've confined our discussion thus far to short-run production costs. *The short run is characterized by fixed costs*—a commitment to specific plants and equipment. A factory, an office building, or some other plants and equipment have been leased or purchased: We're stuck with *fixed costs.* In the short run, our objective is to make the best use of those fixed costs by choosing the appropriate rate of production.

The long run opens up a whole new range of options. In the **long run,** we have no lease or purchase commitments. We're free to start all over again with whatever scale of plants and equipment we desire and whatever technology is available. Quite simply, *there are no fixed costs in the long run.* Nor are there any commitments to existing technology.

That's what excited Elon Musk when he started thinking about mass-producing Tesla electric cars. Although Tesla had sold only 30,000 vehicles in its first 6 years, Musk envisioned his company selling as many as 500,000 vehicles by the year 2020. To do so, he decided he needed to get into the battery business as well. So he built a "gigafactory" of gigantic proportions to produce the lithium-ion batteries he'd need for mass production of Tesla cars. To build this factory, he incurred fixed costs of $4.5 *billion!* Since the factory was opened in 2016, Tesla has focused on the short-run production decision of how many batteries and cars to produce from its gigafactory.

Tesla is now going through the same sequence of long- and short-run decisions in China. In 2019 it constructed a $2 billion gigafactory in Shanghai (see World View "Tesla Starts Rolling Out Cars from Shanghai Gigafactory"). Now Tesla has to decide how many cars it wants to produce from that (fixed-cost) facility.

long run: A period of time long enough for all inputs to be varied (no fixed costs).

Long-Run Average Costs

The opportunities available in the long run include building a plant of any desired size, including "gigafactories." Suppose we still wanted to go into the jeans business. In the long run, we could build or lease any size factory we wanted and could lease as many sewing machines as we desired. Figure 7.8 illustrates three choices: a small factory (ATC_1), a medium-sized factory (ATC_2), and a large factory (ATC_3). All three factories have the common U-shaped average total cost curves. But there are important differences. As we observed earlier, it's very expensive to produce lots of jeans with a small factory. The ATC curve for a small factory (ATC_1) starts to head straight up at relatively low rates of output. In the long run, we'd lease or build such a factory only if we anticipated a continuing low rate of output.

The ATC_2 curve illustrates how costs might fall if we leased or built a medium-sized factory. With a small factory, ATC becomes prohibitive at an output of 50 to 60 pairs of jeans

WORLD VIEW

TESLA STARTS ROLLING OUT CARS FROM SHANGHAI GIGAFACTORY

Elon Musk gambled a fortune in Reno, Nevada, when he built a "gigafactory" to manufacture lithium batteries for Tesla electric vehicles. Together with battery-maker Panasonic, he invested $4.5 billion in the factory. When fully completed, the Reno facility will be the largest factory in the world, capable of producing enough battery packs for 500,000 cars a year. Musk says the sheer scale of the factory will enable Tesla to bring down the cost of battery packs by as much as 30 percent, the most expensive component of electric vehicles.

Musk has made the same bet again—this time in China. At a cost of $2 billion, Tesla has built another gigafactory in Shanghai and is already producing Model 3 vehicles. In 2020 Tesla hopes to build at least 35,000 cars, then ramp up to 500,000 cars annually in a few years. Given the success of the Reno plant, few investors want to bet against him.

Source: Media reports of December 2019–January 2020.

CRITICAL ANALYSIS: As the size of a factory increases, it may be able to reduce the costs of doing business. Decreasing **long-run costs** (economies of scale) can give a large firm a competitive advantage over smaller firms.

per day. A medium-sized factory can produce these quantities at lower cost. Moreover, ATC continues to drop as jeans production increases in the medium-sized factory—at least for a while. Even a medium-sized factory must contend with resource constraints and therefore rising average costs: Its ATC curve is U-shaped also.

If we expected to sell really large quantities of jeans, we'd want to build or lease a large factory. Beyond the rate of output b, the largest factory offers the lowest average total cost. There's a risk in leasing such a large factory, of course. If our sales don't live up to our high expectations, we'll end up with very high fixed costs and thus very expensive jeans. Look at the high average cost of producing only 60 pairs of jeans per day with the large factory (ATC_3). Then think what Tesla's ATC would look like if it produced only 1,000 cars a year from its Shanghai gigafactory—rather than the 500,000 it hopes to produce in future years!

In choosing an appropriate factory, then, we must decide how many jeans we expect to sell. Once we know our expected output, we can select the right-sized factory. It will be the one that offers the lowest ATC for that rate of output. If we expect to sell fewer jeans than a,

---

FIGURE 7.8

Long-Run Costs with Three Plant Size Options

Long-run cost possibilities are determined by all possible short-run options. In this case, there are three options of varying size (ATC_1, ATC_2, and ATC_3).

In the long run, we'd choose the plant that yielded the lowest average cost for any desired rate of output. The solid portions of the curves (LATC) represent these choices. The smallest factory (ATC_1) is best for output levels below a; the largest (ATC_3), for output rates in excess of b.

we'll choose the small factory in Figure 7.8. If we expect to sell jeans at a rate between *a* and *b,* we'll select a medium-sized factory. Beyond rate *b,* we'll want the largest factory. These choices are reflected in the solid parts of the three ATC curves. The composite "curve" created by these three segments constitutes our long-run cost possibilities. *The long-run cost curve is just a summary of our best short-run cost possibilities, using existing technology and facilities.*

We might confront more than three choices, of course. There's really no reason we couldn't build a factory to *any* desired size. In the long run, we face an infinite number of scale choices, not just three. The effect of all these choices is to smooth out the long-run cost curve. Figure 7.9 depicts the long-run curve that results. Each rate of output is most efficiently produced by some size (scale) of plant. That sized plant indicates the minimum cost of producing a particular rate of output. Its corresponding short-run ATC curve provides one point on the long-run ATC curve.

Long-Run Marginal Costs

Like all average cost curves, the long-run (LATC) curve has its own marginal cost curve. The long-run marginal cost (LMC) curve isn't a composite of short-run marginal cost curves. Rather, it's computed on the basis of the costs reflected in the long-run ATC curve itself. We won't bother to compute those costs here. Note, however, that the long-run MC curve—like all MC curves—intersects its associated average cost curve at its lowest point.

ECONOMIES OF SCALE

Figure 7.8 seems to imply that a producer must choose either a small plant or a larger one. That isn't completely true. The choice is often between one large plant or *several* small ones. Suppose the desired level of output was relatively large, as at point *c* in Figure 7.8. A single small plant (ATC$_1$) is clearly not up to the task. But what about using several small plants rather than one large one (ATC$_3$)? How would costs be affected?

Notice what happens to *minimum ATC* in Figure 7.8 when the size (scale) of the factory changes. When a medium-sized factory (ATC$_2$) replaces a small factory (ATC$_1$), minimum average cost drops (the bottom of ATC$_2$ is below the bottom of ATC$_1$). This implies that a jeans producer who wants to minimize costs should build one medium-sized factory rather than try to produce the same quantity with two small ones. **Economies of scale** exist in this situation: Larger facilities reduce *minimum* average costs.

This is the kind of potential that excited Elon Musk. As he studied alternatives for building a battery factory, he saw several possibilities for bringing minimum average costs down. Innovations in manufacturing, better logistics, co-located processes, and reduced overhead could give a larger plant economies of scale that smaller plants couldn't achieve. So he

economies of scale:
Reductions in minimum average costs that come about through increases in the size (scale) of plant and equipment.

(a) Constant returns to scale

(b) Economies of scale

(c) Diseconomies of scale

FIGURE 7.10

Economies of Scale

A lot of output (Q_m) can be produced from one large plant or many small ones. Here we contrast the average total costs associated with one small plant (ATCs) and three large plants (ATC₁, ATC₂, and ATC₃). If a large plant attains the same *minimum* average costs (point m_1 in part *a*) as a smaller plant (point *c*), there's no advantage to large size (scale). Many small plants can produce the same output just as cheaply. However, either economies (part *b*) or diseconomies (part *c*) of scale may exist.

decided to build a 10-million-square-foot "gigafactory" that could achieve substantial economies of scale (see World View "Tesla Starts Rolling Out Cars from Shanghai Gigafactory").

Larger production facilities don't always result in cost reductions. Suppose that a firm has the choice of producing the quantity Q_m from several small factories or from one large, centralized facility. Centralization may have three different impacts on costs; these are illustrated in Figure 7.10. In each illustration, we see the average total cost (ATC) curve for a typical small firm or plant and the ATC curve for a much larger plant producing the same product.

Constant Returns. Figure 7.10*a* depicts a situation in which there's no economic advantage to centralization of manufacturing operations because a large plant is no more efficient than a lot of small plants. The critical focus here is on the *minimum* average costs attainable for a given rate of output. Note that the lowest point on the smaller plant's ATC curve (point *c*) is no higher or lower than the lowest point on the larger firm's ATC curve (point m_1). Hence, it would be just as cheap to produce the quantity Q_m from a multitude of small plants as it would be to produce Q_m from one large plant. Thus, increasing the size (or *scale*) of individual plants won't reduce minimum average costs: This is a situation of **constant returns to scale.**

constant returns to scale: Increases in plant size do not affect minimum average cost; minimum per-unit costs are identical for small plants and large plants.

Economies of Scale. Figure 7.10*b* illustrates the situation in which a larger plant can attain a lower minimum average cost than a smaller plant. That is, economies of scale (or *increasing returns to scale*) exist. This is evident from the fact that the larger firm's ATC curve falls *below* the dashed line in the graph (m_2 is less than *c*). The greater efficiency of the large factory might come from any of several sources. This is the situation Elon Musk was counting on for his Shanghai gigafactory.

Diseconomies of Scale. Even though large plants may be able to achieve greater efficiencies than smaller plants, there's no guaranty that they actually will. In fact, increasing the size (scale) of a plant may actually *reduce* operating efficiency, as depicted in Figure 7.10*c*. Workers may feel alienated in a plant of massive proportions and feel little commitment to productivity. Creativity may be stifled by rigid corporate structures and off-site management. A large plant may also foster a sense of anonymity that induces workers to underperform. When these things happen, *diseconomies of scale* result. Microsoft tries to avoid such diseconomies of scale by creating autonomous cells of no more than 35 employees ("small plants") within its larger corporate structure.

In evaluating long-run options, then, we must be careful to recognize that *efficiency and size don't necessarily go hand in hand.* Some firms and industries may be subject to economies of scale, but others may not. Bigger isn't always better.

DECISIONS FOR **TOMORROW**

Can U.S. Companies Compete?

From 1900 to 1970, the United States regularly exported more goods and services than it imported. Since then America has had a trade deficit nearly every year. In 2020, U.S. imports exceeded exports by roughly $600 billion. To many people, such trade deficits are a symptom that the United States can no longer compete effectively in world markets. To President Trump, the U.S. trade deficit was proof that the rest of the world—especially China and Mexico—were engaged in "unfair" trading practices. As he saw it, the trade deficit would disappear if every nation played fair, giving American companies equal access to all markets.

In free and open markets, global competition would depend on the costs of production. If international competitors could produce goods more cheaply, they'd be able to undersell U.S. goods and drive up our trade deficit.

Cheap Foreign Labor? Cheap labor keeps costs down in many countries. The average wage in Mexico, for example, ranges from $2 to $3 an hour, compared to more than $24 an hour in the United States. China's manufacturing workers make only $3.50 an hour. Such huge wage gaps certainly suggest that U.S. companies could never compete successfully in global markets.

Low wages are *not,* however, a reliable measure of global competitiveness. To compete in global markets, one must produce more *output* for a given quantity of *inputs.* In other words, labor is "cheap" only if it produces a lot of output in return for the wages paid.

A worker's contribution to output is measured by *marginal physical product (MPP).* What we saw in this chapter was that **a worker's productivity (MPP) depends on the quantity and quality of other resources in the production process.** In this regard, U.S. workers have a tremendous advantage: They work with vast quantities of capital and state-of-the-art technology. They also come to the workplace with more education. Their high wages reflect this greater productivity.

Unit Labor Costs. A true measure of global competitiveness must take into account both factor costs (e.g., wages) and productivity. One such measure is **unit labor cost,** which indicates the labor cost of producing one unit of output. It's computed as

$$\text{Unit labor cost} = \frac{\text{Wage rate}}{\text{MPP}}$$

Suppose that the MPP of a U.S. worker is 10 units per hour and the wage is $24 an hour. The unit labor cost would be

$$\begin{matrix}\text{Unit labor cost} \\ \text{(United States)}\end{matrix} = \frac{\$24/\text{hour}}{10\ \text{units/hour}} = \begin{matrix}\$2.40/\text{unit} \\ \text{of output}\end{matrix}$$

By contrast, assume the average worker in Mexico has an MPP of 1 unit per hour and a wage of $3 an hour. In this case, the unit labor cost would be

$$\begin{matrix}\text{Unit labor cost} \\ \text{(Mexico)}\end{matrix} = \frac{\$3}{1} = \begin{matrix}\$3/\text{unit} \\ \text{of output}\end{matrix}$$

According to these hypothetical examples, "cheap" Mexican labor is no bargain. Mexican labor is actually *more* costly in production despite the much lower wage rate.

Productivity Advance. What these calculations illustrate is how important productivity is for global competitiveness. If we want the United States to stay competitive in global markets, U.S. productivity must increase as fast as that in other nations.

The production function introduced in this chapter helps illustrate the essence of global competitiveness in the economy tomorrow. Until now, we've regarded a firm's production function as a technological fact of life—the *best* we could do, given our state

unit labor cost: Hourly wage rate divided by output per labor-hour.

Continued

(a) When the production function shifts up . . .

TOTAL OUTPUT (units per time period)

RESOURCE INPUTS
(units per time period)

(b) Cost curves shift down

COST (dollars per unit)

ATC₁
ATC₂
MC₁
MC₂

RATE OF OUTPUT
(units per time period)

FIGURE 7.11

Improvements in Productivity Reduce Costs

Advances in technological or managerial knowledge increase our productive capability. This is reflected in upward shifts of the production function (part *a*) and downward shifts of production cost curves (part *b*).

of technological and managerial knowledge. In the real world, however, the best is always getting better. Science and technology are continuously advancing. So is our knowledge of how to organize and manage our resources. These advances keep *shifting* production functions upward: More can be produced with any given quantity of inputs. In the process, the costs of production shift downward, as illustrated in Figure 7.11 by the downward shifts of the MC and ATC curves. These downward shifts imply that we can get more of the goods and services we desire with available resources. We can also compete more effectively in global markets in the economy tomorrow.

SUMMARY

- A production function indicates the maximum amount of output that can be produced with different combinations of inputs.   **LO7-1**
- In the short run, some inputs (e.g., land and capital) are fixed in quantity. Increases in (short-run) output result from more use of variable inputs (e.g., labor).   **LO7-1**
- The contribution of a variable input to total output is measured by its marginal physical product (MPP). This is

the amount by which *total* output increases when one more unit of the input is employed.   **LO7-1**
- The MPP of a factor tends to decline as more of it is used in a given production facility. Diminishing marginal returns result from crowding more of a variable input (e.g., labor) into a production process, reducing the amount of fixed inputs *per unit* of variable input.   **LO7-2**

- Marginal cost is the increase in total cost that results when output is increased by one unit. Marginal cost increases whenever marginal physical product diminishes.   **LO7-3**
- Not all costs go up when the rate of output is increased. Fixed costs such as space and equipment leases don't vary with the rate of output. Only variable costs such as labor and material go up when output is increased.   **LO7-3**
- Average total cost (ATC) equals total cost divided by the quantity of output produced. ATC declines when marginal cost (MC) is less than average cost and rises when MC exceeds it. The MC and ATC curves intersect at minimum ATC (the bottom of the U). That intersection represents least-cost production.   **LO7-3**

- The economic costs of production include the value of *all* resources used. Accounting costs typically include only those dollar costs actually paid (explicit costs).   **LO7-4**
- In the long run there are no fixed costs; the size (scale) of production can be varied. The long-run ATC curve indicates the lowest cost of producing output with facilities of appropriate size.   **LO7-5**
- Economies of scale refer to reductions in *minimum* average cost attained with larger plant size (scale). If minimum ATC rises with plant size, diseconomies of scale exist.   **LO7-5**
- Global competitiveness and domestic living standards depend on productivity advances. Improvements in productivity shift production functions up and push cost curves down.   **LO7-1**

Key Terms

factors of production	profit	explicit cost
production function	marginal cost (MC)	implicit cost
productivity	total cost	economic cost
efficiency	fixed costs	long run
opportunity cost	variable costs	economies of scale
short run	average total cost (ATC)	constant returns to scale
marginal physical product (MPP)	average fixed cost (AFC)	unit labor cost
law of diminishing returns	average variable cost (AVC)	

Questions for Discussion

1. What are the production costs of your economics class? What are the fixed costs? The variable costs? What's the marginal cost of enrolling more students?   **LO7-3**
2. Suppose all your friends offered to help wash your car. Would marginal physical product decline as more friends helped? Why or why not?   **LO7-2**
3. Would an Uber driver have a U-shaped average total cost curve?   **LO7-3**
4. Owner/operators of small gas stations rarely pay themselves an hourly wage. How does this practice affect the economic cost of dispensing gasoline?   **LO7-4**
5. Corporate funeral giants have replaced small family-run funeral homes in many areas, in large part because of the lower costs they achieve. What kind of economies of scale exist in the funeral business? Why doesn't someone build one colossal funeral home and drive costs down further?   **LO7-5**
6. Are colleges subject to economies of scale or diseconomies?   **LO7-5**
7. Why don't more U.S. firms move to Mexico to take advantage of low wages there? Would an *identical* plant in Mexico be as productive as its U.S. counterpart?   **LO7-1**
8. What will happen to the cost of producing Teslas if the Shanghai gigafactory doesn't achieve economies of scale?   **LO7-5**
9. What is the economic cost of doing this homework?   **LO7-4**
10. What causes unit labor costs to rise in some nations and fall in others?   **LO7-3**

LO7-3 1. (*a*) Complete the following cost schedule:

Rate of Output	Total Cost	Marginal Cost	Average Fixed Cost	Average Variable Cost	Average Total Cost
0	$ 600	_____	_____	_____	_____
1	800	_____	_____	_____	_____
2	1,050	_____	_____	_____	_____
3	1,400	_____	_____	_____	_____
4	1,800	_____	_____	_____	_____
5	2,300	_____	_____	_____	_____

(*b*) Use the cost data to plot the ATC and MC curves on a graph.

(*c*) At what output rate is ATC minimized?

LO7-2 2. At what level of labor input in Figure 7.2 does marginal physical product
(*a*) First diminish?
(*b*) Become zero?
(*c*) Turn negative?

LO7-4 3. Suppose a company incurs the following costs: labor, $1,200; equipment, $300; and materials, $200. The company owns the building, so it doesn't have to pay the usual $900 in rent.
(*a*) What is the total accounting cost?
(*b*) What is the total economic cost?
(*c*) If the company sold the building and then leased it back, what would be the change in
  (*i*) Accounting costs?
  (*ii*) Economic costs?

LO7-2 4. Refer to the production table for jeans (Table 7.1). Suppose a firm has two sewing machines and can vary only the amount of labor input.
(*a*) Graph the production function for jeans given the two sewing machines.
(*b*) Compute and graph the marginal physical product curve.
(*c*) At what amount of labor input does the law of diminishing returns first become apparent in your graph of marginal physical product?
(*d*) Is total output still increasing when MPP begins to diminish?
(*e*) What is the value of MPP when output no longer increases?

LO7-5 5. The following table indicates the average total cost of producing varying quantities of output from three different plants:

Rate of output	10	20	30	40	50	60	70	80	90	100
Average total cost										
Small firm	$ 600	$500	$400	$500	$600	$700	$800	$900	$1,000	$1,100
Medium firm	800	650	500	350	200	300	400	500	600	700
Large firm	1,000	900	800	700	600	500	400	300	400	500

(a) Plot the ATC curves for all three firms on the graph.
(b) Which plant(s) should be used to produce 40 units?
(c) Which plant(s) should be used to produce 100 units?
(d) Are there economies of scale in these plant size choices?

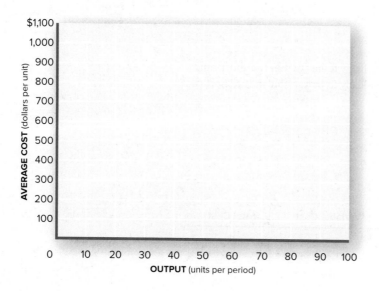

LO7-5 6. Using the information in World View "Tesla Starts Rolling Out Cars from Shanghai Gigafactory,"
(a) Calculate the average fixed cost at the Shanghai factory if the 2020 output level (= 35,000 cars annually) were maintained for 10 years.
(b) Calculate average fixed cost if Tesla ramps up output to 500,000 cars a year for 10 years.
(c) By what percent would average fixed cost decline if this higher level of output was attained?

LO7-2 7. Given the following productivity information,
(a) Calculate marginal physical product.
(b) When does marginal productivity first diminish?

Labor	Output	MP
0	0	_____
1	10	_____
2	22	_____
3	30	_____
4	36	_____
5	38	_____
6	37	_____

LO7-3 8. Table 7.2, repeated here, shows the total cost of production for producing 15 pairs of jeans per day.

TABLE 7.2

The Total Costs of Production (Total Cost of Producing 15 Pairs of Jeans per Day)

The total cost of producing a good equals the market value of all the resources used in its production. In this case, the production of 15 pairs of jeans per day requires resources worth $245.

Resource Input	×	Unit Price of Input	=	Total Cost
1 factory		$100 per day		$100
1 sewing machine		20 per day		20
1 operator		80 per day		80
1.5 bolts of denim		30 per bolt		45
Total cost				$245

(a) Which two inputs are most likely to be fixed in the short run?
(b) Which two inputs are most likely to be variable in the short run?

To produce 15 pairs of jeans, calculate:
(c) Fixed cost
(d) Variable cost
(e) Total cost
(f) Average total cost

LO7-3 9. Complete the following table:

Quantity	Fixed Cost	Variable Cost	Total Cost
0	_____	_____	100
10	_____	40	_____
20	_____	100	_____
30	100	_____	270
40	_____	260	_____

LO7-3 10. Complete the following table:

Quantity	Total Cost	Marginal Cost	Average Variable Cost	Average Total Cost
0	20	—	—	—
1	_____	10	10	_____
2	_____	_____	_____	21
3	_____	16	_____	_____
4	_____	_____	14	_____
5	100	_____	_____	_____

LO7-4 11. Kanesha is an entrepreneur and has recently opened her first coffee shop, The Coffee Cat. She pays $5,000 rent each month, $4,800 for employee payroll, and $1,200 for supplies. She was planning on selling several of her own tables and chairs on Craigslist for $1,500, but instead she brought them to The Coffee Cat. Additionally, she quit working as an accountant where she was earning $52,000 per year to open up the shop. Based on this information identify:

(a) Explicit costs.

(b) Implicit costs.

Calculate annual:

(c) Accounting cost.

(d) Economic cost.

LO7-1 12. *Decisions for Tomorrow:* Suppose the hourly wage rate is $24 in the United States and $3 in China, and productivity is 20 units per hour in the United States and 4 units per hour in China.

(a) What are per unit labor costs in the United States?

(b) What are per unit labor costs in China?

(c) If a company's goal is to minimize per unit labor costs, where would the production facility be located?

Design Credit: Shutterstock

Lars A. Niki

David A. Barnes/Alamy Stock Photo

Library of Congress Prints and Photographs Division [LC-USZ62-63968]

Andrew Resek/McGraw Hill

Jill Braaten/McGraw Hill

PART

3

MARKET STRUCTURE

Market demand curves tell us what products consumers want. And production functions tell us how much it will cost producers to supply those products. What we don't yet know is how many products will actually be supplied—or at what prices. These are *behavioral decisions,* not technological facts. Chapters 8 through 12 examine these behavioral decisions. As we'll see, the *structure* of a market—the number and size of firms in it—has a profound effect on the supply of goods and services—the quantity, quality, and price of specific goods.

CHAPTER 8

The Competitive Firm

After reading this chapter, you should know

LO8-1 How profits are computed.

LO8-2 The characteristics of perfectly competitive firms.

LO8-3 How a competitive firm maximizes profit.

LO8-4 When a firm will shut down.

LO8-5 The difference between production and investment decisions.

LO8-6 What shapes or shifts a firm's supply curve.

Apple Computer would love to raise the price of downloading music from its iTunes store. It isn't likely to do so, however, because too many other firms also offer digital downloads. If Apple raises its prices, customers might sign up with Spotify, Pandora, Amazon Music, Google Play, or some other streaming service.

Your campus bookstore may be in a better position to raise prices. On most college campuses there's only one bookstore. If the campus store increases the price of books or supplies, most of its customers (you) will have little choice but to pay the higher tab.

As we discover in this and the next few chapters, the degree of competition in product markets is a major determinant of product prices, quality, and availability. Although all firms are in business to make a profit, their profit opportunities are limited by the amount of competition they face.

This chapter begins an examination of how businesses make price and production decisions. We first explore the nature of profits and how they're computed. We then observe how one type of firm—a perfectly competitive one—can *maximize* its profits by selecting the right rate of output. The following questions are at the center of this discussion:

- What are *profits?*
- What are the unique characteristics of competitive firms?
- How much output will a competitive firm produce?

The answers to these questions will shed more light on how the *supply* of goods and services is determined in a market economy.

THE PROFIT MOTIVE

The basic incentive for producing goods and services is the expectation of profit. Owning plants and equipment isn't enough. To generate a current flow of income, one must *use* the plants and equipment to produce and sell goods.

Profit is the difference between a firm's sales revenues and its total costs. It's the residual that the owners of a business receive. That profit residual may flow to the sole owner of a corner grocery store, or to the group of stockholders who collectively own a large corporation. In either case, it's the quest for profit that motivates people to own and operate a business (or a piece thereof).

Other Motivations

Profit isn't the only thing that motivates producers. Like the rest of us, producers also worry about social status and crave recognition. People who need to feel important, to control others, or to demonstrate achievement are likely candidates for running a business. Many small businesses are maintained by people who gave up 40-hour weeks, $50,000 incomes, and a sense of alienation in exchange for 80-hour weeks, $45,000 incomes, and a sense of identity and control.

In large corporations, the profit motive may lie even deeper below the surface. Stockholders (the owners) of large corporations rarely visit corporate headquarters. The people who manage the corporation's day-to-day business may have little or no stock in the company. Such nonowner managers may be more interested in their own jobs, salaries, and self-preservation than in the profits that accrue to the stockholding owners. If profits suffer, however, the corporation may start looking for new managers. The "bottom line" for virtually all businesses is the level of profits.

profit: The difference between total revenue and total cost.

Is the Profit Motive Bad?

If it weren't possible to make a profit, few people would choose to supply goods and services. Yet the general public remains suspicious of the profit motive. A Roper survey of adults discovered that one out of four Americans think the profit motive is "bad." An even higher percentage believes that the profit motive results in *inferior* products at inflated prices, As the accompanying Front Page Economics "Too Much Profit?" confirms, nearly 6 out of 10 Americans agree that corporate profits are too high.

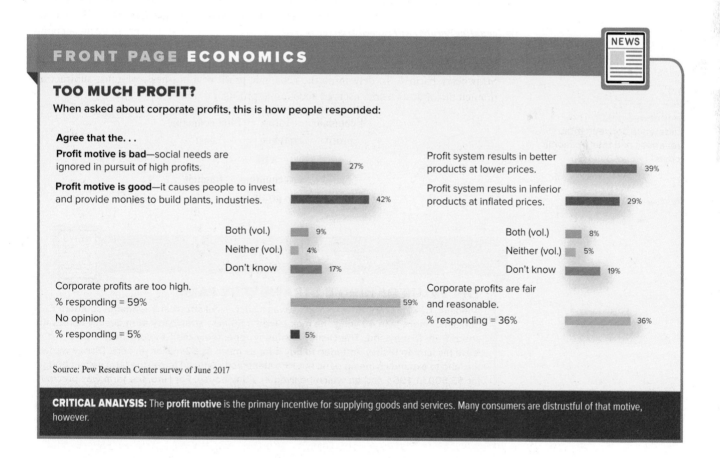

FRONT PAGE ECONOMICS

TOO MUCH PROFIT?

When asked about corporate profits, this is how people responded:

Agree that the. . .

Profit motive is bad—social needs are ignored in pursuit of high profits. 27%

Profit motive is good—it causes people to invest and provide monies to build plants, industries. 42%

Both (vol.) 9%
Neither (vol.) 4%
Don't know 17%

Corporate profits are too high.
% responding = 59% 59%
No opinion
% responding = 5% 5%

Profit system results in better products at lower prices. 39%

Profit system results in inferior products at inflated prices. 29%

Both (vol.) 8%
Neither (vol.) 5%
Don't know 19%

Corporate profits are fair and reasonable.
% responding = 36% 36%

Source: Pew Research Center survey of June 2017

CRITICAL ANALYSIS: The **profit motive** is the primary incentive for supplying goods and services. Many consumers are distrustful of that motive, however.

As we'll see, the profit motive *can* induce business firms to pollute the environment, restrict competition, or maintain unsafe working conditions. However, *the profit motive also encourages businesses to produce the goods and services consumers desire, at prices they're willing to pay.* The profit motive, in fact, moves the "invisible hand" that Adam Smith said orchestrates market outcomes.

ECONOMIC VS. ACCOUNTING PROFITS

Although profits might be a necessary inducement for producers, most consumers feel that profits are too high. And that may be so in many cases. But most consumers have no idea how much profit U.S. businesses actually make. Public *perceptions* of profit are seven or eight times higher than actual profits. The typical consumer believes that 36 cents of every sales dollar goes to profits. In reality, average profit per sales dollar is closer to 5 cents.

Faulty perceptions of profits aren't confined to the general public. As surprising as it might seem, most businesses also measure their profits incorrectly.

Economic Profits

Everyone agrees that *profit represents the difference between total revenues and total costs.* Where people part ways is over the decision of what to include in total costs. Recall from Chapter 7 how economists compute costs. **Economic cost** refers to the value of *all* resources used in production, whether or not they receive an explicit payment. By contrast, most businesses count only **explicit costs**—that is, those they actually write checks for. They typically don't take into account the **implicit costs** of the labor or land and buildings they might own. As a result, they understate costs.

If businesses (and their accountants) understate true costs, they'll overstate true profits. Part of the accounting "profit" will really be compensation to unpaid land, labor, or capital used in the production process. ***Whenever economic costs exceed explicit costs, observed (accounting) profits will exceed true (economic) profits.*** Indeed, what appears to be an accounting profit may actually disguise an economic loss, as illustrated by the Fujishige strawberry farm once located right next to Disneyland (see Front Page Economics "The Value of Hiro's Strawberry Farm"). To determine the **economic profit** of a business, we must subtract all implicit factor costs from observed accounting profits:

economic cost: The value of all resources used to produce a good or service; opportunity cost.

explicit costs: A payment made for the use of a resource.

implicit cost: The value of resources used, for which no direct payment is made.

economic profit: The difference between total revenues and total economic costs.

$$\begin{aligned} \text{Economic profit} &= \text{Total revenue} - \text{Total economic cost} \\ &\text{OR} \\ &= \text{Accounting profit} - \text{Implicit costs} \end{aligned}$$

FRONT PAGE ECONOMICS

THE VALUE OF HIRO'S STRAWBERRY FARM

Anaheim, Ca—Hiroshi ("Hiro") Fujishige was a successful strawberry farmer in southern California. For more than 40 years, he maintained a 56-acre strawberry farm directly across the street from Disneyland. The Disney company repeatedly tried to convince Hiro to sell or lease his farm to Disney—offering to buy it for as much as $2 million an acre. Disney wanted the land to expand its theme park, but Hiro steadfastly refused to sell the farm he had bought for $3,500 in 1954 and on which he lived in a tiny house. For Hiro, the farm was precious, not for the profits it generated but for the security and freedom it provided. Having lost an earlier farm during the World War II internments of Japanese citizens, Hiro vowed not to give up another farm—at any price. "As long as I can make a profit from strawberries," he said, "I'll keep growing them." Which he did until he died in 1998.

Source: News reports, September 1998.

CRITICAL ANALYSIS: Mr. Fujishige's *accounting* profits were in stark contrast to his *economic* losses. The **implicit costs** of his time and land were enormous. After his death, Disney purchased the land for nearly $70 million and built the California Adventure Park.

Total (gross) revenues per month	$27,000
less explicit costs:	
Cost of merchandise sold	$17,000
Wages to cashier, stock, and delivery help	2,500
Rent and utilities	800
Taxes	700
Total explicit costs	$21,000
Accounting profit (revenue minus explicit costs)	$ 6,000
less implicit costs:	
Wages of owner–manager, 300 hours @ $10 per hour	$ 3,000
Return on inventory investment, 10% per year on $120,000	1,000
Total implicit costs	$ 4,000
Economic profit (revenue minus *all* costs)	$ 2,000

TABLE 8.1

The Computation of Economic Profit

To calculate economic profit, we must take account of *all* costs of production. The economic costs of production include the implicit (opportunity) costs of the labor and capital a producer contributes to the production process. The accounting profits of a business take into account only explicit costs paid by the owner. Reported (accounting) profits will exceed economic profits whenever implicit costs are ignored.

Suppose, for example, that Table 8.1 accurately summarizes the revenues and costs associated with a local drugstore. Monthly sales revenues amount to $27,000. Explicit costs paid by the owner-manager include the cost of merchandise bought from producers for resale to consumers ($17,000), wages to the employees of the drugstore, rent and utilities paid to the landlord, and local sales and business taxes. When all these *explicit* costs are subtracted from total revenue, we're left with an *accounting profit* of $6,000 per month.

The owner-manager of the drugstore may be quite pleased with an accounting profit of $6,000 per month. He's working hard for this income, however. To keep his store running, the owner-manager is working 10 hours per day, 7 days a week. This adds up to 300 hours of labor per month. Were he to work this hard for someone else, his labor would be compensated explicitly—with a paycheck. Although he doesn't choose to pay himself this way, his labor still represents a real resource cost. To compute *economic* profit, we must subtract this implicit cost from the drugstore's accounting profits. Suppose that the owner could earn $10 per hour in the best alternative job. Multiplying this wage rate ($10) by the number of hours he works in the drugstore (300), we see that the implicit cost of his labor is $3,000 per month.

The owner has also used his savings to purchase inventory for the store. He purchased the goods on his shelves for $120,000. If he had invested his savings in some other business, he could have earned a return of 10 percent per year. This forgone return represents a real cost. In this case, the implicit return (opportunity cost) on his capital investment amounts to $12,000 per year (10 percent × $120,000), or $1,000 per month.

To calculate the *economic* profit this drugstore generates, we count both explicit and implicit costs. Hence, we must subtract all implicit factor payments (costs) from reported profits. The residual in this case amounts to $2,000 per month. That's the drugstore's *economic* profit.

Note that when we compute the drugstore's economic profit, we deduct the opportunity cost of the owner's capital. Specifically, we assumed that his funds would have reaped a 10 percent return somewhere else. In effect, we've assumed that a "normal" rate of return is 10 percent. This **normal profit** (the opportunity cost of capital) is an economic cost. Rather than investing in a drugstore, the owner could have earned a 10 percent return on his funds by investing in a fast-food franchise, a music store, a steel plant, or some other production activity. By choosing to invest in a drugstore instead, the owner was seeking a *higher* return on his funds—more than he could have obtained elsewhere. In other words, *economic profits represent something over and above "normal profits."*

Our treatment of "normal" returns as an economic cost leads to a startling conclusion: On average, economic profits are zero. Only firms that reap *above-average* returns can claim economic profits. This seemingly strange perspective on profits emphasizes the opportunity costs of all economic activities. *A productive activity reaps an economic profit only if it earns more than its opportunity cost.*

normal profit: The opportunity cost of capital; zero economic profit.

Entrepreneurship

Naturally, everyone in business wants to earn an economic profit. But relatively few people can stay ahead of the pack. To earn economic profits, a business must see opportunities that others have missed, discover new products, find new and better methods of production, or take above-average risks. In fact, economic profits are often regarded as a reward to entrepreneurship, the ability and willingness to take risks, to organize factors of production, and to produce something society desires.

Consider the local drugstore again. People in the neighborhood clearly want such a drugstore, as evidenced by its substantial sales revenue. But why should anyone go to the trouble and risk of starting and maintaining one? We noted that the owner–manager *could* earn $3,000 in wages by accepting a regular job plus $1,000 per month in returns on capital by investing in an "average" business. Why should he take on the added responsibilities and risk of owning and operating his own drugstore?

The inducement to take on the added responsibilities of owning and operating a business is the potential for economic profit, the extra income over and above normal factor payments. In the case of the drugstore owner, this extra income is the economic profit of $2,000 (Table 8.1). In the absence of such additional compensation, few people would want to make the extra effort required.

Risk

Don't forget, however, that the *potential* for profit is not a *guaranty* of profit. Quite the contrary. Substantial risks are attached to starting and operating a business. Tens of thousands of businesses fail every year, and still more suffer economic losses (see Front Page Economics "Risky Business: Start-ups Face High Failure Rates"). From this perspective, profit also represents compensation for the risks incurred in owning or operating a business.

FRONT PAGE ECONOMICS

RISKY BUSINESS: START-UPS FACE HIGH FAILURE RATES

Many people have a glorified view of owning their own business some day. What they don't realize is how many new businesses fail. According to the U.S. Bureau of Labor Statistics, the failure rates are quite high:

Percent of start-ups that fail		
	In first year	20 percent
	Within 5 years	50 percent
	Within 10 years	65 percent

In other words, only 35 percent of new firms survive as long as 10 years. And even those survivors might not be making a profit. Owning a business is not a guarantee for getting rich!

Source: U.S. Bureau of Labor Statistics, Business Employment Dynamics Program (2018).

CRITICAL ANALYSIS: Businesses earn a profit only if they sell products consumers want at prices that exceed costs. Because most start-up businesses fail to do this, entrepreneurship is **risky.**

MARKET STRUCTURE

monopoly: A firm that produces the entire market supply of a particular good or service.

Not all businesses have an equal opportunity to earn an economic profit. The opportunity for profit may be limited by the *structure* of the industry in which the firm is engaged. One of the reasons Google is such a profitable company is that it has long held a near **monopoly** on search engines. As the principal supplier of search engine software, Google can raise software prices without losing many customers. T-shirt shops, by contrast, have to worry about all the other stores that sell similar products in the area (see Front Page Economics "Too Many Sellers: The Woes of T-Shirt Shops"). Faced with so much competition, the owner of a T-shirt shop doesn't have the power to raise prices or accumulate economic profits.

FRONT PAGE ECONOMICS

TOO MANY SELLERS: THE WOES OF T-SHIRT SHOPS

Selling T-shirts is easy. People love T-shirts, especially with custom designs or logos of a special event or favorite band, product, or sports team. Consumers spend at least $15 billion a year on them. Moreover, the inventory is easy to store, doesn't spoil, and is compact. On the surface, a great business.

But there's a catch—everybody and his brother sells T-shirts. Every beach resort has dozens of T-shirt shops. And they sprout like weeds at every major sporting or concert venue. And then there are all the online sites that offer

Mark C. Burnett/McGraw Hill

custom designs and quick delivery. So, the competition is intense. This makes it near impossible for any T-shirt shop to raise the price of its T-shirts, much less hold on to profits. The owner of a T-shirt shop in South Padre Island, Texas, lamented, "Every day you have to compete with other shops. And if you invent something new, they will copy you."

CRITICAL ANALYSIS: The ability to earn a profit depends on how many other firms offer similar products. A **perfectly competitive firm,** facing numerous rivals, has difficulty maintaining prices or profits.

Figure 8.1 illustrates various **market structures.** At one extreme is the monopoly structure in which only one firm produces the entire supply of the good. At the other extreme is **perfect competition.** In perfect competition, a great many firms supply the same good.

There are relatively few monopolies or perfectly competitive firms in the real world. Most of the 30 million businesses in the United States fall between these extremes. They're more accurately characterized by gradations of *imperfect* competition—markets in which competition exists, but individual firms still retain some discretionary power over prices. In a *duopoly,* two firms supply the entire market. In an *oligopoly,* like credit card services, a handful of firms (Visa, MasterCard, American Express) dominate. In *monopolistic competition,* like fast-food restaurants, there are enough firms to ensure some competition, but not so many

market structure: The number and relative size of firms in an industry.

perfect competition: A market in which no buyer or seller has market power.

FIGURE 8.1

Market Structures

The number and relative size of firms producing a good vary across industries. Market structures range from perfect competition (a great many firms producing the same good) to monopoly (only one firm). Most real-world firms are along the continuum of *imperfect* competition. Included in that range are duopoly (two firms), oligopoly (a few firms), and monopolistic competition (many firms).

as to preclude some limited monopoly-type power. We examine all these market structures in later chapters, after we establish the nature of perfect competition.

THE NATURE OF PERFECT COMPETITION

Industries can be classified by their structure—the number and relative size of the firms producing a specific good. As we'll see, the structure of an industry has a profound effect on market outcomes.

Structure

A perfectly competitive industry has several distinguishing characteristics, including

- *Many firms*—lots of firms are competing for consumer purchases.
- *Identical products*—the products of the different firms are identical, or nearly so.
- *Low entry barriers*—it's relatively easy to get into the business.

The T-shirt business has all these traits, which is why store owners have a hard time maintaining profits (see Front Page Economics "Too Many Sellers: The Woes of T-Shirt Shops").

Price Takers

Because they always have to contend with a lot of competition, T-shirt shops can't increase profits by raising T-shirt prices. More than 1 billion T-shirts are sold in the United States each year by tens of thousands of retail outlets. In such a competitive industry, the many individual firms that make up the industry are all *price takers:* They take the price the market sets. A competitive firm can sell all its output at the prevailing market price. If it boosts its price above that level, consumers will shop elsewhere. In this sense, a perfectly competitive firm has no **market power**—no ability to control the market price for the good it sells.

> **market power:** The ability to alter the market price of a good or service.

At first glance, it might appear that all firms have market power. After all, who's to stop a T-shirt shop from raising prices? The important concept here, however, is *market* price—that is, the price at which goods are actually sold. If one shop raises its price to $15 and 40 other shops sell the same T-shirts for $10, it won't sell many shirts, and maybe none at all.

You may confront the same problem if you purchase a bound copy of this book and then try to sell it at the end of the semester. You might want to resell this textbook for $180. But you'll discover that the bookstore won't buy it at that price. With many other students offering to sell their books, the bookstore knows it doesn't have to pay the $180 you're asking. Because you don't have any market power, you have to accept the going price if you want to sell this book. You are a *price taker* in this market.

The same kind of powerlessness is characteristic of the small wheat farmer. Like any producer, the lone wheat farmer can increase or reduce his rate of output by making alternative production decisions. But his decision won't affect the market price of wheat.

Even the largest U.S. wheat farmers can't change the market price of wheat. The largest wheat farm produces nearly 100,000 bushels of wheat per year. But *2 billion* bushels of wheat are brought to market every year, so another 100,000 bushels simply won't be noticed. In other words, ***the output of the lone farmer is so small relative to the market supply that it has no significant effect on the total quantity or price in the market.***

> **competitive firm:** A firm without market power, with no ability to alter the market price of the goods it produces.

A distinguishing characteristic of *powerless* firms is that, individually, they can sell all the output they produce at the prevailing market price. We call all such producers **competitive firms;** they have no independent influence on market prices. *A perfectly competitive firm is one whose output is so small in relation to market volume that its output decisions have no perceptible impact on price.*

Market Demand Curves vs. Firm Demand Curves

It's important to distinguish between the market demand curve and the demand curve confronting a particular firm. T-shirt shops don't contradict the law of demand. The quantity of T-shirts purchased in the market still depends on T-shirt prices. That is, the *market* demand curve for T-shirts

(a) The T-shirt market

(b) Demand facing one shop

FIGURE 8.2

Market vs. Firm Demand

Consumer demand for any product is downward-sloping. The equilibrium price (p_e) of T-shirts is established by the intersection of *market* demand and *market* supply, as in the graph on the left. This market-established price is the only one at which an individual shop can sell T-shirts. If the shop owner asks a higher price (e.g., p_i in the graph on the right), no one will buy his shirts because they can buy identical T-shirts from other shops at p_e. But he can sell all his shirts at the market-set equilibrium price. The shop owner thus confronts a horizontal demand curve for his own output. (Notice the difference in market and individual shop quantities on the horizontal axes of the two graphs.)

is still downward-sloping. A single T-shirt shop faces a *horizontal* demand curve only because its share of the market is so small that changes in its output don't disturb market equilibrium.

Collectively, though, individual firms do count. If all 40 of the T-shirt shops on South Padre Island (see Front Page Economics "Too Many Sellers: The Woes of T-Shirt Shops") were to increase shirt production at the same time, the market equilibrium would be disturbed. That is, a competitive market composed of individually powerless producers still sees a lot of action. The power here resides in the collective action of all the producers, however, not in the individual action of any one. Were T-shirt production to increase so abruptly, the shirts could be sold only at lower prices, in accordance with the downward-sloping nature of the *market* demand curve. Figure 8.2 illustrates the distinction between the actions of a single producer and those of the market. Notice that

- *The market demand curve for a product is always downward-sloping (law of demand).*
- *The demand curve confronting a perfectly competitive firm is horizontal.*

THE PRODUCTION DECISION

A startling implication of Figure 8.2 is that ***perfectly competitive firms don't make pricing decisions;*** the *market* sets the prevailing price. All competitive firms do is *respond* to that market price. As price takers, they have only one decision to make: how much to produce. Choosing a rate of output is a firm's **production decision.** Should it produce all the output it can? Or should it produce at less than capacity?

production decision: The selection of the short-run rate of output (with existing plants and equipment).

Output and Revenues

In searching for the most desirable rate of output, focus on the distinction between total *revenue* and total *profit.* **Total revenue** is the price of the good multiplied by the quantity sold:

$$\text{Total revenue} = \text{Price} \times \text{Quantity}$$

Because a competitive firm can sell all its output at the market price (p_e), total revenue is a simple multiple of p_e. The total revenue of a T-shirt shop, for example, is the price of shirts (p_e)

total revenue: The price of a product multiplied by the quantity sold in a given time period: $p \times q$.

FIGURE 8.3
Total Revenue

Because a competitive firm can sell all its output at the prevailing price, its total revenue curve is linear. In this case, the market (equilibrium) price of T-shirts is assumed to be $8. Hence, a shop's total revenue is equal to $8 multiplied by quantity sold. Total revenue is maximized at capacity output.

Price (per Shirt)	×	Quantity (Shirts per Day)	=	Total Revenue
$8		1		$ 8
8		2		16
8		3		24
8		4		32
8		5		40
8		6		48
8		7		56
8		8		64
8		9		72

short run: The period in which the quantity (and quality) of some inputs can't be changed.

fixed costs: Costs of production that don't change when the rate of output is altered, such as the cost of basic plants and equipment.

variable costs: Costs of production that change when the rate of output is altered, such as labor and material costs.

multiplied by the quantity sold. Figure 8.3 shows the total revenue curve that results from this multiplication. *Note that the total revenue curve of a perfectly competitive firm is an upward-sloping straight line with a slope equal to p_e.*

If a competitive firm wanted to maximize its total *revenue,* its production decision would be simple: It would always produce at capacity. Life isn't that simple, however; *the firm's goal is to maximize profits, not revenues.*

Output and Costs

To maximize profits, a firm must consider how increased production will affect *costs* as well as *revenues.* How do costs vary with the rate of output?

As we observed in Chapter 7, producers are saddled with certain costs in the **short run.** A T-shirt shop has to pay the rent every month, no matter how few shirts it sells. The Low-Rider Jeans Corporation in Chapter 7 had to pay the rent on its factory and lease payments on its sewing machine. These **fixed costs** are incurred even if no output is produced. Once a firm starts producing output, it incurs **variable costs** as well.

Because profits depend on the *difference* between revenues and costs, the costs of added output will determine how much profit a producer can make. Figure 8.4 illustrates a typical

FIGURE 8.4
Total Cost

Total cost increases with output. The rate of increase isn't steady, however. Typically, the rate of cost increase slows initially, then speeds up. After point *z,* diminishing returns (rising marginal costs) cause accelerating costs. These accelerating costs limit the profit potential of increased output.

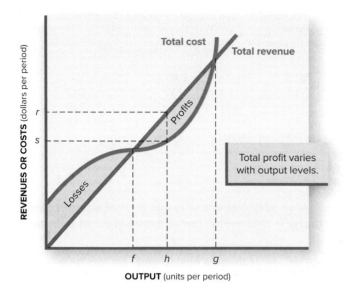

FIGURE 8.5
Total Profit

Profit is the *difference* between total revenue and total cost. It is represented as the vertical distance between the total revenue curve and the total cost curve. At output *h,* profit equals *r* minus *s.* The objective is to find the unique rate of output that *maximizes* profit.

total cost curve. *Total costs increase as output expands, but the rate of cost increase varies.* Hence, the total cost curve is *not* linear. At first total costs rise slowly (notice the gradually declining slope until point *z*), then they increase more quickly (the rising slope after point *z*). This S-shaped curve reflects the *law of diminishing returns.* As we first observed in Chapter 7, **marginal costs (MC)** often decline in the early stages of production and then increase as the available plants and equipment are used more intensively. These changes in marginal cost cause *total* costs to rise slowly at first, and then to pick up speed as output increases.

marginal cost (MC): The increase in total cost associated with a one-unit increase in production.

You may suspect by now that the road to profits is not an easy one. It entails comparing ever-changing revenues with ever-changing costs. Figure 8.5 helps simplify the problem by bringing together typical total revenue and total cost curves. The total revenue line (in orange) is linear because the price is constant. The total cost line, however, is sort of S-shaped, rising slowly at first, then much faster as marginal costs accelerate.

Our focus is on the *vertical distance* between the total revenue and cost curves. That vertical distance represents the *difference* between revenues and costs. Total costs in this case exceed total revenue at low rates of output (below *f*) as well as at very high rates (above *g*). The firm is profitable only at output rates between *f* and *g*.

Although all rates of output between *f* and *g* are profitable, they aren't *equally* profitable. A quick glance at Figure 8.5 confirms that the vertical distance between total revenue and total cost varies considerably within that range. *The primary objective of the producer is to find that one particular rate of output that maximizes total profits.* With a ruler, we could find it in Figure 8.5 by measuring the distance between the revenue and cost curves at all rates of output. In the real world, most producers need more practical guides to profit maximization.

PROFIT-MAXIMIZING RULE

The best single rule for maximizing profits in the short run is straightforward: Never produce a unit of output that costs more than it brings in. By following this simple rule, a producer is likely to make the right production decision. We will see how this rule works by looking first at the revenue side of production ("what it brings in"), then at the cost side ("what it costs").

Marginal Revenue = Price

In searching for the most profitable rate of output, we need to know what an additional unit of output will bring in—that is, how much it adds to the total revenue of the firm. In general,

TABLE 8.2

Total and Marginal Revenue

Marginal revenue (MR) is the *change* in total revenue associated with the sale of one more unit of output. A third bushel increases total revenue from $26 to $39; MR equals $13. If the price is constant (at $13 here), marginal revenue equals price.

Quantity Sold (Bushels per Day)	×	Price (per Bushel)	=	Total Revenue (per Day)	Marginal Revenue (per Bushel)
0	×	$13	=	$ 0	—
1	×	13	=	13	$13
2	×	13	=	26	13
3	×	13	=	39	13
4	×	13	=	52	13

---

marginal revenue (MR): The change in total revenue that results from a one-unit increase in the quantity sold.

---

the contribution to total revenue of an additional unit of output is called **marginal revenue (MR).** Marginal revenue is the *change* in total revenue that occurs when output is increased by one unit:

$$\text{Marginal revenue} = \frac{\text{Change in total revenue}}{\text{Change in output}}$$

To calculate marginal revenue, we compare the total revenues received before and after a one-unit increase in the rate of production; the *difference* between the two totals equals marginal revenue.

When the price of a product is constant, it's easy to compute marginal revenue. Suppose we're operating a catfish farm. Our product is catfish, sold at wholesale at the prevailing price of $13 per bushel. In this case, a one-unit increase in sales (one more bushel) increases total revenue by $13. As illustrated in Table 8.2, as long as the price of a product is constant, price and marginal revenue are the same. Hence, *for perfectly competitive firms, price equals marginal revenue.*

Marginal Cost

Keep in mind why we're breeding and selling catfish. Our goal is not to maximize *revenues* but to maximize *profits.* To gauge profits, we need to know not only the price of fish but also how much each bushel costs to produce. As we saw in Chapter 7, the added cost of producing one more unit of a good is its *marginal cost.* Figure 8.6 summarizes the marginal costs associated with the production of catfish.

The production process for catfish farming is wonderfully simple. The factory is a pond; the rate of production is the number of fish harvested from the pond per day. A farmer can alter the rate of production at will, up to the breeding capacity of the pond. As Calvin Jones, a former schoolteacher now working on a Mississippi catfish farm, says, "You raise fish. You get them out of the pond and you sell them. That's pretty much all you do. There's no genius to it."[1]

Assume that the *fixed* costs of the pond are $10 per day. The fixed costs include the rental value of the pond and the cost of electricity for keeping the pond oxygenated so the fish can breathe. These fixed costs must be paid, no matter how many fish the farmer harvests.

To harvest catfish from the pond, the farmer must incur additional costs. Labor is needed to net and sort the fish. The cost of labor is *variable,* depending on how much output the farmer decides to produce. If no fish are harvested, no variable costs are incurred.

The *marginal costs* of harvesting are the additional costs incurred to harvest *one* more basket of fish. Generally, we expect marginal costs to rise as the rate of production increases. The law of diminishing returns we encountered in Chapter 7 applies to catfish farming as well. As more labor is hired, each worker has less space (pond area) and capital (access to nets, sorting trays) to work with. Accordingly, it takes a little more labor time (marginal cost) to harvest each additional fish.

Analysis: Fish farmers want to maximize profits, not the number of fish caught.

Brian J. Skerry/National Geographic Creative

[1]Shelia Byrd, "Fuel, Feed Costs Crippling US Catfish Industry," Associated Press, June 22, 2008.

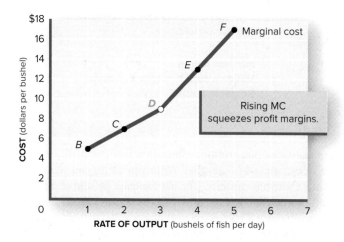

FIGURE 8.6
The Costs of Catfish Production

Marginal cost is the increase in total cost associated with a one-unit increase in production. When production expands from two to three units per day, total costs increase by $9 (from $22 to $31 per day). The marginal cost of the third bushel is therefore $9, as illustrated by point *D* in the graph and row *D* in the table.

	Rate of Output (Bushels per Day)	Total Cost (per Day)	Marginal Cost (per Day)	Average Cost (per Day)
A	0	$10	—	—
B	1	15	$ 5	$15.00
C	2	22	7	11.00
D	3	31	9	10.33
E	4	44	13	11.00
F	5	61	17	12.20

Figure 8.6 illustrates these marginal costs. Notice how the MC rises as the rate of output increases. At the output rate of 4 bushels per day (point *E*), marginal cost is $13. Hence, the fourth bushel *increases* total costs by $13. The fifth bushel is even more expensive, with a marginal cost of $17.

Profit-Maximizing Rate of Output

We're now in a position to make a production decision. The rule about never producing anything that adds more to cost than it brings in can now be stated in more technical terms. Because price equals marginal revenue for competitive firms, we can base the production decision on a comparison of *price* and marginal cost. *There are only three possible scenarios for MC and price:*

- **MC > p.** We don't want to produce an additional unit of output if its MC exceeds its price. If MC exceeds price, we're spending more to produce that extra unit than we're getting back: Total profits will decline if we produce it.
- **p > MC.** The opposite is true when price exceeds MC. If an extra unit brings in more revenue than it costs to produce, it is *adding* to total profit. Total profits must increase in this case. Hence, a competitive firm wants to expand the rate of production whenever price exceeds MC.
- **p = MC.** Because we want to expand output when price exceeds MC and contract output if price is less than MC, the profit-maximizing rate of output is easily found. *For perfectly competitive firms, profits are maximized at the rate of output where price equals marginal cost.* The implications of this **profit maximization rule** are summarized in Table 8.3.

profit-maximization rule: Produce at that rate of output where marginal revenue equals marginal cost.

TABLE 8.3

Short-Run Profit Maximization Rules for Competitive Firm

The relationship between price and marginal cost dictates short-run production decisions. For competitive firms, profits are maximized at that rate of output where price = MC.

Price Level	Production Decision
Price > MC	Increase output
Price = MC	Maintain output (profits maximized)
Price < MC	Decrease output

Figure 8.7 illustrates the application of our profit maximization rule in catfish farming. The prevailing wholesale price of catfish is $13 a bushel. At this price we can sell all the catfish we can produce, up to our short-run capacity. The catfish can't be sold at a higher price because lots of farmers raise catfish and sell them for $13 (see Front Page Economics "The Lure of Catfish"). If we try to charge a higher price, consumers will buy their fish from other vendors. Hence, we confront a horizontal demand curve at the price of $13.

The costs of producing catfish were examined in Figure 8.6. The key concept illustrated here is marginal cost. The MC curve slopes upward in a conventional fashion.

Figure 8.7 also depicts the total revenues, costs, and profits of alternative production rates. Study the table first. Notice that the firm loses $10 per day if it produces no fish (row A). At zero output, total revenue is zero ($p \times q = 0$). However, the firm must still contend with fixed costs of $10 per day. Total profit—total revenue minus total cost—is therefore *minus* $10; the firm incurs a loss.

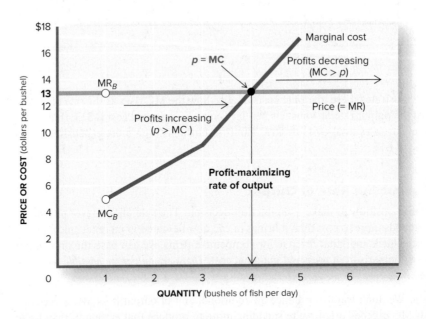

FIGURE 8.7

Maximization of Profits for a Competitive Firm

A competitive firm maximizes total profit at the output rate where MC = p. If MC is less than price, the firm can increase profits by producing more. If MC exceeds price, the firm should reduce output. In this case, profit maximization occurs at an output of 4 bushels per day.

	(1) Number of Bushels (per Day)	(2) Price	(3) Total Revenue	−	(4) Total Cost	=	(5) Total Profit	(6) Marginal Revenue	(7) Marginal Cost
A	0	$13	$ 0		$10		−$10	—	—
B	1	13	13		15		− 2	$13	$ 5
C	2	13	26		22		+ 4	13	7
D	3	13	39		31		+ 8	13	9
E	4	13	52		44		+ 8	13	13
F	5	13	65		61		+ 4	13	17

FRONT PAGE ECONOMICS

THE LURE OF CATFISH

Row-crop farmers throughout the South are taking a liking to catfish. Rising prices for catfish, combined with falling feed prices, have made the lure of catfish farming irresistible. Crop farmers are building ponds, buying aeration equipment, and breeding catfish in record numbers. Production has doubled in the last 15 years—to 340 million pounds this year—and looks to keep increasing as farmers shift from row crops to catfish.

Steve Hollingsworth, a Greensboro, Alabama, farmer, now has ten ponds, each holding about 100,000 fish. He spends $18,000 a week on feed for the 1 million fish in his ponds. But he says the business is good; he takes in about $60,000 a week in sales. Crop farmers in Alabama, Mississippi, Arkansas, and Louisiana are taking the bait.

Source: Media reports, 1993.

CRITICAL ANALYSIS: People go into a competitive business like catfish farming to earn a profit. Once in business, they try to maximize total profits by **equating price and marginal cost.**

Row *B* of the table shows how this loss is reduced when 1 bushel of fish is harvested per day. The production and sale of 1 bushel per day bring in $13 of total revenue (column 3). The total cost of producing 1 bushel per day is $15 (column 4). Hence, the total loss at an output rate of 1 bushel per day is $2 (column 5). This may not be what we hoped for, but it's certainly better than the $10 loss incurred at zero output.

***p* > MC: Expand.** The superiority of harvesting 1 bushel per day rather than none is also evident in columns 6 and 7 of row *B*. The first bushel produced has a *marginal revenue* of $13. Its *marginal cost* is only $5. Hence, it brings in more added revenue than it adds to costs. Under these circumstances—whenever price exceeds MC—output should definitely be expanded. That is one of the decision rules summarized earlier in Table 8.3.

The excess of price over MC for the first unit of output is also illustrated by the graph in Figure 8.7. Point MR_B ($13) lies above MC_B ($5); the *difference* between these two points measures the contribution that the first bushel makes to the total profits of the firm. In this case, that contribution equals $13 − $5 = $8, and production losses are reduced by that amount when the rate of output is increased from zero to 1 bushel per day.

As long as price exceeds MC, additional output increases total profit. Notice what happens to profits when the rate of output is increased from 1 to 2 bushels per day (row *C*). The price (MR) of the second bushel is $13; its MC is $7. Therefore, it *adds* $6 to total profits. Instead of losing $2 per day, the firm is now making a profit of $4 per day.

The firm can make even more profits by expanding the rate of output further. The marginal revenue of the third bushel is $13; its marginal cost is $9 (row *D* of the table). Therefore, the third bushel makes a $4 contribution to profits.

MC = *p*: Max Profit. This firm will never make huge profits. For the fourth unit of output, both price and MC equal $13. It doesn't contribute to total profits, and it doesn't subtract from them. The fourth unit of output represents the highest rate of output the firm desires. *At the rate of output where price = MC, total profits of the firm are maximized.*[2]

---

[2]In this case, profits are the same at output levels of 3 and 4 bushels. Given the choice between the two levels, most firms will choose the higher level. By producing the extra unit of output, the firm increases its customer base. This not only denies rival firms an additional sale but also provides some additional cushion when the economy slumps. Also, corporate size may connote both prestige and power. In any case, the higher output level defines the *limit* to maximum profit production.

MC > p: Contract. Notice what happens if we expand output beyond 4 bushels per day. The price of the fifth bushel is still $13, but its MC is $17. The fifth bushel adds more to costs than to revenue. If we produce that fifth bushel, total profit will decline by $4. In Figure 8.7 the MC curve lies above the price line at all output levels in excess of 4. The lesson here is clear: *Output should not be increased if MC exceeds price.*

The correct production decision—the profit-maximizing decision—is shown in Figure 8.7 by the intersection of the price and MC curves. At this intersection, price equals MC and profits are maximized. If we produced less, we'd be giving up potential profits. If we produced more, total profits would also fall (review Table 8.3).

Adding Up Profits . . .

To reach the right production decision, we've relied on *marginal* revenues and costs. Having found the desired rate of output, however, we may want to take a closer look at the profits we are accumulating. Figure 8.8 provides two different ways of viewing our success.

with Total Revenue and Total Cost. The first view focuses on *total* revenues and *total* costs. Total profits are represented in Figure 8.8*a* by the vertical distance between the total revenue and total cost curves. This is a straightforward interpretation of our definition of total profits:

$$\text{Total profits} = \text{TR} - \text{TC}$$

The vertical distance between the TR and TC curves is maximized at the output of 4 bushels per day.

with Price and Average Cost. A second view of the same profits focuses on *average* costs and price. Total profit is equal to *average* profit per unit multiplied by the number of units produced. Profit *per unit,* in turn, is equal to price *minus* average total cost:

$$\text{Profit per unit} = p - \text{ATC}$$

The price of catfish is illustrated in Figure 8.8*b* by the horizontal price line at $13. The average total cost of producing catfish is shown by the ATC curve. Like the ATC curve we encountered in Chapter 7, this one has a U shape. The *difference* between price and average cost—profit per unit—is illustrated by the vertical distance between the price and ATC curves. At 4 bushels per day, for example, profit per unit equals $13 − $11 = $2.

(a) Computing profits with total revenue and total cost

(b) Computing profits with price and average total cost

FIGURE 8.8
Alternative Views of Total Profit

Total profit can be computed as TR − TC, as in part *a*. Or it can be computed as profit *per unit* (*p* − ATC) multiplied by the quantity sold. This is illustrated in part *b* by the shaded rectangle. To find the profit-maximizing output, we could use either of these graphs or just the price and MC curves in Figure 8.7.

FIGURE 8.9
Different Goals

Businesses seek to maximize total profits, not profit per unit or total revenue. Therefore, they pursue the short-run output rate q_b, not the output rates q_a or q_c.

To compute *total* profits, we note that

$$\text{Total profits} = \text{Profit per unit} \times \text{Quantity}$$
$$= (p - \text{ATC}) \times q$$

In this case, the 4 bushels generate a profit of $2 each, for a *total* profit of $8 per day. *Total* profits are illustrated in Figure 8.8*b* by the shaded rectangle. [Recall that the area of a rectangle is equal to its height (profit per unit) multiplied by its width (the quantity sold).]

Profit per unit is not only used to compute total profits but is often also of interest in its own right. Businesspeople like to cite statistics on "markups," which are a crude index to per-unit profits. However, ***the profit-maximizing producer never seeks to maximize per-unit profits. What counts is* total *profits, not the amount of profit per unit.*** This is the old $5 ice cream problem again. You might be able to maximize profit per unit if you could sell 1 cone for $5, but you would make a lot more money if you sold 100 cones at a per-unit profit of only 50 cents each.

Similarly, ***the profit-maximizing producer has no desire to produce at that rate of output where ATC is at a minimum.*** Minimum ATC does represent least-cost production. But additional units of output, even though they raise average costs, will increase total profits. This is evident in Figure 8.8; price exceeds MC for some output to the right of minimum ATC (the bottom of the U). Therefore, total profits are increasing as we increase the rate of output beyond the point of minimum average costs. Figure 8.9 illustrates the distinctions between these different markers.

THE SHUTDOWN DECISION

The rule established for short-run profit maximization doesn't guarantee any profits. By equating price and marginal cost, the competitive producer is only assured of achieving the *optimal* output. This is the best possible rate of output for the firm, given the existing market price and the (short-run) costs of production.

But what if the best possible rate of output generates a loss? What should the producer do in this case? Keep producing output? Or shut down the factory and find something else to do?

The first instinct may be to shut down the factory to stop the flow of red ink. But this isn't necessarily the wisest course of action. It may be smarter to keep operating a money-losing operation than to shut it down.

The rationale for this seemingly ill-advised course of action resides in the fixed costs of production. ***Fixed costs must be paid even if all output ceases.*** The firm must still pay rent on the factory and equipment even if it doesn't use these inputs. That's why we call such costs "fixed."

The persistence of fixed costs casts an entirely different light on the shutdown deci-sion. Because fixed costs will have to be paid in any case, the question becomes: Which option creates greater losses? Does the firm lose more money by continuing to operate (and incurring a loss) or by shutting down (and incurring a loss equal to fixed costs)? In these terms, the answer becomes clear: *A firm should shut down only if the losses from continuing production exceed fixed costs.* This happens when total revenue is less than total *variable* cost.

Price vs. AVC

The shutdown decision can be made without explicit reference to fixed costs. Figure 8.10 shows how. The relationship to focus on is between the price of a good and its average *variable* cost.

The curves in Figure 8.10 represent the short-run costs and potential demand curves for catfish. As long as the price of catfish is $13 per bushel, the typical firm will produce 4 bushels a day, as determined by the intersection of the MC and MR (= price) curves (point *X* in part *a*). In this case, price ($13) exceeds average *total* cost ($11), and catfish farming is profitable. This is the happy situation we analyzed earlier (Figure 8.7).

The situation wouldn't look so good, however, if the market price of catfish fell to $9. Fol-lowing the rule for profit maximization, the firm would be led to point *Y* in part *b*, where MC intersects the new demand (price) curve. At this intersection, the firm would produce 3 bushels per day. But total revenues would no longer cover total costs, as can be seen from the fact that the ATC curve now lies *above* the price line. The ATC of producing 3 bushels is $10.33 (Figure 8.6); price is $9. Hence, the firm is incurring a loss of $4 per day (3 bushels at a loss of $1.33 each).

Should the firm stay in business under the circumstances? The answer is yes. Recall that the catfish farmer has already dug the pond and installed equipment at a (fixed) cost of $10 per day. The producer will have to pay these fixed costs whether or not the machinery is used. Stopping production would result in a loss amounting to $10 per day. Staying in business, even when catfish prices fall to $9 each, generates a loss of only $4 a day. In this case, *where price exceeds average variable cost but not average total cost, the profit maximization rule minimizes losses.*

FIGURE 8.10

The Firm's Shutdown Point

A firm should cease production only if total revenue is lower than total *variable* cost. The shutdown decision may be based on a comparison of price and AVC. If the price of catfish per bushel was $13, a firm would earn a profit at point *X* in part *a*.

At a price of $9 (point *Y* in part *b*), the firm is losing money (*p* is less than ATC) but is more than covering all variable costs (*p* is greater than AVC). If the price falls to $4 per bushel, as in part *c*, output should cease (*p* is less than AVC).

The Shutdown Point

If the price of catfish falls far enough, the producer may be better off ceasing production altogether. Suppose the price of catfish fell to $4 per bushel (Figure 8.10c). A price this low doesn't even cover the variable cost of producing 1 bushel per day ($5). Continued production of even 1 bushel per day would imply a total loss of $11 per day ($10 of fixed costs *plus* $1 of variable costs). Higher rates of output would lead to still greater losses. Hence, the firm should shut down production, even though that action implies a loss of $10 per day. In all cases *where price doesn't cover average variable costs at any rate of output, production should cease.* Thus, the **shutdown point** occurs where price is equal to minimum average *variable* cost. Any lower price will result in losses larger than fixed costs. In Figure 8.10, the shutdown point occurs at a price of $5, where the MC and AVC curves intersect.

shutdown point: The rate of output where price equals minimum AVC.

THE INVESTMENT DECISION

When a firm shuts down, it doesn't necessarily leave (exit) the industry. General Motors still produces cars even though it idled 5 of its plants in 2017 (see Front Page Economics "GM Shutting 5 Factories This Month"). *The shutdown decision is a short-run response.* It's based on the fixed costs of an established plant and the variable costs of operating it.

Ideally, a producer would never get into a money-losing business in the first place. Entry was based on an **investment decision** that the producer now regrets. *Investment decisions are long-run decisions,* however, and the firm now must pay for its bad luck or poor judgment. The investment decision entails the assumption of fixed costs (e.g., the lease of the factory); once the investment is made, the short-run production decision is designed to make the best possible use of those fixed inputs. The short-run profit maximization rule we've discussed applies only to this second decision; it assumes that a production unit exists. Front Page Economics "Boeing Halts 737 MAX Production" shows the contrast between production and investment decisions: Boeing *idled* its production; GM permanently *closed* its factories.

investment decision: The decision to build, buy, or lease plants and equipment; to enter or exit an industry.

long run: A period of time long enough for all inputs to be varied (no fixed costs).

FRONT PAGE ECONOMICS

BOEING HALTS 737 MAX PRODUCTION

Boeing is halting further production of the troubled 737 MAX as of January 2020. The company already has 400 new 737 MAX planes in inventory, awaiting regulatory approval to resume flying. With backorders for 5,000 planes, Boeing is sure to resume production as soon as the company gets the green light from the FAA and other regulators.

GM CLOSING 5 PLANTS

GM has moved ahead with its planned closings, shuttering 5 plants in Michigan, Ohio, Baltimore, and Canada. The closed plants were producing cars and parts that were not selling well. The closings have resulted in layoffs for 6,000 hourly workers and hundreds of white-collar employees. GM is shifting its investment focus to electric vehicles.

Source: Media reports and company announcements, December 2019–January 2020.

CRITICAL ANALYSIS: Boeing's decision to idle plants was a **short-run** *shutdown* decision; it is still in business. GM, by contrast, made a **long-run** decision to cease operations and *exit* a specific market.

The investment decision is of enormous importance to producers. The fixed costs that we've ignored in the production decision represent the producers' (or the stockholders') investment in the business. If they're going to avoid an economic loss, they have to generate at least enough revenue to recoup their investment—that is, the cost of (fixed) plants and equipment. Failure to do so will result in a net loss, despite allegiance to our profit-maximizing rule.

Whether fixed costs count, then, depends on the decision being made. For producers trying to decide how best to utilize the resources they've purchased or leased, fixed costs no longer enter the decision-making process. For producers deciding whether to enter business, sign a lease, or replace existing machinery and plants, fixed costs count very much. Businesspeople will proceed with an investment only if the *anticipated* profits are large enough to compensate for the effort and risk undertaken.

Long-Run Costs

When businesspeople make an investment decision, they confront not one set of cost figures but many. A plant not yet built can be designed for various rates of production and alternative technologies. In making long-run decisions, a producer isn't bound to one size of plant or to a particular mix of tools and machinery. In the long run, one can be flexible. In general, *a producer will want to build, buy, or lease a plant that's the most efficient for the anticipated rate of output.* This is the (dis)economy of scale phenomenon we discussed in the previous chapter. Once the right plant size is selected, the producer may proceed with the problem of short-run profit maximization. Once production is started, she can only hope that the investment decision was a good one and that a shutdown can be avoided.

DETERMINANTS OF SUPPLY

Whether the time frame is the short run or the long run, the central force in production decisions is the quest for profits. Producers will go into production—incur fixed costs—only if they see the potential for economic profits. Once in business, they'll expand the rate of output so long as profits are increasing. They'll shut down—cease production—when revenues don't at least cover variable costs (operating loss exceeds fixed costs).

Nearly anyone could make money with these principles if given complete information on costs and revenues. What renders the road to fortune less congested is the general absence of such complete information. In the real world, production decisions involve considerably more risk. People often don't know how much profit or loss they'll incur until it's too late to alter production decisions. Consequently, businesspeople are compelled to make a reasoned guess about prices and costs, then proceed. By way of summary, we can identify the major influences that will shape their short- and long-run decisions on how much output to supply to the market.

Short-Run Determinants

A competitive firm's short-run production decisions are dominated by marginal costs. Hence, the quantity of a good supplied will be affected by all forces that alter MC. Specifically, *the determinants of a firm's supply include*

- *The price of factor inputs.*
- *Technology* (the available production function).
- *Expectations* (for costs, sales, technology).
- *Taxes and subsidies.*

Each determinant affects a producer's ability and willingness to supply output at any particular price.

The price of factor inputs determines how much the producer must pay for resources used in production. Technology determines how much output the producer will get from each unit of input. Expectations are critical because they express producers' perceptions of what future costs, prices, sales, and profits are likely to be. And finally, taxes and subsidies may alter costs or the amount of profit a firm gets to keep.

The Short-Run Supply Curve. By using the familiar *ceteris paribus* assumption, we can isolate the effect of price on supply decisions. In other words, we can draw a short-run **supply curve** the same way we earlier constructed consumer demand curves. In this case, the forces we assume constant are input prices, technology, expectations, and taxes. The only variable we allow to change is the price of the product itself.

Figure 8.11 illustrates the response of quantity supplied to a change in price. Notice the critical role of marginal costs: *The marginal cost curve is the short-run supply curve for a competitive firm.* Recall our basic profit maximization rule. A competitive producer wants to supply a good only if its price exceeds its marginal cost. Hence, marginal cost defines the

supply curve: A curve describing the quantities of a good a producer is willing and able to sell (produce) at alternative prices in a given time period, *ceteris paribus.*

FIGURE 8.11

A Competitive Firm's Short-Run Supply Curve

For competitive firms, marginal cost defines the lowest price a firm will accept for a given quantity of output. In this sense, the marginal cost curve *is* the supply curve; it tells us how quantity supplied will respond to price. At $p = \$13$, the quantity supplied is 4; at $p = \$9$, the quantity supplied is 3.

Recall, however, that the firm will shut down if price falls below minimum average variable cost. The supply curve does not exist below minimum AVC (\$5 in this case).

lower limit for an "acceptable" price. A catfish farmer is willing and able to produce 4 bushels per day only if the price of a bushel is \$13 (point X). If the price of catfish dropped to \$9, the *quantity* supplied would fall to 3 (point Y). The marginal cost curve tells us what the quantity supplied would be at all other prices as well. As long as price exceeds minimum AVC (the shutdown point), the MC curve summarizes the response of a producer to price changes: It *is* the short-run supply curve of a perfectly competitive firm.

The shape of the marginal cost curve provides a basic foundation for the *law of supply*. Because marginal costs tend to rise as output expands, an increase in output makes sense only if the price of that output rises. If the price does rise, it's profitable to increase the quantity supplied.

Supply Shifts

All the forces that shape the short-run supply curve are subject to change. Factor prices change; technology changes; expectations change; and tax laws get revised. *If any determinant of supply changes, the supply curve shifts.*

An increase in wage rates, for example, would raise the marginal cost of producing catfish. This would shift the supply curve upward, making it more expensive for producers to supply larger quantities at any given price. An increase in the price of catfish feed has the same effect. Farmed catfish are fed pellets made of corn and soybean meal. Between 2010 and 2012, feed prices rose from \$350 a ton to more than \$450 a ton. This cost spike squeezed profit margins and forced catfish farmers to reduce production dramatically, as Figure 8.12 illustrates.

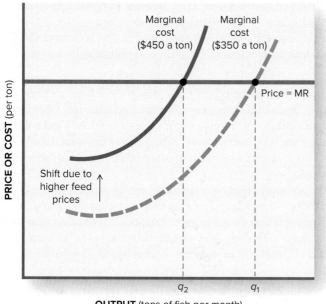

FIGURE 8.12

Rising MC Reduces Desired Output

An increase in feed prices (unit costs) shifts upward the marginal cost curve of a catfish farmer. That shift reduces the profit-maximizing rate of output from q_1 to q_2.

An improvement in technology would have the opposite effect. By increasing productivity, new technology lowers the marginal cost of producing a good. The supply curve shifts downward.

DECISIONS FOR TOMORROW

How Do Taxes Affect Business Decisions?

In this chapter we have looked at how competitive firms make production and investment decisions, relying on sales-revenue and production-cost data. But there is an elephant in the room that we have ignored—namely, government. Governments at all levels levy taxes, fees, and regulations that affect business decisions about what to produce and how to produce. Now its time to look at how taxes—especially *which* taxes—alter production and investment decisions.

Property Taxes. Property taxes are levied by local governments on land and buildings. The tax rate is typically some small fraction (e.g., 1 percent) of total value. Hence, the owner of a $10 million factory might have to pay $100,000 per year in property taxes.

Property taxes have to be paid regardless of whether the factory is used. Hence, *property taxes are a fixed cost* for the firm. These additional fixed costs increase total costs and thus shift the average total cost (ATC) upward, as in Figure 8.13a.

Notice that the MC curve doesn't move when property taxes are imposed. Property taxes aren't based on the quantity of output produced. Accordingly, the production decision of the firm isn't affected by property taxes. The quantity q_1 in Figure 8.13a remains the optimal rate of output even after a property tax is introduced.

Although the optimal output remains at q_1, the profitability of the firm is reduced by the property tax. Profit per unit has been reduced by the upward shift of the ATC curve. If property taxes reduce profits too much, firms may move to a low-tax jurisdiction or another industry (investment decisions).

Payroll Taxes. Payroll taxes have very different effects on business decisions. Payroll taxes are levied on the wages paid by the firm. Employers must pay, for example, a 7.65 percent Social Security tax on the wages they pay (employees pay an identical amount). This tax is used to finance Social Security retirement benefits. Other payroll taxes are levied by federal and state governments to finance unemployment and disability benefits.

All payroll taxes add to the cost of hiring labor. In the absence of a tax, a worker might cost the firm $8 per hour. Once Social Security and other taxes are levied, the cost of labor increases to $8 plus the amount of tax. Hence, $8-per-hour labor might end up costing the firm $9 or more. In other words, *payroll taxes increase marginal costs*. This is illustrated in Figure 8.13b by the upward shift of the MC curve.

Notice how payroll taxes change the production decision. The new MC curve (MC_b) intersects the price line at a lower rate of output (q_b). Thus, payroll taxes tend to reduce output and employment.

Profits Taxes. Taxes are also levied on the profits of a business. Such taxes are very different from either property or payroll taxes because profit taxes are paid only when profits are made. Thus, they are neither a fixed cost nor a variable cost! As Figure 8.13c indicates, neither the MC nor the ATC curve moves when a profits tax is imposed. The only difference is that the firm now gets to keep less of its profits, instead of "sharing" its profits with the government.

Although a profits tax has no direct effect on marginal or average costs, it does reduce the take-home (after-tax) profits of a business. This may reduce investments in new businesses. For this reason, many people urge the government to reduce corporate tax rates and so encourage increased investment. President Trump made the reduction in the corporate income tax rate (from 35 to 21 percent) the centerpiece of his economic programs.

(a) Property taxes affect fixed costs but not marginal costs.

(b) Payroll taxes alter marginal costs.

(c) Profits taxes don't change costs.

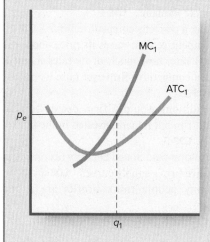

FIGURE 8.13

Impact of Taxes on Business Decisions

(a) **Property taxes** are a fixed cost for the firm. Because they don't affect marginal costs, they leave the optimal rate of output (q_1) unchanged. Property taxes raise average costs, however, and so reduce profits. Lower profits may alter investment decisions.

(b) **Payroll taxes** add directly to marginal costs and so reduce the optimal rate of output (to q_b). Payroll taxes also increase average costs and lower total and per-unit profits.

(c) **Taxes on profits** are neither a fixed cost nor a variable cost because they depend on the existence of profits. They don't affect marginal costs or price and so leave the optimal rate of output (q_1) unchanged. By reducing after-tax profits, however, such taxes lessen incentives to invest.

SUMMARY

- Economic profit is the difference between total revenue and total cost. Total economic cost includes the value (opportunity cost) of *all* inputs used in production, not just those inputs for which an explicit payment is made.   **LO8-1**
- A perfectly competitive firm is a *price taker*. It sells its output at the prevailing market price. It effectively confronts a horizontal demand for its output (even though the *market* demand for the product is downward-sloping).   **LO8-2**
- Competitive firms don't make pricing decisions, only production decisions.   **LO8-2**
- The short-run objective of a firm is to maximize profits from the operation of its existing facilities (fixed costs). For a competitive firm, the profit-maximizing output occurs at the point where marginal cost equals price (marginal revenue).   **LO8-3**
- A firm may incur a loss even at the optimal rate of output. It shouldn't shut down, however, so long as price exceeds average *variable* cost. If revenues at least cover

variable costs, the firm's operating loss is less than its fixed costs.   **LO8-4**
- In the long run there are no fixed costs, and the firm may choose any-sized plant it wants. The decision to incur fixed costs (i.e., build, buy, or lease a plant) or to enter or exit an industry is an investment decision.   **LO8-5**
- A competitive firm's supply curve is identical to its marginal cost curve (above the shutdown point at minimum average variable cost). In the short run, the quantity supplied will rise or fall with price.   **LO8-6**
- The determinants of supply include the price of inputs, technology, taxes, and expectations. Should any of these determinants change, the firm's supply curve will shift.   **LO8-6**
- Business taxes alter business behavior. Property taxes raise fixed costs; payroll taxes increase marginal costs. Profits taxes raise neither fixed costs nor marginal costs but diminish the take-home (after-tax) profits of a business.   **LO8-6**

Key Terms

profit
economic cost
explicit cost
implicit cost
economic profit
normal profit
monopoly
market structure

perfect competition
market power
competitive firm
production decision
total revenue
short run
fixed costs
variable costs

marginal cost (MC)
marginal revenue (MR)
profit-maximization rule
shutdown point
investment decision
long run
supply curve

Questions for Discussion

1. What economic costs will a large corporation likely overlook when computing its profits? How about the owner of a family-run business or farm?   **LO8-1**
2. How can the demand curve facing a firm be horizontal if the market demand curve is downward-sloping?   **LO8-2**
3. How many fish should a commercial fisher try to catch in a day? Should he catch as many as possible or return to dock before filling the boat with fish? Under what economic circumstances should he not even take the boat out?   **LO8-3**
4. If a firm is incurring an economic loss, would society be better off if the firm shut down? Would the firm want to shut down? Explain.   **LO8-4**
5. Why isn't the rate of output that minimizes average total cost the most profitable rate of output?   **LO8-3**
6. What rate of output is appropriate for a nonprofit corporation (such as a hospital)?   **LO8-3**
7. What costs did Boeing eliminate when it shut down its production? (See Front Page Economics "Boeing Halts 737 MAX Production.") How about GM?   **LO8-4**

8. What was the opportunity cost of Hiroshi Fujishige's farm? (See Front Page Economics "The Value of Hiro's Strawberry Farm.") Is society better off with another Disney theme park? Explain.   **LO8-1**
9. Is Apple Computer a perfectly competitive firm?   **LO8-2**
10. If a perfectly competitive firm raises its price above the prevailing market rate, how much of its sales might it lose? Why? Can a competitive firm ever raise its prices? If so, when?   **LO8-2**
11. Under what conditions would a firm decide to shut down in the short run but remain invested in the market in the long run?   **LO8-5**
12. How does an employer-paid Social Security tax on wages affect a competitive firm's supply curve?   **LO8-6**
13. Why do so many people think profits are a bad thing?   **LO8-1**

PROBLEMS FOR CHAPTER 8

LO8-2 1. According to Front Page Economics "The Lure of Catfish,"
   (*a*) How many fish did farmer Hollingsworth have in inventory?
   (*b*) If each of his fish weighed 3 pounds, what percent of the market did he have?

LO8-1 2. If the owner of the Table 8.1 drugstore hired a manager for $10 an hour to take his place, how much of a change would show up in
   (*a*) Accounting profits?   (*b*) Economic profits?

LO8-1 3. Kanesha is an entrepreneur and has recently opened her first coffee shop, The Coffee Cat. She pays $5,000 rent each month, $4,800 for monthly employee payroll, and $1,200 for supplies each month. She was planning on selling several of her own tables and chairs on Craigslist for $1,500, but instead she brought them to The Coffee Cat. Additionally, she quit working as an accountant where she was earning $52,000 per year to open up the shop. If the shop earns $180,000 in revenue this year, calculate annual
   (*a*) Accounting profit.   (*b*) Economic profit.

LO8-1 4. If the price of catfish fell from $13 to $7 per bushel, use Figure 8.7 to determine the
   (*a*) Profit-maximizing output.
   (*b*) Profit or loss per bushel.
   (*c*) Total profit or loss.

LO8-2 5. Complete the following cost and revenue schedules:

Quantity	Price	Total Revenue	Total Cost	Marginal Cost
0	$50	_____	$ 50	—
1	50	_____	60	_____
2	50	_____	90	_____
3	50	_____	140	_____
4	50	_____	200	_____
5	50	_____	280	_____

   (*a*) Graph MC and *p*.
   (*b*) What quantity maximizes profit?
   (*c*) What is MC at that quantity?

LO8-2 6. Complete the following cost schedules:

Quantity	0	1	2	3	4	5	6	7
Total cost	$9	$12	$16	$21	$30	$40	$52	$66
ATC	___	___	___	___	___	___	___	___
MC	—	___	___	___	___	___	___	___

   Assuming the price of this product is $12, at what output rate is
   (*a*) Total revenue maximized?   (*c*) Profit per unit maximized?
   (*b*) ATC minimized?   (*d*) Total profit maximized?

LO8-3 7. Assume the price of silk ties in a perfectly competitive market is $21 and that the typical firm confronts the following costs:

Quantity (ties per day)	0	1	2	3	4	5	6	7	8	9	10
Total cost	$10	$17	$26	$37	$50	$65	$82	$101	$122	$145	$170

   (*a*) What is the profit-maximizing rate of output for the firm?
   (*b*) How much profit does the firm earn at that rate of output?
   (*c*) If the price of ties fell to $15, how many ties should the firm produce?
   (*d*) At what price should the firm shut down?

PROBLEMS FOR CHAPTER 8 (cont'd)

LO8-6 8. Illustrate on the accompanying graph the changes to the cost curves due to
  (a) Higher feed prices.   (c) Higher worker productivity.
  (b) Lower wage rates.

  Does the profit-maximizing rate of output increase, decrease, or stay
  the same with
  (d) Higher feed prices?   (f) Higher worker productivity?
  (e) Lower wage rates?

LO8-4 9. Complete the following table:

Output	Total Cost	Marginal Cost	Average Total Cost	Average Variable Cost
0	$100	—	—	—
5	110			
10	130			
15	170			
20	220			
25	290			
30	380			
35	490			

  According to the table above,
  (a) If the price is $10, how much output will the firm supply?   (c) At what price will the firm shut down?
  (b) How much profit or loss will it make?

LO8-5 10. A firm has leased plant and equipment to produce video games, which can be sold in unlimited
  quantities at $13 each. The following figures describe the firm's costs of production:

Rate of output (per day)	0	1	2	3	4	5	6	7	8
Total cost (per day)	$50	$55	$62	$75	$96	$125	$162	$203	$248

  (a) How much are fixed costs?
  (b) Draw total revenue and cost curves on the first graph.
  (c) Draw the average total cost (ATC), marginal cost (MC), and demand curves of the firm on the second graph.
  (d) What is the profit-maximizing rate of output?
  (e) Calculate profits or losses at this profit-maximizing rate of output.
  (f) How much is lost if the firm shuts down?
  (g) Should the firm produce or shut down in the short run?

LO8-6 11. *Decisions for Tomorrow:* Using the data from Problem 7 (at the original price of $21), determine
  the impact on marginal costs and identify if the profit-maximizing output would increase,
  decrease, or remain unchanged given the following tax changes.
  (a) A tax of $2 per tie were collected from the producer.   (c) Profits were taxed at 50 percent.
  (b) A property tax of $2 were levied.

Design Credit: Shutterstock

David A. Barnes/Alamy Stock Photo

9

Competitive Markets

LEARNING OBJECTIVES

After reading this chapter, you should know

LO9-1 The market characteristics of perfect competition.

LO9-2 How prices are established in competitive markets.

LO9-3 Why long-run economic profits approach zero in competitive markets.

LO9-4 How society benefits from market competition.

Catfish farmers in the South are very upset. Back in 2015–2017 catfish prices were rising and profits increasing. In response, farmers in Mississippi, Alabama, and Arkansas built more fish ponds in cotton fields and upgraded older ponds. Prices peaked at $1.35 a pound in January 2017. When those investment decisions caused catfish production to increase, however, the situation deteriorated. Prices started falling in mid-2017 and got down to $0.93 a pound in 2019. Profits disappeared. With losses mounting, a lot of farmers got out of the catfish business in 2019–2020, filling their ponds with dirt and planting soybeans instead.

The dilemma catfish farmers find themselves in is a familiar occurrence in competitive markets. When profits look good, everybody wants to get in on the act. As more and more firms start producing the good, prices and profits tumble. This helps explain why more than 200,000 new firms are formed each year and why more than 50,000 others fail.

This chapter focuses on the behavior of competitive markets. We have three principal questions:

- **How are prices determined in competitive markets?**
- **How does competition affect the profits of a firm or industry?**
- **What does society gain from market competition?**

The answers to these questions will reveal how markets work when all producers are relatively small and lack market power. In subsequent chapters, we emphasize how market outcomes change when markets are less competitive.

FIGURE 9.1

Competitive Market Supply

A Firm's Supply. The portion of the MC curve that lies above AVC is a competitive firm's short-run supply curve. The curve MC_A tells us that Farmer A will produce 40 pounds of catfish per day if the market price is $3 per pound.

Market Supply. To determine the *market* supply, we add up the quantities supplied at each price by every farmer. The total quantity supplied to the market at the price of $3 is 150 pounds per day ($a + b + c$). Market supply depends on the number of firms and their respective marginal costs.

THE MARKET SUPPLY CURVE

In the previous chapter we examined the supply behavior of a perfectly competitive firm. The perfectly competitive firm is a price taker. It *responds* to the market price by producing that rate of output where marginal cost equals price.

But what about the *market* supply of catfish? We need a market supply curve to determine the **equilibrium price** the individual farmer will confront. In the previous chapter we simply drew a market supply curve arbitrarily to establish a market price. Now our objective is to find out where that **market supply** curve comes from.

Like the market supply curves we first encountered in Chapter 3, we can calculate the market supply of catfish by simple addition. All we have to do is add up the quantities each of America's 1,000 catfish farmers stands ready to supply at each price. Then we'll know the total quantity of fish to be supplied to the market at that price.

Remember the critical role that **marginal cost** plays in the production decision of the competitive firm. As we saw in the previous chapter, a competitive firm will produce where $MC = p$. So, the firm's MC curve is in effect its supply curve. If we know what the MC curves of the firms in an industry look like, we can compute the *market* supply. Figure 9.1 illustrates this summation. Notice that *the market supply curve is the sum of the marginal cost curves of all the firms.* Hence, whatever determines the marginal cost of a typical firm will also affect industry supply. Specifically, *the market supply of a competitive industry is determined by*

- *The price of factor inputs.*
- *Technology.*
- *Expectations.*
- *Taxes and subsidies.*
- *The number of firms in the industry.*

Entry and Exit

If more firms enter an industry, the market supply curve will shift to the right. This is the problem confronting the catfish farmers in Mississippi (see World View "Catfish Farmers Give Up"). It's fairly inexpensive to get into the catfish business: You can start with a pond, some breeding stock, and relatively little capital equipment. These **investment decisions** shift

equilibrium price: The price at which the quantity of a good demanded in a given time period equals the quantity supplied.

market supply: The total quantities of a good that sellers are willing and able to sell at alternative prices in a given time period, *ceteris paribus.*

marginal cost (MC): The increase in total cost associated with a one-unit increase in production.

investment decision: The decision to build, buy, or lease plants and equipment; to enter or exit an industry.

(a) Market entry pushes price down and . . .

(b) Reduces profits of competitive firm.

FIGURE 9.2
Market Entry

If economic profits exist in an industry, more firms will want to enter it. As they do, the market supply curve will shift to the right and cause the market price to drop from p_1 to p_2 (part *a*).

The lower market price, in turn, will reduce the output and profits of the typical firm. In part *b*, the firm's output falls from q_1 to q_2.

the market supply curve to the right and drive down catfish prices. This process is illustrated in Figure 9.2*a*. Notice how the equilibrium price slides down the market demand curve from E_1 to E_2 when more firms enter the market. The entry of Vietnamese and Chinese farmers into the catfish market accelerated the steep decline in catfish prices.

If prices fall too far, profits will disappear. Indeed, profits will turn into losses if the market price falls below a farmer's minimum average total cost. When this happens, some farmers will drain their ponds and plant soybeans instead (see World View "U.S. Catfish Farmers Give Up"). When they do so, they are *exiting* the catfish business and *entering* the soybean business. These exits will shift the market supply curve a bit to the left, helping to stabilize catfish prices and "stop the bleeding" in the industry.

WORLD VIEW

CATFISH FARMERS GIVE UP

Catfish farming used to look good. So good, in fact, that hundreds of crop farmers stopped growing corn and soybeans, choosing instead to dig catfish ponds on their land. As these ponds have matured, the supply of catfish has jumped, outpacing demand. The result has been a depressing decline in prices that has wiped out profits for hundreds of farmers. Wholesale prices for catfish have fallen by 30 percent in the last two years. In 2018 catfish acreage fell by 1,890 acres as farmers switched to other species like redfish and striped bass, or filled in their ponds and planted soybeans.

Source: Media reports, Fall 2019.

CRITICAL ANALYSIS: When economic profits exist in an industry, more producers try to enter. As they do, prices and economic profits decline. When losses are incurred, firms begin to **exit** the industry.

Tendency toward Zero Profits

The profit motive drives these entry and exit decisions. Five years ago catfish farming looked a whole lot more profitable than cotton farming. Farmers responded by flooding their cotton fields to create fish ponds; they *exited* the cotton business and *entered* the catfish industry.

The resulting shift of market supply caused the **economic profits** in catfish farming to disappear. Notice in Figure 9.2b how total profits for the typical firm shrink when price is driven down from p_1 to p_2. If price continued to fall, profits would shrink further. Indeed, if price declines to p_3, profits disappear.

When profits disappear (at the price p_3 in Figure 9.2b) there is no incentive to *enter* the industry. Were price to fall still further—below p_3—the typical catfish farmer would actually be losing money. That would motivate some farmers to *exit* the industry—planting soybeans instead of feeding fish. Eventually, price will settle at p_3, where economic profit is zero. **When economic profit disappears, entry and exit cease and the market stabilizes.** This is exactly what has happened in the catfish industry. At the new equilibrium, catfish farmers earn only a normal (average) rate of return.

Catfish farmers would be happier, of course, if the price of catfish didn't decline to the point where economic profits disappear. But how are they going to prevent it? Farmer Jess King evidently knows all about the laws of supply and demand. He would dearly like to keep all those Vietnamese and Chinese catfish out of this country. He also wishes those farmers in Maine would keep cranberries in their ponds rather than catfish. Jess would also like to get other farmers in the South to slow production a little before all the profits disappear. But King is powerless to stop the forces of a **competitive market.** He can't even afford to reduce his *own* catfish production. Even though he has 200 acres of ponds, nobody would notice the resulting drop in market supplies, and catfish prices would continue to slide. The only one affected would be King, who'd be denying himself the opportunity to share in the (dwindling) fortunes of the catfish market while they lasted.

Farmer King's dilemma goes a long way toward explaining why catfish farming isn't highly profitable. Whenever the profit picture looks good, everybody tries to get in on the action. This kind of pressure on prices and profits is a fundamental characteristic of competitive markets. *As long as it's easy for existing producers to expand production or for new firms to enter an industry, economic profits won't last long.*

Low Barriers to Entry

New producers will be able to enter a profitable industry and help drive down prices and profits as long as they don't encounter significant barriers. Such **barriers to entry** may include patents, control of essential factors of production, control of distribution outlets, well-established brand loyalty, or even governmental regulation. All such barriers make it expensive, risky, or impossible for new firms to enter an industry. In the absence of such barriers, new firms can enter an industry more readily and at less risk. Not surprisingly, firms already entrenched in a profitable industry do their best to keep out newcomers by erecting barriers to entry. Unfortunately for Farmer King, there are few barriers to entering the catfish business; all you need to get started is a pond and a few fish. Recall the Calvin Jones quote from Chapter 8: "You raise fish. You get them out of the pond and you sell them. . . . There's no genius to it."

Market Characteristics of Perfect Competition

This brief review of catfish economics illustrates a few general observations about the structure, behavior, and outcomes of a competitive market:

- *Many firms.* A competitive market includes a great many firms, none of which has a significant share of total output.
- *Identical products.* Products are homogeneous. One firm's product is the same as any other firm's product.

---

economic profit: The difference between total revenues and total economic costs.

competitive market: A market in which no buyer or seller has market power.

barriers to entry: Obstacles such as patents that make it difficult or impossible for would-be producers to enter a particular market.

- *Perfect information.* All buyers and sellers have complete information on available supply, demand, and prices.
- *MC = p.* All competitive firms will seek to expand output until marginal cost equals price, much as price and marginal revenue are identical for such firms.
- *Low barriers.* Barriers to enter the industry are low. If economic profits are available, more firms will enter the industry.
- *Zero economic profit.* The tendency of production and market supplies to expand when profit is high puts heavy pressures on prices and profits in competitive industries. Economic profit will approach zero in the long run as prices are driven down to the level of average production costs.

COMPETITION AT WORK: MICROCOMPUTERS

Few markets have all the characteristics just listed. That is, *few, if any, product markets are perfectly competitive.* However, many industries function much like the competitive model we sketched out. In addition to catfish farming, most other agricultural product markets are characterized by highly competitive market structures, with hundreds or even thousands of producers supplying the market. Other highly competitive, and hence not very profitable, businesses are T-shirt shops, laundromats, retail food, printing, clothing manufacturing and retailing, dry-cleaning establishments, beauty salons, and furniture. Online stockbroker services have also become highly competitive. In these markets, prices and profits are always under the threat of expanded supplies brought to market by existing or new producers.

The electronics industry offers numerous examples of how competition reduces prices and profits. Between 1972 and 1983, the price of small, handheld calculators fell from $200 to under $10. The price of digital watches fell even more dramatically, from roughly $2,000 in 1975 to under $7 in 1990. Videocassette recorders (VCRs) that sold for $2,000 in 1979 fell to less than $30 in 2015. DVD players that cost $1,500 in 1997 now sell for under $30. A TiVo DVR that sold for $999 when introduced in 1999 (with 30 hours of play) now sells for under $195 (with 150 hours of play). Cell phones that sold for $1,000 ten years ago are now given away. The same kind of competitive pressures have reduced the price of flat-screen TVs. New entrants keep bringing better TVs to market while driving prices down (see World View "Flat Panels, Thin Margins").

The driving force behind all these price reductions and quality improvements is *competition.* Do you really believe the price of text messages and movie downloads would be falling if only one firm supplied all cell phone or streaming services? Do you think thousands of software writers would be toiling away right now if popular programs didn't generate enormous profits? Would Apple, Amazon, Facebook, Netflix, and Uber keep rolling out new products and services if other companies weren't always snapping at their heels?

Market Evolution

To appreciate how the process of competition works, we will examine the development of the personal computer industry. *As in other industries, the market structure of the computer industry has evolved over time. It was never a monopoly, nor was it ever perfect competition.* In its first couple of years it was dominated by only a few companies (like Apple) that were enormously successful. The high profits the early microcomputer producers obtained attracted swarms of imitators. More than 250 firms entered the microcomputer industry between 1976 and 1983 in search of high profits. The entry of so many firms transformed the industry's market structure: The industry became *more* competitive, even though not *perfectly* competitive. The increased competition pushed prices downward and improved the product. When prices and profits tumbled, scores of companies went bankrupt. They left a legacy, however, of a vastly larger market, much improved computers, and sharply lower prices.

WORLD VIEW

FLAT PANELS, THIN MARGINS

The TVs keep getting bigger and better and cheaper! In fact, industry experts say there is never a "right time" to buy a TV because TVs will be better and cheaper a couple of months later.

Brutal competition keeps pushing prices down and innovation up. In the last five years alone the number of LCD brands for sale in U.S. stores increased fourfold, from 26 to 102. Parts manufacturers in China, Mexico, and Taiwan make it easy to get into the industry. They will sell the needed parts to anyone—and even assemble all the pieces if asked. So, anyone can create an instant brand and get into TV retailing. At a lower price, of course.

AVERAGE PRICE OF 32-INCH LCD TV

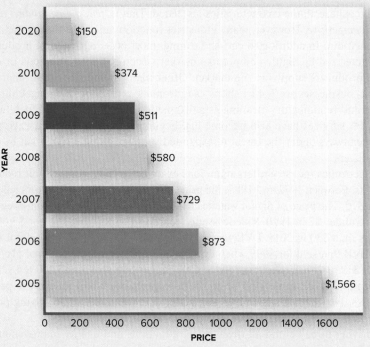

YEAR	PRICE
2020	$150
2010	$374
2009	$511
2008	$580
2007	$729
2006	$873
2005	$1,566

Source: Industry reports (2007–2020).

CRITICAL ANALYSIS: Competitive pressures compel producers of flat-panel TVs to keep improving the product and reducing prices. The lure of profits encourages firms to enter this market even as prices drop.

We'll use the early experiences of the microcomputer industry to illustrate the key behavioral features of a competitive market. As we'll see, many of these competitive features are still at work in the markets for Internet services, content software, digital music, smartphones, ride sharing, cloud storage, streaming services, and 8K television sets.

Initial Conditions: The Apple I

The microcomputer industry really got started in 1977. Prior to that time, microcomputers were essentially a hobby item for engineers and programmers, who bought circuits, keyboards, monitors, and tape recorders and then assembled their own basic computers. Steve Jobs, then working at Atari, and Steven Wozniak, then working at Hewlett-Packard, were among these early computer enthusiasts. They spent their days working on large systems and their nights and weekends trying to put together small computers from mail-order parts.

Analysis: The Apple I pictured here launched the personal computer industry in 1976. Hundreds of firms entered the industry to improve on this first preassembled microcomputer. This competition transformed the industry, the product, and prices.

Eventually, Jobs and Wozniak decided that they had the capability to build commercially attractive small computers. They ordered the parts necessary for building 100 computers and set up shop in the garage of Jobs's parents. Their finished product—the Apple I—was nothing more than a circuit board with a simple, built-in operating system. This first microcomputer was packaged in a wooden box (see the photo). Despite primitive characteristics, the first 100 Apple I computers sold out immediately. This quick success convinced Jobs and Wozniak to package their computers more fully—which they did by enclosing them in plastic housing—and to offer more of them for sale. Shortly thereafter, in January 1977, Apple Computer Inc. was established.

Apple revolutionalized the market by offering a preassembled desktop computer with attractive features and an accessible price. The impact on the marketplace was much like that of Henry Ford's early Model T: Suddenly a newfangled piece of technology came into reach of the average U.S. household, and everybody, it seemed, wanted one. The first mass-produced Apple computer—called the Apple II—was just a basic keyboard with an operating system that permitted users to write their own programs. The computer had no disk drive, no monitor, and only 4K of random access memory (RAM). Consumers had to use their TV sets as screens and audiocassettes for data storage. This primitive Apple II was priced at just under $1,300 when it debuted in June 1977. Apple was producing computers at the rate of 500 per month.

Apple didn't engineer or manufacture chips or semiconductor components. Instead it simply packaged existing components purchased from outside suppliers. Hence, it was easy for other companies to follow Apple's lead. Within a very brief time, other firms also started to assemble computers. By the middle of 1978, the basic small computer was selling for $1,000, and industry sales were about 20,000 a month. Figure 9.3*a* depicts the initial (1978) equilibrium in the computer market, and Figure 9.3*b* illustrates the approximate costs of production for the typical computer manufacturer at that time.

The Production Decision

The short-run goal of every producer is to find the rate of output that maximizes profits. Finding this rate entails making the best possible **production decision.** In this short-run context, *each competitive firm seeks the rate of output at which marginal cost equals price.*

Figure 9.3*b* illustrates the cost and price curves the typical computer producer confronted in 1978. As in most lines of production, the marginal costs of computer production

production decision: The selection of the short-run rate of output (with existing plants and equipment).

(a) The computer industry

(b) The typical firm

FIGURE 9.3

Initial Equilibrium in the Computer Market

(a) **The Industry.** In 1978 the market price of microcomputers was $1,000. This price was established by the intersection of the market supply and demand curves.

(b) **A Firm.** Each competitive producer in the market sought to produce computers at that rate (600 per month) where marginal cost equaled price (point C). Profit per computer was equal to price (point C) minus average total cost (point D). Total profits for the typical firm are indicated by the shaded rectangle.

increased with the rate of output. Marginal costs rose in part because output could be increased in the short run (with existing plants and equipment) only by crowding additional workers onto the assembly line. In 1978 Apple had only 10,000 square feet of manufacturing space. As more workers were hired, each worker had less capital and land to work with, and marginal physical product fell. The law of diminishing returns pushed marginal costs up.

The upward-sloping marginal cost curve intersected the price line at an output level of 600 computers per month (point *C* in Figure 9.3*b*). That was the profit-maximizing rate of output (MC = *p*) for the typical manufacturer. Manufacturing any more than 600 computers per month would raise marginal costs over price and reduce total profits. Manufacturing any fewer would be passing up an opportunity to make another buck.

Profit Calculations

Table 9.1 shows how much *profit* a typical computer manufacturer was making in 1978. As the "total profit" column indicates, the typical computer manufacturer could make a real killing in the computer market, reaping a monthly profit of $180,000 by producing and selling 600 microcomputers.

We could also calculate the computer manufacturers' profits by asking how much the manufacturers make on *each* computer and then multiplying that figure by total output:

Total profit = Profit per unit × Quantity sold

We can compute these profits by studying the first and last columns in Table 9.1 or by using a little geometry in Figure 9.3*b*. In the figure, average costs (total costs divided by the rate of

Output per Month	Price	Total Revenue	Total Cost	Total Profit	Marginal Revenue*	Marginal Cost*	Average Total Cost	Profit per Unit (Price Minus Average Cost)
0	$1,000	$ 0	$ 60,000	−$ 60,000	—	—	—	—
100	1,000	100,000	90,000	10,000	$1,000	$ 300	$ 900	$100
200	1,000	200,000	130,000	70,000	1,000	400	650	350
300	1,000	300,000	180,000	120,000	1,000	500	600	400
400	1,000	400,000	240,000	160,000	1,000	600	600	400
500	1,000	500,000	320,000	180,000	1,000	800	640	360
600	1,000	600,000	420,000	180,000	1,000	1,000	700	300
700	1,000	700,000	546,000	154,000	1,000	1,260	780	220
800	1,000	800,000	720,000	80,000	1,000	1,740	900	100
900	1,000	900,000	919,800	−19,800	1,000	1,998	1,022	−22

*Note that output levels are calibrated in hundreds in this example; that's why we have divided the *change* in total costs and revenues from one output level to another by 100 to calculate marginal revenue and marginal cost. Very few manufacturers deal in units of 1.

TABLE 9.1

Computer Revenues, Costs, and Profits

Producers seek that rate of output where total profit is maximized. This table illustrates the output choices the typical computer producer faced in 1978. The profit-maximizing rate of output occurred at 600 computers per month. At that rate of output, marginal cost was equal to price ($1,000), and profits were $180,000 per month.

output) are portrayed by the **average total cost (ATC)** curve. At the output rate of 600 (the row in white in Table 9.1), the distance between the price line ($1,000 at point *C*) and the ATC curve ($700 at point *D*) is $300, which represents the average **profit per unit.** Multiplying this figure by the number of units sold (600 per month) will give us *total* profit per month. Total profits are represented by the shaded rectangle in Figure 9.3*b* and are equal to our earlier profit figure of $180,000 per month.

average total cost (ATC): Total cost divided by the quantity produced in a given time period.

profit per unit: Total profit divided by the quantity produced in a given time period; price minus average total cost.

The Lure of Profits

While gaping at the computer manufacturer's enormous profits, we should remind ourselves that those profits might not last long. Indeed, the more quick-witted among us already will have seen and heard enough to know they've discovered a good thing. And in fact, the kind of profits the early microcomputer manufacturers enjoyed attracted a lot of entrepreneurial interest. *In competitive markets, economic profits attract new entrants.* This is what happened in the catfish industry and also in the computer industry. Within a very short time, a whole crowd of profit maximizers entered the microcomputer industry in hot pursuit of its fabulous profits. By the end of 1980, Apple had a lot of competition, including new entrants from IBM, Xerox, Digital Equipment, Casio, Sharp, and dozens of other start-up firms.

Low Entry Barriers

A critical feature of the microcomputer market was its lack of entry barriers. A microcomputer is little more than a box containing a microprocessor "brain," which connects to a keyboard (to enter data), a memory (to store data), and a screen (to display data). Although the microprocessors that guide the computer are extremely sophisticated, they can be purchased on the open market. Thus, to enter the computer industry, all one needs is some space, some money to buy components, and some dexterity in putting parts together. Such *low entry barriers permit new firms to enter competitive markets.* This is what facilitated competition in the flat-screen TV market (see the World View "Flat Panels, Thin Margins"). The same low entry barriers existed in computers. According to Table 9.1, the

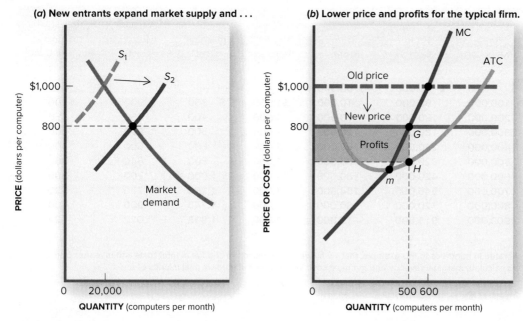

(a) New entrants expand market supply and . . .

(b) Lower price and profits for the typical firm.

FIGURE 9.4

The Competitive Price and Profit Squeeze

(a) **The Industry.** The economic profits in the computer industry encouraged new firms to enter the industry. As they did, the market supply curve shifted from S_1 to S_2. This rightward shift of the supply curve lowered the equilibrium price of computers.

(b) **A Firm.** The lower market price, in turn, forced the typical producer to reduce output to the point where MC and price were equal again (point G). At this reduced rate of output, the typical firm earned less total profit than it had earned before.

typical producer needed only $60,000 of plant and equipment (fixed costs) to get started in the microcomputer market. Jobs and Wozniak had even less when they started making Apples in their garage.

A Shift of Market Supply

Figure 9.4 shows what happened to the computer market and the profits of the typical firm once the word got out. As more and more entrepreneurs heard how profitable computer manufacturing could be, they quickly got hold of a book on electronic circuitry, rushed to the bank, got a little financing, and set up shop. Before many months had passed, scores of new firms had started producing small computers. *The entry of new firms shifts the market supply curve to the right.* In Figure 9.4a, the supply curve shifted from S_1 to S_2. Almost as fast as a computer can calculate a profit (loss) statement, the willingness to supply increased abruptly.

But the new computer companies were in for a bit of disappointment. With so many new firms hawking microcomputers, it became increasingly difficult to make a fast buck. The downward-sloping market demand curve confirms that a greater quantity of microcomputers could be sold only if the price of computers dropped. And drop it did. The price slide began as computer manufacturers found their inventories growing and so offered price discounts to maintain sales volume. The price fell rapidly, from $1,000 in mid-1978 to $800 in early 1980.

The sliding market price squeezed the profits of each firm, causing the profit rectangle to shrink (compare Figure 9.3b to Figure 9.4b). The lower price also changed the production decision of the typical firm. The new price ($800) intersected the unchanged MC curve at the output rate of 500 computers per month (point *G* in Figure 9.4b). With average production costs of $640 (Table 9.1), the firm's total profits in 1980 were only $80,000 per

(a) The computer industry:
continuous entry

(b) The typical firm: price and
profit squeeze

FIGURE 9.5

The Competitive Squeeze Approaching Its Limit

(a) The Industry. Even at a price of $800 per computer, economic profits attracted still more entrepreneurs, shifting the market supply curve further (S_3). The next short-term equilibrium occurred at a price of $700 per computer.

(b) A Firm. At this reduced market price, the typical manufacturer wanted to supply only 430 computers per month (point *J*). Total profits were much lower than they had been earlier, with fewer producers and higher prices.

month [(*p* − ATC) × 500]. Not a paltry sum, to be sure, but nothing like the fantastic fortunes pocketed earlier.

As long as an economic profit is available, it will continue to attract new entrants. Those entrepreneurs who were a little slow in absorbing the implications of Figure 9.3 eventually woke up to what was going on and tried to get in on the action, too. Even though they were a little late, they didn't want to miss the chance to cash in on the $80,000 in monthly profits still available to the typical firm. Hence, the market supply curve continued to shift, and computer prices slid further, as in Figure 9.5. This process squeezed the profits of the typical firm still more, further shrinking the profit rectangle.

As long as economic profits exist in **short-run competitive equilibrium,** that equilibrium won't last. If the rate of profit obtainable in computer production is higher than that available in other industries, new firms will enter the industry. Conversely, if the short-run equilibrium is unprofitable, firms will exit the industry. Profit-maximizing entrepreneurs have a special place in their hearts for economic profits, not computers.

Price and profit declines will cease when the price of computers equals the minimum average cost of production. At that price (point *m* in Figure 9.5*b*), there's no more economic profit to be squeezed out. Firms no longer have an incentive to enter the industry, and the supply curve stops shifting. This situation represents the **long-run competitive equilibrium** for the firm and for the industry. *In long-run equilibrium, entry and exit cease, and zero economic profit (that is, normal profit) prevails* (see Figure 9.6). Table 9.2 summarizes the profit-maximizing rules that bring about this long-run equilibrium.

Once a long-run equilibrium is established, it will continue until market demand shifts or technological progress reduces the cost of computer production. In fact, that's just what happened in the computer market.

short-run competitive equilibrium: *p* = *MC*.

long-run competitive equilibrium: *p* = *MC* = minimum ATC.

(a) Short-run equilibrium (p = MC)

(b) Long-run equilibrium (p = MC = ATC)

FIGURE 9.6

Short- vs. Long-Run Equilibrium for the Competitive Firm

(a) Short Run. Competitive firms strive for the rate of output at which marginal cost (MC) equals price. When they achieve that rate of output, they are in *short-run equilibrium*. Whether profitable or not, there is no incentive to alter the rate of output produced with existing (fixed) plants and equipment; it is the *best* the firm can do in the short run.

(b) Long Run. If the short-run equilibrium (q_s) is profitable (p > ATC), other firms will want to enter the industry. As they do, market price will fall until it reaches the level of minimum ATC. In this *long-run equilibrium* (q_L), economic profits are zero, and nobody wants to enter or exit the industry.

TABLE 9.2

Long-Run Rules for Entry and Exit

Firms will enter an industry if economic profits exist (p > ATC). They will exit if economic losses prevail (p < ATC). Entry and exit cease in long-run equilibrium with zero economic profit (p = ATC). (See Table 8.3 for short-run profit maximization rules.)

Price Level	Result for a Typical Firm	Market Response
p > ATC	Profits	Enter industry (or expand capacity).
p < ATC	Loss	Exit industry (or reduce capacity).
p = ATC	Break even	Maintain existing capacity (no entry or exit).

Personal Computers

As profit margins narrowed to the levels shown in Figure 9.5, quick-thinking entrepreneurs realized that future profits would have to come from product improvements or cost reductions. Microcomputers upgraded with new features came to be known as *personal* computers, or PCs.

Apple was again a pioneer in that transition. It started enlarging the memory of the Apple II in late 1978 (from 4K to as many as 48K). It offered a monitor (produced by Sanyo) for the first time in May 1979. Shortly thereafter, Apple ceased making the basic Apple II and instead produced only upgraded versions (the Apple IIe, the IIc, and the III). Hundreds of other companies followed Apple's lead, touting increasingly sophisticated personal computers.

Price Competition

With so many firms vying for PC sales, price competition was fierce. In addition to innovating new features, companies had to worry about production costs.

FIGURE 9.7

Lower Costs Improve Profits and Stimulate Output

The quest for profits encouraged producers to discover cheaper ways to manufacture computers. The resulting improvements lowered costs and encouraged further increases in the rate of output. The typical computer producer increased output from point *J* (where *p* = old MC) to point *N* (where *p* = new MC).

To reduce costs, firms sought to reduce the number of microprocessor chips installed in the computer's "brain." Fewer chips not only reduce direct materials costs, but more importantly, they decrease the amount of labor required for computer assembly. The key to lower manufacturing costs was more powerful chips. More powerful chips appeared when Intel, Motorola, and Texas Instruments developed 16-bit chips, doubling the computer's "brain" capabilities.

Further Supply Shifts

The impact of the improved chips on computer production costs and profits is illustrated in Figure 9.7, which takes over where Figure 9.5 left off. Recall that the market price of computers had been driven down to $700 by the beginning of 1980. At this price the typical firm maximized profits by producing 430 computers per month, as determined by the intersection of the prevailing price and MC curves (point *J* in Figure 9.7).

The only way for the firm to improve profitability at this point was to reduce costs. The new chips made such cost reductions easy. Such ***technological improvements are illustrated by a downward shift of the ATC and MC curves.*** Notice in Figure 9.7 how the new technology permits 430 computers to be produced for a lower marginal cost (about $500) than previously ($700 at point *J*).

The lower cost structure increases the profitability of computer production and stimulates a further increase in production. Note in particular that the "new MC" curve intersects the price ($700) line at an output of 600 computers per month (point *N*). By contrast, the old, higher MC curve dictated a production rate of only 430 computers per month for the typical firm (point *J*) at that price. Thus, existing producers suddenly had an incentive to *expand* production, and new firms had a greater incentive to *enter* the industry. The great rush into computer production was on again.

The market implications of another entrepreneurial stampede should now be obvious. As more and more firms tried to get in on the action, the market supply curve again shifted to the right. As output increased, computer prices slid further down the market demand curve.

Figure 9.8 illustrates how steeply prices fell after 1980 for the bare-bones computer manufactured by Texas Instruments. In just over three years (December 1979 to January 1983), the price for those computers plunged from $950 to $149. As the price plunged, so did profits. Fourth-quarter profits at Atari, for example, fell from $137 million in 1981 to only $1.2 million in 1983.

FIGURE 9.8

Plummeting Prices

Improved technology and fierce competition forced computer prices down. In the span of only a few years, the price of a basic computer fell from just under $1,000 to only $49. In the process, price fell below average variable cost, and many firms were forced to shut down.

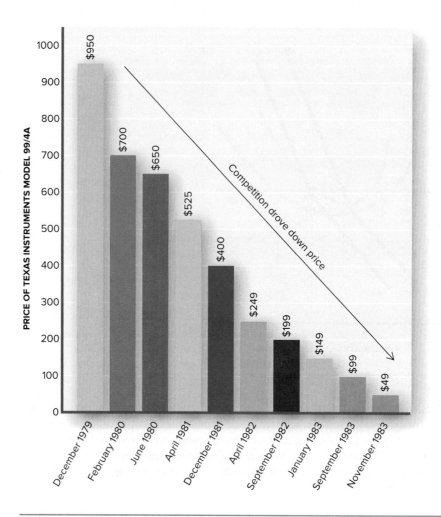

Shutdowns

That didn't stop the competitive process, however. At Texas Instruments, minimum *variable* costs were roughly $100 per computer in January 1983, so TI and other manufacturers could afford to keep producing even at lower prices. And they had little choice but to do so because if they didn't, other companies would quickly take up the slack. Industry output kept increasing despite shrinking profit margins. The increased supply pushed computer prices ever lower.

By the time computer prices reached $99 in September 1983, TI was losing $300 million per year. The company recognized then that the price would no longer even cover average variable costs. ***Once a firm is no longer able to cover variable costs, it should shut down production.*** When the price of basic, entry-level computers dipped below minimum average variable costs, TI had reached the **shutdown point,** and the company ceased production. At the time TI made the shutdown decision, the company had an inventory of nearly 500,000 unsold computers. To unload them, TI reduced its price to $49 (see Figure 9.8), forcing lower prices and losses on other computer firms.

shutdown point: The rate of output where price equals minimum AVC.

Exits

Shortly after Texas Instruments shut down its production, it got out of the computer business altogether. Mattel, Atari, and scores of smaller companies also withdrew from the computer market. The exit rate between 1983 and 1985 matched the entry rate of the period 1979 to 1982.

Product Innovation

The firms that survived the brutal price competition in the PC market largely did so by innovating. Firms added more memory, faster microprocessors, better monitors, expanded operating systems, new applications software, and other features. New entrants into the market—Compaq in 1982; then Dell, AST, Gateway, and more—were the source of most product innovations. They and scores of more recent entrants have created relentless pressure on Apple and other computer manufacturers to continue upgrading their products, improving cost-efficiencies, and reducing prices.

THE COMPETITIVE PROCESS

It is now evident that consumers have reaped substantial benefits from competition in the computer market. More than 2 billion personal computers have been sold. Along the way, technology has made personal computers five thousand times faster than the first Apple IIs, with phenomenal increases in memory. The iMac computer introduced by Apple in 1998 made the Apple I of 1976 look prehistoric. The latest iMacs make even the 1998 model look primitive. And an Apple Watch Series 6 has more power, speed, and features than the 1983 Apple IIe! How did all these innovations come about? When we look back at the evolution of the computer industry, we have to recognize that *competitive market pressures were a driving force in the spectacular growth of the computer industry.* And they still are.

Allocative Efficiency: The Right Output Mix

The squeeze on prices and profits that we've observed in the computer market is a fundamental characteristic of the competitive process. Indeed, the **market mechanism** works best under competitive pressure. The existence of economic profits is an indication that consumers place a high value on a particular product and are willing to pay a comparatively high price to get it. The high price and profits signal this information to profit-hungry entrepreneurs, who come forward to satisfy consumer demands. Thus, *high profits in a particular industry indicate that consumers want a different mix of output* (more of that industry's goods). The competitive squeeze on those same profits indicates that resources are being reallocated to produce that desired mix. In a competitive market, consumers get more of the goods they desire—and at a lower price.

market mechanism: The use of market prices and sales to signal desired outputs (or resource allocations).

iPhone 7 Plus and Apple Watch

Why does Apple keep improving its products?

Analysis: The evolution of personal computers from the Apple I to the latest iPhone, iPad, and Apple Watch was driven by intense competition.

The ability of competitive markets to allocate resources efficiently across industries originates in the way competitive prices are set. To attain the optimal mix of output, we must know the **opportunity cost** of producing different goods. A competitive market gives us the information necessary for making such choices. Why? Because competitive firms always strive to produce at the rate of output at which price equals marginal cost. Hence, *the price signal the consumer gets in a competitive market is an accurate reflection of opportunity cost.* As such, it offers a reliable basis for making choices about the mix of output and attendant allocation of resources. In this sense, the **marginal cost pricing** characteristic of competitive markets permits society to answer the WHAT-to-produce question efficiently. The amount consumers are willing to pay for a good (its price) equals its opportunity cost (marginal cost).

Production Efficiency: Minimum Average Cost

When the competitive pressure on prices is carried to the limit, we also get the right answer to the HOW-to-produce question. Competition drives costs down to their bare minimum—the hallmark of economic **efficiency.** This was illustrated by the tendency of computer prices to be driven down to the level of *minimum* average costs. Figure 9.9 summarizes this competitive process, showing how the industry moves from short-run equilibrium (point *a*) to long-run equilibrium (point *c*). Once the long-run equilibrium has been established, society is getting the most it can from its available (scarce) resources.

Zero Economic Profit

Competitive pressures also affect the FOR WHOM question. At the limit of long-run equilibrium, all economic profit is eliminated. This doesn't mean that producers are left empty-

FIGURE 9.9

Summary of Competitive Process

All competitive firms seek to produce at that output where MC = *p*. Hence, a competitive *industry* will produce at that rate of output where *industry* MC (the sum of all firms' MC curves) intersects market demand (point *a*).

If economic profits exist in the industry short-run equilibrium (as they do here because price exceeds ATC at point *a*), more firms will enter the industry. As they do, the *industry* MC (supply) curve will shift to the right. The shifting MC curve will pull the *industry* ATC curve along with it. As the *industry* MC curve continues to shift rightward, the intersection of MC and ATC (point *b*) eventually will reach the demand curve at point *c*. At point *c,* MC still equals price, but no economic profits exist and entry (shifts) will cease. Point *c* will be the *long-run* equilibrium of the industry.

If competitive pressures reduce costs (i.e., improve technology), the supply (MC) curve will shift further to the right and *down,* reducing long-run prices even more.

Note that MC = *p* in both short- and long-run equilibrium. Notice also that equilibrium must occur on the market demand curve.

handed, however. The zero-profit limit is rarely, if ever, reached because new products are continually being introduced, consumer demands change, and more efficient production processes are discovered. In fact, the competitive process creates strong pressures to pursue product and technological innovation. In a competitive market, the adage about the early bird getting the worm is particularly apt. As we observed in the computer market, the first ones to perceive and respond to the potential profitability of computer production were the ones who made the greatest profits.

Relentless Profit Squeeze

The sequence of events common to competitive markets evolves as follows:

* High prices and profits signal consumers' demand for more output.
* Economic profit attracts new suppliers.
* The market supply curve shifts to the right.
* Prices slide down the market demand curve.
* A new equilibrium is reached at which increased quantities of the desired product are produced and its price is lower. Average costs of production are at or near a minimum, much more of the product is supplied and consumed, and economic profit approaches zero.
* Throughout the process, producers experience great pressure to keep ahead of the profit squeeze by reducing costs, a pressure that frequently results in product and technological innovation.

What is essential to remember about the competitive process is that the ***potential threat of other firms expanding production or of new firms entering the industry keeps existing firms on their toes.*** Even the most successful firm can't rest on its laurels for long. To stay in the game, competitive firms must continually update technology, improve their products, and reduce costs.

DECISIONS FOR TOMORROW

$29 AirPods?

Competition didn't end with computers. Steve Jobs, the guy who started the personal computer business back in 1977, knew that. He introduced another hot consumer product in November 2001—the iPod. The iPod was the first mass-produced portable digital music player. It allowed consumers to download, store, and retrieve up to 1,000 songs. Its compact size, sleek design, and simple functionality made it an instant success: Apple was selling iPods as fast as they could be produced, piling up huge profits in the process.

So what happened? Other entrepreneurs quickly got the scent of iPod's profits. Within a matter of months, competitors were designing their own digital music players. By 2003 the "attack of the iPod clones" was in full force. Competitors were adding new features, shrinking the size, and reducing prices on MP3 players.

Under these circumstances, Apple could not afford to sit back and admire its profits. Steve Jobs knew he'd have to keep running to stay ahead of the MP3 player pack. He kept improving the iPod. Within 2 years Apple had three generations of iPods, each substantially better than the last. Memory capacity increased tenfold (to 10,000 songs), features were added, and the size shrank further. In less than 2.5 years, the iPod's price fell by 40 percent even while quality improved dramatically.

iPads. The same kind of unrelenting competitive dynamic has hounded Apple's iPad. The iPad wasn't the first tablet computer, but it was a huge success: 300,000 iPads were sold on the first day and 15 million in the first year (2010). Apple reaped enormous profits.

Continued

Those profits signaled a slew of companies to enter the tablet market, seeking to get a piece of the new profit pie. More than 100 companies entered the tablet market in 2011 alone, putting enormous pressure on Apple's sales, price, and profits. Apple stayed ahead of the competitive pack by reducing price, adding new features (e.g., built-in cameras, faster processor, four speakers, live video, Bluetooth keyboard), and shrinking the tablet's size and weight.

AirPods. Apple launched another successful product in December 2016: AirPods, the first wireless earbud. They were an immediate hit, with 16 million sold in the first year. And they were insanely profitable: The AirPods cost $59–$69 to produce and were being sold for $159. That was a profit margin of 56–62 percent! Tim Cook, CEO of Apple, was absolutely correct when he called the AirPods "a runaway success."

Tim Cook wasn't the only one who noticed these gigantic profit margins. Within a year's time dozens of other firms started producing wireless earbuds. Some, like Amazon, Microsoft, Sony, Jaybird, and Samsung, focused on creating upmarket styles and features that would compare well with Apple's AirPods. Dozens of other firms, like Fantime, DoingTop, Usams, OnePlus, and Anke, simply produced AirPod knockoffs at lower prices (as low as $29.99 in January 2020).

Once again, Apple couldn't afford to sit back and enjoy its success. With packs of competitors innovating and cutting costs, Apple has to again run fast just to keep ahead of the pack. This kind of competitive pressure will force continuing improvements in earbuds and, who knows, maybe $29 AirPods in the near future.

What will happen to the price of AirPods?
Photographer and videographer/iStock/Getty Images

SUMMARY

- A perfectly competitive firm has no power to alter the market price of the product it sells. The perfectly competitive firm confronts a horizontal demand curve for its own output even though the relevant *market* demand curve is negatively sloped. **LO9-1**

- Profit maximization induces the competitive firm to produce at that rate of output where marginal costs equal price (MC = p). This represents the short-run equilibrium of the firm. **LO9-2**

- If profits exist in short-run equilibrium, new firms will enter the market. The resulting shift of supply will drive market prices down the market demand curve. As prices fall, the profit of the industry and its constituent firms will be squeezed. **LO9-3**

- The limit to the competitive price and profit squeeze is reached when price is driven down to the level of minimum average total cost (MC = p = ATC). At this point (long-run equilibrium), additional output and profit will be attained only if technology is improved (lowering costs) or if market demand increases. **LO9-3**

• Firms will shut down production if price falls below average variable cost. Firms will exit the industry if they foresee continued economic losses. **LO9-3**

• The most distinctive thing about competitive markets is the persistent pressure they exert on prices and profits.

The threat of competition is a tremendous incentive for producers to respond quickly to consumer demands and to seek more efficient means of production. In this sense, competitive markets do best what markets are supposed to do—efficiently allocate resources. **LO9-4**

Key Terms

equilibrium price
market supply
marginal cost (MC)
investment decision
economic profit
competitive market

barriers to entry
production decision
average total cost (ATC)
profit per unit
short-run competitive equilibrium
long-run competitive equilibrium

shutdown point
market mechanism
opportunity cost
marginal cost pricing
efficiency

Questions for Discussion

1. Why would anyone want to enter a profitable industry knowing that profits would eventually be eliminated by competition? **LO9-3**

2. Why wouldn't producers necessarily want to produce output at the lowest average cost? Under what conditions would they end up doing so? **LO9-1**

3. What industries do you regard as being highly competitive? Can you identify any barriers to entry in those industries? **LO9-1**

4. Why do TV prices continue to fall so much? (See World View "Flat Panels, Thin Margins.") **LO9-2**

5. What drives prices down in competitive markets? What stops prices from falling? **LO9-3**

6. As the price of computers fell, what happened to their quality? How is this possible? **LO9-4**

7. Will the price of AirPods really get as low as $29? **LO9-3**

8. Is "long-run" equilibrium permanent? What forces might dislodge it? **LO9-3**

9. Why don't catfish farmers raise the price of their fish and create better profits? **LO9-2**

10. Identify two products that have either (*a*) fallen sharply in price or (*b*) gotten significantly better without price increases. How did these changes come about? **LO9-4**

11. What happens to the factors of production that exit an industry? **LO9-4**

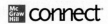
LO9-2 1. According to Table 9.1,
    (*a*) What were the fixed costs of production for the firm?
    (*b*) At what rate of output was profit per computer maximized? (Choose the highest output level.)
    (*c*) At what output rate was total profit maximized?

LO9-2 2. According to Figure 9.3*b*, if the market price for computers is $800,
    (*a*) What is the profit-maximizing quantity?
    (*b*) Calculate the profits (or losses) for this typical firm.
    (*c*) At this market price, will firms enter or exit the market?
    (*d*) Will this entry or exit cause prices to rise or fall?

LO9-1 3. Suppose the following data summarize the costs of a perfectly competitive firm:

Quantity	0	1	2	3	4	5	6	7	8
Total cost	$100	101	103	106	110	115	121	128	136

    (*a*) Draw the firm's MC curve on graph (*a*).
    (*b*) Draw the market supply curve on graph (*b*), assuming there are 8 firms identical to the one just described.
    (*c*) What is the equilibrium price in this market?

LO9-1 4. Suppose the following data describe the demand for fruit smoothies:

Price	$11	$10	$9	$8	$7	$6	$5	$4	$3	$2
Quantity demanded	7	10	13	16	19	22	25	28	31	34

Five identical, perfectly competitive firms are producing these smoothies. The cost of producing these smoothies at each firm is the following:

Quantity produced	0	1	2	3	4	5	6	7	8	9	10
Total cost	$5	$8	$10	$13	$17	$22	$28	$36	$45	$55	$67

    (*a*) What price will prevail in this market?
    (*b*) What quantity is produced?
    (*c*) How much profit (loss) does each firm make?
    (*d*) What happens to price if two more identical firms enter the market?

PROBLEMS FOR CHAPTER 9 (cont'd)

LO9-3 5. Suppose the typical catfish farmer was incurring an economic loss at the prevailing price p_1.
    (*a*) Illustrate these losses on the market and firm graphs. Include the supply and demand curves on the market graph and average total cost, marginal cost, and price in the firm graph.
    (*b*) Identify the price that would prevail in the long-run equilibrium.
    (*c*) What supply forces would raise the price to this long run equilibrium. Illustrate your answer on the graphs.

LO9-2 6. According to Table 9.1,
    (*a*) What was the prevailing computer price in 1978?
    (*b*) How much total profit did the typical firm earn?
    (*c*) At what price would profits have been zero?
    (*d*) At what price would the firm have shut down?

LO9-2 7. If a competitive firm has fixed costs of $15,000 per month and a minimum average variable cost of $26, at what price will it shut down?

LO9-4 8. Suppose that the monthly market demand schedule for Frisbees is

Price	$8	$7	$6	$5	$4	$3	$2	$1
Quantity demanded	1,000	2,000	4,000	8,000	16,000	32,000	64,000	128,000

Suppose further that the marginal and average costs of Frisbee production for every competitive firm are

Rate of output	100	200	300	400	500	600
Marginal cost	$2.00	$3.00	$4.00	$5.00	$6.00	$7.00
Average total cost	2.00	2.50	3.00	3.50	4.00	4.50

Finally, assume that the equilibrium market price is $6 per Frisbee.
    (*a*) Draw the cost curves of the typical firm and identify its profit-maximizing rate of output and its total profits.
    (*b*) Draw the market demand curve and identify market equilibrium.
    (*c*) How many Frisbees are being sold?
    (*d*) How many (identical) firms are initially producing Frisbees?
    (*e*) How much profit is the typical firm making?
    (*f*) In view of the profits being made, more firms will enter into Frisbee production, shift the market supply curve to the right, and push price down. At what equilibrium price are all profits eliminated?
    (*g*) How many firms will be producing Frisbees at this long-term price?

(a) The firm

(b) The market

LO9-3 9. Suppose the competitive tablet market is in the long-run equilibrium. If at this equilibrium, the typical firm produces 20,000 tablets per month, total costs for this production are $1,800,000, and the minimum of the average variable costs is $70, what price will
   (a) Induce entry into the market?
   (b) Cause firms to shut down production in the short run?
   (c) Result in firms exiting the market in the long run?

10. *Decisions for Tomorrow:*
   (a) If the average total cost of producing AirPods was $64 in 2016–2017, how much profit did Apple make that first year of sales? (See "Decisions for Tomorrow" section.)
   (b) Suppose the profit per unit in 2021 was half that of 2016–2017. If Apple sold 100 million AirPods in 2021, how much profit would Apple have made in 2021?

Design Credit: Shutterstock

CHAPTER 10

Monopoly

In 1908 Ford produced the Model T, the car "designed for the common man." It was cheap, reliable, and as easy to drive as the horse and buggy it was replacing. Ford sold 10,000 Model Ts in its first full year of production (1909). After that, sales more than doubled every year. In 1913 nearly 200,000 Model Ts were sold; and Ford was fast changing U.S. patterns of consumption, travel, and living standards.

During this early development of the U.S. auto industry, Henry Ford dominated the field. There were other producers, but the Ford Motor Company was the only producer of an inexpensive "motorcar for the multitudes." In this situation, Henry Ford could dictate the price and the features of his cars. When he opened his new assembly line factory at Highland Park, he abruptly raised the Model T's price by $100—an increase of 12 percent—to help pay for the new plant. Then he decided to paint all Model Ts black. When told of consumer complaints about the lack of colors, Ford advised one of his executives in 1913, "Give them any color they want so long as it's black."[1]

Henry Ford had market power. He could dictate what color car Americans would buy. And he could raise the price of Model Ts without fear of losing all his customers. Such power is alien to competitive firms. Competitive firms are always under pressure to reduce costs, improve quality, and cater to consumer preferences.

In this chapter we examine how market structure influences market outcomes. Specifically, we examine how a market controlled by a single producer—a monopoly—behaves. We're particularly interested in the following questions:

- **What price will a monopolist charge?**
- **How much output will the monopolist produce?**
- **Are consumers better or worse off when only one firm controls an entire market?**

MARKET POWER

The essence of **market power** is the ability to alter the price of a product. The catfish farmers in Chapter 9 had no such power. Because 2,000 farms were producing and selling the same good, each catfish producer had to act as a *price taker*. Each producer could sell all it wanted at the prevailing price but would lose all its customers if it tried to charge a higher price.

[1]Charles E. Sorensen, *My Forty Years with Ford* (New York: W. W. Norton & Co., 1956), p. 127.

FIGURE 10.1
Firm vs. Industry Demand

A competitive firm can sell its entire output at the prevailing market price. In this sense, the firm confronts a horizontal demand curve, as in part *a*. Nevertheless, *market* demand for the product still slopes downward. The demand curve confronting the industry is illustrated in part *b*. Note the difference in the units of measurement (single bushels vs. thousands). A monopolist confronts the *industry* (market) demand curve.

(a) The competitive firm

PRICE (dollars per bushel)

$13 ──────────────── Demand facing competitive firm

0

QUANTITY
(bushels of fish per day)

(b) The industry

PRICE (dollars per bushel)

Market demand

$13 ──── ●

In perfect competition, the **firm** is not the **industry**; in monopoly it is.

0

QUANTITY
(thousands of bushels of fish per day)

market power: The ability to alter the market price of a good or service.

The Downward-Sloping Demand Curve

Firms that have market power *can* alter the price of their output without losing all their customers. Sales volume may drop when price is increased, but the quantity demanded won't drop to zero. In other words, *firms with market power confront downward-sloping demand curves for their own output.*

The distinction between perfectly competitive (powerless) and imperfectly competitive (powerful) firms is illustrated again in Figure 10.1. Figure 10.1*a* re-creates the market situation that confronts a single catfish farmer. In Chapter 8, we assumed that the prevailing price of catfish was $13 a bushel and that a small, competitive firm could sell its entire output at this price. Hence, each individual firm effectively confronted a horizontal demand curve.

We also noted earlier that catfish don't violate the law of demand. As good as catfish taste, people aren't willing to buy unlimited quantities of them at $13 a bushel. To induce consumers to buy more catfish, the market price of catfish must be reduced.

This seeming contradiction between the law of demand and the situation of the competitive firm is resolved in Figure 10.1. There are *two* relevant demand curves. The one on the left, which appears to contradict the law of demand, refers to a single competitive producer. The one on the right refers to the entire *industry,* of which the competitive producer is one very tiny part. The industry or market demand curve *does* slope downward, even though individual competitive firms are able to sell their own output at the going price.

Monopoly

An industry needn't be composed of many small firms. The entire output of catfish could be produced by a single large producer. Such a firm would be a **monopoly**—a single firm that produces the entire market supply of a good.

monopoly: A firm that produces the entire market supply of a particular good or service.

The emergence of a monopoly obliterates the distinction between industry demand and the demand curve facing the firm. A monopolistic firm *is* the industry. Hence, there's only *one* demand curve to worry about, and that's the market (industry) demand curve, as illustrated in Figure 10.1*b*. This simplifies things: *In monopoly situations, the demand curve facing the firm is identical to the market demand curve for the product.*

Price and Marginal Revenue

profit-maximization rule: Produce at that rate of output where marginal revenue equals marginal cost.

Although monopolies simplify the geometry, they complicate the arithmetic of **profit maximization.** The basic rule for maximizing profits is unchanged—that is, produce the rate of output where marginal revenue equals marginal cost. This rule applies to *all* firms. In a competitive industry, however, this general rule was simplified. For competitive firms, marginal revenue is equal to price. Hence, a competitive firm can maximize profits by producing at that rate of output where marginal cost equals *price.*

This special adaptation of the profit-maximizing rule doesn't work for a monopolist. The demand curve facing a monopolist is downward-sloping. Because of this, *marginal revenue isn't equal to price for a monopolist.* On the contrary, marginal revenue is always *less* than price in a monopoly, which makes it just a bit more difficult to find the profit-maximizing rate of output.

Figure 10.2 is a simple illustration of the relationship between price and marginal revenue. The monopolist can sell 1 bushel of fish per day at a price of $13. If he wants to sell a larger quantity of fish, however, he has to reduce his price. According to the demand curve shown here, the price must be lowered to $12 to sell 2 bushels per day. This reduction in price is shown by a movement along the demand curve from point *A* to point *B*.

How much additional revenue does the second bushel bring in? It's tempting to say that it brings in $12 because that's its price. **Marginal revenue (MR),** however, refers to the *change* in *total* revenue that results from a one-unit increase in output. More generally, we use the formula

$$\frac{\text{Marginal}}{\text{revenue}} = \frac{\text{Change in total revenue}}{\text{Change in quantity sold}} = \frac{\Delta \text{TR}}{\Delta q}$$

where the delta symbol Δ denotes "change in." According to this formula, the marginal revenue of the second bushel is

$$\text{MR} = \frac{\$24 - \$13}{1} = \$11.$$

Hence, MR ($11) is less than price ($12) for the second bushel sold.

marginal revenue (MR): The change in total revenue that results from a one-unit increase in the quantity sold.

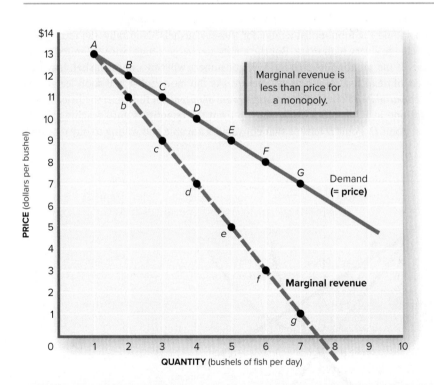

	Quantity	×	Price	=	Total Revenue	Marginal Revenue (= ΔTR ÷ Δq)
A	1		$13		$13	–
B	2		12		24	$11
C	3		11		33	9
D	4		10		40	7
E	5		9		45	5

FIGURE 10.2

Price Exceeds Marginal Revenue in Monopoly

If a firm must lower its price to sell additional output, marginal revenue is less than price. If this monopoly firm wants to increase its sales from 1 to 2 bushels per day, for example, price must be reduced from $13 to $12. The marginal revenue of the second bushel is therefore only $11. This is indicated in row *B* of the table and by point *b* on the graph.

Figure 10.2 summarizes the calculations necessary for computing MR. Row *A* of the table indicates that the total revenue resulting from one sale per day is $13. To increase sales, price must be reduced. Row *B* indicates that total revenue rises to $24 per day when fish sales double. The *increase* in total revenue resulting from the added sales is thus $11. This concept is illustrated in the last column of the table and by point *b* on the marginal revenue curve.

Notice that the MR of the second bushel ($11) is *less* than its price ($12) because both bushels are being sold for $12 apiece. In effect, the firm is giving up the opportunity to sell only 1 bushel per day at $13 to sell a larger quantity at a lower price. In this sense, the firm is sacrificing $1 of potential revenue on the first bushel to increase *total* revenue. Marginal revenue measures the change in total revenue that results.

So long as the demand curve is downward-sloping, MR will always be less than price. Compare columns 2 and 4 of the table in Figure 10.2. At each rate of output in excess of 1 bushel, marginal revenue is less than price. This is also evident in the graph: *The MR curve lies below the demand (price) curve at every point but the first.*

Profit Maximization

Although the presence of market power adds a new wrinkle, the rules of profit maximization remain the same. ***Instead of looking for an intersection of marginal cost and price (as in perfect competition), we now look for the intersection of marginal cost and marginal revenue (monopoly).*** This is illustrated in Figure 10.3 by the intersection of the MR and MC curves (point *d*). Looking down from that intersection, we see that the associated rate of output is 4 bushels per day. Thus, 4 bushels is the profit-maximizing rate of output.

How much should the monopolist charge for these 4 bushels? Naturally, the monopolist would like to charge a very high price. But the ability to charge a high price is limited by the demand curve. If the monopolist charges $13, consumers will buy only 1 bushel, leaving 3 unsold bushels of dead fish. Not a pretty picture. As the monopolist will soon learn, ***only one price is compatible with the profit-maximizing rate of output.*** In this case, the price is $10. This price is found in Figure 10.3 by moving up from the quantity 4 until reaching the demand curve at point *D*. Point *D* tells us that consumers are able and willing to buy 4 bushels

FIGURE 10.3

Profit Maximization (MR = MC)

The most profitable rate of output is indicated by the intersection of marginal revenue and marginal cost (point *d*). This intersection (MC = MR) establishes 4 bushels as the profit-maximizing rate of output. Point *D* indicates that consumers will pay $10 per bushel for this much output.

Total profits equal price ($10) minus average total cost ($8), multiplied by the quantity sold (4).

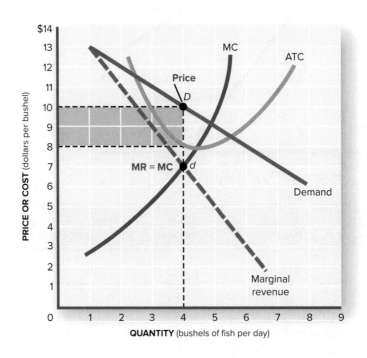

of fish per day only at the price of $10 each. A monopolist who tries to charge more than $10 won't be able to sell all 4 bushels.

Figure 10.3 also illustrates the total profits of the catfish monopoly. To compute total profits, we can first calculate profit per unit—that is, price minus *average* total cost. In this case, profit per unit is $2 at the profit-maximizing rate of output. Multiplying profit per unit by the quantity sold (4) gives us total profits of $8 per day, as illustrated by the shaded rectangle.

MARKET POWER AT WORK: THE COMPUTER MARKET REVISITED

To develop a keener appreciation for the nature of market power, we can return to the computer market of Chapter 9. The computer market wasn't perfectly competitive, but it nearly behaved as though it was. We saw how the continuing entry of new firms kept competitive pressure on computer firms to reduce costs and improve quality. In this chapter, we'll make some different assumptions about market structure. In particular, assume that a single firm, Universal Electronics, acquires an exclusive patent on the production of the microprocessors that function as the computer's "brain." This one firm is now in a position to deny potential competitors access to the basic ingredient of computers. The patent thus functions as a **barrier to entry,** to be erected or set aside at the will of Universal Electronics.

Universal's management is familiar enough with the principles of economics (including W. C. Fields's advice about never giving a sucker an even break) to know when it's onto a good thing. It's not about to let every would-be Horatio Alger have a slice of the profit pie. Even the Russians understood this strategy during the heyday of communism. They made sure no one else could produce sable furs that could compete with their monopoly (see World View "Russia's Sable Monopoly Persists"). Let's assume that Universal Electronics is equally protective of its turf and will refuse to sell or give away any rights to its patent or the chips it produces. That is, Universal Electronics sets itself up as a computer monopoly.

barriers to entry: Obstacles such as patents that make it difficult or impossible for would-be producers to enter a particular market.

WORLD VIEW

RUSSIA'S SABLE MONOPOLY PERSISTS

Ancient Greeks and Romans called the fur of the sable the "Golden Fleece." Unlike any other fur, sable is smooth in all directions, even after stroked. Living in the wilds of Siberia, the sable has always been one of Russia's most valuable exports. In 1697 Peter the Great decreed a monopoly on sable, forbidding the export of live sables or the technology of breeding them. In the 1980s Russia was selling more than 15 million sable pelts a year and reaping monopoly-type profits. Exporting live sables or the breeding technology was a crime punishable by death. The plot of the 1983 movie *Gorky Park* centers on the murder of three men who attempted to export live sables out of Russia.

CRITICAL ANALYSIS: To ward off potential competition, a monopoly must erect **barriers to entry.** By not letting live sables leave the country, to breed elsewhere, Russia maintained a monopoly on sable furs.

Let's also assume that Universal has a multitude of manufacturing plants, each of which is identical to the typical competitive firm in Chapter 9. This is an unlikely situation because a monopolist would probably achieve **economies of scale** by closing at least a few plants and consolidating production in larger plants. Our fictional Universal company

economies of scale: Reductions in minimum average costs that come about through increases in the size (scale) of plant and equipment.

would maintain a multitude of small plants only if constant returns to scale or actual diseconomies of scale were rampant. Nevertheless, by assuming that multiple plants are maintained, we can compare monopoly behavior with competitive behavior on the basis of identical cost structures. In particular, if Universal continues to operate the many plants that once made up the competitive home computer industry, it will confront the same short-run marginal and average cost curves already encountered in Chapter 9. Later in this chapter we relax this assumption of multiplant operations to determine whether, in the long run, a monopolist may actually lower production costs below those of a competitive industry.

Figure 10.4a re-creates the marginal costs the typical competitive firm faced in the early stages of the microcomputer boom (from Figure 9.3 and Table 9.1). We now assume that this MC curve also expresses the costs of operating one of Universal's many (identical) plants. Thus, the extension of monopoly control is assumed to have no immediate effect on production costs.

The market demand for computers is also assumed to be unchanged. There's no reason why people should be less willing to buy computers now than they were when the market was competitive. Most consumers have no notion of how many firms produce a product. Even if they knew, there's no reason why their demand for the product would change. Thus, Figure 10.4b expresses an unchanged market demand for computers.

Our immediate concern is to determine how Universal Electronics, as a monopolist, will respond to these unchanged demand and cost curves. Will it produce exactly as many computers as the competitive industry did? Will it sell the computers at the same price that the competitive industry did? Will it improve the product as much or as fast?

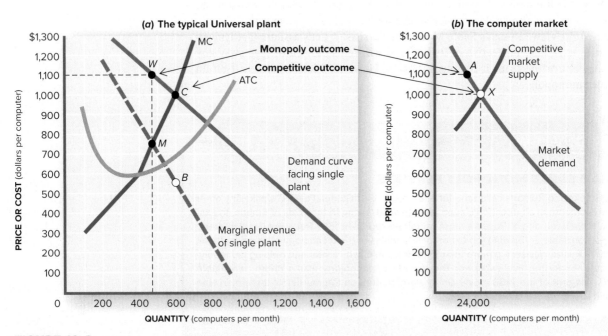

FIGURE 10.4

Initial Conditions in the Monopolized Computer Market

We assume that a monopoly firm (Universal Electronics) would confront the same costs (MC and ATC) and demand as would the competitive industry in Chapter 9. In the initial short-run equilibrium, the competitive price was $1,000 (point C), and each firm (plant) was producing 600 computers (where MC = p).

A monopolist isn't bound by the competitive market price. Instead the monopolist must contend with downward-sloping demand and marginal revenue curves. If each monopoly plant produced where MC = $1,000 (point C in part a), marginal cost (point C) would exceed marginal revenue (point B). To maximize profits, the monopolist must find that rate of output where MC = MR (point M in part a). That rate of output (475) can be sold at the higher monopoly price of $1,100 (point W in part a).

Part b illustrates the market implications of the monopolist's production decision: A reduced quantity is sold at a higher price (point A).

The Production Decision

Like any producer, Universal Electronics will strive to produce its output at the rate that maximizes total profits. But unlike competitive firms, Universal will explicitly take account of the fact that an increase in output will put downward pressure on computer prices. This may threaten corporate profits.

The implications of Universal's market position for the **production decision** of its many plants can be seen in the new price and marginal revenue curves imposed on each of its manufacturing plants. Universal can't afford to let each of its plants compete with the others, expanding output and driving down prices; that's the kind of folly reserved for truly competitive firms. Instead Universal will seek to *coordinate* the production decisions of its plants, instructing all plant managers to expand or contract output simultaneously, to achieve the corporate goal of profit maximization.

A simultaneous reduction of output by each Universal plant will lead to a significant reduction in the quantity of computers supplied to the market. This reduced supply will cause a move up the market demand curve to higher prices. By the same token, an expansion of output by all Universal plants will lead to an increase in the quantity supplied to the market and a slide down the market demand curve. As a consequence, each of the monopolist's plants effectively confronts a downward-sloping demand curve. These downward-sloping demand curves are illustrated in Figure 10.4a.[2]

Notice that in Figure 10.4b the *market* demand for computers is unchanged; only the demand curve confronting each plant (firm) has changed. A competitive *industry,* like a monopoly, must obey the law of demand. But the individual firms that compose a competitive industry all act independently, *as if* they could sell unlimited quantities at the prevailing price. That is, they all act as if they confronted a horizontal demand curve at the market price of $1,000. A competitive firm that doesn't behave in this fashion will simply lose sales to other firms. In contrast, *a monopolist not only foresees the impact of increased production on market price but also can prevent such production increases by its separate plants.*

Marginal Revenue. The downward-sloping demand curve now confronting each Universal plant implies that marginal revenue no longer equals price. Notice that the marginal revenue curve in Figure 10.4a lies *below* the demand curve at every rate of output. Because marginal revenue is less than price for a monopoly, Universal's plants would no longer wish to produce up to the point where marginal cost equals price. *Only firms that confront a horizontal demand curve (perfect competitors) equate marginal cost and price.* Universal's plants must stick to the generic profit-maximizing rule about equating marginal revenue and marginal cost. Should the individual plant managers forget this rule, Universal's central management will fire them.

The output and price implications of Universal's monopoly position become apparent as we examine the new revenue and cost relationships. Recall that the equilibrium price of computers in the early stages of the home computer boom was $1,000. This equilibrium price is indicated in Figure 10.4b by the intersection of the *competitive* market supply curve with the market demand curve (point *X*). Each competitive *firm* produced up to the point where marginal cost (MC) equaled that price (point *C* in Figure 10.4a). At that point, each competitive firm was producing 600 computers a month.

Reduced Output. The emergence of Universal as a monopolist alters these production decisions. Now each Universal plant *does* have an impact on market price because its behavior is imitated simultaneously by all Universal plants. In fact, the marginal revenue associated with the 600th computer is only $575, as indicated by point *B* in Figure 10.4a.

production decision: The selection of the short-run rate of output (with existing plants and equipment).

[2]The demand and marginal revenue curves in Figure 10.4a are illustrative; they're not derived from earlier tables. As discussed here, we're assuming that the central management of Universal determines the profit-maximizing rate of output and then instructs all individual plants to produce equal shares of that output.

At this rate of output, the typical Universal plant would be operating with marginal costs ($1,000) far in excess of marginal revenues ($575). Such behavior is inconsistent with profit maximization.

The enlightened Universal plant manager will soon discover that the profit-maximizing rate of output is less than 600 computers per month. In Figure 10.4*a* we see that the marginal revenue and marginal cost curves intersect at point *M*. This MR = MC intersection occurs at an output level of only 475 computers per month. Accordingly, the typical Universal plant will want to produce *fewer* computers (475) than were produced by the typical competitive firm (600) in the early stages of the home computer boom. Recall that individual competitive firms had no incentive to engage in such production cutbacks. They couldn't alter the market supply curve or price on their own and weren't coordinated by a central management. Thus, the first consequence of Universal's monopoly position is a reduction in the rate of industry output.

The Monopoly Price

The reduction in output at each Universal plant translates automatically into a decrease in the *quantity supplied* to the market. As consumers compete for this reduced market supply, they'll bid computer prices up. We can observe the increased prices in Figure 10.4 by looking at either the typical Universal plant or the computer market. Notice that in Figure 10.4*a* the price is determined by moving directly up from point *M* to the demand curve confronting the typical Universal plant. The demand curve always tells how much consumers are willing to pay for any given quantity. Hence, once we've determined the quantity that's going to be supplied (475 computers per month), we can look at the demand curve to determine the price ($1,100 at point *W*) that consumers will pay for these computers. That is,

- *The intersection of the marginal revenue and marginal cost curves establishes the profit-maximizing rate of output.*
- *The demand curve tells us how much consumers are willing to pay for that specific quantity of output.*

Figure 10.4*a* shows how Universal's monopoly position results in both reduced output and increased prices. This result is also evident in Figure 10.4*b*, where we see that a smaller quantity supplied to the market will force a move up the demand curve to the higher price of $1,100 per computer (point *A*).

Monopoly Profits

Universal's objective was and remains the maximization of profits. That it has succeeded in its effort can be confirmed by scrutinizing Figure 10.5. As you can see, the typical Universal plant ends up selling 475 computers a month at a price of $1,100 each (point *W*). The **average total cost (ATC)** of production at this rate of output is only $630 (point *K*), as was detailed in Table 9.1.

As always, we can compute total profit as

Total profit = Profit per unit × Quantity sold

In this case, we see that

$$\text{Total profit} = (\$1{,}100 - \$630) \times 475$$

$$= \$223{,}250$$

This figure significantly exceeds the monthly profit of $180,000 earned by the typical competitive firm in the early stages of the computer boom (see Table 9.1).

It's apparent from these profit figures that Universal management has learned its economic principles well. By reducing the output of each plant and raising prices a little, it has managed to increase profits. This can be seen again in Figure 10.6, which is an enlarged

FIGURE 10.5
Monopoly Profits: The Typical Universal Plant

The profit-maximizing rate of output occurs where the marginal cost and marginal revenue curves intersect (point *M*). The demand curve indicates the price (point *W*) that consumers will pay for this much output.

Total profit equals price (*W*) minus *average* total cost (*K*), multiplied by the quantity sold (**475**). Total profits are represented by the shaded rectangle.

illustration of the *market* situation for the home computer industry. The figure translates the economics of our single-plant and competitive-firm comparison into the dimensions of the whole industry.

Figure 10.6 reaffirms that the competitive industry in Chapter 9 initially produces the quantity q_c and sells it at a price of $1,000 each. Its profits are equal to the rectangle formed by the points *R, X, U, T.* The monopolist, on the other hand, produces the smaller q_m and charges a higher price, $1,100. The monopoly firm's profits are indicated by the larger profit rectangle shaded in the figure. Thus, *a monopoly receives larger profits than a comparable competitive industry by reducing the quantity supplied and pushing prices up.* The larger

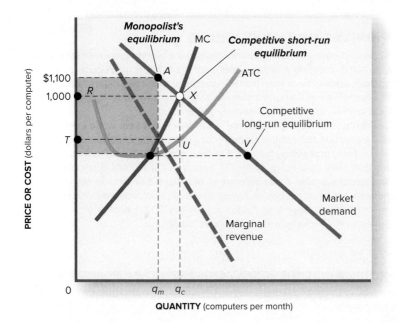

FIGURE 10.6
Monopoly Profit: The Entire Company

Total profits of the monopolist (including all plants) are illustrated by the shaded rectangle. The monopolist's total output q_m is determined by the intersection of the (industry) MR and MC curves. The price of this output is determined by the market demand curve (point *A*).

In contrast, a competitive industry would produce q_c computers in the short run and sell them at a lower price (*X*) and profit per unit (*X − U*). Those profits would attract new entrants until long-run equilibrium (point *V*) was reached. (See Figure 9.9 for a summary of competitive market equilibrium.)

profits make Universal very happy and make consumers a little sadder and wiser. Consumers are now paying more and getting less.

Barriers to Entry

The higher profits Universal Electronics attained as a result of its monopoly position aren't the end of the story. The existence of economic profit tends to bring profit-hungry entrepreneurs swarming like locusts. In the competitive computer industry of Chapter 9, the lure of high profits brought about an enormous expansion of computer output and a steep decline in computer prices. In Figure 10.6 the long-run equilibrium of a competitive industry is indicated by point V. What can we expect to happen in the computer market now that Universal has a monopoly position and is enjoying huge profits?

Remember that Universal is now assumed to have an exclusive patent on microprocessor chips and can use this patent as an impassable barrier to entry. Consequently, would-be competitors can swarm around Universal's profits until their wings drop off; Universal isn't about to let them in on the spoils. By locking out potential competition, Universal can prevent the surge in computer output that pushed prices down the market demand curve. As long as Universal is able to keep out the competition, only the more affluent consumers will be able to use computers.

The same phenomenom explains why ticket prices for live concerts are so high. When Live Nation acquired Ticketmaster in 2010, it became a virtual monopolist for concert sites and ticket distribution. Live Nation controls 500 artists, including U2 and Miley Cyrus, and more than 200 concert venues. It operates 80 of the top 100 venues in the United States. This gives it great power to decide who will sell concert tickets and how they will be distributed. Critics and competitors charge that Live Nation uses its near-monopoly power to pressure venues into using Ticketmaster as the sole ticketing agent. The end result is higher ticket prices and much greater profits for Live Nation (see Front Page Economics "Live Nation Drives Up Ticket Prices").

A monopoly has no incentive to move from point A in Figure 10.6, and there's no competitive pressure to force such a move. Universal may discover ways to reduce the costs of production and thus lower prices, but there's no *pressure* on it to do so, as there was in the competitive situation. Similarly, there's no *competitive pressure* on Live Nation to reduce concert prices.

FRONT PAGE ECONOMICS

LIVE NATION DRIVES UP TICKET PRICES

The world's largest concert promoter, Live Nation, acquired the world's largest ticket distributor, Ticketmaster, in 2010, creating a virtual monopoly on concert production and ticket sales. Bruce Springsteen warned back then that the merger of these two giants "would make the current ticket situation even worse for the fan than it is now" due to the increased monopoly power of the newly created Live Nation Entertainment.

He was right: Concert tickets have gotten more expensive every year while Live Nation's profits have steadily increased. In part, the higher prices have come about through a proliferation of fees: service fees, processing fees, facility fees, etc. A Government Accountablity Office study found that fees now account for 27 percent of a ticket's price and nearly 50 percent of Ticketmaster's profits. As Congressman Bill Pascrell of New Jersey observed, "coveted ticketed events are more expensive, harder to obtain, and larded with hidden fees."

The U.S. Justice Department sued Live Nation in January 2020, accusing it of strong-arming concert venues to hire Ticketmaster as their sole distributor.

Source: Media reports, April 2018–March 2020.

CRITICAL ANALYSIS: Control of concert sites and ticket distribution serves as **entry barriers** that enable Live Nation Entertainment to charge monopoly prices for live concerts.

A COMPARATIVE PERSPECTIVE OF MARKET POWER

The different outcomes of the computer industry under competitive and monopoly conditions illustrate basic features of market structures. We may summarize the sequence of events that occurs in each type of market structure as follows:

COMPETITIVE INDUSTRY	**MONOPOLY INDUSTRY**
• High prices and profits signal consumers' demand for more output.	• High prices and profits signal consumers' demand for more output.
• The high profits attract new suppliers.	• Barriers to entry are erected to exclude potential competition.
• Production and supplies expand.	• Production and supplies are constrained.
• Prices slide down the market demand curve.	• Prices don't move down the market demand curve.
• A new equilibrium is established wherein more of the desired product is produced, its price falls, average costs of production approach their minimum, and economic profits approach zero.	• No new equilibrium is established; average costs aren't necessarily at or near a minimum, and economic profits are at a maximum.
• Price equals marginal cost throughout the process.	• Price exceeds marginal cost at all times.
• Throughout the process, there's great pressure to keep ahead of the profit squeeze by reducing costs or improving product quality.	• There's no squeeze on profits and thus no pressure to reduce costs or improve product quality.

In our discussion, we assumed that both the competitive industry and the monopoly started from the same position—an initial equilibrium in which the price of computers is $1,000. In reality, an industry may manifest concentrations of market power *before* such an equilibrium is established. That is, the sequence of events we've depicted may be altered (with step 3 occurring first, e.g.). Nevertheless, the basic distinctions between competitive and monopolistic behavior are evident.

Productivity Advances. To the extent that monopolies behave as we've discussed, they affect not just the price and output of a specific product but broader economic outcomes as well. Remember that competitive industries tend, in the long run, to produce at minimum average costs. Competitive industries also pursue cost reductions and product improvements relentlessly. These pressures tend to expand our production possibilities. No such forces are at work in the monopoly we've discussed here. Hence, there's a basic tendency for monopolies to inhibit productivity advances and economic growth.

The Mix of Output. Another important feature of competitive markets is their observed tendency toward **marginal cost pricing.** Marginal cost pricing is important to consumers because it permits rational choices among alternative goods and services. In particular, it informs consumers of the true opportunity costs of various goods, thereby allowing them to choose the mix of output that delivers the most utility with available resources. In our monopoly example, however, consumers end up getting fewer computers than they'd like, while the economy continues to produce other, less desired goods. Thus, the mix of output shifted away from computers when Universal took over the industry.

The power to influence prices and product flows may have far-reaching consequences for our economic welfare. Changes in prices and product flows directly influence the level and composition of output, employment and resource allocation, the level and distribution of income, and, of course, the level and structure of prices. Hence, firms that wield significant market power affect all dimensions of economic welfare.

marginal cost pricing: The offer (supply) of goods at prices equal to their marginal cost.

Political Power. Market power isn't the only kind of power wielded in society, of course. Political power, for example, is a different kind of power and important in its own right. Indeed, the power to influence an election or to sway a Senate committee vote may ultimately be more important than the power to increase the price of laundry soap. Nevertheless, market power is a force that influences the way we live, the incomes we earn, and our relationships with other countries. Moreover, market power may be the basis for political power: The individual or firm with considerable market power is likely to have the necessary resources to influence an election or sway a vote on a congressional committee.

The Limits to Power

Even though market power enables a producer to manipulate market outcomes, there's a clear limit to the exercise of power. Even a monopolist can't get everything it wants. Universal, for example, would really like to sell q_m computers at a price of $1,500 each because that kind of price would bring it even greater profits. Yet, despite its monopoly position, Universal is constrained to sell that quantity of computers at the lower price of $1,100 each. Even monopolists have their little disappointments.

The ultimate limit to a monopolist's power is evident in Figure 10.6. Universal's attainment of a monopoly position allows it only one prerogative: the ability to alter the quantity of output *supplied* to the market. This is no small prerogative, but it's far from absolute power. Universal, and every other monopolist, must still contend with the market *demand* curve. Note again that the new equilibrium in Figure 10.6 occurs at a point on the *unchanged* market demand curve. In effect, ***a monopolist has the opportunity to pick any point on the market demand curve and designate it as the new market equilibrium.*** The point it selects will depend on its own perceptions of effort, profit, and risk (in this case point *A,* determined by the intersection of marginal revenue and marginal cost).

The ultimate constraint on the exercise of market power, then, resides in the market demand curve. How great a constraint the demand curve imposes depends largely on the **price elasticity of demand.** The greater the price elasticity of demand, the more a monopolist will be frustrated in attempts to establish both high prices and high volume. Consumers will simply reduce their purchases if price is increased. If, however, consumer demand is highly inelastic—if consumers need or want that product badly and few viable substitutes are available—the monopolist can reap tremendous profits from market power. That was clearly the case for the monopoly that produces a life-saving drug for AIDS patients (see Front Page Economics "Drugmaker Hikes Price of AIDS Drug 5,000 Percent!").

price elasticity of demand: The percentage change in quantity demanded divided by the percentage change in price.

FRONT PAGE ECONOMICS

DRUGMAKER HIKES PRICE OF AIDS DRUG 5,000 PERCENT!

Turing Pharmaceuticals hiked the price of Daraprim, a critical drug for preventing infections in people with the HIV virus, from $13.50 per capsule to $750. Turing, a pharmaceutical start-up, acquired the rights to Daraprim in August. In September, it announced a price hike of 5,000 percent. The company's CEO, Martin Shkreli, defended the price hike, saying, "the companies before us were actually giving it away almost." "We need to turn a profit on this drug," Shkreli told Bloomberg News. Because the cost of producing the drug is only $1 a capsule, Shkreli told his board of directors that the company could earn a cool billion dollars at the higher price.

Source: Media reports of September 2016.

CRITICAL ANALYSIS: If demand is **inelastic**, a monopolist can increase price without losing many sales.

Price Discrimination

Even in situations where the *market* demand is relatively elastic, a monopolist may be able to extract high prices. A monopolist has the power not only to raise the market price of a good (by reducing the quantity supplied) but also to charge various prices for the same good. Recall that the market demand curve reflects the combined willingness of many individuals to buy. Some of those individuals are willing to buy the good at prices higher than the market price, just as other individuals will buy only at lower prices. A monopolist may be able to increase total profits by selling each unit of the good separately, at a price each *individual* consumer is willing to pay. This practice is called **price discrimination.**

The airline industry has practiced price discrimination for many years. Basically, there are two distinct groups of travelers: business and nonbusiness travelers. Business executives must fly from one city to another on a certain day and at a particular time. They typically make flight arrangements on short notice and may have no other way to get to their destination. Nonbusiness travelers, such as people on vacation and students going home during semester break, usually have more flexible schedules. They may plan their trips weeks or months in advance and often have the option of traveling by car, bus, or train.

The different travel needs of business and vacation travelers are reflected in their respective demand curves. Business demand for air travel is less price-elastic than the demand of nonbusiness travelers. Few business executives would stop flying if airfares increased. Higher airfares would, however, discourage air travel by nonbusiness travelers.

What should airlines do in this case? Should they *raise* airfares to take advantage of the relative price inelasticity of business demand, or should they *lower* airfares to attract more nonbusiness travelers?

They should do both. In fact, they *have* done both. The airlines offer a full-fare ride, available at any time, and a discount-fare ride, available only by purchasing a ticket in advance and agreeing to some restrictions on time of departure. The advance purchase and other restrictions on discount fares effectively exclude most business travelers, who end up paying full fare. The higher full fare doesn't, however, discourage most nonbusiness travelers, who can fly at a discount. Consequently, the airlines are able to sell essentially identical units of the same good (an airplane ride) at substantially different prices to different customers. This price discrimination enables the airlines to capture the highest possible *average* price for the quantity supplied.

With *perfect* price discrimination, a monopolist would sell the product to each consumer on the demand curve at the maximum price that individual was willing to pay. If that happened, the monopolist would eliminate all **consumer surplus** and capture the extra revenue that a single price misses. Doctors, lawyers, and car dealers commonly practice this type of price discrimination.

> **price discrimination:** The sale of an individual good at different prices to different consumers.

> **consumer surplus:** The difference between the maximum price a person is willing to pay and the price paid.

Entry Barriers

It's the lack of competitors that gives monopolists such pricing power. Accordingly, *the preservation of monopoly power depends on keeping potential competitors out of the market.* A monopolist doesn't want anyone else to produce an *identical* product or even a *close substitute.* To do that, a monopoly must erect and maintain barriers to market entry. Some of the entry barriers used to repel would-be competitors include the following.

Patents. This was the critical barrier in the mythical Universal Electronics case. A government-awarded patent gives a producer 20 years of exclusive rights to produce a particular product. Turing Pharmaceuticals used those patent rights to hike the price of Daraprim by 5,000 percent overnight (see Front Page Economics "Drugmaker Hikes Price of AIDS Drug 5,000 Percent!"): No one was producing a substitute drug. The Polaroid

Corporation used its patents to keep Eastman Kodak and other potential rivals out of the market for instant development cameras. In 2015 Polaroid sued GoPro for patent infringement in the design of its cube-shaped camera (the Hero4 Session). In 2007 Verizon and Sprint used broad patents to curb the growth of Vonage, the leading provider of Internet phone service.

Monopoly Franchises. The government also creates and maintains monopolies by giving a single firm the exclusive right to supply a particular good or service, even though other firms could produce it. Local cable TV stations and telephone companies are examples. Congress also bestows monopoly privileges to baseball teams and the U.S. Postal Service. Your campus bookstore may have exclusive rights to sell textbooks on campus.

Control of Key Inputs. A company may lock out competition by securing exclusive access to key inputs. Airlines need landing rights and terminal gates to compete. Oil and gas producers need pipelines to supply their products. Utility companies need transmission networks to supply consumers with electricity. Software vendors need to know the features of computer operating systems. Ticket sellers need access to concert venues. If a single company controls these critical inputs, it can lock out potential competition. Intel was accused by the Federal Trade Commission (FTC) of trying to lock out competition by enticing computer makers with hefty discounts to use Intel chips exclusively in their computers. Microsoft was accused of using similar tactics to consolidate its monopoly position in operating systems. Google is under investigation for allegedly using its dominant online search engine to direct consumers to its own vendors (see "Decisions for Tomorrow" section at the end of this chapter).

Lawsuits. In the event that competitors actually surmount other entry barriers, a monopoly may sue them out of existence. Typically, start-up firms are rich in ideas but cash poor. They need to get their products to the market quickly to generate some cash. A timely lawsuit alleging patent or copyright infringement can derail such a company by absorbing critical management, cash, and time. Long before the merits of the lawsuit are adjudicated, the company may be forced to withdraw from the market. In 2019 the My Pillow company, famous for its TV ads, sued a small competitor, I Love My Pillow, for trademark infringement for using the words "my" and "pillow" in Google search ads. The 1,600-employee company, with $44 million in sales, was trying to keep the smaller, 9-employee upstart from gaining market share.

Acquisition. When all else fails, a monopolist may simply purchase a potential competitor. Live Nation's acquisition of Ticketmaster in 2010 (see Front Page Economics "Live Nation Drives Up Ticket Prices") eliminated competition in the ticket distribution system. Mergers tend to raise consumer prices.

Economies of Scale. Last but far from least, a monopoly may persist because of economies of scale. If large firms have a substantial cost advantage over smaller firms, the smaller firms may not be able to compete. We look at this entry barrier again in a moment.

PROS AND CONS OF MARKET POWER

Despite the strong case against market power, it's conceivable that monopolies could also benefit society. One argument made for concentrations of market power is that monopolies have greater ability to pursue research and development. Another argument is that the lure of market power creates a tremendous incentive for invention and innovation. A third argument in defense of monopoly is that large companies can produce goods more efficiently than smaller firms. Finally, it's argued that even monopolies have to worry about *potential* competition and will behave accordingly.

Research and Development

In principle, monopolies are well positioned to undertake valuable research and development. First, such firms are sheltered from the constant pressure of competition. Second, they have the resources (monopoly profits) with which to carry out expensive R&D functions. The manager of a perfectly competitive firm, by contrast, has to worry about day-to-day production decisions and profit margins. As a result, she is unable to take the longer view necessary for significant research and development and couldn't afford to purchase such a view even if she could see it.

The basic problem with the R&D argument is that it says nothing about *incentives*. Although monopolists have a clear financial advantage in pursuing research and development activities, they have no clear incentive to do so. Research and development aren't necessarily required for profitable survival. In fact, research and development that make existing plants and equipment technologically obsolete run counter to a monopolist's vested interest and so may actually be suppressed (see Front Page Economics "Jury Awards $26 Million for Suppressed Technology"). In contrast, a perfectly competitive firm can't continue to make significant profits unless it stays ahead of the competition. This pressure constitutes a significant incentive to discover new products or new and cheaper ways of producing existing products.

FRONT PAGE ECONOMICS

JURY AWARDS $26 MILLION FOR SUPPRESSED TECHNOLOGY

Two Bay Area entrepreneurs won a $25.7 million judgment in Oakland's U.S. district court yesterday for the suppression of their energy-saving technology. In 1984, C. R. Stevens and William Alling sold to Universal Manufacturing Company a new technology that reduces the energy consumption of fluorescent lighting by 70 percent. But Universal never marketed the new technology, as it had promised. Stevens and Alling claimed that Universal suppressed their invention in order to protect its existing, less-efficient technology. The jury agreed and ordered Universal to pay $25.7 million in damages.

Source: News reports, January 10–15, 1990.

CRITICAL ANALYSIS: A monopoly has little **incentive** (due to no competitive pressure) to pursue R&D. In fact, R&D that threatens established products or processes may be suppressed.

Entrepreneurial Incentives

The second defense of market power uses a novel incentive argument. Every business is out to make a buck, and it's the quest for profits that keeps industries running. Thus, it's argued, even greater profit prizes will stimulate more entrepreneurial activity. Little Horatio Algers will work harder and longer if they can dream of one day possessing a whole monopoly.

The incentive argument for market power is enticing but not entirely convincing. After all, an innovator can make substantial profits in a competitive market before the competition catches up. Recall that the early birds did get the worm in the competitive computer industry (see Chapter 9), even though profit margins were later squeezed. It's not evident that the profit incentives available in a competitive industry are at all inadequate.

We must also recall the arguments about research and development efforts. A monopolist has little incentive to pursue R&D. Furthermore, entrepreneurs who might pursue product innovation or technological improvements may be dissuaded by their inability to penetrate a monopolized market. The barriers to entry that surround market power may not only keep out potential competitors but also lock out promising ideas.

Economies of Scale

A third defense of market power is the most plausible. A large firm, it's argued, can produce goods at a lower unit (average) cost than a small firm. If such *economies of scale* exist, we could attain greater efficiency (higher productivity) by permitting firms to grow to market-dominating size.

We sidestepped this argument in our story about the Universal Electronics monopoly. We explicitly assumed that Universal confronted the same production costs as the competitive industry. We simply converted each typical competitive firm into a separate plant owned and operated by Universal. Universal wasn't able to produce computers any more cheaply than its competitive counterpart, and we concerned ourselves only with the different production decisions made by competitive and monopolistic firms.

A monopoly *could*, however, attain greater cost savings. By centralizing various functions, it might be able to eliminate some duplicative efforts. It might also shut down some plants and concentrate production in fewer facilities. If these kinds of efficiencies are attained, a monopoly would offer attractive resource savings.

There's no guarantee, however, of such economies of scale. As we observed in Chapter 7, increasing the size (scale) of a plant may actually *reduce* operating efficiency (see Figure 7.10). In evaluating the economies-of-scale argument for market power, then, we must recognize that ***efficiency and size don't necessarily go hand in hand. Some firms and industries may be subject to economies of scale, but others won't.***

Even when economies of scale are present, there is no guarantee that consumers will benefit. The 2006 merger of Boeing and Lockheed cut the costs of rocket production by $100–150 million a year (see Front Page Economics "US FTC Enables Boeing–Lockheed 'Monopoly'"). But the Defense Department ended up paying higher prices. The Justice Department initially opposed the merger of the nation's only two satellite radio companies in 2007 for the same reason. Even though there were substantial short-run economies of

---

FRONT PAGE ECONOMICS

NEWS

US FTC ENABLES BOEING–LOCKHEED "MONOPOLY"

On 3 October 2006, the Federal Trade Commission (FTC) announced its tentative approval of merging Boeing and Lockheed Martin's space launch divisions to create the United Launch Alliance (ULA). . . . —this decision in essence creates a single-source supplier for putting US satellites in orbit.

In August 2006, Kenneth Krieg, head of acquisitions for the Pentagon, wrote to the FTC to support the proposed merger. He acknowledged that while it "will almost certainly have an adverse effect on competition, including higher prices over the long term, as well as a diminution in innovation and responsiveness," he still thought, "The national security advantages of ULA are paramount to the department's support of the transaction."

Apparently, the FTC took his recommendation to heart.

Samson, Victoria, "US FTC Enables Boeing-Lockheed 'Monopoly'." Center for Defense Information, 2017. ETH Zurich.

CRITICAL ANALYSIS: Mergers eliminate duplicate facilities, thereby reducing total costs. But monopoly power permits the merged entity to retain the cost savings rather than pass them along to the consumer in the form of lower prices.

FRONT PAGE ECONOMICS

A SIRIUS MISTAKE? FCC APPROVES XM–SIRIUS MERGER

The Federal Communications Commission (FCC) has approved the merger of the nation's only two satellite radio companies, XM and Sirius. The merged company, called Sirius XM, will own the entire band of spectrum allocated to satellite radio. The companies said that combining their operations would cut costs by more than $150 million. In its 3-2 decision, the FCC commissioners acknowledged that the merged company would be a monopoly provider of satellite radio. But the majority argued that concessions made by the merged company—including a three-year price freeze and the guarantee of set-asides for minority and nonprofit channels—would generate consumer benefits that outweigh potential anticompetitive effects. And they noted that terrestrial radio would always be a competitor to satellite radio. The dissenting commissioners argued that programming choices would contract and subscription prices would increase after the three-year freeze ended.

Source: News reports, July 25–31, 2008.

CRITICAL ANALYSIS: Monopolies may enjoy **economies of scale.** In the long run, however, consumers may benefit more from competitive pressures to reduce costs, improve product quality, and lower prices.

scale in eliminating duplicate facilities, the Justice Department concluded that even a little competition (two firms) was better than none (a monopoly) in expanding consumer choice and keeping prices low (see Front Page Economics "A Sirius Mistake? FCC Approves XM-Sirius Merger"). Both the Justice Department and the Federal Communications Commission ultimately approved the XMSatellite–Sirius Radio merger, however, in return for their promise not to raise prices for at least three years.

Natural Monopolies. Industries that exhibit economies of scale over the entire range of market output are called **natural monopolies.** In these cases, one single firm can produce the entire market supply more efficiently than any large number of (smaller) firms. As the size (scale) of the one firm increases, its minimum average costs continue to fall. These economies of scale give the one large producer a decided advantage over would-be rivals. Hence, *economies of scale act as a "natural" barrier to entry.*

Local telephone and utility services are classic examples of natural monopoly. A single telephone or utility company can supply the market more efficiently than a large number of competing firms.

Although natural monopolies are economically desirable, they may be abused. We must ask whether and to what extent consumers are reaping some benefit from the efficiency a natural monopoly makes possible. Do consumers end up with lower prices, expanded output, and better service? Or does the monopoly keep most of the benefits for itself, in the form of higher prices and profits? Multiplex movie theaters, for example, achieve economies of scale by sharing operating and concession facilities among as many as 30 screens. But do moviegoers get lower prices for movies or popcorn? Not often. Because megamultiplex theaters tend to drive out competition, they don't have to reduce prices when costs drop.

natural monopoly: An industry in which one firm can achieve economies of scale over the entire range of market supply.

Contestable Market

Governmental regulators aren't necessarily the only force keeping monopolists in line. Even though a firm may produce the entire supply of a particular product at present, it may face *potential* competition from other firms. Potential rivals may be sitting on the sidelines, watching how well the monopoly fares. If it does too well, these rivals may enter

contestable market: An imperfectly competitive industry subject to potential entry if prices or profits increase.

the industry, undermining the monopoly structure and profits. In such **contestable markets,** monopoly behavior may be restrained by potential competition.

How "contestable" a market is depends not so much on its structure as on entry barriers. If entry barriers are insurmountable, would-be competitors are locked out of the market. But if entry barriers are modest, they'll be surmounted when the lure of monopoly profits is irresistible. When CNN's profits from cable news reached irresistible proportions, both domestic and foreign companies (e.g., CNBC, Fox News, Bloomberg News) decided to invade CNN's monopoly market. Since then, CNN hasn't been nearly as profitable.

Structure vs. Behavior. From the perspective of contestable markets, the whole case against monopoly is misconceived. Market *structure* per se isn't a problem; what counts is market *behavior.* If potential rivals force a monopolist to behave like a competitive firm, then monopoly imposes no cost on consumers or on society at large.

The experience with the Model T Ford illustrates the basic notion of contestable markets. At the time Henry Ford decided to increase the price of the Model T and paint them all black, the Ford Motor Company enjoyed a virtual monopoly on mass-produced cars. But potential rivals saw the profitability of offering additional colors and features such as a self-starter and left-hand drive. When rivals began producing cars in volume, Ford's market power was greatly reduced. In 1926 the Ford Motor Company tried to regain its dominant position by again supplying cars in colors other than black. By that time, however, consumers had more choices. Ford ceased production of the Model T in May 1927.

The experience with the Model T suggests that potential competition can force a monopoly to change its ways. Critics point out, however, that even contestable markets don't force a monopolist to act *exactly* like a competitive firm. There will always be a gap between competitive outcomes and those monopoly outcomes likely to entice new entry. That gap can cost consumers a lot. The absence of *existing* rivals is also likely to inhibit product and productivity improvements. From 1913 to 1926, all Model Ts were black, and consumers had few alternatives. Ford changed its behavior only after *potential* competition became *actual* competition. Even after 1927, when the Ford Motor Company could no longer act like a monopolist, it still didn't price its cars at marginal cost.

DECISIONS FOR **TOMORROW**

Microsoft and Google: Bullies or Geniuses?

Ford Motor Company's experience is a useful reminder that monopolies rarely last forever. Potential competitors will always look for ways to enter a profitable market. Eventually they'll surmount entry barriers or develop substitute goods that supplant a monopolist's products.

Consumer advocates assert that we shouldn't have to wait for the invisible hand to dismantle a monopoly. They say the government should intervene to dismantle a monopoly or at least force it to change its behavior. Then consumers would get lower prices and better products a whole lot sooner.

Microsoft's dominant position in the computer industry highlights this issue. Microsoft produces the operating system (Windows) that once powered 9 out of 10 personal computers. It also produces a huge share of applications software, including Internet browsers. Critics fear that this kind of monopoly power is a threat to consumers. They say Microsoft charges too much for its systems software, suppresses substitute technologies, and pushes potential competitors around. In short, Microsoft is a bully. In April 2000 a federal court accepted this argument (see Front Page Economics "Microsoft Guilty of Monopoly Abuse"). To weaken Microsoft's grip on the computer market, courts in both the United States and Europe forced changes in both Microsoft's behavior and structure.

FRONT PAGE ECONOMICS

MICROSOFT GUILTY OF MONOPOLY ABUSE

A federal judge ruled Monday that Microsoft has unfairly used its dominant position in computer operating systems to thwart competition in applications software. At the center of the case was Microsoft's practice of bundling its web browser, Internet Explorer, with its Windows operating system. Competitors charged that this practice made it difficult, if not impossible, for them to sell competing web browsers (like Netscape's Navigator). They also complained that Microsoft designed its Windows operating system to render competing web browsers slow and inefficient.

Microsoft CEO Bill Gates argued that Internet Explorer and Windows were intrinsically related and should be viewed as a single product. But Microsoft sold Internet Explorer as a stand-alone product for MAC OS. Critics also charged that Microsoft forced computer manufacturers to install only Windows on new equipment, shutting the door on competing software.

U.S. district judge Thomas Penfield ruled in favor of the government, declaring that Microsoft violated the Sherman Antitrust Act by "unlawfully tying its Web browser" to its windows operating system. By "placing an oppressive thumb on the scale of competitive forces," Microsoft was guilty of abusing its dominant position in the marketplace to bully competitors, stifle competition, and harm consumers.

Source: Media reports, April 4–6, 2000.

CRITICAL ANALYSIS: A federal court concluded that Microsoft followed the textbook script of **monopoly:** erecting entry barriers, suppressing innovation, and charging high prices.

The AT&T Case. The federal government's authority to mend Microsoft's ways originates in the Sherman, the Clayton, and the Federal Trade Commission Acts. As noted in Table 10.1, these acts give the government broad **antitrust** authority to break up monopolies or compel them to change their behavior. The government used this authority in 1984 to dismantle American Telephone and Telegraph's (AT&T's) phone monopoly. AT&T then supplied 96 percent of all long-distance service and more than 80 percent of local telephone service. AT&T kept long-distance charges high and compelled consumers to purchase hardware from its own subsidiary (Western Electric). Potential competitors claimed they could supply better and cheaper services if the government ended the AT&T monopoly. After four years of antitrust litigation, AT&T agreed to (1) separate its long-distance and local services and (2) turn over the local transmission networks to new "Baby Bell" companies. Since then there has been a competitive revolution in telephone hardware, services, and pricing.

The Microsoft Case. The U.S. Department of Justice filed a similar antitrust action against Microsoft. The first accusation leveled against Microsoft was that it thwarted competitors in operating systems by erecting entry barriers such as exclusive purchase agreements with computer manufacturers. These agreements either forbade manufacturers from installing a rival operating system or made it prohibitively expensive. The second accusation against Microsoft was that it used its monopoly position in *operating* systems to gain an unfair advantage in the *applications* market. It did this by not disclosing operating features that make applications run more efficiently or by bundling software, thereby forcing consumers to accept Microsoft applications along with the

antitrust: Government intervention to alter market structure or prevent abuse of market power.

Continued

- *The Sherman Act (1890).* The Sherman Act prohibits "conspiracies in restraint of trade," including mergers, contracts, or acquisitions that threaten to monopolize an industry. Firms that violate the Sherman Act are subject to fines of up to $1 million, and their executives may be subject to imprisonment. In addition, consumers who are damaged—for example, via high prices—by a "conspiracy in restraint of trade" may recover treble damages. With this act as its principal "trustbusting" weapon, the U.S. Department of Justice has blocked attempted mergers and acquisitions, forced changes in price or output behavior, required large companies to sell some of their assets, and even sent corporate executives to jail for "conspiracies in restraint of trade."
- *The Clayton Act (1914).* The Clayton Act of 1914 was passed to outlaw specific antitrust behavior not covered by the Sherman Act. The principal aim of the act was to prevent the development of monopolies. To this end, the Clayton Act prohibited price discrimination, exclusive dealing agreements, certain types of mergers, and interlocking boards of directors among competing firms.
- *The Federal Trade Commission Act (1914).* The increased antitrust responsibilities of the federal government created the need for an agency that could study industry structures and behavior so as to identify anticompetitive practices. The Federal Trade Commission was created for this purpose in 1914.

Although the Sherman, Clayton, and FTC acts create a legal basis for government antitrust activity, they leave some basic implementation issues unanswered. What, for example, constitutes a "monopoly" in the real world? Must a company produce 100 percent of a particular good to be a threat to consumer welfare? How about 99 percent? Or even 75 percent?

And what specific monopolistic practices should be prohibited? Should we be looking for specific evidence of price gouging? Or should we focus on barriers to entry and unfair market practices?

These kinds of questions determine how and when antitrust laws will be enforced. The first question relates to the *structure* of markets, and the rest to their *behavior.*

operating system. When the latter occurs, consumers have little incentive to buy a competing product. Microsoft also prohibited computer manufacturers from displaying rival product icons on the Windows desktop. Finally, Microsoft was accused of thwarting competition by simply buying out promising rivals.

Microsoft's Defense. Bill Gates, Microsoft's chairman, scoffed at the government's charges. He contends that Microsoft dominates the computer industry only because it continues to produce the best products at attractive prices. Microsoft doesn't need to lock out potential competitors, he argues, because it can and does beat the competition with superior products. Furthermore, Gates argues, the software industry is a highly *contestable* market even if not a perfectly competitive one. So Microsoft has to behave like a competitive firm even though it supplies most of the industry's output. In short,

Microsoft is a genius, not a bully. Therefore, the government should leave Microsoft alone and let the market decide who best serves consumers.

The Verdict. After nine *years* of litigation, a federal court determined that Microsoft was more of a bully than a genius. The court concluded that Microsoft not only held a monopoly position in operating systems but had abused that position in a variety of anticompetitive ways. As a result, consumers were harmed. *The real economic issue, the court asserted, was not whether Microsoft was improving its products (it was) or reducing prices (it was) but instead how much faster products would have improved and prices fallen in a more competitive market.* By limiting consumer choices and stifling competition, Microsoft had denied consumers better and cheaper information technology.

The Remedy. The trial judge suggested that Microsoft might have to be broken into two companies—an operating software company and an applications software company—to ensure enough competition. Such a *structural* remedy would have resembled the court-ordered breakup of AT&T. In November 2001, however, the U.S. Department of Justice decided to seek *behavioral* remedies only. With Windows XP about to be launched, the Justice Department required Microsoft only to lower entry barriers for competing software applications (e.g., disclose middleware specifications, refrain from exclusive contracts, open desktops to competition).

Google a Bully?. The same kind of anticompetitive concerns have been raised about Google. Google now dominates the Internet search market that Microsoft once did with its (bundled) Internet Explorer. Google provides for 88 percent of all online searches (Yahoo! has about 3 percent and Bing about 6 percent of the market). Companies pay big bucks to occupy top positions on Google search pages and to place ads in prominent locations. More than 90 percent of Google's immense profits come from paid advertising.

The core complaint against Google is that it uses its dominant search-engine position to suppress competition. Critics (including, ironically, Microsoft) say Google unfairly steers users to the company's own growing network of services (e.g., maps, travel) at the expense of rival producers. They say this harms consumers by restricting the ability of other companies to put better or cheaper products and services in front of Internet users. They contend Google reinforces its monopoly power with entry barriers such as unique key search words, long-term exclusive advertising contracts, suppression of search results for rival firms, and outright acquisitions of potential competitors.

After a five-year investigation, European trustbusters concluded in June 2017 that Google was more a bully than a genius and had "denied European consumers a genuine choice of services and the full benefits of innovation." European regulators also noted that Google was requiring smartphone makers using Google's Android operating system to preinstall the Google search app and Chrome browser—a bundling tactic that got Microsoft in trouble. The EU imposed a record $9.4 billion in fines on the company for its bullying tactics (see Front Page Economics "EU Levies Record Fines on Google"). In October 2020 the U.S. Justice Department also sued Google, echoing the same monopoly abuses the EU charged.

Continued

FRONT PAGE ECONOMICS

EU LEVIES RECORD FINES ON GOOGLE

After a five-year investigation, the European Commission has formally charged Google with "search bias." In its formal Statement of Objection, the European Union's trust-busters accuse Google of using its dominant position in Internet search to steer consumers to its own services. The Commission said Google "stifles competition and harms consumers" by prominently displaying ads for its own map, travel, and product services over those of rivals. The EU fined Google $2.7 billion for that behavior in 2017, $5 billion in 2018 for requiring smartphone makers to preinstall Google Search on Android phones, and another $1.7 billion in 2019 for restricting access for competitors to third-party websites. Google has promised to change its ways.

Source: Media reports, 2017–2019.

CRITICAL ANALYSIS: Does Google strengthen its dominant position in search with unfair **entry barriers?** Rivals say it does. Google responds that it is just a better competitor.

SUMMARY

- Market power is the ability to influence the market price of goods and services. The extreme case of market power is monopoly, a situation in which only one firm produces the entire supply of a particular product. **LO10-1**
- The distinguishing feature of any firm with market power is the fact that the demand curve it faces is downward-sloping. In the case of monopoly, the demand curve facing the firm and the market demand curve are identical. **LO10-1**
- The downward-sloping demand curve facing a monopolist creates a divergence between marginal revenue and price. To sell larger quantities of output, the monopolist must lower product prices. A firm without market power has no such problem. **LO10-1**
- Like other producers, a monopolist will produce at the rate of output at which marginal revenue equals marginal cost. Because marginal revenue is always less than price in monopoly, the monopolist will produce less output than a competitive industry confronting the same market demand and costs. That reduced rate of output will be sold at higher prices in accordance with the (downward-sloping) market demand curve. **LO10-2**
- A monopoly will attain a higher level of profit than a competitive industry because of its ability to equate industry (that is, its own) marginal revenues and costs. By contrast, a competitive industry ends up equating

marginal costs and price because its individual firms have no control over market supply. **LO10-2**
- Because the higher profits attained by a monopoly will attract envious entrepreneurs, barriers to entry are needed to prohibit other firms from expanding market supplies. Patents are one such barrier to entry. **LO10-2**
- The defense of market power rests on (1) the alleged ability of large firms to pursue long-term research and development, (2) the incentives implicit in the chance to attain market power, (3) the efficiency that larger firms may attain, and (4) the contestability of even monopolized markets. The first two arguments are weakened by the fact that competitive firms are under much greater pressure to innovate and can stay ahead of the profit game only if they do so. The contestability defense at best concedes some amount of monopoly exploitation. **LO10-3**
- A natural monopoly exists when one firm can produce the output of the entire industry more efficiently than can a number of small firms. This advantage is attained from economies of scale. Large firms aren't necessarily more efficient, however, because either constant returns to scale or diseconomies of scale may prevail. **LO10-3**
- Antitrust laws restrain the acquisition and abuse of monopoly power. Where barriers to entry aren't insurmountable, market forces may ultimately overcome a monopoly. **LO10-3**

Key Terms

market power	economies of scale	price discrimination
monopoly	production decision	consumer surplus
profit-maximization rule	average total cost (ATC)	natural monopoly
marginal revenue (MR)	marginal cost pricing	contestable market
barriers to entry	price elasticity of demand	antitrust

Questions for Discussion

1. The objective in the game of Monopoly is to get all the property and then raise the rents. Can this power be explained with market supply and demand curves? **LO10-1**

2. According to the Federal Trade Commission (Front Page Economics "US FTC Enables Boeing–Lockheed 'Monopoly'"), how often do monopolies lead to higher prices? Why, then, did the rocket merger get approved? **LO10-1**

3. Why don't monopolists try to establish "the highest price possible," as many people allege? What would happen to sales? To profits? **LO10-1**

4. How does individualized price discrimination by car dealers affect their total revenue and profits? **LO10-1**

5. What would have happened to iPad prices and features if Apple had not faced competition from iPad clones (Chapter 9)? **LO10-2**

6. What entry barriers helped protect the following? **LO10-2**
    (a) The Russian sable monopoly (World View "Russia's Sable Monopoly Persists").
    (b) The Live Nation monopoly (Front Page Economics "Live Nation Drives Up Ticket Prices").

    (c) Turing Pharmaceutical (Front Page Economics "Drugmaker Hikes Price of AIDS Drug 5,000 Percent!").
    (d) The rocket monopoly (Front Page Economics "US FTC Enables Boeing–Lockheed 'Monopoly'").
    (e) Google's search dominance (Front Page Economics "EU Levies Record Fines on Google").

7. What similarities exist between the AT&T, Microsoft, and Google antitrust cases? **LO10-3**

8. How might consumers have benefited from the merger of XM and Sirius (Front Page Economics "A Sirius Mistake? FCC Approves XM–Sirius Merger")? How might they have lost? **LO10-3**

9. How can concert promoters use price discrimination to increase profits? **LO10-1**

10. Is the demand for a life-saving drug like Daraprim (Front Page Economics "Drugmaker Hikes Price of AIDS Drug 5,000 Percent!") likely to be elastic or inelastic? How does that affect the pricing decision of a monopolist? **LO10-1**

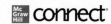
LO10-1 1. Use Figure 10.3 to answer the following questions:
  (*a*) What is the highest price the monopolist could charge and still sell fish?
  (*b*) What is total revenue at that highest price?
  (*c*) What rate of output maximizes total revenue (partial unit okay)?
  (*d*) What rate of output maximizes total profit (use higher rate)?
  (*e*) What is MR at that rate of output?
  (*f*) What is the price at the profit-maximizing rate of output?

LO10-1 2. (*a*) Complete the following table:

Price	$27	$24	$21	$18	$15	$12	$9	$6	$3
Quantity demanded	0	1	2	3	4	5	6	7	8
Marginal revenue	——	——	——	——	——	——	——	——	

  (*b*) At what rate of output does marginal revenue turn negative?
  (*c*) If marginal cost is constant at $12, what is the profit-maximizing rate of output?
  (*d*) What price should this monopolist charge for that rate of output?

LO10-1 3. Given the following information about demand for a local utility service, graph the demand and marginal revenue curves.

Price	$ 6	5	4	3	2
Quantity demanded	10	50	90	150	210

LO10-3 4. Identify the barrier to entry that best matches the following news stories about monopolies:
  (*a*) Front Page Economics "US FTC Enables Boeing–Lockheed 'Monopoly.'"
  (*b*) Front Page Economics "Drugmaker Hikes Price of AIDS Drug 5,000 Percent!"
  (*c*) World View "Russia's Sable Monopoly Persists."

LO10-1 5. Live Nation sold 500 million concert tickets in 2019 at an average price of $96.
  (*a*) How much total revenue did the company take in?
  (*b*) How much of this revenue came from fees (see Front Page Economics "Live Nation Drives Up Ticket Prices")?

LO10-1 6. The following table indicates the prices various buyers are willing to pay for a Ford F-150 truck:

Buyer	Maximum Price	Buyer	Maximum Price
Buyer A	$50,000	Buyer D	$20,000
Buyer B	40,000	Buyer E	10,000
Buyer C	30,000	Buyer F	0

The cost of producing the trucks includes $40,000 of fixed costs and a constant marginal cost of $10,000.
  (*a*) Graph below the demand, marginal revenue, and marginal cost curves.
  (*b*) What is the profit-maximizing rate of output and price for a monopolist?
  (*c*) How much profit does the monopolist make?
  (*d*) If the monopolist can price discriminate, how many trucks will he sell?
  (*e*) How much profit will he make?

LO10-2 7. If the on-campus demand for soda is as follows:

Price (per can)	$2.00	1.75	1.50	1.25	1.00	0.75	0.50	0.25
Quantity demanded (per day)	30	40	50	60	70	80	90	100

and the marginal cost of supplying a soda is 50 cents, what price will students end up paying in
(a) A perfectly competitive market?
(b) A monopolized market?

LO10-3 8. According to Front Page Economics "US FTC Enables Boeing–Lockheed 'Monopoly,'"
(a) What was the annual cost savings for the rocket monopoly (in $ millions)?
(b) How much of this savings did the FTC expect to be reflected in reduced rocket prices?
(c) According to economic theory, which is likely to be higher, the merged monopoly price or the two-firm competitive price?

LO10-2 9. What was the profit per unit for the drug Daraprim (Front Page Economics "Drugmaker Hikes Price of AIDS Drug 5,000 Percent!"):
(a) Before Turing increased the price?
(b) After Turing increased the price?
(c) What barrier to entry typically exists in the pharmaceutical market?

LO10-2 10. In 2019 Google had total profits of approximately $40 billion; ninety percent of this profit came from online advertising.
(a) How much profit did Google make from online ads?
(b) If online search was a perfectly competitive market, how much would annual profits be in the long run?

LO10-2 11. The following table summarizes the weekly sales and cost situation confronting a monopolist:

Price	Quantity Demanded	Total Revenue	Marginal Revenue	Total Cost	Marginal Cost	Average Total Cost
$22	0	_____	—	$ 4	—	_____
20	1	_____	_____	8	_____	_____
18	2	_____	_____	13	_____	_____
16	3	_____	_____	19	_____	_____
14	4	_____	_____	27	_____	_____
12	5	_____	_____	37	_____	_____
10	6	_____	_____	51	_____	_____
8	7	_____	_____	69	_____	_____

(a) Complete the table.
(b) Graph the demand, MR, and MC curves on the following graph.

(*c*) At what rate of output are profits maximized?

(*d*) What are the values of MR and MC at the profit-maximizing rate of output?

(*e*) What price will the firm charge?

(*f*) What are total profits at that output rate?

(*g*) If a competitive industry confronted the same demand and costs, how much output would it produce and what price would it charge in the short run?

LO10-3 **12. *Decisions for Tomorrow:*** Identify the market and the barrier to entry that best matches the case studies presented in Decisions for Tomorrow.

(*a*) Microsoft.

(*b*) AT&T.

(*c*) Google.

Design Credit: Shutterstock

CHAPTER 11

Oligopoly

People of the same trade seldom meet together, but the conversation ends in a conspiracy against the public, or in some diversion to raise prices.

—Adam Smith, The Wealth of Nations, 1776

A lthough it's convenient to think of the economy as composed of the powerful and the powerless, market realities don't always provide such clear distinctions. There are very few perfectly competitive markets in the world, and few monopolies. Market power is an important phenomenon nonetheless; it's just that it's typically shared by several firms rather than monopolized by one. In the soft drink industry, for example, Coca-Cola and Pepsi share tremendous market power, even though neither company qualifies as a pure monopoly. The same kind of power is shared by Kellogg, General Mills, and Ralcorp in the breakfast cereals market, and by Sony, Nintendo, and Microsoft in the video game console market. Apple Computer Inc., too, now shares power in the tablet computer market with Samsung, Lenovo, Huawei, Sony, LG, Microsoft, and other firms. Netflix has to contend with Disney+, HBO Max, Hulu, and other streaming services.

These market structures fall between the extremes of perfect competition and pure monopoly; they represent *imperfect competition*. They contain some elements of competitive rivalry but also exhibit traces of monopoly. In many cases, imperfect competitors behave much like a monopoly: restricting output, charging higher prices, and reaping greater profits than firms in a competitive market. But behavior in imperfectly competitive markets is more complicated than in a monopoly because it involves a number of decision makers (firms) rather than only one.

This chapter focuses on one form of imperfect competition: *oligopoly*. We examine the nature of decision making in this market structure and the likely impacts on prices, production, and profits. What we want to know is

- **What determines how much market power a firm has?**
- **How do firms in an oligopoly set prices and output?**
- **What problems does an oligopoly have in maintaining price and profit?**

LEARNING OBJECTIVES

After reading this chapter, you should know

LO11-1 The unique characteristics of oligopoly.

LO11-2 How oligopolies maximize profits.

LO11-3 How interdependence affects oligopolists' pricing decisions.

LO11-4 The Challenges of Antitrust Policy.

MARKET STRUCTURE

As we saw in Chapter 10, Microsoft is the dominant supplier of computer operating systems and Google dominates the search-engine market. As near monopolies, those companies have tremendous market power. The corner grocery store, on the other hand, must compete with other stores and has less control over prices. But even the corner grocery isn't completely powerless. If it's the only grocery within walking distance or the only one open on Sunday, it too exerts *some* influence on prices and product flows. The amount of power it possesses depends on the availability of *substitute goods*—that is, the proximity and convenience of alternative retail outlets.

Degrees of Power

market structure The number and relative size of firms in an industry.

Between the extremes of monopoly and perfect competition are many gradations of market power. To sort them out, we classify firms into five specific **market structures,** based on the number and relative size of firms in an industry.

Table 11.1 summarizes the characteristics of the five major market structures. At one extreme is the structure of *perfect competition,* the subject of Chapters 8 and 9. At the other extreme of the power spectrum is perfect *monopoly.* A perfect monopoly exists when only one firm is the exclusive supplier of a particular product. Our illustration of Universal Electronics (the imaginary computer monopolist in Chapter 10) exemplifies such a firm.

Between the two extremes of perfect competition and perfect monopoly lies most of the real world, which we call *imperfectly competitive.* ***In imperfect competition, individual firms have some power in a particular product market.*** *Oligopoly* refers to one of these imperfectly competitive market structures. **Oligopoly** is a situation in which only a *few* firms have a great deal of power in a product market. An oligopoly may exist because only a few firms produce a particular product or because a few firms account for most, although not all, of a product's output.

oligopoly A market in which a few firms produce all or most of the market supply of a particular good or service.

Determinants of Market Power

The number of firms in an industry is a key characteristic of market structure. The amount of market power the firms possess, however, depends on several factors. ***The determinants of market power include***

- *Number of producers.*
- *Size of each firm.*
- *Barriers to entry.*
- *Availability of substitute goods.*

When only one or a few producers or suppliers exist, market power is automatically conferred. In addition to the number of producers, however, the size of each firm is also important. More than 600 firms supply long-distance telephone service in the United States. But

Characteristic	Market Structure				
	Perfect Competition	Monopolistic Competition	Oligopoly	Duopoly	Monopoly
Number of firms	Very large number	Many	Few	Two	One
Barriers to entry	None	Low	High	High	High
Market power (control over price)	None	Some	Substantial	Substantial	Substantial
Type of product	Standardized	Differentiated	Standardized or differentiated	Standardized or differentiated	Unique

TABLE 11.1

Characteristics of Market Structures

Market structure varies, depending on the number of producers, their size, barriers to entry, and the availability of substitute goods. An oligopoly is an imperfectly competitive structure in which a few firms dominate the market.

just three of those firms (Verizon, T-Mobile US, AT&T) account for 98 percent of all calls. Hence, it wouldn't make sense to categorize that industry on the basis of only the number of firms; relative size is also important. The same thing is true in the beer industry. There are more than 7,000 breweries in the United States, but only four produce 80 percent of industry output (see Table 11.2).

A third and critical determinant of market power is the extent of barriers to entry. A highly successful monopoly or oligopoly arouses the envy of other profit maximizers. If it's a **contestable market,** potential rivals will seek to enter the market and share in the spoils. Should they succeed, the power of the former monopolist or oligopolists would be reduced. Accordingly, ease of entry into an industry limits the ability of a powerful firm to dictate prices and product flows. In Chapter 10 we saw how monopolies erect barriers to entry (e.g., patents) to maintain their power.

contestable market An imperfectly competitive industry subject to potential entry if prices or profits increase.

A fourth determinant of market power is the availability of substitute goods. If a monopolist or other power baron sets the price of a product too high, consumers may decide to switch to close substitutes. Thus, the price of Coors is kept in check by the price of Coke, the price of sirloin steak is restrained by the price of chicken and pork, and the price of streaming subscriptions (Netflix, Disney+, Amazon Prime Video, etc.) is constrained by the price of conventional cable service. By the same token, a lack of available substitute products keeps the prices of insulin and AZT high.

Measuring Market Power

Although there are many determinants of market power, most observers use just one yardstick to measure the extent of power in an industry.

Concentration Ratio. The standard measure of market power is the **concentration ratio.** This ratio tells the share of output (or combined market share) accounted for by the largest firms in an industry. Using this ratio, one can readily distinguish between an industry composed of hundreds of small, relatively powerless firms and another industry also composed of hundreds of firms but dominated by a few that are large and powerful. Thus, *the concentration ratio is a measure of market power that relates the size of firms to the size of the product market.*

concentration ratio The proportion of total industry output produced by the largest firms (usually the four largest).

Table 11.2 gives the concentration ratios for selected products in the United States. The standard measure used here depicts the proportion of domestic production accounted for by the largest firms, usually the four largest. As a rule of thumb, *an industry with a concentration ratio above 60 percent is considered an oligopoly.* As is apparent from the table, the supply sides of these product markets easily qualify as *oligopolies* because most of these industries' output is produced by just three or four firms. Indeed, in some markets, one single firm is so large that an outright monopoly is nearly attained. For example, 70 percent of all canned soup is produced by Campbell. Gerber produces 80 percent of all prepared baby food. Google accounts for 87 percent of all web searches and Netflix has 87 percent of all video streaming subscribers. All firms that have a market share of at least 40 percent are denoted by **boldface** type in Table 11.2.

Firm Size. We noted before that market power isn't necessarily associated with firm size—in other words, a small firm could possess a lot of power in a relatively small market. Table 11.2, however, should be convincing testimony that we're not talking about small product markets here. Every one of the products listed enjoys a broad-based market. Even the chewing gum market (94 percent concentration ratio) rings up annual sales of $20 billion. The three oligopolists that produce video game consoles (Sony, Microsoft, Nintendo) have 100 percent of a $50 billion market. Accordingly, for most of the firms listed in the table, market power and firm size go hand in hand. Indeed, the largest firms enjoy sales volumes that exceed the entire output of most of the *countries* in the world (see World View "Putting Size in Global Perspective"). Walmart's annual revenues alone would make it the world's 24th largest country!

Product	Largest Firms	Concentration Ratio (%)
Video game consoles	**Sony**, Microsoft, Nintendo	100%
Instant breakfast	**Carnation**, Pillsbury, Dean Foods	100
Laser eye surgery	**VISX**, Summit Technology	100
Tennis balls	**Gen Corp (Penn)**, PepsiCo **(Wilson)**, Dunlop, Spalding	100
Credit cards	**Visa**, MasterCard, American Express, Discover	99
Disposable diapers	**Procter & Gamble**, Kimberly-Clark, Curity, Romar Tissue Mills	99
Cell phone service	Verizon, T-Mobile US, AT&T	98
Razor blades	**Gillette**, Warner-Lambert (Schick; Wilkinson), Bic, American Safety Razor	98
Online food delivery	**DoorDash**, UberEats (Postmates), Grubhub	98
Sports drinks	**PepsiCo** (Gatorade), Coca-Cola (PowerAde), Monarch (All Sport)	98
Internet search engines	**Google**, Bing, Yahoo	98
Scientific calculators	**Texas Instruments**, Casio, Hewlett-Packard	97
Video streaming	**Netflix**, Disney, Amazon	96
Sanitary napkins	**Johnson & Johnson**, Kimberly-Clark, Procter & Gamble	96
Cigarettes	**Altria**, Reynolds American, Imperial, Liggett	96
Baby food	**Gerber Products**, Beech-Nut, DelMonte	95
Online travel service	**Expedia**, Priceline, Orbitz	95
Batteries	**Duracell**, Eveready, Ray-O-Vac, Kodak	94
Chewing gum	**Wm. Wrigley**, Mondelez, Hershey	94
Soft drinks	**Coca-Cola**, PepsiCo, Dr Pepper Snapple, Cott (RC Cola)	94
Breakfast cereals	**Kelloggs**, General Mills, Ralcorp, PepsiCo (Quaker Oats)	92
Toothpaste	Colgate-Palmolive, Procter & Gamble, Church & Dwight, Beecham	91
Detergents	**Procter & Gamble**, Lever Bros., Dial, Colgate-Palmolive	90
Art auctions	**Sotheby's**, Christie's	90
Greeting cards	**Hallmark**, American Greetings, Gibson	88
Canned soup	**Campbell**, Progresso, Heinz	85
Beer	**Anheuser-Busch**, MillerCoors, Constellation, Heineken	80
Computer printers	**Hewlett-Packard**, Canon, Epson, Brother	70

Sources: Data from Federal Trade Commission, *The Wall Street Journal, Advertising Age, Financial World, Standard & Poor's, Fortune,* and industry sources.

Note: Individual corporations with a market share of at least 40 percent are designated in **boldface**. Market shares based on selected years, 2014–2020.

TABLE 11.2

Power in U.S. Product Markets

The domestic production of many familiar products is concentrated among a few firms. These firms have substantial control over the quantity supplied to the market and thus over market price. The concentration ratio measures the share of total output produced by the largest producers in a given market.

Measurement Problems

A high concentration ratio or large firm size isn't the only way to achieve market power. The supply and price of a product can be altered by many firms acting in unison. Even 1,000 small producers can band together to change the quantity supplied to the market, thus exercising market power. Recall how our mythical Universal Electronics (Chapter 10) exercised market power by coordinating the production decisions of its many separate plants. Those plants could have attempted such coordination on their own even if they hadn't all been owned by the same corporation. Lawyers and doctors exercise this kind of power by maintaining uniform fee schedules for members of the American Bar Association (ABA) and the American Medical Association (AMA).[1] Similarly, dairy farmers act

---

[1]The courts have ruled that uniform fee schedules are illegal and that individual lawyers and doctors have the right to advertise their prices (fees). Nevertheless, a combination of inertia and self-interest has effectively maintained high fee schedules and inhibited advertising.

WORLD VIEW

PUTTING SIZE IN GLOBAL PERSPECTIVE

The largest firms in the United States are also the dominant forces in global markets. They export products to foreign markets and produce goods abroad for sale there or to import back into the United States. In terms of size alone, these business giants rival most of the world's nations. Walmart's gross sales, for example, would make it the 24th largest "country" in terms of national GDP.

American corporations aren't the only giants in the global markets. Volkswagen (Germany), Royal Dutch Shell (The Netherlands), and Toyota (Japan) are among the foreign giants that contest global markets.

Rank	Country or Corporation	Sales or GDP (in billions of dollars)	Rank	Country or Corporation	Sales or GDP (in billions of dollars)
1	United States	$20,636	20	Saudi Arabia	728
2	China	13,181	21	Sweden	565
3	Japan	5,227	22	Argentina	551
4	Germany	3,905	23	Poland	536
5	United Kingdom	2,777	24	Walmart Stores	524
6	France	2,752	25	Belgium	523
7	India	2,728	26	Thailand	459
8	Italy	2,038	27	Iran	441
9	Brazil	1,915	28	Austria	436
10	Canada	1,666	29	Norway	428
11	South Korea	1,580	30	Royal Dutch Shell	397
12	Russia	1,502	31	Nigeria	385
13	Spain	1,371	32	Amazon	281
14	Australia	1,330	33	Volkswagen	278
15	Mexico	1,159	34	Toyota	273
16	Indonesia	1,026	35	Finland	266
17	The Netherlands	883	36	ExxonMobil	265
18	Turkey	858	37	Apple	260
19	Switzerland	719	38	Portugal	226

Sources: World Bank Atlas Method and *Fortune*'s annual ranking of the world's largest corporations, 2018–2019.

CRITICAL ANALYSIS: Firm size is a determinant of market power. The size of the largest firms, as measured by total revenue, exceeds the value of total output in most of the world's 200-plus countries.

jointly through three large cooperatives (the American Milk Producers, Mid-America Dairies, and Dairymen, Inc.), which together control 50 percent of all milk production. In 2019, the U.S. Justice Department launched a criminal investigation into chicken pricing, alleging that poultry processors were working in tandem to keep prices high in the $65 billion chicken industry.

Finally, all the figures and corporations cited here refer to *national* markets. They don't convey the extent to which market power may be concentrated in a *local* market. In fact, many industries with low concentration ratios nationally are represented by just one or a few firms locally. Prime examples include milk, newspapers, and transportation (both public and private). For example, fewer than 60 cities in the United States have two or more independently owned daily newspapers, and nearly all those newspapers rely on only two news services (Associated Press and United Press International). Perhaps you've also noticed that most college campuses have only one bookstore. It may not be a *national* powerhouse, but it does have the power to influence what goods are available on campus and how much they cost.

OLIGOPOLY BEHAVIOR

With so much market power concentrated in so few hands, it's unrealistic to expect market outcomes to resemble those of perfect competition. As we observed in Chapter 10, *market structure affects market behavior and outcomes*. In that chapter we focused on the contrast between monopoly and perfect competition. Now we focus on the behavior of a more common market structure: oligopoly.

To isolate the unique character of oligopoly, we'll return to the computer market. In Chapter 9 we observed that the computer market was highly competitive in its early stages, when entry barriers were low and hundreds of firms were producing similar products. In Chapter 10 we created an impassable barrier to entry (a patent on the electronic brain of the computer) that transformed the computer industry into a monopoly of Universal Electronics. Now we'll transform the industry again. This time we'll create an oligopoly by assuming that three separate firms (Universal, World, and International) all possess patent rights. The patent rights permit each firm to produce and sell all the computers it wants and to exclude all other would-be producers from the market. With these assumptions, we create three **oligopolists,** the firms that share an *oligopoly.* Our objective is to see how market outcomes would change in such a market structure.

oligopolist One of the dominant firms in an oligopoly.

The Initial Equilibrium

As before, we'll assume that the initial conditions in the computer market are represented by a market price of $1,000 and market sales of 20,000 computers per month, as illustrated in Figure 11.1.

We'll also assume that the **market share** of each producer is accurately depicted in Table 11.3. Thus, Universal Electronics is assumed to be producing 8,000 computers per month, or 40 percent of total market supply. World Computers has a market share of 32.5 percent, while International Semiconductor has only a 27.5 percent share. The assumed **concentration ratio** is therefore 100.

market share The percentage of total market output produced by a single firm.

The Battle for Market Shares

The first thing to note about this computer oligopoly is that it's likely to exhibit great internal tension. Neither World Computers nor International Semiconductor is really happy playing second or third fiddle to Universal Electronics. Each company would like to be number one in this market. On the other hand, Universal would like a larger market share as well, particularly in view of the huge profits being made on computers. As we observed in Chapter 9, the initial equilibrium in the computer industry yielded an *average* profit of $300 per computer, and total *industry* profits of $6 million per month (20,000 × $300). Universal would love to acquire the market shares of its rivals, thereby grabbing all this industry profit for itself.

FIGURE 11.1

Initial Conditions in the Computer Market

As in Chapters 9 and 10, we assume that the initial equilibrium in the computer market occurs at a price of $1,000 and a quantity of 20,000 per month. How will an oligopoly alter these outcomes?

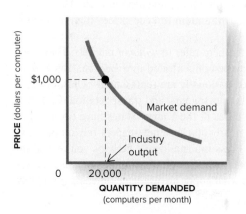

Producer	Output (Computers per Month)	Market Share (%)
Universal Electronics	8,000	40.0%
World Computers	6,500	32.5
International Semiconductor	5,500	27.5
Total industry output	20,000	100.0%

TABLE 11.3

Initial Market Shares of
Microcomputer Producers

The market share of a firm is the
percentage of total market
output it produces. These are
hypothetical market shares of
three fictional oligopolists.

But how does an oligopolist acquire a larger market share? In a truly competitive market, a single producer could expand production at will, with no discernible impact on market supply. That's not possible when there are only three firms in the market. *In an oligopoly, increased sales on the part of one firm will be noticed immediately by the other firms.*

How do we know that increased sales will be noticed so quickly? Because increased sales by one firm will have to take place either at the existing market price ($1,000) or at a lower price. Either of these two events will ring an alarm at the corporate headquarters of the other two firms.

Increased Sales at the Prevailing Market Price. Consider first the possibility of Universal Electronics increasing its sales at the going price of $1,000 per computer. We know from the demand curve in Figure 11.1 that consumers are willing to buy *only* 20,000 microcomputers per month at that price. Hence, any increase in computer sales by Universal must be immediately reflected in *lower* sales by World or International. That is, *increases in the market share of one oligopolist necessarily reduce the shares of the remaining oligopolists.* If Universal were to increase its sales from 8,000 to 9,000 computers per month, the combined monthly sales of World and International would have to fall from 12,000 to 11,000 (see Table 11.3). The *quantity demanded* at $1,000 remains 20,000 computers per month (see Figure 11.1). Thus, any increased sales at that price by Universal must be offset by reduced sales by its rivals.

This interaction among the market shares of the three oligopolists ensures that Universal's sales success will be noticed. It won't be necessary for World Computers or International Semiconductor to engage in industrial espionage. These firms can quickly figure out what Universal is doing simply by looking at their own (declining) sales figures.

Increased Sales at Reduced Prices. Universal could pursue a different strategy. Specifically, Universal could attempt to increase its sales by lowering the price of its computers. Reduced prices would expand total market sales, possibly enabling Universal to increase its sales without directly reducing the sales of either World or International.

But this outcome is most unlikely. If Universal lowered its price from $1,000 to, say, $900, consumers would flock to Universal Computers, and the sales of World and International would plummet. After all, we've always assumed that consumers are rational enough to want to pay the lowest possible price for any particular good. It's unlikely that consumers would continue to pay $1,000 for a World or International machine when they could get basically the same computer from Universal for only $900. If there were no difference, either perceived or real, among the computers of the three firms, a *pure* oligopoly would exist. In that case, Universal would capture the *entire* market if it lowered its price below that of its rivals.

More often, consumers perceive differences in the products of rival oligopolists, even when the products are essentially identical. These perceptions (or any real differences that may exist) create a *differentiated* oligopoly. In this case, Universal would gain many but not all customers if it reduced the price of its computers. That's the outcome we'll assume here. In either case, there simply isn't any way that Universal can increase its sales at reduced prices without causing alarms to go off at World and International.

Retaliation

So what if the alarms do go off at World Computers and International Semiconductor? As long as Universal Electronics is able to enlarge its share of the market and grab more profits, why should it care if World and International find out?

Universal *does* have something to worry about. World and International may not be content to stand by and watch their market shares and profits diminish. On the contrary, World and International are likely to take some action of their own once they discover what's going on.

There are two things World and International can do once they decide to act. In the first case, where Universal is expanding its market share at prevailing prices ($1,000), World and International can retaliate by

- Stepping up their own marketing efforts.
- Cutting prices on their computers.

Advertising. To step up their marketing efforts, World and International might increase their advertising expenditures, repackage their computers, put more sales representatives on the street, or sponsor a college homecoming week. This is the kind of behavior Dr Pepper used to gain market share from Coke and Pepsi (see Front Page Economics "Dr Pepper Targets College Football Fans"). Such attempts at **product differentiation** are designed to make one firm's products appear different and superior to those produced by other firms. The success of its marketing efforts increased Dr Pepper's sales and market share in 2018–2020.

product differentiation
Features that make one product appear different from competing products in the same market.

FRONT PAGE ECONOMICS

DR PEPPER TARGETS COLLEGE FOOTBALL FANS

Dr Pepper, the perennial third place in the U.S. soda market, has scored a touchdown with its new "Fansville" marketing campaign. Launched in time for the 2018 football season, the campaign focuses on the fictional Fansville, where characters "doctor" and "sheriff" duel. The episodes have been a hit with Millenials. With a stepped-up ad spend of $500 million for Fansville, together with its sponsorship of the college football playoffs, Dr Pepper has expanded its market share by 0.3 percentage point in the $250 billion soda market.

Source: Media reports of December 2019–January 2020.

The U.S. Soda Market
Market share of soft drink makers, 2019.

Pepsi 24.9
Dr Pepper Snapple Group 18.2
Coca-Cola 42.6
Others 14.3

CRITICAL ANALYSIS: Because price competition is typically self-defeating in an oligopoly, rival firms in an oligopoly rely on advertising and product differentiation (**nonprice competition**) to gain market share.

Price Cuts. An even quicker way to stop Universal from enlarging its market share is for World and International to lower the price of *their* computers. Such price reductions will destroy Universal's hopes of increasing its market share at the old price. In fact, this is the other side of a story we've already told. If the price of World and International computers drops to, say, $900, it's preposterous to assume that Universal will be able to expand its market share at a price of $1,000. Universal's market share will shrink if it maintains a price of $1,000 per computer after World and International drop their prices to $900. Hence, the threat to Universal's market share grab is that the other two oligopolists will retaliate by reducing *their* prices. Should they carry out this threat, Universal would be forced to cut computer prices too, or accept a greatly reduced market share.

The same kind of threat exists in the second case, where we assumed that Universal Electronics expands its sales by initiating a price reduction. World and International aren't

FIGURE 11.2
Rivalry for Market Shares Threatens an Oligopoly

If oligopolists start cutting prices to capture larger market shares, they'll be behaving much like truly competitive firms. The result will be a slide down the market demand curve to lower prices, increased output, and smaller profits. In this case, the market price and quantity would move from point *F* to point *G* if rival oligopolists cut prices to gain market shares.

going to just sit by and applaud Universal's marketing success. They'll have to respond with price cuts of their own. Universal would then have the highest price on the market, and computer buyers would flock to cheaper substitutes. Accordingly, it's safe to conclude that *an attempt by one oligopolist to increase its market share by cutting prices will lead to a general reduction in the market price*. The three oligopolists will end up using price reductions as weapons in the battle for market shares, the kind of behavior normally associated with competitive firms. Should this behavior continue, not only will oligopoly become less fun, but it will also become less profitable as prices slide down the market demand curve (Figure 11.2). This is why *oligopolists avoid price competition and instead pursue nonprice competition* (e.g., advertising and product differentiation).

The preference for nonprice competition over price competition helps explain how Netflix responded to the entry of Disney into the movie streaming market. When Disney launched Disney+ in November 2019, it offered a subscription price ($6.99 per month) that was half of the Netflix price. Rather than cut its own price in response, Netflix chose to spend more on new programming, hoping to convince consumers that its product was superior. That nonprice response helped preserve industry profits. When Comcast/NBCUniversal joined the streaming wars in 2020, it followed a similar strategy of limited price competition (see Front Page Economics "Streaming Wars Heat Up").

FRONT PAGE ECONOMICS

STREAMING WARS HEAT UP

No one expected Netflix to have the video streaming market all to itself. But the field has gotten more crowded faster than analysts expected. On Tuesday, Comcast/NBCUniversal announced that it is launching Peacock, a video-streaming service that will compete directly with Netflix, Disney+, Amazon Prime Video, Hulu, CBS All Access, Apple TV+, and the coming HBO Max, due in May. Peacock will be free for Comcast's 24 million cable subscribers. For nonsubscribers, the monthly fee will be $4.99 with ads or $9.99 without ads. Although the ad-laden price is near the low end of the market, Comcast's real strength is its vast library (15,000 hours) of programming, including NBC shows like *The Office, Law and Order, and Saturday Night Live*. Peacock will also stream the Tokyo Olympics, for which NBC has the broadcast rights.

Source: Media reports, January 2020.

CRITICAL ANALYSIS: Oligopolies try to avoid price competition by **differentiating their product** when possible. In the streaming wars, the proprietary programming libraries are a source of differentiation and a significant barrier to entry.

THE KINKED DEMAND CURVE

The close interdependence of oligopolists—and the limitations it imposes on individual price and output decisions—is the principal moral of this story. We can summarize the story with the aid of the kinked demand curve in Figure 11.3.

Recall that at the beginning of this oligopoly story Universal Electronics had a market share of 40 percent and was selling 8,000 computers per month at a price of $1,000 each. This output is represented by point *A* in Figure 11.3. The rest of the demand curve illustrates what would happen to Universal's unit sales if it changed its selling price. What we have to figure out is why this particular demand curve has such a strange "kinked" shape.

Rivals' Response to Price Reductions

Consider first what would happen to Universal's sales if it lowered the price of its computers to $900. In general, we expect a price reduction to increase sales. However, *the degree to which an oligopolist's sales increase when its price is reduced depends on the response of rival oligopolists.*

Rivals Don't Match. Suppose World and International *didn't* match Universal's price reduction. In this case, Universal would have the only low-priced computer in the market. Consumers would flock to Universal, and sales would increase dramatically, from point *A* to point *D*.

Rivals Do Match. But point *D* is little more than a dream, as we've observed. World and International are sure to cut their prices to $900 to maintain their market shares. As a consequence, Universal's sales will expand only slightly, to point *C* rather than to point *D*. Universal's increased sales at point *C* reflect the fact that the total quantity demanded in the market has risen as the market price has fallen to $900 (see Figure 11.2). Thus, even though Universal's *market share* may not have increased, its monthly sales have.

The section of the demand curve that runs from point *A* to point *D* is unlikely to exist in an oligopolistic market. Instead, *we expect rival oligopolists to match any price reductions* that Universal initiates, forcing Universal to accept the demand curve that runs from point *A* through point *C*. Front Page Economics "Rivals Match Southwest's Flash Sale" illustrates such behavior in the airline industry, where rivals were forced to match price cuts introduced by Southwest Airlines.

FIGURE 11.3

The Kinked Demand Curve Confronting an Oligopolist

The shape of the demand curve facing an oligopolist depends on the responses of its rivals to its price and output decisions. If rival oligopolists match price reductions but not price increases, the demand curve will be kinked.

Initially, the oligopolist is at point *A*. If it raises its price to $1,100 and its rivals don't raise their prices, it will be driven to point *B*. If its rivals match a price reduction (to $900), the oligopolist will end up at point *C*.

FRONT PAGE ECONOMICS

RIVALS MATCH SOUTHWEST'S FLASH SALE

Rival airlines are quickly matching some—but not all—of the low fares Southwest rolled out on Tuesday as part of its 72-hour flash sale. American, United, and Jet Blue all announced fare cuts to below $100 on the short routes where Southwest is offering sale tickets. Flights between San Francisco and Los Angeles are now priced at $97, if purchased by Thursday midnight.

Source: Media reports, June 8, 2016.

DELTA ROLLS BACK FARE HIKE

Delta's fare increase didn't stick. On Tuesday Delta announced fare increases of $10–$20 per roundtrip ticket. American, United, and USAirways quickly did the same. But Southwest and Jet Blue didn't follow suit. Last night Delta started rolling back its fare hikes.

—David Koenig

Source: Media reports, April 19–22, 2012.

CRITICAL ANALYSIS: If rivals match price cuts but not price increases, the demand curve confronting an oligopolist will be **kinked**. Prices will increase only when all firms agree to raise them at the same time.

Rivals' Response to Price Increases

What about price increases? How will World and International respond if Universal raises the price of its computers to $1,100?

Rivals Don't Match. Recall that the demand for computers is assumed to be price-elastic in the neighborhood of $1,000 and that all computers are basically similar. Accordingly, if Universal raises its price and neither World nor International follows suit, Universal will be out there alone with a higher price and reduced sales. *Rival oligopolists may choose not to match price increases.* In terms of Figure 11.3, a price increase that isn't matched by rival oligopolists will drive Universal from point *A* to point *B*. At point *B*, Universal is selling very few computers at its price of $1,100 each.[2]

Is this a likely outcome? Suffice it to say that World Computers and International Semiconductor wouldn't be unhappy about enlarging their own market shares. Unless they see the desirability of an industrywide price increase, they're not likely to come to Universal's rescue with price increases of their own. This is why other airlines decided not to match the fare hikes announced by Delta (see Front Page Economics "Delta Rolls Back Fare Hike").

Rivals Do Match. Anything is possible, however. When JetBlue increased the fee for checked baggage on August 27, 2018, United did the same four days later. Delta and American followed suit shortly afterwards, giving the airlines a great source of added profits. World and International might do the same thing here—matching Universal's price increase. In this case, the *market price* would rise to $1,100 and the total quantity of computers demanded would diminish. Under such circumstances Universal's sales would diminish, too, in accordance with its (constant) share of a smaller market. This would lead us to point *M* in Figure 11.3.

Kinked Demand Curve. We may draw two conclusions from Figure 11.3:

- *The shape of the demand curve an oligopolist faces depends on the responses of its rivals to a change in the price of its own output.*
- *That demand curve will be kinked if rival oligopolists match price reductions but not price increases.*

[2]Notice again that we're assuming that Universal is able to sell some computers at a higher price (point *B*) than its rivals. The kinked demand curve applies primarily to differentiated oligopolies. As we'll discuss later, such differentiation may result from slight product variations, advertising, customer habits, location, friendly service, or any number of other factors. Most oligopolies exhibit some differentiation.

GAME THEORY

The central message of the kinked demand curve is that oligopolists can't make truly independent price or output decisions. Because only a few producers participate in the market, *each oligopolist has to consider the potential responses of rivals when formulating price or output strategies.* This *strategic interaction* is the inevitable consequence of their oligopolistic position.

Uncertainty and Risk. What makes oligopoly particularly interesting is the *uncertainty* of rivals' behavior. For example, Universal *would* want to lower its prices *if* it thought its rivals wouldn't retaliate with similar price cuts. But it can't be sure of that response. Universal must instead consider the odds of its rivals not matching a price cut. If the odds are low, Universal might decide *not* to initiate a price cut. Or maybe Universal might offer price discounts to just a few select customers, hoping World and International might not notice or react to small changes in market share.

payoff matrix A table showing the risks and rewards of alternative decision options.

The Payoff Matrix. Table 11.4 summarizes the strategic options each oligopolist confronts. In this case, let's assume that Universal is contemplating a price cut. Its rivals have only two options: either reduce their price also or not. Hence, the **payoff matrix** has only four cells, each of which refers to a possible scenario. The payoff matrix in the table summarizes the various profit consequences of each scenario. One thing should be immediately clear: *The payoff to an oligopolist's price cut depends on how its rivals respond.* Indeed, the only scenario that increases Universal's profit is one in which Universal reduces its price and its rivals don't. We visualized this outcome earlier as a move from point *A* to point *D* in Figure 11.3. Note again that this scenario implies losses for Universal's two rival oligopolists.

The remaining cells in the payoff matrix show how profits change with other action/response scenarios. One thing is evident: If Universal *doesn't* reduce prices, it can't increase profits. In fact, it might end up as the big loser if its rivals reduce *their* prices while Universal stands pat.

The option of reducing price doesn't guarantee a profit, but at least it won't ruin Universal's market share or profits. If rivals match a Universal price cut, all three oligopolists will suffer small losses.

So what should Universal do? The *collective* interests of the oligopoly are protected if no one cuts the market price. But an individual oligopolist could lose a lot if it holds the line on price when rivals reduce price. Hence, each oligopolist might decide to play it safe by *initiating* a price cut.

Expected Gain (Loss). The decision to initiate a price cut boils down to an assessment of *risk*. If you thought the risk of a "first strike" was high, you'd be more inclined to reduce price. This kind of risk assessment is the foundation of game theory. You could, in fact, make that decision by *quantifying* the risks involved. Consider again the option of reducing

Universal's Options	Rivals' Actions	
	Reduce Price	Don't Reduce Price
Reduce price	Small loss for everyone	Huge gain for Universal; rivals lose
Don't reduce price	Huge loss for Universal; rivals gain	No change

TABLE 11.4

Oligopoly Payoff Matrix

The payoff to an oligopolist's price cut depends on its rivals' responses. Each oligopolist must assess the risks and rewards of each scenario before initiating a price change. Which option would you choose?

price. As the first row of Table 11.4 shows, rivals can respond in one of only two ways. If they follow suit, a small loss is incurred by Universal. If they don't, there's a huge gain for Universal. To quantify the risk assessment, we need two pieces of information: (1) the size of each "payoff" and (2) the probability of its occurrence.

Suppose the "huge gain" is $1 million and the "small loss" is $20,000. What should Universal do? The huge gain looks enticing, but we now know it's not likely to happen. But *how* unlikely is it? What if there's only a 1 percent chance of rivals not matching a price reduction? In that case, the *expected* payoff to a Universal price cut is

$$\begin{bmatrix} \text{Expected payoff} \\ \text{of price cut} \end{bmatrix} = \begin{bmatrix} \text{Probability of} \\ \text{rival matching} \end{bmatrix} \times \begin{bmatrix} \text{Loss from} \\ \text{price cut} \end{bmatrix} + \begin{bmatrix} \text{Probability} \\ \text{of rival} \\ \text{not matching} \end{bmatrix} \times \begin{bmatrix} \text{Gain} \\ \text{from} \\ \text{price cut} \end{bmatrix}$$

$$= [0.99 \times -\$20,000] + [0.01 \times \$1,000,000]$$

$$= -\$19,800 + \$10,000 = -\$9,800$$

Hence, it's not a good idea. Once potential payoffs and probabilities are taken into account, a unilateral price cut doesn't look promising. The odds say a unilateral price cut will result in a loss (−$9,800).

These kinds of computations underlay the Cold War games that the world's one-time superpowers played. Neither side was certain of the enemy's next move but knew a nuclear first strike could trigger retaliatory destruction. As a consequence, the United States and the former Soviet Union continually probed each other's responses but were quick to retreat from the brink whenever all-out retaliation was threatened. Oligopolists play the same kind of game on a much smaller scale, using price discounts and advertising rather than nuclear warheads as their principal weapons. The reward they receive for coexistence is the oligopoly profits that they continue to share. This reward, together with the threat of mutual destruction, leads oligopolists to limit their price rivalry.

This isn't to say oligopolists won't ever cut prices or use other means to gain market share. They might, given the right circumstances and certain expectations of how rivals will behave. Indeed, there are a host of different price, output, and marketing strategies an oligopolist might want to pursue. The field of **game theory** is dedicated to the study of how decisions are made when such strategic interaction exists—for example, when the outcome of a business strategy depends on the decisions rival firms make. Just as there are dozens of different moves and countermoves in a chess game, so too are there numerous strategies oligopolists might use to gain market share.

game theory The study of decision making in situations where strategic interaction (moves and countermoves) occurs between rivals.

OLIGOPOLY VS. COMPETITION

While contemplating strategies for maximizing their *individual* profits, oligopolists are also mindful of their common interest in maximizing *joint* (industry) profits. They want to avoid behavior that destroys the very profits that they're vying for. Indeed, they might want to coordinate their behavior in a way that maximizes *industry* profits. If they do, how will market outcomes be affected?

Price and Output

Thus far we've focused on a single oligopolist's decision about whether to *change* the price of its output. But how was the initial (market) price determined? In this example, we assumed that the initial price was $1,000 per computer, the price that prevailed initially in a *competitive* market. But the market is no longer competitive. As we saw in the previous chapter, a change in industry structure will affect market outcomes. A monopolist, for example, would try to maximize *industry* profits, all of which it would keep. To do this, it would select that one rate of output where marginal revenue equals marginal cost, and it would charge whatever price consumers were willing and able to pay for that rate of output (see Figure 11.4).

FIGURE 11.4

Maximizing Oligopoly Profits

An oligopoly strives to behave like a monopoly. Industry profits are maximized at the rate of output at which the *industry's* marginal cost equals marginal revenue (point *J*). In a monopoly, this profit all goes to one firm; in an oligopoly, it must be shared among a few firms.

In an oligopoly, the MC and ATC curves represent the combined production capabilities of several firms, rather than only one. The industry MC curve is derived by horizontally summing the MC curves of the individual firms.

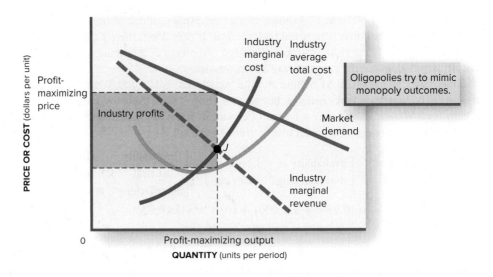

An oligopoly would seek similar profits. An oligopoly is really just a *shared* monopoly. Hence **an oligopoly will want to behave like a monopoly, choosing a rate of industry output that maximizes total industry profit.**

The challenge for an oligopoly is to replicate monopoly outcomes. To do so, the firms in an oligopoly must find the monopoly price and maintain it. This is what the members of OPEC are trying to do when they meet to establish a common price for the oil they sell and agree to limit their output so as to achieve that price. Reaching agreement requires a common view of the industry demand curve, satisfaction with respective market shares, and precise coordination. Those were the prerequisites for the Ivory Coast and Ghana when they formed a new cocoa cartel in October 2020 (see World View "COPEC: The New Cocoa Cartel").

WORLD VIEW

COPEC: THE NEW COCOA CARTEL

The Ivory Coast has banded together with Ghana to limit cocoa supplies and drive cocoa prices higher. Together, the two nations produce 64 percent of the world's cocoa, a $110 billion industry. Cocoa prices have fluctuated wildly in the last five years, falling from a high of $3,270 a ton in 2016 to a low of $1,800 a ton in 2017. Following the OPEC model, the two African nations want to limit and regulate supply, enabling them to charge a $400 premium above the market price of around $2,500 a ton, beginning October 2020. If successful, candy makers like Mars, Nestle, and Hershey will be passing along the cartel premium to chocolate consumers.

Source: Media reports of July 2019–January 2020.

CRITICAL ANALYSIS: A **cartel** entails an explicit agreement among oligopolists to regulate supply and increase price. That is the intent of the new cocoa cartel.

In most years, OPEC was successful in establishing a profitable price for oil. In 2020, however, the coronavirus pandemic severely curtailed world demand for oil, causing oil prices to decline. At their March 2020 meeting, Saudi Arabia proposed a cut in OPEC production of 1.5 million barrels a day to prop up falling oil prices. The 13 members of OPEC were willing to make such cuts, but Russia—the world's second largest oil producer—wasn't. In response, Saudi Arabia *increased* production, igniting a price war that pushed oil prices down from $57.75 a barrel to a low of $24.67 in a single month. That price plunge devastated the finances of not only OPEC nations, but Russia and the U.S. oil industry as well (see World View "Nations Scrambling to End Oil-Price War"). That price war was a stark reminder of how important it is for oligopolists to coordinate their production decisions.

WORLD VIEW

NATIONS SCRAMBLING TO END OIL-PRICE WAR

The coronavirus pandemic has upended the global oil market. Since December 2016, Russia has worked closely with the 13 members of OPEC to limit oil production and maintain high oil prices. But when OPEC proposed to cut production by 1.5 million barrels a day to offset declining global demand, Russia said, "nyet." That sparked a price war with Saudi Arabia that has seen prices fall by more than 50 percent in a month. Iraq and other OPEC nations are working behind the scenes to bring the price war to an end. Even the Texas Railroad Commission that regulates Texas oil has hinted at production cutbacks to help stem the price decline. President Trump also got involved, asking Russia and Saudi Arabia to settle their differences. After a month of devastating losses, the oil-producing nations agreed to collectively cut supply by 9.7 million barrels a day.

Source: Media reports, February–April 2020.

CRITICAL ANALYSIS: An oligopoly tries to act like a shared monopoly. To maximize industry profit, the firms in an oligopoly must concur on what the monopoly price is and agree to maintain it by limiting output and allocating market shares.

The cocoa cartel formed by the Ivory Coast and Ghana in 2020 should be easier to coordinate, as its two founding members control two-thirds of world production. By contrast, OPEC has to deal with the different goals of not only its 13 member nations, but also the behavior of non-OPEC nations like Russia and the United States.

Competitive industries would also like to reap monopoly-like profits. But competitive industries experience relentless pressure on profits as individual firms expand output, reduce costs, and lower prices. To maximize industry profits, competitive firms would have to band together and agree to restrict output and raise prices. If they did, though, the industry would no longer be competitive. Maximizing industry profits is easier in an oligopoly because fewer firms are involved and each is aware of its dependence on the behavior of the others.

COORDINATION PROBLEMS

A successful oligopoly will achieve monopoly-level profits by restricting industry output. As we've observed, however, this outcome depends on mutual agreement and coordination among the oligopolists. This may not come easy. ***There's an inherent conflict in the joint and individual interests of oligopolists.*** Their joint, or collective, interest is in maximizing industry profit. The individual interest of each oligopolist, however, is to maximize its own share of sales and profit. This conflict creates great internal tension within an oligopoly. To avoid self-destructive behavior, ***oligopolists must coordinate their production decisions so that***

* **Industry *output and price are maintained at profit-maximizing levels*.**
* ***Each oligopolistic* firm *is content with its market share*.**

Price-Fixing

To bring about this happy outcome, rival oligopolists could discuss their common interests and attempt to iron out an agreement on both issues. Identifying the profit-maximizing rate of industry output would be comparatively simple, as Figure 11.4 illustrated. Once the optimal rate of output was found, the associated profit-maximizing price would be evident. The only remaining issue would be the division of industry output among the oligopolists—that is, the assignment of market shares.

The most explicit form of coordination among oligopolists is called **price-fixing.** In this case, the firms in an oligopoly explicitly agree to charge a uniform (monopoly) price. This is what the 13 OPEC member-nations try to do when they get together to set oil prices (see World View "Nations Scrambling to End Oil-Price War"). Some other examples of price-fixing include the following.

price-fixing Explicit agreements among producers regarding the price(s) at which a good is to be sold.

Ivy League Colleges. For more than 30 years, Ivy League schools worked together to offer a uniform financial aid package for individual students, eliminating price competition. The Justice Department ordered the schools to end that practice in 1992.

Electric Generators. In 1961 General Electric and Westinghouse were convicted of fixing prices on $2 billion worth of electrical generators that they'd been selling to the Tennessee Valley Authority and commercial customers. Among the corporate executives, 7 went to prison and 23 others were put on probation. In addition, the companies were fined a total of $1.8 million and compelled to pay triple damages in excess of $500 million to their victimized customers. Nevertheless, another suit was filed against General Electric and Westinghouse in 1972, charging these same companies—still the only two U.S. manufacturers of turbine generators—with continued price-fixing.

Perfume. Thirteen companies—including Chanel, Dior, and Yves Saint Laurent—paid $55 million in penalties in 2006 for fixing prices.

Auction Commissions. Sotheby's and Christie's, who together control 90 percent of the world's art auction business, admitted in 2000 to fixing commission rates throughout the 1990s. They paid a $512 million fine when they were caught.

Laser Eye Surgery. The FTC in 2006 charged the two companies that sell the lasers used for corrective eye surgery (VISX and Summit Technology) with price-fixing that inflated the retail price of surgery by $500 per eye.

Memory Chips. In 2005 the world's largest memory chip (DRAM) manufacturers (Samsung, Micron, Infineon, Hynix) admitted to fixing prices in the $16-billion-a-year DRAM market and paid nearly $700 million in criminal fines.

Elevators. In 2007 five companies were fined $1.3 billion for fixing prices on elevators and escalators in Europe for 10 years.

Ebooks. In June 2015 Apple was found guilty of conspiring with five book publishers to fix the price of ebooks. Ebook prices on Amazon went up from $9.99 to $12.99 or $14.99. Apple paid a $450 million fine.

Laundry Detergent. Colgate-Palmolive was found guilty in 2016 of conspiring with its chief rival and a retailer to fix the price of laundry detergent in Australia. The company paid an $18 million fine.

Auto Parts. Bridgestone agreed to pay a $425 million criminal fine in 2016 for conspiring with other firms to fix prices, rig bids, and allocate sales of parts to auto manufacturers in the United States.

Canned Tuna. In 2018 the largest providers of canned tuna (Bumble Bee, Starkist, and Chicken of the Sea) were found guilty of fixing prices and were fined $125 million.

Chicken. In June 2020 the Justice Department indicted the largest chicken producers of fixing prices from 2012 to 2017.

Price Leadership

Although price-fixing agreements are still a reality in many product markets, oligopolies have discovered that they don't need *explicit* agreements to arrive at uniform prices; they can achieve the same outcome in more subtle ways. **Price leadership** rather than price-fixing will suffice. If all oligopolists in a particular product market follow the lead of one firm in raising prices, the result is the same as if they had all agreed to raise prices simultaneously. Instead of conspiring in motel rooms (as in the electrical products and soft drink cases), the firms can achieve their objective simply by reading *The Wall Street Journal* or industry publications and responding appropriately.

According to the U.S. Department of Justice, the major airlines developed a highly sophisticated form of price leadership. They used their shared computer reservation systems to signal *intended* price hikes. Rival oligopolists then responded with their own *intended* price changes. Only after it was clear that all the airlines would match a planned price increase was the price hike announced. The Justice Department argued that this "electronic dialogue" was equivalent to a price-fixing conspiracy that cost consumers $1.9 billion in excessive fares. In response, the major airlines agreed to stop using the reservations system to communicate *planned* fare hikes.

price leadership An oligopolistic pricing pattern that allows one firm to establish the (market) price for all firms in the industry.

Allocation of Market Shares

Whenever oligopolists successfully raise the price of a product, the law of demand tells us that unit sales will decline. Even in markets with highly inelastic demand *some* decrease in sales always accompanies an increase in price. When this happens in a monopolistic industry, the monopolist simply cuts back the rate of output. In an oligopoly, however, no single firm will wish to incur the whole weight of that cutback. Some form of accommodation is required by all the oligopolists.

The adjustment to the reduced sales volume can take many forms. Members of OPEC, for example, assign explicit quotas for the oil output of each member country. Such open and explicit production-sharing agreements transform an oligopoly into a **cartel.**

Because cartels openly violate U.S. antitrust laws, American oligopolies have to be more circumspect in divvying up shared markets. A particularly novel method of allocating market shares occurred in the price-fixing case involving General Electric and Westinghouse. Agreeing to establish high prices on electric generators wasn't particularly difficult. But how would the companies decide who was to get the restricted sales? Their solution was to designate one firm as the "low" bidder for a particular phase of the moon. The "low" bidder would charge the previously agreed-upon (high) price, with the other firm offering its products at even higher prices. The "low" bidder would naturally get the sale. Each time the moon entered a new phase, the order of "low" and "high" bidders changed. Each firm got a share of the business, and the price-fixing scheme hid behind a facade of "competitive" bidding.

Such intricate systems for allocating market shares are more the exception than the rule. More often the oligopolists let the sales and output reduction be divided up according to consumer demands, intervening only when market shares are thrown markedly out of balance. At such times, an oligopolist may take drastic action, such as **predatory pricing.** Predatory price cuts are temporary price reductions intended to drive out new competition or reestablish market shares. The sophisticated use of price cutting can also function as a significant barrier to entry, inhibiting potential competitors from trying to gain a foothold in the price cutter's market. Front Page Economics "Eliminating the Competition with Low Prices" describes how major airlines forced Independence Air out of their market with predatory pricing in 2006.

cartel A group of firms with an explicit, formal agreement to fix prices and output shares in a particular market.

predatory pricing Temporary price reductions designed to alter market shares or drive out competition.

FRONT PAGE ECONOMICS

ELIMINATING THE COMPETITION WITH LOW PRICES

On January 5, 2006, Independence Air ceased flying. CEO Kerry Skeen, armed with $300 million in start-up capital, had positioned Independence as a low-fare entrant at the profitable Washington, DC, Dulles airport. At its launch in June 2004, Skeen observed that the Washington, DC, area was "screaming" for low fares.

The major carriers didn't agree. United Airlines, with a hub at Dulles, slashed fares as soon as Independence took flight. The rest of the "Big Six" (Delta, American, Northwest, US Airways, Continental) did the same. The fare war kept Independence from gaining enough market share to survive. As CEO Skeen concluded, "It's a brutal industry."

The week after Independence ceased flying, the "walk-up" fare between Dulles and Atlanta jumped from $118 to $478. Other fares followed suit.

Source: "Flying Monopoly Air," *McGraw-Hill News Flash*, McGraw-Hill Education, February 2006.

CRITICAL ANALYSIS: To protect their prices and profits, oligopolists must be able to eliminate potential competition. **Predatory pricing** can serve that purpose.

BARRIERS TO ENTRY

If oligopolies succeed in establishing monopoly prices and profits, they'll attract the envy of would-be entrants. To keep potential competitors out of their industry, oligopolists must maintain **barriers to entry.** *Above-normal profits can't be maintained over the long run unless barriers to entry exist.* The entry barriers erected include those monopolists use (Chapter 10).

barriers to entry Obstacles such as patents that make it difficult or impossible for would-be producers to enter a particular market.

Patents

Patents are a very effective barrier to entry. Potential competitors can't set up shop until they either develop an alternative method for producing a product or receive permission from the patent holder to use the patented process. Such permission, when given, costs something, of course. In 2006 Research in Motion paid an extraordinary $612.5 million for the patent rights to produce BlackBerrys. In 2007 a federal court ordered Internet phone provider Vonage to pay $135 million and 5 percent of its future profits to its wired rivals, Verizon and Sprint. Patents and patent litigation scare off a lot of potential competition. Apple and Samsung have sued each other several times over alleged patent violations, always hoping to blunt competition.

Distribution Control

Another way of controlling the supply of a product is to take control of distribution outlets. If a firm can persuade retail outlets not to peddle anyone else's competitive wares, it will increase its market power. This control of distribution outlets can be accomplished through selective discounts, long-term supply contracts, or expensive gifts at Christmas. Recall from Chapter 10 (see Front Page Economics "Live Nation Drives Up Ticket Prices") how Live Nation Entertainment locked up concert arenas and ticket distribution. According to the U.S. Justice Department, Visa and MasterCard prevent banks that issue their credit cards from offering rival cards. Frito-Lay elbows out competing snack companies by paying high fees to "rent" shelf space in grocery stores (see Front Page Economics "Frito-Lay Eats Up Snack-Food Business"). Such up-front costs create an entry barrier for potential rivals. Even if a potential rival can come up with the up-front money, the owner of an arena or grocery store chain may not wish to anger the firm that dominates the market.

FRITO-LAY EATS UP SNACK-FOOD BUSINESS

Anheuser-Busch is throwing in the towel on the snack-food business. The company announced it is selling off its Eagle Snacks subsidiary, after trying in vain to gain market share against Frito-Lay. Frito-Lay dominates the business, with half of all salty snack items. Competitors say Frito-Lay has secured its dominant position with shelf-space rentals in retail stores—paying as much as $40,000 a foot annually to secure prime shelf space in grocery and convenience stores. "Frito can afford it," said a regional rep for a competing company, "but we can't. It's become a real estate business." Such tactics have made Frito-Lay an invincible foe.

Source: News reports, October 1995.

CRITICAL ANALYSIS: **Barriers to entry** such as shelf-space rental and advertising enable a firm to maintain market dominance. Acquisitions also reduce competition.

New car warranties also serve as an entry barrier. The warranties typically require regular maintenance at authorized dealerships and the exclusive use of authorized parts. These provisions limit the ability of would-be competitors to provide cheaper auto parts and service. Frequent flier programs have similar effects in the airline industry.

Input Lock-Ups

Another way to deter competition is to acquire exclusive access to needed or ancillary inputs. Live Nation strengthens its power in the concert business by tying entertainers to exclusive contracts. Microsoft and Sony retain the lion's share of video console sales by contracting with developers to create games exclusively for their consoles. Apple does the same thing with applications software developers. Tesla is building a giga-factory to produce the lithium batteries that are the heart and soul of electric cars. U.S. Steel has exclusive access to coal mines it owns and operates. In all these cases, would-be competitors will find it difficult to acquire the inputs they need to produce competing products.

Access to key inputs has also been a critical factor in the ongoing "streaming war" between Netflix and its many new competitors. Prior to 2019, Netflix had licenses to stream Disney movies (e.g., *Star Wars*) and popular TV shows like *Friends* from Warner (AT&T). Then Disney and AT&T decided to launch their own streaming services. To gain advantage in the streaming wars, both Disney and AT&T terminated the leasing deals with Netflix, denying Netflix access to a critical input (video content). That forced Netflix to invest billions more in original content, reducing its profit margins. By controlling popular movie archives, these three companies thwart potential competitors.

Mergers and Acquisition

Large and powerful firms can also limit competition by outright *acquisition*. A *merger* between two firms amounts to the same thing, although mergers often entail the creation of new corporate identities.

Perhaps the single most dramatic case of acquisition for this purpose occurred in the breakfast cereals industry. In 1946 General Foods acquired the cereal manufacturing facilities of Campbell Cereal Company, a substantial competitor. Following this acquisition, General Foods dismantled the production facilities of Campbell Cereal and shipped them off to South Africa!

Although the General Foods acquisition was more dramatic than most, acquisitions have been the most popular route to increased market power. General Motors attained a dominant share of the auto market largely by its success in merging with and acquiring two dozen independent manufacturers. In the cigarette industry, the American Tobacco Company attained monopoly powers by absorbing 250 independent companies. Later antitrust action (1911) split up the resultant tobacco monopoly into an oligopoly consisting of four companies, which continued to dominate the cigarette market until 2004, when R. J. Reynolds bought Brown & Williamson, leaving only three firms to dominate the cigarette industry. In 2014, Reynolds bought Lorillard, effectively creating an oligopoly (see Front Page Economics "Joe Camel Acquires Newport").

FRONT PAGE ECONOMICS

JOE CAMEL ACQUIRES NEWPORT

In a widely anticipated move, Reynolds American, producer of best-selling brand Camel, announced yesterday that it has agreed to buy Lorillard, maker of Newport, the number 1 menthol cigarette. The $25 billion deal will combine the number 2 and number 3 cigarette manufacturers. The new company, retaining the Reynolds American name, will have 35 percent of the U.S. market, running second to Altria's 47 percent share. As part of the deal, Imperial Tobacco will purchase several of Lorillard's brands, including Blu, its popular e-cigarette, and end up with 10 percent of the market. Liggett Vector will keep 4 percent of the market. Prior to merging, Reynolds had 25 percent of the market and Lorillard had 12 percent, with Imperial at 8 percent.

Reynolds expects to cut annual costs by $800 million through eliminating overlap in sales, production, and overhead costs. Consumers worry that reduced competition will raise cigarette prices and further limit choices. The deal must win antitrust approval before it is finalized.

Source: News reports, July 15–18, 2014.

CRITICAL ANALYSIS: Mergers reduce competition, increase the concentration ratio, and often limit choice and raise price.

Other companies that came to dominate their product markets through mergers and acquisitions include U.S. Steel, U.S. Rubber, General Electric, United Fruit, National Biscuit Company, International Salt, and Live Nation Entertainment. Frito-Lay's 1995 acquisitions of Eagle Snacks (see Front Page Economics "Frito-Lay Eats Up Snack-Food Business") extended its already dominant control of the chip, pretzel, and nuts markets.

Government Regulation

The government often helps companies acquire and maintain control of market supply. Patents are issued and enforced by the federal government and so represent one form of supply-restricting regulation. Barriers to international trade are another government-imposed barrier to entry. By limiting imports of everything from Chinese mushrooms to Japanese cars (see Chapter 21), the federal government reduces potential competition in U.S. product markets. Government regulation also limits *domestic* competition in many industries.

New York City also limits competition—in this case, the number of taxicabs on the streets. The maximum number of cabs was set at 11,787 in 1937 and stayed at that ceiling until 1996. The city's Taxi and Limousine Commission has since raised the ceiling to 13,605 taxis. That didn't do much to eliminate New York's perennial taxi shortage (for a population of more than 8 million people), much less reduce fares. As a result, license holders reaped monopoly-like profits for decades. A good measure of those monopoly profits was the price of the medallions that served as taxi licenses—a price that reached $1.3 million in 2014. When Uber, Lyft, and other ride-sharing services surmounted that entry barrier, the monopoly power of the medallions was shattered. In 2020, medallions were selling for less than

$200,000 and ride-sharing services had 35 percent of the market. Other states and cities are still protecting their taxi oligopolies by prohibiting Uber, Lyft, and other ride-share companies from operating.

Nonprice Competition

Producers who control market supply can enhance their power even further by establishing some influence over market demand. The primary mechanism of control is *advertising.* To the extent that a firm can convince you that its product is essential to your well-being and happiness, it has effectively shifted your demand curve. ***Advertising not only strengthens brand loyalty but also makes it expensive for new producers to enter the market.*** A new entrant must buy both production facilities and advertising outlets.

The cigarette industry is a classic case of high concentration and product differentiation. As Table 11.2 shows, the top four cigarette companies produce 96 percent of all domestic output; small, generic firms produce the rest. Together, the four cigarette companies produce well over 100 brands. To solidify brand loyalties, the cigarette industry spent more than $9 billion on advertising and promotions in 2019.

The breakfast cereal industry also uses nonprice competition to lock in consumers. Although the Federal Trade Commission has suggested that "a corn flake is a corn flake no matter who makes it," the four firms (Kellogg, General Mills, Ralcorp, and Quaker Oats) that supply more than 90 percent of all ready-to-eat breakfast cereals spend more than $1 billion a year—about $1 per box!—to convince consumers otherwise.

Training

In today's technology-driven markets, early market entry can create an important barrier to later competition. Customers of computer hardware and software, for example, often become familiar with a particular system or computer package. Switching to a new product may entail significant cost, including the retraining of user staff. As a consequence, would-be competitors will find it difficult to sell their products even if they offer better quality and lower prices.

Network Economies

The widespread use of a particular product may also heighten its value to consumers, thereby making potential substitutes less viable. The utility of instant messaging—or even a telephone—depends on how many of your friends have telephones. If no one else had a phone, there'd be no reason to own one. In other words, the larger the network of users, the greater the value of the product. Such network economies help explain why software developers prefer to write apps for the iPhone than applications for rival smartphones and why advertisers pay a premium to appear on Facebook.

DECISIONS FOR TOMORROW

Should We Break Up Big Tech?
Examples of market power at work in product markets could be extended for another 10 chapters. The few cases cited here, however, are testimony enough to the fact that market power has some influence on our lives. Market power *does* exist; market power *is* used. Although market power may result in economies of scale, the potential for abuse is evident. Market power contributes to **market failure** when it leads to resource misallocation (restricted output) or greater inequity (monopoly profits, higher prices).

market failure An imperfection in the market mechanism that prevents optimal outcomes.

Continued

What should we do about these abuses? Should we leave it to market forces to find ways of changing industry structure and behavior? Or should the government step in to curb noncompetitive practices? In the 2020 presidential campaign, both Elizabeth Warren and Bernie Sanders proposed to break up monopolies and other large companies.

Industry Behavior. As consumers, our primary concern is the *behavior* of market participants. What ultimately counts is the quantity of goods supplied to the market, their quality, and their price. Few consumers care about the underlying *structure* of markets; what we seek are good market *outcomes*.

In principle, the government could change industry behavior without changing industry structure. We could, for example, explicitly outlaw collusive agreements and cast a wary eye on industries that regularly exhibit price leadership. We could dismantle barriers to entry and thereby promote contestable markets. We might also prohibit oligopolists from extending their market power via such mechanisms as acquisitions, excessive or deceptive advertising, and the financing of political campaigns. In fact, the existing **antitrust** laws—the Sherman Act, the Clayton Act, and the Federal Trade Commission Act (see Table 10.1)—explicitly forbid most of these practices.

There are several problems with this behavioral approach. The first limitation is scarce resources. Policing markets and penalizing noncompetitive conduct require more resources than the public sector can muster. Indeed, the firms being investigated often have more resources than the public watchdogs. The advertising expenditures of just one oligopolist, Procter & Gamble, are more than 10 times as large as the *combined* budgets of both the Justice Department's Antitrust Division and the Federal Trade Commission.

The paucity of antitrust resources is partly a reflection of public apathy. Consumers rarely think about the connection between market power and the price of the goods they buy, the wages they receive, or the way they live. As Ralph Nader discovered, "Antitrust violations are part of a phenomenon which, to the public, is too complex, too abstract, and supremely dull."[3] As a result, there's little political pressure to regulate market behavior.

The behavioral approach also suffers from the "burden-of-proof" requirement. How often will "trustbusters" catch colluding executives in the act? More often than not, the case for collusion rests on such circumstantial evidence as simultaneous price hikes, identical bids, or other market outcomes. The charge of explicit collusion is hard to prove. Even in the absence of explicit collusion, however, consumers suffer. If an oligopoly price is higher than what a competitive industry would charge, consumers get stuck with the bill whether or not the price was "rigged" by explicit collusions. The U.S. Supreme Court recognized that consumers may suffer from *tacit* collusion, even where no *explicit* collusion occurs.

Industry Structure. The concept of tacit collusion directs attention to the *structure* of an industry. It essentially says that oligopolists and monopolists will act in their own best interest. As former Supreme Court Chief Justice Earl Warren observed, "An industry which does not have a competitive structure will not have competitive behavior."[4] To expect an oligopolist to disavow profit opportunities or to ignore its interdependence with fellow oligopolists is naive. It also violates the basic motivations imputed to a market economy. As long as markets are highly concentrated, we must expect to observe oligopolistic behavior. This was the premise of the proposals from Elizabeth Warren and Bernie Sanders to break up Big Tech and other large companies.

Judge Learned Hand used these arguments to dismantle the Aluminum Company of America (Alcoa) in 1945. Alcoa wasn't charged with any illegal *behavior*. Nevertheless, the company controlled more than 90 percent of the aluminum supplied to the market.

antitrust Government intervention to alter market structure or prevent abuse of market power.

[3]Mark J. Green et al., *The Closed Enterprise System: The Report on Antitrust Enforcement* (New York, NY: Grossman, 1972), p. ix.
[4]Ibid., p. 7.

This monopoly structure, the Supreme Court concluded, was itself a threat to the public interest.

Corporate breakups are rarely pursued today. In 2001 the Justice Department withdrew a proposal to break up Microsoft into separate systems and applications companies. The prevalent feeling today, even among antitrust practitioners, is that the powerful firms are too big and too entrenched to make deconcentration a viable policy alternative.

Objections to Antitrust. Some people think *less* antitrust enforcement is actually a good thing. The companies challenged by the public "trustbusters" protest that they're being penalized for their success. Alcoa, for example, attained a monopoly by investing heavily in a new product before anyone else recognized its value. Other firms too have captured dominant market shares by being first, best, or most efficient. Having "won" the game fairly, why should they have to give up their prize? They contend that noncompetitive *behavior,* not industry *structure,* should be the only concern of antitrust enforcers.

Essentially the same argument is made for proposed mergers and acquisitions. The firms involved claim that the increased concentration will enhance productive efficiency (e.g., via economies of scale). This was the argument T-Mobile and Sprint used when they proposed to merge (see Front Page Economics "Feds Approve T-Mobile–Sprint Merger"). Oligopolists also argue that big firms are needed to maintain America's competitive position in international markets (which are themselves often dominated by foreign monopolies and oligopolies). Those same global markets, they contend, ensure that even highly concentrated domestic markets will be contested by international rivals.

FRONT PAGE ECONOMICS

FEDS APPROVE T-MOBILE–SPRINT MERGER

The FCC gave the nod to the merger of T-Mobile and Sprint, creating a combined wireless company the size of AT&T. The Commission's approval was expected, given the Justice Department's approval back in July. The deal also created a fourth wireless company to be created by transferring 9 million cell phone customers from Sprint to Dish Network.

AT&T
33.4%

Verizon
35.5%

T-Mobile
17.1%

Sprint
12.6%

Other 1.4%

Source: Media reports of November 2019–January 2020.

CRITICAL ANALYSIS: Companies argue that **mergers** promote greater efficiency that improves product quality and reduces prices. Critics argue that less competitive market structures inevitably slow innovation and increase prices.

Continued

Finally, critics of antitrust suggest that market forces themselves will ensure competitive behavior. Foreign firms and domestic entrepreneurs will stalk a monopolist's preserve. People will always be looking for ways to enter a profitable market. Monopoly or oligopoly power may slow entry but is unlikely to stop it forever. Eventually competitive forces will prevail.

Structural Guidelines: The Herfindahl-Hirshman Index. There are no easy answers. In theory, competition is valuable, but some mergers and acquisitions undoubtedly increase efficiency. Moreover, some international markets may require a minimum firm size not consistent with perfect competition. Finally, our regulatory resources are limited; not every acquisition or merger is worthy of public scrutiny.

Where would we draw the line? Can a firm hold a 22 percent market share, but not 30 percent? Are five firms too few, but six firms in an industry enough? Someone has to make those decisions. That is, *the broad mandates of the antitrust laws must be transformed into specific guidelines for government intervention.*

In 1982 the Antitrust Division of the U.S. Department of Justice adopted specific guidelines for intervention based on industry *structure* alone. They're based on an index that takes into account the market share of *each* firm rather than just the *combined* market share of the top four firms. Specifically, the **Herfindahl-Hirshman Index (HHI)** of market concentration is calculated as

$$\text{HHI} = \sum_{i=1}^{n} = \left(\frac{\textbf{Share of}}{\textbf{firm 1}}\right)^2 + \left(\frac{\textbf{Share of}}{\textbf{firm 2}}\right)^2 + \cdots + \left(\frac{\textbf{Share of}}{\textbf{firm } n}\right)^2$$

Thus, a three-firm oligopoly like that described in Table 11.3 would have an HHI value of

$$\text{HHI} = (40.0)^2 + (32.5)^2 + (27.5)^2 = 3{,}412.5$$

where the numbers in parentheses indicate the market shares of the three fictional computer companies. The calculation yields an HHI value of 3,412.5.

For policy purposes, the Justice Department decided it would draw the line at 1,800. *Any merger that creates an HHI value over 1,800 will be challenged by the Justice Department.* If an industry has an HHI value between 1,000 and 1,800, the Justice Department will challenge any merger that *increases* the HHI by 100 points or more. Mergers and acquisitions in industries with an HHI value of less than 1,000 won't be challenged.

The HHI is an arbitrary but workable tool for deciding when the government should intervene to challenge mergers and acquisitions. The Justice Department reviews about 2,500 mergers a year but challenges fewer than 50.

The AT&T/T-Mobile Deal. The Justice Department's guidelines were put to the test in 2011. In March 2011 AT&T announced that it planned to purchase T-Mobile, the fourth largest wireless phone company. That acquisition would have sent the Herfindahl-Hirschmann Index through the roof. But AT&T argued that the acquisition of T-Mobile would result in economies of scale that would improve service and reduce costs. Critics said the loss of competition would raise prices and reduce phone service options. The Justice Department sided with the critics and sued in August 2011 to block the merger. AT&T abandoned the idea four months later and now competes with T-Mobile.

The T-Mobile–Sprint Merger. Ironically, T-Mobile has since tried on several occasions to merge with another phone-service provider, Sprint. The first effort to merge the two companies ended in 2014, after objections from the Obama Justice Department. A second attempt failed in 2017 when the companies themselves could not agree on the terms of the merger. In 2018, a third attempt at merger was begun. The argument in favor of the merger was again that the combined company would have the resources to compete more effectively against the two giants in the industry, AT&T and Verizon. They would also have the resources to build out the 5G network. Consumers, they claimed, would benefit from better service and lower prices. Critics objected, expressing the fear that three major wireless companies was definitely less competitive than four, and that slower innovation and less price pressure were sure to follow. In 2019 the Trump Justice Department approved the merger, after requiring Sprint to give 9 million cell phone customers to satellite TV provider Dish Network, a concession that would create a tiny new (fourth) competitor in the wireless market (see Front Page Economics "Feds Approve T-Mobile–Sprint Merger").

SUMMARY

- Imperfect competition refers to markets in which individual suppliers (firms) have some independent influence on the price at which their output is sold. Examples of imperfectly competitive market structures are duopoly, oligopoly, and monopolistic competition. **LO11-1**
- The extent of market power (control over price) depends on the number of firms in an industry, their size, barriers to entry, and the availability of substitutes. **LO11-1**
- The concentration ratio is a measure of market power in a particular product market. It equals the share of total industry output accounted for by the largest firms, usually the top four. **LO11-1**
- An oligopoly is a market structure in which a few firms produce all or most of a particular good or service (a concentration-ratio of 60 or higher); it's essentially a shared monopoly. **LO11-1**
- Because oligopolies involve several firms rather than only one, each firm must consider the effect of its price and output decisions on the behavior of rivals. Such firms are highly interdependent. **LO11-3**
- Game theory attempts to identify different strategies a firm might use, taking into account the consequences of rivals' moves and countermoves. **LO11-3**
- The kinked demand curve illustrates a pattern of strategic interaction in which rivals match a price cut but not a price hike. Such behavior reinforces the oligopolistic aversion to price competition. **LO11-3**
- A basic conflict exists between the desire of each individual oligopolist to expand its market share and the *mutual* interest of all the oligopolists in restricting total output so as to maximize industry profits. This conflict must be resolved in some way, via either collusion or some less explicit form of agreement (such as price leadership). **LO11-3**
- Oligopolists may use price-fixing agreements or price leadership to establish the market price. To maintain that price, the oligopolists must also agree on their respective market shares. **LO11-3**
- To maintain economic profits, an oligopoly must erect barriers to entry. Patents are one form of barrier. Other barriers include predatory price cutting (price wars), control of distribution outlets, government regulations, advertising (product differentiation), training, and network economies. Outright acquisition and merger may also eliminate competition. **LO11-2**
- Market power may cause market failure. The symptoms of that failure include increased prices, reduced output, and a transfer of income from the consuming public to a relatively few powerful corporations and the people who own them. **LO11-2**
- Government intervention may focus on either market structure or market behavior. In either case, difficult decisions must be made about when and how to intervene. **LO11-4**
- The Herfindahl-Hirshman Index is a measure of industry concentration that takes into account the number of firms and the size of each. It is used as a structural guideline to identify cases worthy of antitrust concern. **LO11-4**

Key Terms

market structure	product differentiation	predatory pricing
oligopoly	payoff matrix	barriers to entry
contestable market	game theory	market failure
concentration ratio	price-fixing	antitrust
oligopolist	price leadership	Herfindahl-Hirshman Index (HHI)
market share	cartel	

Questions for Discussion

1. How many bookstores are on or near your campus? If there were more bookstores, how would the price of new and used books be affected? **LO11-1**

2. What entry barriers exist in (*a*) the fast-food industry, (*b*) video streaming service, (*c*) the auto industry, (*d*) marijuana distribution, (*e*) ride-sharing service, and (*f*) beauty salons? **LO11-1**

3. Why does Dr Pepper depend on advertising to gain market share? (See Front Page Economics "Dr Pepper Targets Football Fans.") Why not offer cheaper sodas than Coke or Pepsi? **LO11-3**

4. If an oligopolist knows rivals will match a price cut, would it ever reduce its price? **LO11-3**

5. How might the high concentration ratio in the credit card industry (Table 11.2) affect the annual fees and interest charges for credit card services? **LO11-2**

6. What evidence of economies of scale is cited in the proposed cigarette merger (Front Page Economics "Joe Camel Acquires Newport")? Should the acquisition be approved? **LO11-4**

7. What reasons might rival airlines have for *not* matching Delta's fare increase? (See Front Page Economics "Delta Rolls Back Fare Hike.") **LO11-3**

8. The Ivy League schools defended their price-fixing arrangement (see Ivy League Colleges in Coordination Problems section) by arguing that their coordination assured a fair distribution of scholarship aid. Who was hurt or helped by this arrangement? **LO11-4**

9. Using the payoff matrix in Table 11.4, decide whether Universal should cut its price. What factors will influence the decision? **LO11-3**

10. Would we be better off if Facebook and Google were forced to break up into smaller companies? How could we do that? **LO11-4**

11. Why did the price of NYC taxi medallions decline so much when Uber started ride-sharing service in New York? Why are the medallions still worth $200,000? **LO11-2**

12. What has happened to cocoa prices since COPEC was formed (see World View "COPEC: The New Cocoa Cartel")? **LO11-2**

LO11-1 1. According to Table 11.2, in how many markets do fewer than four firms produce at least 80 percent of total output?

LO11-2 2. Assume that during the oil-price war, global oil production increased from 90 million to 97 million barrels per day, causing the price of oil fall by 50 percent. Calculate the implied price elasticity of oil demand (see World View "Nations Scrambling to End Oil-Price War").

LO11-2 3. (*a*) According to Front Page Economics "Joe Camel Acquires Newport," how many years will it take Reynolds to recoup its purchase price through cost savings?
   (*b*) If Reynolds increases cigarette prices by 10 percent and the price elasticity of demand is 0.4, by how much will its annual revenue of $11 billion increase?

LO11-2 4. According to Front Page Economics "Dr Pepper Targets Football Fans," calculate the sales revenue that comes from Dr Pepper Snapple Group's share of the soda market.

LO11-2 5. If the price of a medallion is a proxy for the profits of the NYC taxi industry, by what percentage did the industry's profits decline when Uber entered the market?

LO11-3 6. Assume an oligopolist confronts *two* possible demand curves for its own output, as illustrated here. The first (*A*) prevails if other oligopolists don't match price changes. The second (*B*) prevails if rivals *do* match price changes.

   (*a*) By how much does quantity demanded increase if the price is reduced from $11 to $9 and
      (*i*) Rivals match the price cut?
      (*ii*) Rivals don't match the price cut?
   (*b*) By how much does quantity demanded change when the price is raised from $11 to $13 and
      (*i*) Rivals match the price hike?
      (*ii*) Rivals don't match the price hike?

LO11-3 7. How large would the probability of a "don't match" outcome have to be to make a Universal price cut statistically worthwhile? (See expected payoff in section "Expected Gain (Loss).")

LO11-3 8. Suppose the payoff to each of four strategic interactions is as follows:

	Rival Response	
Action	**Reduce Price**	**Don't Reduce Price**
Reduce price	Loss = $800	Gain = $50,000
Don't reduce price	Loss = $6,000	No loss or gain

PROBLEMS FOR CHAPTER 11 (cont'd)

    (*a*) If the probability of rivals matching a price reduction is 98 percent, what is the expected payoff of a price cut?

    (*b*) If the probability of rivals reducing price when you don't reduce your price is 5 percent, what is the expected payoff of *not* reducing price?

    (*c*) Based on your answers to (*a*) and (*b*), should the firm cut its price?

LO11-2 9. Suppose that the following schedule summarizes the sales (demand) situation confronting an oligopolist:

Price (per unit)	$20	$19	$18	$17	$16	$14	$12	$10	$ 8
Quantity demanded (units per period)	2	3	4	5	6	7	8	9	10

    (*a*) Draw the demand and marginal revenue curves facing the firm.

    (*b*) Identify the profit-maximizing rate of output and price in a situation where marginal cost is constant at $11 per unit.

LO11-2 10. What is the price elasticity of demand between points *F* and *G* in Figure 11.2 (use the midpoint method)?

LO11-1 11. *Decisions for Tomorrow:* According to Front Page Economics "Joe Camel Acquires Newport," what were the values of

    (*a*) The concentration ratio in the cigarette industry

        (*i*) Prior to the merger?

        (*ii*) After the merger?

    (*b*) The *maximum* value of the Herfindahl-Hirschman Index

        (*i*) Prior to the merger?

        (*ii*) After the merger?

    (*c*) Which measure best reflects the increased market power?

LO11-4 12. *Decisions for Tomorrow:* According to Front Page Economics "Feds Approve T-Mobile–Sprint Merger," calculate the value of the HHI

    (*a*) Prior to the T-Mobile–Sprint merger.

    (*b*) After the merger but prior to the Dish Network transfer.

Design Credit: Shutterstock

STARBUCKS COFFEE

Jill Braaten/McGraw Hill

LEARNING OBJECTIVES

After reading this chapter, you should know

LO12-1 The unique structure of monopolistic competition.

LO12-2 The unique behavior of monopolistically competitive firms.

LO12-3 How monopolistically competitive firms maximize profits.

LO12-4 Why economic profits tend toward zero in monopolistic competition.

CHAPTER 12

Monopolistic Competition

Starbucks is already the biggest coffee bar chain in the world, with roughly 28,000 locations in 70 countries, including 15,000 in the United States. And the company is determined to keep growing by setting up coffee bars in airports, department stores, and just about anywhere consumers congregate. Even if Starbucks achieves such meteoric growth, however, it will never have great market power. There are more than 15,000 other coffee bars in the United States, not to mention a million or so other places you can buy a cup of coffee (e.g., McDonald's, 7-Eleven, Einstein Bros.). With so many other close substitutes, the best Starbucks can hope for is a little brand loyalty. If enough consumers think of Starbucks when they get the caffeine urge, Starbucks will at least be able to charge more for coffee than a perfectly competitive firm. It won't enjoy *monopoly* profits, or even share the kind of monopoly profits *oligopolies* sometimes achieve. It may, however, be able to maintain an economic profit for many years.

Starbucks is an example of yet another market structure—*monopolistic competition.* In this chapter we focus on how such firms make price and output decisions and the market outcomes that result. Our objective is to determine

- **The unique features of monopolistic competition.**
- **How market outcomes are affected by this market structure.**
- **The long-run consequences of different market structures.**

In this chapter we'll also see why we can't escape the relentless advertising that bombards us from every angle.

STRUCTURE

As we first noted in Table 11.1, the distinguishing structural characteristic of **monopolistic competition** is that there are *many* firms in an industry. "Many" isn't an exact specification, of course. It's best understood as lying somewhere between the few that characterize oligopoly and the hordes that characterize perfect competition.

Low Concentration

A more precise way to distinguish monopolistic competition is to examine **concentration ratios.** Oligopolies have very high four-firm concentration ratios. As we saw in Chapter 11 (Table 11.2), concentration ratios of 70 to 100 percent are common in oligopolies. By contrast, there's much less concentration in monopolistic competition. A few firms may stand

Product	Largest Firms (Market Share)	Concentration Ratio (%)
Coffee bars	Starbucks (40%), JAB (Peet's, Caribou, etc.) (13%), Coffee Beanery (3%), Tim Horton (2%)	58
Brewed coffee	McDonald's (14.3%), Dunkin' (13.7%), Starbucks (11.8%), 7-Eleven (6.8%)	47
Sparkling water	La Croix (17.3%), Polar (10.6%), Bubly (9.4%), Perrier (8.8%)	46
Pizza	Domino's (12.6%), Pizza Hut (11.7%), Little Caesars (7.9%), Papa John's (6.4%)	39
Retail food	Walmart (17.3), Kroger (8.9), Safeway (5.6), Costco (5.1)	37
Auto tires (replacement)	Goodyear (16%), Michelin (8%), Firestone (7.5%), General (5%)	37
Bottled water	Coca-Cola (Dasani, 9.9%), PepsiCo (Aquafina, 9.6%), Nestle (8.3%), Glaceau (7.6%)	35
Toys	Lego (12%), Mattel (11%), Hasbro (10%), Tyco (5%)	35
Pet food	PetSmart (12%), Chewy (8%), Petco (8%), Amazon (6%)	34
Casinos	MGM, Caesars, Station, Mohegan Sun	33
Fast-food restaurants	McDonald's (12%), Subway (6%), Starbucks (3%), Taco Bell (3%)	24
Prescription drugs	GlaxoSmithKline (5.8%), Hoechst-Marion Merrell Dow (4.4%), Merck (4.4%), American Home Products (3.8%)	18

Source: Industry sources and business publications (2014–2020 data).

TABLE 12.1

Monopolistic Competition

Monopolistically competitive industries are characterized by modest concentration ratios and low entry barriers. Contrast these four-firm concentration ratios with those of oligopoly (see Table 11.2).

monopolistic competition: A market in which many firms produce similar goods or services but each maintains some independent control of its own price.

concentration ratio: The proportion of total industry output produced by the largest firms (usually the four largest).

above the rest, but the combined market share of the top four firms will typically be in the range of 20 to 40 percent. Hence, *low concentration ratios are common in monopolistic competition.* Table 12.1 illustrates concentration ratios in this range for several popular products.

Defining the Market. Notice the entries in Table 12.1 for the coffee business. Everyone knows that Starbucks is the biggest dedicated coffee bar chain. It has a commanding 40 percent of the coffee-bar business, with its principal rivals accounting for another 18 percent. This would put the concentration ratio for the coffee-bar business at 58 percent, just below the threshold for oligopoly.

But are Peet's, the Coffee Beanery, and Caribou the only significant rivals to Starbucks? No. In fact, people buy more coffee from McDonald's than they do from Starbucks. Indeed, if we look at the broader market of brewed coffee purchases, Starbucks comes in third place, with only an 11.8 percent market share. In that broader market, the concentration ratio is only 47 percent, clearly indicating a monopolistically competitive market.

The same classification problem applies to McDonald's in the fast-food market. McDonald's dwarfs Starbucks in size, with 38,000 outlets in 118 countries. In the United States, it commands close to a 50 percent share of the quickie *hamburger* market. But is that the relevant market? Or should we look at the broader *fast-food* market that includes pizzas, tacos, hot dogs, and Chinese take-out? If consumers view these other food options as close substitutes for a Big Mac, then McDonald's has a lot less market power than its share of the smaller hamburger market implies. In that larger fast-food market, McDonald's has a market share of only 12% (Table 12.1).

The same kind of consumer choice affects how we assess market power in the pizza business. Three companies have 46 percent of the pizza *delivery* business. But they compete with more than 75,000 pizzerias in the United States, as well as all the other fast-food outlets. And those other pizzerias and fast-food outlets now take advantage of third-party delivery services like Uber Eats, DoorDash, and Grubhub. These expanded consumer choices reduce the market shares and power of the biggest, national pizza companies.

Market Power

Although concentration rates are low in monopolistic competition, the individual firms aren't powerless. There is a *monopoly* aspect to monopolistic competition. Each producer in monopolistic competition is large enough to have some **market power.** If a perfectly competitive firm increases the price of its product, it will lose all its customers. Recall that a perfectly competitive firm confronts a horizontal demand curve for its output. Competition is less intense in monopolistic competition. *A monopolistically competitive firm confronts a downward-sloping demand curve for its output.* When Starbucks increases the price of coffee, it loses some customers, but nowhere close to all of them (see Front Page Economics "Starbucks Raises Prices Again"). Starbucks, like other monopolistically competitive firms, has some control over the price of its output. This is the *monopoly* dimension of monopolistic competition.

market power: The ability to alter the market price of a good or service.

FRONT PAGE ECONOMICS

STARBUCKS RAISES PRICES AGAIN

Starbucks has made the morning caffeine jolt a bit more expensive. The company increased the price of brewed coffee from $1.95 to $2.15 for a tall (small) cup, effective June 2018. The response of consumers has been muted, with traffic at Starbucks declining 2 percent in the six months following the price increase. Despite the drop in traffic, sales revenue climbed 1 percent.

Source: Media reports, June–December 2018.

CRITICAL ANALYSIS: A monopolistically competitive firm has the power to increase price unilaterally. The greater the **brand loyalty,** the less unit sales will decline in response.

Independent Production Decisions

In an oligopoly, a firm that increased its price would have to worry about how rivals might respond (like the airlines in Chapter 11, Front Page Economics "Rivals Match Southwest's Flash Sale"). In monopolistic competition, however, there are many more firms. As a result, *modest changes in the output or price of any single firm will have no perceptible influence on the sales of any other firm.* This relative independence results from the fact that the effects of any one firm's behavior will be spread over many other firms (rather than only two or three other firms, as in an oligopoly).

The relative independence of monopolistic competitors means that they don't have to worry about retaliatory responses to every price or output change. As a result, they confront more traditional demand curves with no kinks. Recall that the kink in the oligopolist's curve results from the likelihood that rival oligopolists will match price reductions (to preserve market shares) but not necessarily price increases (to increase their shares). In monopolistic competition, by contrast, the market shares of rival firms aren't perceptibly altered by another firm's price changes.

barriers to entry: Obstacles such as patents that make it difficult or impossible for would-be producers to enter a particular market.

Low entry barriers encourage competition.

Chris Lawrence/Alamy Stock Photo

Low Entry Barriers

Another characteristic of monopolistic competition is the presence of *low* **barriers to entry**—it's relatively easy to get in and out of the industry. To become a coffee vendor, all you need is boiling water, some fresh beans, and cups. You can save on rent by using a pushcart to dispense the brew, which is how Starbucks itself got started on the streets of Seattle (see the photo).

Coinstar has even replaced the pushcart with bright red Rubi kiosks in grocery stores. Such unusually low entry barriers now keep Starbucks and other coffee bars on their toes. Low entry barriers also tend to push economic profits toward zero. In the pizza business, more than 4,000 firms enter and exit every year. This is the *competitive* dimension of monopolistic competition.

BEHAVIOR

Given the unique structural characteristics of monopolistic competition, we should anticipate some distinctive behavior.

Product Differentiation

product differentiation:
Features that make one product appear different from competing products in the same market.

One of the most notable features of monopolistically competitive behavior is **product differentiation.** A monopolistically competitive firm is distinguished from a purely competitive firm by its downward-sloping demand curve. Individual firms in a perfectly competitive market confront horizontal demand curves because consumers view their respective products as interchangeable (virtually identical). As a result, an attempt by one firm to raise its price will drive its customers to other firms.

Brand Image. In monopolistic competition, each firm has a distinct identity—a *brand image.* Its output is perceived by consumers as being somewhat different from the output of all other firms in the industry. Nowhere is this more evident than in the fast-growing bottled water industry. Pepsi and Coke have become the leaders in the bottled water market as a result of effective marketing (see Front Page Economics "Selling 'Pure Water': A $Billion Scam?"). Although Aquafina (Pepsi) and Dasani (Coke) are just filtered municipal water, clever advertising campaigns have convinced consumers that these branded waters are different—and better—than hundreds of other bottled waters. As a result of such product differentiation, Pepsi and Coke can raise the price of their bottled waters without losing all their customers to rival firms.

FRONT PAGE ECONOMICS

SELLING "PURE WATER": A $BILLION SCAM?

The ads for Aquafina claim it has bottled the "purest of waters," while Dasani ads assert that what it bottles is "as pure as water can get." Visual backgrounds of glacial streams and lush woodlands reinforce the image of healthy, pure water.

The reality of bottled waters is very different, however. Every drop of water in Pepsi's Aquafina and Coca-Cola's Dasani comes out of the tap, not some mountain spring or glacial melt. Yes, the two major rivals in the bottled water business do filter the tap water, but it is still tap water. In blind tastings, most consumers either prefer simple tap water or can't tell the difference between the bottled and tap options. Further, the National Resources Defense Council found that bottled (filtered) water is no safer than tap water. The Environmental Protection Agency (EPA) tightly regulates the safety of tap water, while the Food and Drug Administration (FDA) sets less stringent requirements for bottled water and often relies on self-testing.

Despite the absence of any tangible benefits, consumers spend more than $20 billion on bottled water every year. They are driven in large part by the $100 million a year that Pepsi, Coca-Cola, Nestlé, and other bottlers spend on ads touting their "purest of waters."

Source: News reports, 2019.

CRITICAL ANALYSIS: By differentiating their products, monopolistic competitors establish brand loyalty. **Brand loyalty** gives producers greater control over the prices of their products.

Brand Loyalty

At first blush, the demand curve facing a monopolistically competitive firm looks like the demand curve confronting a monopolist. There's a profound difference, however. In a monopoly, there are no other firms. In monopolistic competition, *each firm has a monopoly only on its brand image; it still competes with other firms offering close substitutes.* This implies that the extent of power a monopolistically competitive firm has depends on how successfully it can differentiate its product from those of other firms. The more brand loyalty a firm can establish, the less likely consumers are to switch brands when price is increased. In other words, *brand loyalty makes the demand curve facing the firm less price-elastic.*

Brand loyalty exists even when products are virtually identical. Gasoline of a given octane rating is a very standardized product. Nevertheless, most consumers regularly buy one particular brand. Because of that brand loyalty, Exxon can raise the price of its gasoline by a penny or two a gallon without losing customers to competing companies. Brand loyalty is particularly high for cigarettes, toothpaste, and even laxatives. Consumers of those products say they'd stick with their accustomed brand even if the price of a competing brand was cut by 50 percent. In other words, *brand loyalty implies low* **cross-price elasticity of demand.** Brand loyalty is less strong (and cross-price elasticity higher) for paper towels and virtually nonexistent for tomatoes.

In the computer industry, product differentiation has been used to establish brand loyalty. Although virtually all computers use identical microprocessor "brains" and operating platforms, the particular mix of functions performed on any computer can be varied, as can its appearance (packaging). Effective advertising can convince consumers that one computer is "smarter," more efficient, or more versatile than another.

Even coffee vendors go to great lengths to differentiate their product. Starbucks offers not just coffee, but also WiFi hot spots, mobile payments, and powermats for cordless phone charging. These features give consumers added reason to linger at Starbucks and order more coffee. In Everett, Washington, coffee vendors differentiated themselves in 2014 with "bikini baristas"—baristas attired in skimpy bikinis. Every firm is looking to establish a unique image and greater brand loyalty. If successful in any of these efforts, *each monopolistically competitive firm will establish some consumer loyalty.* With such loyalty a firm can alter its own price somewhat without fear of great changes in unit sales (quantity demanded). In other words, the demand curve facing each firm will slope downward, as in Figure 12.1.

Repurchase Rates. One measure of brand loyalty is consumers' tendency to repurchase the same brand. Nearly 8 out of 10 Apple users stick with Apple products when they upgrade smartphones, computers, or tablets. Repurchase rates are 74 percent for Dell and 72 percent for Hewlett-Packard. Starbucks also counts heavily on return customers. And Amazon Prime retains a phenomenal 93 percent of its members. By contrast, ride-sharing companies

cross-price elasticity of demand: Percentage change in the quantity demanded of *X* divided by the percentage change in the price of *Y*.

The short-run equilibrium for the firm (MC = MR)

FIGURE 12.1

Short-Run Equilibrium in Monopolistic Competition

Brand loyalty makes the demand curve facing a monopolistically competitive firm downward-sloping. This causes MR < price.

In the short run, a monopolistically competitive firm equates marginal revenue and marginal cost (point *K*). In this case, the firm sells the resulting output at a price (point *F*) above marginal cost. Total profits are represented by the shaded rectangle.

have surprisingly low retention rates, with many consumers maintaining both Uber and Lyft apps on their phones.

To maintain such brand loyalty, monopolistically competitive firms must often expand services or product offerings. Remember that entry barriers are low. In the coffee business, it was relatively easy for fast-food companies like McDonald's and Dunkin' to enter once they saw how profitable Starbucks was. When they did, Starbucks had to expand its menu to maintain its market dominance. Although menu expansion is costly, firms often decide that increased service is more cost-effective than price competition, given the low cross-price elasticity of demand in monopolistically competitive markets. In recent years, Starbucks has continued to pursue product differentiation with a new logo, instant coffee, new cup sizes (the 31-ounce "trenta"), single-serve machines, mobile payments, wine bars, and new food items.

Price Premiums. Another symptom of brand loyalty is the price differences between computer brands. Consumers are willing to pay more for an Apple, Lenovo, or Dell computer than a no-name computer with identical features. For the same reason, consumers are willing to pay more for Starbucks coffee, Ben and Jerry's ice cream, or Aquafina water, even when virtually identical products are available at lower prices.

Short-Run Price and Output

production decision: The selection of the short-run rate of output (with existing plants and equipment).

The monopolistically competitive firm's **production decision** is similar to that of a monopolist. Both types of firms confront downward-sloping demand and marginal revenue curves. To maximize profits, both seek the rate of output at which marginal revenue equals marginal cost. This short-run profit-maximizing outcome is illustrated by point K in Figure 12.1. That MC = MR intersection establishes q_a as the profit-maximizing rate of output. The demand curve indicates (point F) that q_a of output can be sold at the price of p_a. Hence, the quantity-price combination q_a, p_a illustrates the short-run equilibrium of the monopolistically competitive firm.

Entry and Exit

economic profit: The difference between total revenues and total economic costs.

Figure 12.1 indicates that this monopolistically competitive firm is earning an **economic profit:** price (p_a) exceeds average total cost (c_a) at the short-run rate of output. These profits are of course a welcome discovery for the firm. They also portend increased competition, however.

Entry Effects. If firms in monopolistic competition are earning an economic profit, other firms will flock to the industry. Remember that *entry barriers are low in monopolistic competition, so new entrants can't be kept out of the market.* If they get wind of the short-run profits depicted in Figure 12.1, they'll come running.

As new firms enter the industry, supply increases and prices will be pushed down the market demand curve, just as in competitive markets. Figure 12.2a illustrates these market changes. The initial price p_1 is set by the intersection of *industry* MC and MR. Because that price generates a profit, more firms enter. This entry shifts the *industry* cost structure to the right, creating a new equilibrium price, p_2.

The impact of this entry on the firms already in the market will be different from that in competitive markets, however. As new firms enter a monopolistically competitive industry, existing firms will lose customers. This is illustrated by the leftward shift of the demand curve facing each firm, as in Figure 12.2b. Accordingly, we conclude that *when firms enter a monopolistically competitive industry,*

- *The industry cost curves shift to the right, pushing down price* (Figure 12.2a).
- *The demand curves facing individual firms shift to the left* (Figure 12.2b).

As the demand curve it faces shifts leftward, the monopolistically competitive firm will have to make a new production decision. It need not charge the same price as its rivals, however, or coordinate its output with theirs. Each monopolistically competitive firm has some independent power over its (shrinking numbers of) captive customers.

(a) Effect of entry on the industry

(b) Effect of entry on the monopolistically competitive firm

FIGURE 12.2

Market vs. Firm Effects of Entry

Barriers to entry are low in monopolistic competition. Hence, new firms will enter if economic profits are available.

(a) The Market. The entry of new firms will shift the *market* cost curves to the right, as in part *a*. This pushes the average price down the *market* demand curve.

(b) The Firm. The entry of new firms also affects the demand curve facing the typical firm. The *firm's* demand curve shifts to the left and becomes more elastic because more close substitutes (other firms) are available.

No Long-Run Profits

Although each firm has some control over its own pricing decisions, *entry-induced leftward shifts of the demand curve facing the firm will ultimately eliminate economic profits.*

Long-Run Equilibrium. Notice in Figure 12.3 where the firm eventually ends up. In long-run equilibrium (point G), marginal cost is again equal to marginal revenue (at the MR = MC intersection directly below G). At that rate of output (q_g), however, there are no economic profits. At that output, price (p_g) is exactly equal to average total cost.

The long-run equilibrium for the firm (MC = MR, *p* = ATC)

FIGURE 12.3

Long-Run Equilibrium in Monopolistic Competition

In the long run, more firms enter the industry. As they do so, the demand curve facing each firm *shifts* to the left as all market shares decline. Firms still equate MR and MC. Ultimately, however, the demand curve will be tangent to the ATC curve (point *G*), at which point price equals average total cost and no economic profits exist.

The profit-maximizing equilibrium (point G) occurs where the demand curve is tangent to the ATC curve. If the demand curve shifted any farther left, price would always be less than ATC and the firm would incur losses. If the demand curve were positioned farther to the right, price would exceed ATC at some rates of output. When the demand curve is *tangent* to the ATC curve, the firm's best possible outcome is to break even. At point G in Figure 12.3, price equals ATC and economic profit is zero.

Will a monopolistically competitive firm end up at point G? As long as other firms can enter the industry, the disappearance of economic profits is inevitable. Existing firms can postpone the day of reckoning by increasing their product differentiation and advertising. But rival firms will enter as long as the demand (price) line lies above ATC at some point. Firms will exit when the demand facing the firm lies to the left of and below the ATC curve. This is a common occurrence in monopolistically competitive industries. In 2017–2019 Tully's, Peet's, Biggby, and FIFA all closed dozens of coffee bars that were losing money. Even Starbucks closed 150 stores in 2019, while opening new stores in more profitable (less competitively congested) locations. Entry and exit cease when the firm's demand curve is *tangent* to the ATC curve. Once entry and exit cease, the long-run equilibrium has been established. ***In the long run, there are no economic profits in monopolistic competition.***

Inefficiency

The zero-profit equilibrium of firms in monopolistic competition, as illustrated in Figure 12.3, differs from the perfectly competitive equilibrium. In perfect competition, long-run profits are also zero. But at that point, a competitive industry produces at the *lowest* point on the ATC curve and thus maximizes efficiency. In monopolistic competition, however, the demand curve facing each firm slopes downward. Hence, it can't be tangent to the ATC curve at its lowest point (the bottom of the U), as in perfect competition. Instead, the demand curve of a monopolistically competitive firm must touch the ATC curve on the *left* side of the U.

Note in Figure 12.3 how point G lies above and to the left of the bottom of the ATC curve. This long-run equilibrium occurs at an output rate that is less than the minimum-cost rate of production. In long-run equilibrium, the monopolistically competitive industry isn't producing at minimum average cost. As a consequence, ***monopolistic competition tends to be less efficient in the long run than a perfectly competitive industry.***

Excess Capacity. One symptom of the inefficiencies associated with monopolistic competition is industrywide excess capacity (see Front Page Economics "Coffee Shops Seeking New Identities"). Each firm tries to gain market share by building more outlets and advertising heavily. In equilibrium, however, the typical firm is producing at a rate of output that's less than its minimum-ATC output rate. This implies that the *same* level of *industry* output could be produced at lower cost with fewer firms. If that happened, the resources used to develop that excess capacity could be used for more desired purposes.

Flawed Price Signals. The misallocation of resources that occurs in monopolistic competition is a by-product of the flawed price signal that is transmitted in imperfectly competitive markets. Because the demand curve facing a firm in monopolistic competition slopes downward, such a firm will violate the principle of **marginal cost pricing.** Specifically, it will always price its output above the level of marginal costs, just like firms in an oligopoly or monopoly. Notice in Figures 12.1 and 12.3 that price lies above marginal cost in both short- and long-run equilibrium. As a consequence, price always exceeds the opportunity cost. Consumers respond to these flawed signals by demanding fewer goods from monopolistically competitive industries than they would otherwise. We end up with the wrong (suboptimal) mix of output and misallocated resources.

Thus, ***monopolistic competition results in both production inefficiency (above minimum average cost) and allocative inefficiency (wrong mix of output).*** This contrasts with the model of perfect competition, which delivers both minimum average total cost and efficient (MC-based) price signals.

marginal cost pricing: The offer (supply) of goods at prices equal to their marginal cost.

NEWS

FRONT PAGE ECONOMICS

COFFEE SHOPS SEEKING NEW IDENTITIES

ALBANY—It's easy to get a good cup of coffee on Wolf Road. And it's getting easier.

With over 35,000 specialty coffee shops in the United States, it isn't easy to brew a profit in the coffee business anymore. To buck that trend, coffee purveyors are trying to create new niches that are less competitive. In 2015 Starbucks debuted its "Starbucks Reserve Roastery and Tasting Room," located just nine blocks up the street from its very first Seattle shop. The Roastery specializes in single-source and often rare coffees, like Peru Chontali and Rwanda Maraba (for $4–$7 a cup). Consumers can observe the in-store roasting process while viewing images of the locations the beans came from. Stumptown and Microlots are pursuing the same niche, striving to preserve profits in a saturated coffee market.

Source: Media reports, 2015–2016.

CRITICAL ANALYSIS: Continued entry will push economic profits to zero and leave the industry with excess capacity.

DECISIONS FOR TOMORROW

Do We Need Truth in Advertising?

Models of oligopoly and monopolistic competition show how industry structure affects market behavior. Of particular interest is the way different kinds of firms "compete" for sales and profits. *In truly (perfectly) competitive industries, firms compete on the basis of price.* Competitive firms win by achieving greater efficiency and offering their products at the lowest possible price.

Firms in imperfectly competitive markets don't "compete" in the same way. In oligopolies, the kink commonly found in the demand curve facing each firm inhibits price reductions. In monopolistic competition, there's also a reluctance to engage in price competition. Because each firm has its own captive market—consumers who prefer its particular brand over competing brands—price reductions by one firm won't induce many consumers to switch brands. As we noted earlier, the cross-price elasticity of demand is low in monopolistically competitive markets. Thus, price reductions aren't a very effective way to increase sales or market share in monopolistic competition.

If imperfectly competitive firms don't compete on the basis of price, do they really compete at all? The answer is evident to anyone who listens to the radio, watches television, reads magazines or newspapers, clicks on the Internet, drives on the highway, or streams free movies. *Imperfectly competitive firms engage in nonprice competition.*

The most prominent form of *nonprice competition* is advertising. An imperfectly competitive firm typically uses advertising to enhance its own product's image, thereby increasing the size of its captive market (consumers who identify with a particular brand). The Coca-Cola Company hires rock stars to create the image that Coke is superior to other soft drinks (see Front Page Economics "The Cola Wars: It's Not All Taste"), thereby creating brand loyalty. In 2020, oligopolies and monopolistically competitive firms spent more than $200 *billion* on advertising for such purposes. Procter & Gamble alone spent $4.3 billion (see Table 12.2). P&G hopes that these expenditures shift the demand for its products (e.g., Ivory Soap, Pampers, Jif peanut butter, Crest, Tide) to the right, while perhaps making it less price-elastic as well. By contrast, perfectly competitive firms have no incentive to advertise because they can individually sell their entire output at the current market price.

Continued

FRONT PAGE ECONOMICS

THE COLA WARS: IT'S NOT ALL TASTE

American consumers gulp nearly 40 million soft drinks per day. The Coca-Cola Company produces about 40 percent of those soft drinks, while Pepsi-Cola produces about 30 percent of the market supply. With nearly 70 percent of the market between them, Pepsi and Coke wage fierce battles for market share.

The major weapon in these "cola wars" is advertising. Coke spends $6 billion a year globally to convince consumers that its products are superior. Pepsi spends about $4 billion to win the hearts and taste buds of American consumers. The advertisements not only tout the superior taste of their respective products but also try to create a distinctive image for each cola.

The advertising apparently works. Half of all soft drink consumers profess loyalty to either Coke or Pepsi. Few of these loyalists can be persuaded to switch cola brands, even when offered lower prices for the "other" cola.

Ironically, few people can identify their favorite cola in blind taste tests. Seventy percent of the people who swore loyalty to either Coke or Pepsi picked the wrong cola in a taste test.

The moral of the story? That in imperfectly competitive markets, product *image* and *perceptions* may be as important as product quality and price in winning market shares.

Source: Media reports, January-March 2020

CRITICAL ANALYSIS: Advertising is intended to create brand loyalty. Loyal consumers are likely to buy the same brand all the time, even if competitors offer nearly identical products.

A company that runs a successful advertising campaign can create enormous *goodwill* value. That value is reflected in stronger brand loyalty—as expressed in greater demand and smaller price elasticity. Often a successful brand image can be used to sell related products as well. According to World View "The Best Global Brands," the most valuable brand name in the world is Apple, whose worldwide name recognition is worth $206 *billion.*

Societal Issues. While it is evident that successful ad campaigns benefit the firms that sponsor them, how much good or harm do they do for society? How about the resources (labor, capital) that ad campaigns absorb? Could those resources be better used in other pursuits?

And what about consumer choice? If Procter & Gamble used that $4 billion now spent on advertising instead on product innovation, maybe we'd be getting better and cheaper

Company	Ad Spending in 2018 ($ billions)
Comcast	6.1
AT&T	5.4
Amazon	4.5
Proctor & Gamble	4.3
General Motors	3.1
Disney	3.1
Charter	3.0
Google	3.0
American Express	2.8
Verizon	2.7

Source: Kantar Media.

TABLE 12.2

Top 10 Advertisers

Firms with market power attempt to preserve and extend that power through advertising. A successful advertising campaign alters the demand curve facing the firm, thus increasing potential profits. Shown here are the advertising outlays of the biggest advertisers in 2018.

WORLD VIEW

THE BEST GLOBAL BRANDS

For companies in almost every industry, brands are important in a way they never were before. Why? For one thing, customers for everything from soda pop to software now have a staggering number of choices. And a quick online search can bring the full array to any computer screen with a click of the mouse. Without trusted brand names as touchstones, shopping for almost anything would be overwhelming. Meanwhile, in a global economy, corporations must reach customers in markets far from their home base. A strong brand acts as an ambassador when companies enter new markets or offer new products.

That's why companies that once measured their worth strictly in terms of tangibles such as factories, inventory, and cash have realized that a vibrant brand, with its implicit promise of quality, is an equally important asset. A brand has the power to command a premium price, increasing profits and sheltering a company from competition.

The World's 10 Most Valuable Brands

Rank	Brand	2020 Brand Value ($ billions)
1	Apple	206
2	Google	168
3	Microsoft	125
4	Amazon	97
5	Facebook	89
6	Coca-Cola	59
7	Samsung	53
8	Disney	52
9	Toyota	45
10	McDonald's	44

Source: Forbes, May 2020.

CRITICAL ANALYSIS: **Brand names** are valuable economic assets and assist a firm in maintaining a base of loyal customers. These brands have worldwide recognition as a result of heavy advertising.

products. And why don't the wireless companies put all that ad money into infrastructure instead, giving us faster, more reliable communications? As it now stands, we pay for those ads indirectly via higher product prices and lower quality.

There is also a privacy issue here. Facebook, Google, and other companies know so much about our search and purchase habits that they can sell *targeted* ad programs to consumer companies. Political ads are also targeted, typically without any explicit consent on our part.

Finally, there is the issue of *truth*. Clearly, both the companies and the politicians who bombard us with ads have selfish interests. They want our dollars or our votes. And they might say anything to get them, whether true or not.

Ad Bans. These many societal concerns have prompted many people to demand not only truth in advertising, but also limits on advertising. Twitter, for example, decided to ban all political advertising, while Facebook beefed up its ad-review staff to weed out false ads. The federal government also polices false advertising.

But there are two sides to this debate. Advertisers argue that they have a free-speech right to promote their products. They also note that free markets assure that any claims they put

Continued

forth can be challenged by rival firms or candidates. Further, the businesses that sponsor successful campaigns note that their success brings in profits that finance product innovation.

Models of imperfect competition imply that advertising wars between powerful corporations won't end anytime soon. As long as markets have the *structure* of oligopoly or monopolistic competition, we expect the *behavior* of nonprice competition. Will their catchy ads continue to shape our consumer choices?

SUMMARY

- There are many (rather than few) firms in monopolistic competition. The concentration ratio in such industries tends to be low (20–40 percent). **LO12-1**
- Each monopolistically competitive firm enjoys some brand loyalty. This brand loyalty, together with its relatively small market share, gives each firm a high degree of independence in price and output decisions. **LO12-1**
- Brand loyalty is reflected in the downward-sloping demand curve facing the firm. Profits are maximized at the rate of output where MR = MC. **LO12-3**
- The amount of market share and power a monopolistically competitive firm possesses depends on how successfully it differentiates its product from similar products. Accordingly, monopolistically competitive firms tend to devote more resources to advertising. **LO12-2**

- The market power bestowed by brand loyalty is measured by low cross-price elasticities of demand, high repurchase rates, and price premiums. **LO12-1**
- Low entry barriers permit new firms to enter a monopolistically competitive industry whenever economic profits exist. Such entry eliminates long-run economic profit and reduces (shifts leftward) the demand for the output of existing firms. **LO12-4**
- Monopolistic competition results in resource misallocations (due to flawed price signals) and inefficiency (above-minimum-average cost). **LO12-3**
- Monopolistic competition encourages nonprice competition instead of price competition. Because the resources used in nonprice competition (advertising, packaging, service, etc.) may have more desirable uses, these industry structures lead to resource misallocation. **LO12-3**

Key Terms

monopolistic competition	barriers to entry	production decision
concentration ratio	product differentiation	economic profit
market power	cross-price elasticity of demand	marginal cost pricing

Questions for Discussion

1. If the price elasticity of demand for Starbucks is less than 1.0, why doesn't it increase prices a lot more? **LO12-2**
2. Why do 4,000 new pizzerias open every year? Why do just as many close? **LO12-4**
3. Name three products each for which you have (a) high brand loyalty and (b) low brand loyalty. **LO12-2**
4. If one gas station reduces its prices, must other gas stations match the price reduction? Why or why not? **LO12-2**
5. Front Page Economics "The Cola Wars: It's Not All Taste" suggests that most consumers can't identify their favorite cola in blind taste tests. Why then do people stick with one brand? What accounts for brand loyalty in bottled water (Front Page Economics "Selling 'Pure Water': A $Billion Scam?")? **LO12-1**
6. Why would Starbucks invest $20 million in a new "Roastery" if the coffee-shop market is already saturated

(Front Page Economics "Coffee Shops Seeking New Identities")? **LO12-4**
7. What happens to the demand curve facing a Starbucks shop when a Dunkin' store opens next to it? What can Starbucks do to maintain its business? **LO12-4**
8. How would our consumption of cereal change if cereal manufacturers stopped advertising? Would we be better or worse off? **LO12-3**
9. Why isn't the video-streaming market considered to be monopolistically competitive (see Front Page Economics "Streaming Wars Heat Up" in Chapter 11)? **LO12-1**
10. Why isn't the video-streaming market considered monopolistically competitive? **LO12-1**
11. According to World View "The Best Global Brands," what gives brand names their value? **LO12-2**

PROBLEMS FOR CHAPTER 12

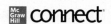

LO12-1 1. What is the concentration ratio in an industry with the following market shares?

Firm A	13.2	Firm C	4.2	Firm E	2.7	Firm G	1.6
Firm B	11.4	Firm D	3.6	Firm F	2.2	Other firms	61.1

LO12-2 2. According to Front Page Economics "Starbucks Raises Prices Again,"
  (*a*) By what percent did Starbucks increase the price of a tall cup of brewed coffee (use the midpoint method)?
  (*b*) Calculate the price elasticity of demand for brewed coffee if 50% of the decline in traffic was due to the increased brewed coffee prices.
  (*c*) Explain the relationship between price elasticity of demand and total revenue.

LO12-2 3. If Starbucks raises its price by 6 percent and McDonald's experiences a 0.3 percent increase in demand for its coffee, what is the cross-price elasticity of demand?

LO12-2 4. In Figure 12.3, at what output rate is economic profit equal to zero?

LO12-3 5. (*a*) Use the accompanying graph to illustrate the short-run equilibrium of a monopolistically competitive firm.
  (*b*) At that equilibrium, what is
     (*i*) Price?   (*ii*) Output?   (*iii*) Total profit?
  (*c*) Identify the long-run equilibrium of the same firm.
  (*d*) In long-run equilibrium, what is (approximately)
     (*i*) Price?   (*ii*) Output?   (*iii*) Total profit?

LO12-4 6. (*a*) In the *short*-run equilibrium of the previous problem, what is
     (*i*) The price of the product?
     (*ii*) The opportunity cost of producing the last unit?
  (*b*) In the *long*-run equilibrium of the previous problem, what is
     (*i*) The price of the product?
     (*ii*) The opportunity cost of producing the last unit?

LO12-4 7. On the accompanying graph, identify each of the following *market* outcomes:
   (*a*) Short-run equilibrium output in competition.
   (*b*) Long-run equilibrium output in competition.
   (*c*) Long-run equilibrium output in monopoly.
   (*d*) Long-run equilibrium output in monopolistic competition.

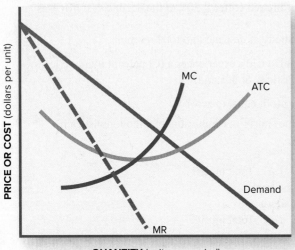

LO12-2 8. *Decisions for Tomorrow:* If Coke sells approximately 2 billion sodas globally per day, according to Front Page Economics "The Cola Wars: It's Not All Taste," how much is Coke spending on advertising per soda?

LO12-2 9. *Decisions for Tomorrow:* On the following graph, show the effect of a successful advertising campaign on the firm's cost, demand, and marginal revenue curves.

Design Credit: Shutterstock

PART

4

REGULATORY ISSUES

Microeconomic theory provides insights into how prices and product flows are determined in unregulated markets. Sometimes those market outcomes are not optimal, and the government intervenes to improve them. In this section we examine government regulation of natural monopolies (Chapter 13), environmental protection (Chapter 14), and farm output and prices (Chapter 15). The goal is to determine whether and how government regulation might improve market outcomes—or possibly worsen them.

BananaStock/Getty Images

Andrew Merry/Getty Images

Fuse/Getty Images

BananaStock/Getty Images

Natural Monopolies: (De)Regulation?

The lights went out in California in 2020—not just once but repeatedly. Offices went dark, air conditioners shut down, assembly lines stopped, and TV screens went blank. Hundreds of thousands of homes and businesses were subjected to these rolling blackouts. Governor Newsom blamed the state's utility regulators for not anticipating the electricity shortfall. He wanted *more* regulation of the power industry. Industry representatives responded that government regulation was itself responsible for throwing California into a new Dark Age. *Less* regulation, not more, would have kept the lights on, they claimed.

The battle over government regulation of the power industry quickly became part of the broader battle over clean energy. Environmentalists urged the pursuit of green energy sources to supplant reliance on fossil fuels. Governor Newsom himself noted that California would not sacrifice its green agenda to avoid future blackouts. Many business groups pointed out that solar and wind power is unreliable and expensive. They stressed the need for reliable and cheaper energy sources, including the nuclear and gas-fired power plants that California had forced to close. President Trump intensified the debate, asserting that excessive regulation had curbed America's energy production and eliminated thousands of jobs. He proposed a massive rollback of federal regulation.

Everyone agrees that markets sometimes fail—that unregulated markets may produce the wrong mix of output, undesirable methods of production, or an unfair distribution of income. But government intervention can fail as well. Hence, we need to ask,

- **When is government regulation necessary?**
- **What form should that regulation take?**
- **When is it appropriate to deregulate an industry?**

In answering these questions, we draw on economic principles as well as recent experience. This will permit us to contrast the theory of (de)regulation with reality.

LEARNING OBJECTIVES

After reading this chapter, you should know

LO13-1 The characteristics of natural monopoly.

LO13-2 The regulatory dilemmas posed by natural monopoly.

LO13-3 The costs associated with regulation.

LO13-4 How deregulation has fared in specific industries.

ANTITRUST VS. REGULATION

A perfectly competitive market provides a model for economic efficiency. As we first observed in Chapter 3, the market mechanism can answer the basic economic questions of WHAT to produce, HOW to produce it, and FOR WHOM. Under ideal conditions, the market's answers may also be optimal—that is, the best possible outcomes. To achieve this **laissez-faire** ideal, all producers must be perfect competitors; people must have full information about tastes, costs, and prices; all costs and benefits must be reflected in market prices; and pervasive economies of scale must be absent.

In reality, these conditions are rarely, if ever, fully attained. Markets may be dominated by large and powerful producers. In wielding their power, these producers may restrict output, raise prices, stifle competition, and inhibit innovation. In other words, market power may cause **market failure**, leaving us with suboptimal market outcomes.

Behavioral Focus

As we observed in Chapter 11, the government has two options for intervention where market power prevails. It may focus on the *structure* of an industry or on its *behavior*. **Antitrust** laws cover both options: They prohibit mergers and acquisitions that reduce potential competition (structures) and forbid market practices (behavior) that are anticompetitive.

Government **regulation** has a different focus. Instead of worrying about industry structure, regulation focuses almost exclusively on *behavior*. In general, regulation seeks to change market outcomes directly by imposing specific limitations on the price, output, or investment decisions of private firms.

NATURAL MONOPOLY

Regulation is almost always the policy choice when dealing with natural monopolies. A **natural monopoly** exists when a single firm has such pervasive economies of scale that it will "naturally" dominate its industry. In natural monopoly, bigger *is* always better—at least in terms of production costs. The larger the firm, the lower its costs. Because of these scale economies, a natural monopoly can produce the products consumers want at the lowest possible price. A single cable company is more efficient than a horde of cable firms developing a maze of cable networks. The same is true of local telephone service and many utilities. In all of these cases, a single company can deliver products at lower cost than a bunch of smaller firms. Dismantling such a natural monopoly would destroy that cost advantage. A natural monopoly is therefore a potentially desirable market *structure*.

But what about behavior? Do we need to regulate natural monopolies? Even though a natural monopoly might enjoy economies of scale, it might not pass those savings along to consumers. In that case, the economies of scale don't do consumers any good, and the government might have to regulate the firm's behavior.

To determine whether regulation is desirable, we first have to determine how an *unregulated* natural monopoly will behave.

Declining ATC Curve

Figure 13.1 illustrates the unique characteristics of a natural monopoly. *The distinctive characteristic of a natural monopoly is its downward-sloping average total cost (ATC) curve.* Because unit costs keep falling as the rate of production increases, a single large firm can underprice any smaller firm. Ultimately, it can produce all the market supply at the lowest attainable cost. In an unregulated market, such a firm will "naturally" come to dominate the industry.

High Fixed Costs. Natural monopolies typically emerge in situations where the fixed costs of production are extremely large. To supply electricity, for example, you first need to build a power source (e.g., a coal-fired plant, hydroelectric dam, or nuclear generator), then a distribution network. It's the same thing with subways and railroads: A lot of infrastructure must be constructed before anyone gets a ride. As a consequence of these high fixed costs, the *average* total cost curve starts out very high (recall that ATC = AFC + AVC).

laissez faire: The doctrine of "leave it alone," of nonintervention by government in the market mechanism.

market failure: An imperfection in the market mechanism that prevents optimal outcomes.

antitrust: Government intervention to alter market structure or prevent abuse of market power.

regulation: Government intervention to alter the behavior of firms—for example, in pricing, output, or advertising.

natural monopoly: An industry in which one firm can achieve economies of scale over the entire range of market supply.

FIGURE 13.1

Declining ATC

A combination of high fixed costs and very low marginal costs generates a unique, downward-sloping ATC curve in natural monopoly. MC lies below ATC at all output levels.

Low Marginal Costs. Once productive capacity is built, the focus turns to *marginal costs*. In natural monopolies, marginal costs are typically low—*very low*. Supplying another kilowatt of electricity entails negligible marginal cost. Carrying one more passenger on a railroad or subway entails similarly negligible costs.

Even if marginal costs rise as production increases (the law of diminishing returns), marginal cost remains less than average total cost over the entire range of output. Notice in Figure 13.1 that *the marginal cost (MC) curve lies below the ATC curve at all rates of output for a natural monopoly.* The ATC curve never rises into its conventional U shape because marginal costs never exceed average costs. Hence, there is no force to pull average total costs up, as in conventional cost structures.

The combination of high fixed costs and low (negligible) marginal costs gives the ATC curve a unique shape. The ATC curve starts out high (due to high AFC) and keeps declining as output increases (because MC < ATC at all times). *The downward-sloping ATC curve is the hallmark of a natural monopoly.*

The declining costs of a natural monopoly are of potential benefit to society. The **economies of scale** offered by a natural monopoly imply that no other market structure can supply the good as cheaply. Hence, *natural monopoly is a desirable market structure.* A competitive market structure—with many smaller firms—would have higher average costs.

economies of scale:
Reductions in minimum average costs that come about through increases in the size (scale) of plant and equipment.

Unregulated Behavior

Although the **structure** *of a natural monopoly may be beneficial, its* **behavior** *may leave something to be desired.* Natural monopolists have the same profit-maximizing motivations as other producers. Moreover, they have the monopoly power to achieve and maintain economic profits. Hence, there's no guarantee that consumers will reap the cost-saving benefits of a natural monopoly. Critics charge that natural monopolies don't pass the cost savings along to consumers, instead keeping most of the benefits for themselves. This has been a recurrent criticism of cable TV operators: Consumers have complained about high prices, poor service, and a lack of programming choices from local cable monopolies.

Figure 13.2 illustrates how we expect an unregulated natural monopolist to behave. Like all other producers, the natural monopolist will follow the **profit-maximization rule,** by producing at that rate of output where marginal revenue equals marginal cost. Point A in Figure 13.2 indicates that an unregulated monopoly will end up producing the quantity q_A and charging the price p_A.

profit-maximization rule:
Produce at that rate of output where marginal revenue equals marginal cost.

Wrong WHAT Outcome. The natural monopolist's preferred outcome isn't the most desirable one for society. This price–output combination violates the competitive principle of

FIGURE 13.2

Natural Monopoly: Price Regulation

If unregulated, a natural monopoly will produce q_A, where MR = MC (point *A*). And it will charge the price p_A, as determined by the demand curve for that rate of output.

Regulation designed to achieve efficient prices will seek point *B*, where p = MC. Still lower average costs (production efficiency) are attainable at higher rates of output (capacity), however. On the other hand, a zero-profit, zero-subsidy outcome exists only at point *C*.

Which price–output combination should be sought?

marginal cost pricing. The intersection of MC and MR at point *A* in Figure 13.2 dictates the output level q_A. At what price will that output be sold? We go up from q_A to the demand curve to find out. There we see that the monopolist will sell the quantity q_A at the price p_A. Hence, price (p_A) greatly exceeds the marginal cost of production (MC$_A$). As a result of this gap, consumers aren't getting accurate information about the **opportunity cost** of this product. This flawed price signal is the cause of market failure. We end up consuming less of this product (and more of other goods) than we would if charged its true opportunity cost. A suboptimal mix of output results.

Wrong HOW Outcome. The natural monopolist's profit-maximizing output (q_A) also fails to minimize average total cost. In a competitive industry, ATC is driven down to its minimum by relentless competition. In this case, however, reductions in ATC cease when the monopolist achieves the profit-maximizing rate of output (q_A). Were output to increase further, average total costs would fall.

Wrong FOR WHOM Outcome. Finally, notice that the higher price (p_A) associated with the monopolist's preferred output (q_A) ensures a fat profit (= per-unit profit of $p_A - p_D$ multiplied by the quantity q_A). This **economic profit** may violate our visions of equity. In 2020 millions of Californians were convinced that this kind of "profiteering" was the root of their electricity woes.

marginal cost pricing: The offer (supply) of goods at prices equal to their marginal cost.

opportunity cost: The most desired goods or services that are forgone in order to obtain something else.

economic profit: The difference between total revenues and total economic costs.

REGULATORY OPTIONS

The suboptimal outcomes likely to emerge from a free-swinging natural monopoly prompt consumers to demand government intervention. The market alone can't overcome the natural advantage of pervasive economies of scale. (New, smaller firms would have higher average total costs and be unable to compete.) But the government could compel different outcomes. Which outcomes do we want? And how will we get them?

Price Regulation

For starters, we might consider price regulation. The natural monopolist's preferred price (p_A) is, after all, a basic cause of market failure. By regulating the firm, the government can compel a lower price. The California legislature did this in 1996 when it set a *maximum* retail price for electricity.

Setting a maximum price for the natural monopoly sounds like a simple solution. But what price should be set? As is apparent from Figure 13.2, there are lots of choices in setting a regulated price. We start with the conviction that the unregulated price p_A is too high. But where on the demand curve below p_A do we want to be? A price of zero (free electricity!) sounds really appealing, but we know that's not going to happen.

Price Efficiency ($p = $ MC). A more realistic possibility might be to set the price at a level consistent with opportunity costs. As we saw earlier, a monopolist's unregulated price sends out a flawed price signal. By charging a price in excess of marginal cost, the monopolist causes a suboptimal allocation of resources (i.e., the wrong mix of output). We could improve market outcomes, therefore, by compelling the monopolist to set the price equal to marginal cost, just as perfectly competitive markets do. Such an efficient price would lead us to point *B* in Figure 13.2, where the demand curve and the marginal cost curve intersect. At that price (p_B), consumers would get optimal use of the good or service produced.

Subsidy. Although the price p_B will give us the right answer to the WHAT question, it will also bankrupt the producer. In a natural monopoly, MC is always less than ATC. Hence, *marginal cost pricing by a natural monopolist implies a loss on every unit of output produced.* In this case, the loss per unit is equal to $B^* - B$. If confronted with the regulated price p_B, the firm will ultimately shut down and exit from the market. This was one of the many problems that plagued California. Unable to charge a price high enough to cover their costs, some of the state's utility companies were forced into bankruptcy.

If we want to require efficient pricing (p = MC), we must provide a subsidy to the natural monopoly. In Figure 13.2 the amount of the subsidy would have to equal the anticipated loss at q_B–that is, the quantity q_B multiplied by the per-unit loss ($B^* - B$). Such subsidies are provided to subway systems. With subsidies, local subway systems can charge fees below *average* cost and closer to *marginal* cost. These subsidized fares increase ridership, thus ensuring greater use of very expensive mass transportation systems.

Despite the advantages of this subsidized pricing strategy, taxpayers always complain about the cost of such subsidies. Taxpayers are particularly loath to provide subsidies for private companies. Hence, political considerations typically preclude efficient (marginal cost) pricing, despite the economic benefits of this regulatory strategy.

Production Efficiency ($p = $ min ATC). Another option is to focus on efficient *production* rather than efficient *pricing*. Production efficiency is attained at the lowest possible average total cost. At q_B we're producing a lot of output but still have some unused capacity. Because ATC falls continuously, we could achieve still lower average costs if we increased output beyond q_B. *In a natural monopoly, production efficiency is achieved at capacity production, where ATC is at a minimum.*

Increasing output beyond q_B raises the same problems we encountered at that rate of output. At production rates in excess of q_B, ATC is always higher than price. Even MC is higher than price to the right of point *B*. Thus, *no regulated price can induce a natural monopolist to achieve minimum average cost. A subsidy would be required to offset the market losses.*

Profit Regulation

Instead of focusing on price, why don't we focus on profits instead? Simply disallow monopoly profits like those of the unregulated monopoly (at q_A and p_A in Figure 13.2). We can achieve this result by mandating a price equal to average total cost. In Figure 13.2 this regulatory objective is achieved at point *C*. In this case, the rate of output is q_C and the regulated price is p_C.

Profit regulation looks appealing for two reasons. First, it eliminates the need to subsidize the monopolist. Second, it allows us to focus on profits only, thus removing the need to develop demand and cost curves. In theory, all we have to do is check the firm's annual profit-and-loss statement to confirm that it's earning a normal (average) profit. If its profits are too high, we can force the firm to reduce its price; if profits are too low, we may permit a price increase.

Bloated Costs. While beautiful in principle, profit regulation can turn ugly in practice. In particular, profit regulation can lead to bloated costs and dynamic inefficiency. *If a firm is permitted a specific profit rate (or rate of return), it has no incentive to limit costs.* On the contrary, higher costs imply higher profits. If permitted to charge 10 percent over unit costs, a monopolist may be better off with average costs of $6 rather than only $5. The higher costs translate into 60 cents of profit per unit rather than only 50 cents, even though the profit *rate* is the same. Hence, there's an incentive to "pad costs." If those costs actually represent improvements in the firm's wages and salaries, executive bonuses, fringe benefits, or the work environment, then cost increases are doubly attractive to the firm and its employees. Cost-efficiency is as welcome as the plague under such circumstances.

Profit regulation can also motivate a firm to inflate its costs by paying above-market prices for products purchased from an unregulated subsidiary. This was the strategy AT&T used to increase its *regulated* cost base while ringing up high profits at Western Electric, its *unregulated* subsidiary (see Chapter 10). The FCC accused Nynex (the "Baby Bell" that provided phone service in New York and New England in the 1980s) of using the same strategy to pad its profits. Nynex used its *un*regulated subsidiary (Material Enterprises Co.) to sell equipment at inflated prices to its *regulated* phone company subsidiaries (New England Telephone & Telegraph and New York Telephone). Profits in all three companies increased.

Output Regulation

Given the difficulties in regulating prices and profits, regulators may choose to regulate output instead. The natural monopolist's preferred output rate is q_A, as illustrated again in Figure 13.3. We could compel this monopolist to provide a minimum level of service

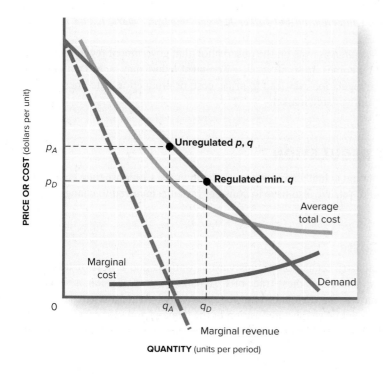

FIGURE 13.3

Minimum Service Regulation

Regulation may seek to ensure some minimal level of service. In this case, the required rate of output is arbitrarily set at q_D. Consumers are willing to pay p_D per unit for that output.

Regulated output q_D is preferable to the unregulated outcome (q_A, p_A) but may induce a decline in quality. Cost cutting is the only way to increase profits when the rate of output is fixed and price is on the demand curve.

in excess of q_A. This regulated minimum is designated q_D in Figure 13.3. At q_D consumers get the benefit not only of more output but also of a lower price (p_D). At q_D total monopoly profit must also be less than at q_A because q_A was the profit-maximizing rate of output.

It appears, then, that compelling any rate of output in excess of q_A can only benefit consumers. Moreover, output regulation is an easy rule to enforce.

Quality Deterioration. Unfortunately, minimum-service regulation can also cause problems. If forced to produce at the rate of q_D, the monopolist may seek to increase profits by cutting cost corners. This can be accomplished by deferring plant and equipment maintenance, reducing quality control, or otherwise lowering the quality of service. ***Regulation of the quantity produced may induce a decline in quality.*** Because a monopolist has no direct competition, consumers pretty much have to accept whatever quality the monopolist offers. This structural reality may explain why consumers complain so much about the services of local cable monopolies.

In addition to encouraging quality deterioration, output regulation at q_D also violates the principle of marginal cost pricing. Because an economic profit exists at q_D, equity goals may be jeopardized as well. Hence, minimum service (output) regulation isn't a panacea for the regulatory dilemma. In fact, there is no panacea. ***Goal conflicts are inescapable, and any regulatory rule may induce undesired producer responses.***

Imperfect Answers

The call for public regulation of natural monopolies is based on the recognition that the profit motive doesn't generate optimal outcomes in any monopoly environment. If unregulated, a natural monopolist will charge too much and produce too little. The regulatory remedy for these market failures isn't evident, however. Regulators can compel efficient prices or least-cost production only by offering a subsidy. Profit regulation is likely to induce cost-inflating responses. Output regulation is an incentive for quality deterioration. No matter which way we turn, regulatory problems result.

There's not much hope for transforming unregulated market failure into perfect regulated outcomes. In reality, regulators must choose a strategy that balances competing objectives (e.g., price efficiency and equity). A realistic goal for regulation is to *improve* market outcomes, not to *perfect* them. In the real world, ***the choice isn't between imperfect markets and flawless government intervention but rather between imperfect markets and imperfect intervention.***

The argument for *deregulation* rests on the observation that government regulation sometimes worsens market outcomes. In some cases, **government failure** may be worse than market failure. Specifically, regulation may lead to price, cost, or production outcomes that are inferior to those of an unregulated market.

government failure:
Government intervention that fails to improve economic outcomes.

THE COSTS OF REGULATION

Let's *assume* that regulation actually improves market outcomes. Could we then claim regulatory success? Not quite yet. We also have to consider the *costs* incurred to change market outcomes.

Administrative Costs

As we've observed, industry regulation entails various options and a host of trade-offs. Someone must sit down and assess these trade-offs. To make a sound decision, a regulatory administration must have access to lots of information. At a minimum, the regulator must have some clue as to the actual shape and position of the demand and cost curves depicted in Figures 13.2 and 13.3. Crude illustrations won't suffice when decisions about the prices,

Agency	Number of Employees (2020)
SOCIAL REGULATION	
Consumer Safety and Health	44,296
• Food and Drug Administration (FDA)	
• Food Safety and Inspection Service, etc.	
Homeland Security	154,896
• Transportation Security Administration (TSA)	
• Customs and Border Security	
• Immigration and Customs, etc.	
Transportation	9,381
• Federal Aviation Administration (FAA)	
• Federal Motor Carriers Safety Administration	
• Federal Railroad Administration, etc.	
Workplace	9,822
• Occupational Safety and Health Administration (OSHA)	
• Mine Safety and Health Administration	
• Employment Standards Administration, etc.	
Environment	22,484
• Environmental Protection Agency (EPA)	
• Forest and Rangeland Research	
• Fish and Wildlife Service, etc.	
ECONOMIC REGULATION	
General Business	21,410
• Patent and Trademark Office	
• Securities and Exchange Commission (SEC)	
• Federal Trade Commission (FTC), etc.	
Finance and Banking	18,340
• Federal Reserve System	
• Federal Deposit Insurance Corporation (FDIC)	
• Comptroller of the Currency, etc.	
Industry-Specific Regulation	6,434
• Agricultural Marketing Service	
• Federal Communications Commission (FCC), etc.	
Total Regulatory Employment:	**287,063**

Source: Mark Fabrizio, Melinda Warren, and Susan Dudley. *Regulators' Budget*. Weidenbaum Center, Washington University, October 2019.

TABLE 13.1

Employment in Federal Regulatory Agencies

The human and capital resources the bureaucracy employs represent a real opportunity cost. The 287,063 people employed in 63 federal agencies—and tens of thousands more employed in state and local bureaucracies—could be producing other goods and services. These and other costs must be compared to the benefits of regulation.

output, or costs of a multibillion-dollar industry are being made. The regulatory commission needs volumes of details about actual costs and demand and a platoon of experts to collect and analyze the needed data. All this labor represents a real cost to society because the regulatory lawyers, accountants, and economists could be employed elsewhere.

As Table 13.1 illustrates, more than 280,000 people are employed in the more visible regulatory agencies of the federal government. That's more employees than General Motors employs to build cars. On top of that, thousands more have regulatory responsibilities in smaller federal agencies and executive departments. Tens of thousands more people are employed by state and local regulatory agencies. By using all these workers to regulate private industry, we are forgoing their use in the production of desired goods and services. This is a significant economic cost.

Compliance Costs

The administrative costs of regulation focus on resources used in the public sector. By its very nature, however, regulation also changes resource use in the private sector. Regulated industries must expend resources to educate themselves about the regulations, to change their production behavior, and often to file reports with the regulatory authorities. The human and capital resources used for these purposes represent the *compliance* cost of regulation.

New rules on trucking illustrate how regulation can increase production costs. In 2013 the U.S. Department of Transportation reduced the amount of driving time permitted for interstate truckers (see Front Page Economics "Sleep Rules Raise Trucking Costs"). This rule requires freight companies to use more trucks and more labor to transport goods, thereby raising economic costs. Although the resultant gain in safety is desired, the cost of achieving that gain is not inconsequential.

FRONT PAGE ECONOMICS

SLEEP RULES RAISE TRUCKING COSTS

The Federal Motor Carrier Safety Administration (FMCSA) now monitors the sleep hours and practices of long-haul truck drivers. As of July 1, 2013, the FMCSA insists that drivers

- Drive no more than 11 hours a day.
- Work no more than 14 hours a day.
- Work no more than 70 hours a week.
- Take a 30-minute break in their first 8 hours of driving.
- Rest for 34 consecutive hours after completing a 70-hour week, including at least two nights between the hours of 1 and 5 a.m.

According to FMCSA, the new sleep rules will reduce chronic fatigue and related crashes, saving 19 lives per year. But the trucking industry says the new rules are too costly and even dangerous. They force drivers to sleep when they're not tired and to drive when they are tired. They also force trucks onto the road at commute times. The $700 billion industry says shipping costs will rise 2 to 6 percent, upward of $2 billion.

Source: Federal Motor Carrier Safety Administration and news reports of July 2013.

CRITICAL ANALYSIS: Regulations designed to improve market outcomes typically impose higher costs. The challenge is to balance benefits and costs.

Efficiency Costs

Finally, we have to consider the potential costs of changes in output. Most regulation alters the mix of output, either directly or indirectly. Ideally, regulation will always improve the mix of output. But it's possible that bad decisions, incomplete information, or faulty implementation may actually *worsen* the mix of output. If this occurs, then the loss of utility associated with an inferior mix of output imposes a further cost on society, over and above administrative and compliance costs.

Dynamic Losses. Efficiency costs may increase significantly over time. Consumer tastes change, demand and marginal revenue curves shift, costs change, and new technologies emerge. Can regulatory commissions respond to these changes as fast as the market mechanism does? If not, even optimal regulations may soon become obsolete and counterproductive. Worse still, the regulatory process itself may impede new technology, new marketing approaches, or improved production processes. These losses may be the most important. As Robert Hahn of the American Enterprise Institute observed,

> [t]he measurable costs of regulation pale against the distortions that sap the economy's dynamism. The public never sees the factories that weren't built, the new products that didn't appear, or the entrepreneurial idea that drowned in a cumbersome regulatory process.[1]

These kinds of dynamic efficiency losses are a drag on economic growth, limiting outward shifts of the production possibilities curve while perpetuating an increasingly undesired mix of output.

Balancing Benefits and Costs

The economic costs of regulation are a reminder of the "no free lunch" maxim. Although regulatory intervention may improve market outcomes, that intervention isn't without cost. The real resources used in the regulatory process could be used for other purposes. Hence, even if we could achieve perfect outcomes with enough regulation, the cost of achieving perfection might outweigh the benefits. ***Regulatory intervention must balance the anticipated improvements in market outcomes against the economic cost of regulation.*** In principle, the marginal benefit of regulation must exceed its marginal cost. If this isn't the case, then additional regulation isn't desirable, even if it would improve short-run market outcomes.

DEREGULATION IN PRACTICE

The push to *de*regulate is prompted by two concerns. The first concern focuses on the dynamic inefficiencies that regulation imposes, stifling innovation and rendering regulated industries less productive than desired. The other push for deregulation comes from advancing technology, which often destroys the structural basis for natural monopoly. A brief review of the resulting deregulation illustrates the impact of these forces.

Railroads

The railroad industry was the federal government's first broad regulatory target. Railroads are an example of natural monopoly, with high fixed costs and negligible marginal costs. Furthermore, there were no airports or interstate highways to compete with the railroads in 1887, when Congress created the Interstate Commerce Commission (ICC). The ICC was established to limit monopolistic exploitation of this situation while assuring a fair profit to railroad owners. The ICC established rates and routes for the railroads while limiting both entry to and exit from the industry.

With the advent of buses, trucks, subways, airplanes, and pipelines as alternative modes of transportation, railroad regulation became increasingly obsolete. Regulated cargoes, routes, and prices prevented railroads from adapting their prices or services to meet changing consumer demands. With regulation-protected routes, they also had little incentive to invest in new technologies or equipment. As a result, railroad traffic and profits declined while other transportation industries flourished.

The Railroad Revitalization and Regulatory Reform Act of 1976 was a response to this crisis. Its major goal was to reduce the scope of government regulation. Reinforced by the Staggers Rail Act of 1980, railroads were granted much greater freedom to adapt their prices and service to market demands.

Railroad companies used that flexibility to increase their share of total freight traffic. Fresh fruits and vegetables, for example, were exempted from ICC rate regulation in 1979. Railroads responded by *reducing* their rates and improving service. In the first year of deregulated rates, fruits and vegetable shipments increased more than 30 percent, a dramatic reversal of earlier trends. Deregulation of coal traffic (in 1980) and piggyback (trucks on

---

[1]Louis S. Richman and John Labate, "Bringing Reason to Regulation," *Fortune,* October 19, 1992, p. 94.

railroad flatcars) traffic (in 1982) prompted similar turnarounds. The railroads prospered by reconfiguring routes and services, cutting operating costs, and offering lower rates. Between 1986 and 1993, the average cost of moving freight by rail dropped by 69 percent.

Not all rates have fallen. Indeed, one worrisome effect of deregulation is the increased concentration in the rail industry. After a series of mergers and acquisitions, the top four railroads (Burlington-Northern, Union Pacific, CSX, and Norfolk-Southern) now move nearly 90 percent of all rail freight—an extremely high **concentration ratio.** Moreover, these same firms hold monopoly positions on specific routes. Shippers in these captive markets pay rates 20 to 30 percent higher than in nonmonopoly routes.

concentration ratio: The proportion of total industry output produced by the largest firms (usually the four largest).

Telephone Service

The telephone industry has long been the classic example of a natural monopoly. Although enormous fixed costs are necessary to establish a telephone network, the marginal cost of an additional telephone call approaches zero. Hence, it made economic sense to have a single network of telephone lines and switches rather than a maze of competing ones. Recognizing these economies of scale, Congress permitted AT&T to maintain a monopoly on both long-distance and most local telephone service for decades. To ensure that consumers would benefit from this natural monopoly, the Federal Communications Commission (FCC) regulated phone services and prices.

Once again, technology outpaced regulation. Communications satellites made it much easier and less costly for new firms to provide long-distance telephone service. Moreover, the rate structure that AT&T and the Federal Communications Commission had established made long-distance service highly profitable. Accordingly, start-up firms clamored to get into the industry, and consumers petitioned for lower rates.

Long Distance. In 1982, the courts put an end to AT&T's monopoly, transforming long-distance telecommunications into a more competitive industry with more firms and less regulation. Soon thereafter, more than 800 firms entered the industry, and long-distance telephone rates dropped sharply. The quality of service also improved with fiber optic cable, advanced switching systems, cell phones, and myriad new phone line services such as fax transmissions, remote access, Internet access, texting, mobile computing, gaming, and payments. All these changes contributed to a quadrupling of long-distance telephone use in the United States.

Local Service. The deregulation of long-distance services was so spectacularly successful that observers wondered whether *local* telephone service might be deregulated as well. As competition in *long-distance* services increased, the monopoly nature of *local* rates became painfully apparent: Local rates kept increasing after 1983 while long-distance rates were tumbling.

The Baby Bells that held monopolies on local service defended their high rates based on the high costs of building and maintaining transmission networks. But new technologies permitted wireless companies to offer local service if they could gain access to the monopoly networks. Congress responded in 1996. The Telecommunications Act of 1996 required the Baby Bells to grant rivals access to their transmission networks. The Baby Bells kept rivals at bay, however, by charging excessive access fees, imposing overly complex access codes, requiring unnecessary capital equipment, and raising other entry barriers. The battle for local access continues.

Airlines

The Civil Aeronautics Board (CAB) was created in 1938 to regulate airline routes and fares. From its inception, the primary concern of the CAB was to ensure a viable system of air transportation for both large and small communities. Such a system would be ensured, the CAB believed, only if a fair level of profits was maintained by entry and price regulations. Thus, the focus of the CAB was on *profit* regulation.

P = ATC. To ensure fair profits, the CAB set fares in accordance with airline costs. This required the CAB to undertake intensive cost studies, based on accounting data provided by the airlines. Once the average cost of service and capital equipment was established, the CAB then set an average price that would ensure a fair rate of return (profit) (much like point *C* in Figure 13.2).

The CAB also wanted to ensure air service to smaller, less-traveled communities. Short hauls entail higher average costs and therefore justify higher fares. To avoid high fares on such routes, the CAB permitted airlines to charge prices well in excess of average costs on longer routes as long as they maintained service on shorter, unprofitable routes. This **cross-subsidization** was similar to that of the telephone industry, in which long-distance profits helped keep local telephone charges low.

To maintain this price and profit structure, the CAB had to regulate routes and limit entry into the airline industry. Otherwise, established carriers would abandon short, unprofitable routes, and new carriers would offer service only on more profitable routes. Unregulated entry thus threatened both cross-subsidization and the CAB's vision of a fair profit.

No Entry. The CAB was extremely effective in restricting entry into the industry. Would-be entrants had to demonstrate to the CAB that their proposed service was required by "public convenience and necessity" and was superior to that of established carriers. Established carriers could oppose a new application by demonstrating sufficient service, offering to expand their service, or claiming superior service. In view of the fact that new applicants had no airline experience, established carriers easily won the argument. From 1938 until 1977, the CAB *never* awarded a major route to a new entrant.

No Price Competition. The CAB also eliminated price competition between established carriers. The CAB fixed airfares on all routes. Airlines could reduce fares no more than 5 percent and couldn't increase them more than 10 percent without CAB approval.

Bloated Costs. Ironically, the established airlines failed to reap much profit from these high fares. Unable to compete on the basis of price, the established carriers had to engage in nonprice competition. The most costly form of nonprice competition was frequency of service. Once the CAB authorized service between any two cities, a regulated carrier could provide as many flights as desired. This enticed the regulated carriers to purchase huge fleets of planes and provide frequent departures. In the process, load factors (the percentage of seats filled with passengers) fell and average costs rose.

The regulated carriers also pursued **product differentiation** by offering special meals, first-run movies, free drinks, better service, and wider seats. This nonprice competition further inflated average costs and reduced profits.

New Entrants. The Airline Deregulation Act of 1978 changed the structure and behavior of the airline industry. Entry regulation was effectively abandoned. With the elimination of this **barrier to entry**, the number of carriers increased greatly. Between 1978 and 1985, the number of airline companies increased from 37 to 174! The new entrants intensified competition on nearly all routes. The share of domestic markets with four or more carriers grew from 13 percent in May 1978 to 73 percent in May 1981. All those new entrants pushed airfares down sharply.

The CAB's authority over airfares ended January 1, 1983. Since then, airlines have been able to adapt their fares to market supply and demand. The CAB itself was eliminated in 1984.

Increasing Concentration. Although airline deregulation is hailed as one of the greatest policy achievements of the 1980s, airline industry structure and behavior remain imperfect. In the competitive fray spawned by deregulation, lots of new entrants and even some established airlines went broke. Unable to match lower fares and increased service, scores of airline companies exited the industry in the period 1985–1995. In the process, a handful of major carriers

cross-subsidization: Use of high prices and profits on one product to subsidize low prices on another product.

product differentiation: Features that make one product appear different from competing products in the same market.

barriers to entry: Obstacles such as patents that make it difficult or impossible for would-be producers to enter a particular market.

increased their market share. The combined market share of the four largest carriers (American, Delta, Southwest, United) increased from 35 percent in 1985 to 60 percent in 2014. In many cases, firms gained near-monopoly power in specific hub airports. Not surprisingly, a study by the U.S. Government Accountability Office found that ticket prices are 45 to 85 percent higher on monopolized routes than on routes where at least two airlines compete.

The concentration ratio in the airline industry spiked even higher in 2013 when American Airlines merged with U.S. Airways. The merged airline became the largest U.S. carrier, and the concentration ratio jumped to 80 percent. Although U.S. Attorney General Eric Holder warned that the American/U.S. Air merger "would result in consumers paying the price—in higher fares, higher fees, and fewer choices," the Justice Department approved the merger three months after suing to block it.

Entry Barriers. To exploit their hub dominance, major carriers must keep out rivals. One of the most effective entry barriers is their ownership of landing slots. Air traffic is limited by the number of these slots, or authorized landing permits. In 1998, United Airlines controlled 82 percent of the slots at Chicago's O'Hare; Delta controls 83 percent of the slots at New York's Kennedy Airport. Smaller airlines complain that they can't get access to these slots, even when the slots aren't being used.

The Justice Department forced American and U.S. Airways to give up 52 slots at Washington, DC's Reagan airport; 17 at La Guardia; and 2 each at five other airports as a condition for approving their merger. Justice said it would make those slots available to low-cost carriers in order to create more competitive pricing situations.

When entry barriers (including slot access) are lowered, new competitors emerge and push down airfares as one would expect in a **contestable market.** A 2013 MIT study estimated that the entry of JetBlue into a new air travel market caused one-way air fares to drop an average of $32. JetBlue is hoping to bring the same kind of limited price competition to London (see World View "JetBlue Looks to London")

contestable market: An imperfectly competitive industry subject to potential entry if prices or profits increase.

WORLD VIEW

JETBLUE LOOKS TO LONDON

JetBlue announced that it is going to start service between Boston/New York and London, beginning in 2021. The New York–London route carries over 2.5 million passengers a year. With roundtrip business fares at $7,800, it is a very profitable route. JetBlue wants in. CEO Robin Hayes promised that JetBlue would "drastically" reduce the "obscene" fares being charged by American, Delta, and other established carriers. But he has one big problem: landing slots. As he put it, "We will bring the airplanes, we will bring the low fares, we will bring the service, we will bring everything else. The thing we can't bring are the slots." With most of the landing slots at Heathrow controlled by its competitors, JetBlue is exploring the possibility of flying to Gatwick, south of London.

Source: Media reports of April 2019.

When JetBlue enters a market, prices drop.

DANIEL SLIM/Getty Images

CRITICAL ANALYSIS: Slot ownership by rival carriers at Heathrow proved to be an effective **entry barrier** to potential competitors.

Cable TV

The cable TV industry offers examples of both deregulation and *re*regulation. Up until 1986, city and county governments had the authority to franchise (approve) local cable TV operators and regulate their rates. In almost all cases, local governments franchised only one operator, thus establishing local monopolies. The monopoly structure was justified by pervasive economies of scale and the desire to avoid the cost and disruption of laying multiple cable systems. The rationale behind local regulation of cable prices (rates) was to ensure that consumers shared in the cost advantages of natural monopoly.

Deregulation. By 1984 Congress was convinced that broadcast TV and emerging technologies (such as microwave transmissions and direct satellite broadcasts) offered sufficient competition to ensure consumers fair prices and quality service. The Cable Communications Policy Act of 1984 *de*regulated cable TV by stripping local governments of the authority to regulate prices. From 1986 to 1992, cable TV was essentially unregulated.

Soon after price regulation ended, cable companies began increasing their rates sharply. As Figure 13.4 shows, the rate of price acceleration nearly doubled after the cable industry was deregulated. Consumers also complained that local cable companies offered poor service. They demanded that Congress *re*regulate the industry.

Reregulation. In 1992 Congress responded with the Cable Television Consumer Protection and Competition Act. That act gave the Federal Communications Commission authority to reregulate cable TV rates. The FCC required cable operators to *reduce* prices by nearly 17 percent in 1993–1994. It then issued 450 pages of new rules that would limit future price increases. As Figure 13.4 illustrates, these interventions had a dramatic effect on cable prices.

While consumers applauded the new price rules, cable operators warned of unwelcome long-term effects. The rate cuts reduced cable industry revenues by nearly $4 billion between 1993 and 1995. The cable companies say they would have used that revenue to invest in improved networks and services. The cable companies also argued that increased competition from satellite transmissions and the Internet made government regulation of (wired) cable TV increasingly unnecessary.

Deregulation. Congress responded to these industry complaints by *de*regulating the cable industry again. The Telecommunications Act of 1996 mandated that rate regulation be phased out and ended completely by March 1999. Almost immediately, cable prices soared again, as Figure 13.4 shows.

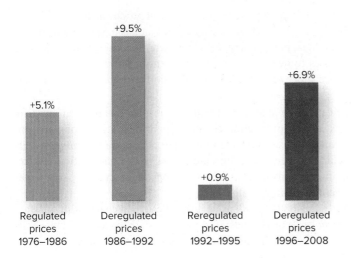

FIGURE 13.4

Annual Increase in Price of Basic Cable Service

After cable TV prices were deregulated in 1986, monthly charges moved up sharply. In 1992 Congress reregulated cable TV and prices stabilized. The Telecommunications Act of 1996 again deregulated prices and they surged, as shown in these annual averages.

Satellite Technology. The surge in cable TV prices was a boon to satellite TV providers. Satellite transmissions became a **substitute good** for cable TV—a substitute that also enjoyed pervasive economies of scale. So you suddenly had *competing* natural monopolies in a *contestable* market. Satellites won. In 1993, when cable prices were still relatively low, cable had 93 percent of the pay TV market. By 2011 the cable market share had declined to 65 percent. The high prices and profits of the cable industry ultimately spawned effective competition, first in satellite technology, then in broadband TV services (e.g., Netflix, Hulu, Blu-ray). Cable prices are still high and service below par, but at least the cable companies are now compelled by competition to improve the customer experience.

Electricity

The electric utility industry is the latest target for deregulation. Here again, the industry is a natural monopoly. The enormous fixed costs of a power plant and transmission network, combined with negligible marginal costs for delivering another kilowatt of electricity, give electric utilities a downward-sloping average total cost curve. The focus of government intervention was therefore on rate regulation (behavior) rather than promoting competition (structure).

Bloated Costs, High Prices. Critics of local utility monopolies complained that local rate regulation wasn't working well enough. To get higher (retail) prices, the utility companies allowed costs to rise. They also had no incentive to pursue new technologies that would reduce the costs of power generation or distribution. Big power users like steel companies complained that high electricity prices were crippling their competitive position. The only viable option for consumers was to move from a state with a high-cost power monopoly to a state with a low-cost power monopoly.

Demise of Power Plant Monopolies. Advances in transmission technology gave consumers a new choice. High-voltage transmission lines can carry power thousands of miles with negligible power loss. Utility companies used these lines to link their power grids, thereby creating backup power sources in the event of regional blackouts. In doing so, however, they created a new entry point for potential competition. Now a Kentucky power plant with surplus capacity can supply electricity to consumers in California. There's no longer any need to rely on a regional utility monopoly. At the wholesale level, utility companies have been trading electricity across state lines since 1992.

Local Distribution Monopolies. Although technology destroyed the basis for natural monopolies in power *production,* local monopolies in power *distribution* remain. Electricity reaches consumers through the wires attached to every house and business. As with TV cables, there is a natural monopoly in electricity distribution; competing wire grids would be costly and inefficient.

To deliver the benefits of competition in power *production,* rival producers must be able to access these local distribution grids. This is the same problem that has plagued competition in local telephone service. The local power companies that own the local distribution grids aren't anxious to open the wires to new competition. The central problem for electricity deregulation has been to assure wider access to local distribution grids.

Why is electric power regulated?

Nora Carol Photography/Getty Images

California's Mistakes. The California legislature decided to resolve this problem by stripping local utility monopolies of their production capacity. By forcing utility companies to sell their power plants, California transformed its utilities into pure power *distributors.* This seemed to resolve the conflict between ownership and access to the distribution system. However, it also made California's utility companies totally dependent on third-party power producers, many of which were then out of state.

California also put a **price ceiling** on the *retail* price its utilities could charge. But the state had no power to control the *wholesale* price of electricity in interstate markets. When wholesale prices rose sharply in 2000, ***California's utilities were trapped between rising costs and a*** *fixed price ceiling.* Fearful of a political backlash, the governor refused to raise the retail price ceiling. As a result, some of the utility companies were forced into bankruptcy and power supplies were interrupted leading to widespread blackouts.

In the wake of the 2001 blackouts, the state took over management of the power grid and pursued an ambitious goal of replacing "dirty" power sources with "clean" ones. Gas-fired and nuclear plants were closed while wind and solar facilities were constructed. This proved to be expensive: in 2020 the retail price of electricity in California was 18.78 cents per kilowatt hour, seventy percent higher than the national average (10.97 cents). Worse yet, when a heat wave engulfed the West in the summer of 2020, the quantity of electricity demanded exceeded the quantity supplied, resulting in rolling blackouts. Solar panels and farms provide no power when the sun sets, so couldn't bridge the market shortage. And the state didn't want to raise consumer prices or pay more for electricity from other states. So, rolling blackouts became the victim of the market disequilibrium. Governor Newsom himself recognized the problem and noted that the state would have to depend on market forces as a backup reserve while it continued to pursue a 100 percent renewable power grid.

DECISIONS FOR TOMORROW

Should We Deregulate Everything?

Deregulation of the railroad, telephone, airline, and electricity industries has yielded substantial benefits: more competition, lower prices, and improved services. Such experiences bolster the case for laissez faire. Nevertheless, we shouldn't jump to the conclusion that all regulation of business should be dismantled. All we know from experience is that the regulation of certain industries became outmoded. Changing consumer demands, new technologies, and substitute goods simply made existing regulations obsolete, even counterproductive. A combination of economic and political forces doomed them to extinction.

But were these regulations ever necessary? In the 1880s there were no viable alternatives to railroads for overland transportation. The forces of natural monopoly could easily have exploited consumers and retarded economic growth. The same was largely true for long-distance telephone service prior to the launching of communications satellites. Even the limitations on competition in trucking and banking made some sense in the depths of the Great Depression. One shouldn't conclude that regulatory intervention never made sense just because the regulations themselves later became obsolete.

Even today, most people recognize the need for regulation of many industries. The transmission networks for local telephone service and electricity delivery are still natural monopolies. The government can force owners to permit greater access. But an unregulated network owner could still extract monopoly profits through excessive prices. Hence, even a deregulated industry may still require some regulation at critical entry or supply junctures. Existing regulations may not be optimal, but they probably generate better outcomes than totally unregulated monopolies.

Likewise, few people seriously propose relying on competition and the good judgment of consumers to determine the variety or quality of drugs on the market. Regulations imposed by the Food and Drug Administration restrain competition in the drug industry, raise production costs, and inhibit new technology. But they also make drugs safer. Here, as in other industries, there's a trade-off between the virtues of competition and those of regulation. *The basic policy issue, as always, is whether the benefits of regulation exceed their administrative, compliance, and efficiency costs.* The challenge for public policy in the economy tomorrow is to adapt regulations—or to discard them (i.e., deregulate)—as market conditions, consumer demands, or technology changes.

SUMMARY

- Antitrust and regulation are alternative options for dealing with market power. Antitrust focuses on market structure and anticompetitive practices. Regulation stipulates specific market behavior. **LO13-2**
- High fixed costs and negligible marginal costs create a downward-sloping ATC curve, the hallmark of natural monopoly. **LO13-1**
- Natural monopolies offer pervasive economies of scale. Because of this potential efficiency, a more competitive market *structure* may not be desirable. **LO13-2**
- Regulation of natural monopoly can focus on price, profit, or output *behavior*. Price regulation may require subsidies; profit regulation may induce cost escalation; and output regulation may lead to quality deterioration. These problems compel compromises and second-best solutions. **LO13-2**
- The demand for deregulation rests on the argument that the costs of regulation exceed the benefits. These costs include the opportunity costs associated with regulatory administration and compliance as well as the (dynamic) efficiency losses that result from inflexible pricing and production rules. **LO13-3**
- Deregulation of the railroad, telephone, and airline industries has been a success. In all these industries, regulation became outmoded by changing consumer demands, products, and technology. As regulation was relaxed, these industries became more competitive, output increased, and prices fell. **LO13-4**
- Recent experiences with deregulation don't imply that all regulation should end. Regulation is appropriate if market failure exists *and* if the benefits of regulation exceed the costs. As benefits and costs change, decisions about what and how to regulate must be reevaluated. **LO13-3**

Key Terms

laissez faire
market failure
antitrust
regulation
natural monopoly
economies of scale

profit-maximization rule
marginal cost pricing
opportunity cost
economic profit
government failure
concentration ratio

cross-subsidization
product differentiation
barriers to entry
contestable market
substitute goods
price ceiling

Questions for Discussion

1. Why are railroads natural monopolies? What limits their pricing power? **LO13-1**
2. New York City has limited the number of taxicabs for decades. Were taxi companies natural monopolies? What was the purpose of such regulation? Why were Uber, Lyft, and other ride-sharing companies so eager to enter the industry? **LO13-1**
3. What makes cable companies natural monopolies? How did cable profits affect the emergence of satellite transmissions? **LO13-1**
4. Given the inevitable limit on airplane landings, how should available airport slots be allocated? How would market outcomes be altered? **LO13-2**
5. Why would a profit-regulated firm want to sell itself inputs at inflated prices? Or increase wages? **LO13-3**
6. Prior to 1982, AT&T kept local phone rates low by subsidizing them from long-distance profits. Was such cross-subsidization in the public interest? Explain. **LO13-1**
7. How would you put dollar values on the benefits and costs of truck safety regulations (Front Page Economics "Sleep Rules Raise Trucking Costs")? Do benefits exceed costs? **LO13-2**
8. The Telecommunications Act of 1996 requires local phone companies to charge "reasonable" rates for transmission access. What is a "reasonable" rate? **LO13-4**
9. How could a local phone or cable company reduce service quality if forced to accept price ceilings? **LO13-2**
10. Has JetBlue started service to London? What has happened to air fares on the New York–London route? **LO13-4**

PROBLEMS FOR CHAPTER 13

LO13-1 1. Suppose a company has $500 of fixed costs and a constant marginal cost of $0.05. What are average total costs (ATC) at
  (*a*) Output of 10 units?
  (*b*) Output of 100 units?
  (*c*) Output of 1,000 units?

LO13-2 2. In Figure 13.2,
  (*a*) How much profit does an unregulated monopolist earn?
  (*b*) How much profit would be earned if price efficiency (marginal cost pricing, $p = MC$) were imposed?

LO13-2 3. Using the graph, identify output and price and calculate profits for
  (*a*) An unregulated natural monopoly.
  (*b*) A monopoly that is regulated according to price-efficiency ($p = MC$).
  (*c*) A monopoly that is required to provide a minimum service of 60.

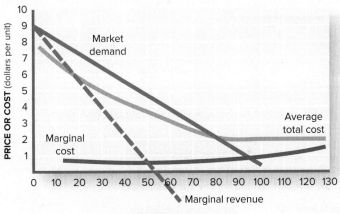

LO13-1 4. What happens to profits (or losses) when new technology reduces average total costs (shifts ATC downward in Figure 13.2) in
  (*a*) An unregulated natural monopoly?
  (*b*) A price-regulated natural monopoly without a subsidy?
  (*c*) A profit-regulated natural monopoly?

LO13-2 5. Suppose a natural monopolist has fixed costs of $15 and a constant marginal cost of $3. The demand for the product is as follows:

Price (per unit)	$10	$9	$8	$7	$6	$5	$4	$3	$2	$1
Quantity demanded (units per day)	0	2	4	6	8	10	12	14	16	18

Under these conditions,
  (*a*) What price and quantity will prevail if the monopolist isn't regulated?
  (*b*) What price-output combination would exist with efficient pricing ($p = MC$)?
  (*c*) What price-output combination would exist with profit regulation (zero economic profits)?

Illustrate your answers on the following graph:

LO13-3 6. According to Front Page Economics "Sleep Rules Raise Trucking Costs," how much will annual shipping costs increase for each saved life?

LO13-3 7. If the average U.S. worker produces $120,000 of output per year, what is the annual opportunity cost of the federal regulatory workforce (Table 13.1)?

LO13-4 8. Suppose a corporation has two subsidiaries, one of which is unregulated and sells all of its output to the other, regulated subsidiary. Permitted profits at the regulated subsidiary are equal to 10 percent of total costs. Here is the initial profit picture for the subsidiaries:

	Unregulated Subsidiary	Regulated Subsidiary
Total revenue	$600,000	$1,100,000
Total costs	$400,000	$1,000,000
Total profit	$200,000	$100,000

If the unregulated subsidiary doubles its selling price and continues to sell the same quantity, what happens to profits at
(*a*) The unregulated subsidiary?
(*b*) The regulated subsidiary?

LO13-4 9. According to World View "JetBlue Looks to London," if a landing slot in London costs $20,000 per flight and each flight carries 300 passengers, calculate the percent of the per-person ticket price allocated to the slot fee for
(*a*) JetBlue if the average price of a JetBlue flight is $800.
(*b*) American if the average price of an American flight is $1,400.

LO13-3 10. *Decisions for Tomorrow:* Suppose the benefits of a regulation related to workplace safety is $10 million per year and the associated administrative costs are $200,000, compliance costs are $4 million, and efficiency costs are $5 million per year. Should deregulation occur?

Andrew Merry/Getty Images

CHAPTER 14

Environmental Protection

Progress in environmental problems is impossible without a clear understanding of how the economic system works in the environment and what alternatives are available to take away the many roadblocks to environmental quality.

—Council on Environmental Quality, First Annual Report

What good is a clean river if you've got no jobs?

—Steelworkers union official in Youngstown, Ohio

Environmental protection, what they do is a disgrace; every week they come out with new regulations

—Donald Trump, 45th president of the United States

LEARNING OBJECTIVES

After reading this chapter, you should know

LO14-1 How markets encourage pollution.

LO14-2 Alternative strategies for reducing pollution.

LO14-3 Why *zero* pollution may not be desirable.

A hole in the ozone layer is allowing increased ultraviolet radiation to reach the earth's surface. The hole is the result of excessive release of chlorine gases (chlorofluorocarbons, or CFCs) from air conditioners, plastic foam manufacture, industrial solvents, and aerosol spray cans such as deodorants and insecticides. The resulting damage to the stratosphere is causing skin cancer, cataracts, and immune system disorders.

Skin cancer may turn out to be one of our less serious problems. As carbon dioxide is building up in the atmosphere, it is creating a gaseous blanket around the earth that is trapping radiation and heating the atmosphere. Scientists predict that this greenhouse effect will melt the polar ice caps, raise sea levels, flood coastal areas, and turn rich croplands into deserts within 60 years.

Everyone wants a cleaner and safer environment. So why don't we stop polluting the environment with CFCs, carbon dioxide, toxic chemicals, and other waste?

Economics is part of the answer. To reduce pollution, we have to change our patterns of production and consumption. This entails economic costs, in terms of restricted consumption choices, more expensive ways of producing goods, higher prices, and jobs. Thus, we have to weigh the benefits of a cleaner, safer environment against the costs of environmental protection.

Instinctively, most people don't like the idea of measuring the value of a cleaner environment in dollars and cents. But most people might also agree that spending $2 trillion to avoid a few cataracts is awfully expensive. There has to be *some* balance between the benefits of a cleaner environment and the cost of cleaning it up.

This chapter assesses our environmental problems from this economic perspective, considering three primary concerns:

- **How do (unregulated) markets encourage pollution?**
- **What are the costs of greater environmental protection?**
- **How can government policy best ensure an *optimal* environment?**

To answer these questions, we first survey the major types and sources of pollution. Then we examine the benefits and costs of environmental protection, highlighting the economic incentives that shape market behavior.

THE ENVIRONMENTAL THREAT

Water, air, and solid waste pollution, and the earth's rising temperature are at the top of the list of environmental concerns. The list is much longer, however, and very old as well. As early as A.D. 61, the statesman and philosopher Seneca was complaining about the smoky air emitted from household chimneys in Rome. Lead emissions from ancient Greek and Roman silver refineries poisoned the air in Europe and the remote Arctic. And historians are quick to remind us that open sewers running down the street were once the principal mode of urban waste disposal. Typhoid epidemics were a recurrent penalty for water pollution. So we can't say that environmental damage is a new phenomenon or that it's now worse than ever before.

But we do know more about the sources of environmental damage than our ancestors did, and we can better afford to do something about it. Our understanding of the economics of pollution has increased as well. We've come to recognize that pollution impairs health, reduces life expectancy, and thus reduces labor force activity and output. Pollution also destroys capital (such as the effects of air pollution on steel structures) and diverts resources to undesired activities (like car washes, laundry, and cleaning). Not least of all, pollution directly reduces our social welfare by denying us access to clean air, water, and beaches.

Air Pollution

Air pollution is as familiar as a smoggy horizon. But smog is only one form of air pollution.

Acid Rain. Sulfur dioxide (SO_2) is an acrid, corrosive, and poisonous gas that's created by burning high-sulfur fuels such as coal. As a contributor to acid rain, it destroys vegetation and forests. Electric utilities and industrial plants that burn high-sulfur coal or fuel oil are the prime sources of SO_2. Coal burning alone accounts for about 60 percent of all emissions of sulfur oxides. As World View "Polluted Cities" illustrates, pollution is a serious problem not only in U.S. cities but all over the world: The air is much dirtier in Mexico City, Bangkok, and Delhi than in New York City—and virtually unbreathable in heavy industrial cities like Shenyang, China.

Smog. Nitrogen oxides (NO_x), another ingredient in the formation of acid rain, are also a principal ingredient in the formation of smog. Smog not only irritates the eyes and spoils the view, but it also damages plants, trees, and human lungs. Automobile emissions account for 40 percent of urban smog. Bakeries, dry cleaners, and production of other consumer goods account for an equal amount of smog. The rest comes from electric power plants and industrial boilers.

The Greenhouse Effect. The prime villain in the greenhouse effect is the otherwise-harmless carbon dioxide (CO_2) that we exhale. Unfortunately, we and nature now release so much CO_2 that the earth's oceans and vegetation can no longer absorb it all. The excess CO_2 is creating a gaseous blanket around the earth that may warm the earth to disastrous levels. The burning of fossil fuels is a significant source of CO_2 buildup. The destruction of rain forests, which absorb CO_2, also contributes to the greenhouse effect.

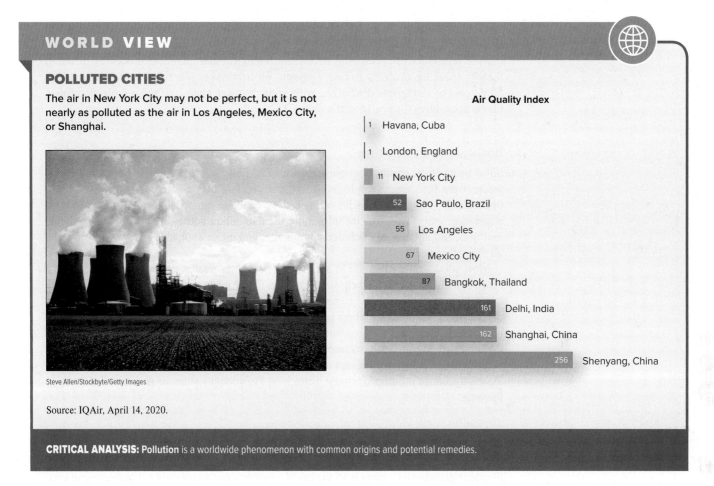

WORLD VIEW

POLLUTED CITIES

The air in New York City may not be perfect, but it is not nearly as polluted as the air in Los Angeles, Mexico City, or Shanghai.

Air Quality Index

1   Havana, Cuba

1   London, England

11   New York City

52   Sao Paulo, Brazil

55   Los Angeles

67   Mexico City

87   Bangkok, Thailand

161   Delhi, India

162   Shanghai, China

256   Shenyang, China

Steve Allen/Stockbyte/Getty Images

Source: IQAir, April 14, 2020.

CRITICAL ANALYSIS: Pollution is a worldwide phenomenon with common origins and potential remedies.

Water Pollution

Water pollution is another environmental threat. Its effects are apparent in the contamination of drinking water, restrictions on swimming and boating, foul-smelling waterways, swarms of dead fish, and floating debris.

Organic Pollution. The most common form of water pollution occurs in the disposal of organic wastes from toilets and garbage disposals. The wastes that originate there are collected in sewer systems and ultimately discharged into the nearest waterway. The key question is whether the wastes are treated (separated and decomposed) before ultimate discharge. Sophisticated waste treatment plants can reduce organic pollution up to 99 percent. Unfortunately, only 70 percent of the U.S. population is served by a system of sewers and adequate (secondary) treatment plants. Inadequate treatment systems often result in the closure of waterways and beaches due to excessive levels of bacteria.

In addition to household wastes, our waterways must also contend with industrial wastes. More than half the volume of industrial discharge comes from just a few industries—principally paper, organic chemicals, petroleum, and steel. Finally, there are all those farm animals: The 7.5 billion chickens and 161 million cows and hogs raised each year generate 1.4 billion tons of manure (whew!). If improperly managed, that organic waste will contaminate water supplies and trigger algae blooms that can choke waterways and kill fish. Animal wastes don't cause too great a problem in Boston or New York City, but they can wreak havoc on the water supplies of towns in California, Texas, Kansas, and Iowa.

Thermal Pollution. Thermal pollution is an increase in the temperature of waterways brought about by the discharge of steam or heated water. Heat discharges can kill fish, upset marine reproductive cycles, and accelerate biological and chemical processes in water, thereby reducing its ability to retain oxygen. Electric power plants account for more than 80 percent of all thermal discharges, with primary metal, chemical, and petroleum-refining plants accounting for nearly all the rest.

Solid Waste Pollution

Solid waste is yet another environmental threat. Solid waste pollution is apparent everywhere, from the garbage can to litter on the streets and beaches, to debris in the water, to open dumps. According to EPA estimates, we generate more than 5 billion tons of solid waste each year. This figure includes more than 30 billion bottles, 60 billion cans, 100 million tires, and millions of discarded automobiles and major appliances. Where do you think all this refuse goes?

Most solid wastes originate in agriculture (slaughter wastes, orchard prunings, harvest residues) and mining (slag heaps, mill tailings). The much smaller amount of solid waste originating in residential and commercial use is considered more dangerous, however, simply because it accumulates where people live. New York City alone generates 38,000 tons of trash a day, three times more than any other city in the world. Because it has neither the land area nor the incinerators needed for disposal, it must ship its garbage to other states. Seattle ships its trash to Oregon; Los Angeles transports its trash to the Mojave Desert; New York City sludge is dumped in west Texas; and Philadelphia ships its garbage all the way to Panama.

POLLUTION DAMAGES

Shipping garbage to Panama is an expensive answer to our waste disposal problem. But even those costs are a small fraction of the total cost of environmental damage. Much greater costs are associated with the damage to our health (labor), buildings (capital), and land. Even the little things count, like being able to enjoy a clear sunset, swim in the ocean, or just take a deep breath.

Although many people don't like to put a price on the environment, some monetary measure of environmental damage is important in decision making. Unless we value the environment above everything else, we have to establish some method of ranking the importance of environmental damage. Although it's tempting to say that clean air is priceless, *we won't get clean air, clean water, or clean beaches unless we spend resources to get them.* This economic reality suggests that we begin by determining how much cleaner air is worth to us.

Assigning Prices

In some cases, it's fairly easy to put a price on environmental damage. Scientists can measure the increase in cancer, heart attacks, and other disorders attributable to air pollution, as the EPA does for air toxins (see Front Page Economics "Air Pollution Kills"). Engineers can also measure the rate at which buildings decay or forests and lakes die. Economists can then estimate the dollar value of this damage by assessing the economic value of lives, forests, lakes, and other resources. For example, if people are willing to pay $5,000 for a cataract operation, then the avoidance of such eye damage is worth at least $5,000. Saving a tree is worth whatever the marketplace is willing to pay for the products of that tree. According to the EPA, a human life is worth $9.2 million. The EPA uses that benchmark to compute the damages due to premature deaths caused by pollution-related illnesses.

AIR POLLUTION KILLS

More than 100,000 Americans die each year due to heart attacks, strokes, and other illnesses caused by air pollution. The primary culprit is particulate matter emitted into the air from factories, mines, autos, power plants, and farms. The number of pollution-related deaths is just about equal to the number of Americans killed in auto accidents each year.

Air pollution kills.

imantsu/Shutterstock

Source: National Academy of Sciences, April 2019.

CRITICAL ANALYSIS: Pollution entails real costs, as measured by impaired health, reduced life spans, and other **pollution damages.**

The job of pricing environmental damage is much more difficult with intangible losses like sunsets. Nevertheless, when governmental agencies and courts are asked to assess the damages of oil spills and other accidents, they must try to inventory *all* costs, including polluted sunsets, reduced wildlife, and lost recreation opportunities. The science of computing such environmental damage is very inexact. Nevertheless, crude but reasonable procedures generate pollution-related damage estimates in the hundreds of billions of dollars per year.

Cleanup Possibilities

One of the most frustrating things about all this environmental damage is that it can be avoided. The EPA estimates that *95 percent of current air and water pollution could be eliminated by known and available technology.* Nothing very exotic is needed: just simple things like auto emission controls, smokestack cleaners, improved sewage and waste treatment facilities, and cooling towers for electric power plants. Even solid waste pollution could be reduced by comparable proportions if we used less packaging, recycled more materials, or transformed our garbage into a useful (relatively low-polluting) energy source. Why don't we do these things? Why do we continue to pollute so much?

MARKET INCENTIVES

Previous chapters emphasized how market incentives influence the behavior of individual consumers, firms, and government agencies. Incentives in the form of price reductions can be used to change consumer buying habits. Incentives in the form of high profit margins encourage production of desired goods and services. And market incentives in the form of cost differentials help allocate resources efficiently. Accordingly, we shouldn't be too surprised to learn that *market incentives play a major role in pollution behavior.*

The Production Decision

Imagine that you're the majority stockholder and manager of an electric power plant. Such plants are responsible for a significant amount of air pollution (especially sulfur dioxide and particulates) and nearly all thermal water pollution. Hence, your position immediately puts you on the most-wanted list of pollution offenders. But suppose you're civic minded and would truly like to help eliminate pollution. Let's consider the alternatives.

Profit Maximization. As the owner–manager of an electric power plant, you'll strive to make a profit-maximizing **production decision.** That is, you'll seek the rate of output at which marginal revenue equals marginal cost. Let's assume that the electric power industry is still regulated by the state power commission so that the price of electricity is fixed, at least in the short run. The effect of this assumption is to render marginal revenue equal to price, thus giving us a horizontal price line, as in Figure 14.1a.

Figure 14.1a also depicts the marginal and average total costs (MC and ATC) associated with the production of electricity. By equating marginal cost (MC) to price (marginal revenue, MR), we observe (point A) that profit maximization occurs at an output of 1,000 kilowatt-hours per day. Total profits are illustrated by the shaded rectangle between the price line and the average total cost (ATC) curve.

production decision: The selection of the short-run rate of output (with existing plants and equipment).

The Efficiency Decision

The profits illustrated in Figure 14.1a are achieved in part by use of the cheapest available fuel under the boilers (which create the steam that rotates the generators). Recall that the construction of a marginal cost curve presumes some knowledge of alternative production processes. Recall too that the **efficiency decision** requires a producer to choose that production process (and its associated cost curve) that minimizes costs for any particular rate of output.

efficiency decision: The choice of a production process for any given rate of output.

Cut Profits to Pollute Less?. Unfortunately, the efficiency decision in this case leads to the use of high-sulfur coal, the prime villain in SO_2 and particulate pollution. Other fuels, such as low-sulfur coal, fuel oil, natural gas, and nuclear energy, cost considerably more.

(a) Maximizing profits by using cheap but polluting process

(b) Protecting the environment by using more expensive but less polluting process

FIGURE 14.1

Profit Maximization in Electric Power Production

Production processes that control pollution may be more expensive than those that don't. If they are, the MC and ATC curves will shift upward (to MC_2 and ATC_2). At the new profit-maximizing rate of output (point B), output and total profit shrink. Hence, a producer has an incentive to continue polluting, using cheaper technology.

Were you to switch to one of them, the ATC and MC curves would both shift upward, as in Figure 14.1*b*. Under these conditions, the most profitable rate of output would be lower than before (point *B* on the graph), and total profits would decline (note the smaller profit rectangle in Figure 14.1*b*). Thus, *pollution abatement can be achieved, but only at significant cost to the plant.*

The same kind of cost considerations lead the plant to engage in thermal pollution. Cool water must be run through an electric utility plant to keep the turbines from overheating. Once the water has run through the plant, it's too hot to recirculate. It must be either dumped back into the adjacent river or cooled off by being circulated through cooling towers. As you might expect, it's cheaper to simply dump the hot water in the river, as the Indian Point nuclear plant in New York does (see Front Page Economics "Cut the Power to Save the Fish?"). The fish don't like it, but they don't have to pay the construction costs associated with cooling towers.

FRONT PAGE ECONOMICS

CUT THE POWER TO SAVE THE FISH?

New York State started its attack on the Indian Point nuclear plant in 2001. The State was worried about the safety of nuclear plants and also the impact of the plant's operations on fish. The Indian Point plant sucked in 2.5 billion gallons of water out of the Hudson River every day to cool its generators. It also sucked up and killed millions of fish and larvae. More fish were killed when the heated water was returned to the river. The State's Department of Environmental Conservation (DEC) wanted at least a temporary shutdown in the spawning and migration season (May 10–August 10). Better yet, they wanted Entergy Corp., the plant's owner, to reengineer a closed-circuit cooling system that would end the fish kills.

The DEC faced two problems. First, Entergy said it would be far too costly to reengineer the cooling system; no chance of that happening. Second, electricity consumers needed the power Indian Point provides. The plant supplied 2,000 megawatts of electricity a day—about 25 percent of New York City's daily use. New Yorkers weren't willing to risk blackouts, brownouts, or higher electricity prices to save a few fish.

The State couldn't convince Entergy to change its ways, but economics did. A sharp decline in the price of natural gas in 2018–2020 made nuclear power uneconomical. As electricity consumers switched to natural gas power, Entergy decided to shut down its Indian Point plant. Final shutdown is expected in 2021, at which time the plant will be disassembled and moved to Michigan.

Source: Media reports, 2019–2020.

CRITICAL ANALYSIS: Profits dictate producer decisions. When producers consider only *private* costs, they may select production processes that impose high *external* costs.

The big question here is whether you and your fellow stockholders would be willing to incur higher costs to cut down on pollution. Eliminating the water pollution emanating from the electric plant will cost a lot of money. And to whose benefit? To the people who live downstream? We don't expect profit-maximizing producers to take such concerns into account. *The behavior of profit maximizers is guided by comparisons of revenues and costs, not by philanthropy, aesthetic concerns, or the welfare of fish.*

MARKET FAILURE: EXTERNAL COSTS

The moral of this story—and the critical factor in pollution behavior—is that *people tend to maximize their personal welfare, balancing private benefits against private costs.* For the electric power plant, this means making production decisions on the basis of revenues received and costs incurred. The fact that the power plant imposes costs on others, in the form of air and water pollution, is irrelevant to its profit-maximizing decisions. Those costs are *external* to the firm and don't appear on its profit-and-loss statement. Those **external costs**—or *externalities*—are no less real, but they're incurred by society at large rather than by the firm.

Externalities in Production

Whenever external costs exist, a private firm won't allocate its resources and operate its plant in such a way as to maximize social welfare. In effect, society permits the power plant the free use of valued resources—clean air and clean water. The power plant has a tremendous incentive to substitute those resources for others (such as high-priced fuel or cooling towers) in the production process. The inefficiency of such an arrangement is obvious when we recall that the function of markets is to allocate scarce resources in accordance with the consumer's expressed demands. Yet here we are, proclaiming a high value for clean air and clean water and encouraging the power plant to use up both resources by offering them at zero cost to the firm.

The inefficiency of this market arrangement can be expressed in terms of a distinction between social costs and private costs. **Social costs** are the total costs of all the resources used in a particular production activity. On the other hand, **private costs** are the resource costs incurred by the specific producer.

Ideally, a producer's private costs will encompass all the attendant social costs, and production decisions will be consistent with our social welfare. Unfortunately, this happy identity doesn't always exist, as our experience with the power plant illustrates. *When social costs differ from private costs, external costs exist. In fact, external costs are equal to the difference between the social and private costs:*

$$\text{External costs} = \text{Social costs} - \text{Private costs}$$

When external costs are present, the market mechanism won't allocate resources efficiently. This is a case of **market failure.** The price signal confronting producers is flawed. By not conveying the full (social) cost of scarce resources, the market encourages excessive pollution. We end up with a suboptimal mix of output (too much electricity, too little clean air) and the wrong production processes.

The consequences of this market failure are illustrated in Figure 14.2, which again depicts the cost situation confronting the electric power plant. Notice that we use *two* different marginal cost curves this time. The lower one, the *private* MC curve, reflects the private costs incurred by the power plant when it operates on a profit maximization basis, using high-sulfur coal or without cooling towers. It's identical to the MC curve in

external costs: Costs of a market activity borne by a third party; the difference between the social and private costs of a market activity.

social costs: The full resource costs of an economic activity, including externalities.

private costs: The costs of an economic activity directly borne by the immediate producer or consumer (excluding externalities).

market failure: An imperfection in the market mechanism that prevents optimal outcomes.

FIGURE 14.2
Market Failure

Social costs exceed private costs by the amount of external costs. Production decisions based on private costs alone will lead us to point *B*, where private MC = MR. At point *B*, the rate of output is q_p.

To maximize social welfare, we equate *social* MC and MR, as at point *A*. Only q_s of output is socially desirable. The failure of the market to convey the full costs of production keeps us from attaining this outcome.

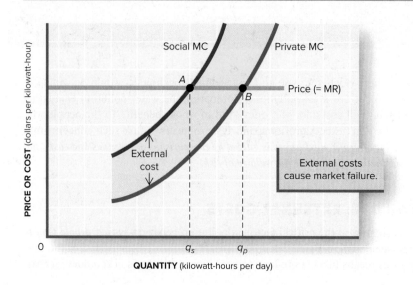

Figure 14.1*a*. We now know, however, that such operations impose external costs on others in the form of air and water pollution. These external costs must be added to private marginal costs. When this is done, we get a *social* marginal cost curve that lies above the private MC curve.

To maximize profits, private firms seek the rate of output that equates private MC to MR (price). ***To maximize social welfare, we need to equate social marginal cost to marginal revenue (price).*** This social optimum occurs at point *A* in Figure 14.2 and results in output of q_s. By contrast, the firm's private profit maximization occurs at point *B*, where q_p is produced. Hence, the private firm ends up producing more output than socially desired, while earning more profit and causing more pollution. As a general rule, ***if pollution costs are external, firms will produce too much of a polluting good.***

Externalities in Consumption

A divergence between private and social costs can also be observed in consumption. Consumers try to maximize their personal welfare. We buy and use more of those goods and services that yield the highest satisfaction (marginal utility) per dollar expended. By implication (and the law of demand), we tend to use more of a product if we can get it at a discount—that is, pay less than the full price. Unfortunately, the "discount" often takes the form of an external cost imposed on neighbors and friends.

Automobile driving illustrates the problem. The amount of driving one does is influenced by the price of a car and the marginal costs of driving it. People buy smaller cars and drive less when the attendant marginal costs (for instance, gasoline prices) increase substantially. But automobile use involves not only *private costs* but *external costs* as well. Auto emissions (carbon monoxide, hydrocarbons, and nitrogen oxides) are a principal cause of air pollution. In effect, automobile drivers have been able to use a valued resource, clean air, at no cost to themselves. Few motorists see any personal benefit in installing exhaust control devices because the quality of the air they breathe would be little affected by their efforts. Hence, low private costs lead to excessive pollution when high social costs are dictating cleaner air.

A divergence between social and private costs can be observed even in the simplest of consumer activities, such as throwing an empty soda can out the window of your car. Hanging onto the can and later disposing of it in a trash barrel involve personal effort and thus private marginal costs. Throwing it out the window not only is more exciting but also effectively transfers the burden of disposal costs to someone else. The resulting externality ends up as roadside litter.

The same kind of divergence between private and social costs helps explain why people abandon old cars in the street rather than haul them to scrapyards. It also explains why people use vacant lots as open dumps. In all these cases, ***the polluter benefits by substituting external costs for private costs.*** In other words, market incentives encourage environmental damage.

REGULATORY OPTIONS

The failure of the market to include external costs in production and consumption decisions creates a basis for government intervention. As always, however, we confront a variety of policy options. We may define these options in terms of ***two general strategies for environmental protection:***

- ***Alter market incentives*** in such a way that they discourage pollution.
- ***Bypass market incentives*** with some form of regulatory intervention.

Market-Based Options

Insofar as market incentives are concerned, the key to environmental protection is to eliminate the divergence between private costs and social costs. The opportunity to shift some costs onto others lies at the heart of the pollution problem. If we could somehow compel producers to *internalize* all costs—pay for both private and external costs—the divergence would disappear, along with the incentive to pollute.

Emission Charges. One possibility is to establish a system of **emission charges:** direct costs attached to the act of polluting. Suppose that we let you keep your power plant and permit you to operate it according to profit-maximizing principles. The only difference is that we no longer supply you with clean air and cool water at zero cost. From now on, we'll charge you for these scarce resources. We might, say, charge 2 cents for every gram of noxious emission discharged into the air. In addition we might charge 3 cents for every gallon of water you use, heat, and discharge back into the river.

Confronted with such emission charges, you'd have to rethink your production decision. *An emission charge increases private marginal cost and encourages lower output and cleaner technology.* Figure 14.3 illustrates this effect. Notice how the fee raises private marginal costs and induces a lower rate of (polluting) production (q_1 rather than q_0).

Once an emission fee is in place, a producer may also reevaluate the efficiency decision. Consider again the choice of fuels to be used in our fictional power plant. We earlier chose high-sulfur coal because it was the cheapest fuel available. Now, however, there's an additional cost attached to burning such fuel, in the form of an emission charge. This added cost may encourage the firm to switch to cleaner sources of energy, which would increase private marginal costs but reduce emission fees.

An emission charge might also persuade a firm to incur higher *fixed* costs. Rather than continuing to pay emission charges, it might be more economical to install scrubbers and other smokestack controls that reduce the volume of emissions. This would entail additional capital outlays for the necessary abatement equipment but might reduce variable costs (including emission charges). In this case, the fee-induced change in fixed costs might reduce pollution without any reduction in output.

The actual response of producers will depend on the relative costs involved. If emission charges are too low, it may be more profitable to continue burning and polluting with high-sulfur coal and pay a nominal fee. This is a simple pricing problem. We could set the emission price higher, prompting the behavioral responses we desire.

Economic incentives can also change consumer behavior. At one time, beverage producers imposed deposits to encourage consumers to bring bottles back so they could be used again. But producers discovered that such deposits discouraged sales and yielded little cost savings. Today returnable bottles are rarely used. One result is the inclusion of more than 30 billion glass bottles and 60 billion cans in our solid waste disposal problem. We could reverse this trend by imposing a deposit on all beverage containers. Many states

FIGURE 14.3

Emission Fees

Emission charges can close the gap between marginal social costs and marginal private costs. Faced with an emission charge of *t,* a private producer will reduce output from q_0 to q_1. Emission charges may also induce different investment and efficiency decisions.

do this, at least for certain cans and bottles. Such deposits internalize pollution costs for the consumer and render the throwing of a soda can out the window equivalent to throwing away money.

Some communities have also tried to reduce solid waste processing by charging a fee for each container of garbage collected. In Charlotte, Virginia, a fee of 80 cents per 32-gallon bag of garbage had a noticeable impact on consumer behavior. Economists Don Fullerton and Thomas Kinnaman observed that households reduced the weight of their garbage by 14 percent and the volume by 37 percent. As they noted, "Households somehow stomped their garbage to get more in a container and trim their garbage bill." Here again, the use of the market mechanism (higher prices) brought about the desired environmental protection.

Recycling Materials. An important bonus that emission charges offer is an increased incentive for the recycling of materials. The glass and metal in used bottles and cans can be recycled to produce new bottles and cans. Such recycling not only eliminates a lot of unsightly litter but also diminishes the need to mine new resources from the earth, a process that often involves its own environmental problems. The critical issues are once again relative costs and market incentives. *A container producer has no incentive to use recycled materials unless they offer superior cost efficiency and thus greater profits.* The largest component in the costs of recycled materials is usually the associated costs of collection and transportation. In this regard, an emission charge such as the 5-cent container deposit lowers collection costs because it motivates consumers to return all their bottles and cans to a central location.

Higher User Fees. Another market alternative is to raise the price consumers pay for scarce resources. If people used less water, we wouldn't have to build so many sewage treatment plants. In most communities, however, the price of water is so low that people use it indiscriminately. Higher water fees would encourage water conservation.

A similar logic applies to auto pollution. The cheapest way to cut down on auto pollution is to drive less. Higher gasoline prices would encourage people to use alternative transportation and drive more fuel-efficient cars. Consumers would complain, of course, about higher taxes on gasoline, but at least they'd be able to breathe cleaner air.

"Green" Taxes. Automakers don't want gasoline prices to go up; neither do consumers. So the government may have to impose *green taxes* to get the desired response. A green tax on gasoline, for example, raises the price of gasoline. The taxes not only curb auto emissions (less driving) but also create a revenue source for other pollution abatement efforts. Other nations impose far more green taxes than does the United States.

Pollution Fines. Not far removed from the concept of emission and user charges is the imposition of fines or liability for cleanup costs. In some situations, such as the April 2010 BP oil spill in the Gulf of Mexico or the 2019 Pertamina spill in Indonesia, the pollution is so sudden and concentrated that society has little choice but to clean it up quickly. The costs for such cleanup can be imposed on the polluter, however, through appropriate fines. Such fines place the cost burden where it belongs.

Although pollution fines are inevitably imposed after the damage is done, the *expectation* of a fine can encourage more environmentally conscious behavior. To avoid a potential fine, oil companies may invest in double-hulled oil tankers and more efficient safety mechanisms on offshore oil wells. When Carnival Cruises was fined $20 million in 2019 for dumping plastic waste from its cruise ships, the firm decided to monitor waste disposal practices more closely. In the absence of such fines, firms have little incentive to invest in environmental protection.

Tradable Pollution Permits ("Cap and Trade")

Another environmental policy option makes even greater use of market incentives. Rather than penalize firms that have already polluted, let firms *purchase* the right to continue polluting. As crazy as this policy might sound, it can be effective in limiting environmental damage.

TABLE 14.1

Pricing Pollution Permits

If both firms reduce emissions by one ton each, the cost is $300. If the utility instead reduces emissions by two tons, the cost is only $250. A permit system allows the smelter to pay the utility for assuming the added abatement responsibility.

	Marginal Cost of Pollution Abatement	
Reduction in Emissions (in Tons)	Copper Smelter	Electric Utility
1	$200	$100
2	250	150
3	300	200

The key to the success of pollution permits is that they're bought and sold among private firms. The system starts with a government-set standard for pollution reduction. Firms that reduce pollution by more than the standard earn pollution credits. They may then sell these credits to other firms, who are thereby relieved of cleanup chores. ***The principal advantage of pollution permits is their incentive to minimize the cost of pollution control.***

To see how the permits work, suppose the policy objective is to reduce sulfur dioxide emissions by two tons. There are only two major polluters in the community: a copper smelter and an electric utility. Should each company be required to reduce its SO_2 emissions by one ton? Or can the same SO_2 reduction be achieved more cheaply with marketable pollution rights?

Focus on Marginal Abatement Costs. Table 14.1 depicts the assumed cost of pollution abatement at each plant. The copper smelter would have to spend $200 to achieve a one-ton reduction in SO_2 emissions. The utility can do it for only $100. Table 14.1 also indicates that the utility can attain a *second* ton of SO_2 abatement for $150. Even though its marginal cost of pollution control is increasing, the utility still has lower abatement costs than the smelter. This cost advantage creates an interesting economic opportunity.

Recall that the policy goal is to reduce emissions by two tons. The copper smelter would have to spend $200 to achieve its one-ton share of the policy target. But the utility can abate a *second* ton for $150. Accordingly, the smelter would save money by *paying* the utility for additional pollution abatement.

How much would the smelter have to pay? The utility would want at least $150 to cover its own marginal costs of additional pollution abatement. The smelter would save money at any price below $200. Accordingly, the price of this transaction would be somewhere between $150 (the utility's marginal cost of a second ton) and $200 (the smelter's marginal cost of the first ton). If they do the deal—trade pollution rights—the smelter would continue to pollute, but total SO_2 emissions would still drop by two tons (all at the electric utility). Both firms would be better off (the smelter with lower costs, the utility with more revenue).

Society also benefits from this cap-and-trade system: The social goal of pollution abatement is achieved at lower cost. Without tradable permits, the resource cost of a two-ton reduction was $300. With the cap-and-trade option, the resource cost falls to $250. So society ends up with $50 of "extra" resources to produce other desired goods and services.

Cap and Trade in California. California has made cap and trade the linchpin of its battle against climate change. It launched its program in 2013, targeting carbon dioxide and other greenhouse-gas emissions (see Front Page Economics "Paying to Pollute in California"). The power plants, industrial plants, and fuel distributors that account for 80 percent of the state's greenhouse emissions are required to participate in the cap-and-trade program. Each year, the state lowers the maximum level of allowable emissions and increases the price of emission "allowances." The escalating price is intended to spur firms to find more ways to reduce emissions.

Environmental Innovation. Pollution permits also encourage third-party innovation in abatement technology. Entrepreneurs now have an incentive to discover cheaper methods

FRONT PAGE ECONOMICS

PAYING TO POLLLULTE IN CALIFORNIA

California has been a leader in the battle against climate change. One of its major weapons is its cap-and-trade program. The state has set an ambitious goal: a reduction in greenhouse emissions of 40 percent below 1990 levels by 2030. Each year the California Air Resources Board (CARB) lowers the maximum allowable level of CO_2 emissions (the "cap") generated by power companies, large industrial plants, and fuel distributors. Then it gives these firms free "allowances" that permit the holder to emit one ton of greenhouse gases per year. The companies are then free to trade these allowances, an exchange that is facilitated by quarterly auctions. At the latest auction, over 65 million one-ton allowances were traded, at an average price of roughly $17. Companies with abatement costs greater than $17 per ton are the principal buyers.

Source: California Air Resources Board and media reports, January–February 2020.

CRITICAL ANALYSIS: **Marketable pollution permits** encourage firms with more efficient pollution control technologies to overachieve, thereby earning pollution permits that can be sold to firms with more expensive pollution control technologies. Such trades reduce the *average* cost of pollution control.

for pollution abatement. They don't have to own a smelter or utility; they can now *sell* their pollution control expertise to the highest bidder. As the market for permits expanded, the profit opportunities for environmental engineering firms increased. This accelerated productivity and reduced the cost of pollution abatement by 25 to 34 percent.

Command-and-Control Options

Public policy needn't rely on tradable permits or other market incentives to achieve desired pollution abatement. The government could instead simply *require* firms to reduce pollutants by specific amounts and even specify which abatement technology must be used. This approach is often referred to as the "command-and-control" option. The government *commands* firms to reduce pollution and then *controls* the process for doing so.

The potential inefficiency of the command-and-control strategy was already revealed in Table 14.1. Had the government required *each* firm to reduce pollution by one ton, the total cost would have been $300. By allowing firms to use tradable permits, the cost of obtaining the same level of pollution abatement was only $250. The cost saving of $50 represents valuable resources that could be used to produce other desired goods and services.

Despite the superior efficiency of market-based environmental policies, the government often relies on the command-and-control approach. The Clean Air Acts of 1970 and 1990, for example, mandated not only fewer auto emissions but also specific processes such as catalytic converters and lead-free gasoline for attaining them. Specific processes and technologies are also required for toxic waste disposal and water treatment. Laws requiring the sorting and recycling of trash are other examples of process regulation.

Although such command-and-control regulation can be effective, this policy option also entails risks. By requiring all market participants to follow specific rules, the regulations may impose excessive costs on some activities and too low a constraint on others. Some communities may not need the level of sewage treatment the federal government prescribes. Individual households may not generate enough trash to make sorting and separate pickups economically sound. Some producers may have better or cheaper ways of attaining environmental standards. ***Excessive process regulation may raise the costs of environmental protection and discourage cost-saving innovation.*** There's also the risk of regulated processes becoming entrenched long after they are obsolete. When that happens, we may end up with worse outcomes than a less regulated market would have generated—that is, **government failure.**

government failure:
Government intervention that fails to improve economic outcomes.

BALANCING BENEFITS AND COSTS

Protecting the environment entails costs as well as benefits. Installing smokestack scrubbers on factory chimneys and catalytic converters on cars requires the use of scarce resources. Taking the lead out of gasoline wears out engines faster and requires expensive changes in technology. Switching to clean fuels requires enormous investments in technology, plants, and equipment. The EPA estimates that a 10-year program to achieve national air and water standards would cost more than $2 trillion. Restoring the ozone layer, removing hazardous wastes, and cleaning up the rest of the environment would cost trillions more.

Opportunity Costs

opportunity cost: The most desired goods or services that are forgone in order to obtain something else.

Although cleaning up the environment is a worthwhile goal, we must remind ourselves that those resources could be used to fulfill other goals as well. The multitrillion-dollar tab would buy a lot of subways and parks or build decent homes for the poor. If we devote those resources instead to pollution abatement, we'll have to forgo other goods and services. Remember the basic principle about "no free lunch"? Well, for the same reason there is no free environmental protection. This isn't to say that environmental goals don't deserve priority but simply to remind us that any use of our scarce resources involves an **opportunity cost.**

Fortunately, the amount of additional resources required to clean up the environment is relatively modest in comparison to our productive capacity. Over a 10-year period we'll produce more than $250 trillion of goods and services (GDP). On this basis, the environmental expenditures contemplated by present environmental policies and goals represent only 1 percent of total output.

The Optimal Rate of Pollution

optimal rate of pollution: The rate of pollution that occurs when the marginal social benefit of pollution control equals its marginal social cost.

Spending even a small percentage of GDP on environmental protection nevertheless entails value judgments. The **optimal rate of pollution** occurs at the point at which the opportunity costs of further pollution control equal the benefits of further reductions in pollution. *To determine the optimal rate of pollution, we need to compare the marginal social benefits of additional pollution abatement with the marginal social costs of additional pollution control expenditure.* The optimal rate of pollution is achieved when we've satisfied the following equality:

$$\begin{matrix} \text{Optimal} \\ \text{rate of} \\ \text{pollution} \end{matrix} : \begin{matrix} \text{Marginal benefit} \\ \text{of pollution} \\ \text{abatement} \end{matrix} = \begin{matrix} \text{Marginal cost of} \\ \text{pollution} \\ \text{abatement} \end{matrix}$$

This formulation is analogous to the utility-maximizing rule in consumption. If another dollar spent on pollution control yields less than a dollar of social benefits, then additional pollution control expenditure isn't desirable. In such a situation, the goods and services that would be forsaken for additional pollution control are more valued than the environmental improvements that would result.

Cost–Benefit Analysis

A 2003 White House study concluded that past efforts to clean up the air have yielded far more benefits than costs: The benefits of a 10-year (1992–2002) air pollution abatement program were five to seven times greater than its cost. Although pollution abatement has been an economic success, that doesn't mean *all* pollution controls are desirable. The focus must still be on *marginal* benefits and costs. In that context, a surprising conclusion emerges: *A totally clean environment isn't economically desirable.* The marginal benefit of achieving zero pollution is infinitesimally small. But the marginal cost of eliminating that last particle of pollution will be very high. As we weigh the marginal benefits and costs, we'll inevitably conclude that *some* pollution is cost-effective.

Mayor Bloomberg performed the same kind of analysis for New York City's recycling program. Everyone thinks recycling is a good idea. But Mayor Bloomberg started looking at the cost of the recycling program and decided it didn't make economic sense (see Front Page Economics "Recycling Wastes Money"). He figured the city could use the $57 million cost of recycling for higher-priority programs, yielding greater (marginal) benefits to NYC residents.

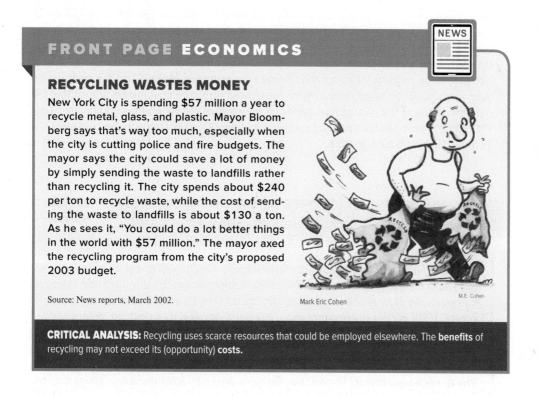

FRONT PAGE ECONOMICS

RECYCLING WASTES MONEY

New York City is spending $57 million a year to recycle metal, glass, and plastic. Mayor Bloomberg says that's way too much, especially when the city is cutting police and fire budgets. The mayor says the city could save a lot of money by simply sending the waste to landfills rather than recycling it. The city spends about $240 per ton to recycle waste, while the cost of sending the waste to landfills is about $130 a ton. As he sees it, "You could do a lot better things in the world with $57 million." The mayor axed the recycling program from the city's proposed 2003 budget.

Source: News reports, March 2002.

Mark Eric Cohen

M.E. Cohen

CRITICAL ANALYSIS: Recycling uses scarce resources that could be employed elsewhere. The **benefits** of recycling may not exceed its (opportunity) **costs.**

Who Will Pay?

The costs of pollution control aren't distributed equally. In New York City, the cost of the recycling program is borne by those who end up with fewer city services and amenities (opportunity costs). A national pollution abatement program would target the relatively small number of economic activities—like coal-fired power plants, paper mills, steel plants—that account for the bulk of emissions and effluents. These activities will have to bear a disproportionate share of the cleanup burden.

Higher Costs. To ascertain how the burden of environmental protection will be distributed, consider first the electric power plant discussed earlier. As we observed (Figure 14.2), the plant's output will decrease if production decisions are based on social rather than private marginal costs—that is, if environmental consequences are considered. If the plant itself is compelled to pay full social costs, in the form of either compulsory investment or emission charges, its profits will be reduced. Were no other changes to take place, the burden of environmental improvements would be borne primarily by the producer.

Higher Prices. Such a scenario is unlikely, however. Rather than absorb all the costs of pollution controls themselves, producers will pass some of this burden on to their customers in the form of higher prices. Their ability to do so will depend on the extent of competition in their industry, their relative cost position in it, and the price elasticity of consumer demand. In reality, the electric power industry isn't very competitive, and its prices are still subject to government regulation. In addition, consumer demand is relatively price-inelastic. Accordingly, the profit-maximizing producer will appeal to the state or local power commission for an increase in electricity prices based on the costs of pollution control. Electric power consumers are likely to end up footing the environmental bill. Critics of government intervention point out that Californians pay higher prices for electricity and gasoline due in part to the cost burdens imposed on private companies by the state's cap-and-trade program (see Front Page Economics "Paying to Pollute in California").

Job Losses. Workers in impacted industries are likely to suffer as well. All of the policy options we have looked at end up reducing the production and consumption of the polluting good. That implies job losses for the affected workers. According to the government itself, environmental regulations enacted in 2011 and 2014 eliminated thousands of coal-mining jobs across the country. Although the Obama administration claimed that the resulting decline in air pollution saved thousands of lives, those displaced coal miners argued that the economic costs of the mining regulations far outweighed the environmental benefits. They were quick to embrace the promises made by candidate Donald Trump in the 2016 elections to "put coal miners back to work."

DECISIONS FOR **TOMORROW**

Can We Afford a Green New Deal?

Forget about littered beaches, smelly landfills, eye-stinging smog, and contaminated water. The really scary problem for the economy tomorrow is much more serious: Scientists know that the carbon emissions we're spewing into the air are warming the earth's atmosphere. If the earth's temperature rises only a few degrees, they contend, polar caps will melt, continents will flood, and weather patterns will go haywire. If things get bad enough, there may not be any economy tomorrow.

The Greenhouse Effect. The earth's climate is driven by solar radiation. The energy the sun absorbs must be balanced by outgoing radiation from the earth and the atmosphere. Scientists fear that a flow imbalance is developing. Of particular concern is a buildup of carbon dioxide (CO_2) that traps heat in the earth's atmosphere, warming the planet.

The natural release of CO_2 dwarfs the emissions from human activities. But there's a concern that the steady increase in man-made CO_2 emissions—principally from burning fossil fuels like gasoline and coal—is tipping the balance.

The Green New Deal. Governments at all levels are already using a variety of techniques to require or encourage emission reductions. But those piecemeal efforts may not be enough to thwart climate change. Perhaps a more comprehensive approach is needed. That thought has inspired proposals for a Green New Deal that would eliminate carbon-based emissions altogether.

The Green Party first proposed a Green New Deal in 2006 and has included that proposal in every one of its political campaign platforms since then. In 2019, a 14-page proposal was introduced in the U.S. Congress by Congresswoman Alexandria Ocasio-Cortez and Sen. Edward Markey. That proposal called for a 40–60 percent reduction in carbon-based emissions by 2030 (from 2010 levels) and a 100 percent reduction by 2050 (i.e., a zero-emissions economy).

The notion of a zero-emissions economy is enticing. But critics quickly asked how much it would cost to achieve that goal. Seventy percent of U.S. energy comes from carbon-based sources and another 13 percent comes from nuclear generation. Transitioning to a carbon-free energy grid is an enormous challenge that would cost trillions of dollars.

In addition to remaking the entire power grid, the Green New Deal would require massive investments in the retrofitting of transportation, manufacturing, and agricultural systems. Critics estimate that a carbon-free program would cost $6-7 trillion over the course of ten years – a tab that would cost the average American household $50,000-70,000.

Opportunity Cost Again. Could we possibly afford such a program? Yes. As we've noted, the U.S. economy will generate somewhere around $250 trillion in income over the next decade. But that begs a critical question. How and who will we pay for the Deal? Proponents say we can raise taxes on the rich a lot and on the rest of us a little. That implies significant changes in consumption patterns and political will. And labor unions have expressed concern about the thousands of jobs that will be lost in carbon-based industries. The decision we have to make is how much sacrifice (opportunity cost) we are willing to absorb in order to achieve lower, or zero, emissions levels.

SUMMARY

- Air, water, and solid waste pollution impose social and economic costs. The costs of pollution include the direct damages inflicted on our health and resources, the expense of cleaning up, and the general aesthetic deterioration of the environment.   **LO14-1**
- Pollution is an external cost, a cost of a market activity imposed on someone (a third party) other than the immediate producer or consumer.   **LO14-1**
- Producers and consumers generally operate on the basis of private benefits and costs. A private producer or consumer has an incentive to minimize his own costs by transforming private costs into external costs. One way of making such a substitution is to pollute—to use "free" air and water rather than install pollution control equipment, or to leave the job of waste disposal to others.   **LO14-1**
- Social costs are the total amount of resources used in a production or consumption process. When social costs are greater than private costs, the market's price signals are flawed. This market failure will induce people to harm the environment by using suboptimal processes and products.   **LO14-1**
- One way to correct the market inefficiency created by externalities is to compel producers and consumers to internalize all (social) costs. This can be done by imposing emission charges and higher user fees. Such charges create an incentive to invest in pollution abatement equipment,

recycle reusable materials, and conserve scarce elements of the environment.   **LO14-2**
- Tradable pollution permits help minimize the cost of pollution control by (a) promoting low-cost controls to substitute for high-cost controls and (b) encouraging innovation in pollution control technology.   **LO14-2**
- An alternative approach to cleaning up the environment is to require specific pollution controls or to prohibit specific kinds of activities. Direct regulation runs the risk of higher cost and discouraging innovations in environmental protection.   **LO14-2**
- The opportunity costs of pollution abatement are the most desired goods and services given up when factors of production are used to control pollution. The optimal rate of pollution is reached when the marginal social benefits of further pollution control equal associated marginal social costs.   **LO14-3**
- In addition to diverting resources, pollution control efforts alter relative prices, change the mix of output, and redistribute incomes. These outcomes cause losses for particular groups and may thus require special economic or political attention.   **LO14-3**
- The greenhouse effect represents a global externality. Reducing global emissions requires consensus on optimal pollution levels (i.e., the optimal balance of pollution abatement costs and benefits) and the distribution of attendant costs.   **LO14-2**

Key Terms

production decision	private costs	opportunity cost
efficiency decision	market failure	optimal rate of pollution
external cost	emission charge	
social costs	government failure	

Questions for Discussion

1. If "green" gasoline were sold for 20 cents per gallon more than "dirty" gasoline, would you buy it? How much of a premium per gallon do you think most people would pay? **LO14-1**

2. What are the *economic* costs of the externalities caused by air toxins (Front Page Economics "Air Pollution Kills"), beach closings, or thermal pollution (Front Page Economics "Cut the Power to Save the Fish?")? How would you measure their value? **LO14-1**

3. Should we try to eliminate *all* pollution? What economic considerations might favor permitting some pollution? **LO14-3**

4. Why would auto manufacturers resist higher fuel efficiency standards? How would their costs, sales, and profits be affected? **LO14-1**

5. Does anyone have an incentive to maintain auto exhaust control devices in good working order? How can we ensure that they will be maintained? Are there any costs associated with this policy? **LO14-1**

6. Who benefited from the closure of the Indian Point nuclear plant (Front Page Economics "Cut the Power to Save the Fish?")? Is the environment now better? **LO14-3**

7. What economic costs are imposed by mandatory sorting of trash (Front Page Economics "Recycling Wastes Money")? **LO14-2**

8. "The issuance of a pollution permit is just a license to destroy the environment." Do you agree? Explain. **LO14-2**

9. If a high per-bag fee were charged for garbage collection, how would consumers respond? **LO14-2**

10. Should coal mining be prohibited in order to reduce carbon emissions? **LO14-2**

11. Over 1 billion people in the world don't have access to electricity, relying mostly on fire for heat and cooking. Discuss the benefits and costs of carbon caps that limit the construction of new power plants in less developed countries. **LO14-2**

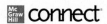
LO14-2 1. (*a*) If the Indian Point nuclear plant (Front Page Economics "Cut the Power to Save the Fish") were charged one-tenth of a mill (0.01 cent) for every gallon of water it used, how much would it have paid in annual emission fees?

(*b*) If the cost of building and operating a closed-cycle cooling system was $100 million per year, would the plant prefer to reengineer the plant or pay the emission fees?

LO14-2 2. EPA says the value of a human life is $9.4 million, measured from birth to death. If life expectancy is 78 years, what is the value of the remaining life of an 18-year-old person?

LO14-2 3. How high would its pollution control costs have to be before a California power plant would "pay to pollute" a ton of carbon dioxide (Front Page Economics "Paying to Pollute in California")?

LO14-1 4. Use the graph to answer the following questions:

(*a*) What is the profit maximizing quantity?

   Suppose that there are external costs equal to $0.01 per kilowatt-hour.

(*b*) Calculate the social marginal cost to produce the profit-maximizing quantity.

(*c*) What is the socially optimal quantity?

(*d*) How much of an emission fee should be charged to close the gap between the private and social marginal costs?

LO14-1 5. Many people pay nothing for each extra pound of garbage they create, yet the garbage is a type of solid waste pollution. In view of this, we can view garbage collection as creating external benefits to society. So what's an appropriate price for garbage collection? Answer the questions based on the following graph.

(*a*) What is the quantity of (free) garbage collection now demanded?

(*b*) How much would be demanded if a fee of $4 per pound were charged?

(*c*) Draw the social demand curve when an external benefit of $2 per pound exists.

(*d*) If the marginal cost of collecting garbage were constant at $6 per pound, what would be the optimal level of garbage collection?

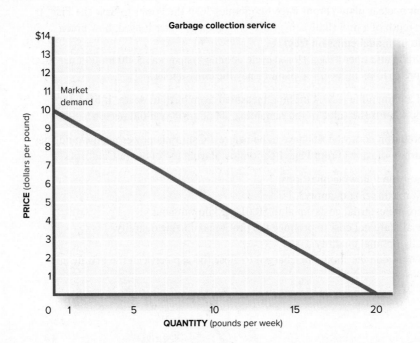

LO14-3 6. How much more per ton is New York City paying to recycle rather than just dump its garbage (Front Page Economics "Recycling Wastes Money")?

LO14-2 7. Suppose three firms confront the following costs for pollution control:

	Total Costs of Control		
Emissions Reduction (Tons per Year)	Firm A	Firm B	Firm C
1	$ 30	$ 40	$ 50
2	70	100	120
3	120	180	210
4	190	280	320

(*a*) If each firm must reduce emissions by one ton, how much will be spent in total by all three firms?

(*b*) If the firms can trade pollution rights, what would be the cheapest way of attaining a net three-ton reduction?

(*c*) How much would a pollution permit trade for (price range)?

Now suppose the goal is to reduce pollution by six tons.

(*d*) What is the marginal cost of a second abatement ton at
   (*i*) Firm A?
   (*ii*) Firm B?
   (*iii*) Firm C?

(*e*) If each firm must reduce emissions by two tons, how much will be spent in total by all three firms?

(*f*) If the firms can trade permits, what is the cheapest way of attaining a six-ton reduction?

(*g*) How much will a permit cost (price range)?

LO14-3 8. The table shows the total benefits and total costs to reduce solid waste pollution in a local river.

Quantity of Pollution Abatement (Tons of Trash Removed per Week)	Benefits	Costs
0	0	0
1	60	10
2	100	30
3	130	60
4	150	100
5	160	155
6	165	220

(a) Calculate the marginal benefits of pollution abatement.

(b) Calculate the marginal costs of pollution abatement.

(c) What is the optimal level of pollution abatement?

LO14-1 9. The following cost schedule depicts the private and social costs associated with the weekly use of dicamba, a strong fertilizer that can damage nearby crops that are not genetically modified to resist the fertilizer. The sales price of dicamba is $26 per ton.

Output (in tons)	0	1	2	3	4	5	6	7	8
Total private cost	$ 5	7	13	23	37	55	77	103	133
Total social cost	$45	63	85	111	141	175	213	255	301

(a) Graph the private and social marginal costs associated with dicamba production.

(b) What is the profit-maximizing rate of output for this competitive firm?

(c) How much profit is earned at that output level?

(d) What is the socially optimal rate of output?

(e) How much profit is there at that output level?

(f) How much of a "green tax" per ton would have to be levied to induce the firm to produce the socially optimal rate of output?

LO14-2 10. Suppose the marginal cost of pollution abatement is constant and equal to 3% of GDP for each 10% increase in pollution control. Given the following data for a $22 trillion economy,

Level of Pollution Abatement (%)	Marginal Benefit ($ trillions)
0 (no pollution control)	—
10	2.0
20	1.7
30	1.3
40	1.0
50	0.8
60	0.6
70	0.4
80	0.3
90	0.2
100% (no emissions)	0.1

(a) identify the optimal rate of pollution abatement.

Now suppose that the marginal costs of pollution abatement decrease to 2% of GDP for each 10% increase in pollution control because of improved pollution control technology and more efficient sources of renewable energy.

(b) Identify the new optimal rate of pollution abatement.

LO14-3 11. *Decisions for Tomorrow:* Calculate the annual household cost of a carbon-free program if the program costs $6.5 trillion evenly spread over 10 years (assume there are 110 million households).

Design Credit: Shutterstock

Fuse/Getty Images

CHAPTER 15

The Farm Problem

In 1996 the U.S. Congress charted a new future for U.S. farmers. No longer would they look to Washington, DC, for decisions on what crops to plant or how much farmland to leave fallow. The Freedom to Farm Act would get the government out of the farm business and let "laissez faire" dictate farm outcomes. Farmers would lose their federal subsidies but could earn as much as they wanted in the marketplace. Taxpayers loved the idea. So did most farmers, who were enjoying unusually high prices and bumper profits in 1996.

The Asian crisis that began in mid-1997 dealt farmers a severe blow. U.S. farms export 25–50 percent of all the wheat, corn, soybeans, and cotton they grow. When Asia's economies plunged into recession, those export sales evaporated. With sales, prices, and profits all declining, farmers lost their enthusiasm for the "freedom to farm"; they wanted Uncle Sam to jump back into the farm business with price and income guarantees. The U.S. Congress obliged by passing the Farm Security Act of 2001. That act not only increased farm subsidies, but also extended them to peanut farmers, hog farmers, and horse breeders. The Farm Act of 2008 spread federal subsidies to still more farmers, abandoning any notion of "free-market" agriculture. The Farm Act of 2014 continued that trend, extending subsidies to hemp and organic farmers. The 2018 Farm Act broadened subsidies for hemp farmers and even made limited CBD products legal. But the dependence on government continued.

This chapter examines the rationale for continuing farm subsidies and their effects on farm production, prices, and exports. In particular, we confront these questions:

- **Why do farmers need any subsidies?**
- **How do government subsidies affect farm production, prices, and incomes?**
- **Who pays for farm subsidies?**

DESTABILIZING FORCES

The agriculture industry is one of the most competitive of all U.S. industries. First, there are 2 million farms in the United States. Although some of these farms are immense—with tens of thousands of acres—no single farm has the power to affect the market supply or price of farm products. That is, individual farmers have no **market power.**

Competition in Agriculture

Competition in agriculture is maintained by low **barriers to entry.** Although farmers need large acreages, expensive farm equipment, substantial credit, hard work, and hired labor, all these resources become affordable when farming is generating **economic profits.** When farming is profitable, existing farmers expand their farms and farmers' children are able to start new farms. It would be much harder to enter the automobile industry, the airline business, or even the farm machinery market than it would be to enter farming. Because of these low barriers to entry, economic profits don't last long in agriculture.

Given the competitive structure of U.S. agriculture, *individual farmers tend to behave like perfect competitors.* They take the existing market price as an established fact, over which they have no control. Individual farmers then seek to expand their rate of output until marginal cost equals price. By following this rule, each farmer makes as much profit as possible from existing resources, prices, and technology.

Like other competitive firms, U.S. farmers can maintain economic profits only if they achieve continuing cost reductions. Above-normal profits obtained from current production techniques and prices aren't likely to last. Such economic profits will entice more people into agriculture and will stimulate greater output from existing farmers. That is exactly the kind of dilemma that confronted catfish farmers in the South and the early producers of microcomputers (Chapter 23). To stay ahead, individual farms must continue to improve their productivity.

Technological Advance

The rate of technological advance in agriculture has, in fact, been spectacular. Since 1929, the farm labor force has shrunk by two-thirds, yet farm output has increased by 80 percent. Between the early 1950s and today,

* Annual egg production has jumped from 183 to 289 eggs per laying chicken.
* Milk output has increased from 5,400 to 23,510 pounds per cow annually.
* Wheat output has increased from 17 to 56 bushels per acre.
* Corn output has jumped from 39 to 175 bushels per acre.

Farm output per labor-hour has grown even faster, having increased 10 times over in the same period. Such spectacular rates of productivity advance rival those of our most high-tech industries. These technological advances resulted from the development of higher-yielding seeds (the "green revolution"), advanced machinery (mechanical feeders and milkers), improved animal breeding (crossbreeding), improved plants (rust-resistant wheat), better land use practices (crop rotation and fertilizers), and computer-based management systems.

Inelastic Demand

In most industries, continuous increases in technology and output would be most welcome. The agricultural industry, however, confronts a long-term problem. Simply put, there's a limit to the amount of food people want to eat.

This constraint on the demand for agricultural output is reflected in the relatively inelastic demand for food. Consumers don't increase their food purchases very much when farm prices fall. The **price elasticity** of food demand is low. As a consequence, when harvests are good, farmers must reduce prices a lot to sell all that extra food. Recall the formula for the price elasticity of demand:

$$E = \frac{\text{Percentage change in quantity demanded}}{\text{Percentage change in price}}$$

Rearranging this formula gives us a guide to how far prices must fall for farmers to unload a bumper crop:

$$\text{Required percentage change in price} = \frac{\text{Percentage change in quantity (harvest)}}{\text{Price elasticity of demand}}$$

market power: The ability to alter the market price of a good or service.

barriers to entry: Obstacles such as patents that make it difficult or impossible for would-be producers to enter a particular market.

economic profit: The difference between total revenues and total economic costs.

price elasticity of demand: The percentage change in quantity demanded divided by the percentage change in price.

FIGURE 15.1

Short-Term Instability

Changes in weather cause abrupt shifts of the food supply curve. When combined with the relatively inelastic demand for food, these supply shifts result in wide price swings. Notice how the price of grain jumps from p_1 to p_2 when bad weather reduces the harvest. If good weather follows, prices may fall to p_2.

Even if the price elasticity of demand were as high as 0.2, the percentage change in price would have to be five times as large as the percentage change in quantity produced. Hence, prices would have to fall 25 percent to sell a bumper crop that was 5 percent larger than normal:

$$\%\Delta p = \frac{0.05}{0.20} = 0.25$$

In 2016 the corn crop was 11 percent *larger* than the year before. In 2008 the corn crop *decreased* by 7 percent. As Figure 15.1 illustrates, ***with low price elasticity of demand, abrupt changes in farm output have a magnified effect on market prices.*** Between 2005 and 2020, corn prices ranged from a low of $1.96 a bushel to a high of $6.80 (see Figure 15.2). That's a *lot* of price instability.

The **income elasticity** of food demand is also low. The income elasticity of demand for food refers to the responsiveness of food demand to changes in income. Specifically,

income elasticity of demand: Percentage change in quantity demanded divided by percentage change in income.

$$\text{Income elasticity of demand} = \frac{\substack{\%\text{ change in quantity demanded} \\ \text{(at constant price)}}}{\%\text{ change in income}}$$

Since 1929, per capita income has quadrupled. But per capita food consumption has increased only 85 percent. Hence, ***neither lower prices nor higher incomes significantly increase the quantity of food demanded.***

In the long run, then, the increasing ability of U.S. agriculture to produce food must be reconciled with very slow growth of U.S. demand for food. Over time, this implies that farm prices will fall, relative to nonfarm prices. And they have. Between the years 1910–1914 and 2020, the ratio of farm prices to nonfarm prices fell 67 percent. In the absence of government price support programs and foreign demand for U.S. farm products, farm prices would have fallen still further.

Abrupt Shifts of Supply

The long-term downtrend in (relative) farm prices is only one of the major problems confronting U.S. agriculture. The second major problem is short run. Prices of farm products are subject to abrupt short-term swings. If the weather is good, harvests are abundant. Normally, this might be a good thing. In farming, however, abundant harvests imply a severe drop in prices. On the other hand, a late or early freeze, a drought, or an infestation by disease or insect pests can reduce harvests and push prices sharply higher (see Figure 15.1).

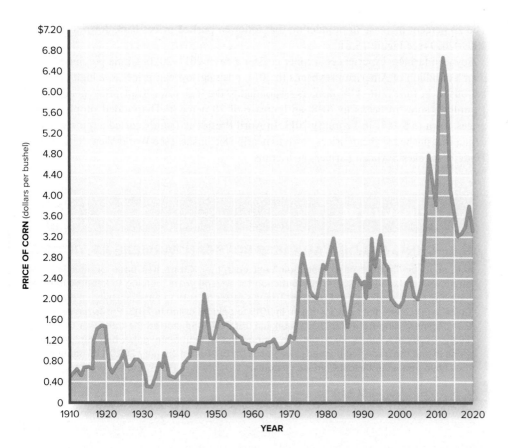

PRICE OF CORN (dollars per bushel)

YEAR

FIGURE 15.2

Unstable Corn Prices

Most agricultural prices are subject to abrupt short-term changes. Notice how corn prices rose dramatically during World Wars I and II, then fell sharply. Poor harvests in the rest of the world increased demand for U.S. food in 1973–1974. Since then prices have moved sharply in both directions.

Source: U.S. Department of Agriculture.

Response Lags. Time lags between the production decision and the resultant harvest also contribute to price instability. If prices are high one year, farmers have an incentive to increase their rate of output. In this sense, prices serve the same signaling function in agriculture as they do in nonfarm industries. What distinguishes the farmers' response is the lack of inventories and the fixed duration of the production process. In the computer industry, a larger quantity of output can be supplied to the market fairly quickly by drawing down inventories or stepping up the rate of production. In farming, supply can't respond so quickly. In the short run, the farmer can only till more land, plant additional seed, or breed more livestock. No additional food supplies will be available until a new crop or herd grows. Hence, *the agricultural supply response to a change in prices is always one harvest (or breeding period) later.*

This lagged supply response intensifies short-term price swings. Suppose corn prices are exceptionally high at the end of a year because of a reduced harvest. High prices will make corn farming appear unusually profitable. Farmers will want to expand their rate of output—plant more corn acreage—to share in these high profits. But the corn won't appear on the market until the following year. By that time, there's likely to be an abundance of corn on the market, as a result of both better weather and increased corn acreage. Hence, corn prices are likely to plummet. This is what happened in 2013–2014, in 2016–2017, and again in 2020.

No single farmer can avoid these boom-or-bust movements of prices. Even a corn farmer who has mastered the principles of economics has little choice but to plant more corn when prices are high. If he doesn't plant additional corn, prices will fall anyway because his own production decisions don't affect market prices. By not planting additional corn, he only denies himself a share of corn market sales. *In a highly competitive market, each producer acts independently.*

Corn prices spiked to $4.20 per bushel after President Bush proposed expanded use of corn-based ethanol as an alternative fuel source. Farmers rushed to plant additional acreage.

The 24 percent increase in production that followed pushed prices back down to $3.55 in 2009–2010 (see Figure 15.2).

Soybean farmers experienced a roller coaster ride in 2017–2020. China purchased more than $14 billion of American soybeans in 2016, pushing soybean prices to a high of $11.78 per bushel in June 2016. U.S. farmers responded to the high price by planting an additional 15 million acres of beans in 2018, an increase of 20 percent. That added supply pushed prices down to $10.71 in February 2018. In April President Trump started a trade war with China that pushed soybean prices down to nearly $8 a bushel (see World View "U.S.–China Trade War Takes Soybean Farmers as Victims").

WORLD VIEW

U.S.–CHINA TRADE WAR TAKES SOYBEAN FARMERS AS VICTIMS

U.S. soybean farmers have lost their best customer. China has been purchasing over one-fourth of American soybean production for several years, helping to keep bean prices high. But China retaliated to President Trump's tariffs by cutting back on soybean purchases. Chinese purchases fell from $14 billion in 2016 to only $3 billion in 2018. Prices have mirrored that decline, falling from $10.71 a bushel just before Trump started the trade war to a low of $8.09. Soybean farmers have taken enormous losses, with many going bankrupt. Although steps to end the trade war pushed prices back up to $9.41 in January 2020, U.S. farmers fear they have permanently lost Chinese customers to farmers in Brazil and elsewhere.

Source: Media reports, 2018–2020.

CRITICAL ANALYSIS: Abrupt changes in the weather or demand for the farm output cause big swings in farm prices. Those price swings, in turn, alter **supply decisions.**

The coronavirus pandemic that swept across the globe in 2020 added to farmers' woes. With restaurants closed, incomes depressed, and consumers ordered to stay home, the demand for farm products declined significantly. Dairy farmers dumped thousands of gallons of milk, while crop farmers left lots of food unharvested. As Figure 15.2 illustrates, farm prices took another hit.

THE FIRST FARM DEPRESSION, 1920–1940

The U.S. agricultural industry operated without substantial government intervention until the 1930s. In earlier decades, an expanding population, recurrent wars, and less advanced technology had helped maintain a favorable supply–demand relationship for farm products. There were frequent short-term swings in farm prices, but these were absorbed by a generally healthy farm sector. The period 1910–1919 was particularly prosperous for farmers, largely because of the expanded foreign demand for U.S. farm products by countries engaged in World War I.

The two basic problems of U.S. agriculture grew to crisis proportions after 1920. In 1919 most farm prices were at historical highs (see Figures 15.2 and 15.3). After World War I ended, however, European countries no longer demanded as much American food. U.S. exports of farm products fell from nearly $4 billion in 1919 to $1.9 billion in 1921. Farm exports were further reduced in the following years by increasing restrictions on international trade. At home, the end of the war implied an increased availability of factors of production and continuing improvement in farm technology.

The impact of reduced demand and increasing supply is evident in Figure 15.3. In 1919 farm prices were more than double their levels of the period 1910–1914. Prices then fell abruptly. In 1921 alone, farm prices fell nearly 40 percent.

FIGURE 15.3

**Farm Prices, 1910–1940
(1910–1914 = 100)**

Farm prices are less stable than nonfarm prices. During the 1930s, relative farm prices fell 50 percent. This experience was the catalyst for government price supports and other agricultural assistance programs.

Size of Farm	Number, 1910	Percent	Number, 2002	Percent
Under 100 acres	3,691,611	58.0%	943,118	44.3%
100–499 acres	2,494,461	39.2	847,322	39.8
500–999 acres	125,295	2.0	161,552	7.6
1,000 acres and over	50,135	0.8	176,990	8.3
Total	6,361,502	100.0%	2,128,982	100.0%

Source: U.S. Department of Agriculture.

TABLE 15.1

Size Distribution of U.S. Farms, 1910 and 2002

Inelastic food demand, combined with increasing agricultural productivity, implies a declining number of farmers. Small farmers are particularly vulnerable because they don't have the resources to maintain a high rate of technological improvement. As a result, the number of small farms has declined dramatically while the number of large farms has grown.

Farm prices stabilized in the mid-1920s but resumed a steep decline in 1930. In 1932 average farm prices were 75 percent lower than they had been in 1919. At the same time, the average income per farmer from farming fell from $2,651 in 1919 to $855 in 1932.

The Great Depression hit small farmers particularly hard. They had fewer resources to withstand consecutive years of declining prices and income. Even in good times, small farmers must continually expand output and reduce costs just to maintain their incomes. Hence, the Great Depression accelerated an exodus of small farmers from agriculture, a trend that continues today.

Table 15.1 shows that the number of small farms has declined dramatically. In 1910 there were 3.7 million farms under 100 acres in size. Today there are fewer than 1 million small farms. During the same period, the number of huge farms (1,000 acres or more) has more than tripled. This loss of small farmers, together with the increased mechanization of larger farms, has reduced the farm population by 23 million people since 1910.

U.S. FARM POLICY

The U.S. Congress has responded to these agricultural problems with a variety of programs. Most seek to raise and stabilize the price of farm products. Other programs seek to reduce the costs of production. When all else fails, the federal government also provides direct income support to farmers.

Price Supports

Price supports have always been the primary focus of U.S. farm policy. As early as 1926, Congress decreed that farm products should sell at a fair price. By "fair," Congress meant a

FIGURE 15.4

Fair Prices and Market Surplus

The interaction of market supply and demand establishes an equilibrium price (p_e) for any product, including food. If a higher price (p_f) is set, the quantity of food supplied (q_s) will be larger than the quantity demanded (q_d). Hence, attempts to establish a "fair" (higher) price for farm products must cope with resultant market surpluses.

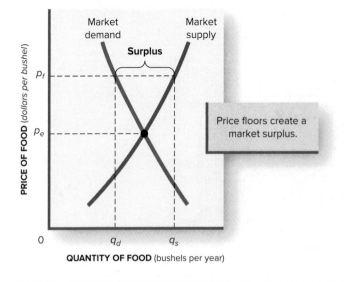

market surplus: The amount by which the quantity supplied exceeds the quantity demanded at a given price; excess supply.

parity: The relative price of farm products in the period 1910–1914.

acreage set-aside: Land withdrawn from production as part of policy to increase crop prices.

price higher than the market equilibrium. The consequences of this policy are evident in Figure 15.4: *a price floor creates a* **market surplus.**

Once it set an above-equilibrium price for food, Congress had to find some way of disposing of the resultant food surplus. Initially, Congress proposed to get rid of this surplus by selling it abroad at world market prices. President Calvin Coolidge, a staunch opponent of government intervention, vetoed this legislation both times Congress passed it.

The notion of fair prices resurfaced in the Agricultural Adjustment Act of 1933. During the Great Depression farmers were going bankrupt in droves. To help them, Congress sought to restore the purchasing power of farm products to the 1909–1914 level (see Figure 15.3). The farm–nonfarm price relationships of 1909–1914 were regarded by Congress as fair and came to be known as **parity** prices. If parity prices could be restored, Congress reasoned, farm incomes would improve.

Supply Restrictions

The goal of parity pricing couldn't be attained without altering market supply and demand in some way.

Set-Asides. The easiest way to increase farm prices without creating a surplus is to reduce the production of food. Congress does this by paying farmers for voluntary reductions in crop acreage. These **acreage set-asides** shift the food supply curve to the left. In 2007 nearly 40 *million* acres of farmland—one-sixth of the nation's wheat, corn, sorghum, rice, and cotton acreage—were idled by government set-asides. If farmers didn't agree to these set-asides, they couldn't participate in the price support programs.

Dairy Termination Program. To prop up dairy prices, the federal government also started a Dairy Termination Program in 1985. This is analogous to a set-aside program. In this case, however, the government pays dairy farmers to slaughter or export dairy cattle. Between 1985 and 1987 the government paid dairy farmers more than $1 billion to "terminate" 1.6 million cows. The reduction in dairy herds boosted prices for milk and other dairy products.

Marketing Orders. The federal government also permits industry groups to limit the quantity of output brought to market. By themselves, individual farmers can't raise the market price by withholding output. If they act collectively, however, they can. If a quantity greater than authorized is actually grown, the "surplus" is disposed of by individual farmers. In the 1980s these *marketing orders* forced farmers to waste each year roughly 500 million lemons,

Commodity	Loan Rate
Corn	$2.20 per bushel
Wheat	3.38
Soybeans	6.20
Cotton (upland)	0.52 per pound
Rice	7.00 per hundredweight
Peanuts	360.00 per ton
Honey	0.69 per pound
Sugar (beet)	0.25 per pound

Source: U.S. Department of Agriculture (2020).

TABLE 15.2

2019–2023 Loan Rates

The Commodity Credit Corporation lends money to farmers at fixed "loan rates" that are implicit price floors. If the market price falls below the CCC loan rate, the government keeps the crop as full payment of the loan or *pays* farmers a "loan deficiency payment."

1 billion oranges, 70 million pounds of raisins, 70 million pounds of almonds, and millions of plums, nectarines, and other fruits. This wholesale destruction of crops gave growers market power and kept farm prices artificially high.

Import Quotas. The market supply of farm products is also limited by import restrictions. Imports of sugar, dairy products, cotton, and peanuts are severely limited by import quotas. Imports of beef are limited by "voluntary" export limits in foreign countries. Import taxes (duties) limit the foreign supply of other farm products.

Demand Distortions

While trying to limit the *supply* of farm products, the government also inflates the *demand* for selected farm products.

Government Stockpiles. An executive order signed by President Franklin Roosevelt in 1933 altered the demand for farm products. The Commodity Credit Corporation (CCC) created at that time became a buyer of last resort for selected farm products.

The CCC becomes a buyer of last resort through its loan programs. Farmers can borrow money from the CCC at **loan rates** set by Congress (see Table 15.2). In 2020, for example, a wheat farmer could borrow $3.38 in cash for every bushel of wheat he relinquished to the CCC. If the market price of wheat goes above $3.38, the farmer can sell the wheat in the open market, repay the CCC, and pocket the difference. If, instead, the price falls below the loan rate, the farmer can simply let the CCC keep the wheat and repay nothing. Hence, *whenever market prices are below CCC loan rates, the government ends up buying surplus crops.*

Figure 15.5 illustrates the effect of CCC price supports on individual farmers and the agricultural market. In the absence of price supports, competitive farmers would confront a horizontal demand curve at price p_e, itself determined by the intersection of market supply and demand (in part *b*). The CCC's offer to buy ("loan") unlimited quantities at a higher price shifts the demand curve facing each farmer upward to the guaranteed price p_2. This higher price induces individual farmers to increase their rate of output from q_1 to q_2.

As farmers respond to price supports, the agriculture market is pushed out of equilibrium. At the support level p_2, more output is supplied than demanded. The market surplus created by government price supports creates an additional policy dilemma. *The market surplus induced by price supports must be eliminated in one of three ways:*

- *Government purchases* and stockpiling of surplus food.
- *Export sales.*
- *Restrictions on supply.*

Government purchases of surplus crops have led to massive stockpiles of wheat, cotton, corn, and dairy products. At one time, the excess wheat was stored in old ammunition

loan rate: The implicit price paid by the government for surplus crops taken as collateral for loans to farmers.

(a) Impact of price supports on the agricultural market

(b) Impact of price supports on the individual farmer

FIGURE 15.5

The Impact of Price Supports

In the absence of price supports, the price of farm products would be determined by the intersection of market supply and demand. In this case, the equilibrium price would be p_e, as shown in part *a*. All individual farmers would confront this price and produce up to the point where MC $= p_e$, as in part *b*.

Government price supports raise the price to p_2. By offering to buy (or "loan") unlimited quantities at this price, the government shifts the demand curve facing each farmer upward. Individual farmers respond by increasing their output from q_1 to q_2. As farmers increase their output, a market surplus develops.

bunkers in Nebraska and scrubbed-out oil tanks in Texas while surplus nonfat dry milk was stored in limestone caverns under Kansas City. In 2020 government stockpiles of surplus farm output included 2.1 *billion* bushels of corn, 2.3 billion bushels of wheat, 1.8 billion bushels of corn, and 6.4 million bales of cotton.

Deficiency Payments. To keep these stockpiles from growing further, Congress amended the CCC loan program in 2001. When market prices fall below CCC loan rates (Table 15.2), farmers don't have to turn over their crops to the government. Instead the government pays them a *loan deficiency payment* equal to the *difference* between the loan rate and the market price. The farmer can then sell his crop on the open market. By dumping excess supply on the market rather than stockpiling it, this policy tends to aggravate downward price swings.

Because farm prices are artificially high in the United States, export sales are sometimes difficult. As a result, the federal government must give away lots of food to poor nations and even subsidize exports to developed nations. The United States isn't alone in this regard: The European Union maintains even higher prices and subsidies (see World View "EU Farm Subsidies").

Price Supports

The government's loan program is an indirect mechanism for establishing a price floor for agricultural products. In 2014, Congress reintroduced more explicit and more generous price supports. The Farm Act of 2014 set **reference prices** for major commodities. As Table 15.3 reveals, the reference price for corn is now $3.70 per bushel. If the market price for corn falls below $3.70, the government pays farmers the difference. Thus, farmers are guaranteed to get the stipulated reference prices, regardless of how abundant the

reference price: Government-guaranteed price floor for specific agricultural commodities.

WORLD VIEW

EU FARM SUBSIDIES

In Europe, believe it or not, the subsidy for every cow is greater than the personal income of half the people in the world.

—Former British Prime Minister Margaret Thatcher

U.S. farm policy isn't unique. Most industrialized countries go to even greater lengths to protect domestic agriculture. For example, France, Germany, and Switzerland all shield their farmers from international competition while subsidizing their exports. Japan protects its inefficient rice producers, while the Netherlands subsidizes greenhouse vegetable farmers.

The motivations for farm subsidies are pretty much the same in every country in the world. Every country wants a secure source of food in the event of war. Most nations also want to maintain a viable farm sector, which is viewed as a source of social stability. Finally, politicians in every country must be responsive to a well-established and vocal political constituency.

The European Union (EU) imposes high tariffs on imported food, keeping domestic prices high. The member governments also agree to purchase any surplus production. To get rid of the surplus, the governments then subsidize exports. In 2016 direct EU farm subsidies exceeded $75 billion, triple the size of U.S. farm subsidies. All this protection costs the average EU consumer more than $150 a year.

CRITICAL ANALYSIS: Farm subsidies are common around the world. Such subsidies alter not only domestic output decisions but international trade patterns as well.

Commodity	Reference Price
Corn	$ 3.70 per bushel
Barley	4.95
Wheat	5.50
Soybeans	8.40
Rice	14.00 per hundredweight
Peanuts	535.00 per ton

Source: U.S. Department of Agriculture (2020).

TABLE 15.3

2019–2023 Reference Prices

Congress sets reference prices for selected commodities. If the market price falls below the reference price, a *deficiency payment* is made directly to the farmer.

national crop may be. These reference prices serve as price floors, with the same effect on output depicted in Figure 15.5.

Cost Subsidies

The market surplus induced by price supports is exacerbated by cost subsidies. Irrigation water, for example, is delivered to many farmers by federally funded reclamation projects. The price farmers pay for the water is substantially below the cost of delivering it; the difference amounts to a subsidy. This water subsidy costs taxpayers more than $500 million a year. The Department of Agriculture also distributes an additional $150 million to $200 million a year to farmers to help defray the costs of fertilizer, drainage, and other production costs.

The federal government also provides basic research, insurance, marketing, grading, and inspection services to farmers at subsidized prices. All these subsidies serve to lower fixed or variable costs. Their net impact is to stimulate additional output, as illustrated in Figure 15.6.

FIGURE 15.6

The Impact of Cost Subsidies

Cost subsidies lower the marginal cost of producing at any given rate of output, thereby shifting the marginal cost curve downward. The lower marginal costs make higher rates of output more profitable and thus increase output. At price p_2, lower marginal costs increase the farmer's profit-maximizing rate of output from q_2 to q_3.

---

profit: The difference between total revenue and total cost.

CONTINUING INCOME VOLATILITY

With so many price supports, supply restrictions, cost subsidies, and income transfers, one would think that farming is a riskless and profitable business. But this hasn't been the case. Incomes remain low and unstable, especially for small farmers.

1980–1986 Depression

In fact, the entire agricultural sector experienced another setback in the 1980s. In 1980 the net income of U.S. farmers fell 42 percent. As Figure 15.7 shows, farm incomes recovered somewhat in 1981 but then resumed their steep decline in 1982. In 1983 farmers' net income was only one-third the level of 1979. This income loss was steeper than that of the Great Depression. Real farm income was actually lower in 1983 than in 1933. This second depression of farm incomes accelerated the exodus of small farmers from agriculture, severely weakened rural economies, and bankrupted many farm banks and manufacturers of farm equipment and supplies.

This second depression of farm incomes was not caused by abrupt price declines. Prices for farm products increased slightly between 1979 and 1983. But production costs rose much faster, led by higher fuel, fertilizer, and interest rate costs. Average farm production costs rose 30 percent between 1979 and 1983 while the average price of farm products increased only 1.5 percent. As a result, the **profit** (net income) of farmers fell abruptly.

2008–2013 Surge

The period 2008–2013 was a much more prosperous time for farmers. Even though the U.S. economy suffered a Great Recession in 2008–2009, American farmers did very well. A multiyear drought curtailed crop production and sent crop prices to record highs, with the price of corn approaching $7 a bushel (see Figure 15.2). At the same time, the recession in the rest of the economy brought down the price of farm inputs. A weak dollar also helped farmers sell exports. Farm incomes peaked at $124 billion in 2013 (Figure 15.7).

Another Price Slide

As we noted earlier, high prices encourage farmers to plant more crops. That is what happened after crop prices rose to record highs in 2012–2013. Farm plantings and harvests increased significantly, driving crop prices down. The price of corn fell from almost $7 a bushel in 2012 to close to $3 in 2016–2017. Weak foreign economies and a strong dollar

FIGURE 15.7

Net Farm Income, 1977–2020

Between 1979 and 1983 net farm income fell 64 percent. This decline was steeper than the income slide that occurred during the Great Depression (when net farm income fell 45 percent between 1929 and 1933). Farm incomes rose sharply from 1983 to 1989 but were unstable between 2007 and 2020.

Source: U.S. Department of Agriculture.

worsened the situation further by depressing farm exports. The net result was a decline in farm incomes of roughly 50 percent between 2013 and 2016. A good thing didn't last long.

U.S.–China Trade War

In March 2018 President Trump introduced tariffs on Chinese imports into the United States. He complained that China engaged in unfair trade practices and that tariffs would convince them to change their ways. In April China retaliated with tariffs of its own, targeting U.S. agricultural exports in particular. By September 2019 the Chinese had imposed tariffs of 15–25 percent on American farm exports. U.S. exports to China of soybeans and cotton fell by 74 percent, wheat by 70 percent, and pork by 14 percent. Falling export sales were accompanied by a sharp decline in prices, severely impacting U.S. farmers. Only when China and the United States took limited steps to end the trade war in December 2019 did farmers get some relief.

Coronavirus Pandemic

Unfortunately, that relief from the trade war didn't last long. The coronavirus pandemic significantly reduced the demand for farm products. People were still eating, but schools were closed, eliminating an important outlet for farm products. And restaurants were closed, eliminating another important outlet for farm products. The net result was a left-ward shift in the demand for farm products, a decline in the parity price ratio, and a blow to farm incomes.

DECISIONS FOR TOMORROW

Should We Keep Farmers on the Dole?

It is apparent that farming continues to be a volatile business. Small variations in production—whether caused by the weather, global economic forces, or farmer's lagged planting responses–cause wild swings in crop prices. Furthermore, unceasing advances in agricultural technology, combined with low income and price elasticities for food, pretty much guarantee that farm prices will continue to lag behind general price inflation. Politicians also emphasize how important it is to have a secure source of food in the event of war. Given these realities, it seems certain that farmers will stay on the government dole in the future.

The 2018 Farm Bill. The specifics of government programs to assist farmers are spelled out in congressional legislation. The 2014 Farm Bill eliminated direct payments to farmers and replaced them with payments based on price or revenue deficiencies. But the core system of crop subsidies was left intact.

The legal authority of the 2014 Farm Bill expired in September 2018. That required Congress to write a new piece of legislation, the 2018 Farm Bill. Given the 2014–2018 decline in farm incomes (see Figure 15.7), no one expected Congress to cut subsidy programs.

Most of the additional help farmers want lies outside the authority of the Farm Bill. Farmers are particularly angry about environmental regulations mandated by the Obama administration in 2011. Those restrictions redefine the concept of "waterways" to include ponds, creeks, and other small water accumulations, subjecting them to federal regulation. New EPA rules also require expensive water testing, a requirement that small farmers say is very burdensome. President Trump repealed some of these regulations.

Farmers are also very concerned about immigration and trade policies. Farmers depend heavily on immigrant workers to harvest their crops. They also export as much as 30 percent of their harvests to other nations, so they are hopeful that America doesn't upend international trade flows.

Although farmers are sure to get continuing subsidies in the future, there is still a lot of opposition to these programs. Environmentalists emphasize that farming is the source of some of our worst pollution problems, especially the discharges of animal waste and other debris into waterways. They insist that if farmers are going to be subsidized, they should be required to protect the environment better. Others want stricter safeguards on food processing and safety as a condition of continuing subsidies.

Last but not least, free marketers continue to insist that the whole system of farm subsidies is inefficient and inequitable. Why do only a handful of crops (e.g., corn, wheat, sugar, honey, etc.) get subsidies while others don't? Are the prices of lemons, chickens, and strawberries any less volatile than cotton or corn prices? Aren't they subject to the same internal and external forces that dictate incomes for subsidized farmers? As they see it, the current system is not only inequitable, but inefficient because it causes farmers to make uneconomical production decisions and forces the government to stockpile farm surpluses.

Given the history of farm programs and farmers' dependence on them, American farmers are sure to be on the dole for the foreseeable future. The brief experiment in *less* government intervention (the Freedom to Farm Act of 1996) has long been forgotten. The challenge for the future is to adjust farm policy to the many competing interests of producers, consumers, environmentalists, and broader government policies.

SUMMARY

- The agricultural sector has a highly competitive structure, with approximately 2 million farms. Many crops are regulated, however, by government restrictions and subsidies. **LO15-1**
- Most farm output is produced by the small percentage of large farms that enjoy economies of scale. Most small farmers rely on nonfarm employment for their income. **LO15-1**
- In a free market, farm prices tend to decline over time because of increasing productivity and low-income elasticity of demand. Variations in harvests, combined with a low price elasticity of demand, make farm prices unstable. **LO15-1**
- Most of today's farm policies originated during the Great Depression in response to low farm prices and incomes. **LO15-3**
- The government uses price supports and cost subsidies to raise farm prices and profits. These policies cause resource misallocations and create market surpluses of specific commodities. **LO15-2**
- The 1996 Farm Act called for a phaseout of farm subsidies. Falling prices and incomes during 1997–2001 stalled and eventually reversed that process, as reflected in the 2008 and 2014 Farm Acts. **LO15-2**
- Farm prices and incomes continue to be highly volatile, despite government subsidy programs. **LO15-3**
- The U.S.–China trade war dealt a financial blow to U.S. farmers, increasing their dependence on government subsidies and risking long-term customer losses. **LO15-1**
- Critics demand that farmers assume more environmental responsibility in return for their subsidies. Other critics want to dismantle the whole system of farm subsidies and let farmers depend on market forces. **LO15-3**

Key Terms

market power	income elasticity of demand	loan rate
barriers to entry	market surplus	reference price
economic profit	parity	profit
price elasticity of demand	acreage set-aside	

Questions for Discussion

1. Would the U.S. economy be better off without government intervention in agriculture? Who would benefit? Who would lose? **LO15-3**
2. Are large price movements inevitable in agricultural markets? What other mechanisms might be used to limit such movement? **LO15-1**
3. Why doesn't the United States just give its crop surpluses to poor countries? What problems might such an approach create? **LO15-3**
4. Farmers can eliminate the uncertainties of fluctuating crop prices by selling their crops in futures markets (agreeing to a fixed price for crops to be delivered in the future). Who gains or loses from this practice? **LO15-2**
5. How do farmers of unsubsidized crops survive and thrive? **LO15-2**
6. You need a government permit (allotment) to grow tobacco. Who gains or loses from such regulation? **LO15-2**
7. Why are the price and income elasticities for food so low? **LO15-1**
8. How have farmers increased milk production per cow so much (see section Technological Advance)? How does this affect milk prices? **LO15-1**
9. Identify at least four groups that were hurt by the Chinese tariffs on soybeans and two that were helped. **LO15-3**

PROBLEMS FOR CHAPTER 15

LO15-1 1. The number of bushels of corn produced decreased from 14.3 billion bushels in 2018 to 13.7 billion bushels in 2019.
 (*a*) By what percent did the quantity of corn supplied decrease in 2019?
 (*b*) If the price elasticity of demand for corn is 0.15, by how much did price rise?

LO15-1 2. If this year's harvest is greater than last year's by 6 percent, to sell all of the crop, how much does price have to change if the price elasticity of demand is 0.2?

LO15-1 3. According to Figure 15.2, how much did corn prices change between 2000 and 2012 in percentage terms?

LO15-1 4. According to the World View "U.S.-China Trade War Takes Soybean Farmers as Victims," in 2016–2018,
 (*a*) By how much did soybean prices fall as a result of the trade war?
 (*b*) What was this decline in percentage terms?
 After steps were taken to end the trade war in January 2020,
 (*c*) What was the ultimate decline in soybean prices since 2016?
 (*d*) What was this decline in percentage terms?

LO15-2 5. The following table shows the market demand and supply for soybeans.

Price ($ per Bushel)	Quantity Demanded (Bushels per Year)	Quantity Supplied (Bushels per Year)
10	0	120
9	10	110
8	20	100
7	30	90
6	40	80
5	50	70
4	60	60
3	70	50
2	80	40
1	90	30
0	100	20

 (*a*) What is the equilibrium price?
 (*b*) What is the equilibrium quantity?
 Suppose the CCC loan rate is $6.
 (*c*) What is the new quantity supplied?
 (*d*) What is the new quantity demanded?
 (*e*) How much is this shortage or surplus?

LO15-2 6. Suppose the market price of corn is $2.00 per bushel.
 (*a*) Would a farmer sell corn to the market or use it for loans from the government (CCC)? (See Table 15.2.)
 (*b*) If the market price rose to $2.50, what would the farmer do with her corn?

PROBLEMS FOR CHAPTER 15 (cont'd)

LO15-1 7. Suppose that consumers' incomes increase 10 percent, which results in a 0.4 percent increase in consumption of farm goods at current prices. What is the income elasticity of demand for farm goods?

LO15-3 8. Assume that the unregulated supply schedule for milk is the following:

Price ($ per pound)	0.18	0.24	0.30	0.36	0.42
Quantity supplied (billions of pounds per year)	43	53	63	73	83

(*a*) Draw the supply and demand curves for milk, assuming that the demand for milk is perfectly inelastic (vertical) and consumers will buy 53 billion pounds of it.

(*b*) What is the equilibrium price?

Now suppose the government pays milk producers to set aside production by 20 billion pounds per year.

(*c*) Draw this new supply curve that reflects the government's action.

(*d*) What is the equilibrium price following the government's action?

(*e*) How much more money are consumers paying for the 53 billion pounds of milk because of the higher equilibrium price?

LO15-3 9. Suppose there are 100 grain farmers, each with identical cost structures, as shown in the following tables:

Production Costs (per Farm)		Demand	
Output (Bushels per Day)	Total Cost (per Day)	Price (per Bushel)	Quantity Demanded (Bushels per Day)
0	$ 5	$1	600
1	7	2	500
2	10	3	400
3	14	4	300
4	19	5	200
5	25	6	100
6	33	7	50

Under these circumstances, graph the market supply and demand.

(*a*) What is the equilibrium price for grain?

(*b*) How much grain will be produced at the equilibrium price?

(*c*) How much total profit will each farmer earn at that price?

(*d*) If the government gives farmers a cost subsidy equal to $1 a bushel, what will happen to
   (*i*)   Output?
   (*ii*) Price?
   (*iii*) Profit?

(*e*) What will happen to total output if the government additionally guarantees a price of $5 per bushel?

(*f*) What price is required to sell this output?

(*g*) What is the cost to the government in *d?*

(*h*) Show your answers on the accompanying graph.

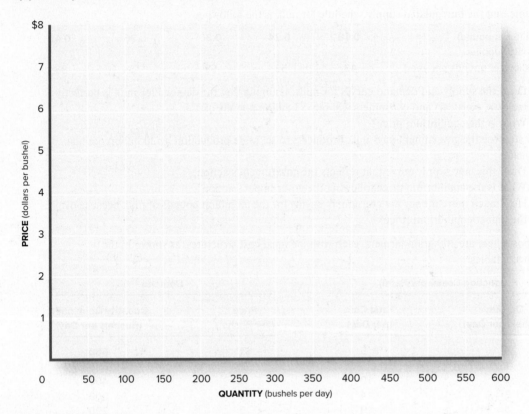

L015-3 10. ***Decisions for Tomorrow:***

(*a*) According to Figure 15.7, how much did farm incomes change (in percentage terms) in 2016–2019?

(*b*) If a law is passed that limits immigration, what is the predicted impact on farm incomes?

(*c*) If subsidies are extended to agricultural products like strawberries, chickens, and lemons, what is the predicted impact on farm incomes?

PART

5

John Rawlston/Chattanooga Times Free Press/AP Images

Bill Pugliano/Getty Images

Steve Allen/Brand X Pictures/Getty Images

FACTOR MARKETS: BASIC THEORY

Factor markets operate like product markets, with supply and demand interacting to determine prices and quantities. In factor markets, however, resource inputs rather than products are exchanged. Those exchanges determine the wages paid to workers and the rent, interest, and profits paid to other inputs. The micro theories presented in Chapters 16, 17, and 18 explain how those factor payments are determined.

John Rawlston/Chattanooga Times Free Press/AP Images

CHAPTER 16

The Labor Market

Dwayne "The Rock" Johnson was paid $89 million in 2019 for starring in movies like *Jumanji: The Next Level* and HBO's *Ballers*. LeBron James received $37 million for playing basketball and another $55 million in product endorsements. Yet the president of the United States was paid only $400,000. And the administrative assistant who typed the manuscript of this book was paid just $19,000. What accounts for these tremendous disparities in earnings?

Why does the average college graduate earn close to $60,000 while the average high school graduate earns just $30,000? Are such disparities simply a reward for enduring four years of college, or do they reflect real differences in talent?

Surely we can't hope to explain these earnings disparities on the basis of the willingness to work. After all, my administrative assistant would be more than willing to work day and night for $89 million per year. For that matter, so would I. Accordingly, the earnings disparities can't be attributed to differences in the quantity of labor supplied. If we're going to explain why some people earn a great deal of income while others earn very little, we must consider both the *supply* and the *demand* for labor. In this regard, the following questions arise:

- **How do people decide how much time to spend working?**
- **What determines the wage rate an employer is willing to pay?**
- **Why are some workers paid so much and others so little?**

To answer these questions, we must examine the behavior of labor *markets*.

LEARNING OBJECTIVES

After reading this chapter, you should know

LO16-1 What factors shape labor supply and demand.

LO16-2 How market wage rates are established.

LO16-3 How wage floors alter labor market outcomes.

LABOR SUPPLY

The following two ads recently appeared in the campus newspaper of a well-known university:

> Will do ANYTHING for money: able-bodied liberal-minded male needs money, will work to get it. Have car. Call Josh 765-3210.

> Web architect. Experienced website designer. Looking for part-time or consulting position on or off campus. Please call Danielle, ext. 0872, 9–5.

Although placed by individuals of very different talents, the ads clearly expressed Josh's and Danielle's willingness to work. Although we don't know how much money they were asking for their respective talents or whether they ever found jobs, we can be sure that they were prepared to take a job at some wage rate. Otherwise they wouldn't have paid for the ads in the "Jobs Wanted" column of their campus newspaper.

The advertised willingness to work represents a **supply of labor.** These individuals are offering to sell their time and talents to anyone who's willing to pay the right price. Their explicit offers are similar to those of anyone who looks for a job. Job seekers who check the current job openings at the student employment office, tap into Monster.com, or e-mail résumés to potential employers are demonstrating a willingness to accept employment—that is, to *supply* labor. The 5,000 people who applied for jobs at Amazon's Career Day (see Front Page Economics "Thousands Line Up for Amazon Jobs") were also offering to supply labor. That was equally true of the 300,000 people who applied online for Amazon's 2020 virtual Career Day, when 33,000 jobs were available.

labor supply: The willingness and ability to work specific amounts of time at alternative wage rates in a given time period, *ceteris paribus.*

FRONT PAGE ECONOMICS

THOUSANDS LINE UP FOR AMAZON JOBS

CRYSTAL CITY, VA—Crystal City is the site of Amazon's second headquarters (HQ2) and one of the six sites for Amazon's Career Day event. Amazon is looking to fill 2,000 jobs here immediately and as many as 25,000 over the next few years. With starting wages of $15 an hour and salaried jobs paying as much as $100,000, job seekers have flocked to the job fair. More than 5,000 applicants showed up for the one-day event, standing in lines that stretched for several blocks in midday heat and humidity.

Source: Media reports of September 17–19, 2019.

CRITICAL ANALYSIS: The **quantity of labor supplied** at any given wage rate depends on the value of leisure and the desire for income. These Amazon job seekers were all willing to supply labor.

Our first concern in this chapter is to explain these labor supply decisions. How do people decide how many hours to supply at any given wage rate? Do people try to maximize their total wages? If they did, we'd all be holding three jobs and sleeping on the commuter bus. Because most of us don't behave this way, other motives must be present.

Income vs. Leisure

The reward for working comes in two forms: (1) the intrinsic satisfaction of working and (2) a paycheck. MBA grads say they care more about the intrinsic satisfaction than the pay (see Front Page Economics "MBA Grads Willing To Sacrifice Money for Corporate Responsibility"). They also get huge paychecks, however. Those big paychecks are explained in part by the quantity of labor supplied: MBA grads often end up working 60 or more hours a week. The reason people are willing to work so many hours is that they want more income.

Not working obviously has some value, too. In part, we need some nonwork time just to recuperate from working. We also want some leisure time to watch television, go to a soccer game, or enjoy other goods and services we've purchased.

The Trade-Off. Because both working and *not* working are rewarding, we have a dilemma: the more time we spend working, the more income we have but also less time to enjoy it. Working, like all activities, involves an opportunity cost: ***The opportunity cost of working is the amount of leisure time that must be given up in the process.***

This inevitable trade-off between labor and leisure explains the shape of individual labor supply curves. As we work more hours, our leisure time becomes more scarce—and thus more valuable. Hence, ***higher wage rates are required to compensate for the increasing opportunity cost of labor*** (forgone leisure). We'll work more—supply a larger quantity of

MBA GRADS WILLING TO SACRIFICE MONEY FOR CORPORATE RESPONSIBILITY

MBA grads looking for their first jobs say money isn't everything. If they are to be believed, intellectual challenge is the most important job attribute they covet, with salary a secondary consideration. 759 graduating MBAs from 11 of the country's top business schools also said that a company's stance on social responsibility was an important consideration in their job acceptance. Indeed, an overwhelming 97.3 percent of the grads said they would be willing to forego some salary in order to work for a company with a strong social conscience. With first-year starting salaries averaging nearly $107,000 in 2019, MBA grads can afford to sacrifice a bit of their paychecks to pursue corporate responsibility.

While expressing a commitment to social responsibility, these MBA grads weren't saying they'd give up a big chunk of their salaries to pursue that goal. According to the study conducted by professors David Montgomery and Catherine Ramus of the University of California at Santa Barbara, the MBA grads said they'd be willing to take a pay cut of only 14.4 percent to take a more socially-responsible job than a less socially responsible one. While that amounts to an average sacrifice of $ 14,902 in first-year salary, that still leaves the MBA grads with enviable starting salaries and excellent career prospects.

People already in the workforce also say they'd sacrifice some salary for other goals. Nearly half of all workers say they'd give up some of their salary for more time off. Yet, most workers still jump at the opportunity to earn overtime pay, either by working longer hours or sacrificing holidays. So, people's decisions about how to balance work and income are hard to predict.

What MBAs at Some Top Schools Earn

School	Starting Salaries in 2019
University of Pennsylvania	$181,927
Stanford	180,831
Harvard	176,928
Columbia	175,725
New York University	173,513
Chicago	173,438
Dartmouth	169,947
Northwestern	168,924
MIT	168,745
University of Virginia	168,626

Source: Global MBA Rankings 2019, U.S. News & World Report, 2019.

Source: Bill Snyder, "For MBA Grads, Corporate Responsibility Trumps Salary," Stanford Graduate School of Business, June 1, 2008.

CRITICAL ANALYSIS: The quantity of **labor supplied** depends on the intrinsic satisfaction of working and the wages paid. MBA grads apparently work long hours for both high wages and job satisfaction. Would they work just as hard for *less* pay?

labor—only if offered a higher wage rate. This is reflected in the upward slope of the labor supply curve in Figure 16.1.

The upward slope of the labor supply curve is reinforced with the changing value of income. Those first few dollars earned on the job are really precious, especially if you have bills to pay. As you work and earn more, however, your most urgent needs will be satisfied. You may still want more things, but the urgency of your consumption desires is likely to diminish. Another dollar of wages doesn't mean as much. In other words, *the marginal utility of income may decline as you earn more.* If this happens, you may not be willing to work more hours unless offered a still higher wage rate.

The upward slope of an individual's labor supply curve is therefore explained by the fact that *as hours worked increase,*

- *The value of leisure time increases.*
- *The marginal utility of income decreases.*

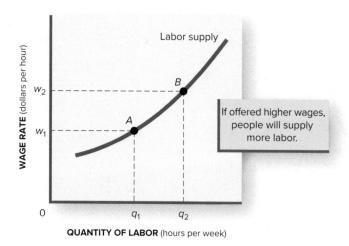

FIGURE 16.1
The Supply of Labor
The quantity of any good or service offered for sale typically increases as its price rises. Labor supply responds in the same way. At the wage rate w_1, the quantity of labor supplied is q_1 (point A). At the higher wage w_2, workers are willing to work more hours per week—that is, to supply a larger quantity of labor (q_1).

Money isn't necessarily the only thing that motivates people to work. People *do* turn down higher-paying jobs in favor of lower-wage jobs that they like. Many parents forgo high-wage "career" jobs to have more flexible hours and time at home. Volunteers offer their services just for the sense of contributing to their communities; they don't need a paycheck. Even MBA graduates say they're motivated more by the challenge of high-paying jobs than the money (see the previous Front Page Economics). But money almost always makes a difference: *People do supply more labor when offered higher wages.*

A Backward Bend?

The force that drives people up the labor supply curve is the lust for more income. Higher wages enable people to buy more goods and services. To achieve higher levels of consumption, people decide to *substitute* labor for leisure. This is the **substitution effect of higher wages.**

At some point, however, higher wages may not be so persuasive. Working added hours just to accumulate a few more toys may not seem so compelling. In fact, higher wages might create the opportunity to work *less*—without giving up any toys. Muhammad Ali once announced that he wouldn't spend an hour in the ring for less than $1 million and would box *less*, not more, as the pay for his fights exceeded $3 million. For him, the added income from one championship fight was so great that he felt he didn't have to fight more to satisfy his income and consumption desires.

A low-wage worker might also respond to higher wage rates by working *less*, not more. People receiving very low wages (such as migrant workers, household help, and babysitters) have to work really long hours just to pay the rent. The increased income made possible by higher wage rates might permit them to work *fewer* hours. These *negative* labor supply responses to increased wage rates are referred to as the **income effect of higher wages.**

The conflict between income and substitution effects shapes an individual's labor supply curve. The *substitution effect* of higher wages encourages people to work more hours. The *income effect,* on the other hand, allows them to reduce work hours without losing income. If substitution effects dominate, the labor supply curve will be upward-sloping. *If income effects outweigh substitution effects, an individual will supply less labor at higher wages.* This kind of reaction is illustrated by the backward-bending portion of the supply curve in Figure 16.2.

Backward-bending labor supply curves are more the exception than the rule. Most Americans do want more leisure. But given the choice between more leisure or more income, Americans choose added income. In other words, substitution effects outweigh income effects in the U.S. labor force. This explains why Americans work such long hours despite their comparatively high incomes. Workers in China, Brazil, and Mexico, by contrast, are more likely to choose (leisure) time over money (see World View "More Time or More Money?").

substitution effect of higher wages: An increased wage rate encourages people to work more hours (to substitute labor for leisure).

income effect of higher wages: An increased wage rate allows a person to reduce hours worked without losing income.

FIGURE 16.2

**The Backward-Bending
Supply Curve**

Increases in wage rates make
additional hours of work more
valuable but also less necessary.
Higher wage rates increase the
quantity of labor supplied as
long as substitution effects
outweigh income effects. At the
point where income effects
begin to outweigh substitution
effects, the labor supply curve
starts to bend backward.

MORE TIME OR MORE MONEY?

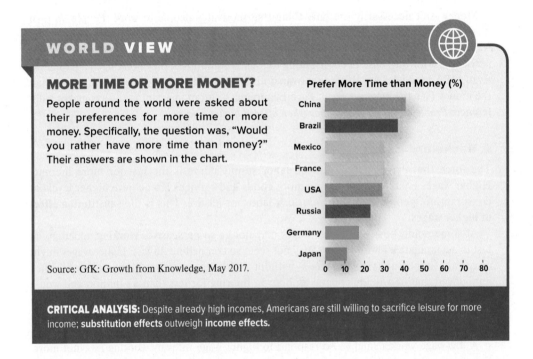

WORLD VIEW

MORE TIME OR MORE MONEY?

People around the world were asked about
their preferences for more time or more
money. Specifically, the question was, "Would
you rather have more time than money?"
Their answers are shown in the chart.

Prefer More Time than Money (%)

Source: GfK: Growth from Knowledge, May 2017.

CRITICAL ANALYSIS: Despite already high incomes, Americans are still willing to sacrifice leisure for more
income; **substitution effects** outweigh **income effects.**

MARKET SUPPLY

market supply of labor: The
total quantity of labor that
workers are willing and able to
supply at alternative wage rates
in a given time period, *ceteris
paribus.*

The **market supply of labor** represents the sum of all individual labor supply decisions.
Although some individuals have backward-bending supply curves, these negative responses
to higher wages are swamped by positive responses from the 166 million individuals who
participate in the U.S. labor market. As a result, the *market* supply curve is upward-sloping.

The upward slope of the labor supply curve doesn't imply that we'll all be working longer
hours in the future. As time passes, the labor supply curve can *shift*. And it will whenever one
of the underlying determinants of supply changes. *The determinants of labor supply include*

- *Tastes* (for leisure, income, and work).
- *Income and wealth.*
- *Expectations* (for income or consumption).
- *Prices* of consumer goods.
- *Taxes.*

These shift factors determine the position and slope of the labor supply curve at any point in time. As time passes, however, these underlying determinants change, causing the labor supply curve to shift. This has evidently happened. In 1890 the average U.S. worker was employed 60 hours a week at a wage rate of 20 cents an hour. In 2020 the average worker worked fewer than 35 hours per week at a wage rate of $29 an hour. Contributing to this long-run leftward shift has been (1) the spectacular rise in living standards (a change in income and wealth), (2) the growth of income transfer programs that provide economic security when one isn't working (a change in income and expectations), and (3) the increased diversity and attractiveness of leisure activities (a change in tastes and other goods).

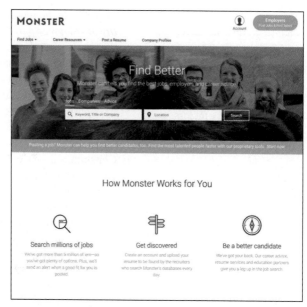

Monster.com brings together the supply and demand for labor.
www.monster.com

Elasticity of Labor Supply

Despite the evident *long*-run shifts of the labor supply curve, workers still respond positively to higher wage rates in the *short* run. To measure the resulting movements along the labor supply curve, we use the familiar concept of elasticity. Specifically, the **elasticity of labor supply** is the percentage change in the quantity of labor supplied divided by the percentage change in the wage rate:

$$\text{Elasticity of labor supply} = \frac{\%\ \text{change in quantity of labor supplied}}{\%\ \text{change in wage rate}}$$

The elasticity of labor tells us how much *more* labor will be available if a higher wage is offered. If the elasticity of labor is 0.2, a 10 percent increase in wage rates will induce a 2 percent increase in the quantity of labor supplied.

The actual responsiveness of workers to a change in wage rates depends on the determinants of labor supply. Time is also important for labor supply elasticity because individuals can't always adjust their schedules or change jobs instantaneously.

elasticity of labor supply: The percentage change in the quantity of labor supplied divided by the percentage change in wage rate.

Institutional Constraints

The labor supply curve and its related elasticities tell us how much time people would like to allocate to work. We must recognize, however, that people seldom have the opportunity to adjust their hours of employment at will. True, a Mark Zuckerberg or a Lady Gaga can easily choose to work more or fewer hours. Most workers, however, face more rigid choices. They must usually choose to work at a regular job for eight hours a day, five days a week, or not to work at all. Very few firms are flexible enough to accommodate a desire to work only between the hours of 11 a.m. and 3 p.m. on alternate Thursdays. Adjustments in work hours are more commonly confined to choices about overtime work or secondary jobs (moonlighting) and vacation and retirement. Families may also alter the labor supply by varying the number of family members sent into the labor force at any given time. Students, too, can often adjust their work hours. The flow of immigrants into the U.S. labor market also increases when U.S. wages rise.

LABOR DEMAND

Regardless of how many people are *willing* to work, it's up to employers to decide how many people will *actually* work. That is, there must be a **demand for labor.** What determines the number of workers employers are willing to hire at various wage rates?

demand for labor: The quantities of labor employers are willing and able to hire at alternative wage rates in a given time period, *ceteris paribus*.

Derived Demand

In earlier chapters we emphasized that employers are profit maximizers. In their quest for maximum profits, firms seek the rate of output at which marginal revenue equals marginal cost. Once they've identified the profit-maximizing rate of output, firms enter factor markets to purchase the required amounts of labor, equipment, and other resources. Thus, *the quantity of resources purchased by a business depends on the firm's expected sales and output.* In this sense, the demand for factors of production, including labor, is a **derived demand**; it's derived from the demand for goods and services.

Consider the plight of strawberry pickers. Strawberry pickers are paid very low wages and are employed only part of the year. But their plight can't be blamed on the greed of the strawberry growers. Strawberry growers, like most producers, would love to sell more strawberries at higher prices. If they did, the growers would hire more pickers and might even pay them higher wages. But the growers must contend with the market demand for strawberries: Consumers aren't willing to buy more strawberries at higher prices. As a consequence, the growers can't afford to hire more pickers or pay them higher wages. In contrast, information technology (IT) firms are always looking for more workers and offer very high wages to get them. This helps explain why college students who major in engineering, math, or computer science get paid a lot more than philosophy majors. IT specialists benefit from the growing demand for Internet services, while philosophy majors suffer because the search for the meaning of life is not a growth industry.

The principle of derived demand suggests that if consumers really want to improve the lot of strawberry pickers, they should eat more strawberries. An increase in the demand for strawberries will motivate growers to plant more berries and hire more labor to pick them. Until then, the plight of the pickers isn't likely to improve.

The Labor Demand Curve

The number of strawberry pickers hired by the growers isn't completely determined by the demand for strawberries. The number of pickers hired will also depend on the wage rate. That is, *the quantity of labor demanded depends on its price (the wage rate).* In general, we expect that strawberry growers will be *willing to hire* more pickers at low wages than at higher wages. Hence, the demand for labor looks very much like the demand for any good or service (see Figure 16.3).

Marginal Physical Product

The fact that the demand curve for labor slopes downward doesn't tell us what quantity of labor will be hired. Nor does it tell us what wage rate will be paid. To answer such questions, we need to know what determines the particular shape and position of the labor demand curve.

A strawberry grower will be willing to hire another picker only if that picker contributes more to output than he or she costs. Growers, as rational businesspeople, recognize that *every* sale and *every* expenditure have some impact on total profits. Hence, the truly profit-maximizing grower will evaluate each picker's job application in terms of the applicant's potential contribution to profits.

Fortunately, a strawberry picker's contribution to output is easy to measure: It's the number of boxes of strawberries he or she picks. Suppose for the moment that Marvin, a college

FIGURE 16.3

The Demand for Labor

The higher the wage rate, the smaller the quantity of labor demanded (*ceteris paribus*). At the wage rate W_1, only L_1 of labor is demanded. If the wage rate falls to W_2, a larger quantity of labor (L_2) will be demanded. The labor demand curve obeys the law of demand.

Demand for labor

More workers are sought at lower wages.

W_1 ⋯⋯ A

W_2 ⋯⋯⋯⋯ B

WAGE RATE (dollars per hour)

L_1 L_2

QUANTITY OF LABOR (hours per month)

dropout with three summers of experience as a canoe instructor, is able to pick five boxes per hour. These five boxes represent Marvin's **marginal physical product (MPP)**. In other words, Marvin's MPP is the *addition* to total output that occurs when the grower hires him for an hour:

$$\text{Marginal physical product} = \frac{\text{Change in total output}}{\text{Change in quantity of labor}}$$

marginal physical product (MPP): The change in total output associated with one additional unit of input.

Marginal physical product establishes an *upper* limit to the grower's willingness to pay. Clearly the grower can't afford to pay Marvin more than five boxes of strawberries for an hour's work; the grower won't pay Marvin more than he produces.

Marginal Revenue Product

Most strawberry pickers don't want to be paid in strawberries. At the end of a day in the fields, the last thing a picker wants to see is another strawberry. Marvin, like the rest of the pickers, wants to be paid in cash. To find out how much cash he might be paid, we need to know what a box of strawberries is worth. This is easy to determine. The market value of a box of strawberries is simply the price at which the grower can sell it. Thus, Marvin's contribution to output can be measured by either marginal *physical* product (five boxes per hour) or the dollar *value* of that product.

The dollar value of a worker's contribution to output is called **marginal revenue product (MRP)**. Marginal revenue product is the *change* in total revenue that occurs when more labor is hired:

marginal revenue product (MRP): The change in total revenue associated with one additional unit of input.

$$\text{Marginal revenue product} = \frac{\text{Change in total revenue}}{\text{Change in quantity of labor}}$$

In Marvin's case, the "change in quantity of labor" is one extra hour of picking strawberries. The "change in total revenue" is the *value* of the extra five boxes of berries Marvin picks in that hour. If the grower can sell strawberries for $2 a box, Marvin's marginal revenue product is simply 5 boxes per hour × $2 per box, or $10 per hour.

We could have come to the same conclusion by multiplying marginal *physical* product times *price:*

$$\text{MRP} = \text{MPP} \times \rho$$

or

$$\$10 \text{ per hour} = 5 \text{ boxes per hour} \times \$2 \text{ per box}$$

In compliance with the rule about not paying anybody more than he or she contributes, the profit-maximizing grower should be willing to pay Marvin *up to* $10 an hour. In other words, *marginal revenue product sets an upper limit to the wage rate an employer will pay.*

But what about a lower limit? Suppose the pickers aren't organized and Marvin is desperate for money. Under such circumstances, he might be willing to work—to supply labor—for only $4 an hour.

Should the grower hire Marvin for such a low wage? The profit-maximizing answer is obvious. If Marvin's marginal revenue product is $10 an hour and his wages are only $4 an hour, the grower will be eager to hire him. The difference between Marvin's marginal revenue product ($10) and his wage ($4) implies additional profits of $6 an hour. In fact, the grower will be so elated by the economics of this situation that he'll want to hire everybody he can find who's willing to work for $4 an hour. After all, if the grower can make $6 an hour by hiring Marvin, why not hire 1,000 pickers and accumulate profits at an even faster rate?

The Law of Diminishing Returns

The exploitative possibilities suggested by Marvin's picking are too good to be true. It isn't at all clear, for example, how the grower could squeeze 1,000 workers onto one acre of land and have any room left over for strawberry plants. There must be some limit to the profit-making potential of this situation.

A few moments' reflection on the absurdity of trying to employ 1,000 people to pick one acre of strawberries should be ample warning of the limits to profits here. You don't need two years of business school to recognize this. But some grasp of economics may help

We can measure a worker's output in *physical* terms (e.g., boxes of strawberries) or *dollar* terms (value of those boxes).

Photodisc/Getty Images

to explain exactly why the grower's eagerness to hire additional pickers will begin to fade long before 1,000 are hired. The operative concept here is *marginal productivity.*

Diminishing MPP. The decision to hire Marvin originated in his marginal physical product—that is, the five boxes of strawberries he can pick in an hour's time. To assess the wisdom of hiring still more pickers, we have to *consider how total output will change if additional labor is employed.* To do so, we need to keep track of marginal physical product.

Figure 16.4 shows how strawberry output changes as additional pickers are hired. Marvin picks five boxes of strawberries per hour. Total output and his marginal physical product are identical because he's initially the only picker employed. When the grower hires George, Marvin's old college roommate, we observe that the total output increases to 10 boxes per hour (point *B* in Figure 16.4). This figure represents another increase of five boxes per hour. Accordingly, we may conclude that George's *marginal physical product* is

FIGURE 16.4

Diminishing Marginal Physical Product

The marginal physical product (MPP) of labor is the *increase* in total production that results when one additional worker is hired. MPP tends to fall as additional workers are hired in any given production process. This decline occurs because each worker has increasingly less of other factors (e.g., land) with which to work. When the second worker (George) is hired, total output increases from 5 to 10 boxes per hour. Hence, the second worker's MPP equals 5 boxes per hour. Thereafter, capital and land constraints diminish marginal physical product.

	Number of Pickers (per Hour)	Total Strawberry Output (Boxes per Hour)	Marginal Physical Product (Boxes per Hour)
	0	0	—
A	1 (Marvin)	5	5
B	2 (George)	10	5
C	3	14	4
D	4	17	3
E	5	19	2
F	6	20	1
G	7	20	0
H	8	18	−2
I	9	15	−3

five boxes per hour, the same as Marvin's. Given such productivity, the grower will want to hire George and continue looking for more pickers.

As more workers are hired, total strawberry output continues to increase but not nearly as fast. Although the later hires work just as hard, the limited availability of land and capital constrain their marginal physical product. One problem is the number of boxes. There are only a dozen boxes, and the additional pickers often have to wait for an empty box. The time spent waiting depresses marginal physical product. The worst problem is space: As additional workers are crowded onto the one-acre patch, they begin to get in one another's way. The picking process is slowed, and marginal physical product is further depressed. Note that the MPP of the fifth picker is two boxes per hour, while the MPP of the sixth picker is only one box per hour. By the time we get to the seventh picker, marginal physical product actually falls to zero because no further increases in total strawberry output take place.

Things get even worse if the grower hires still more pickers. If eight pickers are employed, total output actually *declines.* The pickers can no longer work efficiently under such crowded conditions. The MPP of the eighth worker is *negative,* no matter how ambitious or hardworking this person may be. Figure 16.4 illustrates this decline in marginal physical product, beyond point *G* on the total output curve and beyond point *g* on the MPP curve.

Our observations on strawberry production are similar to those made in most industries. In the short run, the availability of land and capital is limited by prior investment decisions. Hence, additional workers must share existing facilities. As a result, *the marginal physical product of labor eventually declines as the quantity of labor employed increases.* This is the **law of diminishing returns** we first encountered in Chapter 7. It's based on the simple observation that an increasing number of workers leaves each worker with less land and capital to work with. At some point, this "crowding" causes MPP to decline.

Diminishing MRP. *As marginal physical product (MPP) diminishes, so does marginal revenue product (MRP).* As noted earlier, marginal revenue product is the increase in the *value* of total output associated with an added unit of labor (or other input). In our example, it refers to the increase in strawberry revenues associated with one additional picker and is calculated as MPP × *p*.

The decline in marginal revenue product mirrors the drop in marginal physical product. Recall that a box of strawberries sells for $2. With this price and the output statistics in Figure 16.4, we can readily calculate marginal revenue product, as summarized in Table 16.1. As the growth of output diminishes, so does marginal revenue product. Marvin's marginal revenue product of $10 an hour has fallen to $6 by the time four pickers are employed and reaches zero when seven pickers are employed.[1]

law of diminishing returns: The marginal physical product of a variable input declines as more of it is employed with a given quantity of other (fixed) inputs.

Number of Pickers (per Hour)	Total Strawberry Output (in Boxes per Hour)	×	Price of Strawberry (per Box)	=	Total Strawberry Revenue (per Hour)	Marginal Revenue Product
0	0		$2		0	—
1 (Marvin)	5		2		$10	$10
2 (George)	10		2		20	10
3	14		2		28	8
4	17		2		34	6
5	19		2		38	4
6	20		2		40	2
7	20		2		40	0
8	18		2		36	−4
9	15		2		30	−6

TABLE 16.1

Diminishing Marginal Revenue Product

Marginal revenue product (MRP) measures the change in total revenue that occurs when one additional worker is hired. At constant product prices, MRP equals MPP × price. Hence, MRP declines along with MPP.

[1]Marginal revenue product would fall even faster if the price of strawberries declined as increasing quantities were supplied. We're assuming that the grower's output doesn't influence the market price of strawberries and hence that the grower is a *competitive* producer.

A FIRM'S HIRING DECISION

The tendency of marginal revenue product to diminish will cool the strawberry grower's eagerness to hire 1,000 pickers. We still don't know, however, how many pickers will be hired.

The Firm's Labor Supply

Our earlier discussion of labor supply indicated that more workers are available only at higher wage rates. But that's true only for the *market* supply. A single producer may be able to hire an unlimited number of workers at the prevailing wage rate—if the firm is perfectly competitive in the labor market. This happens when the single firm (or farm) is just a bit player in a much larger labor market. Like small firms in big product markets, it has no market power. In other words, *a firm that's a perfect competitor in the labor market can hire all the labor it wants at the prevailing market wage.*

Let's assume that the strawberry grower is so small that his hiring decisions have no effect on local wages. As far as he's concerned, there's an unlimited supply of strawberry pickers willing to work for $4 an hour. His only decision is how many of these willing pickers to hire at that wage rate.

MRP = Firm's Labor Demand

Figure 16.5 provides the answer. We already know that the grower is eager to hire pickers whose marginal revenue product exceeds their wage. He'll therefore hire at least one worker at that wage because the MRP of the first picker is $10 an hour (point *A* in Figure 16.5). A second worker will be hired as well because that picker's MRP (point *B* in Figure 16.5) also exceeds the going wage rate. In fact, *the grower will continue hiring pickers until the MRP has declined to the level of the market wage rate.* Figure 16.5 indicates that this intersection (point *C*) occurs when five pickers are employed. Accordingly the grower will be willing to hire—will *demand*—five pickers if wages are $4 an hour.

The folly of hiring more than five pickers is also apparent in Figure 16.5. The marginal revenue product of the sixth worker is only $2 an hour (point *D*). Hiring a sixth picker will cost more in wages ($4) than the picker brings in as revenue ($2). That makes no sense. The *maximum* number of pickers the grower will employ at prevailing wages is five (point *C*).

FIGURE 16.5

The Marginal Revenue Product Curve Is the Labor Demand Curve

An employer is willing to pay a worker no more than the marginal revenue product. In this case, a grower would gladly hire a second worker because that worker's MRP (point *B*) exceeds the wage rate ($4). The sixth worker won't be hired at that wage rate, however, because the MRP (at point *D*) is less than $4. The MRP curve is the labor demand curve.

Equal Pay. The law of diminishing returns also implies that all five pickers will be paid the same wage. Once five pickers are employed, we can't say that any single picker is responsible for the observed decline in marginal revenue product. Marginal revenue product of labor diminishes because each worker has less capital and land to work with, not because the last worker hired is less able than the others. Accordingly, the "fifth" picker can't be identified as any particular individual. Once five pickers are hired, Marvin's MRP is no higher than any other picker's. *Each (identical) worker is worth no more than the marginal revenue product of the last worker hired, and all workers are paid the same wage rate.*

The principles of marginal revenue product apply to baseball players as well as strawberry pickers. When the Los Angeles Angels agreed to pay Mike Trout $426 million (see Front Page Economics "Angels Sign Mike Trout for $426 Million"), they had his MRP in mind. Mike had been the American League's MVP three times and was a league leader in home runs, runs scored, bases stolen, and slugging percentage. His popularity also caused a spike in attendance and in sales of souvenirs. The Angels decided Trout's potential MRP justified his extraordinary salary.

FRONT PAGE ECONOMICS

ANGELS SIGN MIKE TROUT FOR $426 MILLION

Free agency has served Mike Trout well. The star center fielder for the Los Angeles Angels became a free agent when his contract with the Angels expired. The Angels decided they didn't want to lose one of baseball's greatest players and offered him a 12-year contract worth $426.5 million—with a $20 million signing bonus! That is the richest contract ever given to an American athlete. Trout—nicknamed the "Millville Meteor"—was the Rookie of the Year in 2012 and has since played in 8 All-Star games, been the league's MVP three times, and has the highest slugging percent (.581).

Sean M. Haffey/Getty Images

Source: News reports, March 2019.

CRITICAL ANALYSIS: Marginal revenue product measures what a worker is worth to an employer. The Los Angeles Angels expect a high MRP from Mike Trout.

Whatever the explanation for the disparity between the incomes of baseball players and strawberry pickers, the enormous gap between them seems awfully unfair. An obvious question then arises: Can't the number of pickers or their wages be increased?

Changes in Wage Rates

Suppose the government were to set a minimum wage for strawberry pickers at $6 an hour. At first glance this action would appear to boost the wages of pickers, who have been earning only $4 an hour. This isn't all good news for the strawberry pickers, however. *There's a trade-off between wage rates and the number of workers demanded.* If wage rates go up, growers will hire fewer pickers.

Figure 16.6a illustrates this trade-off. The grower's earlier decision to hire five pickers was based on a wage of $4 an hour (point *C*). If the wage jumps to $6 an hour, it no longer makes economic sense to keep five pickers employed. The MRP of the fifth worker is only

(a) Lower wages spur more hires.

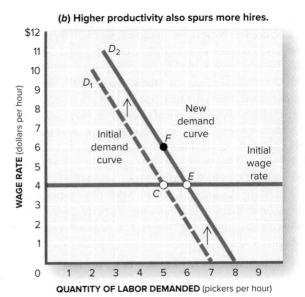

(b) Higher productivity also spurs more hires.

FIGURE 16.6

Incentives to Hire

(*a*) **Lower wage** If the wage rate drops, an employer will be willing to hire more workers, *ceteris paribus*. At $4 an hour, only five pickers per hour would be demanded (point *C*). If the wage rate dropped to $2 an hour, six pickers per hour would be demanded (point *D*).

(*b*) **Higher productivity** If the marginal revenue product of labor improves, the employer will hire a greater quantity of labor at any given wage rate. The labor demand curve will shift up (from D_1 to D_2). In this case, an increase in MRP leads the employer to hire six workers (point *E*) rather than only five workers (point *C*) at $4 per hour.

$4 an hour. The grower will respond to higher wage rates by moving up the labor demand curve to point *G*. At point *G*, only four pickers are hired, and MRP again equals the wage rate. If more workers are to be hired, the wage rate must drop.

Changes in Productivity

The downward slope of the labor demand curve doesn't doom strawberry pickers to low wages. It does emphasize, however, the inevitable link between workers' productivity and wages. *To get higher wages without sacrificing jobs, productivity (MRP) must increase.*

Suppose Marvin and his friends all enroll in a local agricultural extension course and learn new methods of strawberry picking. With these new methods, the marginal physical product of each picker increases by one box per hour. With the price of strawberries still at $2 a box, this productivity improvement implies an increase in marginal *revenue* product of $2 per worker. This change causes an upward *shift* of the labor demand (MRP) curve, as in Figure 16.6*b*.

Notice how the improvement in productivity has altered the value of strawberry pickers. The MRP of the fifth picker is now $6 an hour (point *F*) rather than $4 (point *C*). Hence, the grower can now afford to pay higher wages. Or the grower could employ more pickers than before, moving from point *C* to point *E*. *Increased productivity implies that workers can get higher wages without sacrificing jobs or more employment without lowering wages.* Historically, increased productivity has been the most important source of rising wages and living standards.

Changes in Price

An increase in the price of strawberries would also help the pickers. Marginal revenue product reflects the interaction of productivity and product prices. If strawberry prices were to double, strawberry pickers would become twice as valuable, even without an increase in physical productivity. Such a change in product prices depends, however, on changes in the market supply and demand for strawberries.

MARKET EQUILIBRIUM

The principles that guide the hiring decisions of a single strawberry grower can be extended to the entire labor market. This suggests that *the market demand for labor depends on*

- *The number of employers.*
- *The marginal revenue product of labor in each firm and industry.*

Increases in either the demand for final products or the productivity of labor will tend to increase marginal revenue productivity and therewith the demand for labor.

On the supply side of the labor market we have already observed that *the market supply of labor depends on*

- *The number of available workers.*
- *Each worker's willingness to work at alternative wage rates.*

The supply decisions of workers are in turn a reflection of tastes, income, wealth, expectations, other prices, and taxes.

Equilibrium Wage

Figure 16.7 brings these market forces together. *The intersection of the market supply and demand curves establishes the* **equilibrium wage.** This is the only wage rate at which the quantity of labor supplied equals the quantity of labor demanded. Everyone who's willing and able to work for this wage will find a job.

If the labor market is perfectly competitive, all employers will be able to hire as many workers as they want at the equilibrium wage. Like our strawberry grower, every competitive firm is assumed to have no discernible effect on market wages. *Competitive employers act like price takers with respect to wages as well as prices.* This phenomenon is also portrayed in Figure 16.7.

equilibrium wage: The wage rate at which the quantity of labor supplied in a given time period equals the quantity of labor demanded.

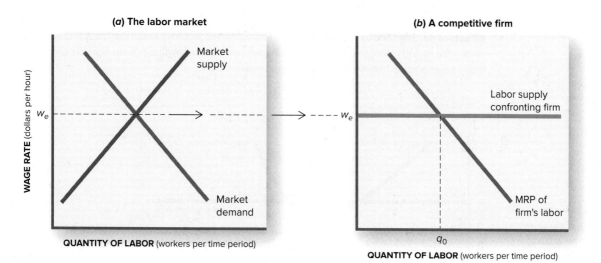

(a) The labor market

(b) A competitive firm

WAGE RATE (dollars per hour)

Market supply

Market demand

w_e

w_e

Labor supply confronting firm

MRP of firm's labor

q_0

QUANTITY OF LABOR (workers per time period)

QUANTITY OF LABOR (workers per time period)

FIGURE 16.7

Equilibrium Wage

The intersection of *market* supply and demand determines the equilibrium wage in a competitive labor market. All the firms in the industry can then hire as much labor as they want at that

equilibrium wage. In this case, the firm can hire all the workers it wants at the equilibrium wage, w_e. It chooses to hire q_0 workers, as determined by their marginal revenue product within the firm.

TABLE 16.2

Minimum Wage History

The federal minimum wage has been increased periodically since first set in 1938. In 2007 Congress raised the minimum to $7.25, effective July 2009.

Oct. 1938	$0.25	Jan. 1978	$2.65
Oct. 1939	0.30	Jan. 1979	2.90
Oct. 1945	0.40	Jan. 1980	3.10
Jan. 1950	0.75	Jan. 1981	3.35
Mar. 1956	1.00	Apr. 1990	3.80
Sept. 1961	1.15	Apr. 1991	4.25
Sept. 1963	1.25	Oct. 1996	4.75
Feb. 1967	1.40	Sept. 1997	5.15
Feb. 1968	1.60	July 2007	5.85
May 1974	2.00	July 2008	6.55
Jan. 1975	2.10	July 2009	7.25
Jan. 1976	2.30		

price floor: Lower limit set for the price of a good.

market surplus: The amount by which the quantity supplied exceeds the quantity demanded at a given price; excess supply.

Minimum Wages

Some people will be unhappy with the equilibrium wage. Employers may grumble that wages are too high. Workers may complain that wages are too low. They may seek government intervention to change market outcomes. This is the goal of Congress when it establishes a legal *minimum* wage—a **price floor** in the labor market (see Table 16.2).

Figure 16.8 illustrates the effects of such government intervention. The market-determined equilibrium wage is W_e, and q_e workers are employed. A government-imposed minimum wage of W_M is then set, above the market equilibrium. So, what happens?

There are changes on both the supply side of the labor market and the demand side. On the supply side, the higher wage W_M encourages more low-skilled workers to seek employment; the quantity supplied *increases* from q_e to q_s. On the demand side, however, the number of available jobs *declines* from q_e to q_d. This leaves a **market surplus** at the wage W_M. As a result of the increased wage, some workers have lost jobs ($q_e - q_d$) and some new entrants fail to find employment ($q_s - q_e$). Only those workers who remain employed (q_d) benefit from the higher wage.

Government-imposed wage floors thus have three distinct effects: *A legal minimum wage*

- *Reduces the quantity of labor demanded, and*
- *Increases the quantity of labor supplied, and thereby*
- *Creates a market surplus.*

Effective vs. Ineffective Minimums. The extent of job loss resulting from a minimum wage hike is hotly debated. How many jobs are lost obviously depends on how far the minimum wage is raised above the market equilibrium.

FIGURE 16.8

Minimum Wage Effects

If the minimum wage exceeds the equilibrium wage, a labor surplus will result: More workers will be willing to work at that wage rate than employers will be willing to hire. Some workers will end up with higher wages, but others will end up unemployed.

In some cases, a hike in the minimum wage may have no impact at all. This would certainly be the case if the minimum wage were set *below* the equilibrium market wage. Likewise, an *increase* in the minimum that stayed at or below the market wage would have no impact on labor demand or supply. Such wage hikes would be *ineffective*. A minimum wage hike is *effective* only if it exceeds the equilibrium market wage.

Most observers agree that the minimum wage of $7.25, set in 2009, has fallen behind market wages. In 2009, the average hourly wage was $20.90. In 2020, the average was $28.81. Yet, the federal minimum remained at $7.25 for those 11 years. This general wage growth has rendered the federal minimum ineffective. Recognizing that, 29 states and many cities have increased their own minimum wages above the federal floor. The ineffective federal floor also gives Congress an easy option to score political points without significant job loss by raising the federal minimum wage a bit.

Demand Elasticity

When a legislated wage hike is effective (above market equilibrium), the elasticity of labor demand becomes critical. Democrats argue that labor demand is inelastic, so few jobs will be lost. Republicans assert that labor demand is elastic, so more jobs will be lost. In the early 1980s the elasticity of labor demand was found to be 0.10. Hence, a 10 percent increase in the minimum wage would cause a 1 percent reduction in employment.

In 2019 the Congressional Budget Office reviewed studies of the minimum wage and estimated the extent of job losses that would occur if the federal minimum was hiked to $10, $12, or $15 an hour. All three of these options entailed *effective* wage hikes, according to the CBO. The smallest job losses, of course, accompanied the smallest wage hikes. A hike to $15 an hour, over a period of five years, would generate a loss of 1.3 million jobs (see Front Page Economics "House Approves $15 Minimum Wage").

What we know for sure is **the extent of job losses following a minimum-wage hike will be larger when**

- **The legislated floor is farther above the market equilibrium.**
- **The elasticity of labor demand is greater.**

FRONT PAGE ECONOMICS

HOUSE APPROVES $15 MINIMUM WAGE

WASHINGTON, DC—The House of Representatives voted today to increase the minimum wage from $7.25 an hour to $15. The "Raise the Wage Act" notches the minimum up annually over the next seven years, hitting $15 an hour in 2024. The Act passed on a partisan basis, with nearly all Democrats and only 3 Republicans contributing to the 231-199 approval. The Republican-led Senate is not expected to take up the bill before next year's election.

Source: News reports, July 18–19, 2019.

CRITICAL ANALYSIS:: A higher minimum wage encourages firms to hire fewer workers. How many jobs are lost depends on the size of the wage hike and the **price elasticity of labor demand.**

CHOOSING AMONG INPUTS

One of the options employers have when wage rates rise is to utilize more machinery in place of labor. In most production processes there are possibilities for substituting capital inputs for labor inputs. In the long run, there are still more possibilities for redesigning the whole production process. Given these options, how should the choice of inputs be made?

Suppose a mechanical strawberry picker can pick berries twice as fast as Marvin. Which will the grower hire, Marvin or the mechanical picker? At first it would seem that the grower would choose the mechanical picker. But the choice isn't so obvious. So far, all we know is that the mechanical picker's MPP is twice as large as Marvin's. But we haven't said anything about the *cost* of the mechanical picker.

Cost Efficiency

Suppose that a mechanical picker can be rented for $10 an hour, while Marvin is still willing to work for $4 an hour. Will this difference in hourly cost change the grower's input choice?

To determine the relative desirability of hiring Marvin or renting the mechanical picker, the grower must compare the ratio of their marginal physical products to their cost. This ratio of marginal product to cost expresses the **cost efficiency** of an input:

$$\text{Cost efficiency} = \frac{\text{Marginal physical product of an input}}{\text{Cost of an input}}$$

Marvin's MPP is five boxes of strawberries per hour and his cost (wage) is $4. Thus, the return on each dollar of wages paid to Marvin is

$$\text{Cost efficiency of labor} = \frac{\text{MPP}_{\text{labor}}}{\text{Cost}_{\text{labor}}} = \frac{5 \text{ boxes}}{\$4} = 1.25 \text{ boxes per } \$1 \text{ of cost}$$

By contrast, the mechanical picker has an MPP of 10 boxes per hour and costs $10 per hour:

$$\begin{array}{l} \text{Cost efficiency} \\ \text{of mechanical picker} \end{array} = \frac{\text{MPP}_{\text{mechanical picker}}}{\text{Cost}_{\text{mechanical picker}}} = \frac{10 \text{ boxes}}{\$10} = 1 \text{ box per } \$1 \text{ of cost}$$

These calculations indicate that Marvin is more cost-effective than the mechanical picker. From this perspective, the grower is better off hiring Marvin than renting a mechanical picker.

From the perspective of cost efficiency, the cheapness of a productive input is measured not by its price but by the amount of output it delivers for that price. Thus, *the most cost-efficient factor of production is the one that produces the most output per dollar.*

The concept of cost efficiency helps explain why American firms don't move en masse to Haiti, where peasants are willing to work for as little as 80 cents an hour. Although this wage rate is far below the minimum wage in the United States, the marginal physical product of Haitian peasants is even further below American standards. American workers remain more cost-efficient than the "cheap" labor available in Haiti, making it unprofitable to **outsource** U.S. jobs. So long as U.S. workers deliver more output per dollar of wages, they will remain cost-effective in global markets.

Alternative Production Processes

Typically a producer doesn't choose between individual inputs but rather between alternative production processes. General Motors, for example, can't afford to compare the cost efficiency of each job applicant with the cost efficiency of mechanical tire mounters. Instead GM compares the relative desirability of a **production process** that is labor-intensive (uses a lot of labor) with others that are less labor-intensive. GM ignores individual differences in marginal revenue product. Nevertheless, the same principles of cost efficiency guide the decision.

The Efficiency Decision

Let's return to the strawberry patch to see how the choice of an entire production process is made. We again assume that strawberries can be picked by either human or mechanical hands. Now, however, we assume that one ton of strawberries can be produced by only one of the three production processes described in Table 16.3. Process A is most *labor-intensive;* it uses the most labor and thus keeps more human pickers employed. By contrast, process C is *capital-intensive;* it uses the most mechanical pickers and provides the least employment to human pickers. Process B falls between these two extremes.

cost efficiency: The amount of output associated with an additional dollar spent on input; the MPP of an input divided by its price (cost).

outsourcing: The relocation of production to foreign countries.

production process: A specific combination of resources used to produce a good or service.

	Alternative Processes for Producing One Ton of Strawberries		
Input	**Process A**	**Process B**	**Process C**
Labor (hours)	400	270	220
Machinery (hours)	13	15	18
Land (acres)	1	1	1

TABLE 16.3

Alternative Production Processes

One ton of strawberries can be produced with varying input combinations. Which process is most efficient? What information is missing?

Which of these three production processes should the grower use? If he used labor-intensive process A, he'd be doing the pickers a real favor. But his goal is to maximize profits, so we assume he'll choose the production process that best serves this objective. That is, he'll choose the *least-cost* process to produce one ton of strawberries.

But which of the production processes in Table 16.3 is least expensive? We really can't tell on the basis of the information provided. To determine the relative cost of each process—and thus to understand the producer's choice—we must know something more about input costs. In particular, we have to know how much an hour of mechanical picking costs and how much an hour of human picking (labor) costs. Then we can determine which combination of inputs is least expensive in producing one ton of strawberries—that is, which is most *cost-efficient*. Note that we don't have to know how much the land costs because the same amount of land is used in all three production processes. Thus, land costs won't affect our efficiency decision.

Suppose that strawberry pickers are still paid $4 an hour and that mechanical pickers can be rented for $10 an hour. The acre of land rents for $500 per year. With this information we can now calculate the total dollar cost of each production process and quickly determine the most cost-efficient. Table 16.4 summarizes the required calculations.

The calculations performed in Table 16.4 clearly identify process C as the least expensive way of producing one ton of strawberries. Process A entails a total cost of $2,230, whereas the capital-intensive process C costs only $1,560 to produce the same quantity of output. As a profit maximizer, the grower will choose process C, even though it implies less employment for strawberry pickers.

The choice of an appropriate production process—the decision about *how* to produce—is called the **efficiency decision.** As we've seen, a producer seeks to use the combination of resources that produces a given rate of output for the least cost. The efficiency decision requires the producer to find that particular least-cost combination.

efficiency decision: The choice of a production process for any given rate of output.

Input	Cost Calculation
Process A (labor-intensive)	
Labor	400 hours at $4 per hour = $1,600
Machinery	13 hours at $10 per hour = 130
Land	1 acre at $500 = 500
	Total cost $2,230
Process B (intermediate)	
Labor	270 hours at $4 per hour = $1,080
Machinery	15 hours at $10 per hour = 150
Land	1 acre at $500 = 500
	Total cost $1,730
Process C (capital-intensive)	
Labor	220 hours at $4 per hour = $ 880
Machinery	18 hours at $10 per hour = 180
Land	1 acre at $500 = 500
	Total cost $1,560

TABLE 16.4

The Least-Cost Combination

A producer wants to produce a given rate of output for the least cost. Choosing the least expensive production process is the efficiency decision. In this case, process C represents the most cost-efficient production process for producing one ton of strawberries.

DECISIONS FOR **TOMORROW**

Should We Cap CEO Pay?

When Disney revealed that it was paying Bob Iger, its CEO, as much as $423 million over four years, Senator Bernie Sanders was outraged. He tweeted the question, "Does Disney CEO Bob Iger have a good explanation for why he is being compensated more than $400 million, while workers at Disneyland are homeless and relying on food stamps to feed their families?" As Sanders saw it, the enormous disparity between executive pay and employee pay was a symptom of what is wrong in America.

Senator Sanders and other critics conclude that many CEO paychecks are out of line with realities of supply and demand. They want corporations to reduce CEO pay and revise the process used for setting CEO pay levels. President Obama moved in this direction by setting a pay cap of $500,000 for executives of corporations receiving government aid.

Pay Ratios. Aside from the absolute size of CEO paychecks, what really bothers critics is the *ratio* of CEO pay to the pay of the average employee. That pay ratio is seen as a critical measure of inequality, even unfairness. On average, the pay ratio is 144 to 1 at U.S. corporations. At Disney, however, Bob Iger's salary in 2018 was 1,424 times larger than the median Disney worker's paycheck. At Chipotle the pay ratio was even larger, at 2,438. At the Gap it was 3,566! Elizabeth Warren often points to these huge pay ratios as a symptom of free-market failure. The city of Portland, Oregon, in 2016 introduced an income surtax on CEO pay that exceed 100 times the pay of the median employee.

Defenders of high CEO compensation argue that Bob Iger's decisions on which movies to produce and to enter the video streaming business contribute way more to the company and the economy than the services of a tour guide at Disney World. They also ask why CEO pay is singled out when similar incomes of baseball players (e.g., Mike Trout) and entertainers (e.g., Beyoncé) are applauded. Does anyone worry about the pay ratio between Beyoncé and the people who set up her sound equipment?

Unmeasured MRP. One of the difficulties in determining the appropriate level of CEO pay is the elusiveness of marginal revenue product. It's easy to measure the MRP of a strawberry picker or even a salesclerk. But a corporate CEO's contributions are less well defined. A CEO is supposed to provide strategic leadership and a sense of mission. These are critical to a corporation's success but hard to quantify.

Congress confronts the same problem in setting the president's pay. We noted earlier that the president of the United States is paid $400,000 a year. Can we argue that this salary represents the president's marginal revenue product? It has been estimated that the president's pay would be in the range of $38–58 million if he were paid on performance (MRP). The wage we actually pay a president is less a reflection of contribution to total output than a matter of custom. The salary also reflects the price that voters believe is required to induce competent individuals to forsake private sector jobs and assume the responsibilities of the presidency. In this sense, the wage paid to the president and other public officials is set by their **opportunity wage**—that is, the wage they could earn in private industry.

The same kinds of considerations influence the wages of college professors. The marginal revenue product of a college professor isn't easy to measure. Is it the number of students she teaches, the amount of knowledge conveyed, or something else? Confronted with such problems, most universities tend to pay college professors according to their opportunity wage—that is, the amount the professors could earn elsewhere.

Opportunity wages help explain CEO pay but don't fully justify such high pay levels. If Disney's CEO pay is justified by opportunity wages, that means another company would be willing to pay him that much. But what would justify such high pay at another company? Would his MRP be any easier to measure? Maybe *all* CEO paychecks have been inflated.

opportunity wage: The highest wage an individual would earn in his or her best alternative job.

Critics of CEO pay conclude that the process of setting CEO pay levels should be changed. All too often, executive pay scales are set by self-serving committees composed of executives of the same or similar corporations. Critics want a more independent assessment of pay scales, with nonaffiliated experts and stockholder representatives.

Some critics want to go a step further and set mandatory "caps" on CEO pay. President Clinton rejected legislated caps but convinced Congress to limit the tax deductibility of CEO pay. Any "unjustified" CEO pay in excess of $1 million a year can't be treated as a business expense but instead must be paid out of after-tax profits. This change put more pressure on corporations to examine the rationale for multimillion-dollar paychecks. President Obama wanted even stricter limits on CEO pay, especially for banks and other companies getting government "bailout" money.

If markets work efficiently, such government intervention shouldn't be necessary. Corporations that pay their CEOs excessively will end up with smaller profits than companies that pay market-based wages. Over time, "lean" companies will be more competitive than "fat" companies, and excessive pay packages will be eliminated. Legislated CEO pay caps imply that CEO labor markets aren't efficient or that the adjustment process is too slow. To forestall more government intervention in pay decisions, companies may tie executive pay more explicitly to performance (marginal revenue product) in the economy tomorrow.

SUMMARY

- The motivation to work arises from social, psychological, and economic forces. People need income to pay their bills, but they also need a sense of achievement. As a consequence, people are willing to work—to supply labor. **LO16-1**
- There's an opportunity cost involved in working—namely, the amount of leisure time one sacrifices. By the same token, the opportunity cost of not working (leisure) is the income and related consumption possibilities thereby forgone. Everyone confronts a trade-off between leisure and income. **LO16-1**
- Higher wage rates induce people to work more—that is, to substitute labor for leisure. But this substitution effect may be offset by an income effect. Higher wages also enable a person to work fewer hours with no loss of income. When income effects outweigh substitution effects, the labor supply curve bends backward. **LO16-2**
- A firm's demand for labor reflects labor's marginal revenue product. A profit-maximizing employer won't pay a worker more than the worker produces. **LO16-2**

- The marginal revenue product of labor diminishes as additional workers are employed on a particular job (the law of diminishing returns). This decline occurs because additional workers have to share existing land and capital, leaving each worker with less land and capital to work with. **LO16-2**
- A producer seeks to get the most output for every dollar spent on inputs. This means getting the highest ratio of marginal product to input price. A profit-maximizing producer will choose the most cost-efficient input (not necessarily the one with the cheapest price). **LO16-1**
- The efficiency decision involves the choice of the least-cost productive process and is also made on the basis of cost efficiency. A producer seeks the least expensive process to produce a given rate of output. **LO16-3**
- Differences in marginal revenue product are an important explanation of wage inequalities. But the difficulty of measuring MRP in some jobs leaves many wage rates to be determined by opportunity wages or other mechanisms. **LO16-3**

Key Terms

labor supply	derived demand	market surplus
substitution effect of higher wages	marginal physical product (MPP)	cost efficiency
income effect of higher wages	marginal revenue product (MRP)	outsourcing
market supply of labor	law of diminishing returns	production process
elasticity of labor supply	equilibrium wage	efficiency decision
demand for labor	price floor	opportunity wage

Questions for Discussion

1. Why are you doing this homework? What are you giving up? What utility do you expect to gain?   **LO16-1**

2. Would you continue to work after winning a lottery prize of $100,000 a year for life? Would you change schools, jobs, or career objectives? What factors besides income influence work decisions?   **LO16-1**

3. Why might Chinese and Brazilian workers have a stronger preference for leisure time over money than American workers (see World View "More Time or More Money")?   **LO16-1**

4 Explain why marginal physical product would diminish as   **LO16-2**

    (*a*) More waiters are hired in a restaurant.

    (*b*) More professors are hired in the economics department.

    (*c*) More carpenters are hired to build a house.

5. Is this course increasing your marginal productivity? If so, in what way?   **LO16-2**

6. How might you measure the marginal revenue product of (*a*) a quarterback and (*b*) the team's coach?   **LO16-2**

7. Who is hurt and who is helped by an increase in the legal minimum wage? Under what circumstances might a higher minimum *not* reduce employment?   **LO16-3**

8. In 2020 the president of the University of Michigan was paid $900,000 and the football coach was paid $9 million. Does this make any sense?   **LO16-2**

9. Why is Mike Trout's $426 million pay package admired while Bob Iger's $423 million pay package is criticized?   **LO16-2**

10. The minimum wage in Mexico is less than $1 an hour. Does this make Mexican workers more cost-effective than U.S. workers? Explain.   **LO16-3**

11. The Congressional Budget Office (CBO) estimated the job losses that would result from minimum-wage hikes to $10, $12, and $15 an hour. Why didn't CBO look at $8 an hour or $20 an hour?   **LO16-3**

PROBLEMS FOR CHAPTER 16

LO16-1 1. According to the Front Page Economics "Thousands Line Up for Amazon Jobs,"
   (*a*) How many jobs were immediately available?
   (*b*) How many job applicants were there?
   (*c*) Was there a surplus or shortage in this market?

LO16-1 2. According to the Front Page Economics "Thousands Line Up for Amazon Jobs," if Amazon increased wages to $16 per hour, what do you predict will happen to that market surplus?

LO16-2 3. By what percentage did the federal minimum wage increase between
   (*a*) September 1997 and July 2009? (See Table 16.2.)
   (*b*) July 2009 and January 2019?
   (*c*) If the "Raise the Wage Act" (see Front Page Economics "House Approves $15 Minimum Wage") becomes law, by what percent will the minimum wage increase between 2019 and 2024?

LO16-1 4. Suppose a wage increase from $12 to $16 an hour for Disney tour guides increases the number of daily job applicants from 48 to 58. What is the price elasticity of labor supply?

LO16-1 5. If the price of strawberries doubled, how many pickers would be hired at $4 an hour, according to Table 16.1?

LO16-3 6. Apples can be harvested by hand or machine. Handpicking yields 80 pounds per hour; mechanical pickers yield 120 pounds per hour.
   (*a*) If the wage rate of human pickers is $8 an hour and the rental on a mechanical picker is $15 an hour, which is more cost effective?
   (*b*) If the wage rate increased to $12 an hour, which would be more cost-effective?

LO16-3 7. According to Figure 16.8,
   (*a*) How many workers are unemployed at the equilibrium wage?
   (*b*) How many workers are unemployed at the minimum wage?

LO16-3 8. Illustrate on the graph below
   (*a*) An ineffective hike in the minimum wage.   (*b*) An effective hike in the minimum wage.

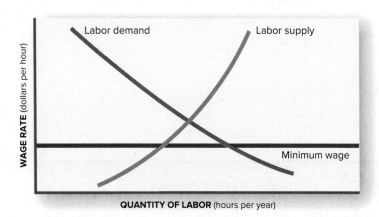

LO16-3 9. Assume that the following data describe labor market conditions:

Wage rate (per hour)	$3	$4	$5	$6	$7	$8	$9	$10
Labor demanded	50	45	40	35	30	25	20	15
Labor supplied	20	30	40	50	60	70	80	90

On a graph, illustrate
(*a*) The equilibrium wage.   (*b*) A government-set minimum wage of $6 per hour.

When the minimum wage is implemented,
(*c*) How many workers lose jobs?
(*d*) How many additional workers seek jobs?
(*e*) How many workers end up unemployed?

LO16-2 10. The following table depicts the number of grapes that can be picked in an hour with varying amounts of labor:

Number of pickers (per hour)	1	2	3	4	5	6	7	8
Output of grapes (in flats)	20	38	53	64	71	74	74	70

   (a) Illustrate the supply and demand of labor for a single farmer, assuming that the local wage rate is $6 an hour and a flat of grapes sells for $2.

   (b) How many pickers will be hired?

   (c) If the wage rate doubles, how many pickers will be hired?

   (d) If the productivity of all workers doubles, how many pickers will be hired at a wage of $12 an hour?

   (e) Illustrate your answers on the following graph.

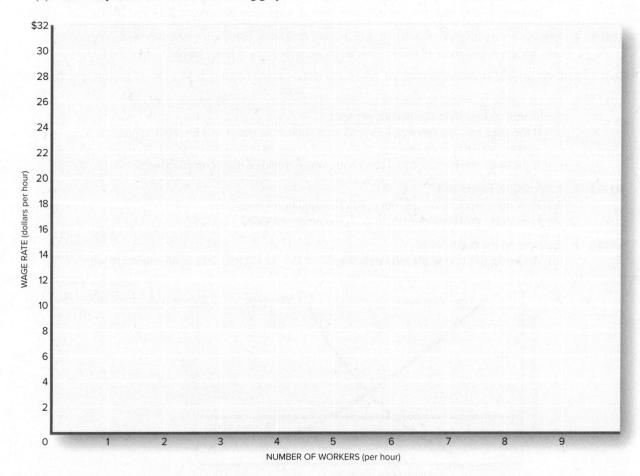

11. The Los Angeles Angels agreed to pay Mike Trout $426.5 million over 12 years (see Front Page Economics "Angels Sign Mike Trout for $426 Million"). If this salary were to be covered by ticket sales only, how many tickets per game would the Angels have to sell to cover Trout's salary if there are 81 home games per year and the average ticket price is $65?

LO16-3 12. By how much would the quantity of labor demanded decrease if a minimum wage hike raised prevailing wages from $8 to $10 an hour and if the elasticity of labor demand were 0.15?

LO16-2 13. *Decisions for Tomorrow:* If the typical Disney worker is paid an annual salary of $25,000, how much higher is the CEO's annual salary in percentage terms?

Design Credit: Shutterstock

Bill Pugliano/Getty Images

CHAPTER 17

Labor Unions

LEARNING OBJECTIVES

After reading this chapter, you should know

LO17-1 How unions secure higher wages.

LO17-2 The factors that affect collective bargaining outcomes.

LO17-3 How unions affect nonunion wages.

The United Auto Workers Union (UAW) launched a strike against Caterpillar, Inc., in November 1991. The union wanted the manufacturer of construction machinery to increase pay, benefits, and job security. *Four years* later, Caterpillar hadn't budged; it continued to operate with replacement workers, management crews, and union members who crossed the picket line. The union finally capitulated in December 1995, sending its 8,700 members back to work with neither higher pay nor even a new contract. The union struck again in 1996 but relented after 17 months. Seven years after their first strike, the Caterpillar workers still had no contract.

To many observers, the failed UAW strike at Caterpillar climaxed a steady decline in the power of labor unions. This impression was reinforced by the failure of *public* unions in Illinois and Ohio to safeguard benefits in early 2011. But the union movement is far from dead. Labor unions are even expanding in some sectors (especially government employment). Many unions still have considerable influence on employment, wages, and working conditions. This chapter focuses on how unions acquire and use such influence. We address the following questions:

- **How do large and powerful employers affect market wages?**
- **How do labor unions alter wages and employment?**
- **What outcomes are possible from collective bargaining between management and unions?**

In the process of answering these questions, we look at the nation's most powerful unions and their actual behavior.

THE LABOR MARKET

To gauge the impact of labor market power, we must first observe how a competitive labor market sets wages and employment. On the supply side, we have all those individuals who are willing to work—to supply labor—at various wage rates. By counting the number of individuals willing to work at each and every wage rate, we can construct a *market labor supply* curve, as in Figure 17.1.

FIGURE 17.1

Competitive Equilibrium in the Labor Market

The market labor supply curve includes all persons willing to work at various wage rates. The labor demand curve tells us how many workers employers are willing to hire. In a competitive market, the intersection of the labor supply and labor demand curves (point C) determines the equilibrium wage (w_e) and employment (q_e) levels.

labor supply: The willingness and ability to work specific amounts of time at alternative wage rates in a given time period, *ceteris paribus.*

demand for labor: The quantities of labor employers are willing and able to hire at alternative wage rates in a given time period, *ceteris paribus.*

equilibrium wage: The wage rate at which the quantity of labor supplied in a given time period equals the quantity of labor demanded.

The willingness of producers (firms) to hire labor is reflected in the market labor demand curve. The curve itself is constructed by counting the number of workers each firm says it is willing and able to hire at each and every wage rate. The curve illustrates the market **demand for labor.**

Competitive Equilibrium

The intersection of the labor supply and labor demand curves (point *C* in Figure 17.1) reveals the **equilibrium wage** rate (w_e): the wage rate at which the quantity of labor supplied equals the quantity demanded. At this wage rate, every job seeker who's willing and able to work for the wage w_e is employed. In addition, firms are able to acquire all the labor they're willing and able to hire at that wage.

Not everyone is employed in equilibrium. Workers who demand wages in excess of w_e are unable to find jobs. By the same token, employers who refuse to pay a wage as high as w_e are unable to attract workers.

Local Labor Markets

Figure 17.1 appears to suggest that there's only *one* labor market and thus only one equilibrium wage. This is a gross oversimplification. If you were looking for a job in Tulsa, you'd have little interest in employment prospects or power configurations in New York City. You'd be more concerned about the available jobs and wages in Tulsa—that is, the condition of the *local* labor market.

Even within a particular geographical area, interest usually focuses on particular occupations and workers rather than on all the people supplying or demanding labor. If you were looking for work as a dancer, you'd have little interest in the employment situation for carpenters or dentists. Rather, you'd want to know how many nightclubs or dance troupes had job vacancies, and what wages and working conditions they offered.

The distinction among various geographical, occupational, and industrial labor markets provides a more meaningful basis for analyzing labor market power. The tremendous size of the national labor market, with more than 160 million workers, precludes anyone from acquiring control of the entire market. The largest employer in the United States (Walmart) employs less than 1 percent of the labor force. General Motors employs far fewer than that, and the top 500 industrial corporations employ less than 20 percent of all workers.

The situation on the supply side is similar. The largest labor unions (National Education Association and the Service Employees International Union) each represents just 1.5 percent of all workers in the country. All unions together represent less than one out of every nine U.S. workers. This doesn't mean that particular employers or unions have no influence on our economic welfare. It does suggest, however, that **market power** *in labor markets is likely to be more effective in specific areas, occupations, and industries.*

market power: The ability to alter the market price of a good or service.

....

LABOR UNIONS

The immediate objective of labor unions is to alter the equilibrium wage and employment conditions in specific labor markets. ***To be successful, unions must be able to exert control over the market supply curve.***

Types of Unions

That's why workers have organized themselves along either industry or occupational craft lines. *Industrial unions* include workers in a particular industry (the United Auto Workers, for example). *Craft unions* represent workers with a particular skill (like the International Brotherhood of Electrical Workers), regardless of the industry in which they work.

The purpose of both types of labor unions is to coordinate the actions of thousands of individual workers, thereby achieving control of market supply. If a union is able to control the supply of workers in a particular industry or occupation, the union acquires a *monopoly* in that market. Like most monopolies, unions attempt to use their market power to increase their incomes.

Union Objectives

A primary objective of unions is to raise the wages of union members. In the 2012 dispute between pro hockey team owners and players, money was the sole issue. The players, who were already getting an average paycheck of $2.4 million per season, were resisting a salary cap that would restrain wages. The team owners wanted to limit total player salaries to 53–55 percent of league revenues, rather than the existing 57 percent.

An exclusive focus on wages is somewhat unusual. Union objectives also include improved working conditions, job security, and other nonwage forms of compensation, such as retirement (pension) benefits, vacation time, and health insurance. The Players Association and the National Football League have bargained about the use of artificial turf, early retirement, player fines, television revenues, game rules, the use of team doctors, drug tests, pensions, and the number of players permitted on a team. A recurring concern of the United Auto Workers is job security. Consequently, they focus on work rules that may eliminate jobs and unemployment benefits for laid-off workers.

Although union objectives tend to be as broad as the concerns of union members, we focus here on just one objective: wage rates. This isn't too great a simplification because most nonwage issues can be translated into their effective impact on wage rates. In 2016, for example, the National Basketball Association and the players' union agreed to more than a dozen different job provisions ranging from the length of time a player had to stay on the disabled list to the location of games (see Front Page Economics "NBA and Players Strike a Deal"). It was possible, however, to figure out the cost of these many provisions ($1.5 million per worker per year). Hence, the "bottom line" of the compensation package could be expressed in terms of wage costs.

What we seek to determine is whether and how unions can raise effective wage rates in a specific labor market by altering the competitive equilibrium depicted in Figure 17.1. What is the source of union power, and how do unions use it?

NBA AND PLAYERS STRIKE A DEAL

The games will go on. The National Basketball Association and the players' union averted a lockout by finalizing the terms of a new contract early Thursday morning. With overflowing revenues of $10 billion per year to divvy up, neither side wanted to disrupt the season schedule. The new contract will last for five years, from 2017 to 2021. Here's what the two sides got:

The players agreed

- To take a smaller share (51 percent, down from 57 percent) of total basketball income, including lucrative TV deals.
- To let the league schedule games outside the United States, provided players get compensated as much as $100,000 per game for travel and inconvenience.

The owners agreed

- To increase the minimum salary from $507,500 to $555,000 by 2019, with cost-of-living adjustments thereafter.
- To reduce the number of exhibition games.
- To shorten the minimum time on the disabled list from 15 days to 10 days.
- To start the season a week earlier so players can get 4 more days of rest.
- To reduce the number of back-to-back games (consecutive days).
- To shorten the length of contracts so players become free agents more often.
- To raise the payroll limit on individual teams.
- To maintain the existing limits on roster size (40 players).

Despite the reduced revenue share, the players will see fatter paychecks: The average salary is projected to increase from $8.5 million in 2016 to $10 million in the 2020–2021 season.

Source: Media reports of November–December 2016.

CRITICAL ANALYSIS: Labor unions bargain with management over a variety of employment conditions. Most issues, however, can be expressed in terms of their impact on wage costs.

THE POTENTIAL USE OF POWER

In a competitive labor market, each worker makes a labor supply decision on the basis of his or her own perceptions of the relative values of labor and leisure (Chapter 16). Whatever decision is made won't alter the market wage. One worker simply isn't that significant in a market composed of thousands. Once a market is unionized, however, these conditions no longer hold. A *union evaluates job offers on the basis of the collective interests of its members.* In particular, it must be concerned with the effects of increased employment on the wage rate paid to its members.

The Marginal Wage

Like all monopolists, unions have to worry about the downward slope of the demand curve. In the case of labor markets, a larger quantity of labor can be "sold" only at lower wage rates. Suppose the workers in a particular labor market confront the market labor demand schedule depicted in Figure 17.2. This schedule tells us that employers aren't willing to hire any workers at a wage rate of $6 per hour (row S) but will hire one worker per hour if the wage rate is $5 (row T). At still lower rates, the quantity of labor demanded increases; five workers per hour are demanded at a wage of $1 per hour.

An individual worker offered a wage of $1 an hour would have to decide whether such wages merited the sacrifice of an hour's leisure. But a union would evaluate the offer differently. A union must consider how the hiring of one more worker will affect the wages of all the workers.

FIGURE 17.2

The Marginal Wage

The *marginal wage* is the change in *total wages* (paid to all workers) associated with the employment of an additional worker. If the wage rate is $4 per hour, only two workers will be hired (point *U*). The wage rate must fall to $3 per hour if three workers are to be hired (point *V*). In the process, *total* wages paid rise from $8 ($4 × 2 workers) to $9 ($3 × 3 workers). The *marginal* wage of the third worker is only $1 (point *v*).

The graph illustrates the relationship of the marginal wage to labor demand. The marginal wage curve lies below the labor demand curve because the marginal wage is less than the nominal wage. Compare the marginal wage (point *v*) and the nominal wage (point *V*) of the third worker.

Table Summary: Table shows the Items and Data to Compute Total Wages Paid and lists Marginal Wage.

	Wage Rate (per Hour)	×	Number of Workers Demanded (per Hour)	=	Total Wages Paid (per Hour)	Marginal Wage (per Labor-Hour)
S	$6		0		$0	
T	5		1		5	$5
U	4		2		8	3
V	3		3		9	1
W	2		4		8	−1
X	1		5		5	−3

Total Wages Paid. Notice that when four workers are hired at a wage rate of $2 an hour (row *W*), *total* wages are $8 per hour. In order for a fifth worker to be employed, the wage rate must drop to $1 an hour (row *X*). At wages of $1 per hour, the *total* wages paid to the five workers amount to only $5 per hour. Thus, total wages paid to the workers actually *fall* when a fifth worker is employed. Collectively the workers would be better off sending only four people to work at the higher wage of $2 an hour and paying the fifth worker $1 an hour to stay home!

The basic mandate of a labor union is to evaluate wage and employment offers from this *collective* perspective. To do so, ***a union must distinguish the marginal wage from the market wage.*** The market wage is simply the current wage rate paid by the employer; it's the wage received by individual workers. The **marginal wage,** on the other hand, is the change in *total* wages paid (to all workers) when an additional worker is hired:

$$\text{Marginal wage} = \frac{\text{Change in total wages paid}}{\text{Change in quantity of labor employed}}$$

The distinction between marginal wages and market wages arises from the downward slope of the labor demand curve. It's analogous to the distinction we made between marginal revenue and price for monopolists in product markets. The distinction simply reflects the law of demand: If more workers are to be hired, wage rates must fall.

marginal wage: The change in total wages paid associated with a one-unit increase in the quantity of labor employed.

The impact of increased employment on marginal wages is also illustrated in Figure 17.2. According to the labor demand curve, one worker will be hired at a wage rate of $5 an hour (point *T*); two workers will be hired only if the market wage falls to $4 an hour (point *U*), at which point the first and second workers will each be getting $4 an hour. Thus, the increased wages of the second worker (from zero to $4) will be partially offset by the reduction in the wage rate paid to the first worker (from $5 to $4). *Total* wages paid will increase by only $3; this is the *marginal* wage (point *u*). The marginal wage actually becomes negative at some point, when the implied wage loss to workers already on the job begins to exceed the wage of a new hired worker.

The Union Wage Goal

A union never wants to accept a negative marginal wage, of course. At such a point, union members would be better off paying someone to stay home. ***The central question for the union is what level of (positive) marginal wage to accept.***

We can answer this question by looking at the labor supply curve. The labor supply curve tells us how much labor workers are *willing to supply* at various wage rates. Hence, the labor supply curve depicts the lowest wage *individual* union members would accept. If the union adopts a *collective* perspective on the welfare of its members, however, it will view the wage offer differently. From their collective perspective, the wage that union members are getting for additional labor is the *marginal* wage, not the nominal (market) wage. Hence, the marginal wage curve, not the labor demand curve, is decisive in the union's assessment of wage offers.

If the union wants to maximize the *total* welfare of its members, it will seek the level of employment that equates the marginal wage with the supply preferences of union members. In Figure 17.3, ***the intersection of the marginal wage curve with the labor supply curve identifies the desired level of employment for the union.*** This intersection occurs at point *u,* yielding total employment of two workers per hour.

The marginal wage at point *u* is $3. However, the union members will get paid an actual wage higher than that. Look up from point *u* on the marginal wage curve to point *U* on the employer's labor demand curve. Point *U* tells us that the employer is *willing to pay* a wage rate of $4 an hour to employ two workers. The union knows it can demand and get $4 an hour if it supplies only two workers to the firm.

What the union is doing here is choosing a point on the labor demand curve that the union regards as the optimal combination of wages and employment. In a competitive market, point *C* would represent the equilibrium combination of wages and employment. But the union forces employers to point *U,* thereby attaining a higher wage rate and reducing employment.

FIGURE 17.3
The Union Wage Objective

The intersection of the marginal wage and labor supply curves (point *u*) determines the union's desired employment. Employers are willing to pay a wage rate of $4 per hour for that many workers, as revealed by point *U* on the labor demand curve.

More workers (*H*) are willing to work at $4 per hour than employers demand (*U*). To maintain that wage rate, the union must exclude some workers from the market. In the absence of such power, wages would fall to the competitive equilibrium (point *C*).

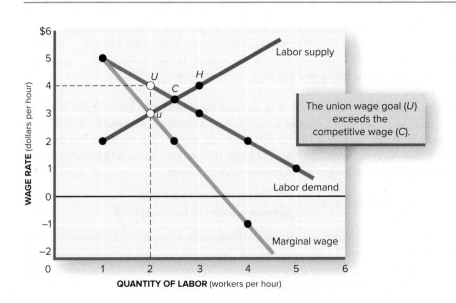

Exclusion

The union's ability to maintain a wage rate of $4 an hour depends on its ability to exclude some workers from the market. Figure 17.3 reveals that three workers are willing and able to work at the union wage of $4 an hour (point *H*), whereas only two are hired (point *U*). If the additional worker were to offer his services, the wage rate would be pushed down the labor demand curve (to $3 per hour). Hence, ***to maintain a noncompetitive wage, the union must be able to exercise some control over the labor supply decisions of individual workers.*** The essential force here is union solidarity. Once unionized, the individual workers must agree not to compete among themselves by offering their labor at nonunion wage rates. Instead, the workers must agree to withhold labor—to strike, if necessary—if wage rates are too low, and to supply labor only at the union-set wage.

Unions can solidify their control of the labor supply by establishing **union shops:** workplaces where workers must join the union within 30 days after being employed. In this way, the unions gain control of all the workers employed in a particular company or industry, thereby reducing the number of replacement workers available for employment during a strike. Stiff penalties (such as loss of seniority or pension rights) and general union solidarity ensure that only nonunion workers will "fink" or "scab"—take the job of a worker on strike.

> **union shop:** An employment setting in which all workers must join the union within 30 days after being employed.

Replacement Workers. Even union shops, however, are subject to potential competition from substitute labor. When the UAW struck Caterpillar in 1991, the company advertised nationally for replacement workers and set up a toll-free phone line for applicants. In the midst of a recession, the company got a huge response. The resulting flow of replacement workers crippled the UAW strike. Professional baseball players faced the same problem in 1995. When the continued strike threatened a second consecutive season, the team owners started hiring new players to replace the regulars. The huge supply of aspiring ball players forced the strikers to reconsider.

Replacement workers are even more abundant in agriculture. The United Farm Workers has been trying for decades to organize California's 20,000 strawberry pickers. But the workers know that thousands of additional workers will flock to California from Mexico if they protest wages and working conditions.

THE EXTENT OF UNION POWER

The first labor unions in America were organized in the 1780s, and the first worker protests as early as 1636. Union power wasn't a significant force in labor markets, however, until the 1900s, when heavily populated commercial centers and large-scale manufacturing became common. Only then did large numbers of workers begin to view their employment situations from a common perspective.

Early Growth

The period 1916–1920 was one of particularly fast growth for labor unions, largely because of the high demand for labor resulting from World War I. All these membership gains were lost, however, when the Great Depression threw millions of people out of work. By 1933 union membership had dwindled to the levels of 1915.

As the Depression lingered on, public attitudes and government policy changed. Too many people had learned the meaning of layoffs, wage cuts, and prolonged unemployment. In 1933 the National Industrial Recovery Act (NIRA) established the right of employees to bargain collectively with their employers. When the NIRA was declared unconstitutional by the Supreme Court in 1935, its labor provisions were incorporated into a new law, the Wagner Act. With this legislative encouragement, union membership doubled between 1933 and 1937. Unions continued to gain in strength as the production needs of World War II increased the demand for labor. Figure 17.4 reflects the tremendous spurt of union activity between the depths of the Depression and the height of World War II.

FIGURE 17.4
Changing Unionization Rates

Unions grew most rapidly during the decade 1935–1945. Since that time, the growth of unions hasn't kept pace with the growth of the U.S. labor force. Most employment growth has occurred in service industries that have traditionally been nonunion.

Source: U.S. Department of Labor.

unionization rate: The percentage of the labor force belonging to a union.

Union Power Today

Union membership stopped increasing in the 1950s, even though the labor force kept growing. As a result, the unionized percentage of the labor force—the **unionization rate**—has been in steady decline for more than 40 years. The current unionization rate of 10.3 percent is less than a third of its post–World War II peak and far below unionization rates in other industrialized nations (see World View "Union Membership").

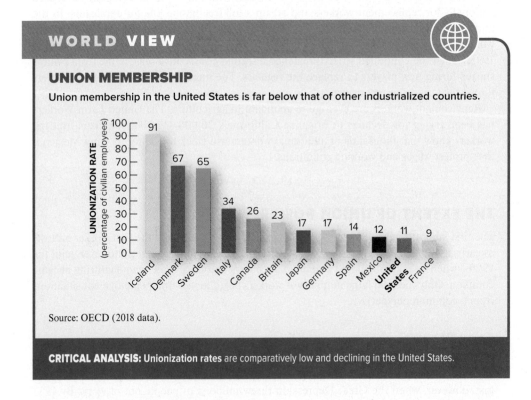

WORLD VIEW

UNION MEMBERSHIP

Union membership in the United States is far below that of other industrialized countries.

Source: OECD (2018 data).

CRITICAL ANALYSIS: Unionization rates are comparatively low and declining in the United States.

Private vs. Public Sector Trends. The decline in the *national* unionization rate conceals two very different trends. Union representation of *private* sector workers has plunged even more sharply than Figure 17.4 suggests. In the last 10 years, the unionization rate in the private sector has fallen from 11.5 percent to only 6.2 percent. At the same time, union membership has increased sharply among teachers, government workers, and nonprofit employees. As of 2020, more than 33 percent of workers on government payrolls were union members. This concentration of unions in the public sector is evident in Figure 17.5. The trend is clear: *The old industrial unions are being supplanted by unions of service workers, especially those employed in the public sector.* Unionization is highest among public schoolteachers, including college professors.

Percentage of workers in unions

FIGURE 17.5

Private vs. Public Unions

Unionization rates have declined sharply in private industry but risen in the public sector. Public sector union membership now exceeds private sector union membership.

Source: U.S. Bureau of Labor Statistics (2020 data).

Although industrial unions have been in general decline, they still possess significant pockets of market power. The Teamsters, the UAW, the United Mine Workers, the Union of Needletrades and Textile Employees, and the Food Workers all have substantial representation in their respective markets. Their strength in those specific markets, not national averages, determines their ability to alter market outcomes.

The AFL-CIO. One labor organization with a decidedly national focus is the AFL-CIO (the American Federation of Labor–Congress of Industrial Organizations). The AFL-CIO is not a separate union but a representational body of more than 50 national unions, representing 12 million workers. It doesn't represent or negotiate for any particular group of workers but focuses instead on issues of general labor interest. The AFL-CIO acts as an advocate for the labor movement and represents labor's interest in legislative areas. It's the primary vehicle for political action. In addition, the AFL-CIO may render economic assistance to member unions or to groups of workers who wish to organize.

Change to Win Coalition. The AFL-CIO's political activity upset member unions who favored more focus on traditional union interests, particularly union organizing. In September 2005, some of these unions (including teamsters, garment workers, food workers, and service workers) quit the AFL-CIO and formed a new multiunion organization, the Change to Win Coalition. By 2017 the coalition included three of the largest unions, representing more than 5 million workers.

EMPLOYER POWER

The power possessed by labor unions in various occupations and industries seldom exists in a power vacuum. Power exists on the demand side of labor markets, too. The United Auto Workers confront GM, Ford, and Chrysler; the Steelworkers confront U.S. Steel and AK Steel; the Teamsters confront the Truckers' Association; the Communications Workers confront AT&T; and so on. An imbalance of power often exists on one side of the market or the other (as with, say, the carpenters versus individual construction contractors). However, *labor markets with significant power on both sides are common.* To understand how wage rates and employment are determined in such markets, we have to assess the market power possessed by employers.

Monopsony

Power on the demand side of a market belongs to a *buyer* who can influence the market price of a good. With respect to labor markets, market power on the demand side implies the ability of a single employer to alter the market wage rate. The extreme case of such

monopsony: A market in which there's only one buyer.

power is a **monopsony,** a situation in which one employer is the only buyer in a particular market. The classic example of a monopsony is a company town—that is, a town that depends for its livelihood on the decisions of a single employer.

Graduate Assistants. Graduate teaching assistants have complained that the universities that employ them are much like company towns. Once they've started taking graduate classes at one university, it's difficult to transfer to another. As they see it, there is only one local labor market for graduate students. They complain that their monopsony employer compels them to work long hours at low wages. In 1998 University of California graduate students went out on strike to protest those conditions. In 1999 more than 10,000 of those graduate students affiliated with the United Auto Workers to gain more power. In November 2000 the National Labor Relations Board decreed that graduate research and teaching assistants are employees with the right to organize and strike.

Pro Athletes. Before 1976 professional sports teams also had monopsony power. Sports contracts prohibited pro players from moving from one team (employer) to another without permission. This gave individual team owners a lot of power to set wages and working conditions. That power was diluted when players got the right to be "free agents" and bargain with more than one team.

Buyer Concentration. There are many degrees of market power, and they can be defined in terms of *buyer concentration.* When buyers are many and of limited market power, the demand for resources is likely to be competitive. When only one buyer has access to a particular resource market, a monopsony exists. Between the two extremes lie the various degrees of imperfect competition, including the awkward-sounding but empirically important case of *oligopsony.* In an oligopsony, only a few firms account for most of the industry's employment.

This was pretty much the situation in Silicon Valley from 2005 to 2009 when Apple, Google, and a few other tech firms were the premier employers. They later admitted to colluding to prevent competitive bidding for programmers, systems engineers, and other tech workers. In other words, they were acting in unison to acquire monopsony powers in the hi-tech labor market (see Front Page Economics "Judge OKs $415 Million Settlement of 'No Poaching' Charges").

FRONT PAGE ECONOMICS

JUDGE OKS $415 MILLION SETTLEMENT OF "NO POACHING" CHARGES

San Jose, CA—Federal judge Lucy Koh yesterday approved a settlement of the five-year litigation that pitted Silicon Valley workers against their corporate employers. Lawyers claimed that some of the Valley's largest employers—Apple, Google, Intel, and Adobe Systems—conspired to suppress competition for engineers and other valued tech workers. They had, it was alleged, a "no poaching" agreement not to recruit workers from each other. The effect of that agreement was to curtail competitive bidding for Valley talent, thereby holding salaries in check. The four companies agreed to pay $415 million to settle the case, which works out to about $6,440 for each of the 64,446 claimants.

Source: Media reports, September 3, 2015.

CRITICAL ANALYSIS: When employers agree not to bid against each other for available workers, they are behaving as an **oligopsony,** attempting to hold wages below competitive levels.

The Potential Use of Power

Firms with power in labor markets generally have the same objective as all other firms—to maximize profits. What distinguishes them from competitive (powerless) firms is their ability to attain and keep economic profits. In labor markets, this means using fewer workers and paying them lower wages.

The distinguishing characteristic of labor market monopsonies is that their hiring decisions influence the market wage rate. In a competitive labor market, no single employer has any direct influence on the market wage rate; each firm can hire as much labor as it needs at the prevailing wage. But a monopsonist confronts the *market* labor supply curve. As a result, any increase in the quantity of labor demanded will force the monopsonist to climb up the labor supply curve in search of additional workers. In other words, *a monopsonist can hire additional workers only if it offers a higher wage rate.*

Marginal Factor Cost. Anytime the price of a resource (or product) changes as a result of a firm's purchases, a distinction between marginal cost and price must be made. Making this distinction is one of the little headaches—and potential sources of profit—of a monopsonist. For labor, we distinguish between the **marginal factor cost (MFC)** of labor and its wage rate.

Suppose that Figure 17.6 accurately describes the labor supply schedule confronting a monopsonist. It's evident that the monopsonist will have to pay a wage of at least $2 an hour if it wants any labor. But even at that wage rate (row *F* of the supply schedule), only one worker will be willing to work. If the firm wants more labor, it will have to offer higher wages.

Two things happen when the firm raises its wage offer to $3 an hour (row *G*). First, the quantity of labor supplied increases (to two workers per hour). Second, the total wages paid

marginal factor cost (MFC): The change in total costs that results from a one-unit increase in the quantity of a factor employed.

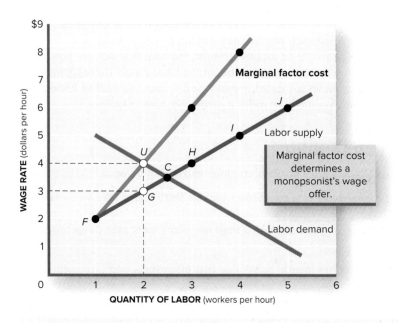

FIGURE 17.6
Marginal Factor Cost

More workers can be attracted only if the wage rate is increased. As it rises, all workers must be paid the higher wage. Consequently, the change in *total* wage costs exceeds the actual wage paid to the last worker. In the table, notice that in row *I,* for example, the marginal factor cost of the fourth worker ($8) exceeds the wage actually paid to that worker ($5). Thus, the marginal factor cost curve lies above the labor supply curve.

In the graph, the intersection of the marginal factor cost and labor demand curves (point *U*) indicates the quantity of labor a monopsonist will want to hire. The labor supply curve (at point *G*) indicates the wage rate that must be paid to attract the desired number of workers. This is the monopsonist's desired wage ($3). In the absence of market power, an employer would end up at point *C* (the competitive equilibrium), paying a higher wage and employing more workers.

Table Summary: Table shows the Items and Data to Compute Total Wage Cost and lists Marginal Factor Cost.

	Wage Rate (per Hour)	×	Quantity of Labor Supplied (Workers per Hour)	=	Total Wage Cost (per Hour)	Marginal Factor Cost (per Labor-Hour)
E	1		0		0	—
F	2		1		2	2
G	3		2		6	4
H	4		3		12	6
I	5		4		20	8
J	6		5		30	10

rise by $4. This *marginal* cost of labor is attributable to the fact that the first worker's wages also rise when the wage rate is increased to attract additional workers. If all the workers perform the same job, the first worker will demand to be paid the new (higher) wage rate. **Thus, the marginal factor cost exceeds the wage rate because additional workers can be hired only if the wage rate for all workers is increased.**

The Monopsony Firm's Goal. The marginal factor cost curve confronting this monopsonist is shown in the upper half of Figure 17.6. It starts at the bottom of the labor supply curve and rises above it. The monopsonist must now decide how many workers to hire, given the impact of its hiring decision on the market wage rate.

Remember from Chapter 16 that the labor demand curve is a reflection of labor's **marginal revenue product (MRP)**—that is, the increase in total revenue attributable to the employment of one additional worker.

As we've emphasized, the profit-maximizing producer always seeks to equalize marginal revenue and marginal cost. Accordingly, the monopsonistic employer will seek to hire the amount of labor at which the marginal revenue product of labor equals its marginal factor cost:

$$\text{Profit-maximizing level of input use}: \quad \substack{\text{Marginal revenue} \\ \text{product of input} \\ \text{(MRP)}} = \substack{\text{Marginal factor} \\ \text{cost of input} \\ \text{(MFC)}}$$

In Figure 17.6, this objective is illustrated by the intersection of the marginal factor cost and labor demand curves at point *U*.

At point *U* the monopsonist is *willing to hire* two workers per hour at a wage rate of $4. But the firm doesn't have to pay this much. The labor supply curve informs us that two workers are *willing to work* for only $3 an hour. Hence, the firm first decides how many workers it wants to hire (at point *U*) and then looks at the labor supply curve (point *G*) to see what it has to pay them. As we suspected, *a monopsonistic employer ends up hiring fewer workers at a lower wage rate than would prevail in a competitive market* (point *C*).

COLLECTIVE BARGAINING

The potential for conflict between a powerful employer and a labor union should be evident:

- *The objective of a labor union is to establish a wage rate that's* **higher** *than the competitive wage* (Figure 17.3).
- *A monopsonist employer seeks to establish a wage rate that's* **lower** *than competitive standards* (Figure 17.6).

The resultant clash generates intense bargaining that often spills over into politics, the courts, and open conflict.

The confrontation of power on both sides of the labor market is a situation referred to as **bilateral monopoly.** In such a market, wages and employment aren't determined simply by supply and demand. Rather, economic outcomes must be determined by **collective bargaining**— that is, direct negotiations between employers and labor unions for the purpose of determining wages, employment, working conditions, and related issues.

Possible Agreements

In a typical labor–business confrontation, the two sides begin by stating their preferences for equilibrium wages and employment. The *demands* laid down by the union are likely to revolve around point *U* in Figure 17.7; the *offer* enunciated by management is likely to be at point *G*.[1] Thus the boundaries of a potential settlement—a negotiated final equilibrium—are

marginal revenue product (MRP): The change in total revenue associated with one additional unit of input.

bilateral monopoly: A market with only one buyer (a monopsonist) and one seller (a monopolist).

collective bargaining: Direct negotiations between employers and unions to determine labor market outcomes.

---

[1] Even though points *U* and *G* may not be identical to the initial bargaining positions, they represent the positions of maximum attainable benefit for both sides. Points outside the demand or supply curve will be rejected out of hand by one side or the other.

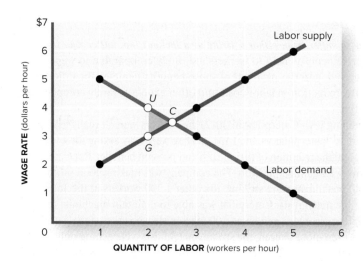

FIGURE 17.7
The Boundaries of Collective Bargaining

Firms with power in the labor market seek to establish wages and employment levels corresponding to point *G* (from Figure 17.6). Unions, on the other hand, seek to establish an equilibrium at point *U* (from Figure 17.3). The competitive equilibrium is at point *C*. The function of collective bargaining is to identify a compromise between these points—that is, to locate an equilibrium somewhere in the shaded area.

usually established at the outset of collective bargaining. Front Page Economics "Caterpillar vs. the IAM" summarizes the points of contention in the 2012 dispute between Caterpillar and the International Association of Machinists.

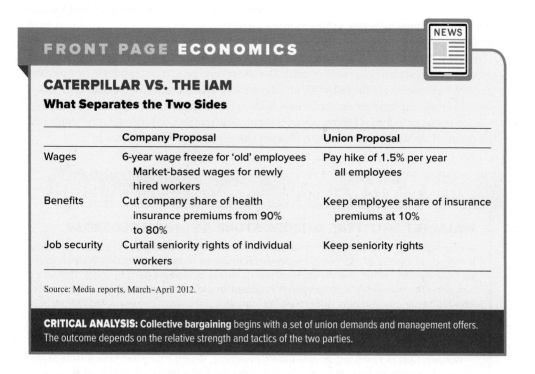

FRONT PAGE ECONOMICS

CATERPILLAR VS. THE IAM
What Separates the Two Sides

	Company Proposal	Union Proposal
Wages	6-year wage freeze for 'old' employees Market-based wages for newly hired workers	Pay hike of 1.5% per year all employees
Benefits	Cut company share of health insurance premiums from 90% to 80%	Keep employee share of insurance premiums at 10%
Job security	Curtail seniority rights of individual workers	Keep seniority rights

Source: Media reports, March–April 2012.

CRITICAL ANALYSIS: Collective bargaining begins with a set of union demands and management offers. The outcome depends on the relative strength and tactics of the two parties.

The interesting part of collective bargaining isn't the initial bargaining positions but the negotiation of the final settlement. The speed with which a settlement is reached and the terms of the resulting compromise depend on the patience, tactics, and resources of the negotiating parties. ***The fundamental source of negotiating power for either side is its ability to withhold labor or jobs.*** The union can threaten to strike, thereby cutting off the flow of union labor to the employer. The employer can impose a lockout, thereby cutting off jobs and paychecks. The effectiveness of those threats depends on the availability of substitute workers or jobs.

The Pressure to Settle

Labor and management both suffer from either a strike or a lockout, no matter who initiates the work stoppage. The strike benefits paid to workers are rarely comparable to wages they would otherwise have received, and the payment of those benefits depletes the union treasury. By the same token, the reduction in labor costs and other expenses rarely compensates the employer for lost profits.

In the machinists' bargaining with Caterpillar in 2012, the workers weren't really asking for much (Front Page Economics "Caterpillar vs. the IAM"). They were only asking for a wage increase of 1.5 percent a year and the retention of their health and pension benefits. But Caterpillar was in an exceptionally strong bargaining position. The company was making good profits and sales were strong. Only 780 machinists were striking; the other 1,200 workers at the Joliet, Illinois, plant weren't joining the machinists. Caterpillar was able to maintain machinist production with supervisors, temporary workers, and about 100 machinists who crossed the picket line to work. To make the battle even more uneven, the striking machinists were getting only $150 a week in strike benefits from their union. They couldn't hold out for long. After three and a half months, the machinists capitulated. They returned to work on the terms Caterpillar set.

Collective bargaining isn't always so favorable to the employer. In 1998 the balance of power was reversed. Car sales were brisk, and inventories were lean. So when the UAW struck a key parts plant in June 1998, GM was under greater pressure to settle. Rather than continuing to lose more than $100 million a day in lost sales, GM relented after 54 days, accepting little more than a UAW promise not to strike again for a year and a half.

Collective bargaining isn't always so lopsided. In 2016 pro basketball teams were enjoying huge and growing revenues. Both the owners and the players recognized that a strike would be foolish. So they were very willing to make a deal that made both sides richer (Front Page Economics "NBA and Players Strike a Deal").

Hockey players weren't so fortunate. Bargaining between the players and the National Hockey League stalled completely in 2012. The owners expressed their frustration by canceling the first three months of the 2012–2013 hockey season. That lockout cost the players $1 *billion* in lost pay and the team owners more than $200 million. Walmart used an extreme version of the lockout tactic to fend off union power: It simply shuttered its Canadian store and eliminated all the jobs (see World View "Walmart Shutters Quebec Store as Union Closes In").

WORLD VIEW

WALMART SHUTTERS QUEBEC STORE AS UNION CLOSES IN

Walmart decided to close its store in Jonquiere, Quebec, rather than give in to union demands. A majority of the store's 145 hourly employees had signed union cards, forcing Walmart to enter into negotiations with the United Food and Commercial Workers (UFCW) union. That was a turn of events Walmart was not prepared to accept. In preliminary negotiations, the union demanded better pay and new work rules. Walmart said the union's demands would force it to hire 30 more workers, which wasn't economically feasible. So Walmart, with a history of fending off unions, decided to close the Jonquiere store. Had the UFCW succeeded in unionizing that store, it would have been the first unionized Walmart in North America.

Walmart CEO H. Lee Scott Jr. defended his decision, saying, "You can't take a store that is a struggling store anyway and add a bunch of people and a bunch of work rules that cause you to even be in worse shape." The Canadian director of UFCW responded that "Walmart is trying to send a message to the rest of their employees that if they join a union the same thing could happen to them. . . ."

Source: News reports, February 9–12, 2005.

CRITICAL ANALYSIS: The power to lock out workers is the ultimate source of employer power in **collective bargaining**. Walmart chose an extreme use of that power.

Sometimes, third parties are critical to pushing for a settlement. In October 2016 the professors at 14 Pennsylvania colleges went on strike. They had been working for more than a year without a contract and wanted the state to come to terms. The state demanded 249 changes in the work rules and pay of the professors. But the faculty resisted the changes and wanted higher wages. On October 14, 2016, they went on strike, canceling classes for more than 100,000 students. The families of the students besieged the governor, who in turn pushed for a settlement. After a three-day strike, the professors and the state settled their differences.

During the 2019 United Auto Workers strike against General Motors, 60,000 other workers lost jobs or hours in the companies that supply GM with parts and services. Restaurants, bars, and other local businesses near GM's 33 plants also suffered losses. Claims for unemployment and welfare benefits increased the fiscal burden on local and state governments as well. All these third parties encouraged the UAW and GM to settle their longest-running nationwide strike in over 50 years (see Front Page Economics "GM Strike Ends").

FRONT PAGE ECONOMICS

GM STRIKE ENDS

The United Auto Workers have voted to end their strike against General Motors. The strike by GM's 48,000 workers was the longest nationwide strike against the automaker in more than 50 years. The key issues were job security and pay. GM promised to invest $7.7 billion in new plants and improvements to its remaining 30 plants, in return for the right to close 3 older plants. UAW members got an $11,000 signing bonus and later a 4% lump-sum bonus and a 3% wage increase. Temporary workers also got a faster path to permanent jobs.

The pressure to settle was intense on both sides. Workers were getting only $275 a week in strike pay, way below their average $630–$1,200 paychecks. And GM lost close to $3 billion in sales, while its parts suppliers laid off or cut hours for another 60,000 workers. As one UAW worker noted, "people were desperate for money."

Source: Media reports of October 25–28, 2019.

CRITICAL ANALYSIS: Strikes and lockouts cause losses for both an employer and its workers. Those losses increase the pressure to settle a **collective bargaining** agreement.

Because potential income losses are usually high, both labor and management try to avoid a strike or lockout if they can. In fact, *more than 90 percent of the 20,000 collective bargaining agreements negotiated each year are concluded without recourse to a strike,* and often without even the explicit threat of one.

The Final Settlement

The built-in pressures for settlement help resolve collective bargaining. They don't tell us, however, what the dimensions of that final settlement will be. All we know is that the settlement will be located within the boundaries established in Figure 17.7. The relative pressures on each side will determine whether the final equilibrium is closer to the union or the management position.

The final settlement almost always necessitates hard choices on both sides. The union usually has to choose between an increase in job security and higher pay. A union must also consider how management will react in the long run to higher wages, perhaps by introducing new technology that reduces its dependence on labor. The employer has to worry whether productivity will suffer if workers are dissatisfied with their pay package.

THE IMPACT OF UNIONS

We know that unions tend to raise wage rates in individual companies, industries, and occupations. But can we be equally sure that unions have raised wages in general? If the UAW is successful in raising wages in the automobile industry, what, if anything, happens to car prices? If car prices rise in step with UAW wage rates, labor and management in the auto industry will get proportionally larger slices of the economic pie. At the same time, workers in other industries will be burdened with higher car prices.

Relative Wages

One measure of union impact is *relative* wages—the wages of union members in comparison with those of nonunion workers. As we've noted, unions seek to control the supply of labor in a particular industry or occupation. This forces the excluded workers to seek work elsewhere. As a result of this labor supply imbalance, wages tend to be higher in unionized industries than in nonunionized industries. Figure 17.8 illustrates this displacement effect.

Although the theoretical impact of union exclusionism on relative wages is clear, empirical estimates of that impact are fairly rare. We do know that union wages in general are significantly higher than nonunion wages ($1,095 versus $892 per week in 2019). But part of this differential is due to the fact that unions are more common in industries that have always been more capital-intensive and paid relatively high wages. When comparisons are made within particular industries or sectors, the differential narrows considerably. Nevertheless, there's a general consensus that unions have managed to increase their relative wages by 15 to 20 percent.

Labor's Share of Total Income

Even though unions have been successful in redistributing some income from nonunion to union workers, the question still remains whether they've increased labor's share of *total*

(a) Unionized labor market

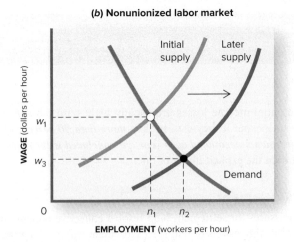

(b) Nonunionized labor market

FIGURE 17.8

The Effect of Unions on Relative Wages

In the absence of unions, the average wage rate would be equal to w_1. As unions take control of the market, however, they seek to raise wage rates to w_2, in the process reducing the amount of employment in that market from l_1 to l_2. The workers displaced from the unionized market will seek work in the nonunionized market, thereby shifting the nonunion supply curve to the right. The result will be a reduction of wage rates (to w_3) in the nonunionized market. Thus, union wages end up higher than nonunion wages.

income. The *labor share* of total income is the proportion of income received by all workers, in contrast to the share of income received by owners of capital (the *capital share*). The labor share of total income will rise only if the gains to union workers exceed the losses to the (excluded) nonunion workers.

Evidence of unions' impact on labor's share is almost as difficult to assemble as evidence on relative wages, and for much the same reasons. Labor's share of national income has risen dramatically, from only 56 percent in 1919 to 75 percent today. But there have been tremendous changes in the mix of output during that same period. The proportion of output composed of personal services (accountants, teachers, electricians) is much larger now than it was in 1919. The labor share of income derived from personal services is and always was close to 100 percent. Accordingly, ***most of the rise in labor's share of total income is due to changes in the structure of the economy rather than to unionization.***

Prices

One way firms can protect their profits in the face of rising union wages is to raise product prices. If firms raise prices along with union wages, consumers end up footing the bill. In that case, profits and the capital share of total income might not be reduced.

The ability of firms to pass along increased union wages depends on the structure of product markets as well as labor markets. If a firm has power in both markets, it's better able to protect itself in this way. There's little evidence, however, that unions have contributed significantly to general cost-push inflation.

Productivity

Unions also affect prices indirectly via changes in **productivity.** Unions bargain not only for wages but also for work rules that specify how goods should be produced. Work rules may limit the pace of production, restrict the type of jobs a particular individual can perform, or require a minimum number of workers to accomplish a certain task. A factory carpenter, for example, may not be permitted to change a lightbulb that burns out in his shop area. And the electrician who is summoned may be required to have an apprentice on all work assignments. Such restrictive work rules would make it very costly to change a burned-out lightbulb.

productivity: Output per unit of input—for example, output per labor-hour.

Not all work rules are so restrictive. In general, however, work rules are designed to protect jobs and maximize the level of employment at any given rate of output. From this perspective, work rules directly restrain productivity and thus inflate costs and prices.

Work rules may also have some beneficial effects. The added job security provided by work rules and seniority provisions tends to reduce labor turnover (quitting) and thus saves recruitment and training costs. Protective rules may also make workers more willing to learn new tasks and to train others in specific skills. Richard Freeman of Harvard asserts that unions have actually accelerated advances in productivity and economic growth.

Political Impact

Perhaps more important than any of these specific union effects is the general impact the union movement has had on our economic, social, and political institutions. Unions are a major political force in the United States. They've not only provided critical electoral and financial support for selected political candidates, but they've also fought hard for important legislation. Unions have succeeded in establishing minimum wage laws, work and safety rules, and retirement benefits. They've also actively lobbied for civil rights legislation and health and education programs. Whatever one may think of any particular union or specific union action, it's clear that our institutions and national welfare would be very different in their absence.

DECISIONS FOR TOMORROW

Will Unions Survive?

Unions have been in retreat for nearly a generation. As shown in Figure 17.4, the unionized share of the labor force has fallen from 35 percent in 1950 to less than 11 percent today. Even that modest share has been maintained only by the spread of unionism among public schoolteachers and other government employees. In the private sector, the unionization rate is less than 7 percent and still declining. The Teamsters, the Auto Workers, and the Steelworkers have lost more than 1 million members in the last 15 years.

The decline in unionization is explained by three phenomena. Most important is the relative decline in manufacturing, coupled with rapid growth in high-tech service industries (like computer software, accounting, and medical technology). The second force is the downsizing of major corporations and the relatively faster growth of smaller companies. These structural changes have combined to shrink the traditional employment base of labor unions.

The third cause of shrinking unionization is increased global competition. The decline of worldwide trade and investment barriers has made it easier for firms to import products from low-wage nations and even to relocate production plants. With more options, firms can more easily resist increased wage demands.

The labor union movement is fully aware of these forces and determined to resist them. To increase their power, unions are merging across craft and industry lines. In 1995 the Rubber Workers merged with the Steelworkers, the two major textile unions combined forces, and the Food Workers and Retail Clerks formed a new union. In 1999 the Grain Millers merged with the Paperworkers Union. By merging, the unions hope to increase representation, gain financial strength, and enhance their political clout. They're also seeking to broaden their appeal by organizing low-wage workers in the service industries. These efforts, together with their political strength, will help unions to play a continuing role in the economy, even if their share of total employment continues to shrink.

SUMMARY

- Power in labor markets is the ability to alter market wage rates. Such power is most evident in local labor markets defined by geographical, occupational, or industrial boundaries. **LO17-1**
- Power on the supply side of labor markets is manifested by unions, organized along industry or craft lines. The basic function of a union is to evaluate employment offers in terms of the *collective* interest of its members. **LO17-1**
- The downward slope of the labor demand curve creates a distinction between the marginal wage and the market wage. The marginal wage is the change in *total* wages occasioned by employment of one additional worker and is less than the market wage. **LO17-1**
- Unions seek to establish that rate of employment at which the marginal wage curve intersects the labor supply curve. The desired union wage is then found on the labor demand curve at that level of employment. **LO17-1**
- Power on the demand side of labor markets is manifested in buyer concentrations such as monopsony and oligopsony. Such power is usually found among the same firms that exercise market power in product markets. **LO17-2**

- By definition, power on the demand side implies some direct influence on market wage rates; additional hiring by a monopsonist will force up the market wage rate. Hence, a monopsonist must recognize a distinction between the marginal factor cost of labor and its (lower) market wage rate. **LO17-2**
- The goal of a monopsonistic employer is to hire the number of workers at which the marginal factor cost of labor equals its marginal revenue product. The employer then looks at the labor supply curve to determine the wage rate that must be paid for that number of workers. **LO17-2**
- The desire of unions to establish a wage rate that's higher than competitive wages directly opposes the desire of powerful employers to establish lower wage rates. In bilateral monopolies, unions and employers engage in collective bargaining to negotiate a final settlement. **LO17-2**
- The impact of unions on the economy is difficult to measure. It appears, however, that they've increased their own relative wages and contributed to rising prices. They've also had substantial political impact. **LO17-3**

Key Terms

labor supply
demand for labor
equilibrium wage
market power
marginal wage

union shop
unionization rate
monopsony
marginal factor cost (MFC)
marginal revenue product (MRP)

bilateral monopoly
collective bargaining
productivity

Questions for Discussion

1. Collective bargaining sessions often start with unreasonable demands and categorical rejections. Why do unions and employers tend to begin bargaining from extreme positions? **LO17-2**

2. Does a strike for a raise of 5 cents an hour make any sense? What kinds of long-term benefits might a union gain from such a strike? **LO17-1**

3. Why do some college professors join a union? What are the advantages or disadvantages of campus unionization? **LO17-1**

4. Are large and powerful firms easier targets for union organization than small firms? Why or why not? **LO17-1**

5. Nonunionized firms tend to offer wage rates that are close to rates paid by unionized firms in the same industry. How do you explain this? **LO17-3**

6. Why are farmworkers much less successful than airplane machinists in securing higher wages? **LO17-2**

7. In 1998 teaching assistants at the University of California struck for higher wages and union recognition, something they had sought for 14 years. How might the availability of replacement workers have affected their power? **LO17-2**

8. Why did the NBA players avert a strike (Front Page Economics "NBA and Players Strike a Deal" and Collective Bargaining Section)? **LO17-2**

9. Why did Walmart choose to close its store rather than hire 30 more workers (World View "Walmart Shutters Quebec Store as Union Closes In")? **LO17-2**

10. Why do pro basketball players want team owners to limit roster size to 40 players (Front Page Economics "NBA and Players Strike a Deal")? Why would owners like larger rosters? **LO17-1**

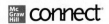
LO17-1   1. Complete the following table:

Wage rate	$14	$13	$12	$11	$10	$9	$8	$7
Quantity of labor demanded	0	5	20	50	75	95	110	120
Marginal wage		——	——	——	——	——	——	——

(a) What is the marginal wage when the nominal wage is $11?

(b) At what wage rate does the marginal wage first become negative?

LO17-1   2. Complete the following table:

Wage rate	$6	$7	$8	$9	$10	$11	$12
Quantity of labor supplied	80	120	155	180	200	210	215
Marginal factor cost		——	——	——	——	——	——

LO17-2   3. Based on the data in Problems 1 and 2 above,

(a) What is the competitive wage rate?

(b) Approximately what wage will the union seek?

(c) How many workers will the union have to exclude in order to get that wage?

LO17-2   4. At the time of the National Football League strike in 1987, the football owners made available the following data:

	Total Team Revenues and Costs	
Source of Revenue or Cost	Before the Strike	During the Strike
Television	$973,000	$973,000
Stadium gate	526,000	126,000
Luxury box seats	255,000	200,000
Concessions	60,000	12,000
Radio	40,000	40,000
Players' salaries and costs	854,000	230,000
Nonplayer costs (coaches' salaries)	200,000	200,000

(a) Compute total revenue, total expense, and profit both before and during the strike.

	Before Strike	During Strike
Total revenue	_____	_____
Total expense	_____	_____
Total profit	_____	_____

(b) Who was better positioned to endure the strike: NFL owners or the players?

LO17-2   5. Suppose the following supply and demand schedules apply in a particular labor market:

Wage rate (per hour)	$4	$5	$6	$7	$8	$9	$10
Quantity of labor supplied (workers per hour)	2	3	4	5	6	7	8
Quantity of labor demanded (workers per hour)	6	5	4	3	2	1	0

Graph the relevant curves and identify the
(*a*) Competitive wage rate.
(*b*) Union wage rate.
(*c*) Monopsonist's wage rate.

LO17-3 6. The graphs show unionized and nonunionized labor markets.
(*a*) Identify a likely wage and employment outcome when the market becomes unionized on the unionized labor market graph.
(*b*) Show the impact of this unionization on the nonunionized labor market.

(*a*) Unionized labor market

(*b*) Nonunionized labor market

LO17-2 7. In the Silicon Valley hiring-conspiracy case (Front Page Economics "Judge OKs $415 Million Settlement of 'No Poaching' Charges"), attorneys for the 64,446 plaintiffs asked for $3 billion in damages.
(*a*) How much did this work out per worker?
(*b*) How much did the judge approve (per worker)?

LO17-2 8. In the 2012 Machinists'-Caterpillar confrontation, the workers' average pay was $26 per hour. If their demand for a 1.5 percent pay hike per year had been granted, what would their hourly wage have been
(*a*) In the following year?
(*b*) Three years later?
Suppose instead that Caterpillar offered the machinists a one-time bonus of $5,000 if they didn't strike. Assuming the machinists worked an average of 2,000 hours per year, was this one-time bonus more or less than the wage demand the union made for
(*c*) The first year?
(*d*) The first three years?

LO17-2 9. *Decisions for Tomorrow:* Identify if the following would likely strengthen or weaken a union membership in the United States.
(*a*) Increase in manufacturing.
(*b*) Faster growth of small companies.
(*c*) Increased global competition.

Design Credit: Shutterstock

Steve Allen/Brand X Pictures/Getty Images

LEARNING OBJECTIVES

After reading this chapter, you should know

LO18-1 How present discounted values are computed.

LO18-2 The difference between stocks and bonds.

LO18-3 Key financial parameters for stocks and bonds.

LO18-4 How risks and rewards are reflected in current values.

CHAPTER 18

Financial Markets

Christopher Columbus had a crazy entrepreneurial idea. He was certain he could find a new route to the Indies by sailing not east from Europe but west—around the world. Such a route, he surmised, would give Europe quicker access to the riches of the East Indies. Whoever discovered that western route could become very, very rich.

To find that route, Columbus needed ships, sailors, and tons of provisions. He couldn't afford to supply these resources himself. He needed financial backers who would put up the money. For several years he tried to convince King Ferdinand of Spain to provide the necessary funds. But the king didn't want to risk so much wealth on a single venture. Twice he turned Columbus down.

Fortunately, Genoese merchant bankers in Seville came to Columbus's rescue. Convinced that Columbus's "enterprise of the Indies" might bring back "pearls, precious stones, gold, silver, spiceries," and other valuable merchandise, they guaranteed repayment of any funds lent to Columbus. With that guarantee in hand, the Duke of Medina Sidonia, in April 1492, offered to lend 1,000 maravedis (about $5,000 in today's dollars) to Queen Isabella for the purpose of funding Columbus's expedition. With no personal financial risk, King Ferdinand then granted Columbus the funds and authority for a royal expedition.

Columbus's experience in raising funds for his expedition illustrates a critical function of financial markets—namely, the management of *risk*. This chapter examines how financial markets facilitate economic activities (like Columbus's expedition) by managing the risks of failure. Three central questions guide the discussion:

- **What is traded in financial markets?**
- **How do the financial markets affect the economic outcomes of WHAT, HOW, and FOR WHOM?**
- **Why do financial markets fluctuate so much?**

THE ROLE OF FINANCIAL MARKETS

A central question for every economy is WHAT to produce. In 1492 all available resources were employed in farming, fishing, food distribution, metalworking, and other basic services. For Columbus to pursue his quest, he needed some of those resources. To get them, he needed money to bid scarce resources from other pursuits and employ them on his expedition.

Financial Intermediaries

Entrepreneurs who don't have great personal wealth must get start-up funds from other people. There are two possibilities: either *borrow* the money or invite other people to *invest* in the new venture.

How might you pursue these options? You could ask your relatives for a loan or go door to door in your neighborhood seeking investors. But such direct fund-raising is costly, inefficient, and often unproductive. Columbus went hat in hand to the Spanish royal court twice, but each time he came back empty-handed.

The task of raising start-up funds is made much easier by the existence of **financial intermediaries**—institutions that steer the flow of savings to cash-strapped entrepreneurs and other investors. Funds flow into banks, pension funds, bond markets, stock markets, and other financial intermediaries from businesses, households, and government entities that have some unspent income. This pool of national savings is then passed on to entrepreneurs, expanding businesses, and other borrowers by these same institutions (see Figure 18.1).

Financial intermediaries provide several important services. They greatly reduce the cost of locating loanable funds. Their pool of savings offers a clear economy of scale compared to the alternative of door-to-door solicitations. They also reduce the cost to savers of finding suitable lending or investment opportunities. Few individuals have the time, resources, or interest to do the searching on their own. With huge pools of amassed savings, however, financial intermediaries have the incentive to acquire and analyze information about lending and investment opportunities. Hence, *financial intermediaries reduce search and information costs* in the financial markets. In so doing, they make the allocation of resources more efficient.

Crowdfunding. Financial intermediaries come in many shapes and sizes. They are not all banks or brick-and-mortar institutions. The Internet has made door-to-door solicitations a thing of the past. Now people can disseminate their entrepreneurial ideas on a crowdfunding platform like GoFundMe, Kickstarter, or Indiegogo and hope that others like the idea enough to contribute some financing. Although **crowdfunding** has become a popular, inexpensive, and efficient method of raising start-up financing, it accounts for a tiny percentage of the funds raised by more traditional intermediaries (see Front Page Economics "Where Do Start-Ups Get Their Money?" later in the chapter).

financial intermediary: Institution (e.g., a bank or the stock market) that makes savings available to dissavers (e.g., investors).

crowdfunding: An internet-based method of raising funds from a large number of people.

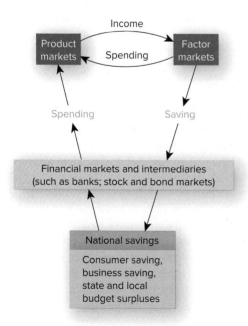

FIGURE 18.1
Mobilizing Savings

The central economic function of financial markets is to channel national savings into new investment and other desired expenditure. Financial intermediaries such as banks, insurance companies, and stockbrokers help transfer purchasing power from savers to spenders.

Although financial intermediaries make the job of acquiring start-up funds a lot easier, there's no guarantee that the funds needed will be acquired. First, there must be an adequate supply of funds available. Second, financial intermediaries must be convinced that they should allocate some of those funds to a project.

The Supply of Loanable Funds

As noted, the supply of loanable funds originates in the decisions of market participants to not spend all their current income. Those saving decisions are influenced by time preferences and interest rates.

Time Preferences. In deciding to *save* rather than *spend,* people effectively reallocate their spending over time. That is, people save *now* in order to spend more *later.* How much to save, then, depends partly on *time preference.* If a person doesn't give any thought to the future, she's likely to save little. If, by contrast, a person wants to buy a car, a vacation, or a house in the future, she's more inclined to save some income now.

Interest Rates. Interest rates also affect saving decisions. If interest rates are high, the future payoff to every dollar saved is greater. A higher return on savings translates into more future income for every dollar of current income saved. Hence, *higher interest rates increase the quantity of available savings (loanable funds).*

Risk. In early 2009, banks in Zimbabwe were offering interest rates on savings accounts of more than 100,000 percent a year. Yet few people rushed to deposit their savings in Zimbabwean banks. Inflation was running at a rate of 230 *million* percent a year, making a 100,000 percent return look pitifully small. Further, people worried that political instability in Zimbabwe might cause the banks to fail, wiping out their savings in the process. In other words, there was a high *risk* attached to those phenomenal interest rates.

Anyone who contemplated lending funds to Columbus confronted a similar risk: The potential payoff was huge, but so was the risk. That was the dilemma King Ferdinand confronted. He had enough funds to finance Columbus's expedition, but he didn't want to risk losing so much on a single venture.

Risk Management. This is why the Genoese bankers were so critical: These financial intermediaries could spread the risk of failure among many individuals. Each investor could put up just a fraction of the needed funds. No one had to put all his eggs in one basket. Once the consortium of bankers agreed to share the risks of Columbus's expedition, the venture had wings. The Genoese merchant bankers could afford to take portions of the expedition's risks because they also financed many less-risky projects. By diversifying their portfolios, they could attain whatever degree of *average* risk they preferred. That is the essence of risk management.

risk premium: The difference in rates of return on risky (uncertain) and safe (certain) investments.

Risk Premiums. Even though diversification permits greater risk management, lenders will want to be compensated for any above-average risks they take. Money lent to local merchants must have seemed a lot less risky than lending funds to Columbus. Thus, no one would have stepped forward to finance Columbus unless promised an *above-average* return upon the expedition's success. The difference between the rates of return on a safe (certain) investment and a risky (uncertain) one is called the **risk premium.** Risk premiums compensate people who finance risky ventures that succeed. Because these ventures are risky, however, investors often lose their money in such ventures too.

Risk premiums help explain why blue-chip corporations such as Microsoft can borrow money from a bank at the low "prime" rate while ordinary consumers have to pay much higher interest rates on personal loans. Corporate loans are less risky because corporations typically have plenty of revenue and assets to cover their debts. Consumers often get overextended, however, and can't pay all their bills. As a result, there's a greater risk that consumers' loans won't be paid back. Banks charge higher interest rates on consumer loans to compensate for this risk.

THE PRESENT VALUE OF FUTURE PROFITS

In deciding whether to assume the *risk* of supplying funds to a new venture, financial intermediaries assess the potential *rewards*. In Columbus's case, the rewards were the fabled treasures of the East Indies. Even if he found those treasures, however, the rewards would only come long after the expedition was financed. When Columbus proposed his East Indies expedition, he envisioned a round trip that would last at least six months. If he located the treasures he sought, he planned subsequent trips to acquire and transport his precious cargoes back home. Although King Ferdinand granted Columbus only one-tenth of any profits from the first expedition, Columbus had a claim on one-eighth of the profits of any subsequent voyages. Hence, even if Columbus succeeded in finding a shortcut to the East, he wouldn't generate any substantial profit for perhaps two years or more. That's a long time to wait.

Suppose for the moment that Columbus expected no profit from the first expedition but a profit of $1,000 at the end of two years from a second voyage. How much was that *future* profit worth to Columbus in 1492?

The success of Columbus's voyage was highly uncertain.

Library of Congress, Prints and Photographs Division (LC-USZ62-105062)

Time Value of Money

To assess the present value of *future* receipts, we have to consider the *time value* of money. A dollar received today is worth more than a dollar received two years from today. Why? Because a dollar received today can earn *interest*. If you have a dollar today and put it in an interest-bearing account, in two years you'll have your original dollar *plus* accumulated interest. *As long as interest-earning opportunities exist, present dollars are worth more than future dollars.*

In 1492 there were plenty of opportunities to earn interest. Indeed, the Genoese bankers were charging high interest rates on their loans and guarantees. If Columbus had had the cash, he too could have lent money to others and earned interest on his funds.

To calculate the present value of future dollars, this forgone interest must be taken into account. This computation is essentially interest accrual in reverse. *We "discount" future dollars by the opportunity cost of money*–that is, the market rate of interest.

Suppose the market rate of interest in 1492 was 10 percent. To compute the **present discounted value (PDV)** of future payment, we discount as follows:

$$PDV = \frac{\text{Future payment}_N}{(1 + \text{Interest rate})^N}$$

where N refers to the number of years into the future when a payment is to be made. If the future payment is to be made in one year, the N in the equation equals 1, and we have

$$PDV = \frac{\$1,000}{1.10}$$
$$= \$909.09$$

Hence, the present discounted value of $1,000 to be paid one year from today is $909.09. If $909.09 were received today, it could earn interest. In a year's time, the $909.09 would grow to $1,000 with interest accrued at the rate of 10 percent per year.

Suppose it would have taken Columbus two years to complete his expeditions and collect his profits, rather than one year. In that case, the present value of the $1,000 payment would be lower. The N in the formula would be 2, and the present value would be

$$PDV = \frac{\$1,000}{(1.10)^2} = \frac{\$1,000}{1.21} = \$826.45$$

Hence, *the longer one has to wait for a future payment, the less present value it has.*

Lottery winners often have to choose between present and future values. In July 2004, for example, Geraldine Williams, a 68-year-old housekeeper in Lowell, Massachusetts, won a $294 million MegaMillions lottery. The $294 million was payable in 26 annual installments

present discounted value (PDV): The value today of future payments, adjusted for interest accrual.

TABLE 18.1

Computing Present Value

The present value of a future payment declines the longer one must wait for a payment. At an interest rate of 4.47 percent, $11.3 million payable in one year is worth only $10.82 million today. A payout of $11.3 million 25 years from now has a present value of only $3.79 million. A string of $11.3 million payments spread out over 25 years has a present value of $168 million (at 4.47 percent interest).

Years in the Future	Future Payment ($ millions)	Present Value ($ millions)
0	$ 11.3	$ 11.30
1	11.3	10.82
2	11.3	10.35
3	11.3	9.91
4	11.3	9.49
5	11.3	8.04
*	*	*
*	*	*
*	*	*
25	11.3	3.79
	$294.0	$168.0

Note: The general formula for computing present values is

$$PDV = \sum \frac{\text{Payment in year } N}{(1 + r)^N},$$

where r is the prevailing rate.

of $11.3 million. If the lucky winner wanted to get her prize sooner, she could accept an immediate but smaller payout rather than 25 future installments.

Table 18.1 shows how the lottery officials figured the present value of the $294 million prize. The first installment of $11.3 million would be paid immediately. Mrs. Williams would have had to wait one year for the second check, however. At the then-prevailing interest rate of 4.47 percent, the *present* value of that second $11.3 million check was only $10.82 million. The *last* payoff check had even less present value because it wasn't due to be paid for 25 years. With so much time for interest to accrue, that final $11.3 million payment had a present value of only $3.79 million. The calculations in Table 18.1 convinced lottery officials to offer an immediate (present) payout of only $168 million on the $294 million (future) prize. Mrs. Williams chose to take the immediate present-value sum—and wasn't too disappointed.

In March 2019 Manuel Franco won a $768.4 million Powerball drawing. The choice again was to take annual payments over 30 years or an immediate lump-sum cashout. Powerball made the 30-year option more attractive by increasing the annual payout by 5 percent a year. So, Manuel would have gotten a payout of $11.6 million the first year and $47.6 million in the 30th year. That wasn't enough to persuade Manuel to wait, however: He took an immediate $477 million cashout.

Interest Rate Effects

Mrs. Williams and Manuel would have received *smaller* cashouts had interest rates been higher. At the time Mrs. Williams won the lottery, the interest rate on bonds was 4.47 percent. Had the interest rate been higher, the discount for immediate payment would have been higher as well. Table 18.2 indicates that Mrs. Williams would have received only $107 million had the prevailing interest rate been 10 percent. What Tables 18.1 and 18.2 illustrate, then, is that *the present discounted value of a future payment declines with*

- *Higher interest rates.*
- *Longer delays in future payment.*

Uncertainty

The valuation of future payments must also consider the possibility of *non*payment. State governments are virtually certain to make promised lottery payouts, so there's little risk in

Interest Rate (%)	Present Discounted Value of $294 Million Lottery Prize ($ millions)
5.0%	$166.3
6.0	150.8
7.0	137.5
8.0	126.0
9.0	115.9
10.0	107.1

TABLE 18.2

Higher Interest Rates Reduce Present Values

Higher interest rates reduce the *present* value of future payments. Shown here is the present discounted value of the July 2004 MegaMillions lottery prize of $294 million at different interest rates.

accepting a promised payout of 25–30 annual installments. But what about the booty from Columbus's expeditions? There was great uncertainty that Columbus would ever return from his expeditions, much less bring back the "pearls, precious stones, gold, silver, and spiceries" that people coveted. Investing in those expeditions was far riskier than deferring a lottery payment.

Expected Value. Whenever an anticipated future payment is uncertain, a risk factor should be included in present value computations. This is done by calculating the **expected value** of a future payment. Suppose there was only a 50:50 chance that Columbus would bring back the goods. In that event, the expected payoff would be

expected value: The probable value of a future payment, including the risk of nonpayment.

$$\text{Expected value} = (1 - \text{Risk factor}) \times \text{Present discounted value}$$

With a 50:50 chance of failure, the expected value of Columbus's first-year profits would have been

$$\text{Expected value} = (1 - 0.5) \times \$909.09$$
$$= \$454.55$$

Expected values also explain why people buy more lottery tickets when the prize is larger. The odds of winning the multistate Powerball lottery are 80 *million*:1. That's about the same odds as getting struck by lightning *14 times* in the same year! So it makes almost no sense to buy a ticket. With a $16 million prize, the *undiscounted* expected value of a $1 lottery ticket is only 20 cents. When the lottery prize increases, however, the expected value of a ticket grows as well (there are still only 80 million possible combinations of numbers). When the grand prize reached $425 million in February 2014, the undiscounted expected value of a lone winning ticket jumped to more than $5. Millions of people decided that the expected value was high enough to justify buying a $1 lottery ticket. People took off from work, skipped classes, and drove across state lines to queue up for lottery tickets. When the prize is only $10 million, far fewer people buy tickets.

The Demand for Loanable Funds

People rarely borrow money to buy lottery tickets. But entrepreneurs and other market participants often use other people's funds to finance their ventures. *How much loanable funds are demanded depends on*

- *The expected rate of return.*
- *The cost of funds.*

The higher the expected return, or the lower the cost of funds, the greater will be the amount of loanable funds demanded.

Figure 18.2 offers a general view of the loanable funds market that emerges from these considerations. From the entrepreneur's perspective, the prevailing interest rate represents the cost of funds. From the perspective of savers, the interest rate represents the payoff to

FIGURE 18.2

The Loanable Funds Market

The market rate of interest (r_e) is determined by the intersection of the curves representing supply of and demand for loanable funds. The rate of interest represents the price paid for the use of money.

savings. When interest rates rise, the quantity of funds supplied goes up and the quantity demanded goes down. The prevailing (equilibrium) interest rate is set by the intersection of these supply and demand curves.

THE STOCK MARKET

The concept of a loanable funds market sounds a bit alien, but the same principles of supply, demand, and risk management go a long way in explaining the action in stock markets. Suppose you had $1,000 to invest. Should you invest it all in lottery tickets that offer a multimillion-dollar payoff? Put it in a savings account that pays next to nothing? Or how about the stock market? The stock market can reward you handsomely, or it can wipe out your savings if the stocks you own tumble. Hence, *stocks offer a higher average return than bank accounts but also entail greater average risk.* People who bought Amazon.com stock in May 1997 got a 1,000 percent profit on their stock in only two years. But people who bought Amazon.com stock in December 1999 lost 90 percent of their investment in even less time.

Corporate Stock

When people buy a share of stock, they're buying partial ownership of a corporation. The three legal forms of business entities are

- Corporations.
- Partnerships.
- Proprietorships.

Limited Liability. Proprietorships are businesses owned by a single individual. The owner–proprietor is entirely responsible for the business, including repayment of any debts. Members of a partnership are typically liable for all business debts and activities as well. By contrast, a **corporation** is a limited liability form of business. The corporation itself, not its individual shareholders, is responsible for all business activity and debts. As a result of this limited liability, you can own a piece of a corporation without worrying about being sued for business mishaps (like environmental damage) or nonpayment of debt. This feature significantly reduces the risk of owning corporate stock.

corporation: A business organization having a continuous existence independent of its members (owners) and power and liabilities distinct from those of its members.

Shared Ownership. The ownership of a corporation is defined in terms of stock shares. Each share of **corporate stock** represents partial ownership of the business. Apple, for example, has 4.6 *billion* shares of stock outstanding (that is, shares held by the public). Hence, each share of Apple stock represents less than one-fifth of one-billionth ownership of the corporation. Potentially, this means that as many as 4.6 billion people could own the Apple

corporate stock: Shares of ownership in a corporation.

Corporation. In reality, many individuals own hundreds of shares, and institutions may own thousands. Indeed, some of the largest pension funds in the United States own more than a million shares of Apple.

In principle, the owners of corporate stock collectively run the business. In practice, the shareholders select a board of directors to monitor corporate activity and protect their interests. The day-to-day business of running a corporation is the job of managers who report to the board of directors.

Stock Returns

If shareholders don't have any direct role in running a corporation, why would they want to own a piece of it? Essentially, for the same reason that the Genoese bankers agreed to finance Columbus's expedition: profits. *Owners (shareholders) of a corporation hope to share in the profits the corporation earns.*

Dividends. Shareholders rarely receive their full share of the company's profits in cash. Corporations typically use some of the profits for investment in new plants or equipment. They may also want to retain some of the profits for operational needs or unforeseen contingencies. *Corporations may choose to retain earnings or pay them out to shareholders as dividends.* Any profits *not* paid to shareholders are referred to as **retained earnings.** Thus,

dividend: Amount of corporate profits paid out for each share of stock.

$$\text{Dividends} = \text{Corporate profits} - \text{Retained earnings}$$

In 2019 Apple paid quarterly dividends amounting to $3.08 per share for the year. But the company earned profits equal to $11.89 per share. Thus, shareholders received only 26 percent of their accrued profits in dividend checks; Apple retained the remaining $8.81 per-share profit earned in 2019 for future investments.

retained earnings: Amount of corporate profits not paid out in dividends.

Capital Gains. If Apple invests its retained earnings wisely, the corporation may reap even larger profits in the future. As a company grows and prospers, each share of ownership may become more valuable. This increase in value would be reflected in higher market prices for shares of Apple stock. Any increase in the value of a stock represents a **capital gain** for shareholders. Capital gains directly increase shareholder wealth.

capital gain: An increase in the market value of an asset.

Total Return. People who own stocks can thus get two distinct payoffs: dividends and capital gains. Together these payoffs represent the total return on stock investments. Hence, *the higher the expected total return (future dividends and capital gains), the greater the desire to buy and hold stocks.* If a stock paid no dividends and had no prospects for price appreciation (capital gain), you'd probably hold your savings in a different form (such as another stock or maybe an interest-earning bank account).

Initial Public Offering

When a corporation is formed, its future sales and profits are most uncertain. When shares are first offered to the public, the seller of stock is the company itself. By *going public,* the corporation seeks to raise funds for investment and growth. A true *start-up* company may have nothing more than a good idea, a couple of dedicated employees, and big plans. To fund these plans, it sells shares of itself in an **initial public offering (IPO).** People who buy the newly issued stock are putting their savings directly into the corporation's accounts.[1] As new owners, they stand to profit from the corporation's business or take their lumps if the corporation fails.

initial public offering (IPO): The first issuance (sale) to the general public of stock in a corporation.

In 2004 Google was still a relatively new company. Although the company had been in operation since 1999, search engine capacities were limited. To expand, it needed more

[1]In reality, some of the initial proceeds will go to stockbrokers and investment bankers as compensation for their services as financial intermediaries. The entrepreneur who starts the company, other company employees, and any venture capitalists who help fund the company before the public offering may also get some of the IPO receipts by selling shares they acquired before the company went public.

computers, more employees, and more technology. To finance this expansion, Google needed more money. The company could have borrowed money from a bank or other financial institution, but that would have saddled the company with debt and forced it to make regular interest payments.

Rather than borrow money, Google's directors elected to sell ownership shares in the company. In August 2004 the company raised $1.7 *billion* in cash by selling 19.6 million shares for $85 per share in its initial public offering. The people who bought those shares were taking a risk: No one back then knew for certain that Google would prosper or fail. As it turned out, early Google investors did well: The $85 they paid for one share of Google in 2004 was worth more than $2,600 in early 2020 (in renamed Alphabet stock). That pushed Google's value (**capitalization**) over $1 *trillion*. Early investors in Uber haven't fared so well (see Front Page Economics "Uber IPO Disappoints").

capitalization: Market value of a publicly traded company; equals number of shares multiplied by the price of the share.

FRONT PAGE ECONOMICS

UBER IPO DISAPPOINTS

Early enthusiasts predicted that Uber Technologies would command a $120 billion capitalization when it went public. But Uber's IPO didn't come close to that valuation. The company sold 180 million shares to the public at a price of $45 a share. That brought in only $8.1 billion for the company and put its market value (with a total of 1.7 billion shares) at a much more modest $76.5 billion. Worse yet, the stock price declined to $41.57 on its first day and hit a low of $25.58 in November, a 43 percent drop from its IPO price. Although Uber notes that it has over 100 million customers in 63 countries, investors are worried that the company's ride-hailing, food-delivery, and other businesses will continue to lose money for a long time.

Source: Media reports, May 2019–January 2020.

CRITICAL ANALYSIS: An **initial public offering** brings in money from investors to help a company operate and expand. The degree of perceived risk is reflected in the IPO price and its aftermath.

Secondary Trading

Why were people eager to buy shares in Google? They certainly weren't buying the stock with expectations of high dividends. The company hadn't earned much profit in its first five years and didn't expect substantial profits for at least another few years.

P/E Ratio. In 2003 Google had earned only 41 cents of profit per share. In 2004 it would earn $1.46 per share. So people who were buying Google stock for $85 per share in August 2004 were paying a comparatively high price for relatively little profit. This can be seen by computing the **price/earnings (P/E) ratio:**

price/earnings (P/E) ratio: The price of a stock share divided by earnings (profit) per share.

$$\text{P/E ratio} = \frac{\text{Price of stock share}}{\text{Earnings (profit) per share}}$$

For Google in 2004,

$$\text{P/E ratio} = \frac{\$85}{\$1.46} = 58.2$$

In other words, investors were paying $58.20 for every $1 of profits. That implies a rate of return of 1 ÷ $58.20, or only 1.7 percent. Compared to the interest rates banks were paying on deposit balances, Google shares didn't look like a very good buy.

Profit Expectation. People weren't buying Google stock just to get a piece of *current* profits. What made Google attractive was its *growth* potential. The company projected that revenues and profits would grow rapidly as its search capabilities expanded, more people used its services, and, most important, more advertisers clamored to get premium spots on the company's web pages. Given these expectations, investors projected that Google's profits would jump from $1.46 per share in 2004 to roughly $10 in four years. From that perspective, the *projected* P/E ratio looked cheap.

Investors who wanted a piece of those future profits rushed to buy Google stock after its IPO. On the first day of trading, the share price rose from the IPO price of $85 to $100. Within a month the price rose to $120. Two years later Google's stock sold for more than $450 a share! A lot of investors racked up huge capital gains.

That post-IPO rise in Google's stock price had no direct effect on the company. A corporation reaps the proceeds of stock sales only when it sells shares to the public (the initial public offering). After the IPO, the company's stock is traded among individuals in the "after market." Virtually all the trading activity on major stock exchanges consists of such after-market sales. Mr. Dow sells his Google shares to Ms. Jones, who may later sell them to Mr. Pitt. Such *secondary* trades may take place at the New York Stock Exchange (NYSE) on Wall Street or in the computerized over-the-counter market (e.g., NASDAQ).

Market Fluctuations

The price of a stock at any moment is the outcome of supply-and-demand interactions. I wouldn't mind owning a piece of Google (Alphabet). But because I think the current share price is too high, I'll buy the stock only if the price falls substantially. Even though I'm not buying any Google stock now, I'm part of the *market demand.* That is, all the people who are willing and able to buy Google stock at *some* price are included in the demand curve in Figure 18.3. The cheaper the stock, the more people will want to buy it, *ceteris paribus.* The opposite is true on the supply side of the market: Ever-higher prices are necessary to induce more shareholders to part with their shares.

Changing Expectations. In early 2006 investors reevaluated the profit prospects for Google and other Internet companies. Several years of experience had shown that earning profits in e-commerce wasn't so easy. Projections of advertising sales growth and future profits were sharply reduced. In two months' time Google's stock price fell from $470 to $340. Figure 18.3 illustrates how this happened. Higher perceived risk reduced the demand for Google stock and increased the willingness of existing shareholders to sell. Such *changes in expectations imply shifts in supply and demand for a company's stock*. As Figure 18.3 illustrates, these combined shifts sent Google (Alphabet) stock plummeting.

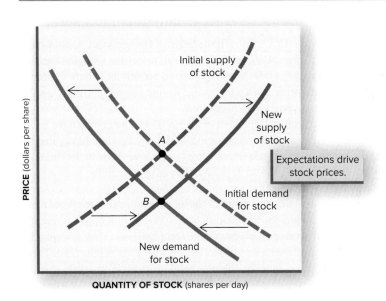

FIGURE 18.3

Worsened Expectations

The supply and demand for stocks is fueled by expectations of future profits. When investors concluded that Google's future profit potential wasn't so great, demand for the stock decreased, supply increased, and the share price fell from point *A* to point *B*.

52 Weeks							Vol				Net
HI	Lo	Stock	Sym	Div	Yld%	P/E	100s	HI	Lo	Close	Chg
318.74	151.00	Apple	APPL	3.08	0.97	26.89	344541	318.74	315.00	318.73	+3.49
47.08	25.58	Uber	UBER	0	0	n/a	172512	35.25	34.65	34.68	+0.45
1480.55	1027.03	Alphabet	GOOGL	0	0	32.19	26211	1480.50	1436.55	1450.16	+29.36

The information provided by this quotation includes the following:

52-Weeks Hi and Lo: The highest and lowest prices paid for a share of stock in the previous year.

Stock: The name of the corporation whose shares are being traded.

Sym: The symbol used as a shorthand description for the stock.

Div: A dividend is the amount of profit paid out by the corporation in the preceding year for each share of stock.

Yld%: The yield is the dividend paid per share divided by the price of a share.

P/E: The price of the stock (P) divided by the earnings (profit) per share (E). This indicates how much a purchaser is effectively paying for each dollar of profits.

Vol 100s: The number of shares traded in hundreds.

Hi: The highest price paid for a share of stock on the previous day.

Lo: The lowest price paid for a share of stock on the previous day.

Close: The price paid in the last trade of the day as the market was closing.

Net Chg: The change in the closing price yesterday vs. the previous day's closing price.

Source: E-Trade (January 17, 2020).

TABLE 18.3

Reading Stock Quotes

The financial pages of the daily newspaper summarize the trading activity in corporate stocks. The quotation here summarizes trading in Apple, Uber, and Google (Alphabet) shares on January 17, 2020.

Table 18.3 summarizes the action in Google stock on a single day. On that day 2.6 million shares of Google (Alphabet) were bought and sold. At the end of the trading day (4 p.m. in New York City) Google shares were selling for $1450.16 apiece (see "Close" in Table 18.3). Along the path to that closing equilibrium, the price had fluctuated between $1,456.55 ("Lo") and $1,480.50 ("Hi"). The stock price fluctuated even more over the preceding year: The "52-week Hi" was $1,480.55, while the "52-week Lo" was only $1,027.03. This huge range in the price of Google shares reflects the changing performance and market expectations for the company.

The Value of Information. The wide fluctuations in the price of Google stock illustrate the value of *information* in financial markets. People who paid high prices for Google shares in 2020 had optimistic expectations for the company's continued growth and share appreciation. Those who *sold* shares at high prices weren't so sure. No one *knew* what future profits would be; everyone was acting on the basis of expectations.

The evident value of information raises a question of access. Do some people have better information than others? Do they get their information fairly? Or do they have "inside" sources (such as company technicians, managers, directors) who give them preferential access to information? If so, these insiders would have an unfair advantage in the marketplace and could alter the distribution of income and wealth in their favor.

The value of information also explains the demand for information services. People pay hundreds and even thousands of dollars for newsletters, wire services, and online computer services that provide up-to-date information on companies and markets. They also pay for the services of investment bankers, advisers, and brokers to help keep them informed. These services help disseminate information quickly, thereby helping financial markets operate efficiently.

TABLE 18.4

Stock Market Averages

More than 1,600 stocks are listed (traded) on the New York Stock Exchange, and many times that number are traded in other stock markets. To gauge changes in so many stocks, people refer to various indexes, such as the Dow Jones Industrial Average. The Dow and similar indexes help us keep track of the market's ups and downs.

Some of the most frequently quoted indexes are

Dow Jones

    Industrial Average: An arithmetic average of the prices of 30 blue-chip industrial stocks traded on the New York Stock Exchange (NYSE) and by computers of the National Association of Securities Dealers (NASD).

    Transportation Average: An average of 20 transportation stocks traded on the NYSE.

    Utilities Average: An average of 15 utility stocks traded on the NYSE.

S&P 500: An index compiled by Standard and Poor of 500 stocks drawn from major stock exchanges as well as over-the-counter stocks. The S&P 500 is made up of 400 industrial companies, 40 utilities, 20 transportation companies, and 40 financial institutions.

NASDAQ Composite: Index of stocks traded in the over-the-counter market among securities dealers.

New York Stock Exchange composite index: The "Big Board" index, which includes all 1,600-plus stocks traded on the NYSE.

Nikkei index: An index of 225 stocks traded on the Tokyo stock market.

Booms and Busts. If stock markets are so efficient at computing the present value of future profits, why does the entire market make abrupt moves every so often? Fundamentally, the same factors that determine the price of a single stock influence the broader stock market averages as well (see Table 18.4). An increase in interest rates, for example, raises the opportunity cost of holding stocks. Hence, higher interest rates should cause stock prices to fall, *ceteris paribus.* Stocks might decline even further if higher interest rates are expected to curtail investment and consumption, thus reducing future sales and profits. Such a double whammy could cause the whole stock market to tumble.

Other factors also affect the relative desirability of holding stock. Congressional budget and deficit decisions, monetary policy, consumer confidence, business investment plans, international trade patterns, and new inventions are just a few of the factors that may alter present and future profits. These *broad changes in the economic outlook tend to push all stock prices up or down at the same time.*

Broad changes in the economic outlook, however, seldom occur overnight. Moreover, these changes are rarely of a magnitude that could precipitate a stock market boom or bust. In reality, the stock market often changes more abruptly than the economic outlook. These *exaggerated movements in the stock market are caused by sudden and widespread changes in expectations.* This was dramatically illustrated in early 2020 when fears of the spreading coronavirus pandemic led to global economic shutdowns. Within a matter of days, the value of nearly all stocks declined sharply. Keep in mind that the value of the stock depends on anticipated *future* profits and *expectations* for interest rates and the economic outlook. No elements of the future are certain. Instead, people use present clues to try to discern the likely course of future events. In other words, *all information must be filtered through people's expectations.* This was dramatically illustrated in early 2020 when fears of the spreading coronavirus pandemic led to global economic shutdowns. Within a matter of days, the value of nearly all stocks declined sharply.

The central role of expectations implies that the economy can change more gradually than the stock market. If, for example, interest rates rise, market participants may regard the increase as temporary or inconsequential: Their expectations for the future may not change. If interest rates keep rising, however, investors may have greater doubts. At some point, the market participants may revise their expectations. Stock prices may falter, triggering an adjustment in expectations. A herding instinct may surface, sending expectations for stock prices abruptly lower.

Resource Allocations

Although it's fascinating and sometimes fun to watch stock market gyrations, we shouldn't lose sight of the *economic* role of financial markets. Columbus needed *real* resources—ships, men, equipment—for his expeditions. Five centuries later, Uber also needed real resources—computers, labor, technology—to expand. To find the necessary economic resources, both Columbus and Uber had to convince society to reallocate resources from other activities to their new ventures.

Financial markets facilitate resource reallocations. In Columbus's case, the Genoese bankers lent the funds that Columbus used to buy scarce resources. The funds obtained from Uber's 2019 initial public offering served the same purpose. In both cases, the funds obtained in the financial markets helped change the mix of output. If the financial markets hadn't supplied the necessary funding, neither Columbus nor Uber would have been able to go forth. The available resources would have been used to produce other goods.

THE BOND MARKET

The bond market is another financial mechanism for transferring the pool of national savings into the hands of would-be spenders. It operates much like the stock market. The major difference is the kind of paper traded. ***In the stock market, people buy and sell shares of corporate ownership. In the bond market, people buy and sell promissory notes (IOUs).*** A **bond** is simply an IOU, a written promise to repay a loan. The bond itself specifies the terms of repayment, noting both the amount of interest to be paid each year and the maturity date (the date on which the borrower is to repay the entire debt). The borrower may be a corporation (corporate bonds), a local government (municipal bonds), the federal government (Treasury bonds), or some other institution.

bond: A certificate acknowledging a debt and the amount of interest to be paid each year until repayment; an IOU.

Bond Issuance

A bond is first issued when an institution wants to borrow money. Recall the situation Google faced in 2004. The company needed additional funds to expand its Internet operations. Rather than sell equity shares in itself, Google could have *borrowed* funds. The advantage of borrowing funds rather than issuing stock is that the owners can keep control of their company. ***Lenders aren't owners, but shareholders are.*** The disadvantage of borrowing funds is that the company gets saddled with a repayment schedule. Lenders want to be paid back—with interest. For a new company like Google, the burden of interest payments may be too great.

Ignoring these problems momentarily, let's assume that Google decided in 2004 to borrow funds rather than sell stock in itself. To do so, it would have *issued* bonds. This simply means that it would have printed formal IOUs called bonds. Typically, each bond certificate would have a **par value** (face value) of $1,000. The bond certificate would also specify the rate of interest to be paid and the promised date of repayment. A Google bond issued in 2004, for example, might specify repayment in 10 years, with annual interest payments of $100. The individual who bought the bond from Google would lend $1,000 for 10 years and receive annual interest payments of $100. Thus, ***the initial bond purchaser lends funds directly to the bond issuer.*** The borrower (such as Google, General Motors, or the U.S. Treasury) can then use those funds to acquire real resources. Thus, ***the bond market also functions as a financial intermediary, transferring available savings (wealth) to those who want to acquire more resources (invest).***

par value: The face value of a bond; the amount to be repaid when the bond is due.

As in the case of IPOs of stock, the critical issue here is the *price* of the bond. How many people are willing and able to lend funds to the company? What rate of interest will they charge?

As we observed in Figure 18.2, the quantity of loanable funds supplied depends on the interest rate. At low interest rates, no one is willing to lend funds to the company. Why lend your savings to a risky venture like Google when more secure bonds and even banks pay higher interest rates? Google might not succeed and later **default** on (not pay) its obligations. Potential lenders would want to be compensated for this extra risk with above-average

default: Failure to make scheduled payments of interest or principal on a bond.

interest rates—that is, a risk premium. Remember that lenders don't share in any profits Google might earn; they get only interest payments. Hence, they'd want a hefty premium to compensate them for the risk of default.

Suppose that market participants will lend the desired amount of money to Google only at 16 percent interest. In this case, Google may agree to pay an interest rate—the so-called **coupon rate**—of 16 percent to secure start-up funding of $50 million. That means Google agrees to pay $160 of interest each year for every $1,000 borrowed and to repay the entire $50 million at the end of 10 years.

coupon rate: Interest rate set for a bond at the time of issuance.

Bond Trading

Once a bond has been issued, the initial lenders don't have to wait 10 years to get their money back. They can't go back to the company and demand early repayment, but they can sell their bonds to someone else. This **liquidity** is an important consideration for prospective bondholders. If a person had no choice but to wait 10 years for repayment, he or she might be less willing to buy a bond (lend funds). *By facilitating resales, the bond market increases the availability of funds to new ventures and other borrowers.* As is the case with stocks, most of the action in the bond markets consists of such after-market trades—that is, the buying and selling of bonds issued at some earlier time. The company that first issued the bonds doesn't participate in these trades.

liquidity: The ability of an asset to be converted into cash.

The portfolio decision in the bond market is motivated by the same factors that influence stock purchases. The *opportunity cost* of buying and selling bonds is the best alternative rate of return—for example, the interest rate on other bonds or money market mutual funds. *Expectations* also play a role in gauging both likely changes in opportunity costs and the ability of the borrower to redeem (pay off) the bond when it's due. *Changes in expectations or opportunity costs shift the bond supply and demand curves,* thereby altering market interest rates.

Current Yields

We've assumed that Google would have had to offer 16 percent interest to induce enough people to lend the company (buy bonds worth) $50 million for its initial operations. This was far higher than the 6 percent the U.S. Treasury was paying on its bonds (borrowed funds). This large risk premium reflected the fear that Google might not succeed and end up defaulting on it loans.

Suppose that Google prospered in the years after bond issuance. The risk of a bond default would diminish, and people would be more willing to lend it funds. This change in the availability of loanable funds is illustrated in the rightward shift of the supply curve in Figure 18.4.

According to the new supply curve in Figure 18.4, Google could now borrow $50 million at 10 percent interest (point *B*) rather than paying 16 percent (point *A*). Unfortunately,

FIGURE 18.4

Shifts in Funds Supply

If lenders decide that a company's future is less risky, they will be more willing to lend it money or hold its bonds. The resulting shift of the loanable funds supply curve reduces the current yield on a bond by raising its price.

Google already borrowed the funds and is obliged to continue paying $160 per year in interest on each bond. Hence, the company doesn't benefit directly from the supply shift.

The change in the equilibrium value of Google bonds must show up somewhere, however. People who hold Google bonds continue to get $160 per year in interest (16 percent of $1,000). Now there are lots of people who would be willing to lend funds to Google at that rate. These people want to hold Google bonds themselves. To get them, they'll have to buy the bonds in the market from existing bondholders. Thus, the *increased willingness to lend funds is reflected in an increased demand for bonds.* This increased demand will push up the price of Google bonds.

current yield: The rate of return on a bond; the annual interest payment divided by the bond's price.

As Google bond prices rise, their effective interest rate (**current yield**) falls. Table 18.5 illustrates this relationship. Google has prospered greatly since its IPO and early bond issuances. As a result, investors are much more willing today to buy Google stock or bonds. This was evident in 2016 when Google decided to borrow $2 billion. This time around it issued 10-year bonds with a coupon rate of only 1.998 percent. Four years later, those bonds were selling very close to par value, with a yield of just 2 percent. The risk premium approached zero.

Changing bond prices and yields are important market signals for resource allocation. In our example, the rising price of Google's bonds reflects increased optimism for the company's sales prospects. The collective assessment of the marketplace is that web search engines will be profitable. The increase in the price of Google bonds makes it easier and less costly for the company to borrow additional funds.

TABLE 18.5

Bond Price and Yields Move in Opposite Directions

Price of Bond	Coupon Rate (Annual Interest Payment)	Current Yield
$ 600	$150	25.0%
800	150	18.8
1,000	150	15.0
1,200	150	12.5

The annual interest payment on a bond—the "coupon rate"—is fixed at the time of issuance. Accordingly, only the market (resale) price of the bond itself can change. An increase in the price of the bond lowers its *effective* interest rate, or yield. The formula for computing the current yield on a bond is

$$\text{Current yield} = \frac{\text{Annual interest payment}}{\text{Market (resale) price of bond}}$$

Thus, higher bond prices imply lower yields (effective interest rates), as confirmed in the table above. Bond prices and yields vary with changes in expectations and opportunity costs.

DECISIONS FOR TOMORROW

Venture Capitalists—Vultures or Angels?

One of the proven paths to high incomes and wealth is entrepreneurship. Most of the great American fortunes originated in entrepreneurial ventures, such as building railroads, mass-producing automobiles, introducing new computers, perfecting mass-merchandising techniques, or pioneering social networking sites (e.g., Facebook). These successful ventures all required more than just a great idea. To convert the original idea into actual output requires the investment of real resources.

Apple. Recall that Apple Computer started in a garage with a minimum of resources (Chapter 9). The idea of packaging a personal computer was novel, and few resources were required to demonstrate that it could be done. But Steven Jobs couldn't have become a multimillionaire by building just a few dozen computers a month. To reap huge economic profits from his idea, he needed much greater production capacity. He also needed resources for marketing the new Apples to a broader customer base. In other words, Steven Jobs needed lots of economic resources—land, labor, and capital—to convert his entrepreneurial dream into a profit-making reality.

Steven Jobs and his partner, Steve Wozniak, had few resources of their own. In fact, they'd sold Jobs's Volkswagen and Wozniak's scientific calculator to raise the finances for the first computer. To go any further, they needed financial support from others. Loans were hard to obtain because the company had no assets, no financial history, and no certainty of success. Jobs needed people who were willing to share the *risks* associated with a new venture. He found one such person in A. C. Markkula, who put up $250,000 and became a partner in the new venture. Shortly thereafter, other venture capitalists provided additional financing. With this start-up financing, Jobs was able to acquire more resources and make the Apple Computer Company a reality.

Facebook. Facebook grew from equally modest origins (Mark Zuckerberg's Harvard dorm room) back in 2004. It went from a small start-up to a national phenomenon only with the help of venture capitalists. Three venture capitalists invested $40 million, giving Facebook the resources to buy its own domain name ($200,000) and build the infrastructure that allowed it to become the premier social networking site.

Uber. Uber, too, needed tons of money to create a nationwide ride-hailing service. The founders, Travis Kalanick and Garrett Camp, had enough money from earlier ventures to start operations with three cars in New York City (their company was then called Uber-Cab). But to grow into a nationwide service they needed a lot more cash. Venture capitalists invested $50 million in 2010–2011. Then the Saudi Arabia Wealth Fund invested a whopping $3.5 *billion* in June 2016, giving Uber enough money to expand. Unfortunately, the later post-IPO decline in Uber stock caused some earlier venture capitalists to lose money. One of those venture capitalists, SoftBank, lost over $1 billion in 2019. The Uber experience reminds us that *risk* is a big part of what venture capitalists finance.

Financing Options. As Front Page Economics "Where Do Start-Ups Get Their Money?" documents, most business start-ups are created with shoestring budgets, averaging less than $20,000 (Apple and Facebook started with even less). The initial seed money typically comes from an entrepreneur's own assets or credit, with a little help from family and friends. If the idea pans out, entrepreneurs need a lot more money to develop their product. This is where venture capitalists come in. Venture capitalists provide initial funding for entrepreneurial ventures. In return for their financial backing, the venture capitalists are entitled to a share of any profits that result. If the venture fails, however, they get nothing. Thus, *venture capitalists provide financial support for entrepreneurial ideas and share in the risks and rewards.* Even Christopher Columbus needed venture capitalists to fund his risky expeditions to the New World.

Venture capital is as important to the economy tomorrow as it was to Columbus. For technology and entrepreneurship to continue growing, market conditions and tax provisions must be amenable to venture capitalists.

Crowdfunding is all the rage these days, but start-ups get relatively little initial capital from throngs of anonymous investors. Personal savings remain the most important source of start-up capital according to a survey of 600 business owners. Initial capital averages less than $20,000. Loans from banks are the second most common source of this start-up funding, as the accompanying chart shows.

Continued

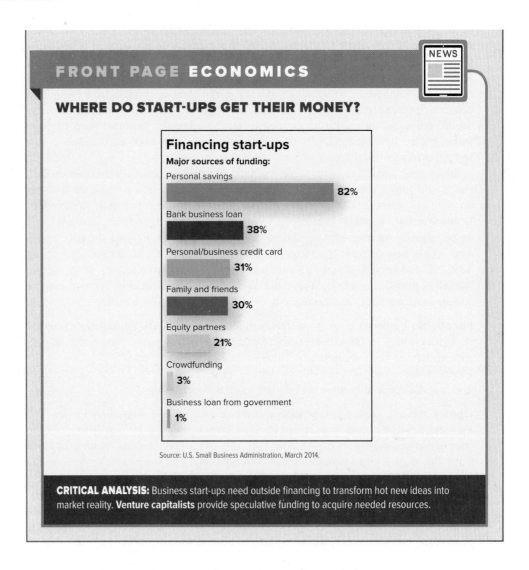

FRONT PAGE ECONOMICS

NEWS

WHERE DO START-UPS GET THEIR MONEY?

Financing start-ups

Major sources of funding:

Personal savings
82%

Bank business loan
38%

Personal/business credit card
31%

Family and friends
30%

Equity partners
21%

Crowdfunding
3%

Business loan from government
1%

Source: U.S. Small Business Administration, March 2014.

CRITICAL ANALYSIS: Business start-ups need outside financing to transform hot new ideas into market reality. **Venture capitalists** provide speculative funding to acquire needed resources.

SUMMARY

- The primary economic function of financial markets is to help allocate scarce resources to desired uses. They do this by providing access to the pool of national savings for entrepreneurs, investors, and other would-be spenders. **LO18-4**

- Financial markets enable individuals to manage risk by holding different kinds of assets. Financial intermediaries also reduce the costs of information and search, thereby increasing market efficiency. **LO18-4**

- Future returns on investments must be discounted to present value. The present discounted value (PDV) of a future payment adjusts for forgone interest accrual. **LO18-1**

- Future returns are also uncertain. The *expected* value of future payments must also reflect the risk of nonpayment. **LO18-1**

- Shares of stock represent ownership in a corporation. The shares are initially issued to raise funds and are then traded on the stock exchanges. **LO18-2**

- Changes in the value of a corporation's stock reflect changing expectations and opportunity costs. Share price changes, in turn, act as market signals to direct more or fewer resources to a company. **LO18-4**

- Bonds are IOUs issued when a company (or government agency) borrows funds. After issuance, bonds are traded in the after (secondary) market. **LO18-2**

- The interest (coupon) rate on a bond is fixed at the time of issuance. The price of the bond itself, however, varies with changes in expectations (perceived risk) and opportunity cost. Yields vary inversely with bond prices. **LO18-3**

- Venture capitalists provide entrepreneurs with the money needed to start or expand a business, thereby assuming some of the risks of new enterprises. **LO18-4**

Key Terms

financial intermediary	dividend	par value
crowdfunding	retained earnings	default
risk premium	capital gain	coupon rate
present discounted value (PDV)	initial public offering (IPO)	liquidity
expected value	capitalization	current yield
corporation	price/earnings (P/E) ratio	
corporate stock	bond	

Questions for Discussion

1. If there were no organized financial markets, how would an entrepreneur acquire resources to develop and produce a new product? **LO18-2**

2. Why would anyone buy shares of a corporation that had no profits and paid no dividends? What's the highest price a person would pay for such a stock? **LO18-3**

3. Why would anyone sell a bond for less than its face (par) value? **LO18-3**

4. If you could finance a new venture with either a stock issue or bonds, which option would you choose? What are their respective (dis)advantages? **LO18-2**

5. Why is it considered riskier to own stock in a software company than to hold U.S. Treasury savings bonds? Which asset will generate a higher return? **LO18-4**

6. How does a successful IPO affect WHAT, HOW, and FOR WHOM the economy produces? **LO18-2**

7. If Uber is so popular, why has the price of its stock declined since its IPO? **LO18-4**

8. Based on the information in Table 18.3, which stock would you prefer to own? **LO18-4**

9. Could Facebook have become a premier social networking site without venture capitalists? How? **LO18-2**

10. Why do people say "a dollar today is worth more than a dollar tomorrow"? **LO18-1**

LO18-3 1. If an $140 stock pays a quarterly dividend of $1, what is the implied annual rate of return?

LO18-3 2. If a $32 per share stock has a P/E ratio of 16 and pays out 40 percent of its profits in dividends,
   (*a*) How much profit is it earning per share?
   (*b*) How large is its dividend?
   (*c*) What is the implied rate of cash return?

LO18-3 3. According to the data in Table 18.3,
   (*a*) How much profit per share did Alphabet (Google) earn?
   (*b*) How much of that profit did it pay out in dividends per share?

LO18-3 4. According to Table 18.3, which company had
   (*a*) The lowest P/E?
   (*b*) The biggest one-day percentage gain?
   (*c*) The biggest percentage gain from the year low to the year high?
   (*d*) A close that was closest to its one-year high?

LO18-3 5. What was the market value (capitalization) of Uber (see Front Page Economics "Uber IPO Disappoints")
   (*a*) At the time of its IPO?
   (*b*) In November 2019?

LO18-1 6. If the market rate of interest is 4 percent, what is the present discounted value of $1,000 that will be paid in
   (*a*) 1 year?
   (*b*) 5 years?
   (*c*) 10 years?

LO18-1 7. What is the present discounted value of $10,000 that is to be received in 2 years if the market rate of interest is
   (*a*) 0 percent?
   (*b*) 4 percent?
   (*c*) 8 percent?

LO18-4 8. What was the expected return on Columbus's expedition, assuming that he had a 50 percent chance of discovering valuables worth $1 million, a 25 percent chance of bringing home only $100,000, and a 25 percent chance of sinking?

LO18-3 9. What is the current yield on a $1,000 bond with a 5 percent coupon if its market price is
   (*a*) $900?
   (*b*) $1,000?
   (*c*) $1,100?

LO18-4 10. How much interest accrued each day on the immediate cash payoff of the MegaMillions jackpot? (See Table 18.1.)

LO18-4 11. Illustrate with demand and supply shifts the impact of the following events on stock prices:
   (*a*) A federal court finds Google guilty of antitrust violations. Which way (right or left) did
      (*i*) Demand shift?
      (*ii*) Supply shift?
   (*b*) Intel announces a new and faster processor. Which way did
      (*i*) Demand shift?
      (*ii*) Supply shift?

(*c*) Corporate executives announce that they intend to sell a large block of stock. Which way did
  (*i*) Demand shift?
  (*ii*) Supply shift?
(*d*) Google enhances its search capabilities. Which way did
  (*i*) Demand shift?
  (*ii*) Supply shift?

LO18-2 12. Which investment has a higher rate of annual cash return? Investment A: $1,000 bond with a coupon rate of 4 percent selling for $1,200 or Investment B: $1,000 stock with a P/E ratio of 10 that pays out half its profits in dividends.

LO18-4 13. ***Decisions for Tomorrow:*** What are the three most important sources of funding for financing a start-up?

PART

6

DISTRIBUTIONAL ISSUES

Of the three core questions in economics, the FOR WHOM issue is often the most contentious. Should the market decide who gets the most output? Or should the government intervene and redistribute market incomes to achieve greater equity?

Tax and transfer systems are designed to redistribute market incomes. The next two chapters survey these systems. In the process, we assess not only how effective they are in achieving greater *equity,* but also what impacts they have on *efficiency.* High taxes and generous transfer payments may blunt work incentives and so reduce the size of the pie being resliced. This creates a fundamental conflict between the goals of equity and efficiency. Chapters 19 and 20 examine this conflict.

alexsl/Getty Images

DreamPictures/Pam Ostrow/Blend Images LLC

411

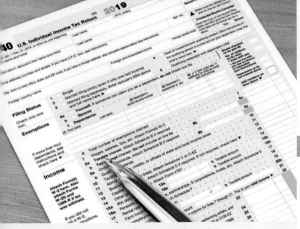

CHAPTER 19

Taxes: Equity versus Efficiency

Insistence on carving the pie into equal slices would shrink the size of the pie. That fact poses the trade-off between economic equality and economic efficiency.

—Arthur M. Okun

LEARNING OBJECTIVES

After reading this chapter, you should know

LO19-1 How the U.S. tax system is structured.

LO19-2 What makes taxes more or less progressive.

LO19-3 The nature of the equity–efficiency trade-off.

Eric Schmidt was rewarded handsomely for his effort in co-founding Google in 2001. When he stepped down as CEO in 2011, Schmidt had amassed 9.2 million shares of Google stock, worth nearly $6 billion. As a parting gift, Google gave him an additional $100 million bonus when he turned the CEO job over to fellow cofounder Larry Page in January 2011. That would have been enough income to lift more than 2 million poor persons out of poverty. But Schmidt didn't share his good fortune with those people, and they remained poor.

The market mechanism generated both Schmidt's extraordinary income and that of so many poor families. Is this the way we want the basic FOR WHOM question to be settled? Should some people own vast fortunes while others seek shelter in abandoned cars? Or do the inequalities that emerge in product and factor markets violate our notions of equity? If the market's answer to the FOR WHOM question isn't right, some form of government intervention to redistribute incomes may be desired.

The tax system is the government's primary lever for redistributing income. But taxing Peter to pay Paul may affect more than just income shares. If taxed too heavily, Peter may stop producing so much. Paul, too, may work less if assured of government support. The end result may be *less* total income to share. In other words, *taxes affect production as well as distribution. This creates a potential trade-off between the goal of equity and the goal of efficiency.*

This chapter examines this equity–efficiency trade-off, with the following questions as a guide:

- **How are incomes distributed in the United States?**
- **How do taxes alter that distribution?**
- **How do taxes affect the rate and mix of output?**

After addressing these questions, we examine some recent and proposed tax changes including proposed "billionaire" wealth taxes.

WHAT IS *INCOME*?

Before examining the distribution of income in the United States, let's decide what to count as *income.* There are several possibilities.

Personal Income

The most obvious choice is **personal income (PI)**—the flow of annual income received by households before payment of personal income taxes. Personal income includes wages and salaries, corporate dividends, rent, interest, Social Security benefits, welfare payments, and any other form of money income.

Personal income isn't a complete measure of income, however. Many goods and services are distributed directly as **in-kind income** rather than through market purchases. Many poor people, for example, live in public housing and pay little or no rent. As a consequence, they receive a larger share of total output than their money incomes imply. People with low incomes also receive food stamps (now called Supplemental Nutrition Assistance Program [SNAP] vouchers) that allow them to purchase more food than their money incomes would allow.

In-kind benefits aren't limited to low-income households. Students who attend public schools and colleges consume more goods and services than they directly pay for: Public education is subsidized by all taxpayers. People over age 65 also get medical services through Medicare that they don't directly pay for. Middle-class workers get noncash fringe benefits (like health insurance, paid vacations, pension contributions) that don't show up in their paychecks or on their tax returns. Even the president of the United States gets substantial in-kind benefits. The president doesn't pay rent at the White House and gets free food, health care, transportation, and security services. Hence, his real income greatly exceeds his $400,000-a-year presidential paycheck.

So long as some goods and services needn't be purchased in the marketplace, *the distribution of money income isn't synonymous with the distribution of goods and services.* This measurement problem is particularly important when comparisons are made over time. For example, the federal government officially classifies people as "poor" if their money income is below a certain threshold. By this standard, we've made no progress against poverty. The Census Bureau counted 34 million Americans as "poor" in 2019, more than it counted in 1965. In both years the Census Bureau counted only money incomes. In 1965 that approach was acceptable because little income was transferred in-kind. In 2019, however, the federal government spent $70 billion on food stamps, $60 billion on housing subsidies, and $600 billion on Medicaid. Had all this in-kind income been counted, 12 million fewer Americans would have been counted as poor in 2019. Although that would still leave a lot of people in poverty, at least more progress in eliminating poverty would be evident.

Wealth

If our ultimate concern is access to goods and services, the distribution of wealth is also important. **Wealth** refers to the market value of assets (such as houses, cars, and bank accounts) people own. Hence, *wealth represents a stock of potential purchasing power; income statistics tell us only how this year's flow of purchasing power (income) is being distributed.* As we saw at the beginning of this chapter, Eric Schmidt walked away from Google with nearly $6 billion. That was a stock of *wealth* (Google stock), not current income. At the beginning of 2021, Elon Musk had over $70 billion in *wealth,* but a modest current income (he refused to take a salary from Tesla). Clearly, both men have a lot more access to goods and services than their *incomes* alone suggest. Accordingly, to provide a complete answer to the FOR WHOM question, we have to know how wealth, as well as income, is distributed. In general, wealth tends to be distributed much less equally than income. The Internal Revenue Service estimates that 10 percent of the adult population own 75 percent of all personal wealth in the United States but earn around 50 percent of total income.

personal income (PI): Income received by households before payment of personal taxes.

in-kind income: Goods and services received directly, without payment, in a market transaction.

wealth: The market value of assets.

THE SIZE DISTRIBUTION OF INCOME

Although incomes aren't a perfect measure of access to goods and services (much less happiness), they're the best single indicator of the FOR WHOM outcomes. In 2019, the *average* income of American households was $90,000. But we know that not every household got that much money. Some households got very little, while others took in millions of dollars. What we want to know is how the total income pie was sliced up. The **size distribution of income** answers that question. It tells us how our total (national) income is *distributed* among our 130 million American households. Specifically, it tells us how large a share of total personal income is received by various households, grouped by income class.

Imagine for the moment that the entire population is lined up in order of income, with lowest-income recipients in front and highest-income recipients at the end of the line. We want to know how much income the people in front get in comparison with those at the back.

We first examined the size distribution of income in Chapter 2. Figure 2.3 showed that households in the lowest quintile received less than $28,000 apiece in 2019. As a group, this class received only 3.1 percent of total income, despite the fact that it included 20 percent of all households (the lowest fifth). Thus, the **income share** of the people in the lowest group (3.1 percent) was much smaller than their proportion in the total population (20 percent).

Moving back to the end of the line, we observed that a household needed $143,000 to make it into the highest income class in 2019. Many families in that class made much more than $143,000—some even millions of dollars. But $143,000 was at least enough to get into the top fifth (quintile).

The top quintile ended up with half of total U.S. income and, by implication, that much of total output. Thus, people in the top quintile of the population got 16 times as much income as people in the lowest quintile. That's a basic measure of inequality.

The Lorenz Curve

The size distribution of income provides the kind of statistical information we need to determine how total income (and output) is distributed. The **Lorenz curve** is a visual summary of that information; it is a graphic illustration of the size distribution.

Figure 19.1 is a Lorenz curve for the United States. Our lineup of individuals is on the horizontal axis, with the lowest-income earners on the left. On the vertical axis we depict the cumulative share of income received by people in our income line. Consider the lowest quintile of the distribution again. They're represented on the horizontal axis at 20 percent.

size distribution of income: The way total personal income is divided up among households or income classes.

income share: The proportion of total income received by a particular group.

Lorenz curve: A graphic illustration of the cumulative size distribution of income; contrasts complete equality with the actual distribution of income.

FIGURE 19.1

The Lorenz Curve

The Lorenz curve illustrates the extent of income inequality. If all incomes were equal, each fifth of the population would receive one-fifth of total income. In that case, the diagonal line through point *C* would represent the cumulative size distribution of income.

In reality, incomes aren't distributed equally. Point *A*, for example, indicates that the 20 percent of the population with the lowest income receive only 3.1 percent of total income.

Source: Figure 2.3.

Analysis: An increase in the size of the economic pie doesn't ensure everyone a larger slice. A goal of the tax system is to attain a fairer distribution of the economic pie.
Robert Graysmith

If their share of income was identical to their share of population, they'd get 20 percent of total income. This would be represented by point *C* in the figure. In fact, the lowest quintile gets only 3.1 percent, as indicated by point *A*. Point *B* tells us that the *cumulative* share of income received by the lowest *three*-fifths of the population was 25.5 percent.

The really handy feature of the Lorenz curve is the way it contrasts the actual distribution of income with an absolutely equal one. If incomes were distributed equally, the first 20 percent of the people in line would be getting exactly 20 percent of all income. In that case, the Lorenz curve would run through point *C*. Indeed, the Lorenz "curve" would be a straight line along the diagonal. The actual Lorenz curve lies below the diagonal because our national income isn't distributed equally. In fact, the area between the diagonal and the actual Lorenz curve (the shaded area in Figure 19.1) is a convenient measure of the degree of inequality. ***The greater the area between the Lorenz curve and the diagonal, the more inequality exists.***

The visual summary of inequality the Lorenz curve provides is also expressed in a mathematical relationship. The ratio of the shaded area in Figure 19.1 to the area of the triangle formed by the diagonal is called the **Gini coefficient.** The higher the Gini coefficient, the greater the degree of inequality. Between 2000 and 2019, the Gini coefficient rose from 0.462 to 0.484. In other words, the shaded area in Figure 19.1 expanded by nearly 4 percent, indicating *increased* inequality. Although the size of the economic pie (real GDP) increased by 45 percent between 2000 and 2019, some people's slices got a lot bigger while other people saw little improvement, or even less (see the cartoon above).

Gini coefficient:
A mathematical summary of inequality based on the Lorenz curve.

The Call for Intervention

To many people, large and increasing inequality represents a form of **market failure:** The market is generating a suboptimal (unfair) answer to the FOR WHOM question. As in other instances of market failure, the government is called on to intervene. The policy lever in this case is taxes. **By levying taxes on the rich and providing transfer payments to the poor, the government** *redistributes* **market incomes.**

market failure: An imperfection in the market mechanism that prevents optimal outcomes.

THE FEDERAL INCOME TAX

The federal income tax is designed for this redistributional purpose. Specifically, the federal income tax is designed to be **progressive**—that is, to impose higher tax *rates* on high incomes than on low ones. Progressivity is achieved by imposing increasing **marginal tax rates** on higher incomes. The *marginal* tax rate refers to the tax rate imposed on the last (marginal) dollar of income.

progressive tax: A tax system in which tax rates rise as incomes rise.

marginal tax rate: The tax rate imposed on the last (marginal) dollar of income.

Tax Brackets and Rates

In 2020, the tax code specified the seven tax brackets shown in Table 19.1. For an individual with less than $9,876 of taxable income, the tax rate was 10 percent. Any income in excess of $9,875 was taxed at a *higher* rate. If an individual's income rose above $85,525, the

TABLE 19.1

Progressive Taxes

The federal income tax is progressive because it levies higher tax rates on higher incomes. The 2020 marginal tax rate started out at 10 percent for incomes below $9,876 and rose to 37 percent for incomes above $518,400.

Tax Bracket	Marginal Tax Rate
$0–9,875	10%
$9,876–40,125	12
$40,126–85,525	22
$85,526–163,300	24
$163,301–207,350	32
$207,351–518,400	35
Over $518,400	37

Source: Internal Revenue Service (2020 tax rates for single individuals).

amount between $85,526 and $163,300 was taxed at 24 percent. Any income greater than $518,400 was taxed at 37 percent.

To understand the efficiency and equity effects of taxes, we must distinguish between the *marginal* tax rate and the *average* tax rate. A person who earned $520,000 taxable income in 2020 paid the 37 percent tax only on the income in excess of $518,400—that is, the last (marginal) $1,600. The first $9,875 was taxed at a marginal rate of only 10 percent.

Here is how taxes are computed on $520,000 of income:

Marginal Tax Rate	Income		Tax
10% of	$ 9,875	=	$ 987.50
12% of	30,250	=	3,630.00
22% of	45,400	=	9,988.00
24% of	77,775	=	18,666.00
33% of	44,050	=	14,096.00
35% of	311,050	=	108,867.50
37% of	1,600	=	592.00
	$520,000		$156,827.00

Notice that the various marginal tax rates apply only to the income in that specific bracket. By adding up the taxes in each bracket, we get a total tax of $156,827. This represents only 30.2 percent of this individual's income. Hence, this person had a

- *Marginal* tax rate of 37 percent.
- *Average* (or nominal) tax rate of 30.2 percent.

By contrast, a person with only $20,000 of taxable income would pay a *marginal* tax of only 12 percent and an *average* tax of 11 percent. The rationale behind this progressive system is to tax ever-larger percentages of higher incomes, thereby reducing income inequalities. **By making the *after-tax* distribution of income more equal than the *before-tax* distribution, *progressive taxes reduce inequality.***

Table 19.2 summarizes the redistributive impact of the federal income tax. Before taxes, the top quintile gets 52.8 percent of all income. After taxes, their share drops to 49.5 percent. Lower quintiles get increased shares in the process. These modest changes in the size distribution of income arise from progressively higher tax *rates* as incomes increase.

Efficiency Concerns

Although the redistributive intent of a progressive tax system is evident, it raises concerns about efficiency. As noted in the chapter-opening quote, attempts to reslice the pie may end up reducing the size of the pie. The central issue here is incentives. Chapter 16 emphasized that the supply of labor is motivated by the pursuit of income. If Uncle Sam takes away ever-larger chunks of income, won't that dampen the desire to work? If so, *the incentive to work more, produce more, or invest more is reduced by higher marginal tax rates.* This suggests that as marginal tax rates increase, total output shrinks, creating a basic conflict between the goals of equity (more progressive taxes) and efficiency (more output).

Quintile	Before-Tax Share	After-Tax Share
Highest	52.8%	49.5%
Second highest	20.6	21.2
Middle	14.1	15.1
Second lowest	8.6	9.7
Lowest	4.0	4.7

Source: Urban-Brookings Tax Policy Center, 2018.

TABLE 19.2

Before- and After-Tax Incomes

Progressive tax rates take larger portions of high incomes, thus making the *after*-tax income distribution more equal than the *before*-tax distribution.

Tax Migration. How great the conflict is between the equity and efficiency depends on how responsive market participants are to higher tax rates. The Rolling Stones left Great Britain off their 1998–1999 world tour because the British marginal tax rate was so high. The band U2 went a step further—moving their home base from Ireland to the Netherlands to avoid paying Irish income taxes (see World View "Bono Says 'Stupid' to Pay Irish Taxes"). A study by the National Bureau of Economic Research (NBER) revealed that international soccer stars choose to live in low-tax nations even while playing for teams in high-tax nations. In the United States, wealthy individuals leave high-tax states like New York and California to resettle in zero-tax states like Florida and Nevada. Businesses also seek out low-tax states and countries.

WORLD VIEW

BONO SAYS "STUPID" TO PAY IRISH TAXES

When Ireland eliminated the tax break for royalty income in 2006, the rock band U2 packed their bags and moved to the Netherlands, where tax rates are much lower. The band has been subjected to criticism ever since. At the Glastonbury Festival in 2011, protesters inflated a huge banner that asked, "U pay tax 2?," which led to a violent skirmish with concert security. In interviews in 2013–2015, Bono, whose real name is Paul Hewson, has repeatedly rejected the charge that the Irish band's tax-exile status is hypocritical, given its well-publicized calls for more aid to the world's poor. Bono says he doesn't have to be "stupid" about taxes; the band is just being "sensible about the way we're taxed."

Source: Media reports and interviews, 2007–2015.

CRITICAL ANALYSIS: High tax rates deter people from supplying resources. In this case, high taxes motivated U2 to move to another country.

Tax Elasticity of Supply. Not everyone can just pack up and move to avoid higher taxes. But people can adjust the amount of work they do. When marginal tax rates climb, people can choose to work less. We measure such responses with the **tax elasticity of supply:**

$$\frac{\text{Tax elasticity}}{\text{of supply}} = \frac{\text{\% change in quantity supplied}}{\text{\% change in tax rate}}$$

tax elasticity of supply: The percentage change in quantity supplied divided by the percentage change in tax rates.

If the tax elasticity of supply were zero, there'd be no conflict between equity and efficiency. But a zero tax elasticity would also imply that people would continue to work, produce, and invest even if Uncle Sam took *all* their income in taxes. In today's range of taxes, the average household's tax elasticity of labor supply is between 0.15 and 0.30. Hence, if tax *rates* go up by 20 percent, the quantity of labor supplied would decline by 3 to 6 percent. In other words, the size of the pie being resliced would shrink by 3–6 percent. Figure 19.2 confirms that the top marginal tax rate has changed by much more than 20 percent in the past, thereby significantly altering the size of the economic pie.

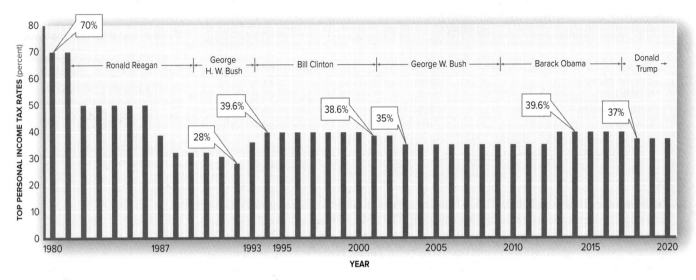

FIGURE 19.2

Changes in Marginal Tax Rates

During the past 40 years, Congress revised the federal income tax system many times. The top marginal tax rate was steadily reduced from 70 percent in 1980 to 28 percent in 1992. It was then raised in 1993–1995. The Bush tax cuts of 2001–2004 reduced marginal tax rates once more. Then President Obama increased the top marginal tax rate to 39.6 again in 2013. President Trump dropped the top tax rate to 37 percent in 2018.

Source: Internal Revenue Service.

Equity Concerns

As if the concern about efficiency weren't enough, critics also raise questions about how well the federal income tax promotes equity. What appears to be a fairly progressive tax in theory turns out to be a lot less progressive in practice. Hundreds of people with $1 million incomes pay no taxes. They aren't necessarily breaking any laws, just taking advantage of loopholes in the tax system.

Loopholes. The progressive *tax rates described in the tax code apply to "taxable" income, not to all income.* The so-called loopholes in the system arise from the way Congress defines taxable income. The tax laws permit one to subtract certain exemptions and deductions from gross income in computing taxable income:

$$\frac{\text{Taxable}}{\text{income}} = \frac{\text{Gross}}{\text{income}} - \text{Exemptions and deductions}$$

Exemptions are permitted for dependent children, spouses, old age, and disabilities. Deductions are permitted for an array of expenses, including home mortgage interest, work-related expenses, child care, depreciation of investments, interest payments, union dues, medical expenses, charitable contributions, and many other items.

The purpose of these many *itemized deductions* is to encourage specific economic activities and reduce potential hardship. The deduction for mortgage interest payments, for example, encourages people to buy their own homes. The deduction for medical expenses helps relieve the financial burden of illness.

Whatever the merits of specific exemptions and deductions, they create potential inequities. *People with high incomes can avoid high taxes by claiming large exemptions and deductions.* In fact, some people with high incomes end up paying *less* tax than people with lower incomes. This violates the principle of **vertical equity,** the progressive intent of taxing people on the basis of their ability to pay.

Table 19.3 illustrates vertical *in*equity. Mr. Jones has an income ($90,000) three times larger than Ms. Smith's ($30,000). However, Mr. Jones also has huge deductions ($70,000) that reduce his *taxable* income dramatically. In fact, Mr. Jones ends up with less *taxable*

vertical equity: Principle that people with higher incomes should pay more taxes.

	Mr. Jones	Ms. Smith
1. Total income	$90,000	$30,000
2. Less exemptions and deductions	−$70,000	−$ 5,000
3. Taxable income	$20,000	$25,000
4. Tax	$ 4,000	$ 5,500
5. Nominal tax rate (= row 4 ÷ row 3)	20%	22%
6. Effective tax rate (= row 4 ÷ row 1)	4.4%	18.3%

TABLE 19.3

Vertical Inequity

Tax exemptions and deductions create a gap between total income and *taxable* income. In this case, Mr. Jones has both a higher income and extensive deductions. He ends up with less *taxable* income than Ms. Smith and so pays less taxes. This vertical inequity is reflected in the lower effective tax rate paid by Mr. Jones (4.4 percent) than Ms. Smith (18.3 percent).

income ($20,000) than Ms. Smith ($25,000). As a result, he also ends up paying lower taxes ($4,000 vs. $5,500). How is this possible? Simply because Mr. Jones has huge itemized deductions for things like mortgage interest, charitable contributions, and the like, and Ms. Smith has nothing comparable.

The deductions that create the vertical inequity between Mr. Jones and Ms. Smith could also violate the principle of **horizontal equity**—as people with the *same* incomes end up paying different amounts of income tax. These horizontal *in*equities also contradict basic notions of fairness.

horizontal equity: Principle that people with equal incomes should pay equal taxes.

Nominal vs. Effective Tax Rates. The "loopholes" created by exemptions, deductions, and tax credits cause a distinction between gross economic income and taxable income. That distinction, in turn, requires us to distinguish between *nominal* tax rates and *effective* tax rates. The term **nominal tax rate** refers to the taxes actually paid as a percentage of *taxable* income. By contrast, the **effective tax rate** is the tax paid divided by *total* economic income without regard to exemptions, deductions, or other intricacies of the tax laws.

nominal tax rate: Taxes paid divided by taxable income.

As Table 19.3 illustrates, someone with a gross income of $90,000 might end up with a much lower *taxable* income, thanks to various tax deductions and exemptions. Mr. Jones ended up with a taxable income of only $20,000 and a tax bill of merely $4,000. As a result, we can characterize Mr. Jones's tax burden in two ways:

effective tax rate: Taxes paid divided by total (gross) income.

$$\frac{\text{Nominal}}{\text{tax rate}} = \frac{\text{Tax paid}}{\text{Taxable income}}$$

$$= \frac{\$4,000}{\$20,000} = 20 \text{ percent}$$

or, alternatively,

$$\frac{\text{Effective}}{\text{tax rate}} = \frac{\text{Tax paid}}{\text{Total economic income}}$$

$$= \frac{\$4,000}{\$90,000} = 4.4 \text{ percent}$$

This huge gap between the nominal tax rate (20 percent) and the effective tax rate (4.4 percent) is a reflection of loopholes in the tax code. It's also the source of the vertical and horizontal inequities discussed earlier. Notice that Ms. Smith, with much less gross income, ends up with an effective tax rate (18.3 percent) that's more than four times higher than Mr. Jones's (4.4 percent).

Front Page Economics "Taxes: Bernie vs. Biden" shows how Bernie Sanders and Joe Biden used these loopholes in 2018. The Bidens had a gross income that was eight times larger than that for the Sanderses. But both families were able to reduce their *taxable income* with deductions for charity, state and local taxes, and home mortgage interest payments.

The Bidens' income clearly put them in the top percent of American households in 2018. But that doesn't mean they paid the top tax rate of 37 percent on all that income. Their tax bill was less than that because (a) they had $314,000 of deductions and (b) taxes are computed on a bracket-by-bracket basis, as shown in Table 19.1. They ended up paying $1,517,831 in federal income taxes, equal to 35.58 percent of their gross income.

FRONT PAGE ECONOMICS

TAXES: BERNIE VS. BIDEN

	The Sanderses	The Bidens
Gross Income	$566,421	$4,580,459
Deductions		
Charitable contributions	$ 18,950	$ 275,796
State and local taxes	10,000	10,000
Mortgage interest	12,814	28,555
Miscellaneous	5,128	22
Taxable Income	$519,529	$4,266,086
Income Tax	$133,124	$1,517,831

Source: 2018 tax returns.

CRITICAL ANALYSIS: Taxes are levied on *taxable* income, not total income. Various deductions reduce taxable income and *effective* **tax rates**.

Bernie Sanders also got a tax break from the same deductions. He paid $133,124 in federal income taxes. That represented 25.62 percent of his *taxable* income but only 23.50 percent of his *gross* income. Other people end up with far lower *effective* tax rates by finding larger tax deductions or, better, receiving *non*taxable income (e.g., interest on municipal bonds).

Tax-Induced Misallocations. Tax loopholes not only foster inequity but encourage inefficiency as well. The optimal mix of output is the one that balances consumer preferences and opportunity costs. Tax loopholes, however, encourage a different mix of output. By offering preferential treatment for some activities, the tax code reduces their relative accounting cost. In so doing, **tax preferences induce resource shifts into tax-preferred activities.** The deduction for mortgage interest, for example, encourages people to purchase homes, thereby changing the mix of output.

These resource allocations are the explicit goal of tax preferences. The accumulation of exemptions, deductions, and credits has become so unwieldy and complex, however, that tax considerations often overwhelm economic considerations in many investment and consumption decisions. The resulting mix of output, many observers feel, is decidedly inferior to a *pure* market outcome. From this viewpoint, the federal income tax promotes both inequity and inefficiency.

tax base: The amount of income or property directly subject to nominal tax rates.

A Shrinking Tax Base. Loopholes in the tax code create yet another problem. As the **tax base** gets smaller and smaller, it becomes increasingly difficult to sustain, much less increase, tax revenues. The tax arithmetic is simple:

$$\text{Tax revenue} = \frac{\text{Average}}{\text{tax rate}} \times \frac{\text{Tax}}{\text{base}}$$

As deductions, exemptions, and credits accumulate, the tax base (taxable income) keeps shrinking. To keep tax rates low—or to reduce them further—Congress has to stop this erosion of the tax base.

The Bush Tax Cuts (2001–2010)

Tax reforms in 1986 and 1993 not only broadened the tax base but also raised tax rates (to a top rate of 39.6 percent). President Bush worried that those higher marginal tax rates would slow economic growth. He also felt that low-income households would gain more from faster economic growth than from progressive tax and transfer policies. After his 2000 election, he made tax *cuts* one of his highest priorities.

Reduced Marginal Rates. As Figure 19.2 illustrated, the 2001 Tax Relief Act reduced the highest marginal tax rate in three steps, to 35 percent from 39.6 percent. That act also reduced the marginal tax rate for the *lowest* income class to only 10 percent (from 15 percent). The goal of this rate cut was to increase the disposable income of low-wage workers (equity) while giving them more incentive to work (efficiency).

New "Loopholes". Aside from encouraging more *work,* President Bush also sought to encourage more *education.* The biggest incentive was a tuition tax deduction of $3,000 per year. This allows students, or their parents, to reduce their taxable income by the amount of tuition payments. In effect, Uncle Sam ends up paying part of the first $3,000 in tuition. In addition, the 2001 legislation allows people to save more money for college in tax-free accounts.

As welcome as these "loopholes" are to college students, they raise the same kind of efficiency and equity concerns as other tax preferences. If most of the students who take the tax deduction would have gone to college anyway, the deduction isn't very *efficient* in promoting education. Furthermore, most of the deductions go to middle-class families who itemize deductions. Hence, the tuition deduction introduces new vertical *inequities.* Few students have protested this particular loophole, however.

The creation of this and other tax preferences raises all the same issues about equity and efficiency. ***The greater the number of loopholes, the wider the distinction between gross incomes and taxable incomes,*** as the previous Front Page Economics reveals.

The Obama Tax Hikes

President Obama vowed to reverse the "Bush tax cuts for the rich." Within a month of his inauguration, Obama proposed to raise the highest marginal tax rate from 35 percent to its former 39.6 percent. He also proposed raising taxes on capital gains, dividends, and estates. Critics objected that the resultant gains in *equity* (Obama's avowed goal) would be more than offset by the loss of *efficiency.* In other words, the pie would shrink when Obama resliced it. When the economy fell into the 2008–2009 recession, President Obama agreed to postpone the proposed tax hikes. In 2011 he again pressed for higher marginal tax rates and Congress complied, raising the top marginal tax rate to 39.6 percent.

Trump Tax Cuts

The tax-rate pendulum swung back again with the election of Donald Trump. President Trump vowed to both simplify the tax code and reduce tax burdens as part of his broad "Make America Great Again" agenda. He convinced Congress to cut the top marginal rate from 39.6 to 37 percent in 2018 and to reduce other rates as well.

President Trump achieved more dramatic reductions in business taxes. He persuaded Congress to reduce the top tax rate on corporations from 35 percent to only 21 percent, a huge drop in tax burdens. The primary motivation for these proposals was *efficiency;* Trump believed such a dramatic drop in business taxes would spur a sharp increase in investment, and ultimately economic growth. Critics, though, worried about the *equity* implications of such tax cutting. The millions of businesses organized as partnerships and subchapter S corporations—disproportionately owned by higher income individuals—would get a windfall tax break.

Biden Tax Hikes

During the 2020 presidential campaign, Joe Biden proposed to reverse some of the Trump tax cuts. Biden felt that the Trump tax cuts unfairly benefited the rich. He was also concerned about the revenue loss from those tax cuts, especially in view of the steep rise in coronavirus-related spending. He proposed increasing the top marginal tax rate from 37 percent back to 39.6 percent, thus affecting only people making more than $400,000. He also proposed to increase the corporate tax rate from 21 percent to 28 percent.

PAYROLL, STATE, AND LOCAL TAXES

The federal income tax is only one of many taxes people must pay. For many families, in fact, the federal income tax is the smallest of many tax bills. Other tax bills come from the Social Security Administration and from state and local governments. These taxes also affect both efficiency and equity.

Sales and Property Taxes

Sales taxes are the major source of revenue for state governments. Many local governments also impose sales taxes, but most cities rely on *property taxes* for the bulk of their tax receipts. Both taxes are **regressive:** They impose higher tax rates on lower incomes.

> **regressive tax:** A tax system in which tax rates fall as incomes rise.

At first glance, a 5 percent sales tax doesn't look very regressive. After all, the same 5 percent tax is imposed on virtually all goods. But we're interested in *people,* not goods and services, so **we gauge tax burdens in relation to people's incomes.** A tax is regressive if it imposes a proportionally *larger* burden on *lower* incomes.

This is exactly what a uniform sales tax does. To understand this concept, we have to look not only at how much tax is levied on each dollar of consumption but also at *what percentage of income* is spent on consumer goods.

Low-income families spend everything they've got (and sometimes more) on basic consumption. As a result, most of their income ends up subject to sales tax. By contrast, higher-income families save more. As a result, a smaller proportion of their income is subject to a sales tax. Table 19.4 illustrates this regressive feature of a sales tax. Notice that the low-income family ends up paying a larger fraction of its income (4.75 percent) than does the high-income family (2.86 percent).

Property taxes are regressive also and for the same reason. Low-income families spend a higher percentage of their incomes for shelter. A uniform property tax thus ends up taking a larger fraction of their income than it does of the incomes of high-income families.

Tax Incidence. It may sound strange to suggest that low-income families bear the brunt of property taxes. After all, the tax is imposed on the landlords who *own* property, not on people who *rent* apartments and houses. However, here again we have to distinguish between the apparent payee and the individual whose income is actually reduced by the tax. **Tax incidence** refers to the actual burden of a tax—that is, who really ends up paying it.

> **tax incidence:** Distribution of the real burden of a tax.

In general, people who rent apartments pay higher rents as a result of property taxes. In other words, landlords pass along to tenants any property taxes they must pay. Thus, to a large extent, **the burden of property taxes is reflected in higher rents.** Tenants pay property taxes *indirectly* via these higher rents. The incidence of the property tax thus falls on renters in the form of higher rents, rather than on the landlords who write checks to the local tax authority.

Payroll Taxes

Payroll taxes also impose effective tax burdens quite different from their nominal appearance. Consider, for example, the Social Security payroll tax, the second-largest source of

TABLE 19.4

The Regressivity of Sales Taxes

A sales tax is imposed on consumer purchases. Although the sales tax itself is uniform (here at 5 percent), the taxes paid represent different proportions of high and low incomes. In this case, the low-income family's *sales tax* bill equals 4.75 percent of its *income.* The high-income family has a sales tax bill equal to only 2.86 percent of its income.

	High-Income Family	Low-Income Family
Income	$70,000	$20,000
Consumption	$40,000	$19,000
Saving	$30,000	$ 1,000
Sales tax paid (5% of consumption)	$ 2,000	$ 950
Effective tax rate (sales tax ÷ income)	2.86%	4.75%

QUANTITY OF LABOR (labor-hours per time period)

FIGURE 19.3
The Incidence of a Payroll Tax
Some portion of a payroll tax imposed on employers may actually be borne by workers. The tax raises the cost of labor and so imposes a tax-burdened supply curve (S + tax) on employers. The intersection of this tax-burdened supply curve with the labor demand curve determines a new equilibrium of employment (L_1). At that level, employers pay w_1 in wages and taxes, but workers get only w_2 in wages. The wage reduction from w_0 to w_2 is a real burden of the payroll tax, and it is borne by workers.

federal tax revenue (see Figure 4.5). Every worker sees a Social Security (FICA) tax taken out of his or her paycheck. The nominal tax rate on workers is 7.65 percent. But there's a catch: Only wages below a legislated ceiling are taxable. In 2020, the taxable wage ceiling was $137,700. Hence, a worker earning $200,000 paid no more tax than a worker earning $137,700. As a result, the effective tax *rate* (tax paid ÷ total wages) is lower for high-income workers than low- and middle-income workers. That's a *regressive* tax.

There is another problem in gauging the impact of the Social Security payroll tax. Nominally, the Social Security payroll tax consists of two parts: half paid by employees and half by employers. But do employers really pay their half? Or do they end up paying lower wages to compensate for their tax share? If so, employees end up paying *both* halves of the Social Security payroll tax.

Figure 19.3 illustrates how the tax incidence of the payroll tax is distributed. The supply of labor reflects the ability and willingness of people to work for various wage rates. Labor demand reflects the **marginal revenue product (MRP)** of labor; it sets a *limit* to the wage an employer is willing to pay.

marginal revenue product (MRP): The change in total revenue associated with one additional unit of input.

Cost of Labor. The employer's half of the payroll tax increases the nominal cost of labor. Thus, the S + tax curve lies *above* the labor supply curve. It incorporates the wages that must be paid to workers *plus* the payroll tax that must be paid to the Social Security Trust Fund. This total labor cost is the one that will determine how many workers are hired. Specifically, the intersection of the S + tax curve and the labor demand curve determines the equilibrium level of employment (L_1). The employer will pay the amount w_1 for this much labor. But part of that outlay ($w_1 - w_2$) will go to the public treasury in the form of payroll taxes. Workers will receive only w_2 in wages. This is less than they'd get in the absence of the payroll tax (compare w_0 and w_2). Thus, *fewer workers are employed, and the net wage is reduced when a payroll tax is imposed.*

Tax Incidence. What Figure 19.3 reveals is how the true incidence of payroll taxes is distributed. The employer share of the Social Security tax is $w_1 - w_2$. This is the amount sent to the Social Security Administration for every hour of labor. Of this amount, the employer incurs higher labor costs ($w_1 - w_0$) and workers lose ($w_0 - w_2$) in the wage rate. Hence, workers end up paying *their* share (7.65 percent) of the Social Security tax *plus* a sizable part ($w_0 - w_2$) of the employer's share ($w_1 - w_2$).

These reflections on tax incidence don't imply that payroll taxes are necessarily bad. They do emphasize, however, that *the apparent taxpayer isn't necessarily the individual who bears the real burden of a tax.*

FIGURE 19.4

Income Tax Shares

Despite loopholes, the federal income tax remains progressive. The richest 1 percent of households pay 37 percent of all federal income taxes, though they receive only 20 percent of all income.

Source: Internal Revenue Service (2016 data).

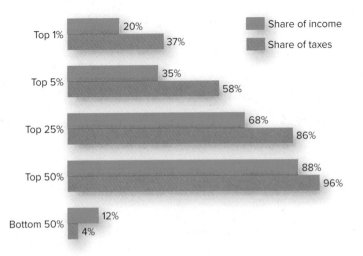

TAXES AND INEQUALITY

The regressivity of the Social Security payroll tax and of many state and local taxes offsets most of the progressivity of the federal income tax. The top 1 percent of income recipients get 20 percent of total income and pay 37 percent of federal income tax (see Figure 19.4). Hence, the federal income tax is still progressive, despite rampant loopholes. Other federal taxes (Social Security, excise), however, reduce the tax share of the rich to only 21 percent. State and local tax incidence reduces their tax share still further.

A Proportional System

The final result is that *the tax system as a whole ends up being nearly proportional.* High-income families end up paying roughly the same percentage of their income in taxes as do low-income families. The tax system does reduce inequality somewhat, but the redistributive impact is quite small.

The Impact of Transfers

The tax system tells only half the redistribution story. It tells whose income was taken away. Equally important is who gets the income the government collects. The government completes the redistribution process by *transferring* income to consumers. The **income transfers** may be explicit, as in the case of welfare benefits, Social Security payments, and unemployment insurance. Or the transfers may be indirect, as in the case of public schools, farm subsidies, and student loans. We'll look more closely at how income transfers alter the distribution of income in the next chapter.

income transfers: Payments to individuals for which no current goods or services are exchanged, such as Social Security, welfare, and unemployment benefits.

WHAT IS *FAIR*?

To many people, the apparent ineffectiveness of the tax system in redistributing income is a mark of **government failure.** They want a much more decisive reslicing of the pie—one in which the top quintile gets a *lot* less than half the pie and the poor get more than 3.1 percent (Figure 2.3). But how much redistribution should we attempt? Rich people can rattle off as many good reasons for preserving income inequalities as poor people can recite for eliminating them.

Economists aren't uniquely qualified to overcome self-interest, much less to divine what a fair distribution of income might look like. But economists can assess some of the costs and benefits of altering the distribution of income.

government failure: Government intervention that fails to improve economic outcomes.

The Costs of Greater Equality

The greatest potential risk to more progressive redistribution is the reduced incentives it might leave in its wake. People *are* motivated by income. In factor markets, higher wages call forth more workers and induce them to work longer hours. In fields where earnings are very high, as in the medical, engineering, and legal professions, people are willing to spend many years and thousands of dollars acquiring the skills such earnings require. Could we really expect people to make such sacrifices in a market that paid everyone the same wage?

The same problem exists in product markets. The willingness of producers to supply goods and services depends on their expectation of profits. Why should they work hard and take risks to produce goods and services if their efforts won't make them any better off? If incomes were distributed equally, producers might just as well sit back and enjoy the fruits of someone else's labor.

The essential economic problem absolute income equality poses is that it breaks the market link between effort and reward. If all incomes were equal, it would no longer pay to make an above-average effort. If people stopped making such efforts, total output would decline, and we'd have less income to share (a smaller pie). Not all high incomes are attributable to great skill or effort. Such factors as luck, market power, and family connections also influence incomes. It remains true, however, that the promise of higher income encourages work effort. Absolute income equality threatens those conditions.

The argument for preserving income inequalities is thus anchored in a concern for productivity. From this perspective, income inequalities are the driving force behind much of our production. By preserving inequalities, we not only enrich the fortunate few, but also provide incentives to take risks, invest more, and work harder. In so doing, we enlarge the economic pie, including the slices available to lower-income groups. Thus, everyone is potentially better off, even if only a few end up rich. This is the rationale that keeps the top marginal tax rate in the United States below those in many other countries (see World View "Top Tax Rates").

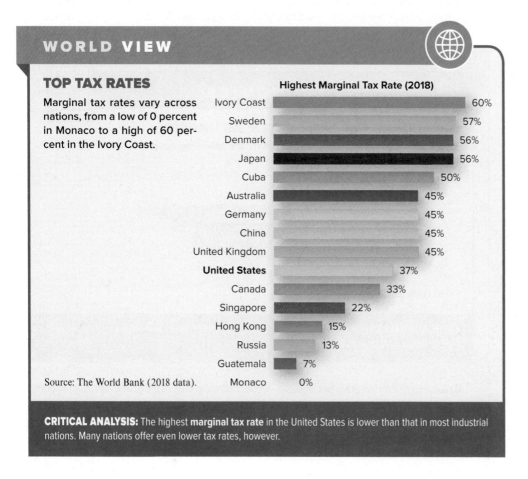

WORLD VIEW

TOP TAX RATES

Marginal tax rates vary across nations, from a low of 0 percent in Monaco to a high of 60 percent in the Ivory Coast.

Highest Marginal Tax Rate (2018)

Country	Rate
Ivory Coast	60%
Sweden	57%
Denmark	56%
Japan	56%
Cuba	50%
Australia	45%
Germany	45%
China	45%
United Kingdom	45%
United States	37%
Canada	33%
Singapore	22%
Hong Kong	15%
Russia	13%
Guatemala	7%
Monaco	0%

Source: The World Bank (2018 data).

CRITICAL ANALYSIS: The highest **marginal tax rate** in the United States is lower than that in most industrial nations. Many nations offer even lower tax rates, however.

The Benefits of Greater Equality

Although the potential benefits of inequality are impressive, ***there's a trade-off between efficiency and equality.*** Moreover, many people are convinced that the terms of the trade-off are exaggerated and the benefits of greater equality are ignored. These rebuttals take the form of economic and noneconomic arguments.

The economic arguments for greater equality also focus on incentives. The first argument is that the present degree of inequality is more than necessary to maintain work incentives. Upper-class incomes needn't be 15 times as large as those of the lowest-income classes; perhaps 4 times as large would do as well.

The second argument is that low-income earners might actually work harder if incomes were distributed more fairly. As matters now stand, the low-income worker sees little chance of making it big. Extremely low income can also inhibit workers' ability to work by subjecting them to poor health, malnutrition, or inadequate educational opportunities. Accordingly, some redistribution of income to the poor might improve the productivity of low-income workers and compensate for reduced productivity among the rich.

Finally, we noted that the maze of loopholes that preserves inequality also distorts economic incentives. Labor and investment decisions are influenced by tax considerations, not just economic benefits and costs. If greater equality were achieved via tax simplification, a more efficient allocation of resources might result.

DECISIONS FOR TOMORROW

Do We Need a Billionaire's Tax?

Public opinion polls reveal that a majority of Americans feel the present tax system isn't doing an adequate job. As Front Page Economics "Americans See Tax System as Unfair" confirms, only 5 percent of American adults feel the tax system is "very fair," while 23 percent feel that it is "not at all fair." The overwhelming sentiment is that the rich simply don't pay enough taxes.

FRONT PAGE ECONOMICS

AMERICANS SEE TAX SYSTEM AS UNFAIR

A March 2019 poll asked American adults the following question: "How fair do you think our present federal tax system is?"

Very fair	5%
Moderately fair	41%
Not too fair	30%
Not at all fair	23%

Source: Pew Research Center.

CRITICAL ANALYSIS: Tax policy must try to balance the goals of **equity and efficiency.** Polls suggest that the public wants more emphasis on equity.

Reforms of the income tax system could increase the tax burden on high-income households. More loopholes could be closed and marginal tax rates increased. But such reforms have had a very mixed record and critics worry about the incentive effects that would accompany higher effective tax rates.

Wealth Tax? An alternative to higher *income* tax rates would be a tax on *wealth*. As we noted earlier, wealth inequality is far more severe than income inequality. By taxing wealth directly, we could reduce that inequality and generate tax revenues that would support public programs that disproportionately benefit the poor (e.g., public schools, transportation, health). A 2020 Reuters/Ipsos opinion poll revealed that 64 percent of American adults agree that "the very rich should contribute an extra share of their total wealth each year to support public programs."

In the 2020 presidential campaign, Elizabeth Warren and Bernie Sanders made wealth tax proposals the center of their platforms. Warren proposed a progressive tax on wealth that would start at 2 percent on wealth of $50 million and rise to 6 percent on wealth in excess of $1 billion. Bernie Sanders proposed an even more progressive tax. After revealing that he thought "billionaires shouldn't exist," he called for a tax that began at 1 percent for wealth of $32 million and rose to 8 percent on wealth in excess of $10 billion. For Amazon CEO Jeff Bezos, that would have required a tax payment of roughly $7 billion in 2020. For Tesla CEO Elon Musk, that would have required a wealth tax of approximately $2 billion.

Equity vs. Efficiency. Proponents of such wealth taxes emphasize two things. First, a wealth tax would go a long way to reducing economic inequality. Second, a wealth tax would raise trillions of dollars over a 10-year period that could fund needed public programs, further reducing lifestyle inequalities. Equity would be served.

Opponents of wealth taxes point to some drawbacks. First, enforcement would be exceedingly difficult, as it would require valuations for businesses, homes, farms, and other assets. Second, it would encourage wealthy individuals to move their wealth to other countries or hide them in various tax shelters. And, most importantly, a wealth tax would blunt the very economic incentives that encouraged Elon Musk, Jeff Bezos, and other entrepreneurs to create spectacularly successful businesses that have benefited consumers.

SUMMARY

- The distribution of income largely determines access to the goods and services we produce. Wealth distribution is important for the same reason. **LO19-3**

- The size distribution of income tells us how incomes are divided up among individuals. The Lorenz curve is a graphic summary of the cumulative size distribution of income. The Gini coefficient is a mathematical summary. **LO19-3**

- Personal incomes are distributed quite unevenly in the United States. At present, the highest quintile (the top 20 percent) gets half of all cash income, and the bottom quintile gets less than 4 percent. **LO19-3**

- The trade-off between equity and efficiency is rooted in supply incentives. The tax elasticity of supply measures how the quantity of available resources (labor and capital) declines when tax rates rise. **LO19-3**

- The progressivity of the federal income tax is weakened by various loopholes (exemptions, deductions, and credits) that create a distinction between nominal and effective tax rates and cause vertical and horizontal inequities. **LO19-2**

- Marginal tax rates were reduced greatly in the 1980s and have alternately risen and fallen since. **LO19-1**

- Mildly progressive federal income taxes are offset by regressive payroll, state, and local taxes. Overall, the tax system redistributes little income; most redistribution occurs through transfer payments. **LO19-2**

- Tax incidence refers to the real burden of a tax. In many cases, reductions in wages, increases in rent, or other real income changes represent the true burden of a tax. **LO19-2**

- There is a trade-off between efficiency and equality. If all incomes are equal, there's no economic reward for superior productivity. On the other hand, a more equal distribution of incomes might increase the productivity of lower-income groups and serve important noneconomic goals as well. **LO19-3**

- Wealth taxes have the potential to achieve greater equality than income taxes. But they raise concerns about enforceability and incentives. **LO19-3**

Key Terms

personal income (PI)	market failure	effective tax rate
in-kind income	progressive tax	tax base
wealth	marginal tax rate	regressive tax
size distribution of income	tax elasticity of supply	tax incidence
income share	vertical equity	marginal revenue product (MRP)
Lorenz curve	horizontal equity	income transfers
Gini coefficient	nominal tax rate	government failure

Questions for Discussion

1. What goods or services do you and your family receive without directly paying for them? How do these goods affect the distribution of economic welfare? **LO19-2**

2. Why are incomes distributed so unevenly? Identify and explain three major causes of inequality. **LO19-3**

3. Do inequalities stimulate productivity? In what ways? Provide two specific examples. **LO19-3**

4. What loopholes reduced the 2018 tax bills of Bernie Sanders and Joe Biden (see Front Page Economics "Taxes: Bernie vs. Biden")? What's the purpose of those loopholes? **LO19-1**

5. If a new tax system not only encouraged more output but also created greater inequality, would it be desirable? **LO19-3**

6. If the tax elasticity of supply were zero, how high could the tax rate go before people reduced their work effort? How do families vary the quantity of labor supplied when tax rates change? **LO19-3**

7. Is a tax deduction for tuition likely to increase college enrollments? How will it affect horizontal and vertical equities? **LO19-3**

8. What share of taxes *should* the rich pay (see Figure 19.4)? Should the poor pay *any* taxes? **LO19-3**

9. How fair do you think the federal tax system is? What answer would you give to the question in Front Page Economics "Americans See Tax System as Unfair"? **LO19-2**

10. How might Jeff Bezos or Elon Musk react if the wealth tax proposed by Bernie Sanders or Elizabeth Warren were enacted? **LO19-3**

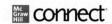
LO19-1 1. How much tax did the Bidens pay in 2018 (Front Page Economics "Taxes: Bernie vs. Biden") on
(*a*) The first $9,000 of taxable income?
(*b*) The last $9,000 of taxable income?

LO19-2 2. For married individuals filing joint returns, the 2018 marginal tax rates were 32 percent for incomes above $315,000, 35 percent for incomes above $400,000, and 37 percent for incomes above $600,000. If deductions for charitable contributions were not allowed, how much more tax would the Sanderses have paid in 2018 (Front Page Economics "Taxes: Bernie vs. Biden")?

LO19-2 3. According to Front Page Economics "Taxes: Bernie vs. Biden," in 2018 what was the Bidens'
(*a*) Nominal tax rate?
(*b*) Effective tax rate?

LO19-1 4. Use Table 19.1 to compute the taxes on a taxable income of $250,000.
(*a*) What is the marginal tax rate?
(*b*) What is the average tax rate?

LO19-1 5. Using Table 19.1, compute the taxable income and taxes for the following taxpayers:

Taxpayer	Gross Income	Deductions	Taxable Income	Tax
A	$ 20,000	$ 4,000	_____	_____
B	40,000	16,000	_____	_____
C	80,000	34,000	_____	_____
D	200,000	110,000	_____	_____

Which taxpayer has
(*a*) The highest nominal (or average) tax rate?
(*b*) The highest effective tax rate?
(*c*) The highest marginal tax rate?

LO19-2 6. If the tax elasticity of supply is 0.15, by how much will the quantity supplied increase when the marginal tax rate decreases from 40 to 36 percent?

LO19-2 7. By how much might the quantity of labor supplied decrease if the tax elasticity of supply were 0.20 and the marginal tax rate increased from 35 to 45 percent?

LO19-3 8. What is the difference in the top marginal tax rate between Germany and Guatemala (World View "Top Tax Rates")?

LO19-2 9. What percentage of income is paid in Social Security taxes by a worker in 2020 with wage earnings of
(*a*) $30,000?
(*b*) $70,000?
(*c*) $200,000?
(*d*) Is this a progressive, regressive, or proportional tax?

PROBLEMS FOR CHAPTER 19 (cont'd)

LO19-2 10. According to Table 19.2, by how many percentage points does the federal income tax
(a) Reduce the income share of the top quintile?
(b) Increase the share of the lowest quintile?

LO19-1 11. Following are hypothetical data on the size distribution of income and wealth for each quintile
(one-fifth) of a population:

Quintile	Lowest	Second	Third	Fourth	Highest
Income	5%	10%	15%	25%	45%
Wealth	2%	8%	12%	20%	58%

(a) On the graph, draw the line of absolute equality; then draw a Lorenz curve for income, and
shade the area between the two curves.
(b) In the same diagram, draw a Lorenz curve for wealth. Is the distribution of wealth more
equal or less equal than the distribution of income?

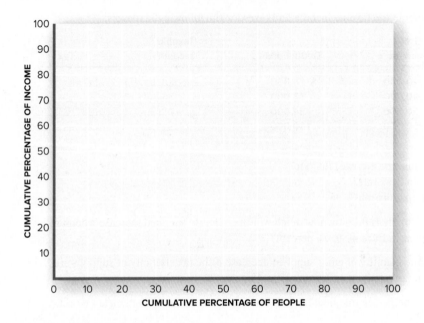

LO19-3 12. (a) On the accompanying graph, draw the supply and demand for labor that are represented by
the following data:

Wage	$12	11	10	9	8	7	6	5	4	3	2	1
Quantity of labor												
Supplied	20	17	14	12	10	8	6	5	4	3	2	1
Demanded	2	3	4	5	6	8	10	12	14	16	18	20

(b) How many workers are employed in equilibrium?
(c) What wage are they paid?
(d) Now suppose a payroll tax of $2 per worker is imposed on the employee. Draw the "supply +
tax" graph that results.
(e) How many workers are now employed?
(f) Now how much is the employer paying for each worker?
(g) Now how much is each worker receiving?
For the incidence of this tax, compared to the initial equilibrium:
(h) What is the increase in the wage paid by the employer?
(i) What is the reduction in the wage received by the workers?

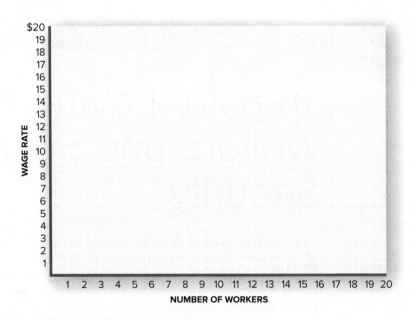

LO19-3 13. *Decisions for Tomorrow:* Identify each of the following as income or wealth
   (*a*) Wages from working as an accountant.
   (*b*) A $350,000 savings account.
   (*c*) $40,000 in Apple stock.

Design Credit: Shutterstock

DreamPictures/Pam Ostrow/Blend Images LLC

CHAPTER 20

Transfer Payments: Welfare and Social Security

Americans are compassionate. Public opinion polls reveal that an overwhelming majority of the public wants to "help the needy." Most Americans say they're even willing to pay more taxes to help fund aid to the poor. But their compassion is tempered by caution: Taxpayers don't want to be ripped off. They want to be sure their money is helping the "truly needy," not being squandered by deadbeats, drug addicts, shirkers, and "welfare queens."

The conflict between compassion and resentment affects not only welfare programs for the poor but also Social Security for the aged, unemployment insurance benefits for the jobless, and even disability benefits for injured workers. In every one of these programs, people are getting money without working. In effect, they're getting a "free ride."

The risk of providing a free ride is that some of the people who take it could have gotten by without it. As the humorist Dave Barry observed, if the government offers $1 million to people with six toes, a lot of people will try to grow a sixth toe or claim they have one. Income transfers create similar incentives: They encourage people to change their behavior in order to get a free ride.

This chapter focuses on how income transfer programs change not only the distribution of income but also work incentives and behavior. We address the following central questions:

- **How much income do income transfer programs redistribute?**
- **How are transfer benefits computed?**
- **How do transfer payments alter market behavior?**

MAJOR TRANSFER PROGRAMS

More than half of every dollar the federal government spends goes to **income transfers** (see Figure 4.5). That amounts to *$2.5 trillion* a year in transfer payments. Who gets all this money?

The easy answer to this question is that almost every household gets some of the transfer money. There are more than 100 federal income transfer programs. Students get tuition grants and subsidized loans. Farmers get crop assistance. Home owners get disaster relief when their homes are destroyed. Veterans get benefit checks and subsidized health

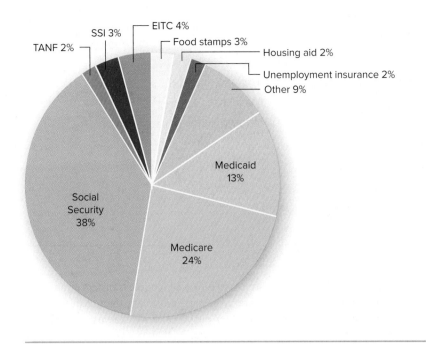

FIGURE 20.1

Income Transfer Programs

There are nearly 100 different federal income transfer programs redistributing more than $2.5 trillion. However, just three programs—Social Security, Medicare, and Medicaid—account for 75 percent of all transfers. Cash welfare benefits (TANF, SSI) absorb only 5 percent of all income transfers.

Source: U.S. Office of Management and Budget (FY 2018 data).

care. People over age 65 get Social Security benefits and subsidized health care. And poor people get welfare checks, food stamps, and subsidized housing.

Although income transfers are widely distributed, not everyone shares equally in the tax-paid bounty. As Figure 20.1 shows, just three of the myriad transfer programs account for 75 percent of total outlays. Social Security, the largest program, alone accounts for 38 percent of the transfer budget. Medicare and Medicaid benefits absorb another 37 percent. By contrast, welfare checks account for only 4 percent of all income transfers.

income transfers: Payments to individuals for which no current goods or services are exchanged, such as Social Security, welfare, and unemployment benefits.

Cash versus In-Kind Benefits

Income transfer doesn't always entail cash payments. The Medicare program, for example, is a health insurance subsidy program that pays hospital and doctor bills for people over age 65. The 60 million people who receive Medicare benefits don't get checks from Uncle Sam; instead Uncle Sam pays the bills for the medical *services* they receive. The same is true for the 75 million people who get Medicaid. Poor people get free health care from the Medicaid program; their benefits are paid *in-kind,* not in cash. Such programs provide **in-kind transfers**—that is, direct transfers of goods and services rather than cash. Food stamps, rent subsidies, legal aid, and subsidized school lunches are all in-kind transfer programs. By contrast, Social Security is a **cash transfer** because it mails benefit checks, not services, to recipients.

in-kind transfers: Direct transfers of goods and services rather than cash, such as food stamps, Medicaid benefits, and housing subsidies.

The provision of in-kind benefits rather than cash is intended to promote specific objectives. Few taxpayers object to feeding the hungry. But they bristle at the thought that welfare recipients might spend the income they receive on something potentially harmful like liquor or drugs or on nonessentials like cars or fancy clothes. To minimize that risk, taxpayers offer electronic food stamps (now called Supplemental Nutrition Assistance Program [SNAP] vouchers), not cash, thereby limiting the recipient's consumption choices. This helps reassure taxpayers that their assistance is being well spent.

cash transfers: Income transfers that entail direct cash payments to recipients, such as Social Security, welfare, and unemployment benefits.

Similar considerations shape the Medicare program. Taxpayers could "cash out" Medicare by simply mailing older people $800 billion now spent on the program every year. But then some healthy older Americans would get cash they didn't need. Some sick people might not get as much money as *they* needed. Or they might choose to spend their new-found income on something other than health care. The end result would be a smaller health care gain than in-kind transfers facilitate.

FIGURE 20.2

Social Insurance versus Welfare

Social insurance programs provide *event*-based transfers—for example, upon reaching age 65 or becoming unemployed or disabled. Welfare programs offer benefits only to those in need; they're *means-tested*. Social insurance transfers greatly outnumber welfare transfers.

Source: U.S. Office of Management and Budget (FY 2018 data).

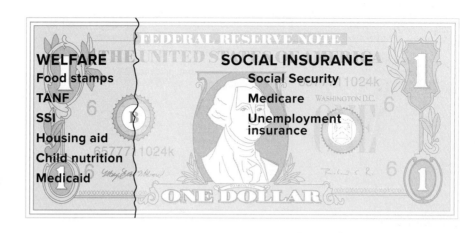

WELFARE
Food stamps
TANF
SSI
Housing aid
Child nutrition
Medicaid

SOCIAL INSURANCE
Social Security
Medicare
Unemployment insurance

---

target efficiency: The percentage of income transfers that go to the intended recipients and purposes.

The **target efficiency** of a transfer program refers to how well income transfers attain their intended purpose. In-kind medical transfers are more target-efficient than cash transfers because recipients can spend cash transfers for other purposes. Food stamps are more target-efficient than cash in reducing hunger for the same reason. If given cash rather than food stamps, recipients would spend less than 70 cents of each dollar on food.

Social Insurance versus Welfare

You may have noted by now that not all income transfers go to the poor. A lot of student loans go to middle-class college students. And disaster relief helps rebuild both mansions and trailer parks. Such income transfers are triggered by specific *events,* not the recipient's income. By contrast, welfare checks are *means-tested:* They go only to families with little income and few assets.

welfare programs: Means-tested income transfer programs, such as welfare and food stamps.

Welfare programs always entail some kind of income eligibility test. To receive welfare payments, a family must prove that it has too little income to fend for itself. Medicaid is an in-kind **welfare program** because only poor people are eligible for the health care benefits of that program. To get food stamps, another in-kind welfare program, a family must also pass an income test.

social insurance programs: Event-conditioned income transfers intended to reduce the costs of specific problems, such as Social Security and unemployment insurance.

Social Security and Medicare aren't *welfare* programs because recipients don't have to be poor. To get Social Security or Medicare benefits you just have to be old enough. The *event* of reaching age 62 makes people eligible for Social Security retirement benefits. At age 65 everyone—whether rich or poor—gets Medicare benefits. These event-conditioned benefits are the hallmark of **social insurance programs:** They insure people against the costs of old age, illness, disability, unemployment, and other specific problems. As Figure 20.2 illustrates, *most income transfers are for social insurance programs, not welfare.*

Transfer Goals

market failure: An imperfection in the market mechanism that prevents optimal outcomes.

If the market sliced up the economic pie in a manner that society deemed fair, there would be no need for all these government-provided income transfers. Hence, the mere existence of such programs implies a **market failure**—an unfair market-generated distribution of income. When the market alone slices up the pie, some people get too much and others get too little. To redress this inequity, we ask the government to play Robin Hood—taking income from the rich and giving it to the poor. Thus, *the basic goal of income transfer programs is to reduce income inequalities*—to change the market's answer to the FOR WHOM question.

Unintended Consequences

Although income transfers try to change the distribution of income in desired ways, they are not costless interventions. The Law of Unintended Consequences rears its ugly head

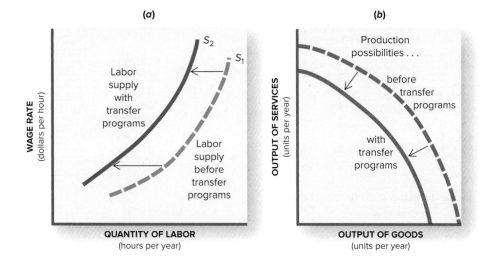

FIGURE 20.3

Reduced Labor Supply and Output

Transfer payments may induce people to supply less labor. If this happens, the supply of labor shifts to the left and the economy's production possibilities shrink. We end up with less total output.

here: *Income transfers often change market behavior and outcomes in unintended (and undesired) ways.*

Reduced Output. Work incentives are a potential problem. If you can get paid for *not* working (via a transfer payment), why would you go to work? Why endure 40 hours of toil for a paycheck when you can stay home and collect a welfare check, an unemployment check, or Social Security? If the income transfers are large enough, I'll stay home too. When people reduce their **labor supply** in response to income transfers, total output will shrink. Figure 20.3 shows that *attempts to redistribute income may reduce total income.* In other words, the pie shrinks when we try to reslice it.

Undesirable Behavior. A reduction in labor supply isn't the only unintended consequence of income transfer programs. People may also change their *nonwork* behavior. Welfare benefits give a (small) incentive to women to have more children and to teen moms to establish their own households. Medicare and Medicaid encourage people to overuse health care services and neglect the associated costs. Unemployment benefits encourage workers to stay jobless longer. And as Dave Barry noted at the beginning of the chapter, disability payments encourage people to grow a sixth toe. Although the actual response to these incentives is hotly debated, the existence of the undesired incentives is unambiguous.

labor supply: The willingness and ability to work specific amounts of time at alternative wage rates in a given time period, *ceteris paribus*.

WELFARE PROGRAMS

To understand how income transfer programs change market behavior and outcomes, let's look closely at how welfare programs operate. The largest federal cash welfare program is called Temporary Aid to Needy Families (TANF). The TANF program was created by congressional welfare reforms in 1996 and replaced an earlier program (AFDC) that had operated since 1935. The new program offers states more discretion to decide who gets welfare, under what conditions, and for how long.

Benefit Determination

The first task of the TANF program is to identify potential recipients. In principle, this task is easy: Find out who is poor. To do this, the federal government has established a poverty line that specifies how much cash income families of different sizes need just to buy basic necessities. In 2020, the federal government estimated that a family of four was

TABLE 20.1

Poverty Lines

The official definition of poverty relates current income to the minimal needs of a family. Poverty thresholds vary with family size. In 2020, a family of four was considered poor if it had less than $26,200 of income.

Number of Family Members	Family Income
1	$12,760
2	17,240
3	21,720
4	26,200
5	30,680
6	35,160
7	39,640
8	44,120

Source: U.S. Bureau of the Census (2020).

poor if its income was less than $26,200. Table 20.1 shows how this poverty threshold varies by family size.

According to Table 20.1, a four-person family with $20,000 of income in 2020 would have had a **poverty gap**—the shortfall between actual income and the poverty threshold—of $6,200. The Jones family needed at least that much *additional* income to purchase what the government deems a "minimally adequate" standard of living.

So how much welfare should the government give this family? Should it give $6,200 to this family, thereby closing its poverty gap? As simple as that proposition sounds, it creates some unintended problems.

poverty gap: The shortfall between actual income and the poverty threshold.

The Work Incentive Problem

Suppose we guaranteed all families enough income to reach their respective poverty line. Any family earning less than the poverty line would receive a welfare check in the amount of their poverty gap. No one would be poor.

This sounds like a simple solution to the poverty problem, but it isn't. First, people who *weren't* poor would have a strong incentive to become poor. Why try to support a family of four with a paycheck of $30,000 when you can quit and get $26,200 in welfare checks? Recall from Chapter 16 that the decision to work is a response to both the financial and psychological rewards associated with employment. People in dull, dirty, low-paying jobs get little of either. By quitting their jobs, declaring themselves poor, and accepting a guaranteed income transfer, they would gain much more leisure at little financial or psychological cost. In the process, total output would shrink (Figure 20.3).

The second potential problem affects the work behavior of people who were poor to begin with. We assumed that the Jones family was earning $20,000 before they got a welfare check. The question now is whether the welfare check will change their work behavior.

Suppose that family gets an opportunity to earn an extra $2,000 a year by working overtime. Should they seize that opportunity? Consider the effect of the higher *wages* on the family's *income*. Before working overtime, the Jones family earned

INCOME WITHOUT OVERTIME WAGES

Wages	$20,000
Welfare benefits	6,200
Total income	$26,200

If they now work overtime, their income is

INCOME WITH OVERTIME WAGES

Wages	$22,000
Welfare benefits	4,200
Total income	$26,200

Something is wrong here: Although *wages* have gone up, the family's *income* hasn't. How would you like to be in this position? How would you react? Would you work overtime?

Implicit Marginal Tax Rates. The failure of income to rise with wages is the by-product of how welfare benefits were computed. *If welfare benefits are set equal to the poverty gap, every additional dollar of wages reduces welfare benefits by the same amount.* In effect, the Jones family confronts a **marginal tax rate** of 100 percent: Every dollar of wages results in a lost dollar of benefits. Uncle Sam isn't literally raising the family's taxes by a dollar. By reducing benefits dollar for dollar, however, the end result is the same.

> **marginal tax rate:** The tax rate imposed on the last (marginal) dollar of income.

With a 100 percent marginal tax rate, a family can't improve its income by working more. In fact, this family might as well work *less.* As wages decline, welfare benefits increase by the same amount. Thus, we end up with a conflict between compassion and work incentives. By guaranteeing a poverty-level income, we destroy the economic incentive of low-income workers to support themselves. This creates a **moral hazard** for welfare recipients; that is, we encourage undesirable behavior. The moral hazard here is the temptation not to support oneself by working–choosing welfare checks instead.

> **moral hazard:** An incentive to engage in undesirable behavior.

Less Compassion

To reduce this moral hazard, Congress and the states changed the way benefits are computed. First, they set a much lower ceiling on welfare benefits. States don't offer to close the poverty gap; instead, they set a maximum benefit far below the poverty line. Hence, we have this amended benefit formula:

$$\frac{\text{Welfare}}{\text{benefit}} = \frac{\text{Maximum}}{\text{benefit}} - \text{Wages}$$

In 2020, the typical state set a maximum benefit of about $10,000 for a family of four. Hence, a family without any other income couldn't get enough money from welfare to stay out of poverty. As a result, *a family totally dependent on welfare is unquestionably poor.* Although the lower benefit ceiling is less compassionate, it reduces the risk of people climbing on the welfare wagon for a free ride.

More Incentives

To encourage welfare recipients to lift their own incomes above the poverty line, welfare departments made another change in the benefit formula. As we just saw, *the rate at which benefits are reduced as wages increase is the marginal tax rate.* The dollar-for-dollar benefit cuts illustrated destroyed the financial incentive to work. To give recipients more incentive to work, the marginal tax rate was cut from 100 to 67 percent. So we now have a new benefit formula:

$$\frac{\text{Welfare}}{\text{benefit}} = \frac{\text{Maximum}}{\text{benefit}} - \frac{2}{3}[\text{Wages}]$$

Figure 20.4 illustrates how this lower marginal tax rate alters the relationship of total income to wages. The black line in the figure shows the total wages Mrs. Jones could earn at $10 per hour. She could earn nothing by not working or as much as $20,000 per year by working full-time (2,000 hours per year, as depicted by point *F* in the figure).

The blue lines in the figure show what happens to her welfare benefits and total income when a 100 percent marginal tax rate is imposed. At point *A* she gets $10,000 in welfare benefits because she's not working at all. That $10,000 is also her total income because she has no wages.

Now consider what happens to the family's total income if Mrs. Jones goes to work. If she works 1,000 hours per year (essentially half-time), she could earn $10,000 (point *B*). But what would happen to her *income?* If the welfare department cuts her benefit by $1 for every dollar she earns, her benefit check slides down the blue "welfare benefits" line to point *C*, where she gets nothing from welfare. By working 1,000 hours per year, all

FIGURE 20.4

Work (Dis)Incentives

If welfare benefits are reduced dollar for dollar as wages increase, the implied marginal tax rate is 100 percent. In that case, total income remains at the benefit limit of $10,000 (point *A*) as work effort increases from 0 to 1,000 hours (point *B*). There is no incentive to work in this range.

When the marginal tax rate is reduced to 67 percent, total income starts increasing as soon as the welfare recipient starts working. At 1,000 hours of work, total income is $13,333 (point *G*).

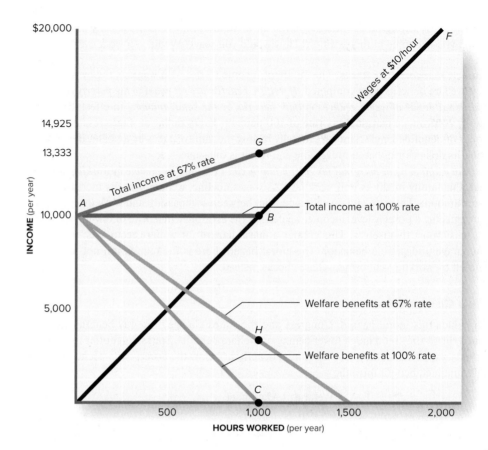

Mrs. Jones has done is replace her welfare check with a paycheck. That might make taxpayers smile, but Mrs. Jones will wonder why she bothered to go to work. With a 100 percent tax rate, her total income doesn't rise above $10,000 until she works more than 1,000 hours.

The green lines in Figure 20.4 show how work incentives improve with a lower marginal tax rate. Now welfare benefits are reduced by only 67 cents for every $1 of wages earned. As a result, total income starts rising as soon as Mrs. Jones goes to work. If she works 1,000 hours, her total income will include

Wages	**$10,000**
Welfare benefit	3,333 = $10,000 − 2/3($10,000)
Total income	**$13,333**

Point *G* on the graph illustrates this outcome.

Incentives versus Costs

It may be comforting to know that the Jones family can now increase its income from $10,000 when not working to $13,333 by working 1,000 hours per year. But they still face a higher marginal tax rate (67 percent) than rich people (the top marginal tax rate on federal income taxes is 37 percent). Why not lower their marginal tax rate even further, thus increasing both their work incentives and their total income?

Unfortunately, a reduction in the marginal tax rate would also increase welfare costs. Suppose we eliminated the marginal tax rate altogether. Then the Jones family could earn wages of $10,000 by working 1,000 hours *and* keep welfare benefits of $10,000. That would boost their total income to $20,000. Sounds great, doesn't it? But should we still be providing $10,000 in welfare payments to someone who earns $10,000 on her own? How about someone earning $20,000 or $30,000? Where should we draw the line? Clearly, *if we don't impose a marginal tax rate at some point, everyone will be eligible for welfare benefits.*

The thought of giving everyone a welfare check might sound like a great idea, but it would turn out to be incredibly expensive. In the end, we'd have to take those checks back, in the form of increased taxes, to pay for the vastly expanded program. We must recognize, then, a basic dilemma:

- *Low marginal tax rates encourage more work effort but make more people eligible for welfare.*
- *High marginal tax rates discourage work effort but make fewer people eligible for welfare.*

The conflict between work incentives and the desire to limit welfare costs and eligibility can be summarized in this simple equation:

$$\text{Breakeven level of income} = \frac{\text{Basic benefits}}{\text{Marginal tax rate}}$$

The **breakeven level of income** is the amount of income a person can earn before losing all welfare benefits. In the Joneses' case, the basic welfare benefit was $10,000 per year and the benefit reduction (marginal tax) rate was 0.67. Hence, the family could earn as much as

$$\text{Breakeven level of income} = \frac{\$10,0000}{0.67} \text{ per year}$$
$$= \$14,925$$

before losing all welfare benefits. Thus, *low marginal tax rates encourage work but make it hard to get completely off welfare.*

If the marginal tax rate were 100 percent, as under the old welfare system, the break-even point would be $10,000 divided by 1.00. In that case, people who earned $10,000 on their own would get no assistance from welfare. Fewer people would be eligible for welfare, but those who drew benefits would have no incentive to work. If the marginal tax rate were lowered to 0, the breakeven point would rise to infinity ($10,000 divided by 0)—and we'd all be on welfare.

As this arithmetic shows, *there's a basic conflict between work incentives (low marginal tax rates) and welfare containment (smaller welfare rolls and outlays).* We can achieve a lower break-even level of income (less welfare eligibility) only by sacrificing low marginal tax rates or higher income floors (basic benefits). Hence, welfare costs can be minimized only if we sacrifice income provision or work incentives.

Tax Elasticity of Labor Supply. The terms of the trade-off between more welfare and less work depend on how responsive people are to marginal tax rates. As we first noted in Chapter 19, the **tax elasticity of labor supply** measures the response to changes in tax rates:

$$\text{Tax elasticity of labor supply} = \frac{\%\text{ change in quantity of labor supplied}}{\%\text{ change in tax rate}}$$

If the tax elasticity of labor supply were zero, it wouldn't matter how high the marginal tax rate was: People would work for nothing (100 percent tax rate). In reality, the tax elasticity of labor supply among low-wage workers is more in the range of 0.2 to 0.3, so marginal tax rates *do* affect work effort. *So long as the tax elasticity of labor supply is greater than zero, there is a conflict between equity (more welfare) and efficiency (more work).*

Time Limits. The 1996 welfare reforms partially sidestepped this dilemma by setting time limits on welfare eligibility. TANF recipients *must* engage in some sort of employment-related activity (e.g., a job, job search, or training) within two years of first receiving benefits. There is also a five-year *lifetime* limit on welfare eligibility. States, however, can still use their own (nonfederal) funds to extend welfare benefits beyond those time limits.

breakeven level of income: The income level at which welfare eligibility ceases.

tax elasticity of labor supply: The percentage change in quantity of labor supplied divided by the percentage change in tax rates.

SOCIAL SECURITY

Like welfare programs, the Social Security program was developed to redistribute incomes. In the case of Social Security, however, *age,* not low income, is the primary determinant of eligibility. The program seeks to provide a financial prop under retirement incomes. Although Social Security is a *social insurance* program rather than a *welfare* program, it has the same kind of conflict between equity and efficiency. Here again we have to confront policy conflicts among the goals of compassion, work incentives, and program costs.

Program Features

The Social Security program is actually a mix of three separate income transfers. The main program is for retired workers, the second for survivors of deceased workers, and the third for disabled workers. Created in 1935, this combined Old Age Survivors and Disability Insurance (OASDI) program is now so large that it accounts for 40 percent of all federal income transfers. The monthly benefit checks distributed to 64 million recipients are financed with a payroll tax on workers and employers.

Retirement Age. As Figure 20.5 confirms, the retirement program is by far the largest component of OASDI. Individuals become eligible for Social Security retirement benefits when they reach certain ages. People can choose either "early" retirement (at age 62 to 64) or "normal" retirement (at age 65 to 67). Those who choose early retirement receive a smaller monthly benefit because they're expected to live longer in retirement.

For people born after 1940, the age threshold for "normal" retirement is increasing each year. By the year 2022, the age threshold for normal retirement will be age 67. This delay in benefit eligibility is intended to keep aging baby boomers working longer, thereby curtailing a surge in benefit outlays.

Progressive Benefits. Retirement benefits are based on an individual's wages. In 2020, the median Social Security retirement benefit for an individual was about $18,000. But high-wage workers could get nearly $36,000 and low-wage workers as little as $8,000 a year.

Although high-wage workers receive larger benefit checks than low-wage workers, the *ratio* of benefits to prior wages isn't constant. Instead, the ***Social Security benefits formula is progressive*** because the ratio of benefits to prior wages declines as wages increase. Social Security replaces 90 percent of the first $960 of prior average monthly earnings but only 15 percent of monthly wages above $5,785 (see Table 20.2). The declining **wage replacement rate** ensures that low-wage workers receive *proportionately* greater benefits.

wage replacement rate: The percentage of base wages paid out in benefits.

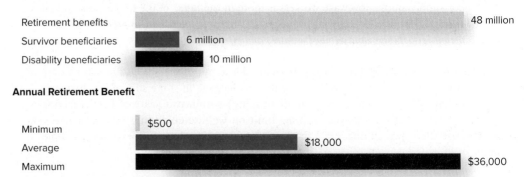

Who Pays Social Security Taxes

Payroll taxes
   7.65% paid by workers
   7.65% paid by employers

Who Gets Social Security Checks

Retirement benefits — 48 million
Survivor beneficiaries — 6 million
Disability beneficiaries — 10 million

Annual Retirement Benefit

Minimum — $500
Average — $18,000
Maximum — $36,000

FIGURE 20.5

Social Security Finances

The Social Security retirement, survivor, and disability programs are financed with payroll taxes. Most benefits go to retired workers, who get an average transfer of $18,000 per year.

Source: U.S. Social Security Administration (2020 data).

Wage Replacement Rate (%)	For Average Monthly Wages of
90%	$1–960
32	$961–5,785
15	over $5,785

Source: U.S. Social Security Administration (2020).

TABLE 20.2

Progressive Benefits

Social Security redistributes income progressively by replacing a larger share of low wages than high wages. Shown here are the wage replacement rates for 2020 (adjusted annually for inflation).

Suppose that two workers are retiring. One had prior wages averaging $9,000 per month; the other had $3,000. These workers will get Social Security benefits of

$$\text{High-wage worker} = 0.90(\$960) + 0.32(\$4,825) + 0.1(\$3,215) = \$2,890.25$$

$$\text{Low-wage worker} = 0.90(\$960) + 0.32(\$2,040) = \$1,516.80$$

Notice how their relative incomes change. When working, the high-wage worker had three times more income than the low-wage worker. In retirement, however, the high-wage worker's benefits are not even two times the low-wage worker's benefits. Thus, ***retirement benefits end up more equally distributed than wages.*** In this sense, Social Security is a *progressive* mechanism of income distribution.

The Earnings Test

In reality, a worker doesn't have to *retire* to receive Social Security benefits. But the government imposes an *earnings test* to determine how much retirement benefits an older person can collect while still working. The earnings test is similar to the formula used to compute welfare benefits. The formula establishes a maximum benefit amount and a marginal tax rate that reduces benefits as wages increase:

$$\frac{\text{Benefit}}{\text{amount}} = \frac{\text{Maximum}}{\text{award}} - 0.5(\text{Wages in excess of ceiling})$$

Consider the case of Leonard, a 62-year-old worker earning $30,000 a year but contemplating retirement. Suppose Leonard's wage history entitles him to a maximum award of $12,000 per year, but he wants to keep working to supplement Social Security benefits with wages. If he could collect full Social Security benefits and continue working, his income would be $42,000 a year. But it isn't that simple. Social Security benefits are *reduced* if a person's wages exceed a set amount.

In 2020 that set amount, called the "earnings test," was $18,240. A person could earn up to that amount with no reduction in Social Security benefits. But if wages exceeded that amount, the Social Security benefit would be reduced: Each dollar earned above that ceiling would reduce Social Security benefits by 50 cents.

Hence, the benefit formula was

$$\frac{\text{Benefit}}{\text{amount}} = \$12,000 - 0.5(\text{Wage} > \$18,240)$$

The Work Disincentive

The formula just described says benefits will drop by 50 cents for every $1 of wages earned more than $18,240. Hence, ***the implicit marginal tax rate is 50 percent.*** Uncle Sam is effectively getting half of any wages Leonard earns in excess of $18,240 per year. Figure 20.6 illustrates this sorry state of affairs.

Notice how many hours Leonard can work before the government starts reducing his Social Security check. At a wage of $20 an hour, Leonard can work 912 hours a year (about 18 hours a week) and keep all his benefits. In that case, he resides at point *C* in Figure 20.6.

FIGURE 20.6

The Social Security Earnings Test

A worker aged 62–64 can earn up to $18,240 (point A) without losing any Social Security benefits. At point C, income includes $12,000 in benefits and $18,240 in wages.

If wages increase beyond $18,240, however, Social Security benefits decline by 50 cents for every $1 earned. After point C, income rises only half as fast as wages.

At the breakeven point D, earnings are $42,240, and there are no Social Security benefits (point B).

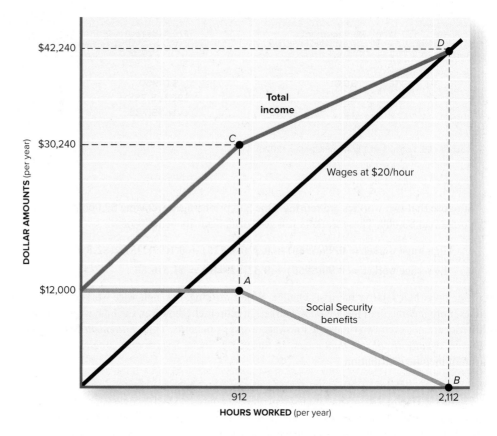

Beyond that, however, every additional hour of work brings in $20 of wages but a $10 reduction in benefits. After point C, his income rises *half* as fast as his wages. That's a real disincentive to work.

In reality, the marginal tax rate on Leonard's wages is even higher and the incentive to work lower. If he works, Leonard will have to pay the Social Security payroll tax (7.65 percent) as well as federal, state, and local income taxes (say, another 15 percent). These additional (explicit) taxes increase the *combined* marginal tax rate to 72.65 percent. In other words, Leonard would get to keep only 27.35 cents out of every additional dollar he earned.

Declining Labor Supply

Like welfare recipients, older people are quick to realize that work no longer pays. Not surprisingly, they've exited the labor market in droves. The **labor force participation rate** measures the percentage of the population that is either employed or actively seeking a job (unemployed). Figure 20.7 shows how precipitously the labor force participation rate has declined among older Americans. This problem isn't unique to the United States. The relative size of the over-65 population is growing everywhere, and more older people are retiring earlier.

Prior to the creation of the Social Security system, most older people had to continue working until advanced age. Many "died with their boots on" because they had no other means of support. Just a generation ago, more than 75 percent of men 62 to 64 were working. Today, less than 50 percent of that group is working.

Compassion, Incentives, and Cost

The primary economic cost of the Social Security program isn't the benefits it pays but the reduction in total output that occurs when workers retire early. In the absence of Social Security benefits, millions of older workers would still be on the job, contributing to the output of goods and services. When they instead retire—or simply work less—total output shrinks.

FIGURE 20.7

Declining Labor Force Participation

In the 1960s and 1970s, the eligibility age for Social Security was lowered for men and benefits were increased. This convinced an increased percentage of older men to leave the labor force and retire. In a single generation the labor force participation rate of men over age **65** was halved.

Source: U.S. Bureau of Labor Statistics.

Trade-offs. Just because the intergenerational redistribution of income shrinks potential output doesn't mean we shouldn't do it. The real economic issue is benefits versus costs. Compassion for older workers is what motivates Social Security transfers. We don't want people who have worked their entire life to end up poor. Presumably, society gains from the more equitable distribution of income that results (a revised FOR WHOM). The economic concern is that we *balance* this gain against the implied costs.

One way of reducing the economic cost of the Social Security program would be to eliminate the earnings test. AARP (formerly known as the American Association of Retired Persons) has advocated this option for many years. If the earnings test were eliminated, the marginal tax rate on the wages of older workers would drop from 50 percent to 0. In a flash, the work disincentive would vanish, and older workers would work more, adding to our total output of goods and services.

There's a downside to this reform, however. If the earnings test were eliminated, all older individuals would get their full retirement benefit, even if they continued to work. This would raise the budgetary cost of the program substantially. To cover that cost, payroll taxes would have to increase. Higher payroll taxes would in turn reduce supply and demand for *younger* workers. Hence, the financial burden of eliminating the earnings test might actually *increase* the economic cost of Social Security.

There's also an equity issue here. Should we increase payroll taxes on younger low-income workers to give higher Social Security benefits to older workers who still command higher salaries? In 2000 Congress gave a very qualified "yes" to this question. The earnings test was eliminated for workers over age 70 and for workers who retired at "normal" age (65–67 depending on year of birth). The marginal tax rate for workers who "retire" early but continue working at ages 65–69 was also reduced to 33.3 percent. The lower earnings test and 50 percent marginal tax rate were left intact, however, for people aged 62–64, the ones for whom the retirement decision is most pressing. The *budget* cost of greater work incentives for "early retirees" (ages 62–64) was regarded as too high.

DECISIONS FOR TOMORROW

Should We Privatize Social Security?

All income transfer programs entail a redistribution of income. In the case of Social Security, the redistribution is largely intergenerational: ***Payroll taxes levied on younger workers finance retirement benefits for older workers.*** The system is financed on a pay-as-you-go basis; future benefits depend on future taxes. This is very different from private pension plans, whereby you salt away some wages while working to finance your own eventual benefits. Such private plans are *advance-funded.*

Continued

Many people say we should run the Social Security system the same way. They want to "privatize" Social Security by permitting workers to establish their own retirement plans. Instead of paying payroll taxes to fund someone else's benefits, you'd make a contribution to your *own* pension fund.

More Output. The case for privatizing Social Security is based on both efficiency and equity. The efficiency argument reflects the core laissez-faire argument that markets know best. In a privatized system, individuals would have the freedom to tailor their consumption and saving choices. The elimination of mandatory payroll taxes and the earnings test would also lessen work disincentives. People would work harder and longer, maximizing total output.

Intergenerational Equity. Advocates of privatization also note how inequitable the existing program is for younger workers. The people now retired are getting a great deal: They paid relatively low payroll taxes when young and now receive substantial benefits. In part this high payoff is due to demographics. Thirty years ago there were four workers for every retired person. As the post–World War II baby boomers retire, the ratio of workers to retirees is declining dramatically. By the year 2030, there will be only two workers for every retiree (see Figure 20.8). As a result, the tax burden on tomorrow's workers will have to be a lot higher, or the baby boomers will have to accept much lower Social Security benefits. Either way, some generation of workers will get a lot less than everyone else. If Social Security is privatized, tomorrow's workers won't have to bear such a demographic tax burden.

More Poverty. As alluring as these suggestions sound, the privatization of Social Security would foster other inequities. The primary goal of Social Security is to fend off poverty among the aged. Social Security does this in two ways: by (1) transferring income from workers to retirees and (2) redistributing income from high-wage workers to low-wage workers in retirement with progressive wage replacement rates. By contrast, a privatized system would let the market alone determine FOR WHOM goods are produced. Low-income workers and other people who saved little while working would end up poor in their golden years. In a privatized system, even some high earners and savers might end up poor if their investments turned sour. Would we turn our collective backs on these people? If not, then the government would have to intervene with *some* kind of transfer program. The real issue, therefore, may not be whether a privatized Social Security system would work but what kind of *public* transfer program we'd have to create to supplement it. Then the choice would be either (1) Social Security or (2) a privatized retirement system plus a public welfare program for the aged poor. Framed in this context, the choice for the economy tomorrow is a lot more complex.

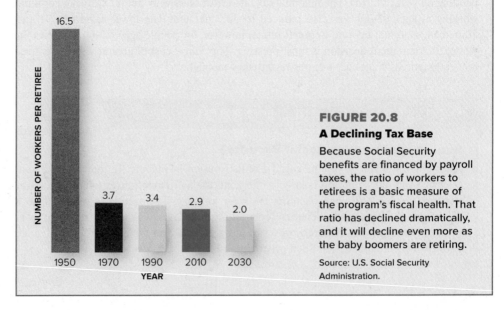

FIGURE 20.8

A Declining Tax Base

Because Social Security benefits are financed by payroll taxes, the ratio of workers to retirees is a basic measure of the program's fiscal health. That ratio has declined dramatically, and it will decline even more as the baby boomers are retiring.

Source: U.S. Social Security Administration.

SUMMARY

- Income transfers are payments for which no current goods or services are exchanged. They include both cash payments such as welfare checks and in-kind transfers such as food stamps and Medicare.   **LO20-1**
- Most transfer payments come from social insurance programs that cushion the income effects of specific events, such as aging, illness, or unemployment. Welfare programs are means-tested; they pay benefits only to the poor.   **LO20-1**
- The basic goal of transfer programs is to alter the market's FOR WHOM outcome. Attempts to redistribute income may, however, have the unintended effect of reducing total income. This is the core equity versus efficiency dilemma.   **LO20-2**
- Welfare programs reduce work incentives in two ways. They offer some income to people who don't work at all, and they also tax the wages of recipients who do work via offsetting benefit reductions.   **LO20-2**
- The benefit reduction that occurs when wages increase is an implicit marginal tax. The higher the marginal tax rate, (1) the less the incentive to work but (2) the smaller the welfare caseload.   **LO20-3**
- The Social Security retirement program creates similar work disincentives. It provides an income floor for people who don't work and imposes a high marginal tax rate on workers aged 62–64.   **LO20-2**
- The core policy dilemma is to find an optimal balance between compassion (transferring more income) and incentives (keeping people at work contributing to total output).   **LO20-3**

Key Terms

income transfers	social insurance programs	moral hazard
in-kind transfers	market failure	break-even level of income
cash transfers	labor supply	tax elasticity of labor supply
target efficiency	poverty gap	wage replacement rate
welfare programs	marginal tax rate	labor force participation rate

Questions for Discussion

1. If we have to choose between compassion and incentives, which should we choose? Do the terms of the trade-off matter?   **LO20-3**
2. What's so hard about guaranteeing everyone a minimal level of income support? What problems arise?   **LO20-2**
3. If poor people don't want to work, should they get welfare? What about their children?   **LO20-3**
4. Once someone has received TANF welfare benefits for a total of five years, he or she is permanently ineligible for more TANF benefits. Should this person receive any further assistance? How will work incentives be affected?   **LO20-2**
5. In what ways do younger workers pay for Social Security benefits received by retired workers?   **LO20-2**
6. Should the Social Security earnings test be eliminated? What are the benefits and costs of doing so?   **LO20-2**
7. How would the distribution of income change if Social Security were privatized?   **LO20-1**
8. Who pays the economic cost of Social Security? In what ways?   **LO20-2**
9. Why don't we give poor people more cash welfare instead of in-kind transfers like food stamps, housing assistance, and Medicaid?   **LO20-3**
10. Why is the increasing ratio of older people to younger people a problem for Social Security? Is there any way to mitigate this demographic problem?   **LO20-3**

PROMBLEMS FOR CHAPTER 20

PROBLEMS FOR CHAPTER 20

LO20-2 1. Suppose the annual welfare benefit formula is

$$\text{Benefit} = \$9,000 - 0.67(\text{Wages} > \$3,000)$$

    (*a*) What is the marginal tax rate on
       (*i*) The first $3,000 of wages?
       (*ii*) Wages above $3,000?
    (*b*) How large is the benefit if wages equal
       (*i*) $0?
       (*ii*) $2,000?
       (*iii*) $6,000?
    (*c*) What is the break-even level of income in this case?

LO20-2 2. A welfare recipient can receive food stamps as well as cash welfare benefits. If the food stamp allotment is set as follows,

$$\text{Food stamps} = \$5,000 - 0.30(\text{Wages})$$

    (*a*) How high can wages rise before all food stamps are eliminated?
    (*b*) If the welfare benefit formula in Problem 1 applies, what is the *combined* marginal tax rate of both welfare and food stamps for wages above $3,000?

LO20-3 3. Draw a graph showing how benefits, total income, and wages change under the following conditions:

$$\text{Wage rate} = \$10 \text{ per hour}$$

$$\text{Welfare benefit} = \$5,000 - 0.5(\text{Wages} > \$3,000)$$

Identify here and label on the graph the following points:
    A—welfare benefit when wages = 0   (*a*) How much is that benefit?   _____
    B—welfare benefit when wages = $10,000 (*b*) How much is that benefit?   _____
    C—break-even level of income   (*c*) What is that income level?   _____

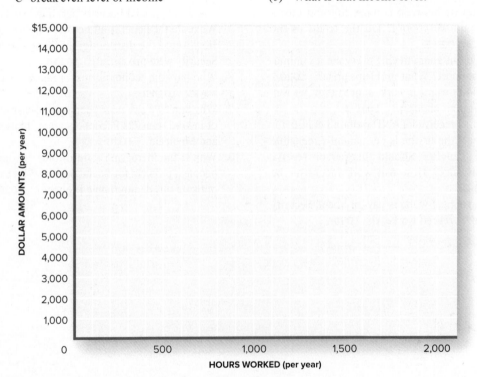

PROBLEMS FOR CHAPTER 20 (cont'd)

LO20-3 4. What is the break-even level of income for Social Security as depicted in Figure 20.6?

LO20-3 5. According to the benefit formula in Table 20.2, how large will the monthly Social Security benefit be for a worker who had prior earnings of
   (*a*) $36,000 a year?
   (*b*) $96,000 a year?
   What is the marginal wage replacement rate for
   (*c*) The $36,000-per-year worker?
   (*d*) The $96,000-per-year worker?

LO20-3 6. How large a monthly Social Security check will a 63-year-old retiree get in 2020 if her maximum benefit is $1,400 per month and she continues working for wages of $2,000 per month?

   7. (*a*) On a graph, depict the wages, total income, and Social Security benefits at different hours of work for a worker in 2020 aged 62–64 who earns $15 per hour and is eligible for $15,000 in Social Security benefits.
   (*b*) What is the total income if the person works 1,000 hours per year?
   (*c*) What is the breakeven level of income?

LO20-3 8. If older workers have a tax elasticity of labor supply equal to 0.30, by how much will their work activity decline when they reach the Social Security earnings test limit (i.e., wage ceiling)?

LO20-1 9. Suppose the benefit formulas for various welfare programs are

> **Food stamps = $400 per month − 0.30(Wages)**
> **Housing assistance = $1,000 per month − 0.25(Wages)**
> **Cash welfare = $400 per month − 0.67(Wages above $500)**

   (*a*) How much will someone earning $700 a month receive in
      (*i*)   Food stamps?
      (*ii*) Housing assistance?
      (*iii*) Cash welfare?
   (*b*) What is the cumulative marginal tax rate at
      (*i*) Wages under $500?
      (*ii*) Wages over $500?

LO20-1 10. *Decisions for Tomorrow:* Social Security tax revenue comes from taxes on current workers' wages up to a cap. Social Security benefits go out to current retirees and are based on age and past earnings. In Decisions for Tomorrow, it is discussed how in the near future tax revenue will be less than the benefits paid out. Identify three ways to keep this program in balance.

INTERNATIONAL ECONOMICS

Our interactions with the rest of the world have a profound impact on the mix of output (WHAT), the methods of production (HOW), and the distribution of income (FOR WHOM). Trade and global money flows can also affect the stability of the macro economy. Chapters 21 and 22 explore the motives, the nature, and the effects of international trade and finance.

Chapter 23 examines one of the world's most urgent problems—the deprivation that afflicts nearly 3 billion people worldwide. In this last chapter, the dimensions, causes, and potential cures for global poverty are discussed.

Ingram Publishing

Don Tonge/Alamy Stock Photo

AFP/Getty Images

CHAPTER 21

International Trade

After reading this chapter, you should know

LO21-1 What comparative advantage is.

LO21-2 What the gains from trade are.

LO21-3 How trade barriers and trade pacts affect prices, output, and incomes.

The 2020 World Series between the Los Angeles Dodgers and the Tampa Bay Rays was played with Japanese gloves, baseballs made in Costa Rica, and Mexican bats. Most of the players were wearing shoes made in Korea or China. And during the regular season, many of the games throughout the major leagues were played on artificial grass made in Taiwan. Baseball, it seems, has become something less than the "all-American" game.

Imported goods have made inroads into other activities as well. All smartphones and video game consoles are imported, as are most televisions, fax machines, personal computers, and iPads. Most of these imported goods could have been produced in the United States. Why did we purchase them from other countries? For that matter, why does the rest of the world buy computers, tractors, chemicals, airplanes, and wheat from us rather than produce such products for themselves? Wouldn't we all be better off relying on ourselves for the goods we consume (and the jobs we need) rather than buying and selling products in international markets? Or is there some advantage to be gained from international trade?

This chapter begins with a survey of international trade patterns—what goods and services we trade, and with whom. Then we address basic issues related to such trade:

- **What benefit, if any, do we get from international trade?**
- **How much harm do imports cause, and to whom?**
- **Should we protect ourselves from "unfair" trade by limiting imports?**

After examining the arguments for and against international trade, we draw some general conclusions about trade policy. As we'll see, international trade tends to increase *average* incomes, although it may diminish the job and income opportunities for specific industries and workers.

U.S. TRADE PATTERNS

The United States is the largest player in global product and resource markets. In 2019 we purchased 13 percent of the world's exports and sold 11 percent of the same total.

Imports

In dollar terms, our imports in 2019 exceeded $3 trillion. These **imports** included the consumer items mentioned earlier as well as capital equipment, raw materials, and food. Table 21.1 identifies some of the goods and services we purchase from foreign suppliers.

Although imports represent only 15 percent of total GDP, they account for larger shares of specific product markets. Coffee is a familiar

Country	Imports from	Exports to
Australia	Beef Alumina Pharmaceuticals	Airplanes Computers Auto parts
Belgium	Jewelry Pharmaceuticals Optical glass	Cigarettes Airplanes Diamonds
Canada	Cars Trucks Paper	Auto parts Cars Computers
China	Computers Clothes Toys	Soybeans Airplanes Cars
Germany	Cars Engines Auto parts	Airplanes Computers Cars
Japan	Cars Computers Telephones	Airplanes Computers Timber
Mexico	Cars Computers Appliances	Computers Cars Chemicals
Russia	Oil Platinum Artworks	Corn Wheat Oil seeds
South Korea	Shoes Cars Computers	Airplanes Leather Iron ingots and oxides

Source: U.S. Department of Commerce.

TABLE 21.1

A U.S. Trade Sampler

The United States imports and exports a staggering array of goods and services. Shown here are some of the top exports and imports with various countries. Notice that we export many of the same goods we import (such as cars and computers). What's the purpose of trading goods we produce ourselves?

example. Because virtually all coffee is imported (except for a tiny amount produced in Hawaii), Americans would have a harder time staying awake without imports. Likewise, there'd be no aluminum if we didn't import bauxite, no chrome bumpers if we didn't import chromium, no tin cans without imported tin, no smartphones, and a lot fewer computers without imported components. We couldn't even play the all-American game of baseball without imports because baseballs are no longer made in the United States.

We import *services* as well as *goods.* If you fly to Europe on Virgin Airways, you're importing transportation services. If you stay in a London hotel, you're importing lodging services. When you go to Barclay's Bank to cash traveler's checks, you're importing foreign financial services. If you go to Mexico for spring break, you are importing tourism services. These and other services now account for one-sixth of U.S. imports.

imports: Goods and services purchased from international sources.

Exports

While we're buying goods (merchandise) and services from the rest of the world, global consumers are buying our **exports.** In 2019 we exported $1.6 trillion of *goods,* including farm products (wheat, corn, soybeans), tobacco, machinery (computers), aircraft, automobiles and auto parts, raw materials (lumber, iron ore), and chemicals (see Table 21.1 for a sample of U.S. merchandise exports). We also exported $845 billion of services (movies, software licenses, tourism, engineering, financial services, etc.).

exports: Goods and services sold to foreign buyers.

Where do the coffee beans come from?

limpido/Getty Images

Although the United States is the world's second largest exporter of goods and services, exports represent a relatively modest fraction of our total output. As World View "Export Ratios" illustrates, other nations export much larger proportions of their GDP. Belgium is one of the most export-oriented countries, with tourist services and diamond exports pushing its export ratio to an incredible 70 percent. By contrast, Afghanistan is basically a closed economy with few exports (other than opium and other drugs traded in the black market).

The low U.S. export ratio (12 percent) disguises our heavy dependence on exports in specific industries. We export 25 to 50 percent of our rice, corn, and wheat production each year, and still more of our soybeans. Clearly a decision by international consumers to stop eating U.S. agricultural products could devastate a lot of American farmers. Such companies as Boeing (planes), Caterpillar Tractor (construction and farm machinery), Weyerhaeuser (logs, lumber), Dow (chemicals), and Oracle (computer workstations) sell more than one-fourth of their output in foreign markets. McDonald's sells hamburgers to nearly 70 million people a day in 120 countries around the world; to do so, the company exports management and marketing services (as well as frozen food) from the United States. The Walt Disney Company produces the most popular TV shows in Russia and Germany,

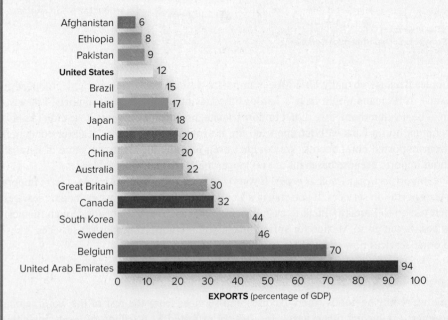

WORLD VIEW

EXPORT RATIOS

Very poor countries often have little to export and thus low export ratios. Saudi Arabia, by contrast, depends heavily on its oil exports. Fast-developing countries in Asia also rely on exports to enlarge their markets and raise incomes. The U.S. export ratio is low by international standards.

Country	Exports (percentage of GDP)
Afghanistan	6
Ethiopia	8
Pakistan	9
United States	12
Brazil	15
Haiti	17
Japan	18
India	20
China	20
Australia	22
Great Britain	30
Canada	32
South Korea	44
Sweden	46
Belgium	70
United Arab Emirates	94

Source: The World Bank, *WDI2019 Data Set.*

CRITICAL ANALYSIS: The relatively low U.S. export ratio reflects the vast size of our domestic market and our relative self-sufficiency in food and resources. European nations are smaller and highly interdependent.

Product Category	Exports ($ billions)	Imports ($ billions)	Surplus (Deficit) ($ billions)
Merchandise	$1,653	$2,519	$(866)
Services	845	595	250
Total trade	$2,498	$3,114	$(616)

Source: U.S. Department of Commerce.

TABLE 21.2

Trade Balances

Both merchandise (goods) and services are traded between countries. The United States typically has a merchandise deficit and a services surplus. When combined, an overall trade deficit remained in 2019.

publishes Italy's best-selling weekly magazine, and has the most popular tourist attraction in Japan (Tokyo Disneyland). The 500,000 foreign students attending U.S. universities are purchasing $5 billion of American educational services. All these activities are part of America's service exports.

Trade Balances

Although we export a lot of products, we usually have an imbalance in our trade flows. The trade balance is the difference between the value of exports and imports:

$$\text{Trade balance} = \text{Exports} - \text{Imports}$$

During 2019 we imported much more than we exported and so had a *negative* trade balance. A negative trade balance is called a **trade deficit.**

Although the overall trade balance includes both goods and services, these flows are usually reported separately, with the *merchandise* trade balance distinguished from the *services* trade balance. As Table 21.2 shows, the United States had a merchandise (goods) trade deficit of $866 billion in 2019 and a *services* trade *surplus* of $250 billion, leaving the overall trade balance in the red.

When the United States has a trade deficit with the rest of the world, other countries must have an offsetting **trade surplus.** On a global scale, imports must equal exports because every good exported by one country must be imported by another. Hence, *any imbalance in America's trade must be offset by reverse imbalances elsewhere.*

Whatever the overall balance in our trade accounts, bilateral balances vary greatly. Table 21.3 shows, for example, that our 2019 aggregate trade deficit ($615 billion) incorporated huge bilateral merchandise trade deficits with China, Germany, Japan, and Mexico. In the same year, however, we had trade surpluses with Brazil, the Netherlands, and Hong Kong.

trade deficit: The amount by which the value of imports exceeds the value of exports in a given time period (negative net exports).

trade surplus: The amount by which the value of exports exceeds the value of imports in a given time period (positive net exports).

Country	Merchandise Exports to ($ billions)	Merchandise Imports from ($ billions)	Trade Balance ($ billions)
Top Deficit Countries			
China	$106	$451	−$345
Mexico	291	399	−108
Japan	124	194	−70
Germany	96	164	−68
Canada	356	390	−32
Top Surplus Countries			
Hong Kong	$ 46	$ 20	+$26
The Netherlands	51	30	+21
Brazil	69	57	+12
United Kingdom	114	138	+6
Singapore	54	49	+5

Source: U.S. Census Bureau (2019 data).

TABLE 21.3

Bilateral Trade Balances

The U.S. trade deficit is the net result of bilateral deficits and surpluses. We had huge trade deficits with China, Germany, and Japan in 2019, for example, but small trade surpluses with Brazil, the Netherlands, and Hong Kong. International trade is *multi*national, with surpluses in some countries being offset by trade deficits elsewhere.

MOTIVATION TO TRADE

Many people wonder why we trade so much, particularly because (1) we import many of the things we also export (like computers, airplanes, cars, clothes), (2) we *could* produce many of the other things we import, and (3) we worry so much about trade imbalances. Why not just import those few things that we can't produce ourselves, and export just enough to balance that trade?

Specialization

Although it might seem strange to be importing goods we could produce ourselves, such trade is entirely rational. Our decision to trade with other countries arises from the same considerations that motivate individuals to specialize in production: satisfying their remaining needs in the marketplace. Why don't you become self-sufficient—growing all your own food, building your own shelter, and recording your own songs? Presumably because you've found that you can enjoy a much higher standard of living (and better music) by working at just one job and then buying other goods in the marketplace. When you do so, you're no longer self-sufficient. Instead you are *specializing* in production, relying on others to produce the array of goods and services you want. When countries trade goods and services, they are doing the same thing—*specializing* in production and then *trading* for other desired goods. Why do they do this? Because **specialization increases total output.**

To see how nations benefit from trade, we'll examine the production possibilities of two countries. We want to demonstrate that two countries that trade can together produce more output than they could in the absence of trade. If they can, *the gain from trade is increased world output and a higher standard of living in all trading countries.* This is the essential message of the *theory of comparative advantage.*

Production and Consumption without Trade

Consider the production and consumption possibilities of just two countries—say, the United States and France. For the sake of illustration, assume that both countries produce only two goods: bread and wine. Let's also set aside worries about the law of diminishing returns and the substitutability of resources, thus transforming the familiar **production possibilities** curve into a straight line, as in Figure 21.1.

The "curves" in Figure 21.1 suggest that the United States is capable of producing much more bread than France. With our greater abundance of labor, land, and other resources, we assume that the United States is capable of producing up to 100 zillion loaves of bread per year. To do so, we'd have to devote all our resources to that purpose. This capability is indicated by point *A* in Figure 21.1*a* and in row *A* of the accompanying production possibilities schedule.

France (Figure 21.1*b*), on the other hand, confronts a *maximum* bread production of only 15 zillion loaves per year (point *G*) because it has little available land, less fuel, and fewer potential workers.

The capacities of the two countries for wine production are 50 zillion barrels for us (point *F*) and 60 zillion for France (point *L*), largely reflecting France's greater experience in tending vines. Both countries are also capable of producing alternative *combinations* of bread and wine, as evidenced by their respective production possibilities curves (points *A–F* for the United States and *G–L* for France).

A nation that doesn't trade with other countries is called a **closed economy.** In the absence of contact with the outside world, the production possibilities curve for a closed economy also defines its **consumption possibilities.** Without imports, a country cannot consume more than it produces. Thus, the only immediate issue in a closed economy is which mix of output to choose—*what* to produce and consume—out of the domestic choices available.

Assume that Americans choose point *D* on their production possibilities curve, producing and consuming 40 zillion loaves of bread and 30 zillion barrels of wine. The French, on the other hand, prefer the mix of output represented by point *I* on their production possibilities curve. At that point they produce and consume 9 zillion loaves of bread and 24 zillion barrels of wine.

production possibilities: The alternative combinations of final goods and services that could be produced in a given period with all available resources and technology.

closed economy: A nation that doesn't engage in international trade.

consumption possibilities: The alternative combinations of goods and services that a country could consume in a given time period.

(a) U.S. production possibilities

(b) French production possibilities

FIGURE 21.1

Consumption Possibilities without Trade

In the absence of trade, a country's consumption possibilities are identical to its production possibilities. The assumed production possibilities of the United States and France are illustrated in the graphs and the corresponding schedules. Before entering into trade, the United States chose to produce and consume at point *D*, with 40 zillion loaves of bread and 30 zillion barrels of wine. France chose point *I* on its own production possibilities curve. By trading, each country hopes to increase its consumption beyond these levels.

> In a closed economy, production possibilities and consumption possibilities are identical.

U.S. Production Possibilities					French Production Possibilities			
	Bread (Zillions of Loaves)	+	Wine (Zillions of Barrels)			Bread (Zillions of Loaves)	+	Wine (Zillions of Barrels)
A	100	+	0		G	15	+	0
B	80	+	10		H	12	+	12
C	60	+	20		I	9	+	24
D	40	+	30		J	6	+	36
E	20	+	40		K	3	+	48
F	0	+	50		L	0	+	60

To assess the potential gain from trade, we must focus the *combined* output of the United States and France. In this case, total world output (points *D* and *I*) comes to 49 zillion loaves of bread and 54 zillion barrels of wine. What we want to know is whether world output would increase if France and the United States abandoned their isolation and started trading. Could either country, or both, consume *more* output by engaging in a little trade?

Production and Consumption with Trade

Because both countries are saddled with limited production possibilities, trying to eke out a little extra wine and bread from this situation might not seem possible. Such a conclusion is unwarranted, however.

Change U.S. Production. Take another look at the production possibilities confronting the United States, as reproduced in Figure 21.2. Suppose the United States were to produce at point *C* rather than point *D*. At point *C* we could produce 60 zillion loaves of bread and 20 zillion barrels of wine. That combination is clearly *possible* because it lies on the production possibilities curve. We didn't choose that point earlier because we assumed the mix of output at point *D* was preferable. The mix of output at point *C could* be produced, however.

FIGURE 21.2

Consumption Possibilities with Trade

A country can increase its consumption possibilities through international trade. Each country alters its mix of domestic output to produce more of the good it produces best. As it does so, total world output increases, and each country enjoys more consumption. In this case, trade allows U.S. consumption to move from point *D* to point *N*. France moves from point *I* to point *M*.

(a) U.S. production and consumption

(b) French production and consumption

In open economies, consumption can exceed production.

Change French Production. We could also change the mix of output in France. Assume that France moved from point *I* to point *K*, producing 48 zillion barrels of wine and only 3 zillion loaves of bread.

Increased World Output. Two observations are now called for. The first is simply that output mixes have changed in each country. The second, and more interesting, is that total world output has *increased*. Notice how this works. When the United States and France were at points *D* and *I*, their *combined* output consisted of

A: Initial Production Choices		
	Bread **(Zillions of Loaves)**	**Wine** **(Zillions of Barrels)**
United States (at point D)	40	30
France (at point I)	9	24
Total pre-trade output	49	54

After they moved along their respective production possibilities curves to points *C* and *K*, the combined world output became

B: Revised Production Choices		
	Bread **(Zillions of Loaves)**	**Wine** **(Zillions of Barrels)**
United States (at point C)	60	20
France (at point K)	3	48
Total output with trade	63	68

Total world output has increased by 14 zillion loaves of bread and 14 zillion barrels of wine. ***Just by changing the mix of output in each country, we've increased total world output.*** This additional output creates the potential for making both countries better off than they were in the absence of trade.

This almost seems like a magic trick, but it isn't. Here's what happened. The United States and France weren't initially producing at points *C* and *K* before because they simply didn't want to *consume* those particular output combinations. Nevertheless, our discovery that points *C* and *K* allow us to produce *more* output suggests that everybody can consume more goods and services if we change the mix of output in each country. This is our first clue as to how specialization and trade can benefit an **open economy**—a nation that engages in international trade.

open economy: A nation that engages in international trade.

Start Trading. Suppose that we Americans are the first to discover the potential benefits from trade. Using Figure 21.2 as our guide, we suggest to the French that they move their mix of output from point *I* to point *K*. As an incentive for making such a move, we promise to give them 6 zillion loaves of bread in exchange for 20 zillion barrels of wine. This would leave them at point *M*, with as much bread to consume as they used to have, plus an extra 4 zillion barrels of wine. At point *I* they had 9 zillion loaves of bread and 24 zillion barrels of wine. At point *M* they can have 9 zillion loaves of bread and 28 zillion barrels of wine. Thus, by altering their mix of output (from point *I* to point *K*) and then trading (point *K* to point *M*), the French end up with more goods and services than they had in the beginning. Notice in particular that this new consumption possibility (point *M*) lies *outside* France's domestic production possibilities curve.

The French will be quite pleased with the extra output they get from trading. But where does this leave us? Does France's gain imply a loss for us? Or do we gain from trade as well?

Mutual Gains

As it turns out, *both* the United States and France gain by trading. The United States, too, ends up consuming a mix of output that lies outside our production possibilities curve.

Note that at point *C* we *produce* 60 zillion loaves of bread per year and 20 zillion barrels of wine. We then *export* 6 zillion loaves to France. This leaves us with 54 zillion loaves of bread to *consume*.

In return for our exported bread, the French give us 20 zillion barrels of wine. These imports, plus our domestic production, permit us to *consume* 40 zillion barrels of wine. Hence, we end up consuming at point *N*, enjoying 54 zillion loaves of bread and 40 zillion barrels of wine. Thus, by first changing our mix of output (from point *D* to point *C*), then trading (point *C* to point *N*), we end up with 14 zillion more loaves of bread and 10 zillion more barrels of wine than we started with. Time to celebrate! International trade has made us better off, too.

Table 21.4 recaps the gains from trade for both countries. Notice that U.S. imports match French exports and vice versa. Also notice how the ***trade-facilitated consumption in each country exceeds no-trade levels.***

	Production and Consumption with Trade							Production and Consumption with No Trade
	Production	**+**	**Imports**	**−**	**Exports**	**=**	**Consumption**	
United States at	Point *C*						Point *N*	Point *D*
Bread	60	+	0	−	6	=	54	compare	40
Wine	20	+	20	−	0	=	40		30
France at	Point *K*						Point *M*	Point *I*
Bread	3	+	6	−	0	=	9	compare	9
Wine	48	+	0	−	20	=	28		24

TABLE 21.4

Gains from Trade

When nations specialize in production, they can export one good and import another and end up with *more* total goods to consume than they had without trade. In this case, the United States specializes in bread production. Notice how

U.S. *consumption* of both goods increases (compare total U.S. consumption of bread and wine at point *N* [with trade] to consumption at point *D* [no trade]).

Specialization Is the Key. All these numbers do indeed look like some kind of magic trick, but there's no sleight of hand going on here; the gains from trade are due to specialization in production. When each country goes it alone, it's a prisoner of its own production possibilities curve; it must make production decisions on the basis of its own consumption desires. When international trade is permitted, however, each country can concentrate on the exploitation of its production capabilities. *Each country produces those goods it makes best and then trades with other countries to acquire the goods it desires to consume.*

The resultant specialization increases total world output. In the process, each country is able to escape the confines of its own production possibilities curve, to reach beyond it for a larger basket of consumption goods. *When a country engages in international trade, its consumption possibilities always exceed its production possibilities.* These enhanced consumption possibilities are emphasized by the positions of points *N* and *M outside* the production possibilities curves (Figure 21.2). If it weren't possible for countries to increase their consumption by trading, there'd be no incentive for trading, and thus no trade.

PURSUIT OF COMPARATIVE ADVANTAGE

Although international trade can make everyone better off, it's not so obvious which goods should be traded, or on what terms. In our previous illustration, the United States ended up trading bread for wine in terms that were decidedly favorable to us. Why did we export bread rather than wine, and how did we end up getting such a good deal?

Opportunity Costs

comparative advantage: The ability of a country to produce a specific good at a lower opportunity cost than its trading partners.

opportunity cost: The most desired goods or services that are forgone in order to obtain something else.

The decision to export bread is based on **comparative advantage**—that is, the *relative* cost of producing different goods. Recall that we can produce a maximum of 100 zillion loaves of bread per year or 50 zillion barrels of wine. Thus, the domestic **opportunity cost** of producing 100 zillion loaves of bread is the 50 zillion barrels of wine we forsake in order to devote all our resources to bread production. In fact, at every point on the U.S. production possibilities curve (Figure 21.2a), the opportunity cost of a loaf of bread is ½ barrel of wine. We're effectively paying half a barrel of wine to get a loaf of bread.

Although the cost of bread production in the United States might appear outrageous, even higher opportunity costs prevail in France. According to Figure 21.2b, the opportunity cost of producing a loaf of bread in France is a staggering 4 barrels of wine. To produce a loaf of bread, the French must use factors of production that could otherwise be used to produce 4 barrels of wine.

How much bread is a bottle of wine worth?
robeo/Getty Images

Comparative Advantage. A comparison of the opportunity costs prevailing in each country exposes the nature of comparative advantage. The United States has a comparative advantage in bread production because less wine has to be given up to produce bread in the United States than in France. In other words, the opportunity costs of bread production are lower in the United States than in France. *Comparative advantage refers to the relative (opportunity) costs of producing particular goods.*

A country should specialize in what it's *relatively* efficient at producing—that is, goods for which it has the lowest opportunity costs. In this case, the United States should produce bread because its opportunity cost (½ barrel of wine) is less than France's (4 barrels of wine). Were you the production manager for the whole world, you'd certainly want each country to exploit its relative abilities, thus maximizing world output. Each country can arrive at that same decision itself by comparing its own opportunity costs to those prevailing elsewhere.

World output, and thus the potential gains from trade, will be maximized when each country pursues its comparative advantage. To do so, each country

- *Exports goods with relatively low opportunity costs.*
- *Imports goods with relatively high opportunity costs.*

That's the kind of situation depicted in Table 21.4.

Absolute Costs Don't Count

In assessing the nature of comparative advantage, notice that we needn't know anything about the actual costs involved in production. Have you seen any data suggesting how much labor, land, or capital is required to produce a loaf of bread in either France or the United States? For all you and I know, the French may be able to produce both bread and wine with fewer resources than we're using. Such an **absolute advantage** in production might exist because of their much longer experience in cultivating both grapes and wheat or simply because they have more talent.

We can envy such productivity, and even try to emulate it, but it shouldn't alter our production or trade decisions. All we really care about are *opportunity costs*—what *we* have to give up in order to get more of a desired good. If we can get a barrel of wine for less bread in trade than in production, we have a comparative advantage in producing bread. As long as we have a *comparative* advantage in bread production, we should exploit it. It doesn't matter to us whether France could produce either good with fewer resources. For that matter, even if France had an absolute advantage in *both* goods, we'd still have a *comparative* advantage in bread production, as we've already confirmed. The absolute costs of production were omitted from the previous illustration because they were irrelevant.

To clarify the distinction between absolute advantage and comparative advantage, consider this example. When Charlie Osgood joined the Willamette Warriors football team, he was the fastest runner ever to play football in Willamette. He could also throw the ball farther than most people could see. In other words, he had an *absolute advantage* in both throwing and running. Charlie would have made the greatest quarterback or the greatest end ever to play football. *Would have.* The problem was that he could play only one position at a time. Thus, the Willamette coach had to play Charlie either as a quarterback or as an end. He reasoned that Charlie could throw only a bit farther than some of the other top quarterbacks but could far outdistance all the other ends. In other words, Charlie had a *comparative advantage* in running and was assigned to play as an end.

absolute advantage: The ability of a country to produce a specific good with fewer resources (per unit of output) than other countries.

TERMS OF TRADE

It definitely pays to pursue one's comparative advantage by specializing in production. It may not yet be clear, however, how we got such a good deal with France. We're clever traders; but beyond that, is there any way to determine the **terms of trade**—the quantity of good A that must be given up in exchange for good B? In our previous illustration, the terms of trade were very favorable to us; we exchanged only 6 zillion loaves of bread for 20 zillion barrels of wine (Table 21.4). The terms of trade were thus 6 loaves = 20 barrels.

terms of trade: The rate at which goods are exchanged; the amount of good A given up for good B in trade.

Limits to the Terms of Trade

The terms of trade with France were determined by our offer and France's ready acceptance. But why did France accept those terms?

France was willing to accept our offer because the terms of trade permitted France to increase its wine consumption without giving up any bread consumption. Our offer of 6 loaves for 20 barrels was an improvement over France's domestic opportunity costs. France's domestic possibilities required it to give up 24 barrels of wine in order to produce 6 loaves of bread (see Figure 21.2b). Getting bread via trade was simply cheaper for France than producing bread at home. France ended up with an extra 4 zillion barrels of wine (take another look at the last two columns in Table 21.4).

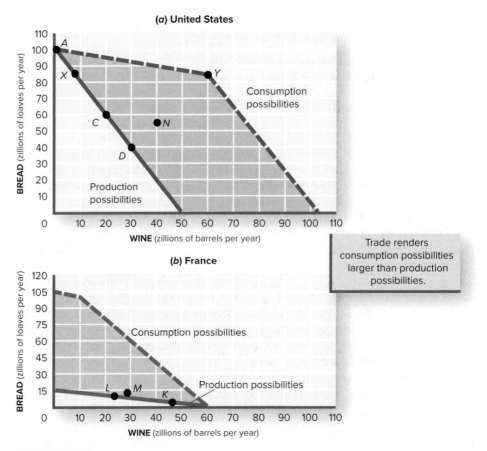

(a) United States

(b) France

Trade renders consumption possibilities larger than production possibilities.

FIGURE 21.3

Searching for the Terms of Trade

Assume the United States can produce 100 zillion loaves of bread per year (point *A*). If we reduce output to only 85 zillion loaves, we could move to point *X*. At point *X* we have 7.5 zillion barrels of wine and 85 zillion loaves of bread.

Trade increases consumption possibilities. If we continued to produce 100 zillion loaves of bread, we could trade 15 zillion loaves to France in exchange for as much as 60 zillion barrels of wine. This would leave us *producing* at point *A* but *consuming* at point *Y*. At point *Y* we have more wine and no less bread than we had at point *X*. This is our motivation to trade.

A country will end up on its consumption possibilities curve only if it gets *all* the gains from trade. It will remain on its production possibilities curve only if it gets *none* of the gains from trade. The terms of trade determine how the gains from trade are distributed, and thus at what point in the shaded area each country ends up.

Note: The kink in the consumption possibilities curve at point Y occurs because France is unable to produce more than 60 zillion barrels of wine.

Our first clue to the terms of trade, then, lies in each country's domestic opportunity costs. *A country won't trade unless the terms of trade are superior to domestic opportunities.* In our example, the opportunity cost of 1 barrel of wine in the United States is 2 loaves of bread. Accordingly, we won't *export* bread unless we get at least 1 barrel of wine in exchange for every 2 loaves of bread we ship overseas.

All countries want to gain from trade. Hence, we can predict that *the terms of trade between any two countries will lie somewhere between their respective opportunity costs in production.* That is, a loaf of bread in international trade will be worth at least ½ barrel of wine (the U.S. opportunity cost), but no more than 4 barrels (the French opportunity cost). In our example, the terms of trade ended up at 1 loaf = 3.33 barrels (that is, at 6 loaves = 20 barrels). This represented a very large gain for the United States and a small gain for France. Figure 21.3 illustrates this outcome and several other possibilities.

The Role of Markets and Prices

Relatively little trade is subject to such direct negotiations between countries. More often than not, the decision to import or export a particular good is left up to the market decisions of individual consumers and producers.

Individual consumers and producers aren't much impressed by such abstractions as comparative advantage. Market participants tend to focus on prices, always trying to allocate their resources in order to maximize profits or personal satisfaction. Consumers tend to buy the products that deliver the most utility per dollar of expenditure, while producers try to get the most output per dollar of cost. Everybody's looking for a bargain.

The Lone Trader. So what does this have to do with international trade? Well, suppose that Henri, an enterprising Frenchman, visited the United States before the advent of international trade. He observed that bread was relatively cheap while wine was relatively expensive—the opposite of the price relationship prevailing in France. These price comparisons brought to his mind the opportunity for making a fast euro. All he had to do was bring over some French wine and trade it in the United States for a large quantity of bread. Then he could return to France and exchange the bread for a greater quantity of wine. *Alors!* Were he to do this a few times, he'd amass substantial profits.

Trade "Winners". Henri's entrepreneurial exploits will not only enrich him but also move each country toward its comparative advantage. The United States ends up exporting bread to France, and France ends up exporting wine to the United States, exactly as the theory of comparative advantage suggests. The activating agent isn't the Ministry of Trade and its 620 trained economists but simply one enterprising French trader. He's aided and encouraged, of course, by consumers and producers in each country. American consumers are happy to trade their bread for his wines. They thereby end up paying less for wine (in terms of bread) than they'd otherwise have to. In other words, the terms of trade Henri offers are more attractive than the prevailing (domestic) relative prices. On the other side of the Atlantic, Henri's welcome is equally warm. French consumers are able to get a better deal by trading their wine for his imported bread than by trading with the local bakers.

Even some producers are happy. The wheat farmers and bakers in the United States are eager to deal with Henri. He's willing to buy a lot of bread and even to pay a premium price for it. Indeed, bread production has become so profitable in the United States that a lot of people who used to grow and mash grapes are now growing wheat and kneading dough. This alters the mix of U.S. output in the direction of more bread, exactly as suggested in Figure 21.2a.

In France the opposite kind of production shift is taking place. French wheat farmers are planting more grape vines so they can take advantage of Henri's generous purchases. Thus, Henri is able to lead each country in the direction of its comparative advantage while raking in a substantial profit for himself along the way.

Where the terms of trade and the volume of exports and imports end up depends partly on how good a trader Henri is. It will also depend on the behavior of the thousands of individual consumers and producers who participate in the market exchanges. In other words, trade flows depend on both the supply and the demand for bread and wine in each country. *The terms of trade, like the price of any good, depend on the willingness of market participants to buy or sell at various prices.* All we know for sure is that the terms of trade will end up somewhere between the limits set by each country's opportunity costs.

PROTECTIONIST PRESSURES

Although the potential gains from world trade are impressive, not everyone will be cheering at the Franco-American trade celebration. On the contrary, some people will be upset about the trade routes that Henri has established. They'll not only boycott the celebration but actively seek to discourage us from continuing to trade with France.

Trade "Losers"

Consider, for example, the winegrowers in western New York. Do you think they're going to be happy about Henri's entrepreneurship? Americans can now buy wine more cheaply from France than they can from New York. Before long we may hear talk about unfair foreign competition or about the greater nutritional value of American grapes (see World View "Imported Wine Squeezing U.S. Vintners"). The New York winegrowers may also emphasize the importance of maintaining an adequate grape supply and a strong wine industry at home, just in case of terrorist attacks.

WORLD VIEW

IMPORTED WINE SQUEEZING U.S. VINTNERS

American consumers are sipping increasing quantities of Italian and French wines. In 2018 U.S. wine consumption barely inched up to 348 million cases, an increase of less than 1 percent. Imports accounted for 23.7 percent of that total consumption, up 1.7 percent from 2017. That increasing import competition is keeping wine prices low and encouraging domestic vintners to convert their vineyards into almond or avocado farms.

Source: Industry reports, November 2019–February 2020.

CRITICAL ANALYSIS: Although **trade** increases consumption possibilities, imports typically compete with a domestic industry. The affected industries will try to restrict imports in order to preserve their own jobs and incomes.

Import-Competing Industries. Joining with the growers will be the farmworkers and the other merchants whose livelihood depends on the New York wine industry. If they're clever enough, the growers will also get the governor of the state to join their demonstration. After all, the governor must recognize the needs of his people, and his people definitely don't include the wheat farmers in Kansas who are making a bundle from international trade, much less French vintners. New York consumers are, of course, benefiting from lower wine prices, but they're unlikely to demonstrate over a few cents a bottle. On the other hand, those few extra pennies translate into millions of dollars for domestic wine producers.

The wheat farmers in France are no happier about international trade than are the winegrowers in the United States. They'd dearly love to sink all those boats bringing cheap wheat from America, thereby protecting their own market position.

If we're to make sense of trade policies, then we must recognize one central fact of life: Some producers have a vested interest in restricting international trade. In particular, *workers and producers who compete with imported products—who work in import-competing industries—have an economic interest in restricting trade.* This helps explain why GM, Ford, and Chrysler are unhappy about auto imports and why shoe workers in Massachusetts want to end the importation of Italian shoes. It also explains why textile producers in South Carolina think China is behaving irresponsibly when it sells cheap cotton shirts and dresses in the United States.

Export Industries. Although imports typically mean fewer jobs and less income for some domestic industries, exports represent increased jobs and income for other industries. Producers and workers in export industries gain from trade. Thus, on a microeconomic level there are identifiable gainers and losers from international trade. *Trade not only alters the mix of output but also redistributes income from import-competing industries to export industries.* This potential redistribution is the source of political and economic friction.

Net Gain. We must be careful to note, however, that the microeconomic gains from trade are greater than the microeconomic losses. It's not simply a question of robbing Peter to enrich Paul. We must remind ourselves that consumers enjoy a higher standard of living as a result of international trade. As we saw earlier, trade increases world efficiency and total output. Accordingly, we end up slicing up a larger pie rather than just reslicing the same old smaller pie.

The gains from trade will mean little to workers who end up with a smaller slice of the (larger) pie. It's important to remember, however, that the gains from trade are large enough to make everybody better off. Whether we actually choose to distribute the gains from trade in this way is a separate question, to which we shall return shortly. Note here, however, that *trade restrictions designed to protect specific microeconomic interests reduce the total gains from trade.* Trade restrictions leave us with a smaller pie to split up.

Additional Pressures

Import-competing industries are the principal obstacle to expanded international trade. Selfish micro interests aren't the only source of trade restrictions, however. Other arguments are also used to restrict trade.

National Security. The national security argument for trade restrictions is twofold. We can't depend on foreign suppliers to provide us with essential defense-related goods, it is said, because that would leave us vulnerable in time of war. The machine tool industry used this argument to protect itself from imports. In 1991 the Pentagon again sided with the tool-makers, citing the need for the United States to "gear up military production quickly in case of war," a contingency that couldn't be assured if weapons manufacturers relied on imported lathes, milling machines, and other tools. After the September 11, 2001, terrorist attacks on the World Trade Center and Pentagon, U.S. farmers convinced Congress to safeguard the nation's food supply with additional subsidies. The steel industry emphasized the importance of not depending on foreign suppliers.

The national security argument surfaced again in 2019. Huawei Technologies is the world's largest producer of telecommunications equipment and a leader in the development of base stations for 5G networks. But it is closely affiliated with the Chinese government. This raised concerns that Huawei's equipment could be used to facilitate cyber espionage or, worse, cripple a nation's telecommunications network in a time of crisis. Several nations, including the United States, have restricted the use (imports) of Huawei equipment.

Variants of the national security argument arose in 2020. The COVID-19 pandemic increased the need for medical supplies dramatically and abruptly. As it turned out, a high percentage of the needed face masks, gloves, swabs, and even medicines needed to fight the pandemic were manufactured in China, then imported into the United States. Trade hawks used that situation to demand that America limit future dependence on imported medical supplies by restricting imports and building up American production capacity. The Trump also used the national security argument to block access to the popular TikTok video-sharing app. President Trump said he was worried that the personal data of TikTok users would be accessible to the Chinese government, which was the majority owner of the app's corporate structure.

Dumping. Another argument against free trade arises from the practice of **dumping.** Foreign producers "dump" their goods when they sell them in the United States at prices lower than those prevailing in their own country, perhaps even below the costs of production.

dumping: The sale of goods in export markets at prices below domestic prices.

Dumping may be unfair to import-competing producers, but it isn't necessarily unwelcome to the rest of us. As long as foreign producers continue dumping, we're getting foreign products at low prices. How bad can that be? There's a legitimate worry, however. Foreign producers might hold prices down only until domestic producers are driven out of business. Then we might be compelled to pay the foreign producers higher prices for their products. In that case, dumping could consolidate market power and lead to monopoly-type pricing. The fear of dumping, then, is analogous to the fear of predatory pricing.

The potential costs of dumping are serious. It's not always easy to determine when dumping occurs, however. Those who compete with imports have an uncanny ability to associate any and all low prices with predatory dumping. The United States has used dumping *charges* to restrict imports of Chinese shrimp, furniture, lingerie, solar panels, and other products in which China has an evident comparative advantage. The Chinese have retaliated with dozens of their own dumping investigations, including the fiber optic cable case. In 2020 the U.S. Commerce Department launched an investigation of alleged dumping by South Korean cigarette manufacturers (see World View "U.S. Accuses South Korea of Dumping Cigarettes").

WORLD VIEW

U.S. ACCUSES SOUTH KOREA OF DUMPING CIGARETTES

The U.S. Commerce Department is investigating charges that the Korean Tobacco and Ginseng Corporation (KT&G) is illegally selling cigarettes in the United States at unfair prices. Sales of the company's THIS brand have skyrocketed from 1.36 million packs in December 2017 to over 220 million packs in December 2019. Domestic competitors claim KT&G is selling its Carnival, THIS, and other brands—a total of $80 million in 2019—at prices "below fair value." If the charge is corroborated, the U.S Trade Representative will propose countervailing duties.

Source: Media reports, January 2020.

CRITICAL ANALYSIS: Dumping means that a foreign producer is selling exports at prices below cost or below prices in the home market, putting import-competing industries at a competitive disadvantage. Accusations of dumping are an effective trade barrier.

Infant Industries. Actual dumping threatens to damage already established domestic industries. Even normal import prices, however, may make it difficult or impossible for a new domestic industry to develop. Infant industries are often burdened with abnormally high start-up costs. These high costs may arise from the need to train a whole workforce, build production infrastructure, and establish new marketing channels. With time to grow, however, an infant industry might experience substantial cost reductions and establish a comparative advantage. When this is the case, trade restrictions might help nurture an industry in its infancy. Trade restrictions are justified, however, only if there's tangible evidence that the industry can develop a comparative advantage reasonably quickly.

Improving the Terms of Trade. A final argument for restricting trade rests on how the gains from trade are distributed. As we observed, the distribution of the gains from trade depends on the terms of trade. If we were to buy fewer imports, foreign producers might lower their prices. If that happened, the terms of trade would move in our favor, and we'd end up with a larger share of the gains from trade.

One way to bring about this sequence of events is to put restrictions on imports, making it more difficult or expensive for Americans to buy foreign products. Such restrictions will reduce the volume of imports, thereby inducing foreign producers to lower their prices. Unfortunately, this strategy can easily backfire. Retaliatory restrictions on imports, each designed to improve the terms of trade, will ultimately eliminate all trade and therewith all the gains people were competing for in the first place.

BARRIERS TO TRADE

The microeconomic losses associated with imports give rise to a constant clamor for trade restrictions. People whose jobs and incomes are threatened by international trade tend to organize quickly and air their grievances. When France signed new trade deals with Canada,

Brazil, and Argentina in October 2019, French farmers drove their tractors into Paris, clogging major highways and dumping hay on critical thoroughfares (see World View "French Tractors Roll into Paris"). Within days, the French government agreed to respond to farmers' concerns about cheap imports. More often than not, governments grant the wishes of these well-organized and well-financed special interests.

WORLD VIEW

FRENCH TRACTORS ROLL INTO PARIS

French farmers drove 1,000 tractors into Paris to protest new trade deals that threaten their livelihood. Trade deals with Canada, Brazil, and Argentina threaten to bring in wheat imports that will crush French farmers. As Joffrey Beaudot, president of the Young Farmers of Saone-et-Loire lamented, "The cost of production for French farmers is higher than that of South American countries; we can't compete, so we will disappear." Farmers used their tractors to clog the highway ring around Paris and to disrupt major arteries in central Paris.

Julien Mattia/ Getty Images

Source: Media reports, November 27–29, 2019.

CRITICAL ANALYSIS: Import-competing industries cite lots of reasons for restricting trade. Their primary concern, however, is to protect their own jobs and profits.

Embargoes

The surefire way to restrict trade is simply to eliminate it. To do so, a country need only impose an embargo on exports or imports, or both. An **embargo** is nothing more than a prohibition against trading particular goods.

embargo: A prohibition on exports or imports.

In 1951 Senator Joseph McCarthy convinced the U.S. Senate to impose an embargo on Soviet mink, fox, and five other furs. He argued that such imports helped finance world communism. Senator McCarthy also represented the state of Wisconsin, where most U.S. minks are raised. The Reagan administration tried to end the fur embargo in 1987 but met with stiff congressional opposition. By then U.S. mink ranchers had developed a $120 million per year industry.

The United States has also maintained an embargo on Cuban goods since 1959, when Fidel Castro took power there. This embargo severely damaged Cuba's sugar industry and deprived American smokers of the famed Havana cigars. It also fostered the development of U.S. sugar beet and tobacco farmers, who now have a vested interest in maintaining the embargo.

Tariffs

A more frequent trade restriction is a **tariff,** a special tax imposed on imported goods. Tariffs, also called *customs duties,* were once the principal source of revenue for governments. In the 18th century, tariffs on tea, glass, wine, lead, and paper were imposed on the American colonies to provide extra revenue for the British government. The tariff on tea led to the Boston Tea Party in 1773 and gave added momentum to the American independence movement.

In modern times, tariffs have been used primarily as a means to protect specific industries from import competition. The current U.S. tariff code specifies tariffs on more than 9,000 different products—nearly 50 percent of all U.S. imports. Although the average tariff is less than 5 percent, individual tariffs vary widely. The tariff on cars, for example, is only 2.5 percent, while cotton sweaters confront a 17.8 percent tariff.

The attraction of tariffs to import-competing industries should be obvious. *A tariff on imported goods makes them more expensive to domestic consumers and thus less competitive with domestically produced goods.* Among familiar tariffs in effect in 2020 were 50 cents per gallon on Scotch whisky and 76 cents per gallon on imported champagne. These tariffs made American-produced spirits look relatively cheap and thus contributed to higher sales and profits for domestic distillers and grape growers. In the same manner, imported baby food is taxed at 34.6 percent, maple sugar at 9.4 percent, golf shoes at 8.5 percent, and imported sailboats at 1.5 percent. In 2009 President Obama imposed a 35 percent tariff on imported Chinese tires and a 26 percent tariff on Chinese solar panels in 2014. In 2017, President Trump announced a 24 percent tariff on Canadian lumber. In each case, domestic producers in import-competing industries gain. The losers are domestic consumers, who end up paying higher prices. The tariff on orange juice, for example, raises the price of drinking orange juice by $525 million a year. The tariff on Canadian lumber raises the price of a new home by $3,000. Tariffs also hurt foreign producers, who lose business, and world efficiency, as trade is reduced.

"Beggar Thy Neighbor". Microeconomic interests aren't the only source of pressure for tariff protection. Imports represent leakage from the domestic circular flow and a potential loss of jobs at home. From this perspective, reducing imports looks like an easy solution to the problem of domestic unemployment. Just get people to "buy American" instead of buying imported products, so the argument goes, and domestic output and employment will surely expand. President Obama used this argument to include "buy American" rules in his 2009 stimulus package. President Trump was even more insistent about "bringing jobs home" by restricting imports and signing "buy American" orders.

Congressman Willis Hawley used this same argument in 1930. He assured his colleagues that higher tariffs would "bring about the growth and development in this country that has followed every other tariff bill, bringing as it does a new prosperity in which all people, in all sections, will increase their comforts, their enjoyment, and their happiness."[1] Congress responded by passing the Smoot-Hawley Tariff Act of 1930, which raised tariffs to an average of nearly 60 percent, effectively cutting off most imports.

Tariffs designed to expand domestic employment are more likely to fail than to succeed. If a tariff wall does stem the flow of imports, it effectively transfers the unemployment problem to other countries, a phenomenon often referred to as "beggar thy neighbor." The resultant loss of business in other countries leaves them less able to purchase our exports. The imported unemployment also creates intense political pressures for retaliatory action. That's exactly what happened in the 1930s. Other countries erected trade barriers to compensate for the effects of the Smoot-Hawley tariff. World trade subsequently fell from $60 billion in 1928 to a mere $25 billion in 1938. This trade contraction increased the severity of the Great Depression (see World View "'Beggar-Thy-Neighbor' Policies in the 1930s").

The same kind of macroeconomic threat surfaced in 2009. The "buy American" provisions introduced by the Obama administration angered foreign nations that would lose export sales. When they threatened to retaliate with trade barriers of their own, President Obama had to offer reassurances about America's commitment to "free trade." When

---

[1] *The New York Times,* June 15, 1930, p. 25.

WORLD VIEW

"BEGGAR-THY-NEIGHBOR" POLICIES IN THE 1930S

President Herbert Hoover signed the Smoot-Hawley Tariff Act on June 17, 1930, despite the pleas from 1,028 economists to veto it. The Act raised the effective tariff on imports by 50 percent between 1929 and 1932. Although designed to limit import competition and boost domestic employment, the Act triggered quick retaliation from America's trading partners:

- Spain passed the Wais tariff in July in reaction to U.S. tariffs on grapes, oranges, cork, and onions.
- Switzerland, objecting to new U.S. tariffs on watches, embroideries, and shoes, boycotted American exports.
- Italy retaliated against tariffs on hats and olive oil with high tariffs on U.S. and French automobiles in June 1930.
- Canada reacted to high duties on many food products, logs, and timber by raising tariffs threefold in August 1932.
- Australia, Cuba, France, Mexico, and New Zealand also joined in the tariff wars.

From 1930 to 1931 U.S. imports dropped 29 percent, but U.S. exports fell even more, 33 percent, and continued their collapse to a modern-day low of $2.4 billion in 1933. World trade contracted by similar proportions, spreading unemployment around the globe.

In 1934 the U.S. Congress passed the Reciprocal Trade Agreements Act to empower the president to reduce tariffs by half the 1930 rates in return for like cuts in foreign duties on U.S. goods. The "beggar-thy-neighbor" policy was dead. Since then, the nations of the world have been reducing tariffs and other trade barriers.

Source: "'Beggar-Thy-Neighbor' Policies in the 1930s," *World Development Report 1987,* p. 139, box 8.4.

CRITICAL ANALYSIS: Tariffs inflict harm on foreign producers. If foreign countries retaliate with tariffs of their own, world trade will shrink and unemployment will increase in all countries.

President Trump imposed tariffs on Chinese goods in 2018 in order to "bring jobs home," China retaliated in kind, igniting a trade war between the two nations.

Quotas

Tariffs reduce the flow of imports by raising import prices. The same outcome can be attained more directly by imposing import **quotas,** numerical restrictions on the quantity of a particular good that may be imported. The United States limits the quantity of ice cream imported from Jamaica to 950 gallons a year. Only 1.4 million kilograms of Australian cheddar cheese and no more than 7,730 tons of Haitian sugar can be imported. Additional quotas are imposed on brooms, tuna, tobacco, and cotton. Textile quotas are imposed on every country that wants to ship textiles to the U.S. market. According to the U.S. Department of State, approximately 12 percent of our imports are subject to import quotas.

quota: A limit on the quantity of a good that may be imported in a given time period.

Comparative Effects

Quotas, like all barriers to trade, reduce world efficiency and invite retaliatory action. Moreover, their impact can be even more damaging than tariffs. To see this, we may compare market outcomes in four different contexts: no trade, free trade, tariff-restricted trade, and quota-restricted trade.

No-Trade Equilibrium. Figure 21.4*a* depicts the supply-and-demand relationships that would prevail in an economy that imposed a trade *embargo* on foreign textiles. In this situation, the **equilibrium price** of textiles is completely determined by domestic demand and supply curves. The no-trade equilibrium price is p_1, and the quantity of textiles consumed is q_1.

FIGURE 21.4

The Impact of Trade Restrictions

In the *absence of trade,* the domestic price and sales of a good will be determined by domestic supply and demand curves (point *A* in part *a*). Once trade is permitted, the market supply curve will be altered by the availability of imports. With *free trade* and unlimited availability of imports at price p_2, a new market equilibrium will be established at world prices (point *B*).

Tariffs raise domestic prices and reduce the quantity sold (point *C*). *Quotas* put an absolute limit on imported sales and thus give domestic producers a great opportunity to raise the market price (point *D*).

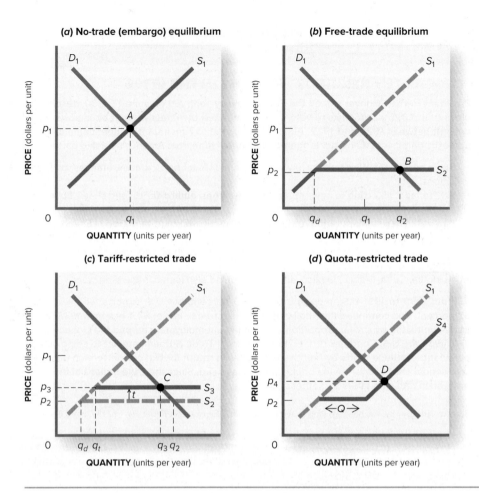

(a) No-trade (embargo) equilibrium

(b) Free-trade equilibrium

(c) Tariff-restricted trade

(d) Quota-restricted trade

Free-Trade Equilibrium. Suppose now that the embargo is lifted. The immediate effect of this decision will be a rightward shift of the market supply curve, as foreign supplies are added to domestic supplies (Figure 21.4*b*). If an unlimited quantity of textiles can be bought in world markets at a price of p_2, the new supply curve will look like S_2 (infinitely elastic at p_2). The new supply curve (S_2) intersects the old demand curve (D_1) at a new equilibrium price of p_2 and an expanded consumption of q_2. At this new equilibrium, domestic producers are supplying the quantity q_d while foreign producers are supplying the rest ($q_2 - q_d$). Comparing the new equilibrium to the old one, we see that *free trade results in reduced prices and increased consumption.*

Domestic textile producers are unhappy, of course, with their foreign competition. In the absence of trade, the domestic producers would sell more output (q_1) and get higher prices (p_1). Once trade is opened up, the willingness of foreign producers to sell unlimited quantities of textiles at the price p_2 puts a lid on domestic prices. Domestic producers hate this.

Tariff-Restricted Trade. Figure 21.4*c* illustrates what would happen to prices and sales if the United Textile Producers were successful in persuading the government to impose a tariff. Assume that the tariff raises imported textile prices from p_2 to p_3, making it more difficult for foreign producers to undersell domestic producers. Domestic production expands from q_d to q_t, imports are reduced from $q_2 - q_d$ to $q_3 - q_t$, and the market price of textiles rises. Domestic textile producers are clearly better off. So is the U.S. Treasury, which will collect increased tariff revenues. Unfortunately, domestic consumers are worse off (higher prices), as are foreign producers (reduced sales).

Quota-Restricted Trade. Now consider the impact of a textile *quota.* Suppose we eliminate tariffs but decree that imports can't exceed the quantity *Q.* Because the quantity of imports can never exceed *Q,* the supply curve is effectively shifted to the right by that amount. The new curve S_4 (Figure 21.4*d*) indicates that no imports will occur below the world price p_2 and above that price the quantity Q will be imported. Thus, the *domestic* demand curve determines subsequent prices. Foreign producers are precluded from selling greater quantities as prices rise further. This outcome is in marked contrast to that of tariff-restricted trade (Figure 21.4*c*), which at least permits foreign producers to respond to rising prices. Accordingly, ***quotas are a greater threat to competition than tariffs because quotas preclude additional imports at any price.*** The actual quotas on textile imports raise the prices of shirts, towels, and other textile products by 58 percent. As a result, a $10 shirt ends up costing consumers $15.80. All told, U.S. consumers end up paying an extra $25 billion a year for textile products.

The sugar industry is one of the greatest beneficiaries of quota restrictions. By limiting imports to 15 percent of domestic consumption, sugar quotas keep U.S. prices artificially high (see Front Page Economics "Sugar Quotas a Sour Deal for U.S. Consumers"). This costs consumers nearly $3 billion a year in higher prices. Candy and soda producers lose sales and profits. According to the U.S. Department of Commerce, more than 6,000 jobs have been lost in sugar-using industries (e.g., candy manufacturing) due to high sugar costs. Hershey alone closed plants in Pennsylvania, Colorado, and California and moved candy production to Canada. Foreign sugar producers (mainly in poor nations) also lose sales, profits, and jobs. Who gains? Domestic sugar producers—who, coincidentally, are highly concentrated in key electoral states like Florida.

FRONT PAGE ECONOMICS

SUGAR QUOTAS A SOUR DEAL FOR U.S. CONSUMERS

U.S. sugar farmers have enjoyed protection from imports since 1789 when Congress enacted the first tariff on imported sugar. The Sugar Act of 1934 gave U.S. farmers an even better deal by creating a quota on the amount of sugar that can be imported into the United States. The Farm Bill of 2018 continued that protection, limiting sugar imports to 1.2 million tons per year—just a fraction of the 11 million tons Americans consume. As a result of that quota, U.S. sugar prices in early 2020 were about 10 cents a pound higher than world prices.

That's great news for America's 4,700 sugar farmers but a sour deal for U.S. consumers and manufacturers, who pay more for all sugar products. U.S. candy producers have cut thousands of jobs and moved manufacturing plants to Canada and elsewhere, where sugar is cheaper. Analysts estimate that 3 manufacturing jobs have been lost for every 1 sugar job saved and consumers are paying more than $2 billion a year in higher sugar prices.

Source: Industry and media reports, January 2020.

CRITICAL ANALYSIS: Import quotas preclude increased foreign competition when domestic prices rise. Protected domestic producers enjoy higher prices and profits while consumers pay higher prices.

Voluntary Restraint Agreements

A slight variant of quotas has been used in recent years. Rather than impose quotas on imports, the U.S. government asks foreign producers to "voluntarily" limit their exports. These so-called **voluntary restraint agreements** have been negotiated with producers in Japan, South Korea, Taiwan, China, the European Union, and other countries. Korea, for example, agreed to reduce its annual shoe exports to the United States from 44 million pairs to 33 million pairs. Taiwan reduced its shoe exports from 156 million pairs to 122 million pairs per year. In 2005 China agreed to slow its exports of clothing, limiting its sales growth to 8–17 percent a year. For their part, the Japanese agreed to reduce sales of color TV sets in the United States from 2.8 million to 1.75 million per year. In 2006 Mexico agreed to limit its cement exports to the United States to 3 million tons a year. In 2014 Mexico also agreed to curtail its sugar exports to the United States, forsaking its unique treaty rights to unrestricted exports.

voluntary restraint agreement (VRA): An agreement to reduce the volume of trade in a specific good; a "voluntary" quota.

All these voluntary export restraints, as they're often called, represent an informal type of quota. The only difference is that they're negotiated rather than imposed. But these differences are lost on consumers, who end up paying higher prices for these goods. The voluntary limit on Japanese auto exports to the United States alone cost consumers $15.7 billion in only four years.

Nontariff Barriers

Tariffs and quotas are the most visible barriers to trade, but they're only the tip of the iceberg. Indeed, the variety of protectionist measures that have been devised is testimony to the ingenuity of the human mind. At the turn of the century, the Germans were committed to a most-favored-nation policy: a policy of extending equal treatment to all trading partners. The Germans, however, wanted to lower the tariff on cattle imports from Denmark without extending the same break to Switzerland. Such a preferential tariff would have violated the most-favored-nation policy. Accordingly, the Germans created a new and higher tariff on "brown and dappled cows reared at a level of at least 300 meters above sea level and passing at least one month in every summer at an altitude of at least 800 meters." The new tariff was, of course, applied equally to all countries. But Danish cows never climb that high, so they weren't burdened with the new tariff.

With the decline in tariffs over the last 20 years, nontariff barriers have increased. The United States uses product standards, licensing restrictions, restrictive procurement practices, and other nontariff barriers to restrict roughly 15 percent of imports. In 1999–2000 the European Union banned imports of U.S. beef, arguing that the use of hormones on U.S. ranches created a health hazard for European consumers. Although both the U.S. government and the World Trade Organization disputed that claim, the ban was a highly effective nontariff trade barrier. The United States responded by slapping 100 percent tariffs on dozens of European products.

Mexican Trucks. One of the more flagrant examples of nontariff barriers is the use of safety regulations to block Mexican trucking companies from using U.S. roads to deliver goods. The resulting trade barrier forced Mexican trucks to unload their cargoes at the U.S. border, and then reload them into U.S. (Teamster-driven) trucks for shipment to U.S. destinations. The U.S. agreed to lift that restriction in 1995, but didn't. In 2009 President Obama actually solidified the Mexican roadblock, despite the fact that Mexican trucks passed all 22 safety (nontariff) regulations the U.S. Department of Transportation had imposed. In so doing, President Obama secured more jobs for Teamster-union drivers but raised costs for U.S. shippers and consumers and drove down sales and employment for Mexican trucking companies. Fed up with U.S. protectionism, Mexico retaliated by slapping tariffs on 90 U.S. export products. By early 2011, U.S. exports to Mexico of those products had declined by 81 percent. This prompted President Obama to offer Mexico a new round of negotiations, which ended in January 2015 with the U.S. declaring Mexican trucks to be safe enough to travel U.S. roads and Mexico repealing the tariffs on U.S. exports. The 2019 U.S-Mexico-Canada Agreement (USMCA) ratified that understanding, prompting a significant increase in cross-border trade.

MULTILATERAL TRADE DEALS

Proponents of free trade and import-competing industries are in constant conflict. Most of the time the trade policy deck seems stacked in favor of the special interests. Because import-competing firms and workers are highly concentrated, they're quick to mobilize politically. By contrast, the benefits of freer trade are less direct and spread over millions of consumers. As a consequence, the beneficiaries of freer trade are less likely to monitor trade policy—much less lobby actively to change it. Hence, the political odds favor the spread of trade barriers.

Multilateral Trade Pacts

Despite these odds, the long-term trend is toward *lowering* trade barriers, thereby increasing global competition. Two forces encourage this trend. ***The principal barrier to protectionist*** *policies is worldwide recognition of the gains from freer trade.* Because world nations now understand that trade barriers are ultimately self-defeating, they're more willing to rise above the din of protectionist cries and dismantle trade barriers. They diffuse political opposition by creating across-the-board trade pacts that seem to spread the pain (and gain) from freer trade across a broad swath of industries. Such pacts also incorporate multiyear timetables that give affected industries time to adjust.

Trade liberalization has also been encouraged by firms that *export* products or use imported inputs in their own production. Candy manufacturers don't want to pay more for sugar, auto companies don't want to pay more for steel, and shippers don't want to pay more for transportation. They, too, can organize and petition governments for relief from trade barriers.

Global Pacts: GATT and WTO

The granddaddy of the multilateral, multiyear free-trade pacts was the 1947 *General Agreement on Tariffs and Trade (GATT).* Twenty-three nations pledged to reduce trade barriers and give all GATT nations equal access to their domestic markets.

Since the first GATT pact, seven more "rounds" of negotiations have expanded the scope of GATT; 117 nations signed the 1994 pact. As a result of these GATT pacts, average tariff rates in developed countries have fallen from 40 percent in 1948 to less than 4 percent today.

WTO

The 1994 GATT pact also created the *World Trade Organization (WTO)* to enforce free-trade rules. If a nation feels its exports are being unfairly excluded from another country's market, it can file a complaint with the WTO. This is exactly what the United States did when the EU banned U.S. beef imports. The WTO ruled in favor of the United States. When the EU failed to lift its import ban, the WTO authorized the United States to impose retaliatory tariffs on European exports.

The EU turned the tables on the United States in 2003. It complained to the WTO that U.S. tariffs on imported steel violated trade rules. The WTO agreed and gave the EU permission to impose retaliatory tariffs on $2.2 billion of U.S. exports. That prompted the Bush administration to scale back the tariffs in December 2003. The U.S. was chastised again in September 2020 for unfairly imposing tariffs on Chinese goods in 2018.

In effect, the WTO is now the world's trade police force. It is empowered to cite nations that violate trade agreements and even to impose remedial action when violations persist. Why do sovereign nations give the WTO such power? Because they are all convinced that free trade is the surest route to GDP growth.

Regional Pacts

Because worldwide trade pacts are so complex, many nations have also pursued *regional* free-trade agreements.

NAFTA. In December 1992 the United States, Canada, and Mexico signed the *North American Free Trade Agreement (NAFTA),* a 1,000-page document covering more than 9,000 products. The ultimate goal of NAFTA was to eliminate all trade barriers between these three countries. At the time of signing, intraregional tariffs averaged 11 percent in Mexico, 5 percent in Canada, and 4 percent in the United States.

The NAFTA-initiated reduction in trade barriers substantially increased trade flows between Mexico, Canada, and the United States. It also prompted a wave of foreign investment in Mexico, where both cheap labor and NAFTA access were available. Overall, NAFTA accelerated economic growth and reduced inflationary pressures in all three nations. Some industries (like construction and apparel) suffered from the freer trade, but others (like trucking, farming, and finance) reaped huge gains.

USMCA. NAFTA was revised and updated with a new trade agreement called the U.S.-Mexico-Canada Agreement (USMCA), signed by President Trump in January 2020. The USMCA continued the free-trade commitments of NAFTA, while adding more labor and environmental standards. It also gives U.S. dairy farmers more access to Canada's market and increases country-of-origin requirements for autos. The International Trade Commission estimated that the new regional pact will add 0.35 percent to U.S. GDP growth over its first six years.

TPP. The Trans-Pacific Partnership was intended to be another regional trade pact, linking 12 nations that border the Pacific Ocean in a multiyear commitment to freer trade. After eight years of negotiations, those 12 nations signed a tentative TPP agreement in February 2016. That 2,000-page agreement not only called for reductions in tariffs and nontariff trade barriers among the member nations, but also sought greater coordination of policies on environmental protection, workers' rights, and regulatory practices. To become effective, the legislatures of the 12 nations had to ratify the agreement by February 2018. President Trump called TPP a particularly "bad deal" and vowed to kill it. He kept that vow by officially withdrawing the United States from the TPP on his very first day of office. Henceforth, he said, he only wanted bilateral deals that "put America first." Critics warned that he was ignoring the benefits of freer trade and risking the perception that America was an unreliable trading partner.

DECISIONS FOR TOMORROW

WHO WINS TRADE WARS?

President Trump's "America first" approach to trade policy put him at odds with the global trend toward lower trade barriers. Indeed, he proclaimed himself to be "a tariff man" who had long advocated using tariffs to offset the "unfair trade practices" of other nations. He singled out China as one of the worst trading partners, claiming that it unfairly promoted huge bilateral trade deficits, engaged in theft of intellectual property, and forced U.S. companies doing business in China to transfer technology secrets.

Retaliatory Tariff Rounds. On March 22, 2018, President Trump announced that he was imposing tariffs on as many as 1,300 Chinese products as "a response to the unfair trade practices of China over the years." Those tariffs, he argued, would force China to reform its trade practices, "leveling the field" for American companies to compete. Advised that China might retaliate with tariffs on American goods, President Trump shrugged that "trade wars are good and easy to win."

China did retaliate. After the U.S. tacked on tariffs to $34 billion of Chinese exports, China did the same to $34 billion of U.S. exports. Three additional rounds of tariffs initiated by Trump made over $250 billion of Chinese products subject to tariffs as high as 25 percent in early 2019. In June 2019 China responded again with 25 percent tariffs on another $60 billion of U.S. exports.

Economic Effects. The tariff escalations sharply reduced trade flows between the United States and China. U.S. agricultural exports to China were particularly hard hit as China sharply cut purchases of American soybeans, pork, and wheat. The uncertainties created by the trade war also caused businesses to defer investment. The Congressional Budget Office estimated that the trade war reduced GDP growth in 2019 by 0.3 percent, trimmed investment spending by 1.3 percent, and reduced the income of the average U.S. household by $580. The International Monetary Fund noted that the effects of the U.S.–China trade war spilled over to other nations, causing a global GDP slowdown from 3.6 percent to 3.3 percent.

A Cease Fire. Recognizing the increasing damage inflicted on both countries, the U.S. and China called for a truce in December 2019. In "Phase One" of that truce, signed on January 15, 2020, the two nations agreed to roll back some of their tariffs, resume some bilateral purchases, and rethink disputed trade practices. As a November 2019 United Nations report noted, there was no winner in the U.S.–China trade war.

SUMMARY

- International trade permits each country to specialize in areas of relative efficiency, increasing world output. For each country, the gains from trade are reflected in consumption possibilities that exceed production possibilities. **LO21-2**

- One way to determine where comparative advantage lies is to compare the quantity of good A that must be given up in order to get a given quantity of good B from domestic production. If the same quantity of B can be obtained for less A by engaging in world trade, we have a comparative advantage in the production of good A. Comparative advantage rests on a comparison of relative opportunity costs. **LO21-1**

- The terms of trade—the rate at which goods are exchanged—are subject to the forces of international supply and demand. The terms of trade will lie somewhere between the opportunity costs of the trading partners. The terms of trade determine how the gains from trade are shared. **LO21-2**

- Resistance to trade emanates from workers and firms that must compete with imports. Even though the country as a whole stands to benefit from trade, these individuals and companies may lose jobs and incomes in the process. **LO21-3**

- Trade barriers take many forms. Embargoes are outright prohibitions against import or export of particular goods. Quotas limit the quantity of a good imported or exported. Tariffs discourage imports by making them more expensive. Other nontariff barriers make trade too costly or time-consuming. **LO21-3**

- The World Trade Organization (WTO) seeks to reduce worldwide trade barriers and enforce trade rules. Regional accords such as the USMCA pursue similar objectives among fewer countries. **LO21-3**

- Trade wars inflict economic losses on the feuding nations and the broader global economy. Such losses create an incentive to resolve disputed issues. **LO21-3**

Key Terms

imports	consumption possibilities	dumping
exports	open economy	embargo
trade deficit	comparative advantage	tariff
trade surplus	opportunity cost	quota
production possibilities	absolute advantage	equilibrium price
closed economy	terms of trade	voluntary restraint agreement (VRA)

Questions for Discussion

1. Suppose a lawyer can type faster than any secretary. Should the lawyer do her own typing? Can you demonstrate the validity of your answer? **LO21-1**

2. What would be the effects of a law requiring bilateral trade balances? **LO21-2**

3. If a nation exported much of its output but imported little, would it be better or worse off? How about the reverse—that is, exporting little but importing a lot? **LO21-2**

4. How does international trade restrain the price behavior of domestic firms? **LO21-3**

5. Suppose we refused to sell goods to any country that reduced or halted its exports to us. Who would benefit and who would lose from such retaliation? **LO21-2**

6. Domestic producers often base their demands for import protection on the fact that workers in country X are paid substandard wages. Is this a valid argument for protection? **LO21-1**

7. Who will benefit or gain if the U.S. slaps tariffs on South Korean cigarettes (see World View "U.S. Accuses South Korea of Dumping Cigarettes")? **LO21-3**

8. According to the National Association of Home Builders, the 2017 tariff on Canadian lumber resulted in the loss of 8,000 U.S. construction jobs. How does this happen? **LO21-3**

9. Would France be better or worse off importing cheap Argentinian wheat? (see World View "French Tractors Roll into Paris")? **LO21-2**

10. If trade wars inflict economic damage on both nations, why do they occur? **LO21-3**

PROBLEMS FOR CHAPTER 21

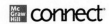

LO21-2 1. Which countries are
    (*a*) The two largest export markets for the United States? (See Table 21.3.)
    (*b*) The two biggest sources of imports?

LO21-1 2. Suppose a country can produce a maximum of 12,000 jumbo airliners or 2,000 aircraft carriers.
    (*a*) What is the opportunity cost of an aircraft carrier?
    (*b*) If another country offers to trade eight planes for one aircraft carrier, should the offer be accepted?
    (*c*) What is the implied "price" of the carrier in trade?

LO21-1 3. If it takes 10 farmworkers to harvest 1 ton of strawberries and 3 farmworkers to harvest 1 ton of wheat, what is the opportunity cost of 6 tons of strawberries?

LO21-2 4. Alpha and Beta, two tiny islands in the Pacific, produce pearls and pineapples. The following production possibilities schedules describe their potential output in tons per year:

Alpha		Beta	
Pearls	**Pineapples**	**Pearls**	**Pineapples**
0	30	0	20
2	25	10	16
4	20	20	12
6	15	30	8
8	10	40	4
10	5	45	2
12	0	50	0

    (*a*) Graph the production possibilities confronting each island.
    (*b*) What is the opportunity cost of pineapples on each island (before trade)?
    (*c*) Which island has a comparative advantage in pineapple production?
    (*d*) Which island has a comparative advantage in pearl production?
Now suppose Alpha and Beta specialize according to their comparative advantages and trade.
If one pearl is traded for 1.5 pineapples,
    (*e*) How many pearls would have to be exported to get 15 pineapples in return?
After this trade,
    (*f*) What is Alpha's consumption?
    (*g*) What is Beta's consumption?

PROBLEMS FOR CHAPTER 21 (cont'd)

LO21-3 5. (*a*) How much more are U.S. consumers paying for the 11 million tons of sugar they consume each year as a result of the quotas on sugar imports? (See Front Page Economics "Sugar Quotas a Sour Deal.")
(*b*) How much is this per person (population = 330 million)?
(*c*) How much would each person save if the quota was lifted?

LO21-2 6. Suppose the two islands in Problem 4 agree that the terms of trade will be one for one and exchange 10 pearls for 10 pineapples.
(*a*) If Alpha produced 6 pearls and 15 pineapples while Beta produced 30 pearls and 8 pineapples before they decided to trade, how many pearls would each be producing after trade? Assume that the two countries specialize according to their comparative advantage.
(*b*) How much would the combined production of pineapples increase for the two islands due to specialization?
(*c*) How much would the combined production of pearls increase?
(*d*) What is the post trade consumption for each island?

LO21-3 7. If there are 12 bottles in a case of wine,
(*a*) How many bottles of wine did Americans consume in 2018?
(*b*) How many of those were imported? (See World View "Imported Wine Squeezing U.S. Vintners.")

LO21-3 8. Suppose the following table reflects the domestic supply and demand for Bluetooth headphones:

Price ($)	60	55	50	45	40	35	30	25
Quantity supplied (in millions per year)	8	7	6	5	4	3	2	1
Quantity demanded (in millions per year)	2	4	6	8	10	12	14	16

(*a*) Graph these market conditions and identify
(*i*) The equilibrium price.
(*ii*) The equilibrium quantity.
(*b*) Now suppose that foreigners enter the market, offering to sell an unlimited supply of Bluetooth headphones for $35 apiece. Illustrate and identify
(*i*) The new market price.
(*ii*) Domestic consumption.
(*iii*) Domestic production.
(*c*) If a tariff of $5 per unit is imposed, what will be
(*i*) The market price?
(*ii*) Domestic consumption?
(*iii*) Domestic production?
Graph your answers.

LO21-3 9. (*a*) Which regional trade pact was in force in 2015 among Canada, the United States, and Mexico?
(*b*) Which industries have gained from this trade pact?
(*c*) Which industries have lost from this trade pact?

LO21-3 10. *Decisions for Tomorrow:*
(*a*) Graphically show the impact of the retaliatory tariff in the Chinese market for soybeans.
(*b*) What happened to the market price in China for these imported soybeans from the U.S.?

Design Credit: Shutterstock

Don Tonge/Alamy Stock Photo

International Finance

Textile, furniture, and shrimp producers in the United States want China to increase the value of the yuan. They say China's undervalued currency makes Chinese exports too cheap, undercutting American firms. President Trump agreed, calling China a "currency manipulator" that kept its currency cheap to undercut American producers. He demanded that China increase the value of its currency so as to "bring jobs back from China."

Walmart disagrees. Walmart thinks a cheap yuan is a good thing because it keeps prices low for the *$100 billion* of toys, tools, linens, and other goods it buys from China each year. Those low import prices help Walmart keep its own prices low and its sales volume high. Walmart is also the largest employer in the United States, providing more than 1.5 million jobs.

This chapter examines how currency values affect trade patterns and ultimately the core questions of WHAT, HOW, and FOR WHOM to produce. We focus on the following questions:

- **What determines the value of one country's money compared to the value of another's?**
- **What causes the international value of currencies to change?**
- **How and why do governments intervene to alter currency values?**

EXCHANGE RATES: THE GLOBAL LINK

As we saw in Chapter 21, the United States exports and imports a staggering volume of goods and services. Although we trade with nearly 200 nations around the world, we seldom give much thought to where imports come from and how we acquire them. Most of the time, all we want to know is which products are available and at what price.

Suppose that you want to buy Apple AirPods. You don't have to know that AirPods are manufactured in China. And you certainly don't have to fly to China to pick them up. All you have to do is drive to the nearest electronics store; or you can just "click and buy" at the Internet's virtual mall.

But you may wonder how the purchase of an imported product was so simple. Chinese companies sell their products in yuan, the currency of China. But you purchase the AirPods in dollars. How is this possible?

There's a chain of distribution between your dollar purchase in the United States and the yuan-denominated sale in China. Somewhere along that chain someone has to convert your dollars into yuan. The critical question for everybody concerned is how many yuan we can get for our dollars—that is, what the **exchange rate** is. If we can get eight yuan for every dollar, the exchange rate is 8 yuan = 1 dollar. Alternatively, we could note that the price of a yuan is 12.5 U.S. cents when the exchange rate is 8 to 1. Thus, *an exchange rate is the price of one currency in terms of another.*

FOREIGN EXCHANGE MARKETS

Most exchange rates are determined in foreign exchange markets. Stop thinking of money as some sort of magical substance, and instead view it as a useful commodity that facilitates market exchanges. From that perspective, an exchange rate—the price of money—is subject to the same influences that determine all market prices: demand and supply.

The Demand for Dollars

When the Chinese company Shuanghui International bought Smithfield Foods in 2013, it paid $4.7 billion. When Belgian beer maker InBev bought Anheuser-Busch (Budweiser, etc.) in 2008, it also needed dollars—more than 50 billion of them. When Fiat acquired control of Chrysler in 2011, it also needed U.S. dollars. In all three cases, the objective of the foreign investor was to acquire an American business. To attain their objectives, however, the buyers first had to buy *dollars.* The Chinese, Belgian, and Italian buyers had to exchange their own currency for American dollars.

Canadian tourists also need American dollars. Few American restaurants or hotels accept Canadian currency as payment for goods and services; they want to be paid in U.S. dollars. Accordingly, Canadian tourists must buy American dollars if they want to warm up in Florida.

Some foreign investors also buy U.S. dollars for speculative purposes. When Argentina's peso started losing value in 2012–2013, many Argentinians feared that its value would drop further and preferred to hold U.S. dollars; they *demanded* U.S. dollars. Ukrainians clamored for U.S. dollars when Russia invaded its territory in 2014. In 2017 Venezuelans were desperately trying to sell their worthless bolivars for pennies.

All these motivations give rise to a demand for U.S. dollars. Specifically, *the market demand for U.S. dollars originates in*

- *Foreign demand for American exports* (including tourism).
- *Foreign demand for American investments.*
- *Speculation.*

Governments also create a demand for dollars when they operate embassies, undertake cultural exchanges, or engage in intergovernment financial transactions.

The Supply of Dollars

The *supply* of dollars arises from similar sources. On the supply side, however, it's Americans who initiate most of the exchanges. Suppose you take a trip to Mexico. You'll need to buy Mexican pesos at some point. When you do, you'll be offering to *buy* pesos by offering to *sell* dollars. In other words, *the* **demand** *for foreign currency represents a* **supply** *of U.S. dollars.*

When Americans buy BMW cars, they also supply U.S. dollars. American consumers pay for their BMWs in dollars. Somewhere down the road, however, those dollars will be exchanged for European euros. At that exchange, dollars are being *supplied* and euros *demanded.*

American corporations demand foreign exchange too. General Motors builds cars in Germany, Coca-Cola produces Coke in China, and Exxon produces and refines oil all over the world. In nearly every such case, the U.S. firm must first build or buy some plants and equipment, using another country's factors of production. This activity requires foreign currency and thus becomes another component of our demand for foreign currency. When Elon Musk wanted to build a gigafactory in Shanghai in 2019, he needed $2 billion worth

How do AirPods (made in China) end up selling for U.S. dollars?

Photographer and videographer/ iStock/Getty Images

exchange rate: The price of one country's currency expressed in terms of another's; the domestic price of a foreign currency.

Which currency is most valuable? It depends on exchange rates.

Maria Toutoudaki/Getty Images

of Chinese yuan to pay construction companies, workers, and suppliers. Now that the factory is open, he needs a constant stream of yuan to pay local Tesla workers and suppliers.

We may summarize these market activities by noting that *the supply of dollars originates in*

- *American demand for imports* (including tourism).
- *American investments in foreign countries.*
- *Speculation.*

As on the demand side, government intervention can also contribute to the supply of dollars.

The Value of the Dollar

Whether American consumers will choose to buy an imported BMW depends partly on what the car costs. The price tag isn't always apparent in international transactions. Remember that the German BMW producer and workers want to be paid in their own currency, the euro. Hence, the *dollar* price of an imported BMW depends on two factors: (1) the German price of a BMW and (2) the *exchange rate* between U.S. dollars and euros. Specifically, the U.S. price of a BMW is

$$\frac{\text{Dollar price}}{\text{of BMW}} = \frac{\text{Euro price}}{\text{of BMW}} \times \frac{\text{Dollar price}}{\text{of euro}}$$

Suppose the BMW company is prepared to sell a German-built BMW for 100,000 euros and that the current exchange rate is 2 euros = \$1. At these rates, a BMW will cost you

$$\frac{\text{Dollar price}}{\text{of BMW}} = 100,000 \text{ euros} \times \frac{\$1}{2 \text{ euros}}$$
$$= \$50,000$$

If you're willing to pay this much for a shiny new German-built BMW, you may do so at current exchange rates.

Now suppose the exchange rate changes from 2 euros = \$1 to 1 euro = \$1. Now you're getting only 1 euro for your dollar rather than 2 euros. In other words, euros have become more expensive. *A higher dollar price for euros will raise the dollar costs of European goods.* In this case, the dollar price of a euro increases from \$0.50 to \$1. At this new exchange rate, the BMW plant in Germany is still willing to sell BMWs at 100,000 euros apiece. And German consumers continue to buy BMWs at that price. But this constant euro price now translates into a higher *dollar* price. That same BMW that you previously could buy for \$50,000 now costs you \$100,000—not because the cost of manufacturing the car in Germany went up, but simply because the exchange rate changed.

As the dollar price of a BMW rises, the number of BMWs sold in the United States will decline. As BMW sales decline, the quantity of euros demanded may decline as well. Thus, the quantity of foreign currency demanded declines when the exchange rate rises because foreign goods become more expensive and imports decline. When the dollar price of European currencies actually increased in 1992, BMW decided to start producing cars in South Carolina. A year later, Mercedes-Benz decided to produce cars in the United States as well. Sales of American-made BMWs and Mercedes no longer depend on the exchange rate of the U.S. dollar. But the dollar price of German-made Audis, French wine, and Italian shoes does.

The Supply Curve. These market responses suggest that the supply of dollars is upward-sloping. If the value of the dollar rises, Americans will be able to buy more euros. As a result, the dollar price of imported BMWs will decline. American consumers will respond by demanding more imports, thereby supplying a larger quantity of dollars. The supply curve in Figure 22.1 shows how the quantity of dollars supplied rises as the value of the dollar increases.

The Demand Curve. The demand for dollars can be explained in similar terms. Remember that the demand for dollars arises from the foreign demand for U.S. exports and investments. If the exchange rate moves from 2 euros = \$1 to 1 euro = \$1, the euro price of dollars falls. As

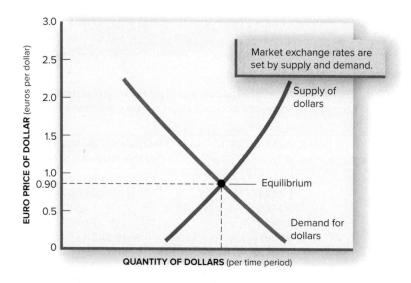

FIGURE 22.1

The Foreign Exchange Market

The foreign exchange market operates like other markets. In this case, the "good" bought and sold is dollars (foreign exchange). The price and quantity of dollars actually exchanged are determined by the intersection of market supply and demand.

dollars become cheaper for Germans, all American exports effectively fall in price. Germans will buy more American products (including trips to Disney World) and therefore demand a greater quantity of dollars. In addition, foreign investors will perceive in a cheaper dollar the opportunity to buy U.S. stocks, businesses, and property at fire-sale prices. Accordingly, they join foreign consumers in demanding more dollars. Not all these behavioral responses will occur overnight, but they're reasonably predictable over a brief period of time.

Equilibrium

Given market demand and supply curves, we can predict the **equilibrium price** of any commodity—that is, the price at which the quantity demanded will equal the quantity supplied. This occurs in Figure 22.1 where the two curves cross. At that equilibrium, the value of the dollar (the exchange rate) is established. In this case, the euro price of the dollar turns out to be 0.90.

The value of the dollar can also be expressed in terms of other currencies. World View "Foreign Exchange Rates" displays a sampling of dollar exchange rates in March 2020. Notice how many Indonesian rupiah you could buy for $1: A dollar was worth 16,222 rupiah. By contrast, a U.S. dollar was worth only 0.90 euro. **The *average* value of the dollar is a weighted mean of the exchange rates between the U.S. dollar and all these currencies.** The value of the dollar is "high" when its foreign exchange price is above recent levels, and it is "low" when it is below recent averages.

equilibrium price: The price at which the quantity of a good demanded in a given time period equals the quantity supplied.

The Balance of Payments

The equilibrium depicted in Figure 22.1 determines not only the *price* of the dollar, but also a specific *quantity* of international transactions. Those transactions include the exports, imports, international investments, and other sources of dollar supply and demand. A summary of all those international money flows is contained in the **balance of payments**—an accounting statement of all international money flows in a given period of time.

Trade Balance. Table 22.1 depicts the U.S. balance of payments for 2019. Notice first how the millions of separate transactions are classified into a few summary measures. The trade balance is the difference between exports and imports of goods (merchandise) and services. In 2019 the United States imported more than $3.1 trillion of goods and services but exported only $2.5 trillion. This created a **trade deficit** of $616 billion. That trade deficit represents a net outflow of dollars to the rest of the world.

balance of payments: A summary record of a country's international economic transactions in a given period of time.

trade deficit: The amount by which the value of imports exceeds the value of exports in a given time period (negative net exports).

$$\text{Trade balance} = \text{Exports} - \text{Imports}$$

WORLD VIEW

FOREIGN EXCHANGE RATES

The foreign exchange midrange rates here show (a) how many U.S. dollars are needed to buy one unit of foreign currency and (b) how many units of foreign currency are needed to buy one U.S. dollar.

Country	(a) U.S. Dollar per Unit (Dollar Price of Foreign Currency)	(b) Currency per U.S. Dollar (Foreign Price of U.S. Dollar)
Brazil (real)	0.1961	5.1006
Britain (pound)	1.2453	0.8030
Canada (dollar)	0.7145	1.4000
China (yuan)	0.1409	7.0950
Indonesia (rupiah)	0.0001	16,222.435
Japan (yen)	0.0092	107.9112
Mexico (peso)	0.0429	23.3313
Russia (ruble)	0.0127	78.7265
Eurozone (euro)	1.1144	0.8973
Venezuela (bolivar)	0.1001	9.9875

Source: March 2020 data from Federal Reserve Board of Governors.

CRITICAL ANALYSIS: The exchange rates between currencies are determined by supply and demand in foreign exchange markets. The rates reported here represent the equilibrium exchange rates on a particular day.

Current Account Balance. The current account balance is a second subtotal in Table 22.1. It includes the trade balance as well as private transfers such as wages sent home by foreign citizens working in the United States (like Mexican strawberry pickers in California). It also includes the income flows from international investments.

$$\text{Current account balance} = \text{Trade balance} + \text{Unilateral transfers} + \text{Net investment income}$$

The current account balance is the most comprehensive summary of our trade relations. As indicated in Table 22.1, the United States had a current account deficit of $498 billion in 2019.

TABLE 22.1

The U.S. Balance of Payments

The balance of payments is a summary statement of a country's international transactions. The major components of that activity are the trade balance (merchandise exports minus merchandise imports), the current account balance (trade, services, and transfers), and the capital account balance. The net total of these balances must equal zero because the quantity of dollars paid must equal the quantity of dollars received.

Item	Amount ($ billions)
1. Merchandise exports	$1,653
2. Merchandise imports	(2,519)
3. Service exports	845
4. Service imports	(595)
Trade balance (items 1–4)	−616
5. Income from U.S. overseas investments	1,123
6. Income outflow for foreign-owned U.S. investments	(866)
7. Net transfers and pensions	(139)
Current account balance (items 1–7)	−498
8. U.S. capital inflow	822
9. U.S. capital outflow	(427)
Capital account balance (items 8–9)	395
10. Statistical discrepancy	103
Net balance (items 1–10)	0

Source: U.S. Department of Commerce (2019 data).

Capital Account Balance. The current account deficit is offset by the capital account surplus. The capital account balance takes into consideration assets bought and sold across international borders:

$$\frac{\text{Capital account}}{\text{balance}} = \frac{\text{Foreign purchases}}{\text{of U.S. assets}} - \frac{\text{U.S. purchases}}{\text{of foreign assets}}$$

As Table 22.1 shows, foreign consumers demanded $822 billion in 2019 to buy farms and factories as well as U.S. bonds, stocks, and other investments (item 8). This exceeded the flow of U.S. dollars going overseas to purchase foreign assets (item 9).

The net capital inflows were essential in financing the U.S. trade deficit (negative trade balance). As in any market, the number of dollars demanded must equal the number of dollars supplied. Thus, *the capital account surplus must equal the current account deficit.* In other words, there can't be any dollars left lying around unaccounted for. Item 10 in Table 22.1 reminds us that our accounting system isn't perfect—we can't identify every transaction. Nevertheless, all the accounts must eventually "balance out":

$$\frac{\text{Net balance}}{\text{of payments}} = \frac{\text{Current account}}{\text{balance}} + \frac{\text{Capital account}}{\text{balance}} = 0$$

That's the character of a market *equilibrium:* The quantity of dollars demanded equals the quantity of dollars supplied.

MARKET DYNAMICS

The interesting thing about markets isn't their character in equilibrium but the fact that prices and quantities are always changing in response to shifts in demand and supply. The U.S. demand for BMWs shifted overnight when Japan introduced a new line of sleek, competitively priced cars (e.g., Lexus). The reduced demand for BMWs shifted the supply of dollars leftward. That supply shift raised the value of the dollar vis-à-vis the euro, as illustrated in Figure 22.2. (It also increased the demand for Japanese yen, causing the yen value of the dollar to *fall.*)

FIGURE 22.2

Shifts in Foreign Exchange Markets

When the Japanese introduced luxury autos into the United States, the American demand for German cars fell. As a consequence, the supply of dollars in the dollar–euro market (part *a*) shifted to the left and the euro value of the dollar rose.

At the same time, the increased American demand for Japanese cars shifted the dollar supply curve in the yen market (part *b*) to the right, reducing the yen price of the dollar.

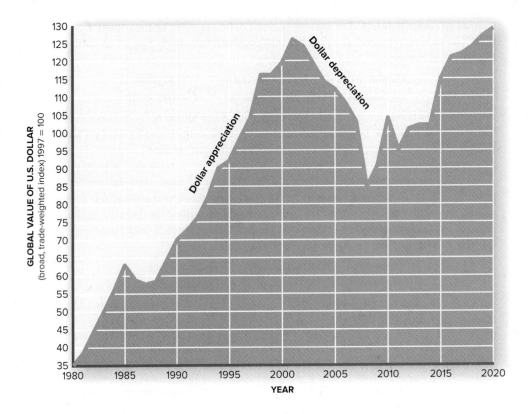

Depreciation and Appreciation

depreciation (currency): A fall in the price of one currency relative to another.

appreciation: A rise in the price of one currency relative to another.

If the dollar is rising in value (appreciating), the euro must be depreciating.

Exchange rate changes have their own terminology. **Depreciation** of a currency occurs when one currency becomes cheaper in terms of another currency. In our earlier discussion of exchange rates, for example, we assumed that the exchange rate between euros and dollars changed from 2 euros = $1 to 1 euro = $1, making the euro price of a dollar cheaper. In this case, the dollar *depreciated* with respect to the euro.

The other side of depreciation is **appreciation,** an increase in value of one currency as expressed in another country's currency. ***Whenever one currency depreciates, another currency must appreciate.*** When the exchange rate changed from 2 euros = $1 to 1 euro = $1, not only did the euro price of a dollar fall, but also the dollar price of a euro rose. Hence, the euro appreciated as the dollar depreciated. It's like a seesaw relationship (see the figure).

Figure 22.3 illustrates actual changes in the exchange rate of the U.S. dollar since 1980. The trade-adjusted value of the U.S. dollar is the (weighted) average of all exchange rates for the dollar. Between 1980 and 1985, the U.S. dollar appreciated more than 80 percent. This appreciation greatly reduced the price of imports and thus increased their quantity. At the same time, the dollar appreciation raised the foreign price of U.S. exports and so reduced their volume. U.S. farmers, aircraft manufacturers, and tourist services suffered huge sales losses. The trade deficit ballooned.

The value of the dollar briefly reversed course after 1985 but started appreciating again, slowing export growth and increasing imports throughout the 1990s. After a long steep appreciation, the dollar started losing value in 2003. Between 2003 and 2011, the U.S. dollar depreciated by 25 percent. This was good for U.S. exporters but bad for U.S. tourists and foreign producers.

The value of the U.S. dollar reversed course again in 2014. From 2014 to 2020 the dollar appreciated by 25 percent. This put a lot of pressure on U.S. companies that competed with imported products. It also made winter vacations in Florida more expensive for Canadians. But Walmart loved the stronger dollar, as it made the price of the imported goods that it sells much less expensive (see World View "Who Gains, Who Loses from Strong Dollar").

WORLD VIEW

WHO GAINS, WHO LOSES FROM STRONG DOLLAR

Between 2014 and 2020, the international value of the U.S. dollar increased by 25 percent. Was that dollar appreciation a good thing? It depends where you were positioned in global markets. Here is a sampling of winners and losers in the United States:

The winners:
Consumers of imported goods
Producers like Apple that use imported parts and equipment
Retailers like Walmart that sell imported goods
Investors in foreign stocks and production facilities
American tourists

The losers:
U.S. exporters like Boeing, Caterpillar, farmers
Import-competing industries like steel, autos, solar panels
Companies like Disney that attract foreign visitors
Companies with overseas factories and outlets

CRITICAL ANALYSIS: Depreciation of a nation's currency is good for that nation's exporters but bad for that nation's importers (including its tourists).

Market Forces

Exchange rates change for the same reasons that any market price changes: The underlying supply or demand (or both) has shifted. Among the more important sources of such shifts are

- *Relative income changes.* If incomes are increasing faster in country A than in country B, consumers in A will tend to spend more, thus increasing the demand for B's exports and currency. B's currency will appreciate (and A's will depreciate).
- *Relative price changes.* If domestic prices are rising rapidly in country A, consumers will seek out lower-priced imports. The demand for B's exports and currency will increase. B's currency will appreciate (and A's will depreciate).
- *Changes in product availability.* If country A experiences a disastrous wheat crop failure, it will have to increase its food imports. B's currency will appreciate.
- *Relative interest rate changes.* If interest rates rise in country A, people in country B will want to move their deposits to A. Demand for A's currency will rise and it will appreciate.
- *Speculation.* If speculators anticipate an increase in the price of A's currency, for the preceding reasons or any other, they'll begin buying it, thus pushing its price up. A's currency will appreciate.

All these various changes are taking place every minute of every day, thus keeping **foreign exchange markets** active. On an average day, more than *$5 trillion* of foreign exchange is bought and sold in the market. Significant changes occur in currency values, however, only when several of these forces move in the same direction at the same time.

foreign exchange markets: Places where foreign currencies are bought and sold.

Ukraine Crisis of 2014

Exchange values are also subject to abrupt changes when an unexpected political or natural upheaval occurs. The Russian invasion of Ukraine in early 2014 was a classic case of an external shock. Foreign exchange markets reacted quickly, sending the value of the hryvnia (Ukraine's currency) into a prolonged depreciation. The dollar value of the hryvnia plunged from 12.3 cents to 7.6 cents in a couple of months. That 40 percent depreciation in the value of the hryvnia substantially increased the cost of badly needed food, oil, and weapons imports.

Venezuelan Currency Collapse, 2016–2018

The collapse of the Venezuelan bolivar was a bit less abrupt, but no less dramatic. Hyperinflation in 2016 eroded the value of the bolivar. People needed wads of bolivars just to buy everyday staples like bread. Worse yet, few goods were available to buy as the economy contracted. People needed U.S. dollars to buy goods from other countries or in the black markets. Venezuelans were desperate to buy U.S. dollars at any price. In 2016 Venezuelans could buy one U.S. dollar for 10 bolivars. By mid-2018 a single dollar cost a staggering 248,210 bolivars! The bolivar was all but worthless. The Venezuelan government then created a new currency, the bolivar soberano, that was worth 100,000 of the old currency (bolivar fuerte).

RESISTANCE TO EXCHANGE RATE CHANGES

Given the scope and depth of currency crises, it's easy to understand why people crave *stable* exchange rates. The resistance to exchange rate fluctuations originates in various micro- and macroeconomic interests.

Micro Interests

The microeconomic resistance to changes in the value of the dollar arises from two concerns. First, people who trade or invest in world markets want a solid basis for forecasting future costs, prices, and profits. Forecasts are always uncertain, but they're even less dependable when the value of money is subject to change. An American firm that invests $2 million in a ski factory in Sweden expects not only to make a profit on the production there but also to return that profit to the United States. If the Swedish krona depreciates sharply in the interim, however, the profits amassed in Sweden may dwindle to a mere trickle, or even a loss, when the kronor are exchanged back into dollars. Imagine how devastated foreign investors in Venezuela were when the bolivar collapsed: They saw not only their profits but their investments evaporate. General Motors recorded a loss of $720 million on its Venezuelan factory due to the abrupt depreciation of the bolivar.

The World View "Weakest Currencies of 2019" illustrates how much some other currencies depreciated in 2019. The new Venezuelan currency essentially became worthless in that year. But a lot of other nations experienced substantial weakness in their currencies, making exports cheaper but needed imports more expensive. For international investors and travelers, these kinds of currency fluctuations are an unwanted headache.

WORLD VIEW

WEAKEST CURRENCIES OF 2019

The U.S. dollar continued its upward move in 2019, gaining strength against most other currencies. But the global 2 percent appreciation of the dollar disguised dramatic changes in the exchange rates for specific countries. These are some of the biggest depreciations of 2019:

Venezuela	Argentina	Haiti	Pakistan	Sweden	South Korea
bolivar	peso	gourde	rupee	krona	won
−97.7%	−31.9%	−19.0%	−10.4%	−7.9%	−6.6%

Source: Forex market, January–September 2019.

CRITICAL ANALYSIS: The global value of a currency changes with shifts of demand and supply. The appreciation of the U.S. dollar is reflected in the **depreciation** of other currencies.

Even when the direction of an exchange rate move is certain, those who stand to lose from the change are prone to resist. *A change in the price of a country's money automatically alters the price of all its exports and imports.* When the Russian ruble and Japanese yen depreciated in 2015–2016, for example, the dollar price of Russian and Japanese steel declined as well. This prompted U.S. steelmakers to accuse Russia and Japan of "dumping" steel. Steel companies and unions appealed to Washington to protect their sales and jobs.

Even in the country whose currency becomes cheaper, there will be opposition to exchange rate movements. When the U.S. dollar appreciates, Americans buy more foreign products. This increased U.S. demand for imports may drive up prices in other countries. In addition, foreign firms may take advantage of the reduced American competition by raising their prices. In either case, some inflation will result. The consumer's insistence that the government "do something" about rising prices may turn into a political force for "correcting" foreign exchange rates.

Macro Interests

Any microeconomic problem that becomes widespread enough can turn into a macroeconomic problem. The huge U.S. trade deficits of the 1980s effectively exported jobs to foreign nations. Although the U.S. economy expanded rapidly in 1983–1985, the unemployment rate stayed high, partly because American consumers were spending more of their income on imports.

This is the kind of scenario that prompted President Trump to castigate "currency manipulators" like China. In his view, the strong dollar of 2014–2017 was in part due to other nations keeping their currencies artificially low. Those low values encouraged American consumers to buy more imports and American businesses to build more factories abroad. He vowed "to bring jobs back to America" by imposing tariffs (Chapter 21) that would offset the cheap price of foreign currencies.

The U.S. trade deficits are typically offset by capital account surpluses. Foreign investors participate in the U.S. economic expansion by buying land, plants, and equipment and by lending money in U.S. financial markets. These capital inflows complicate monetary policy, however, and increase U.S. foreign debt and interest costs.

U.S. a Net Debtor

The inflow of foreign investment also raised anxieties about "selling off" America. When Japanese and other foreign investors increased their purchases of farmland, factories, and real estate (e.g., Rockefeller Center), many Americans worried that foreign investors were taking control of the U.S. economy.

Fueling these fears was the dramatic change in America's international financial position. From 1914 to 1984, the United States had been a net creditor in the world economy. We owned more assets abroad than foreign investors owned in the United States. Our financial position changed in 1985. Continuing trade deficits and offsetting capital inflows transformed the United States into a net debtor in that year. Since then foreigners have owned more U.S. assets than Americans own of foreign assets.

America's debtor status can complicate domestic policy. A sudden flight from U.S. assets could severely weaken the dollar and disrupt the domestic economy. To prevent that from occurring, policymakers must consider the impact of their decisions on foreign investors. This may necessitate difficult policy choices.

There's a silver lining to this cloud, however. The inflow of foreign investment is a reflection of confidence in the U.S. economy. Foreign investors want to share in our growth and profitability. In the process, their investments (like BMW's auto plant) expand America's production possibilities and stimulate still more economic growth.

Foreign investors actually assume substantial risk when they invest in the United States. If the dollar falls, the foreign value of *their* U.S. investments will decline. Hence, foreigners who've already invested in the United States have no incentive to start a flight from the dollar. On the contrary, a strong dollar protects the value of their U.S. holdings.

EXCHANGE RATE INTERVENTION

Given the potential opposition to exchange rate movements, governments often feel compelled to intervene in foreign exchange markets. The intervention is usually intended to achieve greater exchange rate stability. But such stability may itself give rise to undesirable micro- and macroeconomic effects.

Fixed Exchange Rates

One way to eliminate fluctuations in exchange rates is to fix a currency's value. The easiest way to do this is for each country to define the worth of its currency in terms of some common standard. Under a **gold standard**, each country declares that its currency is worth so much gold. In so doing, it implicitly defines the worth of its currency in terms of all other currencies that also have a fixed gold value. In 1944 the major trading nations met at Bretton Woods, New Hampshire, and agreed that each currency was worth so much gold. The value of the U.S. dollar was defined as being equal to 0.0294 ounce of gold, while the British pound was defined as being worth 0.0823 ounce of gold. Thus, the exchange rate between British pounds and U.S. dollars was effectively fixed at $1 = 0.357 pound, or 1 pound = $2.80 (or $2.80/0.0823 = $1/0.0294).

Balance-of-Payments Problems. It's one thing to proclaim the worth of a country's currency; it's quite another to *maintain* the fixed rate of exchange. As we've observed, foreign exchange rates are subject to continual and often unpredictable changes in supply and demand. Hence, two countries that seek to stabilize their exchange rate at some fixed value will have to somehow neutralize such foreign exchange market pressures.

Suppose the exchange rate officially established by the United States and Great Britain is equal to e_1, as illustrated in Figure 22.4. As is apparent, that particular exchange rate is consistent with the then-prevailing demand and supply conditions in the foreign exchange market (as indicated by curves D_1 and S_1).

Now suppose that Americans suddenly acquire a greater taste for British cars and start spending more income on Jaguars, Bentleys, and Mini Coopers. This increased desire for British goods will *shift* the demand for British currency from D_1 to D_2 in Figure 22.4. Were exchange rates allowed to respond to market influences, the dollar price of a British pound would rise, in this case to the rate e_2. But we've assumed that government intervention has *fixed* the exchange rate at e_1. Unfortunately, at e_1, American consumers want to buy more pounds (q_D) than the British are willing to supply (q_S). The difference between the quantity demanded and the quantity supplied in the market at the rate e_1 represents a **market shortage** of British pounds.

gold standard: An agreement by countries to fix the price of their currencies in terms of gold; a mechanism for fixing exchange rates.

market shortage: The amount by which the quantity demanded exceeds the quantity supplied at a given price; excess demand.

FIGURE 22.4

Fixed Rates and Market Imbalance

If exchange rates are fixed, they can't adjust to changes in market supply and demand. Suppose the exchange rate is initially fixed at e_1. When the demand for British pounds increases (shifts to the right), an excess demand for pounds emerges. More pounds are demanded (q_D) at the rate e_1 than are supplied (q_S). This causes a balance-of-payments deficit for the United States.

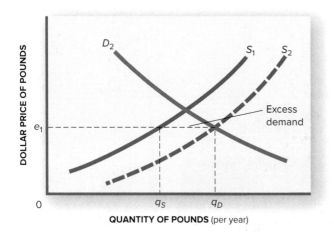

FIGURE 22.5

The Impact of Monetary Intervention

If the U.S. Treasury holds reserves of British pounds, it can use them to buy U.S. dollars in foreign exchange markets. As it does so, the supply of pounds will shift to the right, to S_2, thereby maintaining the desired exchange rate, e_1. The Bank of England could bring about the same result by offering to buy U.S. dollars with pounds (i.e., *supplying* pounds).

The excess demand for pounds implies a **balance-of-payments deficit** for the United States: More dollars are flowing out of the country than into it. The same disequilibrium represents a **balance-of-payments surplus** for Britain because its outward flow of pounds is less than its incoming flow.

Basically, there are only two solutions to balance-of-payments problems brought about by the attempt to fix exchange rates:

- Allow exchange rates to rise to e_2 (Figure 22.4), thereby eliminating the excess demand for pounds.
- Alter market supply or demand so they intersect at the fixed rate e_1.

Because fixed exchange rates were the initial objective of this intervention, only the second alternative is of immediate interest.

The Need for Reserves. One way to alter market conditions would be for someone simply to supply British pounds to American consumers. The U.S. Treasury could have accumulated a reserve of foreign currency in earlier periods. By selling some of those **foreign exchange reserves** now, the Treasury would be *supplying* British pounds, helping to offset excess demand. The rightward shift of the pound supply curve in Figure 22.5 illustrates the sale of accumulated British pounds—and related purchase of U.S. dollars—by the U.S. Treasury.

Although foreign exchange reserves can be used to fix exchange rates, such reserves may not be adequate. Indeed, Figure 22.6 should be testimony enough to the fact that today's deficit isn't always offset by tomorrow's surplus. A principal reason that fixed exchange rates didn't live up to their expectations is that the United States had balance-of-payments deficits for 22 consecutive years. This long-term deficit overwhelmed the government's stock of foreign exchange reserves.

The Role of Gold. Gold reserves are a potential substitute for foreign exchange reserves. As long as each country's money has a value defined in terms of gold, we can use gold to buy British pounds, thereby restocking our foreign exchange reserves. Or we can simply use the gold to purchase U.S. dollars in foreign exchange markets. In either case, the exchange value of the dollar will tend to rise. However, we must have **gold reserves** available for this purpose. Unfortunately, the continuing U.S. balance-of-payments deficits recorded in Figure 22.6 exceeded even the hoards of gold buried under Fort Knox. As a consequence, our gold reserves lost their credibility as a guarantor of fixed exchange rates. When it appeared that foreigners would demand more gold than the U.S. government possessed, President Nixon simply ended the link between the U.S. dollar and gold. As of August 15, 1971, the U.S. dollar had no guaranteed value.

balance-of-payments deficit: An excess demand for foreign currency at current exchange rates.

balance-of-payments surplus: An excess demand for domestic currency at current exchange rates.

foreign exchange reserves: Holdings of foreign currencies by official government agencies, usually the central bank or treasury.

gold reserves: Stocks of gold held by a government to purchase foreign exchange.

FIGURE 22.6

The U.S. Balance of Payments, 1950–1973

The United States had a balance-of-payments deficit for 22 consecutive years. During this period, the foreign exchange reserves of the U.S. Treasury were sharply reduced. Fixed exchange rates were maintained by the willingness of foreign countries to accumulate large reserves of U.S. dollars. However, neither the Treasury's reserves nor the willingness of foreigners to accumulate dollars was unlimited. In 1973 fixed exchange rates were abandoned.

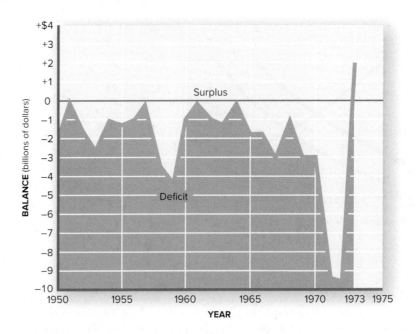

Domestic Adjustments. Government can also use fiscal, monetary, and trade policies to achieve a desired exchange rate. With respect to trade policy, *trade protection can be used to prop up fixed exchange rates.* We could eliminate the excess demand for pounds (Figure 22.4), for example, by imposing quotas and tariffs on British goods. Such trade restrictions would reduce British imports to the United States and thus the demand for British pounds. In August 1971 President Nixon imposed an emergency 10 percent surcharge on all imported goods to help reduce the payments deficit that fixed exchange rates had spawned. Such restrictions on international trade, however, violate the principle of comparative advantage and thus reduce total world output. Trade protection also invites retaliatory trade restrictions.

Fiscal policy is another way out of the imbalance. An increase in U.S. income tax rates will reduce disposable income and have a negative effect on the demand for all goods, including imports. A reduction in government spending will have similar effects. In general, *deflationary (or restrictive) policies help correct a balance-of-payments deficit by lowering domestic incomes and thus the demand for imports.*

Monetary policies in a deficit country could follow the same restrictive course. A reduction in the money supply raises interest rates. The balance of payments will benefit in two ways. The resultant slowdown in spending will reduce import demand. In addition, higher interest rates may induce international investors to move more of their funds into the deficit country. Such moves will provide immediate relief to the payments imbalance.[1] Russia tried this strategy in 1998, tripling key interest rates (to as much as 150 percent). But even that wasn't enough to restore confidence in the ruble, which kept depreciating. Within three months of the monetary policy tightening, the ruble lost half its value.

A surplus country could help solve the balance-of-payments problem. By pursuing expansionary—even inflationary—fiscal and monetary policies, a surplus country could stimulate the demand for imports. Moreover, any inflation at home will reduce the competitiveness of exports, thereby helping to restrain the inflow of foreign demand. Taken together, such efforts would help reverse an international payments imbalance.

---

[1]Before 1930, not only were foreign exchange rates fixed, but domestic monetary supplies were tied to gold stocks as well. Countries experiencing a balance-of-payments deficit were thus forced to contract their money supply, and countries experiencing a payments surplus were forced to expand their money supply by a set amount. Monetary authorities were powerless to control domestic money supplies except by erecting barriers to trade. The system was abandoned when the world economy collapsed into the Great Depression.

Even under the best of circumstances, domestic economic adjustments entail significant costs. In effect, ***domestic adjustments to payments imbalances require a deficit country to forsake full employment and a surplus country to forsake price stability.*** China has had to grapple with these domestic consequences of fixing the value of its currency. The artificially low value of the yuan promoted Chinese exports and accelerated China's GDP growth. But it also created serious macro problems. To keep the value of the yuan low, the Chinese had to keep buying dollars. By 2020 China had more than $3 trillion of foreign currency reserves. It paid for those dollars with yuan, adding to China's money supply. All that money stoked inflation in China. Ultimately, the Chinese government had to adopt restrictive monetary and fiscal policies to keep inflation in check. The Chinese government also had to be willing to keep accumulating U.S. dollars and other currencies.

As we noted earlier, President Trump pursued another approach to correct market imbalances. He blamed the huge trade deficit with China on the intentional manipulation of the value of the yuan by the Chinese government. He called China the "grand champion of currency manipulation" for its alleged role in keeping the value of the yuan low. To offset that "unfair" exchange rate, Trump imposed tariffs on all Chinese imports. He was hoping that the resulting economic pain would force China to appreciate its currency. But China retaliated with tariffs on U.S. exports, and a trade war ensued (Chapter 21). China maintained that it was not manipulating its currency; the cheap yuan was a product of market forces.

There's no easy way out of this impasse. Market imbalances caused by fixed exchange rates can be corrected only with abundant supplies of foreign exchange reserves or deliberate changes in fiscal, monetary, or trade policies. At some point, it may become easier to let a currency adjust to market equilibrium.

The Euro Fix. The original 12 nations of the European Monetary Union (EMU) fixed their exchange rates in 1999. They went far beyond the kind of exchange rate fix we're discussing here. Members of the EMU *eliminated* their national currencies, making the euro the common currency of Euroland. They don't have to worry about reserve balances or domestic adjustments. However, they do have to reconcile their varied national interests to a single monetary authority, which has proven to be difficult politically in times of economic stress.

Flexible Exchange Rates

Balance-of-payments problems wouldn't arise in the first place if exchange rates were allowed to respond to market forces. Under a system of **flexible exchange rates** (often called floating exchange rates), the exchange rate moves up or down to choke off any excess supply of or demand for foreign exchange. Notice again in Figure 22.4 that the exchange rate move from e_1 to e_2 prevents any excess demand from emerging. ***With flexible exchange rates, the quantity of foreign exchange demanded always equals the quantity supplied,*** and there's no imbalance. For the same reason, there's no need for foreign exchange reserves.

Although flexible exchange rates eliminate balance-of-payments and foreign exchange reserves problems, they don't solve all of a country's international trade problems. ***Exchange rate movements associated with flexible rates alter relative prices and may disrupt import and export flows.*** As noted before, depreciation of the dollar raises the price of all imported goods, contributing to domestic cost-push inflation. Also, domestic businesses that sell imported goods or use them as production inputs may suffer sales losses. On the other hand, appreciation of the dollar raises the foreign price of U.S. goods and reduces the sales of American exporters. Hence, ***someone is always hurt, and others are helped, by exchange rate movements.*** The resistance to flexible exchange rates originates in these potential losses. Such resistance creates pressure for official intervention in foreign exchange markets or increased trade barriers.

The United States and its major trading partners abandoned fixed exchange rates in 1973. Although exchange rates are now able to fluctuate freely, it shouldn't be assumed that they necessarily undergo wild gyrations. On the contrary, experience with flexible rates since 1973 suggests that some semblance of stability is possible even when exchange rates are free to change in response to market forces.

flexible exchange rates: A system in which exchange rates are permitted to vary with market supply-and-demand conditions; floating exchange rates.

Speculation. One force that often helps maintain stability in a flexible exchange rate system is—surprisingly—speculation. Speculators often counteract short-term changes in foreign exchange supply and demand. If a currency temporarily rises above its long-term equilibrium, speculators will move in to sell it. By selling at high prices and later buying at lower prices, speculators hope to make a profit. In the process, they also help stabilize foreign exchange rates.

Speculation isn't always stabilizing, however. Speculators may not correctly gauge the long-term equilibrium. Instead they may move "with the market" and help push exchange rates far out of kilter. This kind of destabilizing speculation sharply lowered the international value of the U.S. dollar in 1987, forcing the Reagan administration to intervene in foreign exchange markets, borrowing foreign currencies to buy U.S. dollars. In 1997 the Clinton administration intervened for the opposite purpose: stemming the rise in the U.S. dollar. The Bush administration was more willing to stay on the sidelines, letting global markets set the exchange rates for the U.S. dollar.

These kinds of interventions are intended to *narrow* rather than *eliminate* exchange rate movements. Such limited intervention in foreign exchange markets is often referred to as **managed exchange rates,** or, popularly, "dirty floats."

Although managed exchange rates would seem to be an ideal compromise between fixed rates and flexible rates, they can work only when some acceptable "rules of the game" and mutual trust have been established. As Sherman Maisel, a former governor of the Federal Reserve Board, put it, "Monetary systems are based on credit and faith: If these are lacking, a . . . crisis occurs."[2]

managed exchange rates: A system in which governments intervene in foreign exchange markets to limit but not eliminate exchange rate fluctuations; "dirty floats."

DECISIONS FOR TOMORROW

Are Currency Bailouts a Good Thing?

The world has witnessed a string of currency crises, including the one in Asia during 1997–1998, the Brazilian crisis of 1999, the Argentine crisis of 2001–2002, the Greek and Portuguese crises of 2010–2012, Venezuela in 2016–2018, and recurrent ruble crises in Russia. In every instance, the country in trouble pleads for external help. In most cases, a currency "bailout" is arranged, whereby global monetary authorities lend the troubled nation enough reserves (such as U.S. dollars) to defend its currency. Typically the International Monetary Fund (IMF) heads the rescue party, joined by the central banks of the strongest economies.

The Case for Bailouts. The argument for currency bailouts typically rests on the domino theory. Weakness in one currency can undermine another. This seemed to be the case during the 1997–1998 Asian crisis. After the **devaluation** of the Thai baht, global investors began worrying about currency values in other Asian nations. Choosing to be safe rather than sorry, they moved funds out of Korea, Malaysia, and the Philippines and invested in U.S. and European markets (notice in Figure 22.3 the 1997–1998 appreciation of the U.S. dollar).

The initial baht devaluation also weakened the competitive trade position of these same economies. Thai exports became cheaper, diverting export demand from other Asian nations. To prevent loss of export markets, Thailand's neighbors felt they had to devalue as well. Speculators who foresaw these effects accelerated the domino effect by selling the region's currencies.

When Brazil devalued its currency (the *real*) in January 1999, global investors worried that a "samba effect" might sweep across Latin America. The domino effect could reach

devaluation: An abrupt depreciation of a currency whose value was fixed or managed by the government.

[2]Sherman Maisel, *Managing the Dollar* (New York: W. W. Norton, 1973), p. 196.

across the ocean and damage U.S. and European exports as well. The Greek crisis of 2010 threatened the common currency (euro) of 28 nations. Hence, richer, more stable countries often offer a currency bailout as a form of self-defense.

The Case against Bailouts. Critics of bailouts argue that such interventions are ultimately self-defeating. They say that once a country knows for sure that currency bailouts are in the wings, it doesn't have to pursue the domestic policy adjustments that might stabilize its currency. A nation can avoid politically unpopular options such as high interest rates, tax hikes, or cutbacks in government spending. It can also turn a blind eye to trade barriers, monopoly power, lax lending policies, and other constraints on productive growth. Hence, the expectation of readily available bailouts may foster the very conditions that cause currency crises.

Future Bailouts? The decision to bail out a depreciating currency isn't as simple as it appears. To minimize the ill effects of bailouts, the IMF and other institutions typically require the nation in crisis to pledge more prudent monetary, fiscal, and trade policies. Usually there's a lot of debate about what kinds of adjustments will be made—and how soon. As long as the nation in crisis is confident of an eventual bailout, however, it has a lot of bargaining power to resist policy changes. Only after the IMF finally said no to further bailouts in Greece did the Greek parliament pass austerity measures that reduced its fiscal imbalances.

SUMMARY

- Money serves the same purposes in international trade as it does in the domestic economy—namely, to facilitate specialization and market exchanges. The basic challenge of international finance is to create acceptable standards of value from the various currencies maintained by separate countries.   **LO22-1**

- Exchange rates are the mechanism for translating the value of one national currency into the equivalent value of another. An exchange rate of $1 = 2$ euros means that one dollar is worth two euros in foreign exchange markets.   **LO22-1**

- Foreign currencies have value because they can be used to acquire goods and resources from other countries. Accordingly, the supply of and demand for foreign currency reflect the demands for imports and exports, for international investment, and for overseas activities of governments.   **LO22-2**

- The balance of payments summarizes a country's international transactions. Its components are the trade balance, the current account balance, and the capital account balance. The current and capital accounts must offset each other.   **LO22-2**

- The equilibrium exchange rate is subject to any and all shifts of supply and demand for foreign exchange. If relative incomes, prices, or interest rates change, the demand for foreign exchange will be affected. A depreciation is a change in market exchange rates that makes one country's currency cheaper in terms of another currency. An appreciation is the opposite kind of change.   **LO22-3**

- Changes in exchange rates are often resisted. Producers of export goods don't want their currencies to rise in value (appreciate); importers and tourists dislike it when their currencies fall in value (depreciate).   **LO22-4**

- Under a system of fixed exchange rates, changes in the supply and demand for a specific currency can't be expressed in exchange rate movements. Instead, such shifts will be reflected in excess demand for or supply of that currency. Such market imbalances are referred to as balance-of-payments deficits or surpluses.   **LO22-3**

- To maintain fixed exchange rates, monetary authorities must enter the market to buy and sell foreign exchange. To do so, deficit countries must have foreign exchange reserves. In the absence of sufficient reserves, a country can maintain fixed exchange rates only if it's willing to alter basic fiscal, monetary, or trade policies.   **LO22-4**

- Flexible exchange rates eliminate balance-of-payments problems and the crises that accompany them. But complete flexibility can lead to disruptive changes. To avoid this contingency, many countries prefer to adopt managed exchange rates—that is, rates determined by the market but subject to government intervention.   **LO22-4**

Key Terms

exchange rate	foreign exchange markets	gold reserves
equilibrium price	gold standard	flexible exchange rates
balance of payments	market shortage	managed exchange rates
trade deficit	balance-of-payments deficit	devaluation
depreciation (currency)	balance-of-payments surplus	
appreciation	foreign exchange reserves	

Questions for Discussion

1. Why would a rise in the value of the dollar prompt U.S. manufacturers to build production plants in Mexico? **LO22-4**

2. How do changes in the value of the U.S. dollar affect foreign enrollments at U.S. colleges? **LO22-4**

3. How would rapid inflation in Canada affect U.S. tourism travel to Canada? Does it make any difference whether the exchange rate between Canadian and U.S. dollars is fixed or flexible? **LO22-3**

4. Under what conditions would a country welcome a balance-of-payments deficit? When would it *not* want a deficit? **LO22-4**

5. In what sense do fixed exchange rates permit a country to "export its inflation"? **LO22-4**

6. Why did the value of the Ukrainian hryvnia depreciate so much when Russia invaded (see section Ukraine Crisis of 2014)? **LO22-3**

7. If a nation's currency depreciates, are the reduced export prices that result "unfair"? **LO22-4**

8. How would each of these events affect the supply or demand for Japanese yen? **LO22-3**
   (*a*) Stronger U.S. economic growth.
   (*b*) A decline in Japanese interest rates.
   (*c*) Higher inflation in the United States.
   (*d*) A Japanese tsunami.

9. According to the World View "Weakest Currencies of 2019," which nation got the cheapest for American tourists in 2019? Why did it get so cheap? **LO22-4**

10. How could Venezuela have slowed the depreciation of the bolivar? Would an international bailout have solved the problem? **LO22-3**

L022-1 1. According to World View "Foreign Exchange Rates," which nation had
(*a*) The cheapest currency?
(*b*) The most expensive currency?

L022-1 2. If a euro is worth $1.20, what is the euro price of a dollar?

L022-3 3. How many Ukrainian hryvnia (see section Ukraine Crisis of 2014) could you buy with one U.S. dollar
(*a*) Before the Russian invasion?
(*b*) After the Russian invasion?

L022-1 4. If a McDonald's Big Mac meal sold for $5.00 in March 2020, how much would it cost in the currencies of
(*a*) Brazil?
(*b*) Japan?
(*c*) Indonesia?
(See World View "Foreign Exchange Rates.")

L022-3 5. By what percent did the cost of visiting Argentina decline in 2019 for American tourists? (See World View "Weakest Currencies of 2019.")

L022-4 6. If an admission ticket to Disney World in Florida costs $120, how much more expensive was the ticket to a person from Sweden after the 2019 currency depreciation (see World View "Weakest Currencies of 2019")?

L022-1 7. Between 2014 and 2017, did the U.S. dollar appreciate or depreciate (see Figure 22.3)?

L022-1 8. If a PlayStation 5 costs 40,000 yen in Japan, how much will it cost in U.S. dollars if the exchange rate is
(*a*) 110 yen = $1?
(*b*) 1 yen = $0.009?
(*c*) 100 yen = $1?

L022-1 9. Between 1990 and 2000, by how much did the dollar appreciate (Figure 22.3)?

L022-1 10. If inflation raises U.S. prices by 2 percent and the U.S. dollar appreciates by 3 percent, by how much does the foreign price of U.S. exports change?

L022-1 11. According to World View "Foreign Exchange Rates," what was the peso price of a euro in March 2020?

L022-2 12. For each of the following possible events, indicate whether the global value of the U.S. dollar will rise or fall.
(*a*) American cars become suddenly more popular abroad.
(*b*) Inflation in the United States accelerates.
(*c*) The United States falls into a recession.
(*d*) Interest rates in the United States drop.
(*e*) The United States experiences rapid increases in productivity.

L022-3 13. The following schedules summarize the supply and demand for trifflings, the national currency of Tricoli:

Triffling price (U.S. dollars per triffling)	0	$4	$8	$12	$16	$20	$24
Quantity demanded (per year)	40	38	36	34	32	30	28
Quantity supplied (per year)	1	11	21	31	41	51	61

Use these schedules for the following:
(*a*) Graph the supply and demand curves.
(*b*) Determine the equilibrium exchange rate.

(*c*) Determine the size of the excess supply or excess demand that would exist if the Tricolian government fixed the exchange rate at $20 = 1 triffling.

(*d*) Which of the following events would help reduce the payments imbalance? Which would not?

(*i*) Domestic inflation.

(*ii*) Foreign inflation.

(*iii*) Slower domestic growth.

(*iv*) Faster domestic growth.

LO22-3 14. *Decisions for Tomorrow:* Show graphically the impact on the South Korean currency (won) when the Thai baht was devalued.

AFP/Getty Images

CHAPTER 23

Global Poverty

B ono, the lead singer for the rock group U2, has performed concerts around the world to raise awareness of global poverty. He doesn't have a specific agenda for eradicating poverty. He does believe, though, that greater awareness of global poverty will raise assistance levels and spawn more ideas for combating global hunger, disease, and isolation.

The dimensions of global poverty are staggering. According to the World Bank, more than a third of the world's population lacks even the barest of life's necessities. *Billions* of people are persistently malnourished, poorly sheltered, minimally clothed, and at constant risk of debilitating diseases. Life expectancies among the globally poor population still hover in the range of 40–50 years, far below the norm (70–80 years) of the rich, developed nations.

In this chapter we follow Bono's suggestion and take a closer look at global poverty. We address the following issues:

- **What income thresholds define "poverty"?**
- **How many people are poor?**
- **What actions can be taken to reduce global poverty?**

In the process of answering these questions, we get another opportunity to examine what makes economies "tick"—particularly what forces foster faster economic growth for some nations and slower economic growth for others.

AMERICAN POVERTY

Poverty, like beauty, is often in the eye of the beholder. Many Americans feel "poor" if they can't buy a new car, live in a fancy home, or take an exotic vacation. Indeed, the average American asserts that a family needs at least $58,000 a year "just to get by." With that much income, however, few people would go hungry or be forced to live in the streets.

Official Poverty Thresholds

To develop a more objective standard of poverty, the U.S. government assessed how much money a U.S. family needs to purchase a "minimally adequate" diet. Back in 1963 it concluded that $1,000 per year was needed for that purpose alone. Then it asked how much income was needed to purchase other basic necessities like housing, clothes, transportation, and so on. It figured all those *non*food necessities would cost twice as much as the food staples. So it concluded that a budget of $3,000 per year would fund a "minimally adequate" living standard for a U.S. family of four. That standard became the official **U.S. poverty threshold** in 1963.

Inflation Adjustments. Since 1963, prices have risen every year. As a result, the price of the poverty "basket" has risen as well. In 2020, it cost roughly $26,000 to purchase those same basic necessities for a family of four that cost only $3,000 in 1963.

Twenty-six thousand dollars might sound like a lot of money, especially if you're not paying your own rent or feeding a family. If you break the budget down, however, it doesn't look so generous. Only a third of the budget goes for food. And that portion has to feed four people. So the official U.S. poverty standard provides less than $6 per day for an individual's food. That just about covers a single Big Mac combo at McDonald's. There's no money in the poverty budget for dining out. And the implied rent money is only $850 a month (for the whole family). So the official U.S. poverty standard isn't that generous—certainly not by *American* standards (where the *average* family has an income of nearly $85,000 per year and eats outside their $250,000 home three times a week).

U.S. Poverty Count

poverty rate: Percentage of the population counted as poor.

The Census Bureau counted more than 34 million Americans as "poor" in 2019 according to the official U.S. thresholds (as adjusted for family size). This was one out of nine U.S. households, for a **poverty rate** of roughly 11 percent. According to the Census Bureau, the official U.S. poverty rate has been in a narrow range of 11–15 percent for the last 40 years.

How Poor Is U.S. "Poor"?

Many observers criticize these official U.S. poverty statistics. On the one hand, liberals assert that the official poverty thresholds are ridiculously low. They also contend that the number of households in "near poverty" (incomes of $26,000–$34,000 for a family of four) is too high and too often ignored. Conservatives respond that the official poverty count is overstated—that there are far fewer poor people in America than the Census Bureau claims.

in-kind transfers: Direct transfers of goods and services rather than cash, such as food stamps, Medicaid benefits, and housing subsidies.

In-Kind Income. A major flaw in the official tally is that the government counts only *cash* income in defining poverty. Since the 1960s, however, the United States has developed an extensive system of **in-kind transfers** that augment cash incomes. Food stamps, for example, can be used just as easily as cash to purchase groceries. Medicaid and Medicare pay doctor and hospital bills, reducing the need for cash income. Government rent subsidies and public housing allow poor families to have more housing than their cash incomes would permit. These in-kind transfers allow "poor" families to enjoy a higher living standard than their cash incomes imply. Adding those transfers to cash incomes would bring the U.S. poverty count down into the 8–10 percent range.

Material Possessions. Even those families who remain "poor" after counting in-kind transfers aren't necessarily destitute. More than 40 percent of America's "poor" families own their homes, 70 percent own a car or truck, and 30 percent own at least *two* vehicles. Telephones, color TVs, dishwashers, clothes dryers, air conditioners, and microwave ovens are commonplace in America's poor households.

America's poor families themselves report few acute problems in everyday living. Fewer than 14 percent report missing a rent or mortgage payment, and fewer than 8 percent report a food deficiency. So American poverty isn't synonymous with homelessness, malnutrition, chronic illness, or even social isolation. These problems exist among America's poverty population, but they don't define American poverty.

GLOBAL POVERTY

Poverty in the rest of the world is much different from poverty in America. *American poverty is more about* relative *deprivation than* absolute *deprivation. In the rest of the world, poverty is all about* absolute *deprivation.*

Low Average Incomes

As a starting point for assessing global poverty, consider how *average* incomes in the rest of the world stack up against U.S. levels. By global standards, the United States is unquestionably a very rich nation. As we observed in Chapter 2 (see World View "GDP per Capita around the World"), U.S. GDP per capita is five times larger than the world average. More than three-fourths of the world's population lives in what the World Bank calls "low-income" or "lower-middle-income" nations. In those nations the *average* income is under $4,000 a year, less than *one-tenth* of America's per capita GDP. Average incomes are lower yet in Haiti, Nigeria, Ethiopia, and other desperately poor nations. By American standards, virtually all the people in these nations would be poor. By *their* standards, no American would be poor.

World Bank Poverty Thresholds

Because national poverty lines are so diverse and culture-bound, the World Bank decided to establish a uniform standard for assessing global poverty. And it set the bar amazingly low. In fact, the World Bank regularly uses two thresholds, namely $1.90 per day for **"extreme" poverty** and a higher $3.10 per day standard for less **"severe" poverty**.

The World Bank thresholds are incomprehensibly low by American standards. The $1.90 standard works out to $2,774 per year for a family of four—a mere tenth of America's poverty standard. Think about it. How much could you buy for $1.90 a day? A little rice, maybe, and perhaps some milk? Certainly not a Big Mac. Not even a grande coffee at Starbucks. And part of that $1.90 would have to go for rent. Clearly this isn't going to work. Raising the World Bank standard to $3.10 per day (severe poverty) doesn't reach a whole lot further.

The World Bank, of course, wasn't defining "poverty" in the context of American affluence. They were instead trying to define a rock-bottom threshold of absolute poverty—a threshold of physical deprivation that people everywhere would acknowledge as the barest "minimum"—a condition of "unacceptable deprivation."

Global Poverty Counts

On the basis of household surveys in more than 100 nations, *the World Bank classifies 700 million people as being in "extreme" poverty (<$1.90/day) and nearly 2 billion people as being in "severe" poverty (<$3.10/day).*

Figure 23.1 shows where concentrations of extreme poverty are the greatest. Concentrations of extreme poverty are alarmingly high in dozens of smaller, less developed nations like Mali, Haiti, and Zambia, where average incomes are also shockingly low. However, the greatest *number* of extremely poor people reside in the world's largest countries.

Table 23.1 reveals that the distribution of severe poverty (<$3.10/day) is similar. The incidence of this higher poverty threshold is, of course, much greater. Severe poverty afflicts more than 80 percent of the population in dozens of nations and even reaches more than 90 percent of the population in some (e.g., Burundi). By contrast, less than 15 percent of the U.S. population falls below the official *American* poverty threshold, and **virtually no American household has an income below the global poverty threshold.**

extreme poverty (world): World Bank income standard of less than $1.90 per day per person (inflation adjusted).

severe poverty (world): World Bank income standard of $3.10 per day per person (inflation adjusted).

Analysis: Global poverty is defined in terms of absolute deprivation.
Stockbyte/Getty Images

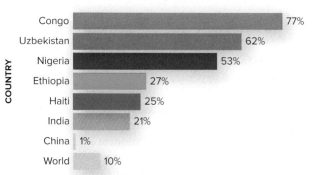

POPULATION IN EXTREME POVERTY (<$1.90/DAY)

FIGURE 23.1

Geography of Extreme Poverty

Over 700 million people around the world are in "extreme" poverty. In smaller, poor nations, deprivation is commonplace.

Source: The World Bank, *WDR2019 Data Set.*

TABLE 23.1

Population in Severe Poverty
(<$3.10/day)

A fourth of the world's
population has income of less
than $3.10 per person per day.
Such poverty is pervasive in
low-income nations.

Country	Living in Severe Poverty (Percent)
Congo	91%
Burundi	89
Uzbekistan	86
Sierra Leone	81
Nigeria	78
Ethiopia	62
India	60
Haiti	51
China	7
United States	1.5
World	25%

Source: The World Bank, *WDR2019 Data Set.*

The COVID-19 Surge

The coronavirus pandemic that swept across the globe in 2020 made an already desperate situation worse for the global poor. The United Nations estimated that the illnesses, deaths, and economic disruptions caused by COVID-19 pushed an additional 71 million people into extreme poverty in 2020. That was the first increase in global poverty since 1998. The pandemic also caused significant setbacks in education and health for the world's poor.

Social Indicators

The levels of poverty depicted in Figure 23.1 and Table 23.1 imply levels of physical and social deprivation few Americans can comprehend. Living on less than two or three dollars a day means always being hungry, malnourished, ill-clothed, dirty, and unhealthy. The problems associated with such deprivation begin even before birth. Pregnant women often fail to get enough nutrition or medical attention. In low-income countries, only a third of all births are attended by a skilled health practitioner. If something goes awry, both the mother and the baby are at fatal risk. Nearly all of the children in global poverty are in a state of chronic malnutrition. At least 1 out of 10 children in low-income nations will actually die before reaching age 5. In the poorest sectors of the population, infant and child mortality rates are often two to three times higher than that. Children often remain unimmunized to preventable diseases. And AIDS is rampant among both children and adults in the poorest nations. All of these factors contribute to a frighteningly short life expectancy—less than half that in the developed nations.

Fewer than one out of two children from extremely poor households is likely to stay in school past the eighth grade. Women and minority ethnic and religious groups are often wholly excluded from educational opportunities. As a consequence, great stocks of human capital remain undeveloped: In low-income nations, only one out of two women and only two out of three men are literate.

Persistent Poverty

Global poverty is not only more desperate than American poverty, but also more permanent. In India a rigid caste system still defines differential opportunities for millions of rich and poor villagers. Studies in Brazil, South Africa, Peru, and Ecuador document barriers that block access to health care, education, and jobs for children of poor families. Hence, inequalities in poor nations not only are more severe than in developed nations but also tend to be more permanent.

Economic stagnation also keeps a lid on upward mobility. President John F. Kennedy observed that "a rising tide lifts all boats," referring to the power of a growing economy to raise everyone's income. In a growing economy, one person's income *gain* is not another person's *loss*. By contrast, a stagnant economy intensifies class warfare, with everyone jealously protecting whatever gains they have made. The *haves* strive to keep the *have-nots* at bay. Unfortunately, this is the reality in many low-income nations. As we observed in Chapter 2 (Table 2.1), in some of the poorest nations in the world, output grows more slowly than the population, intensifying the competition for resources.

GOALS AND STRATEGIES

Global poverty is so extensive that no policy approach offers a quick solution. Even the World Bank doesn't see an end to global poverty. The United Nations set a much more modest goal back in 2000.

The UN Millennium Goals

The UN established a Millennium Poverty Goal of cutting the incidence of extreme global poverty in half by 2015 (from 30 percent in 1990 to 15 percent in 2015). That goal was attained. But that didn't significantly decrease the *number* of people in poverty. The world's population keeps growing at upward of 80–100 million people a year. In 2020, there were 7.8 billion people on this planet. Fifteen percent of that population would still have left more than a *billion* people in extreme global poverty. In 2015, the World Bank set a new and more ambitious goal of *eliminating* extreme poverty by 2030.

Why should we care? After all, America has its own poverty problems and a slew of other domestic concerns. So why should an American—or, for that matter, an affluent Canadian, French, or German citizen—embrace the **UN and World Bank Poverty Goal?**

For starters, one might embrace the notion that a poor child in sub-Saharan Africa or Borneo is no less worthy than a poor child elsewhere. And a child's death in Bangladesh is just as tragic as a child's death in Buffalo, New York. In other words, humanitarianism is a starting point for *global* concern for poor people.

Then there are pragmatic concerns. Poverty and inequality sow the seeds of social tension both within and across national borders. Poverty in other nations also limits potential markets for international trade. Last but not least, undeveloped human capital anywhere limits human creativity. For all these reasons, the World Bank feels its Poverty Goal should be universally embraced.

UN and World Bank Poverty Goal: UN goal of eliminating extreme poverty by 2030.

Policy Strategies

Eliminating severe poverty around the world won't be easy. In principle, ***there are only two general approaches to global poverty reduction:***

- *Redistribution* of incomes within and across nations.
- *Economic growth* that raises average incomes.

The following sections explore the potential of these strategies for eliminating global poverty.

INCOME REDISTRIBUTION

Many people suggest that the quickest route to eliminating global poverty is simply to *redistribute* incomes and assets, both within and across countries. The potential for redistribution is often exaggerated, however, and its risks are underestimated.

Within-Nation Redistribution

Take another look at those nations with the highest concentrations of extreme poverty. Nigeria is near the top of the list in Figure 23.1 and Table 23.1, with an incredible 54 percent of its population in extreme poverty and 78 percent in severe poverty. Yet the other 22 percent of the population lives fairly well, taking more than half of that nation's income. So what would happen if we somehow forced Nigeria's richest households to share that wealth? Sure,

WORLD VIEW

GLARING INEQUALITIES

Inequality tends to diminish as a country develops. In some developing nations, the richest tenth of the population can get 40 to 50 percent of all income—sometimes even more. In more developed countries, the richest tenth gets 20 to 30 percent of total income.

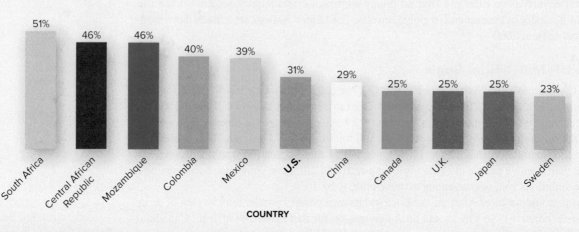

Income Share of Richest Tenth of Population

South Africa 51%
Central African Republic 46%
Mozambique 46%
Colombia 40%
Mexico 39%
U.S. 31%
China 29%
Canada 25%
U.K. 25%
Japan 25%
Sweden 23%

COUNTRY

Source: The World Bank, *WDI2019 Data Set,* data.worldbank.org.

CRITICAL ANALYSIS: The FOR WHOM question is reflected in the distribution of income. Although the U.S. income distribution is very unequal, inequalities loom even larger in most poor countries.

Nigeria's poorest households would be better off. But the gains wouldn't be spectacular: The *average* income in Nigeria is only $5,500 a year. Haiti, Zambia, and Madagascar also have such low *average* incomes that outright redistribution doesn't hold great hope for income gains by the poor. (See World View "Glaring Inequalities.")

Economic Risks. Then there's the downside to direct redistribution. How is the income pie going to be resliced? Will the incomes or assets of the rich be confiscated? How will underlying jobs, stocks, land, and businesses be distributed to the poor? How will *total* output (and income) be affected by the redistribution?

If savings are confiscated, people will no longer want to save and invest. If large, efficient farms are divided up into small parcels, who will manage them? After Zimbabwe confiscated and fragmented that nation's farms in 2000, its agricultural productivity plummeted and the economy collapsed. Cuba experienced the same kind of economic decline after the government seized and fragmented sugar and tobacco plantations. If the government expropriates factories, mills, farms, or businesses, who will run them? If the *rewards* to saving, investment, entrepreneurship, and management are expropriated, who will undertake these economic activities?

This is not to suggest that *no* redistribution of income or assets is appropriate. More progressive taxes and land reforms can reduce inequalities and poverty. But the potential of direct within-nation redistribution is often exaggerated. Historically, nations have often been forced to reverse land, tax, and property reforms that have slowed economic growth and reduced average incomes.

Expenditure Reallocation. In addition to directly redistributing private income and wealth, governments can also reduce poverty by reallocating direct government expenditures. As we observed in Chapter 1 (Figure 1.3), some poor nations devote a large share of output to the military. If more of those resources were channeled into schools, health services, and infrastructure, the poor would surely benefit. Governments in poor nations

Country	Total Aid ($ billions)	Percentage of Donor Total Income
United States	$ 34	0.17%
United Kingdom	19	0.70
Germany	25	0.61
France	12	0.43
Japan	14	0.28
Sweden	6	1.04
Canada	5	0.28
Italy	5	0.19
Australia	3	0.23
24-Nation Total	$153	0.31%

Source: OECD (2018 data).

TABLE 23.2

Foreign Aid

Rich nations give roughly $150 billion to poor nations every year. This is a tiny fraction of donor GDP, however.

also tend to give priority to urban development (where the government and middle class reside), to the neglect of rural development (where the poor reside). Redirecting more resources to rural development and core infrastructure (roads, electricity, and water) would accelerate poverty reduction.

Across-Nation Redistribution

Redistribution *across* national borders could make even bigger dents in global poverty. After all, the United States and other industrialized nations are so rich that they could transfer a lot of income to the globally poor if they chose to.

Foreign Aid. Currently, developed nations give poorer nations around $150 billion a year in "official development assistance." That's a lot of money. But even if it were distributed exclusively to globally poor households, it would amount to only $50 per year per person.

Developed nations have set a goal of delivering more aid. The United Nations' **Millennium Aid Goal** is to raise foreign aid levels to 0.7 percent of donor-country GDP. That may not sound too ambitious, but it's a much larger flow than at present. As Table 23.2 reveals, few "rich" nations now come close to this goal. Although the United States is by far the world's largest aid donor, its aid equals only 0.17 percent of U.S. total output. For all developed nations, the aid ratio averages 0.31 percent.

Given the history of foreign aid, the UN goal is unlikely to be met anytime soon. But what if it were? What if foreign aid *tripled?* Would that cure global poverty? No. Tripling foreign aid would generate only $200 a year for each of the 2 billion people now in global poverty. Even that figure is optimistic, as it assumes all aid is distributed to the poor in a form (e.g., food, clothes, and medicine) that directly addresses their basic needs.

Millennium Aid Goal: United Nations goal of raising foreign aid levels to 0.7 percent of donor-country GDP.

Nongovernmental Aid. Official development assistance is augmented by private charities and other nongovernmental organizations (NGOs). The Gates Foundation, for example, spends upward of $1 billion a year on health care for the globally poor, focusing on treatable diseases like malaria, tuberculosis, and HIV infection (see World View "The Way We Give"). Religious organizations operate schools and health clinics in areas of extreme poverty. The International Red Cross brings medical care, shelter, and food in emergencies.

As with official development assistance, the content of NGO aid can be as important as its level. Relatively low-cost immunizations, for example, can improve health conditions more than an expensive, high-tech health clinic can. Teaching basic literacy to a community of young children can be more effective than equipping a single high school with Internet capabilities. Distributing drought-resistant seeds to farmers can be more effective than donating advanced farm equipment (which may become useless when it needs to be repaired).

WORLD VIEW

THE WAY WE GIVE

Philanthropy Can Step in Where Market Forces Don't

One day my wife Melinda and I were reading about millions of children dying from diseases in poor countries that were eliminated in this country. . . .

Malaria has been known for a long time. In 1902, in 1907, Nobel Prizes were given for advances in understanding the malaria parasite and how it was transmitted. But here we are a hundred years later and malaria is setting new records, infecting more than 400 million people every year, and killing more than a million people every year. That's a number that's increasing every year, and every day it's more than 2,000 African children. . . .

And this would extend to tuberculosis, yellow fever, AIDS vaccine, acute diarrheal illnesses, respiratory illnesses; you know, millions of children die from these things every year, and yet the advances we have in biology have not been applied because rich countries don't have these diseases. The private sector really isn't involved in developing vaccines and medicines for these diseases because the developing countries can't buy them. . . .

And so if left to themselves, these market forces create a world, which is the situation today, where more than 90 percent of the money spent on health research is spent on those who are the healthiest. An example of that is the billion a year spent on combating baldness. That's great for some people, but perhaps it should get behind malaria in terms of its priority ranking. . . .

So philanthropy can step in where market forces are not there. . . . It can get the people who have the expertise and draw them in. It can use awards, it can use novel arrangements with private companies, it can partner with the universities. . . . And every year the platform of science that we have to do this on gets better.

—Bill Gates

Source: Gates, Bill. "Speech at The Tech Museum." Bill & Melinda Gates Foundation, November 15, 2006.

CRITICAL ANALYSIS: When markets fail to provide for basic human needs, additional institutions and incentives may be needed (such as **nongovernmental aid**).

ECONOMIC GROWTH

No matter how well designed foreign aid and philanthropy might be, across-nation transfers alone cannot eliminate global poverty. As Bill Gates observed, the entire endowment of the Gates Foundation would meet the health needs of the globally poor for only one year. The World Bank concurs: "Developing nations hold the keys to their prosperity; global action cannot substitute for equitable and efficient domestic policies and institutions."[1] So as important as international assistance is, it will never fully suffice.

Increasing Total Income

economic growth: An increase in output (real GDP); an expansion of production possibilities.

The "key" to ending global poverty is, of course, **economic growth.** As we've observed, *redistributing existing incomes doesn't do the job;* **total** *income has to increase.* This is what economic growth is all about.

Unique Needs. The generic prescription for economic growth is simple: more resources and better technology. But this growth formula takes on a new meaning in the poorest nations. Rich nations can focus on research, technology, and the spread of "brain power." Poor nations need the basics—the "bricks and mortar" elements of an economy such as water systems, roads, schools, and legal systems. Bill Gates learned this firsthand in his early philanthropic efforts. In 1996 Microsoft donated a computer for a community center in Soweto, one of the poorest areas in South Africa. When he visited the center in 1997, he

[1]World Bank, *World Development Report, 2006* (Washington, DC: World Bank, 2006), p. 206.

discovered the center had no electricity. He quickly realized that growth policy priorities for poor nations are different from those for rich nations.

Growth Potential

The potential of economic growth to reduce poverty in poor nations is impressive. The 40 nations classified as "low-income" by the World Bank have a combined output of only $600 billion. That's just a shade more than the annual sales revenue of Walmart. "Lower-middle-income" nations like China, Brazil, Egypt, and Sri Lanka produce another $7 trillion or so of annual output. Hence, every percentage point of economic growth increases total income in these combined nations by nearly $75 billion. According to the World Bank, if these nations could grow their economies by just 3.8 percent a year, that would generate an extra $285 billion of output in the first year and increasing thereafter. That "growth dividend" is twice the amount of foreign aid (Table 23.2).

China has demonstrated just how effective economic growth can be in reducing poverty. Since 1990 China has been the world's fastest-growing economy, with annual GDP growth rates routinely in the 8–10 percent range. This sensational growth has not only raised *average* incomes but has also dramatically reduced the incidence of poverty. In fact, *the observed success in reducing extreme global poverty from 30 percent in 1990 to 10 percent in 2019 is almost entirely due to the decline in Chinese poverty.* By contrast, slow economic growth in Africa, Latin America, and South Asia has *increased* their respective poverty populations.

Growth of Per Capita Output

The really critical factor in reducing poverty is the relationship of output growth to population growth. China has been spectacularly successful in this regard: Not only does it have one of the fastest GDP growth rates, but it also has one of the world's slowest population growth rates. As a result, its per capita output has grown by an incredible 9 percent a year.

Notice in Table 23.3 how slow population growth rates in high-income nations allow them to achieve ever-rising living standards. Japan is the ultimate example: With zero population growth, it is pretty easy to achieve an increase in per capita income.

	Average Annual Growth Rate (2000–2018) of		
	GDP	**Population**	**Per Capita GDP**
High-income countries			
United States	1.7	0.8	0.9
Canada	1.9	1.0	0.9
Japan	0.7	0.0	0.7
France	1.1	0.6	0.5
Middle-income countries			
China	9.5	0.5	9.0
India	6.8	1.4	5.4
West Bank/Gaza	5.2	2.5	2.7
Libya	−1.2	1.2	−2.4
Zimbabwe	1.4	1.1	0.3
Low-income countries			
Burundi	3.1	3.1	0.0
Madagascar	2.9	2.8	0.1
Haiti	1.4	1.5	−0.1
Central African Republic	0.4	1.4	−1.0
Ethiopia	9.8	2.8	7.0

Source: The World Bank, *WDR2019 Data Set.*

TABLE 23.3

Growth Rates in Selected Countries, 2000–2018

The relationship between GDP growth and population growth is very different in rich and poor countries. The populations of rich countries are growing very slowly, and gains in per capita GDP are easily achieved. In the poorest countries, population is still increasing rapidly, making it difficult to raise living standards. Notice how per capita incomes are declining in many poor countries (such as Libya and Haiti).

Libya, Haiti, and the Central African Republic don't fare so well. Their output didn't grow as fast as their populations. As a consequence, the average citizen had *less* output to consume every year: extreme poverty spread.

Investing in Human Capital

human capital: The knowledge and skills possessed by the workforce.

While the math of global poverty is simple, the strategies for reducing poverty are many and diverse. A common observation, however, is the need to invest more in **human capital.**

Education. In poor nations, the need for human capital development is evident. Only 71 percent of the population in low-income nations completes even elementary school. Even fewer people are *literate*—that is, able to read and write a short, simple statement about everyday life (e.g., "We ate rice for breakfast"). Educational deficiencies are greatest for females, who are often prevented from attending school by cultural, social, or economic concerns (see World View "The Female 'Inequality Trap'"). In Chad and Liberia, fewer than one out of six girls completes primary school. Primary school completion rates for girls are in the 25–35 percent range in most of the poor nations of sub-Saharan Africa.

WORLD VIEW

THE FEMALE "INEQUALITY TRAP"

In many poor nations, women are viewed as such a financial liability that female fetuses are aborted, female infants are killed, and female children are so neglected that they have significantly higher mortality rates. The "burden" females pose results from social norms that restrict the ability of women to earn income, accumulate wealth, or even decide their own marital status. In many of the poorest nations, women

- Have restricted property rights.
- Can't inherit wealth.
- Are prohibited or discouraged from working outside the home.
- Are prohibited or discouraged from going to school.
- Are prevented from voting.
- Are denied the right to divorce.
- Are paid less than men if they do work outside the home.
- Are often expected to bring a financial dowry to the marriage.
- May be beaten if they fail to obey their husbands.

These social practices create an "inequality trap" that keeps returns on female human capital investment low. Without adequate education or training, they can't get productive jobs. Without access to good jobs, they have no incentive to get an education or training. This kind of vicious cycle creates an inequality trap that keeps women and their communities poor.

Source: The World Bank, *World Development Report 2006*, pp. 51–54.

CRITICAL ANALYSIS: Denying women economic rights not only is discriminatory but reduces the amount of **human capital** available for economic growth.

inequality trap: Institutional barriers that impede human and physical capital investment, particularly by the poorest segments of society.

In Niger and Mali, only one out of five *teenage* girls is literate. This lack of literacy creates an **inequality trap** that restricts the employment opportunities for young women to simple, routine, manual jobs (e.g., carpet weaving and sewing). With so few skills and little education, they are destined to remain poor.

The already low levels of *average* education are compounded by unequal access to schools. Families in extreme poverty typically live in rural areas, with primitive transportation and communication facilities. *Physical* access to school itself is problematic. On top of that, the poorest families often need their children to work, either within the family or in paid employment. In Somalia, only 8 percent of poor young children attend primary schools; in Ethiopia, Yemen, and Mali, about 50 percent attend. These forces often foreclose school attendance for the poorest children.

Health. In poor nations, basic health care is also a critical dimension of human capital development. Immunizations against measles, diphtheria, and tetanus are more the exception than the rule in Somalia, Nigeria, Afghanistan, Congo, the Central African Republic, and many other poor nations. For all low-income nations taken together, the child immunization rate is only 67 percent (versus 96 percent in the United States). Access and education—not money—are the principal barriers to greater immunizations.

Water and sanitation facilities are also in short supply. The World Bank defines "adequate water access" as a protected water source of at least 20 liters per person a day within 1 kilometer of the home dwelling. We're not limited to indoor plumbing with this definition: A public water pipe a half mile from one's home is considered adequate. Yet only three out of four households in low-income nations meet even this minimum threshold of water adequacy. In Afghanistan, Ethiopia, and Somalia, only one out of four households has even that much water access. Access to sanitation facilities (ranging from pit latrines to flush toilets) is less common still (on average one out of three low-income-nation households). In Ethiopia only 6 percent of the population is so privileged.

When illness strikes, professional health care is hard to find. In the United States, there is one doctor for every 180 people. In Sierra Leone, there is one doctor for every 10,000 people! For low-income nations as a group, there are 2,500 people for every available doctor.

These glaring inadequacies in health conditions breed high rates of illness and death. In the United States, only 8 out of every 1,000 children die before age 5. In Angola, 260 of every 1,000 children die that young. For all low-income nations, the under-5 mortality rate is 13.5 percent (nearly one out of seven). Those children who live are commonly so malnourished (severely underweight and/or short) that they can't develop fully (another inequality trap).

AIDS takes a huge toll as well. Only 0.6 percent of the U.S. adult population has HIV. In Botswana, Lesotho, Swaziland, and Zimbabwe, more than 25 percent of the adult population is HIV-infected. As a result of these problems, life expectancies are inordinately low. In Zambia, only 16 percent of the population lives to age 65. In the Central African Republic, life expectancy at birth is 52 years (versus 79 years in the United States). For low-income nations as a group, life expectancy is a mere 63 years.

Analysis: Unsafe water is a common problem for the globally poor.
Frank Bienewald/Getty Images

Capital Investment

If they are ever going to eradicate poverty and its related social ills, poor nations need sharply increased capital investment in both the public and private sectors. Transportation and communications systems must be expanded and upgraded so markets can function. Capital equipment and upgraded technology must flow into both agricultural and industrial enterprises.

Internal Financing. Acquiring the capital resources needed to boost productivity and accelerate economic growth is not an easy task. Domestically, freeing up scarce resources for capital investment requires cutbacks in domestic consumption. In the 1920s Stalin used near-totalitarian powers to cut domestic consumption in Russia (by limiting output of consumer goods) and raise Russia's **investment rate** to as much as 30 percent of output. This elevated rate of investment accelerated capacity growth, but at a high cost in terms of consumer deprivation.

Other nations haven't had the power or the desire to make such a sacrifice. China spent two decades trying to raise consumption standards before it gave higher priority to investment. Once it did so, however, economic growth accelerated sharply. Unfortunately, low investment rates continue to plague other poor nations.

Pervasive poverty in poor nations sharply limits the potential for increased savings. Nevertheless, governments can encourage more saving with improved banking facilities, transparent capital markets, and education and saving incentives. And there is mounting evidence that even small dabs of financing can make a big difference. Extending a small loan that

investment rate: The percentage of total output (GDP) allocated to the production of new plants, equipment, and structures.

microfinance: The granting of small ("micro"), unsecured loans to small businesses and entrepreneurs.

enables a poor farmer to buy improved seeds or a plow can have substantial effects on productivity. Financing small equipment or inventory for an entrepreneur can get a new business rolling. Such **microfinance** can be a critical key to escaping poverty. The Bangladesh economist Muhammad Yunus won the Nobel Peace Prize for his early demonstrations of how micro lending could create "development from below" in poor, rural areas.

Some nations have also used inflation as a tool for shifting resources from consumption to investment. By financing public works projects and private investment with an increased money supply, governments can increase the inflation rate. As prices rise faster than consumer incomes, households are forced to curtail their purchases. This "inflation tax" ultimately backfires, however, when both domestic and foreign market participants lose confidence in the nation's currency. Periodic currency collapses have destabilized many South and Central American economies and governments. Inflation financing also fails to distinguish good investment ideas from bad ones.

External Financing. Given the constraints on internal financing, poor nations have to seek external funding to lift their investment rate. In fact, Columbia University economist Jeffrey Sachs has argued that external financing is not only necessary but, if generous enough, also sufficient for *eliminating* global poverty (see World View "Jeffrey Sachs: Big Money, Big Plans"). As we've observed, however, actual foreign aid flows are far below the "Big Money" threshold that Sachs envisions. Skeptics also question whether more foreign aid would really solve the problem, given the mixed results of previous foreign aid flows. They suggest that more emphasis should be placed on increasing *private* investment flows. Private investment typically entails *direct foreign investment* in new plants, equipment, and technology, or the purchase of ownership stakes in existing enterprises.

WORLD VIEW

JEFFREY SACHS: BIG MONEY, BIG PLANS

Columbia University economics professor Jeffrey Sachs has seen the ravages of poverty around the world. As director of the UN Millennium Project, he is committed to attaining the UN's goal of reducing global poverty rates by half by 2015. In fact, Professor Sachs thinks we can do even better: the complete *elimination* of extreme poverty by 2025.

How will the world do this? First, rich nations must double their foreign aid flows now, and then double them again in 10 years. Second, poor nations must develop full-scale, comprehensive plans for poverty reduction. This "shock therapy" approach must address all dimensions of the poverty problem simultaneously and quickly, sweeping all inequality traps out of the way.

Critics have called Sachs's vision utopian. They point to the spotty history of foreign aid projects and the failure of many top-down, Big Plan development initiatives. But they still applaud Sachs for mobilizing public opinion and economic resources to fight global poverty.

Source: Jeffrey Sachs, *The End of Poverty* (New York, NY: Penguin Random House, 2006).

CRITICAL ANALYSIS: World poverty can't be eliminated without committing far more resources. Jeffrey Sachs favors an **external finance** option: the comprehensive Big Plan approach.

Agricultural Development

When we think about capital investment, we tend to picture new factories, gleaming office buildings, and computerized machinery. In discussing global poverty, however, we have to remind ourselves of how dependent poor nations are on agriculture. As Figure 23.2 illustrates, nearly 50 percent of Somalia's income originates in agriculture. Agricultural shares in the range of 30–45 percent are common in the poorest nations. By contrast, only 1 percent of America's output now comes from farms.

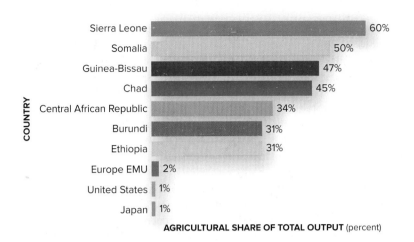

FIGURE 23.2

Agricultural Share of Output

In poor nations, agriculture accounts for a very large share of total output.

Source: The World Bank, *WDR2019 Data Set.*

Low Farm Productivity. What keeps poor nations so dependent on agriculture is their incredibly low **productivity**. Subsistence farmers are often forced to plow their own fields by hand with wooden plows. Irrigation systems are primitive and farm machinery is scarce or nonexistent. While high-tech U.S. farms produce nearly $100,000 of output per worker, Ugandan farms produce a shockingly low $690 of output per worker (see Figure 23.3). Farmers in Somalia produce only 500 kilograms of cereal per hectare, compared with 8,200 kilos per hectare in the United States.

To grow their economies, poor nations have to invest in agricultural development. Farm productivity has to rise beyond subsistence levels so that workers can migrate to other industries and expand production possibilities. One of the catapults to China's growth was an exponential increase in farm productivity that freed up labor for industrial production. (China now produces 6,000 kilos of cereal per hectare.) To achieve greater farm productivity, poor nations need capital investment, technological know-how, and improved infrastructure.

productivity: Output per unit of input—for example, output per labor-hour.

Institutional Reform

Clearly, poor nations need a lot more investment. But more resources alone may not suffice. To attract and keep capital, **a** *nation needs an institutional structure that promotes economic growth.*

Property Rights. Land, property, and contract rights have to be established before farmers will voluntarily improve their land or invest in agricultural technology. China saw how agricultural productivity jumped when it transformed government-run communal farms into local enterprises and privately managed farms, beginning in 1978. China is using the lessons of that experience to now extend ownership rights to farmers.

Analysis: Lack of capital, technology, and markets keeps farm productivity low.
Barry Barker/McGraw Hill

FIGURE 23.3

Low Agricultural Productivity

Farmers in poor nations suffer from low productivity. They are handicapped by low education, inferior technology, primitive infrastructure, and a lack of machinery.

Source: The World Bank, *WDR2019 Data Set.*

Entrepreneurial Incentives. Unleashing the "animal spirits" of the marketplace is also critical. People *do* respond to incentives. If farmers see the potential for profit—and the opportunity to keep that profit—they will pursue productivity gains with more vigor. To encourage that response, governments need to assure the legitimacy of profits and their fair tax treatment. In 1992 the Chinese government acknowledged the role of profits and entrepreneurship in fostering economic advancement. Before then, successful entrepreneurs ran the risk of offending the government with conspicuous consumption that highlighted growing inequalities. The government even punished some entrepreneurs and confiscated their wealth. Once "profits" were legitimized, however, entrepreneurship and foreign investment accelerated, raising China's growth rate significantly.

Cuba stopped short of legitimizing private property and profits. Although Fidel Castro periodically permitted some private enterprises (e.g., family restaurants), he always withdrew that permission when entrepreneurial ventures succeeded. As a consequence, Cuba's economy stagnated for decades. Venezuela has recently moved further in that direction, expropriating and nationalizing private enterprises (see World View "Maduro: 'Bourgeois Parasites' Thwart Growth"), thereby discouraging private investment and entrepreneurship. In the first five years of the Maduro presidency, Venezuela's GDP contracted by more than 50 percent.

WORLD VIEW

MADURO: "BOURGEOIS PARASITES" THWART GROWTH

When he won a third presidential term in 2006, Hugo Chávez made his intentions clear. Venezuela, he said, is "heading toward socialism, and no one can prevent it." He embarked on a policy of nationalization, price controls, and a political takeover of Venezuela's central bank. Since then, the Venezuelan economy has stalled; factories, oil fields, and farms have shut down; inflation has soared; and food and energy shortages have become commonplace.

Chávez's successor, Nicolas Maduro, blames the nation's economic woes not on government policy but on the "bourgeois parasites" who have conspired to raise prices, hoard commodities, and strangle the economy. He ordered the nation's largest electronic retailer, Daka, to cut its prices in half and sent the military into its stores to enforce those price cuts. He urged Venezuelans to "leave nothing on the shelves, nothing in the warehouses" and threatened store managers with arrest if they interfered. Critics called the action "government-sanctioned looting." Maduro also levied fines and threatened jail sentences for General Motors executives who he accused of cutting back production and charging "exploitive" prices for new cars.

President Maduro's policies drove the Venezuelan economy into a downward spiral. Output shrank every year and inflation skyrocketed. In the wake of increasing popular protests and a disputed election, President Maduro in late 2019 agreed to relax some of his most anti-capitalism rhetoric and policies.

Source: News reports, September 2014 and January 2020.

CRITICAL ANALYSIS: By restricting private ownership and market freedom, governments curb the **entrepreneurship** and investment that may be essential for economic development.

Equity. What disturbed both Castro and Venezuelan President Chávez was the way capitalism intensified income inequalities. Entrepreneurs got rich while the mass of people remained poor. For Castro, the goal of equity was more important than the goal of efficiency. A nation where everyone was equally poor was preferred to a nation of haves and have-nots.

In many of today's poorest nations, policy interests are not so noble. A small elite often holds extraordinary political power and uses that power to protect its privileges. Greed

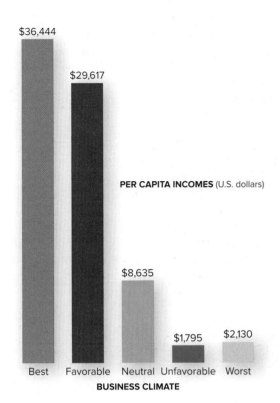

PER CAPITA INCOMES (U.S. dollars)

$36,444
$29,617
$8,635
$1,795
$2,130

| Best | Favorable | Neutral | Unfavorable | Worst |

BUSINESS CLIMATE

FIGURE 23.4

Business Climates Affect Growth

Nations that offer more secure property rights, less regulation, and lower taxes grow faster and enjoy higher per capita incomes.

Note: Business climate in 183 nations gauged by 50 measures of government tax, regulatory, and legal policy.

2011 Index of Economic Freedom, Washington, DC: The Heritage Foundation, p. 7, 2011.

restricts the flow of resources to the poorest segments of the population, leaving them to fend for themselves. These inequalities in power, wealth, and opportunity create inequality traps that restrain human capital development, capital investment, entrepreneurship, and ultimately economic growth.

Business Climate. To encourage capital investment and entrepreneurship, governments have to assure a secure and supportive business climate. Investors and business start-ups want to know what the rules of the game are and how they will be enforced. They also want assurances that contracts will be enforced and that debts can be collected. They want their property protected from crime and government corruption. They want minimal interference from government regulation and taxes.

As the annual surveys by the Heritage Foundation document, nations that offer a more receptive business climate grow at a faster pace. Figure 23.4 illustrates this connection. Notice that nations with the most pro-business climate (e.g., Hong Kong, Singapore, Iceland, the United States, and Denmark) enjoy living standards far superior to those in nations with hostile business climates (e.g., North Korea, Cuba, Congo, Sudan, Zimbabwe, and Myanmar). This is no accident; *pro-business climates encourage the capital investment, the entrepreneurship, and the human capital investment that drive economic growth.*

Unfortunately, some of the poorest nations still fail to provide a pro-business environment. Figure 23.5 illustrates how specific dimensions of the business climate differ across fast-growing nations (China) and perpetually poor ones (Cambodia and Kenya). A biannual survey of 26,000 international firms elicits their views of how different government policies restrain their investment decisions. Notice how China offers a more certain policy environment, less corruption, more secure property rights, and less crime. Given these business conditions, where would you invest?

The good news about the business climate is that it doesn't require huge investments to fix. It does require, however, a lot of political capital.

FIGURE 23.5

Investment Climate

International investors gravitate toward nations with business-friendly policies. Shown here are the percentages of international firms citing specific elements of the business climate that deter their investment in the named countries.

Source: The World Bank, *World Development Indicators 2006.*

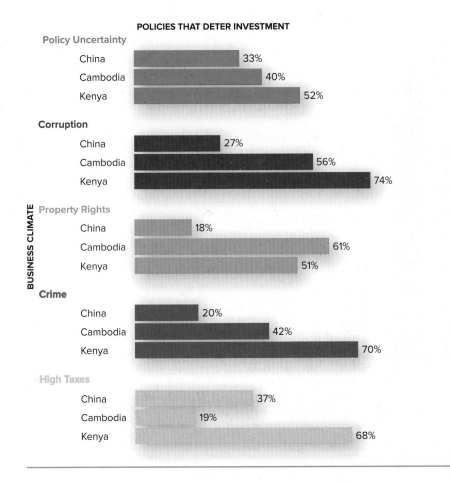

POLICIES THAT DETER INVESTMENT

comparative advantage: The ability of a country to produce a specific good at a lower opportunity cost than its trading partners.

import quota: A limit on the quantity of a good that may be imported in a given time period.

World Trade

When it comes to political capital, poor nations have a complaint of their own. They say that rich nations lock them out of their most important markets—particularly agricultural export markets. Poor nations typically have a **comparative advantage** in the production of agricultural products. Their farm productivity may be low (see Figure 23.3), but their low labor costs keep their farm output competitive. They can't fully exploit that advantage in export markets, however. The United States, the European Union, and Japan heavily subsidize their own farmers. This keeps farm prices low in the rich nations, eliminating the cost advantage of farmers in poor nations. To further protect their own farmers from global competition, rich nations erect trade barriers to stem the inflow of Third World products. The United States, for example, enforces an **import quota** on foreign sugar. This trade barrier has fostered a high-cost, domestic beet sugar industry while denying poor nations the opportunity to sell more sugar and grow their economies faster.

Poor nations need export markets. Export sales generate the hard currency (dollars, euros, and yen) that is needed to purchase capital equipment in global markets. Export sales also allow farmers in poor nations to expand production, exploit economies of scale, and invest in improved technology. Ironically, *trade barriers in rich nations impede poor nations from pursuing the agricultural development that is a* **prerequisite** *for growth.* The latest round of multilateral trade negotiations dragged on forever because of the resistance of rich nations to opening their agricultural markets. Poor nations plead that "trade, not aid" is their surest path to economic growth.

DECISIONS FOR **TOMORROW**

Can Entrepreneurship Alleviate Poverty?

The traditional approach to economic development emphasizes the potential for government policy to reallocate resources and increase capital investment. External financing of capital investment was always at or near the top of the policy agenda (see World View "Jeffrey Sachs: Big Money, Big Plans"). This approach has been criticized for neglecting the power of people and markets.

One of the most influential critics is the Peruvian economist Hernando de Soto. When he returned to his native Peru after years of commercial success in Europe, he was struck by the dichotomy in his country. The "official" economy was mired in bureaucratic red tape and stagnant. Most of the vitality of the Peruvian economy was contained in the unofficial "underground" economy. The underground economy included trade in drugs but was overwhelmingly oriented to meeting the everyday demands of Peruvian consumers and households. The underground economy wasn't hidden from view; it flourished on the streets, in outdoor markets, and in transport services. The only thing that forced this thriving economy underground was the failure of the government to recognize it and give it legitimate status. Government restrictions on prices, business activities, finance, and trade—a slew of inequality traps—forced entrepreneurs to operate "underground."

De Soto concluded that countries like Peru could grow more quickly if governments encouraged rather than suppressed these entrepreneurial resources. In his best-selling book *The Other Path,* he urged poor countries to refocus their development policies. This "other path" entails improving the business climate by

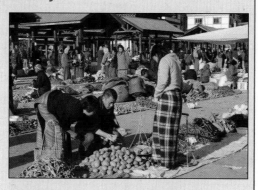

Analysis: Markets exist but struggle in poor nations.
Lissa Harrison

- Reducing bureaucratic barriers to free enterprise.
- Spreading private ownership.
- Developing and enforcing legal safeguards for property, income, and wealth.
- Developing infrastructure that facilitates business activity.

Muhammad Yunus's "microloans" would also fit comfortably on this other path.

De Soto's book has been translated into several languages and has encouraged market-oriented reforms in Peru, Argentina, Mexico, Russia, Vietnam, and elsewhere. In India the government is drastically reducing both regulation and taxes to pursue De Soto's other path. The basic message of his other path is that poor nations should exploit the one resource that is abundant in even the poorest countries—entrepreneurship.

SUMMARY

- Definitions of "poverty" are culturally based. Poverty in the United States is defined largely in *relative* terms, whereas global poverty is tied more to *absolute* levels of subsistence. **LO23-1**

- About 11 percent of the U.S. population (more than 37 million people) is officially counted as poor. Poor people in America suffer from *relative* deprivation, not *absolute* deprivation, as in global poverty. **LO23-1**

- Global poverty thresholds are about one-tenth of U.S. standards. "Extreme" poverty is defined as less than $1.90 per day per person; "severe" poverty is less than $3.10 per day (inflation adjusted). **LO23-1**
- More than 700 million people around the world are in extreme poverty; 2 billion are in severe poverty. In low-income nations, global poverty rates are as high as 70–90 percent. **LO23-2**
- The United Nations' Millennium Poverty Goal is to eliminate severe poverty by 2030. **LO23-3**
- Redistribution of incomes *within* poor nations doesn't have much potential for reducing poverty, given their low *average* incomes. *Across*-nation redistributions (e.g., foreign aid) can make a small dent, however. **LO23-3**

- Economic growth is the key to global poverty reduction. Many poor nations are held back by undeveloped human capital, primitive infrastructure, and subsistence agriculture. To grow more quickly, they need to meet basic human needs (health and education), increase agricultural productivity, and encourage investment. **LO23-3**
- To move into sustained economic growth, poor nations need capital investment and institutional reforms that promote both equity and entrepreneurship. **LO23-3**
- Poor nations also need "trade, not aid"—that is, access to rich nation markets, particularly in farm products. **LO23-3**

Key Terms

poverty threshold (U.S.)	UN and World Bank Poverty Goal	investment rate
poverty rate	Millennium Aid Goal	microfinance
in-kind transfers	economic growth	productivity
extreme poverty (world)	human capital	comparative advantage
severe poverty (world)	inequality trap	import quota

Questions for Discussion

1. Why should Americans care about extreme poverty in Haiti, Ethiopia, or Bangladesh? **LO23-2**
2. If you had only $18 to spend per day (the U.S. poverty threshold), how would you spend it? What if you had only $1.90 a day (the World Bank "extreme poverty" threshold)? **LO23-1**
3. If a poor nation must choose between building an airport, some schools, or a steel plant, which one should it choose? Why? **LO23-3**
4. How do more children per family either restrain or expand income-earning potential? **LO23-3**
5. Are property rights a prerequisite for economic growth? Explain. **LO23-3**
6. How do unequal rights for women affect economic growth? **LO23-3**
7. How does microfinance alter prospects for economic growth? The distribution of political power? **LO23-3**
8. Why is the agricultural share of total output so high in poor nations? (See Figure 23.2.) **LO23-3**
9. Would you invest in Cambodia or Kenya on the basis of the information in Figure 23.5? **LO23-3**
10. Why do economists put so much emphasis on entrepreneurship? How can poor nations encourage it? **LO23-3**
11. If economic growth reduced poverty but widened inequalities, would it still be desirable? **LO23-3**

LO23-1 1. The World Bank's threshold for "extreme" poverty is $1.90 per person per day.
    (*a*) How much *annual* income does this imply for a family of four?
    (*b*) What portion of the official U.S. poverty threshold (roughly $26,000 for a family of four) is met by the World Bank's measure?

LO23-2 2. There are 2 billion people in "severe" poverty with less than $3.10 of income per day.
    (*a*) What is the maximum *combined* income of this "severely" poor population?
    (*b*) What percentage of the world's *total* income (roughly $90 trillion) does this represent?

LO23-2 3. In Mozambique,
    (*a*) What percentage of total output is received by the richest 10 percent of households? (See World View "Glaring Inequalities.")
    (*b*) How much output did this share amount to in 2018, when Mozambique's GDP was $14 billion?
    (*c*) With a total population of 30 million, what was the implied per capita income of
        (*i*) The richest 10 percent of the population?
        (*ii*) The remaining 90 percent?

LO23-3 4. (*a*) How much foreign aid did the United States provide in 2018? (See Table 23.2.)
    (*b*) How much more is required to satisfy the UN's Millennium Aid Goal if U.S. GDP was $20 trillion?

LO23-3 5. If the 24 industrialized nations were to satisfy the UN's Millennium Aid Goal, how much *more* foreign aid would they give annually? (See Table 23.2.)

LO23-3 6. According to Table 23.3, how many years will it take for per capita GDP to double in
    (*a*) China?
    (*b*) Madagascar?
    (*c*) Burundi?

LO23-3 7. According to World View "The Way We Give,"
    (*a*) How much money is spent annually to combat baldness?
    (*b*) How much medical care would that money buy for each child who dies from malaria each year?

LO23-3 8. Foreign aid to poor nations amounted to $20 per year per person. What percentage did this aid cover of
    (*a*) The extreme poverty annual budget?
    (*b*) The severe poverty annual budget?

LO23-3 9. *Decisions for Tomorrow:* Identify the four key paths identified by De Soto to improve business climate in less-developed countries.

Design Credit: Shutterstock

GLOSSARY

A

absolute advantage: The ability of a country to produce a specific good with fewer resources (per unit of output) than other countries.

acreage set-aside: Land withdrawn from production as part of policy to increase crop prices.

AD excess: The amount by which aggregate demand must be reduced to achieve full-employment equilibrium after allowing for price-level changes.

AD shortfall: The amount of additional aggregate demand needed to achieve full employment after allowing for price-level changes.

adjustable-rate mortgage (ARM): A mortgage (home loan) that adjusts the nominal interest rate to changing rates of inflation.

aggregate demand (AD): The total quantity of output (real GDP) demanded at alternative price levels in a given time period, *ceteris paribus*.

aggregate expenditure: The rate of total expenditure desired at alternative levels of income, *ceteris paribus*.

aggregate supply (AS): The total quantity of output (real GDP) producers are willing and able to supply at alternative price levels in a given time period, *ceteris paribus*.

antitrust: Government intervention to alter market structure or prevent abuse of market power.

appreciation: A rise in the price of one currency relative to another.

arithmetic growth: An increase in quantity by a constant amount each year.

asset: Anything having exchange value in the marketplace; wealth.

automatic stabilizer: Federal expenditure or revenue item that automatically responds countercyclically to changes in national income, like unemployment benefits and income taxes.

autonomous consumption: Consumer spending not dependent on current income.

average fixed cost (AFC): Total fixed cost divided by the quantity produced in a given time period.

average propensity to consume (APC): Total consumption in a given period divided by total disposable income.

average total cost (ATC): Total cost divided by the quantity produced in a given time period.

average variable cost (AVC): Total variable cost divided by the quantity produced in a given time period.

B

balance of payments: A summary record of a country's international economic transactions in a given period of time.

balance-of-payments deficit: An excess demand for foreign currency at current exchange rates.

balance-of-payments surplus: An excess demand for domestic currency at current exchange rates.

bank reserves: Assets held by a bank to fulfill its deposit obligations.

barriers to entry: Obstacles such as patents that make it difficult or impossible for would-be producers to enter a particular market.

barter: The direct exchange of one good for another, without the use of money.

base year: The year used for comparative analysis; the basis for indexing price changes.

bilateral monopoly: A market with only one buyer (a monopsonist) and one seller (a monopolist).

bond: A certificate acknowledging a debt and the amount of interest to be paid each year until repayment; an IOU.

bracket creep: The movement of taxpayers into higher tax brackets (rates) as nominal incomes grow.

breakeven level of income: The income level at which welfare eligibility ceases.

budget constraint: A line depicting all combinations of goods that are affordable with a given income and given prices.

budget deficit: The amount by which government spending exceeds government revenue in a given time period.

budget surplus: An excess of government revenues over government expenditures in a given time period.

business cycle: Alternating periods of economic growth and contraction.

C

capital: Final goods produced for use in the production of other goods, such as equipment and structures.

capital gain: An increase in the market value of an asset.

capital gains tax: A tax levied on the profit from the sale of property.

capital-intensive: Production processes that use a high ratio of capital to labor inputs.

capitalization: Market value of a publicly traded company; equals number of shares multiplied by the price of the share.

cartel: A group of firms with an explicit, formal agreement to fix prices and output shares in a particular market.

cash transfers: Income transfers that entail direct cash payments to recipients, such as Social Security, welfare, and unemployment benefits.

ceteris paribus: The assumption of nothing else changing.

closed economy: A nation that doesn't engage in international trade.

collective bargaining: Direct negotiations between employers and unions to determine labor market outcomes.

comparative advantage: The ability of a country to produce a specific good at a lower opportunity cost than its trading partners.

competitive firm: A firm without market power, with no ability to alter the market price of the goods it produces.

competitive market: A market in which no buyer or seller has market power.

complementary goods: Goods frequently consumed in combination; when the price of good x rises, the demand for good y falls, *ceteris paribus*.

concentration ratio: The proportion of total industry output produced by the largest firms (usually the four largest).

constant returns to scale: Increases in plant size do not affect minimum average cost; minimum per-unit costs are identical for small plants and large plants.

Consumer Price Index (CPI): A measure (index) of changes in the average price of consumer goods and services.

consumer surplus: The difference between the maximum price a person is willing to pay and the price paid.

consumption: Expenditure by consumers on final goods and services.

consumption function: A mathematical relationship indicating the rate of desired consumer spending at various income levels.

consumption possibilities: The alternative combinations of goods and services that a country could consume in a given time period.

contestable market: An imperfectly competitive industry subject to potential entry if prices or profits increase.

core inflation rate: Changes in the CPI, excluding food and energy prices.

corporate stock: Shares of ownership in a corporation.

corporation: A business organization having a continuous existence independent of its members (owners) and power and liabilities distinct from those of its members.

cost efficiency: The amount of output associated with an additional dollar spent on input; the MPP of an input divided by its price (cost).

cost-of-living adjustment (COLA): Automatic adjustments of nominal income to the rate of inflation.

coupon rate: Interest rate set for a bond at time of issuance.

cross-price elasticity of demand: Percentage change in the quantity demanded of X divided by the percentage change in the price of Y.

cross-subsidization: Use of high prices and profits on one product to subsidize low prices on another product.

crowdfunding: The financing of a project through individual contributions from a large number of people, typically via an Internet platform.

crowdfunding: An internet-based method of raising funds from a large number of people.

crowding in: An increase in private sector borrowing (and spending) caused by decreased government borrowing.

crowding out: A reduction in private sector borrowing (and spending) caused by increased government borrowing.

current yield: The rate of return on a bond; the annual interest payment divided by the bond's price.

cyclical deficit: That portion of the budget deficit attributable to unemployment or inflation.

cyclical unemployment: Unemployment attributable to a lack of job vacancies—that is, to an inadequate level of aggregate demand.

D

debt ceiling: An explicit, legislated limit on the amount of outstanding national debt.

debt service: The interest required to be paid each year on outstanding debt.

default: Failure to make scheduled payments of interest or principal on a bond.

deficit ceiling: An explicit, legislated limitation on the size of the budget deficit.

deficit spending: The use of borrowed funds to finance government expenditures that exceed tax revenues.

deflation: A decrease in the average level of prices of goods and services.

demand: The willingness and ability to buy specific quantities of a good at alternative prices in a given time period, *ceteris paribus*.

demand curve: A curve describing the quantities of a good a consumer is willing and able

to buy at alternative prices in a given time period, *ceteris paribus*.

demand for labor: The quantities of labor employers are willing and able to hire at alternative wage rates in a given time period, *ceteris paribus*.

demand for money: The quantities of money people are willing and able to hold at alternative interest rates, *ceteris paribus*.

demand schedule: A table showing the quantities of a good a consumer is willing and able to buy at alternative prices in a given time period, *ceteris paribus*.

demand-pull inflation: An increase in the price level initiated by excessive aggregate demand.

deposit creation: The creation of transactions deposits by bank lending.

depreciation: The consumption of capital in the production process; the wearing out of plant and equipment.

depreciation (currency): A fall in the price of one currency relative to another.

derived demand: The demand for labor and other factors of production results from (depends on) the demand for final goods and services produced by these factors.

devaluation: An abrupt depreciation of a currency whose value was fixed or managed by the government.

discount rate: The rate of interest the Federal Reserve charges for lending reserves to private banks.

discounting: Federal Reserve lending of reserves to private banks.

discouraged worker: An individual who isn't actively seeking employment but would look for or accept a job if one were available.

discretionary fiscal spending: Those elements of the federal budget not determined by past legislative or executive commitments.

disposable income (DI): After-tax income of households; personal income less personal taxes.

dissaving: Consumption expenditure in excess of disposable income; a negative saving flow.

dividend: Amount of corporate profits paid out for each share of stock.

dumping: The sale of goods in export markets at prices below domestic prices.

E

economic cost: The value of all resources used to produce a good or service; opportunity cost.

economic growth: An increase in output (real GDP); an expansion of production possibilities.

economic profit: The difference between total revenues and total economic costs.

economics: The study of how best to allocate scarce resources among competing uses.

economies of scale: Reductions in minimum average costs that come about through increases in the size (scale) of plant and equipment.

effective tax rate: Taxes paid divided by total (gross) income.

efficiency: Maximum output of a good from the resources used in production.

efficiency decision: The choice of a production process for any given rate of output.

elasticity of labor supply: The percentage change in the quantity of labor supplied divided by the percentage change in wage rate.

embargo: A prohibition on exports or imports.

emission charge: A fee imposed on polluters, based on the quantity of pollution.

employment rate: The percentage of the adult population that is employed.

employment targeting: The use of an unemployment-rate threshold (6.5 percent) to signal the need for monetary stimulus.

entrepreneurship: The assembling of resources to produce new or improved products and technologies.

equation of exchange: Money supply (M) times velocity of circulation (V) equals level of aggregate spending ($P \times Q$).

equilibrium (macro): The combination of price level and real output that is compatible with both aggregate demand and aggregate supply.

equilibrium GDP: The value of total output (real GDP) produced at macro equilibrium (AS = AD).

equilibrium price: The price at which the quantity of a good demanded in a given time period equals the quantity supplied.

equilibrium rate of interest: The interest rate at which the quantity of money demanded in a given time period equals the quantity of money supplied.

equilibrium wage: The wage rate at which the quantity of labor supplied in a given time period equals the quantity of labor demanded.

excess reserves: Bank reserves in excess of required reserves.

exchange rate: The price of one country's currency expressed in terms of another's; the domestic price of a foreign currency.

expected value: The probable value of a future payment, including the risk of nonpayment.

expenditure equilibrium: The rate of output at which desired spending equals the value of output.

explicit costs: A payment made for the use of a resource.

exports: Goods and services sold to foreign buyers.

external costs: Costs of a market activity borne by a third party; the difference between the social and private costs of a market activity.

external debt: U.S. government debt (Treasury bonds) held by foreign households and institutions.

externalities: Costs (or benefits) of a market activity borne by a third party; the difference between the social and private costs (benefits) of a market activity.

extreme poverty (world): World Bank income standard of less than $1.90 per day per person (inflation adjusted).

F

factor market: Any place where factors of production (e.g., land, labor, capital) are bought and sold.

factors of production: Resource inputs used to produce goods and services, e.g., land, labor, capital, entrepreneurship.

federal funds rate: The interest rate for inter-bank reserve loans.

financial intermediary: Institution (e.g., a bank or the stock market) that makes savings available to dissavers (e.g., investors).

fine-tuning: Adjustments in economic policy designed to counteract small changes in economic outcomes; continuous responses to changing economic conditions.

fiscal policy: The use of government taxes and spending to alter macroeconomic outcomes.

fiscal restraint: Tax hikes or spending cuts intended to reduce (shift) aggregate demand.

fiscal stimulus: Tax cuts or spending hikes intended to increase (shift) aggregate demand.

fiscal year (FY): The 12-month period used for accounting purposes; begins October 1 for the federal government.

fixed costs: Costs of production that don't change when the rate of output is altered, such as the cost of basic plants and equipment.

flexible exchange rates: A system in which exchange rates are permitted to vary with market supply-and-demand conditions; floating exchange rates.

foreign exchange markets: Places where foreign currencies are bought and sold.

foreign exchange reserves: Holdings of foreign currencies by official government agencies, usually the central bank or treasury.

free rider: An individual who reaps direct benefits from someone else's purchase (consumption) of a public good.

frictional unemployment: Brief periods of unemployment experienced by people moving between jobs or into the labor market.

full employment: The lowest rate of unemployment compatible with price stability, variously estimated at between 4 percent and 6 percent unemployment.

full-employment GDP: The value of total market output (real GDP) produced at full employment.

G

game theory: The study of decision making in situations where strategic interaction (moves and countermoves) occurs between rivals.

GDP deflator: A price index that refers to all goods and services included in GDP.

GDP per capita: Total GDP divided by total population; average GDP.

geometric growth: An increase in quantity by a constant proportion each year.

Gini coefficient: A mathematical summary of inequality based on the Lorenz curve.

gold reserves: Stocks of gold held by a government to purchase foreign exchange.

gold standard: An agreement by countries to fix the price of their currencies in terms of gold; a mechanism for fixing exchange rates.

government failure: Government intervention that fails to improve economic outcomes.

gross business saving: Depreciation allowances and retained earnings.

gross domestic product (GDP): The total market value of all final goods and services produced within a nation's borders in a given time period.

gross investment: Total investment expenditure in a given time period.

growth rate: Percentage change in real output from one period to another.

growth recession: A period during which real GDP grows but at a rate below the long-term trend of 3 percent.

H

Herfindahl-Hirshman Index (HHI): Measure of industry concentration that accounts for number of firms and size of each.

horizontal equity: Principle that people with equal incomes should pay equal taxes.

human capital: The knowledge and skills possessed by the workforce.

hyperinflation: Inflation rate in excess of 200 percent, lasting at least one year.

I

implicit cost: The value of resources used, for which no direct payment is made.

import quota: A limit on the quantity of a good that may be imported in a given time period.

imports: Goods and services purchased from international sources.

in-kind income: Goods and services received directly, without payment, in a market transaction.

in-kind transfers: Direct transfers of goods and services rather than cash, such as food stamps, Medicaid benefits, and housing subsidies.

income effect of higher wages: An increased wage rate allows a person to reduce hours worked without losing income.

income elasticity of demand: Percentage change in quantity demanded divided by percentage change in income.

income quintile: One-fifth of the population, rank-ordered by income (e.g., top fifth).

income share: The proportion of total income received by a particular group.

income transfers: Payments to individuals for which no current goods or services are exchanged, such as Social Security, welfare, and unemployment benefits.

indifference curve: A curve depicting alternative combinations of goods that yield equal satisfaction.

indifference map: The set of indifference curves that depicts all possible levels of utility attainable from various combinations of goods.

inequality trap: Institutional barriers that impede human and physical capital investment, particularly by the poorest segments of society.

inferior good: Goods for which demand decreases when income rises.

inflation: An increase in the average level of prices of goods and services.

inflation rate: The annual percentage rate of increase in the average price level; (Price Level$_{Year 2}$ − Price Level$_{Year 1}$)/Price Level$_{Year 1}$.

inflation targeting: The use of an inflation ceiling ("target") to signal the need for monetary-policy adjustments.

inflationary flashpoint: The rate of output at which inflationary pressures intensify; the point on the AS curve where slope increases sharply.

inflationary gap: The amount by which aggregate spending at full employment exceeds full-employment output.

inflationary GDP gap: The amount by which equilibrium GDP exceeds full-employment GDP.

infrastructure: The transportation, communications, education, judicial, and other institutional systems that facilitate market exchanges.

initial public offering (IPO): The first issuance (sale) to the general public of stock in a corporation.

injection: An addition of spending to the circular flow of income.

interest rate: The price paid for the use of money.

intermediate goods: Goods or services purchased for use as input in the production of final goods or in services.

internal debt: U.S. government debt (Treasury bonds) held by U.S. households and institutions.

investment: Expenditures on (production of) new plants, equipment, and structures (capital) in a given time period, plus changes in business inventories.

investment decision: The decision to build, buy, or lease plants and equipment; to enter or exit an industry.

investment rate: The percentage of total output (GDP) allocated to the production of new plants, equipment, and structures.

item weight: The percentage of total expenditure spent on a specific product; used to compute inflation indexes.

L

labor force: All persons over age 16 who are either working for pay or actively seeking paid employment.

labor force participation rate: The percentage of the working-age population working or seeking employment.

labor productivity: Amount of output produced by a worker in a given period of time; output per hour (or day, etc.).

labor supply: The willingness and ability to work specific amounts of time at alternative wage rates in a given time period, *ceteris paribus*.

laissez faire: The doctrine of "leave it alone," of nonintervention by government in the market mechanism.

law of demand: The quantity of a good demanded in a given time period increases as its price falls, *ceteris paribus*.

law of diminishing marginal utility: The marginal utility of a good declines as more of it is consumed in a given time period.

law of diminishing returns: The marginal physical product of a variable input declines as more of it is employed with a given quantity of other (fixed) inputs.

law of supply: The quantity of a good supplied in a given time period increases as its price increases, *ceteris paribus*.

leakage: Income not spent directly on domestic output but instead diverted from the circular flow—for example, saving, imports, taxes.

liability: An obligation to make future payment; debt.

liquidity: The ability of an asset to be converted into cash.

liquidity trap: The portion of the money demand curve that is horizontal; people are willing to hold unlimited amounts of money at some (low) interest rate.

loan rate: The implicit price paid by the government for surplus crops taken as collateral for loans to farmers.

long run: A period of time long enough for all inputs to be varied (no fixed costs).

long-run competitive equilibrium: $p = MC =$ minimum ATC.

Lorenz curve: A graphic illustration of the cumulative size distribution of income; contrasts complete equality with the actual distribution of income.

M

macroeconomics: The study of aggregate economic behavior, of the economy as a whole.

managed exchange rates: A system in which governments intervene in foreign exchange markets to limit but not eliminate exchange rate fluctuations; "dirty floats."

marginal cost (MC): The increase in total cost associated with a one-unit increase in production.

marginal cost pricing: The offer (supply) of goods at prices equal to their marginal cost.

marginal factor cost (MFC): The change in total costs that results from a one-unit increase in the quantity of a factor employed.

marginal physical product (MPP): The change in total output associated with one additional unit of input.

marginal propensity to consume (MPC): The fraction of each additional (marginal) dollar of disposable income spent on consumption; the change in consumption divided by the change in disposable income.

marginal propensity to save (MPS): The fraction of each additional (marginal) dollar of disposable income not spent on consumption; $1 - MPC$.

marginal rate of substitution: The rate at which a consumer is willing to exchange one good for another; the relative marginal utilities of two goods.

marginal revenue (MR): The change in total revenue that results from a one-unit increase in the quantity sold.

marginal revenue product (MRP): The change in total revenue associated with one additional unit of input.

marginal tax rate: The tax rate imposed on the last (marginal) dollar of income.

marginal utility: The change in total utility obtained by consuming one additional (marginal) unit of a good or service.

marginal wage: The change in total wages paid associated with a one-unit increase in the quantity of labor employed.

market demand: The total quantities of a good or service people are willing and able to buy at alternative prices in a given time period; the sum of individual demands.

market failure: An imperfection in the market mechanism that prevents optimal outcomes.

market mechanism: The use of market prices and sales to signal desired outputs (or resource allocations).

market power: The ability to alter the market price of a good or service.

market share: The percentage of total market output produced by a single firm.

market shortage: The amount by which the quantity demanded exceeds the quantity supplied at a given price; excess demand.

market structure: The number and relative size of firms in an industry.

market supply: The total quantities of a good that sellers are willing and able to sell at alternative prices in a given time period, *ceteris paribus*.

market supply of labor: The total quantity of labor that workers are willing and able to supply at alternative wage rates in a given time period, *ceteris paribus*.

market surplus: The amount by which the quantity supplied exceeds the quantity demanded at a given price; excess supply.

merit good: A good or service society deems everyone is entitled to some minimal quantity of.

microeconomics: The study of individual behavior in the economy, of the components of the larger economy.

microfinance: The granting of small ("micro"), unsecured loans to small businesses and entrepreneurs.

Millennium Aid Goal: United Nations goal of raising foreign aid levels to 0.7 percent of donor-country GDP.

misery index: The sum of inflation and unemployment rates.

mixed economy: An economy that uses both market signals and government directives to allocate goods and resources.

monetary policy: The use of money and credit controls to influence macroeconomic outcomes.

money: Anything generally accepted as a medium of exchange.

money illusion: The use of nominal dollars rather than real dollars to gauge changes in one's income or wealth.

money multiplier: The number of deposit (loan) dollars that the banking system can create from $1 of excess reserves; equal to 1 ÷ required reserve ratio.

money supply (M1): Currency held by the public, plus balances in transactions accounts.

money supply (M2): M1 plus balances in most savings accounts and money market funds.

monopolistic competition: A market in which many firms produce similar goods or services but each maintains some independent control of its own price.

monopoly: A firm that produces the entire market supply of a particular good or service.

monopsony: A market in which there's only one buyer.

moral hazard: An incentive to engage in undesirable behavior.

multiplier: The multiple by which an initial change in aggregate spending will alter total expenditure after an infinite number of spending cycles; $1/(1 - MPC)$.

N

national debt: Accumulated debt of the federal government.

national income (NI): Total income earned by current factors of production: GDP less depreciation and indirect business taxes, plus net foreign factor income.

national income accounting: The measurement of aggregate economic activity, particularly national income and its components.

natural monopoly: An industry in which one firm can achieve economies of scale over the entire range of market supply.

natural rate of unemployment: The long-term rate of unemployment determined by structural forces in labor and product markets.

net domestic product (NDP): GDP less depreciation.

net exports: The value of exports minus the value of imports: $(X - M)$.

net investment: Gross investment less depreciation.

nominal GDP: The value of final output produced in a given period, measured in the prices of that period (current prices).

nominal income: The amount of money income received in a given time period, measured in current dollars.

nominal tax rate: Taxes paid divided by taxable income.

normal good: Good for which demand increases when income rises.

normal profit: The opportunity cost of capital; zero economic profit.

O

Okun's law: One percent more unemployment is estimated to equal 2 percent less output.

oligopolist: One of the dominant firms in an oligopoly.

oligopoly: A market in which a few firms produce all or most of the market supply of a particular good or service.

open economy: A nation that engages in international trade.

open market operations: Federal Reserve purchases and sales of government bonds for the purpose of altering bank reserves.

opportunity cost: The most desired goods or services that are forgone in order to obtain something else.

opportunity wage: The highest wage an individual would earn in his or her best alternative job.

optimal consumption: The mix of consumer purchases that maximizes the utility attainable from available income.

optimal mix of output: The most desirable combination of output attainable with existing resources, technology, and social values.

optimal rate of pollution: The rate of pollution that occurs when the marginal social benefit of pollution control equals its marginal social cost.

outsourcing: The relocation of production to foreign countries.

P

par value: The face value of a bond; the amount to be repaid when the bond is due.

parity: The relative price of farm products in the period 1910–1914.

payoff matrix: A table showing the risks and rewards of alternative decision options.

per capita GDP: The dollar value of GDP divided by total population; average GDP.

perfect competition: A market in which no buyer or seller has market power.

personal income (PI): Income received by households before payment of personal taxes.

Phillips curve: A historical (inverse) relationship between the rate of unemployment and the rate of inflation; commonly expresses a trade-off between the two.

portfolio decision: The choice of how (where) to hold idle funds.

poverty gap: The shortfall between actual income and the poverty threshold.

poverty rate: Percentage of the population counted as poor.

poverty threshold (U.S.): Annual income of less than $26,200 for a family of 4 (2020).

precautionary demand for money: Money held for unexpected market transactions or for emergencies.

predatory pricing: Temporary price reductions designed to alter market shares or drive out competition.

present discounted value (PDV): The value today of future payments, adjusted for interest accrual.

price ceiling: An upper limit imposed on the price of a good.

price discrimination: The sale of an individual good at different prices to different consumers.

price elasticity of demand: The percentage change in quantity demanded divided by the percentage change in price.

price elasticity of supply: The percentage change in quantity supplied divided by the percentage change in price.

price floor: Lower limit set for the price of a good.

price leadership: An oligopolistic pricing pattern that allows one firm to establish the (market) price for all firms in the industry.

price stability: The absence of significant changes in the average price level; officially defined as a rate of inflation of less than 3 percent.

price-fixing: Explicit agreements among producers regarding the price(s) at which a good is to be sold.

price/earnings (P/E) ratio: The price of a stock share divided by earnings (profit) per share.

private costs: The costs of an economic activity directly borne by the immediate producer or consumer (excluding externalities).

private good: A good or service whose consumption by one person excludes consumption by others.

product differentiation: Features that make one product appear different from competing products in the same market.

product market: Any place where finished goods and services (products) are bought and sold.

production decision: The selection of the short-run rate of output (with existing plants and equipment).

production function: A technological relationship expressing the maximum quantity of a good attainable from different combinations of factor inputs.

production possibilities: The alternative combinations of final goods and services that could be produced in a given period with all available resources and technology.

production process: A specific combination of resources used to produce a good or service.

productivity: Output per unit of input—for example, output per labor-hour.

profit: The difference between total revenue and total cost.

profit per unit: Total profit divided by the quantity produced in a given time period; price minus average total cost.

profit-maximization rule: Produce at that rate of output where marginal revenue equals marginal cost.

progressive tax: A tax system in which tax rates rise as incomes rise.

proportional tax: A tax that levies the same rate on every dollar of income.

public choice: Theory of public sector behavior emphasizing rational self-interest of decision makers and voters.

public good: A good or service whose consumption by one person does not exclude consumption by others.

Q

quota: A limit on the quantity of a good that may be imported in a given time period.

R

rational expectations: Hypothesis that people's spending decisions are based on all available information, including the anticipated effects of government intervention.

real GDP: The value of final output produced in a given period, adjusted for changing prices.

real income: Income in constant dollars; nominal income adjusted for inflation.

real interest rate: The nominal interest rate minus the anticipated inflation rate.

recession: A decline in total output (real GDP) for two or more consecutive quarters.

recessionary gap: The amount by which aggregate spending at full employment falls short of full-employment output.

recessionary GDP gap: The amount by which equilibrium GDP falls short of full-employment GDP.

reference price: Government-guaranteed price floor for specific agricultural commodities.

refinancing: The issuance of new debt in payment of debt issued earlier.

regressive tax: A tax system in which tax rates fall as incomes rise.

regulation: Government intervention to alter the behavior of firms—for example, in pricing, output, or advertising.

relative price: The price of one good in comparison with the price of other goods.

required reserves: The minimum amount of reserves a bank is required to hold; equal to required reserve ratio times transactions deposits.

reserve ratio: The ratio of a bank's reserves to its total transactions deposits.

retained earnings: Amount of corporate profits not paid out in dividends.

risk premium: The difference in rates of return on risky (uncertain) and safe (certain) investments.

S

saving: That part of disposable income not spent on current consumption; disposable income less consumption.

Say's law: Supply creates its own demand.

scarcity: Lack of enough resources to satisfy all desired uses of those resources.

seasonal unemployment: Unemployment due to seasonal changes in employment or labor supply.

severe poverty (world): World Bank income standard of $3.10 per day per person (inflation adjusted).

shift in demand: A change in the quantity demanded at any (every) price.

short run: The period in which the quantity (and quality) of some inputs can't be changed.

short-run competitive equilibrium: $p = \text{MC}$.

shutdown point: The rate of output where price equals minimum AVC.

size distribution of income: The way total personal income is divided up among households or income classes.

social costs: The full resource costs of an economic activity, including externalities.

social insurance programs: Event-conditioned income transfers intended to reduce the costs of specific problems, such as Social Security and unemployment insurance.

speculative demand for money: Money held for speculative purposes, for later financial opportunities.

stagflation: The simultaneous occurrence of substantial unemployment and inflation.

structural deficit: Federal revenues at full employment minus expenditures at full employment under prevailing fiscal policy.

structural unemployment: Unemployment caused by a mismatch between the skills (or location) of job seekers and the requirements (or location) of available jobs.

substitute goods: Goods that substitute for each other; when the price of good x rises, the demand for good y increases, *ceteris paribus*.

substitution effect of higher wages: An increased wage rate encourages people to work more hours (to substitute labor for leisure).

supply: The ability and willingness to sell (produce) specific quantities of a good at alternative prices in a given time period, *ceteris paribus*.

supply curve: A curve describing the quantities of a good a producer is willing and able to sell (produce) at alternative prices in a given time period, *ceteris paribus*.

supply-side policy: The use of tax incentives, (de)regulation, and other mechanisms to increase the ability and willingness to produce goods and services.

T

T-accounts: The accounting ledgers used by banks to track assets and liabilities.

target efficiency: The percentage of income transfers that go to the intended recipients and purposes.

tariff: A tax (duty) imposed on imported goods.

tax base: The amount of income or property directly subject to nominal tax rates.

tax elasticity of labor supply: The percentage change in quantity of labor supplied divided by the percentage change in tax rates.

tax elasticity of supply: The percentage change in quantity supplied divided by the percentage change in tax rates.

tax incidence: Distribution of the real burden of a tax.

tax rebate: A lump-sum refund of taxes paid.

terms of trade: The rate at which goods are exchanged; the amount of good A given up for good B in trade.

total cost: The market value of all resources used to produce a good or service.

total revenue: The price of a product multiplied by the quantity sold in a given time period: $p \times q$.

total utility: The amount of satisfaction obtained from entire consumption of a product.

trade deficit: The amount by which the value of imports exceeds the value of exports in a given time period (negative net exports).

trade surplus: The amount by which the value of exports exceeds the value of imports in a given time period (positive net exports).

transactions account: A bank account that permits direct payment to a third party—for example, with a check or debit card.

transactions demand for money: Money held for the purpose of making everyday market purchases.

transfer payments: Payments to individuals for which no current goods or services are exchanged, like Social Security, welfare, and unemployment benefits.

Treasury bonds: Promissory notes (IOUs) issued by the U.S. Treasury.

U

UN and World Bank Poverty Goal: UN goal of eliminating extreme poverty by 2030.

underemployment: People seeking full-time paid employment who work only part-time or are employed at jobs below their capability.

unemployment: The inability of labor force participants to find jobs.

unemployment rate: The proportion of the labor force that is unemployed.

union shop: An employment setting in which all workers must join the union within 30 days after being employed.

unionization rate: The percentage of the labor force belonging to a union.

unit labor cost: Hourly wage rate divided by output per labor-hour.

utility: The pleasure or satisfaction obtained from a good or service.

V

value added: The increase in the market value of a product that takes place at each stage of the production process.

variable costs: Costs of production that change when the rate of output is altered, such as labor and material costs.

velocity of money (V): The number of times per year, on average, that a dollar is used to purchase final goods and services; $PQ \div M$.

vertical equity: Principle that people with higher incomes should pay more taxes.

voluntary restraint agreement (VRA): An agreement to reduce the volume of trade in a specific good; a "voluntary" quota.

W

wage replacement rate: The percentage of base wages paid out in benefits.

wealth: The market value of assets.

wealth effect: A change in consumer spending caused by a change in the value of owned assets.

welfare programs: Means-tested income transfer programs, such as welfare and food stamps.

Y

yield: The rate of return on a bond; the annual interest payment divided by the bond's price.

Note: **Bold** page numbers indicate definitions; page numbers followed by *n* indicate material in notes.